Jean–Christophe, Vol. I

Romain Rolland

JEAN–CHRISTOPHE VOLUME I

DAWN, MORNING, YOUTH, REVOLT

by Romain Rolland

Translated by Gilbert Cannan

PREFACE

"Jean–Christophe" is the history of the development of a musician of genius. The present volume comprises the first four volumes of the original French, viz.: "L'Aube," "Le Matin," "L'Adolescent," and "La Revolte," which are designated in the translation as Part I—The Dawn; Part II—Morning; Part III—Youth; Part IV—Revolt. Parts I and II carry Jean–Christophe from the moment of his birth to the day when, after his first encounter with Woman, at the age of fifteen, he falls back upon a Puritan creed. Parts III and IV describe the succeeding five years of his life, when, at the age of twenty, his sincerity, integrity, and unswerving honesty have made existence impossible for him in the little Rhine town of his birth. An act of open revolt against German militarism compels him to cross the frontier and take refuge in Paris, and the remainder of this vast book is devoted to the adventures of Jean–Christophe in France.

His creator has said that he has always conceived and thought of the life of his hero and of the book as a river. So far as the book has a plan, that is its plan. It has no literary artifice, no "plot." The words of it hang together in defiance of syntax, just as the thoughts of it follow one on the other in defiance of every system of philosophy. Every phase of the book is pregnant with the next phase. It is as direct and simple as life itself, for life is simple when the truth of it is known, as it was known instinctively by Jean–Christophe. The river is explored as though it were absolutely uncharted. Nothing that has ever been said or thought of life is accepted without being brought to the test of Jean–Christophe's own life. What is not true for him does not exist; and, as there are very few of the processes of human growth or decay which are not analysed, there is disclosed to the reader the most comprehensive survey of modern life which has appeared in literature in this century.

Jean–Christophe, Vol. I

Romain Rolland

Table of Contents

To leave M. Rolland's simile of the river, and to take another, the book has seemed to me like a, mighty bridge leading from the world of ideas of the nineteenth century to the world of ideas of the twentieth. The whole thought of the nineteenth century seems to be gathered together to make the starting–point for Jean–Christophe's leap into the future. All that was most religious in that thought seems to be concentrated in Jean–Christophe, and when the history of the book is traced, it appears that M. Rolland has it by direct inheritance.

M. Rolland was born in 1866 at Clamecy, in the center of France, of a French family of pure descent, and educated in Paris and Rome. At Rome, in 1890, he met Malwida von Meysenburg, a German lady who had taken refuge in England after the Revolution of 1848, and there knew Kossuth, Mazzini, Herzen, Ledin, Rollin, and Louis Blanc. Later, in Italy, she counted among her friends Wagner, Liszt, Lenbach, Nietzsche, Garibaldi, and Ibsen. She died in 1908. Rolland came to her impregnated with Tolstoyan ideas, and with her wide knowledge of men and movements she helped him to discover his own ideas. In her "Memoires d'une Idealiste" she wrote of him: "In this young Frenchman I discovered the same idealism, the same lofty aspiration, the same profound grasp of every great intellectual manifestation that I had already found in the greatest men of other nationalities."

The germ of "Jean–Christophe" was conceived during this period—the "Wanderjahre"—of M. Rolland's life. On his return to Paris he became associated with a movement towards the renascence of the theater as a social machine, and wrote several plays. He has since been a musical critic and a lecturer on music and art at the Sorbonne. He has written Lives of Beethoven, Michael Angelo, and Hugo Wolf. Always his endeavor has been the pursuit of the heroic. To him the great men are the men of absolute truth. Jean–Christophe must have the truth and tell the truth, at all costs, in despite of circumstance, in despite of himself, in despite even of life. It is his law. It is M. Rolland's law. The struggle all through the book is between the pure life of Jean–Christophe and the common acceptance of the second–rate and the second–hand by the substitution of civic or social morality, which is only a compromise, for individual morality, which demands that every man should be delivered up to the unswerving judgment of his own soul. Everywhere Jean–Christophe is hurled against compromise and untruth, individual and national. He discovers the German lie very quickly; the French lie grimaces at him as soon as he sets foot in Paris.

The book itself breaks down the frontier between France and Germany. If one frontier is broken, all are broken. The truth about anything is universal truth, and the experiences of Jean–Christophe, the adventures of his soul (there are no other adventures), are in a greater or less degree those of every human being who passes through this life from the tyranny of the past to the service of the future.

The book contains a host of characters who become as friends, or, at least, as interesting neighbors, to the reader. Jean–Christophe gathers people in his progress, and as they are all brought to the test of his genius, they appear clearly for what they are. Even the most unpleasant of them is human, and demands sympathy.

The recognition of Jean–Christophe as a book which marks a stage in progress was instantaneous in France. It is hardly possible yet to judge it. It is impossible to deny its vitality. It exists. Christophe is as real as the gentlemen whose portraits are posted outside the Queen's Hall, and much more real than many of them. The book clears the air. An open mind coming to it cannot fail to be refreshed and strengthened by its voyage down the river of a man's life, and if the book is followed to its end, the voyager will discover with Christophe that there is joy beneath sorrow, joy through sorrow ("Durch Leiden Freude").

Those are the last words of M. Rolland's life of Beethoven; they are words of Beethoven himself: "La devise de tout ame heroique."

In his preface, "To the Friends of Christophe," which precedes the seventh volume, "Dans la Maison," M. Rolland writes:

"I was isolated: like so many others in France I was stifling in a world morally inimical to me: I wanted air: I wanted to react against an unhealthy civilization, against ideas corrupted by a sham elite: I wanted to say to them: 'You lie! You do not represent France!' To do so I needed a hero with a pure heart and unclouded vision, whose soul would be stainless enough for him to have the right to speak; one whose voice would be loud enough for him to gain a hearing, I have patiently begotten this hero. The work was in conception for many years before I set myself to write a word of it. Christophe only set out on his journey when I had been able to see the end of it for him."

If M. Rolland's act of faith in writing Jean–Christophe were only concerned with France, if the polemic of it were not directed against a universal evil, there would be no reason for translation. But, like Zarathustra, it is a book for all and none. M. Rolland has written what he believes to be the truth, and as Dr. Johnson observed: "Every man has a right to utter what he thinks truth, and every other man has a right to knock him down for it...."

By its truth and its absolute integrity—since Tolstoy I know of no writing so crystal clear—"Jean–Christophe" is the first great book of the twentieth century. In a sense it begins the twentieth century. It bridges transition, and shows us where we stand. It reveals the past and the present, and leaves the future open to us....

GILBERT CANNAN

THE DAWN

Dianzi, nell'alba che precede al giorno,
Quando l'anima tua dentro dormia....
    Purgatorio, ix.

I

Come, quando i vapori umidi e spessi
A diradar cominciansi, la spera
Del sol debilemente entra per essi....
    Purgatorio, xvii.

From behind the house rises the murmuring of the river. All day long the rain has been beating against the window–panes; a stream of water trickles down the window at the corner where it is broken. The yellowish light of the day dies down. The room is dim and dull.

The new–born child stirs in his cradle. Although the old man left his sabots at the door when he entered, his footsteps make the floor creak. The child begins to whine. The mother leans out of her bed to comfort it; and the grandfather gropes to light the lamp, so that the child shall not be frightened by the night when he awakes. The flame of the lamp lights up old Jean Michel's red face, with its rough white beard and morose expression and quick eyes. He goes near the cradle. His cloak smells wet, and as he walks he drags his large blue list slippers, Louisa signs to him not to go too near. She is fair, almost white; her features are drawn; her gentle, stupid face is marked with red in patches; her lips are pale and' swollen, and they are parted in a timid smile; her eyes devour the child—and her eyes are blue and vague; the pupils are small, but there is an infinite tenderness in them.

The child wakes and cries, and his eyes are troubled. Oh! how terrible! The darkness, the sudden flash of the lamp, the hallucinations of a mind as yet hardly detached from chaos, the stifling, roaring night in which it is enveloped, the illimitable gloom from which, like blinding shafts of light, there emerge acute sensations, sorrows, phantoms—those enormous faces leaning over him, those eyes that pierce through him, penetrating, are beyond his comprehension!... He has not the strength to cry out; terror holds him motionless, with eyes and mouth wide open and he rattles in his throat. His large head, that seems to have swollen up, is wrinkled with the grotesque and lamentable grimaces that he makes; the skin of his face and hands is brown and purple, and spotted with yellow....

"Dear God!" said the old man with conviction: "How ugly he is!"

He put the lamp down on the table.

Louisa pouted like a scolded child. Jean Michel looked at her out of the corner of his eye and laughed.

"You don't want me to say that he is beautiful? You would not believe it. Come, it is not your fault. They are all like that."

The child came out of the stupor and immobility into which he had been thrown by the light of the lamp and the eyes of the old man. He began to cry. Perhaps he instinctively felt in his mother's eyes a caress which made it possible for him to complain. She held out her arms for him and said:

"Give him to me."

The old man began, as usual, to air his theories:

"You ought not to give way to children when they cry. You must just let them cry."

But he came and took the child and grumbled:

"I never saw one quite so ugly."

Louisa took the child feverishly and pressed it to her bosom. She looked at it with a bashful and delighted smile.

"Oh, my poor child!" she said shamefacedly. "How ugly you are—how ugly! and how I love you!"

Jean Michel went back to the fireside. He began to poke the fire in protest, but a smile gave the lie to the moroseness and solemnity of his expression.

"Good girl!" he said. "Don't worry about it. He has plenty of time to alter. And even so, what does it matter? Only one thing is asked of him: that he should grow into an honest man."

The child was comforted by contact with his mother's warm body. He could be heard sucking her milk and gurgling and snorting. Jean Michel turned in his chair, and said once more, with some emphasis:

"There's nothing finer than an honest man."

He was silent for a moment, pondering whether it would not be proper to elaborate this thought; but he found nothing more to say, and after a silence he said irritably:

"Why isn't your husband here?"

"I think he is at the theater," said Louisa timidly. "There is a rehearsal."

"The theater is closed. I passed it just now. One of his lies."

"No. Don't be always blaming him. I must have misunderstood. He must have been kept for one of his lessons."

"He ought to have come back," said the old man, not satisfied. He stopped for a moment, and then asked, in a rather lower voice and with some shame:

"Has he been ... again?"

"No, father—no, father," said Louisa hurriedly.

The old man looked at her; she avoided his eyes.

"It's not true. You're lying."

She wept in silence.

"Dear God!" said the old man, kicking at the fire with his foot. The poker fell with a clatter. The mother and the child trembled.

"Father, please—please!" said Louisa. "You will make him cry."

The child hesitated for a second or two whether to cry or to go on with his meal; but not being able to do both at once, he went on with the meal.

Jean Michel continued in a lower tone, though with outbursts of anger:

"What have I done to the good God to have this drunkard for my son? What is the use of my having lived as I have lived, and of having denied myself everything all my life! But you—you—can't you do anything to stop it? Heavens! That's what you ought to do.... You should keep him at home!..."

Louisa wept still more.

"Don't scold me!... I am unhappy enough as it is! I have done everything I could. If you knew how terrified I am when I am alone! Always I seem to hear his step on the stairs. Then I wait for the door to open, or I ask myself: 'O God! what will he look like?' ... It makes me ill to think of it!"

She was shaken by her sobs. The old man grew anxious. He went to her and laid the disheveled bedclothes about her trembling shoulders and caressed her head with his hands.

"Come, come, don't be afraid. I am here."

She calmed herself for the child's sake, and tried to smile.

"I was wrong to tell you that."

The old man shook his head as he looked at her.

"My poor child, it was not much of a present that I gave you."

"It's my own fault," she said. "He ought not to have married me. He is sorry for what he did."

"What, do you mean that he regrets?..."

"You know. You were angry yourself because I became his wife."

"We won't talk about that. It is true I was vexed. A young man like that—I can say so without hurting you—a young man whom I had carefully brought up, a distinguished musician, a real artist—might have looked higher than you, who had nothing and were of a lower class, and not even of the same trade. For more than a hundred years no Krafft has ever married a woman who was not a musician! But, you know, I bear you no grudge, and am fond of you, and have been ever since I learned to know you. Besides, there's no going back on a choice once it's made; there's nothing left but to do one's duty honestly."

He went and sat down again, thought for a little, and then said, with the solemnity in which he invested all his aphorisms:

"The first thing in life is to do one's duty."

9

* * * * *

Night was fully come. Louisa's voice roused old Jean Michel from the torpor into which he had sunk by the fireside as he thought of the sorrows of the past and present.

"It must be late, father," said the young woman affectionately. "You ought to go home; you have far to go."

"I am waiting for Melchior," replied the old man.

"Please, no. I would rather you did not stay."

"Why?"

The old man raised his head and looked fiercely at her.

She did not reply.

He resumed.

"You are afraid. You do not want me to meet him?"

"Yes, yes; it would only make things worse. You would make each other angry, and I don't want that. Please, please go!"

The old man sighed, rose, and said:

"Well ... I'll go."

He went to her and brushed her forehead with his stiff beard. He asked if she wanted anything, put out the lamp, and went stumbling against the chairs in the darkness of the room. But he had no sooner reached the staircase than he thought of his son returning drunk, and he stopped at each step, imagining a thousand dangers that might arise if Melchior were allowed to return alone....

In the bed by his mother's side the child was stirring again. An unknown sorrow had arisen from the depths of his being. He stiffened himself against her. He twisted his body, clenched his fists, and knitted his brows. His suffering increased steadily, quietly, certain of its strength. He knew not what it was, nor whence it came. It appeared immense,—infinite, and he began to cry lamentably. His mother caressed him with her gentle hands. Already his suffering was less acute. But he went on weeping, for he felt it still near, still inside himself. A man who suffers can lessen his anguish by knowing whence it comes. By thought he can locate it in a certain portion of his body which can be cured, or, if necessary, torn away. He fixes the bounds of it, and separates it from himself. A child has no such illusive resource. His first encounter with suffering is more tragic and more true. Like his own being, it seems infinite. He feels that it is seated in his bosom, housed in his heart, and is mistress of his flesh. And it is so. It will not leave his body until it has eaten it away.

His mother hugs him to her, murmuring: "It is done—it is done! Don't cry, my little Jesus, my little goldfish...." But his intermittent outcry continues. It is as though this wretched, unformed, and unconscious mass had a presentiment of a whole life of sorrow awaiting, him, and nothing can appease him....

The bells of St. Martin rang out in the night. Their voices are solemn and slow. In the damp air they come like footsteps on moss. The child became silent in the middle of a sob. The marvelous music, like a flood of milk, surged sweetly through him. The night was lit up; the air was moist and tender. His sorrow disappeared, his heart began to laugh, and he slid, into his dreams with a sigh of abandonment.

The three bells went on softly ringing in the morrow's festival. Louisa also dreamed, as she listened to them, of her own past misery and of what would become in the future of the dear little child sleeping by her side. She had been for hours lying in her bed, weary and suffering. Her hands and her body were burning; the heavy eiderdown crushed her; she felt crushed and oppressed by the darkness; but she dared not move. She looked at the child, and the night did not prevent her reading his features, that looked so old. Sleep overcame her; fevered images passed through her brain. She thought she heard Melchior open the door, and her heart leaped. Occasionally the murmuring of the stream rose more loudly through the silence, like the roaring of some beast. The window once or twice gave a sound under the beating of the rain. The bells rang out more slowly, and then died down, and Louisa slept by the side of her child.

All this time Jean Michel was waiting outside the house, dripping with rain, his beard wet with the mist. He was waiting for the return of his wretched son: for his mind, never ceasing, had insisted on telling him all sorts of tragedies brought about by drunkenness; and although he did not believe them, he could not hate slept a wink if he had gone away without having seen his son return. The sound of the bells made him: melancholy, for he remembered all his shattered hopes. He thought of what he was doing at such an hour in the street, and for very shame he wept.

* * * * *

The vast tide of the days moves slowly. Day and night come up and go down with unfailing regularity, like the ebb and low of an infinite ocean. Weeks and months go by, and then begin again, and the succession of days is like one day.

The day is immense, inscrutable, marking the even beat of light and darkness, and the beat of the life of the torpid creature dreaming in the depths of his cradle—his imperious needs, sorrowful or glad—so regular that the night and the day which bring them seem by them to be brought about.

The pendulum of life moves heavily, and in its slow beat the whole creature seems to be absorbed. The rest is no more than dreams, snatches of dreams, formless and swarming, and dust of atoms dancing aimlessly, a dizzy whirl passing, and bringing laughter or horror. Outcry, moving shadows, grinning shapes, sorrows, terrors, laughter, dreams, dreams.... All is a dream, both day and night.... And in such chaos the light of friendly eyes that smile upon him, the flood of joy that surges through his body from his mother's body, from her breasts filled with milk—the force that is in him, the immense, unconscious force gathering in him, the turbulent ocean roaring in the narrow prison of the child's body. For eyes that could see into it there would be revealed whole worlds half buried in the darkness, nebulae taking shape, a universe in the making. His being is limitless. He is all that there is....

Months pass.... Islands of memory begin to rise above the river of his life. At first they are little uncharted islands, rocks just peeping above the surface of the waters. Round about them and behind in the twilight of the dawn stretches the great untroubled sheet of water; then new islands, touched to gold by the sun.

So from the abyss of the soul there emerge shapes definite, and scenes of a strange clarity. In the boundless day which dawns once more, ever the same, with its great monotonous beat, there begins to show forth the round of days, hand in hand, and some of their forms are smiling, others sad. But ever the links of the chain are broken, and memories are linked together above weeks and months....

The River ... the Bells ... as long as he can remember—far back in the abysses of time, at every hour of his life—always their voices, familiar and resonant, have rung out....

Night—half asleep—a pale light made white the window.... The river murmurs. Through the silence its voice rises omnipotent; it reigns over all creatures. Sometimes it caresses their sleep, and seems almost itself to die away in the roaring of its torrent. Sometimes it grows angry, and howls like a furious beast about to bite. The clamor ceases. Now there is a murmuring of infinite tenderness, silvery sounds like clear little bells, like the laughter of children, or soft singing voices, or dancing music—a great mother voice that never, never goes to sleep! It rocks the child, as it has rocked through the ages, from birth to death, the generations that were before him; it fills all his thoughts, and lives in all his dreams, wraps him round with the cloak of its fluid harmonies, which still will be about him when he lies in the little cemetery that sleeps by the water's edge, washed by the Rhine....

The bells.... It is dawn! They answer each other's call, sad, melancholy, friendly, gentle. At the sound of their slow voices there rise in him hosts of dreams—dreams of the past, desires, hopes, regrets for creatures who are gone, unknown to the child, although he had his being in them, and they live again in him. Ages of memory ring out in that music. So much mourning, so many festivals! And from the depths of the room it is as though, when they are heard, there passed lovely waves of sound through the soft air, free winging birds, and the moist soughing of the wind. Through the window smiles a patch of blue sky; a sunbeam slips through the curtains to the bed. The little world known to the eyes of the child, all that he can see from his bed every morning as he awakes, all that with so much effort he is beginning to recognize and classify, so that he may be master of it—his kingdom is lit up. There is the table where people eat, the cupboard where he hides to play, the tiled floor along which he crawls, and the wall–paper which in its antic shapes holds for him so many humorous or terrifying stories, and the clock which chatters and stammers so many words which he alone can understand. How many things there are in this room! He does not know them all. Every day he sets out on a voyage of exploration in this universe which is his. Everything is his. Nothing is immaterial; everything has its worth, man or fly, Everything lives—the cat, the fire, the table, the grains of dust which dance in a sunbeam. The room is a country, a day is a lifetime. How is a creature to know himself in the midst of these vast spaces? The world is so large! A creature is lost in it. And the faces, the actions, the movement, the noise, which make round about him an unending turmoil!... He is weary; his eyes close; he goes to sleep. That sweet deep sleep that overcomes him suddenly at any time, and wherever he may be—on his mother's lap, or under the table, where he loves to hide!... It is good. All is good....

These first days come buzzing up in his mind like a field of corn or a wood stirred by the wind, and cast in shadow by the great fleeting clouds....

* * * * *

The shadows pass; the sun penetrates the forest. Jean–Christophe begins to find his way through the labyrinth of the day.

It is morning. His parents are asleep. He is in his little bed, lying on his back. He looks at the rays of light dancing on the ceiling. There is infinite amusement in it. Now he laughs out loud with one of those jolly children's laughs which stir the hearts of those that hear them. His mother leans out of her bed towards him, and says: "What is it, then, little mad thing?" Then he laughs again, and perhaps he makes an effort to laugh because he has an audience. His mamma looks severe, and lays a finger on her lips to warn him lest he should wake his father: but her weary eyes smile in spite of herself. They whisper together. Then there is a furious growl from his father. Both tremble. His mother hastily turns her back on him, like a naughty little girl: she pretends to be asleep. Jean–Christophe buries himself in his bed, and holds his breath.... Dead silence.

After some time the little face hidden under the clothes comes to the surface again. On the roof the weathercock creaks. The rain–pipe gurgles; the Angelus sounds. When the wind comes from the east, the distant bells of the villages on the other bank of the river give answer. The sparrows foregathered in the ivy–clad wall make a deafening noise, from which three or four voices, always the same, ring out more shrilly than the others, just as in the games of a band of children. A pigeon coos at the top of a chimney. The child abandons himself to the lullaby of these sounds. He hums to himself softly, then a little more loudly, then quite loudly, then very loudly, until once more his father cries out in exasperation: "That little donkey never will be quiet! Wait a little, and I'll pull your ears!" Then Jean–Christophe buries himself in the bedclothes again, and does not know whether to laugh or cry. He is terrified and humiliated; and at the same time the idea of the donkey with which his father has compared him makes him burst out laughing. From the depths of his bed he imitates its braying. This time he is whipped. He sheds every tear that is in him. What has he done? He wanted so much to laugh and to get up! And he is forbidden to budge. How do people sleep forever? When will they get up?...

One day he could not contain himself. He heard a cat and a dog and something queer in the street. He slipped out of bed, and, creeping awkwardly with his bare feet on the tiles, he tried to go down the stairs to see what it was; but the door was shut. To open it, he climbed on to a chair; the whole thing collapsed, and he hurt himself and howled. And once more at the top of the stairs he was whipped. He is always being whipped!...

   * * * * *

He is in church with his grandfather. He is bored. He is not very comfortable. He is forbidden to stir, and all the people are saying all together words that he does not understand. They all look solemn and gloomy. It is not their usual way of looking. He looks at them, half frightened. Old Lena, their neighbor, who is sitting next to him, looks very cross; there are moments when he does not recognize even his grandfather. He is afraid a little. Then he grows used to it, and tries to find relief from boredom by every means at his disposal. He balances on one leg, twists his neck to look at the ceiling, makes faces, pulls his grandfather's coat, investigates the straws in his chair, tries to make a hole in them with his finger, listens to the singing of birds, and yawns so that he is like to dislocate his jaw.

Suddenly there is a deluge of sound; the organ is played. A thrill goes down his spine. He turns and stands with his chin resting on the back of his chair, and he looks very wise. He does not understand this noise; he does not know the meaning of it; it is dazzling, bewildering, and he can hear nothing clearly. But it is good. It is as though he were no longer sitting there on an uncomfortable chair in a tiresome old house. He is suspended in mid–air, like a bird; and when the flood of sound rushes from one end of the church to the other, filling the arches, reverberating from wall to wall, he is carried with it, flying and skimming hither and thither, with nothing to do but to abandon himself to it. He is laughed aloud at its contortions.

It occurred to him also to tie a piece of string to his magic wand, and gravely cast it into the river, and wait for a fish to come and bite. He knew perfectly well that fish do not usually bite at a piece of string without bait or hook; but he thought that for once in a way, and for him, they might make an exception to their rule; and in his inexhaustible confidence, he carried it so far as to fish in the street with a whip through the grating of a sewer. He would draw up the whip from time to time excitedly, pretending that the cord of it was more heavy, and that he had caught a treasure, as in a story that his grandfather had told him....

And always in the middle of all these games there used to occur to him moments of strange dreaming and complete forgetfulness. Everything about him would then be blotted out; he would not know what he was doing, and was not even conscious of himself. These attacks would take him unawares. Sometimes as he walked or went upstairs a void would suddenly open before him. He would seem then to have lost all thought. But when he came back to himself, he was shocked and bewildered to find himself in the same place on the dark staircase. It was as though he had lived through a whole lifetime—in the space of a few steps.

His grandfather used often to take him with him on his evening walk. The little boy used to trot by his side and give him his hand. They used to go by the roads, across plowed fields, which smelled strong and good. The grasshoppers chirped. Enormous crows poised along the road used to watch them approach from afar, and then fly away heavily as they came up with them.

His grandfather would cough. Jean–Christophe knew quite well what that meant. The old man was burning with the desire to tell a story; but he wanted it to appear that the child had asked him for one. Jean–Christophe did not fail him; they understood each other. The old man had a tremendous affection for his grandson, and it was a great joy to find in him a willing audience. He loved to tell of episodes in his own life, or stories of great men, ancient and modern. His voice would then become emphatic and filled with emotion, and would tremble with a childish joy, which he used to try to stifle. He seemed delighted to hear his own voice. Unhappily, words used to fail him when he opened his mouth to speak. He was used to such disappointment, for it always came upon him with his outbursts of eloquence. And as he used to forget it with each new attempt, he never succeeded in resigning himself to it.

He used to talk of Regulus, and Arminius, of the soldiers of Luetzow, of Koerner, and of Frederic Stabs, who tried to kill the Emperor Napoleon. His face would glow as he told of incredible deeds of heroism. He used to pronounce historic words in such a solemn voice that it was impossible to hear them, and he used to try artfully to keep his hearer on tenterhooks at the thrilling moments. He would stop, pretend to choke, and noisily blow his nose; and his heart would leap when the child asked, in a voice choking with impatience: "And then, grandfather?"

There came a day, when Jean–Christophe was a little older, when he perceived his grandfather's method; and then he wickedly set himself to assume an air of indifference to the rest of the story, and that hurt the poor old man. But for the moment Jean–Christophe is altogether held by the power of the story–teller. His blood leaped at the dramatic passages. He did not know what it was all about, neither where nor when these deeds were done, or whether his grandfather knew Arminius, or whether Regulus were not—God knows why!—some one whom he had seen at church last Sunday. But his heart and the old man's heart swelled with joy and pride in the tale of heroic deeds, as though they themselves had done them; for the old man and the child were both children.

Jean–Christophe was less happy when his grandfather interpolated in the pathetic passages one of those abstruse discourses so dear to him. There were moral thoughts generally traceable to some idea, honest enough, but a little trite, such as "Gentleness is better than violence," or "Honor is the dearest thing in life," or "It is better to be good than to be wicked"—only they were much more involved. Jean–Christophe's grandfather had no fear of the criticism of his youthful audience, and abandoned himself to his habitual emphatic manner; he was not afraid of repeating the same phrases, or of not finishing them, or even, if he lost himself in his discourse, of saying anything that came into his head, to stop up the gaps in his thoughts; and he used to punctuate his words, in order to give them greater force, with inappropriate gestures. The boy used to listen with profound respect, and he thought his grandfather very eloquent, but a little tiresome.

Both of them loved to return again and again to the fabulous legend of the Corsican conqueror who had taken Europe. Jean–Christophe's grandfather had known him. He had almost fought against him. But he was a man to admit the greatness of his adversaries: he had said so twenty times. He would have given one of his arms for such a man to have and when with his heel he crushed the dried top of a clod of earth, and filled up the valley at the foot of it, it seemed to him that his day had not been wasted.

Sometimes they would meet a peasant in his cart on the highroad, and, if the peasant knew Jean–Christophe's grandfather they would climb up by his side. That was a Paradise on earth. The horse went fast, and Jean–Christophe laughed with delight, except when they passed other people walking; then he would look serious and indifferent, like a person accustomed to drive in a carriage, but his heart was filled with pride. His grandfather and the man would talk without bothering about him. Hidden and crushed by their legs, hardly sitting, sometimes not sitting at all, he was perfectly happy. He talked aloud, without troubling about any answer to what he said. He watched the horse's ears moving. What strange creatures those ears were! They moved in every direction—to right and left; they hitched forward, and fell to one side, and turned backwards in such a ridiculous way that he: burst out laughing. He would pinch his grandfather to make him look at them; but his grandfather was not interested in them. He would repulse Jean–Christophe, and tell him to be quiet. Jean–Christophe would ponder. He thought that when people grow up they are not surprised by anything, and that when they are strong they know everything; and he would try to be grown up himself, and to hide his curiosity, and appear to be indifferent.

He was silent them The rolling of the carriage made him drowsy. The horse's little bells danced—ding, ding; dong, ding. Music awoke in the air, and hovered about the silvery bells, like a swarm of bees. It beat gaily with the rhythm of the cart—an endless source of song, and one song came on another's heels. To Jean–Christophe they were superb. There was one especially which he thought so beautiful that he tried to draw his grandfather's attention to it. He sang it aloud. They took no heed of him. He began it again in a higher key, then again shrilly, and then old Jean Michel said irritably: "Be quiet; you are deafening me with your trumpet–call!" That took away his breath. He blushed and was silent and mortified. He crushed with his contempt the two stockish imbeciles who did not understand the sublimity of his song, which opened wide the heavens! He thought them very ugly, with their week–old beards, and they smelled very ill.

He found consolation, in watching the horse's shadow. That an astonishing sight. The beast ran along with them lying on its side. In the evening, when they returned, it covered a part of the field. They came upon a rick, and the shadow's head would rise up and then return to its place when they had passed. Its snout was flattened out like a burst balloon;

its ears were large, and pointed like candles. Was it really a shadow or a creature? Jean–Christophe would not have liked to encounter it alone. He would not have run after it as he did after his grandfather's shadow, so as to walk on its head and trample it under foot. The shadows of the trees when the sun was low were also objects of meditation. They made barriers along the road, and looked like phantoms, melancholy and grotesque, saying, "Go no farther!" and the creaking axles and the horse's shoes repeated, "No farther!"

Jean–Christophe's grandfather and the driver never ceased their endless chatter. Sometimes they would raise their voices, especially when they talked of local affairs or things going wrong. The child would cease to dream, and look at them uneasily. It seemed to him that they were angry with each other, and he was afraid that they would come to blows. However, on the contrary, they best understood each other in their common dislikes. For the most part, they were without haired or the least passion; they talked of small matters loudly, just for the pleasure of talking, as is the joy of the people. But Jean–Christophe, not understanding their conversation, only heard the loud tones of their voices and saw their agitated faces, and thought fearfully: "How wicked he looks! Surely they hate each other! How he rolls his eyes, and how wide he opens his mouth! He spat on my nose in his fury. O Lord, he will kill my grandfather!..."

The carriage stopped. The peasant said: "Here you are." The two deadly enemies shook hands. Jean–Christophe's grandfather got down first; the peasant handed him the little boy. The whip flicked the horse, the carriage rolled away, and there they were by the little sunken road near the Rhine. The sun dipped down below the fields. The path wound almost to the water's edge. The plentiful soft grass yielded under their feet, crackling. Alder–trees leaned over the river, almost half in the water. A cloud of gnats danced. A boat passed noiselessly, drawn on by the peaceful current, striding along. The water sucked the branches of the willows with a little noise like lips. The light was soft and misty, the air fresh, the river silvery gray. They reached their home, and the crickets chirped, and on the threshold smiled his mother's dear face....

Oh, delightful memories, kindly visions, which will hum their melody in their tuneful flight through life!... Journeys in later life, great towns and moving seas, dream countries and loved faces, are not so exactly graven in the soul as these childish walks, or the corner of the garden seen every day through the window, through the steam and mist made by the child's mouth glued to it for want of other occupation....

Evening now, and the house is shut up. Home ... the refuge from all terrifying things—darkness, night, fear, things unknown. No enemy can pass the threshold.... The fire flares. A golden duck turns slowly on the spit; a delicious smell of fat and of crisping flesh scents the room. The joy of eating, incomparable delight, a religious enthusiasm, thrills of joy! The body is too languid with the soft warmth, and the fatigues of the day, and the familiar voices. The act of digestion plunges it in ecstasy, and faces, shadows, the lampshade, the tongues of flame dancing with a shower of stars in the fireplace—all take on a magical appearance of delight. Jean–Christophe lays his cheek on his plate, the better to enjoy all this happiness....

He is in his soft bed. How did he come there? He is overcome with weariness. The buzzing of the voices in the room and the visions of the day are intermingled in his mind. His father takes his violin; the shrill sweet sounds cry out complaining in the night. But the crowning joy is when his mother comes and takes Jean–Christophe's hands. He is drowsy, and, leaning over him, in a low voice she sings, as he asks, an, old song with words that have no meaning. His father thinks such music stupid, but Jean–Christophe never wearies of it. He holds his breath, and is between laughing and crying. His heart is intoxicated. He does not know where he is, and he is overflowing with tenderness. He throws his little arms round his mother's neck, and hugs her with all his strength. She says, laughing:

"You want to strangle me?"

He hugs her close. How he loves her! How he loves everything! Everybody, everything! All is good, all is beautiful.... He sleeps. The cricket on the hearth cheeps. His grandfather's tales, the great heroes, float by in the happy night.... To be a hero like them!... Yes, he will be that ... he is that.... Ah, how good it is to live!

* * * * *

What an abundance of strength, joy, pride, is in that little creature! What superfluous energy! His body and mind never cease to move; they are carried round and round breathlessly. Like a little salamander, he dances day and night in the flames. His is an unwearying enthusiasm finding its food in all things. A delicious dream, a bubbling well, a treasure of inexhaustible hope, a laugh, a song, unending drunkenness. Life does not hold him yet; always he escapes it. He swims in the infinite. How happy he is! He is made to be happy! There is nothing in him that does not believe in happiness, and does not cling to it with all his little strength and passion!...

Life will soon see to it that he is brought to reason.

II

L'alba vinceva l'ora, mattutina.
Che fuggia 'nnanzi, si che di lontano
Conobbi il tremolar della marina....
            Purgatorio, i.

The Kraffts came originally from Antwerp. Old Jean Michel had left the country as a result of a boyish freak, a violent quarrel, such as he had often had, for he was devilish pugnacious, and it had had an unfortunate ending. He settled down, almost fifty years ago, in the little town of the principality, with its red–pointed roofs and shady gardens, lying on the slope of a gentle hill, mirrored in the pale green eyes of *Vater Rhein*. An excellent musician, he had readily gained appreciation in a country of musicians. He had taken root there by marrying, forty years ago, Clara Sartorius, daughter of the Prince's *Kapellmeister*, whose duties he took over. Clara was a placid German with two passions—cooking and music. She had for her husband a veneration only equaled by that which she had for her father, Jean Michel no less admired his wife. They had lived together in perfect amity for fifteen years, and they had four children. Then Clara died; and Jean Michel bemoaned her loss, and then, five months later, married Ottilia Schuetz, a girl of twenty, with red cheeks, robust and smiling. After eight years of marriage she also died, but in that time she gave him seven children—eleven children in all, of whom only one had survived. Although he loved them much, all these bereavements had not shaken his good–humor. The greatest blow had been the death of Ottilia, three years ago, which had come to him at an age when it is difficult to start life again and to make a new home. But after a moment's confusion old Jean Michel regained his equilibrium, which no misfortune seemed able to disturb.

He was an affectionate man, but health was the strongest thing in him. He had a physical repugnance from sadness, and a need of gaiety, great gaiety, Flemish fashion—an enormous and childish laugh. Whatever might be his grief, he did not drink one drop the less, nor miss one bite at table, and his band never had one day off. Under his direction the Court orchestra won a small celebrity in the Rhine country, where Jean Michel had become legendary by reason of his athletic stature and his outbursts of anger. He could not master them, in spite of all his efforts, for the violent man was at bottom timid and afraid of compromising himself. He loved decorum and feared opinion. But his blood ran away with him. He used to see red, and he used to be the victim of sudden fits of crazy impatience, not only at rehearsals, but at the concerts, where once in the Prince's presence he had hurled his baton and had stamped about like a man possessed, as he apostrophized one of the musicians in a furious and stuttering voice. The Prince was amused, but the artists in question were rancorous against him. In vain did Jean Michel, ashamed of his outburst, try to pass it by immediately in exaggerated obsequiousness. On the next occasion he would break out again, and as this extreme irritability increased with age, in the end it made his position very difficult. He felt it himself, and one day, when his outbursts had all but caused the whole orchestra to strike, he sent in his resignation. He hoped that in consideration of his services they would make difficulties about accepting it, and would ask him to stay. There was nothing of the kind, and as he was too proud to go back on his offer, he left, brokenhearted, and crying out upon the ingratitude of mankind.

Since that time he had not known how to fill his days. He was more than seventy, but he was still vigorous, and he went on working and going up and down the town from morning to night, giving lessons, and entering into discussions, pronouncing perorations, and entering into everything. He was ingenious, and found all sorts of ways of keeping himself occupied. He began to repair musical instruments; he invented, experimented, and sometimes discovered improvements. He composed also, and set store by his compositions. He had once written a *Missa Solennis*, of which he used often to talk, and it was the glory of his family. It had cost him so much trouble that he had all but brought about a congestion of the mind in the writing of it. He tried to persuade himself that it was a work of genius, but he knew perfectly well with what emptiness of thought it had been written, and he dared not look again at the manuscript, because every time he did so he recognized in the phrases that he had thought to be his own, rags taken from other authors, painfully pieced together haphazard. It was a great sorrow to him. He had ideas sometimes which he thought admirable. He would run tremblingly to his table. Could he keep his inspiration this time? But hardly had he taken pen in hand than he found himself alone in silence, and all his efforts to call to life again the vanished voices ended only in bringing to his ears familiar melodies of Mendelssohn or Brahms.

"There are," says George Sand, "unhappy geniuses who lack the power of expression, and carry down to their graves the unknown region of their thoughts, as has said a member of that great family of illustrious mutes or stammerers—Geoffrey Saint–Hilaire." Old Jean Michel belonged to that family. He was no more successful in expressing himself in music than in words, and he always deceived himself. He would so much have loved to talk, to write, to be a great musician, an eloquent orator! It was his secret sore. He told no one of it, did not admit it to himself, tried not to think of it; but he did think of it, in spite of himself, and so there was the seed of death in his soul.

Poor old man! In nothing did he succeed in being absolutely himself. There were in him so many seeds of beauty and power, but they never put forth fruit; a profound and touching faith in the dignity of Art and the moral value of life, but it was nearly always translated in an emphatic and ridiculous fashion; so much noble pride, and in life an almost servile admiration of his superiors; so lofty a desire for independence, and, in fact, absolute docility; pretensions to strength of mind, and every conceivable superstition; a passion for heroism, real courage, and so much timidity!—a nature to stop by the wayside.

* * * * *

Jean Michel had transferred all his ambitions to his son, and at first Melchior had promised to realize them. From childhood he had shown great musical gifts. He learned with extraordinary facility, and quickly acquired as a violinist a virtuosity which for a long time made him the favorite, almost the idol, of the Court concerts. He played the piano and other instruments pleasantly. He was a fine talker, well, though a little heavily, built, and was of the type which passes in Germany for classic beauty; he had a large brow that expressed nothing, large regular features, and a curled beard—a Jupiter of the banks of the Rhine. Old Jean Michel enjoyed his son's success; he was ecstatic over the virtuoso's *tours de force*, he who had never been able properly to play any instrument. In truth, Melchior would have had no difficulty in expressing what he thought. The trouble was that he did not think; and he did not even bother about it. He had the soul of a mediocre comedian who takes pains with the inflexions of his voice without caring about what they express, and, with anxious vanity, watches their effect on his audience.

The odd thing was that, in spite of his constant anxiety about his stage pose, there was in him, as in Jean Michel, in spite of his timid respect for social conventions, a curious,

way at every turn, and he had never the least idea but that his parents were completely their own masters. It was a shock to his whole being when, for the first time, he perceived that among men there are those who command, and those who are commanded, and that his own people were not of the first class; it was the first crisis of his life.

It happened one afternoon. His mother had dressed him in his cleanest clothes, old clothes given to her which Louisa's ingenuity and patience had turned to account. He went to find her, as they had agreed, at the house in which she was working. He was abashed at the idea of entering alone. A footman was swaggering in the porch; he stopped the boy, and asked him patronizingly what he wanted. Jean-Christophe blushed, and murmured that he had come to see "Frau Krafft"—as he had been told to say.

"Frau Krafft? What do you want with Frau Krafft?" asked the footman, ironically emphasizing the word *Frau*, "Your mother? Go down there. You will find Louisa in the kitchen at the end of the passage."

He went, growing redder and redder. He was ashamed to hear his mother called familiarly *Louisa*. He was humiliated; he would have liked to run away down to his dear river, and the shelter of the brushwood where he used to tell himself stories.

In the kitchen he came upon a number of other servants, who greeted him with noisy exclamations. At the back, near the stove, his mother smiled at him with tender embarrassment. He ran to her, and clung to her skirts. She was wearing a white apron, and holding a wooden spoon. She made him more unhappy by trying to raise his chin so as to look in his face, and to make him hold out his hand to everybody there and say good-day to them. He would not; he turned to the wall and hid his face in his arms. Then gradually he gained courage, and peeped out of his hiding-place with merry bright eyes, which hid again every time any one looked at him. He stole looks at the people there. His mother looked busy and important, and he did not know her like that; she went from one saucepan to another, tasting, giving advice, in a sure voice explaining recipes, and the cook of the house listened respectfully. The boy's heart swelled with pride as he saw how much his mother was appreciated, and the great part that she played in this splendid room, adorned with magnificent objects of gold and silver.

Suddenly conversation ceased. The door opened. A lady entered with a rustling of the stuffs she was wearing. She cast a suspicious look about her. She was no longer young, and yet she was wearing a light dress with wide sleeves. She caught up her dress in her hand, so as not to brush against anything. It did not prevent her going to the stove and looking at the dishes, and even tasting them. When she raised her hand a little, her sleeve fell back, and her arm was bare to the elbow. Jean–Christophe thought this ugly and improper. How dryly and abruptly she spoke to Louisa! And how humbly Louisa replied! Jean–Christophe hated it. He hid away in his corner, so as not to be observed, but it was no use. The lady asked who the little boy might be. Louisa fetched him and presented him; she held his hands to prevent his hiding his face. And, though he wanted to break away and flee, Jean–Christophe felt instinctively that this time he must not resist. The lady looked at the boy's scared face, and at first she gave him a kindly, motherly smile. But then she resumed her patronizing air, and asked him about his behavior, and his piety, and put questions to him, to which he did not reply. She looked to see how his clothes fitted him, and Louisa eagerly declared that they were magnificent. She pulled down his waistcoat to remove the creases. Jean–Christophe wanted to cry, it fitted so tightly. He did not understand why his mother was giving thanks.

The lady took him by the hand and said that she would take him to her own children. Jean–Christophe cast a look of despair at his mother; but she smiled at the mistress so eagerly that he saw that there was nothing to hope for from her, and he followed his guide like a sheep that is led to the slaughter.

They came to a garden, where two cross–looking children, a boy and a girl, about the same age as Jean–Christophe, were apparently sulky with each other. Jean–Christophe's advent created a diversion. They came up to examine the new arrival. Jean–Christophe, left with the children by the lady, stood stock–still in a pathway, not daring to raise his eyes. The two others stood motionless a short distance away, and looked him up and down, nudged each other, and tittered. Finally, they made up their minds. They asked him who he was, whence he came, and what his father did. Jean–Christophe, turned to stone, made no reply; he was terrified almost to the point of tears, especially of the little girl, who had fair hair in plaits, a short skirt, and bare legs.

They began to play. Just as Jean–Christophe was beginning to be a little happier, the little boy stopped dead in front of him, and touching his coat, said:

"Hullo! That's mine!"

Jean-Christophe did not understand. Furious at this assertion that his coat belonged to some one else, he shook his head violently in denial.

"I know it all right," said the boy. "It's my old blue waistcoat. There's a spot on it."

And he put his finger on the spot. Then, going on with his inspection, he examined Jean-Christophe's feet, and asked what his mended-up shoes were made of. Jean-Christophe grew crimson. The little girl pouted and whispered to her brother—Jean-Christophe heard it—that it was a little poor boy. Jean-Christophe resented the word. He thought he would succeed In combating the insulting opinions, as he stammered in a choking voice that he was the son of Melchior Krafft. and that his mother was Louisa the cook. It seemed to him that this title was as good as any other, and he was right. But the two children, interested in the news, did not seem to esteem him any the more for it. On the contrary, they took on a patronizing tone. They asked him what he was going to be—a cook or a coachman. Jean-Christophe revolted. He felt an iciness steal into his heart.

Encouraged by his silence, the two rich children, who had conceived for the little poor boy one of those cruel and unreasoning antipathies which children have, tried various amusing ways of tormenting him, The little girl especially was implacable. She observed that Jean-Christophe could hardly run, because his clothes were so tight, and she conceived the subtle idea of making him jump. They made an obstacle of little seats, and insisted on Jean-Christophe clearing it. The wretched child dared not say what it was that prevented his jumping. He gathered himself together, hurled himself through, the air, and measured his length on the ground. They roared with laughter at him. He had to try again. Tears in his eyes, he made a desperate attempt, and this time succeeded in jumping. That did not satisfy his tormentors, who decided that the obstacle was not high enough, and they built it up until it became a regular break-neck affair. Jean-Christophe tried to rebel, and declared that he would not jump. Then the little girl called him a coward, and said that he was afraid. Jean-Christophe could not stand that, and, knowing that he must fall, he jumped, and fell. His feet caught in the obstacle; the whole thing toppled over with him. He grazed his hands and almost broke his head, and, as a crowning misfortune, his trousers tore at the knees and elsewhere. He was sick with shame; he heard the two children dancing with delight round him; he suffered horribly. He felt that they, despised and hated him. Why? Why? He would gladly have died! There is no more cruel suffering than that of a child who discovers for the first time the wickedness of others; he believes then that he is persecuted by the—whole world, and there is nothing to support him; there is nothing then—nothing!... Jean–Christophe tried to get up; the little boy pushed him down again; the little girl kicked him. He tried again, and they both jumped on him, and sat on his back and pressed his face down into the ground. Then rage seized him—it was too much. His hands were bruised, his fine coat was torn—a catastrophe for him!—shame, pain, revolt against the injustice of it, so many misfortunes all at once, plunged him in blind fury. He rose to his hands and knees, shook himself like a dog, and rolled his tormentors over; and when they returned to the assault he butted at them, head down, bowled over the little girl, and, with one blow of his fist, knocked the boy into the middle of a flower–bed.

They howled. The children ran into the house with piercing cries. Doors slammed, and cries of anger were heard. The lady ran out as quickly as her long dress would let her. Jean–Christophe saw her coming, and made no attempt to escape. He was terrified at what he had done; it was a thing unheard of, a crime; but he regretted nothing. He waited. He was lost. So much the better! He was reduced to despair.

The lady pounced on him. He felt her beat him. He heard her talking in a furious voice, a flood of words; but he could distinguish nothing. His little enemies had come back to see his shame, and screamed shrilly. There were servants—a babel of voices. To complete his downfall, Louisa, who had been summoned, appeared, and, instead of defending him, she began to scold him—she, too, without knowing anything—and bade him beg pardon. He refused angrily. She shook him, and dragged him by the hand to the lady and the children, and bade him go on his knees. But he stamped and roared, and bit his mother's hand. Finally, he escaped among the servants, who laughed.

He went away, his heart beating furiously, his face burning with anger and the slaps which he had received. He tried not to think, and he hurried along because he did not want to cry in the street. He wanted to be at home, so as to be able to find the comfort of tears. He choked; the blood beat in his head; he was at bursting–point.

Finally, he arrived; he ran up the old black staircase to his usual nook in the bay of a window above the river; he hurled himself into it breathlessly, and then there came a flood of tears. He did not know exactly why he was crying, but he had to cry; and when the first flood of them was done, he wept again because he wanted, with a sort of rage, to make himself suffer, as if he could in this way punish the others as well as himself. Then

35

he thought that his father must be coming home, and that his mother would tell him everything, and that his own miseries were by no means at an end. He resolved on flight, no matter whither, never to return.

Just as he was going downstairs, he bumped into his father, who was coming up.

"What are you doing, boy? Where are you going?" asked Melchior.

He did not reply.

"You are up to some folly. What have you done?"

Jean–Christophe held his peace.

"What have you done?" repeated Melchior. "Will you answer?"

The boy began to cry and Melchior to shout, vying with each other until they heard Louisa hurriedly coming up the stairs. She arrived, still upset. She began with violent reproach and further chastisement, in which Melchior joined as soon as he understood—and probably before—with blows that would have felled an ox. Both shouted; the boy roared. They ended by angry argument. All the time that he was beating his son, Melchior maintained that he was right, and that this was the sort of thing that one came by, by going out to service with people who thought they could do everything because they had money; and as she beat the child, Louisa shouted that her husband was a brute, that she would never let him touch the boy, and that he had really hurt him. Jean–Christophe was, in fact, bleeding a little from the nose, but he hardly gave a thought to it, and he was not in the least thankful to his mother for stopping it with a wet cloth, since she went on scolding him. In the end they pushed him away in a dark closet, and shut him up without any supper.

He heard them shouting at each other, and he did not know which of them he detested most. He thought it must be his mother, for he had never expected any such wickedness from her. All the misfortunes of the day overwhelmed him: all that he had suffered—the injustice of the children, the injustice of the lady, the injustice of his parents, and—this he felt like an open wound, without quite knowing why—the degradation of his parents, of whom he was so proud, before these evil and contemptible people. Such cowardice, of which for the first time he had become vaguely conscious, seemed ignoble to him. Everything was upset for him—his admiration for his own people, the religious respect with which they inspired him, his confidence in life, the simple need that he had of loving others and of being loved, his moral faith, blind but absolute. It was a complete cataclysm. He was crushed by brute force, without any means of defending himself or of ever again escaping. He choked. He thought himself on the point of death. All his body stiffened in desperate revolt. He beat with fists, feet, head, against the wall, howled, was seized with convulsions, and fell to the floor, hurting himself against the furniture.

His parents, running up, took him in their arms. They vied with each other now as to who should be the more tender with him. His mother undressed him, carried him to his bed, and sat by him and remained with him until he was calmer. But he did not yield one inch. He forgave her nothing, and pretended to be asleep to get rid of her. His mother seemed to him bad and cowardly. He had no suspicion of all the suffering that she had to go through in order to live and give a living to her family, and of what she had borne in taking sides against him.

After he had exhausted to the last drop the incredible store of tears that is in the eyes of a child, he felt somewhat comforted. He was tired and worn out, but his nerves were too much on stretch for him to sleep. The visions that had been with him floated before him again in his semi–torpor. Especially he saw again the little girl with her bright eyes and her turned–up, disdainful little nose, her hair hanging down to her shoulders, her bare legs and her childish, affected way of talking. He trembled, as it seemed to him that he could hear her voice. He remembered how stupid he had been with her, and he conceived a savage hatred for her. He did not pardon her for having brought him low, and was consumed with the desire to humiliate her and to make her weep. He sought means of doing this, but found none. There was no sign of her ever caring about him. But by way of consoling himself he supposed that everything was as he wished it to be. He supposed that he had become very powerful and famous, and decided that she was in love with him. Then he began to tell himself one of those absurd stories which in the end he would regard as more real than reality.

She was dying of love, but he spurned her. When he passed before her house she watched him pass, hiding behind the curtains, and he knew that she watched him, but he pretended to take no notice, and talked gaily. Even he left the country, and journeyed far to add to her anguish. He did great things. Here he introduced into his narrative fragments chosen from his grandfather's heroic tales, and all this time she was falling ill of grief. Her mother, that proud dame, came to beg of him: "My poor child is dying. I beg you to come!" He went. She was in her bed. Her face was pale and sunken. She held out her arms to him. She could not speak, but she took his hands and kissed them as she wept. Then he looked at her with marvelous kindness and tenderness. He bade her recover, and consented to let her love him. At this point of the story, when he amused himself by drawing out the coming together by repeating their gestures and words several times, sleep overcame him, and he slept and was consoled.

But when he opened his eyes it was day, and it no longer shone so lightly or so carelessly as its predecessor. There was a great change in the world. Jean–Christophe now knew the meaning of injustice.

* * * * *

There were now times of extremely straitened circumstances at home. They became more and more frequent. They lived meagerly then. No one was more sensible of it than Jean–Christophe. His father saw nothing. He was served first, and there was always enough for him. He talked noisily, and roared with laughter at his own jokes, and he never noticed his wife's glances as she gave a forced laugh, while she watched him helping himself. When he passed the dish it was more than half empty. Louisa helped the children—two potatoes each. When it came to Jean–Christophe's turn there were sometimes only three left, and his mother was not helped. He knew that beforehand; he had counted them before they came to him. Then he summoned up courage, and said carelessly:

"Only one, mother."

She was a little put out.

"Two, like the others."

"No, please; only one."

"Aren't you hungry?"

"No, I'm not very hungry."

But she, too, only took one, and they peeled them carefully, cut them up in little pieces, and tried to eat them as slowly as possible. His mother watched him. When he had finished:

"Come, take it!"

"No, mother."

"But you are ill?"

"I am not ill, but I have eaten enough."

Then his father would reproach him with being obstinate, and take the last potato for himself. But Jean-Christophe learned that trick, and he used to keep it on his plate for Ernest, his little brother, who was always hungry, and watched him out of the corner of his eyes from the beginning of dinner, and ended by asking:

"Aren't you going to eat it? Give it me, then, Jean-Christophe."

Oh, how Jean-Christophe detested his father, how he hated him for not thinking of them, or for not even dreaming that he was eating their share! He was so hungry that he hated him, and would gladly have told him so; but he thought in his pride that he had no right, since he could not earn his own living. His father had earned the bread that he took. He himself was good for nothing; he was a burden on everybody; he had no right to talk. Later on he would talk—if there were any later on. Oh, he would die of hunger first!...

He suffered more than another child would have done from these cruel fasts. His robust stomach was in agony. Sometimes he trembled because of it; his head ached. There was a hole in his chest—a hole which turned and widened, as if a gimlet were being twisted in it. But he did not complain. He felt his mother's eyes upon him, and assumed an expression of indifference. Louisa, with a clutching at her heart, understood vaguely that her little boy was denying himself so that the others might have more. She rejected the idea, but always returned to it. She dared not investigate it or ask Jean-Christophe if it were true, for, if it were true, what could she do? She had been used to privation since her childhood. What is the use of complaining when there is nothing to be done? She never suspected, indeed—she, with her frail health and small needs—that the boy might suffer more than herself. She did not say anything, but once or twice, when the others were gone, the children to the street, Melchior about his business, she asked her eldest son to stay to do her some small service. Jean-Christophe would hold her skein while she unwound it. Suddenly she would throw everything away, and draw him passionately to her. She would take him on her knees, although he was quite heavy, and would hug and hug him. He would fling his arms round her neck, and the two of them would weep desperately, embracing each other.

"My poor little boy!..."

"Mother, mother!..."

They said no more, but they understood each other.

* * * * *

It was some time before Jean-Christophe realized that his father drank. Melchior's intemperance did not—at least, in the beginning—exceed tolerable limits. It was not brutish. It showed itself rather by wild outbursts of happiness. He used to make foolish remarks, and sing loudly for hours together as he drummed on the table, and sometimes he insisted on dancing with Louisa and the children. Jean-Christophe saw that his mother looked sad. She would shrink back and bend her face over her work; she avoided the drunkard's eyes, and used to try gently to quiet him when he said coarse things that made her blush. But Jean-Christophe did not understand, and he was in such need of gaiety that these noisy home-comings of his father were almost a festival to him. The house was melancholy, and these follies were a relaxation for him. He used to laugh heartily at Melchior's crazy antics and stupid jokes; he sang and danced with him; and he was put out when his mother in an angry voice ordered him to cease. How could it be wrong, since his father did it? Although his ever keen observation, which never forgot anything it had seen, told him that there were in his father's behavior several things which did not accord with his childish and imperious sense of justice, yet he continued to admire him. A child has so much need of an object of admiration! Doubtless it is one of the eternal forms of self-love. When a man is, or knows himself to be, too weak to accomplish his desires and satisfy his pride, as a child he transfers them to his parents, or, as a man who has failed, he transfers them to his children. They are, or shall be, all that he dreamed of being—his champions, his avengers—and in this proud abdication in their favor, love and egoism are mingled so forcefully and yet so gently as to bring him keen delight. Jean–Christophe forgot all his grudges against his father, and cast about to find reasons for admiring him. He admired his figure, his strong arms, his voice, his laugh, his gaiety, and he shone with pride when he heard praise of his father's talents as a virtuoso, or when Melchior himself recited with some amplification the eulogies he had received. He believed in his father's boasts, and looked upon him as a genius, as one of his grandfather's heroes.

One evening about seven o'clock he was alone in the house. His little brothers had gone out with Jean Michel. Louisa was washing the linen in the river. The door opened, and Melchior plunged in. He was hatless and disheveled. He cut a sort of caper to cross the threshold, and then plumped down in a chair by the table. Jean–Christophe began to laugh, thinking it was a part of one of the usual buffooneries, and he approached him. But as soon as he looked more closely at him the desire to laugh left him. Melchior sat there with his arms hanging, and looking straight in front of him, seeing nothing, with his eyes blinking. His face was crimson, his mouth was open, and from it there gurgled every now and then a silly laugh. Jean–Christophe stood stock–still. He thought at first that his father was joking, but when he saw that he did not budge he was panic–stricken.

"Papa, papa!" he cried.

Melchior went on gobbling like a fowl. Jean–Christophe took him by the arm in despair, and shook him with all his strength.

"Papa, dear papa, answer me, please, please!"

Melchior's body shook like a boneless thing, and all but fell. His head flopped towards Jean–Christophe; he looked at him and babbled incoherently and irritably. When Jean–Christophe's eyes met those clouded eyes he was seized with panic terror. He ran away to the other end of the room, and threw himself on his knees by the bed, and buried his face in the clothes. He remained so for some time. Melchior swung heavily on the chair, sniggering. Jean–Christophe stopped his ears, so as not to hear him, and trembled. What was happening within him was inexpressible. It was a terrible upheaval—terror, sorrow, as though for some one dead, some one dear and honored.

41

No one came; they were left alone. Night fell, and Jean–Christophe's fear grew as the minutes passed. He could not help listening, and his blood froze as he heard the voice that he did not recognize. The silence made it all the more terrifying; the limping clock beat time for the senseless babbling. He could bear it no longer; he wished to fly. But he had, to pass his father to get out, and Jean–Christophe shuddered, at the idea of seeing those eyes again; it seemed to him that he must die if he did. He tried to creep on hands and knees to the door of the room. He could not breathe; he would not look; he stopped at the least movement from Melchior, whose feet he could see under the table. One of the drunken man's legs trembled. Jean–Christophe reached the door. With one trembling hand he pushed the handle, but in his terror he let go. It shut to again. Melchior turned to look. The chair on which he was balanced toppled over; he fell down with a crash. Jean–Christophe in his terror had no strength left for flight. He remained glued to the wall, looking at his father stretched there at his feet, and he cried for help.

His fall sobered Melchior a little. He cursed and swore, and thumped on the chair that had played him such a trick. He tried vainly to get up, and then did manage to sit up with his back resting against the table, and he recognized his surroundings. He saw Jean–Christophe crying; he called him. Jean–Christophe wanted to run away; he could not stir. Melchior called him again, and as the child did not come, he swore angrily. Jean–Christophe went near him, trembling in every limb. Melchior drew the boy near him, and made him sit on his knees. He began by pulling his ears, and in a thick, stuttering voice delivered a homily on the respect due from a son to his father. Then he went off suddenly on a new train of thought, and made him jump in his arms while he rattled off silly jokes. He wriggled with laughter. From that he passed immediately to melancholy ideas. He commiserated the boy and himself; he hugged him so that he was like to choke, covered him with kisses and tears, and finally rocked him in his arms, intoning the *De Profundis*. Jean–Christophe made no effort to break loose; he was frozen with horror. Stifled against his father's bosom, feeling his breath hiccoughing and smelling of wine upon his face, wet with his kisses and repulsive tears, he was in an agony of fear and disgust. He would have screamed, but no sound would come from his lips. He remained in this horrible condition for an age, as it seemed to him, until the door opened, and Louisa came in with a basket of linen on her arm. She gave a cry, let the basket fall, rushed at Jean–Christophe, and with a violence which seemed incredible in her she wrenched Melchior's arm, crying:

"Drunken, drunken wretch!"

Her eyes flashed with anger.

Jean–Christophe thought his father was going to kill her. But Melchior was so startled by the threatening appearance of his wife that he made no reply, and began to weep. He rolled on the floor; he beat his head against the furniture, and said that she was right, that he was a drunkard, that he brought misery upon his family, and was ruining his poor children, and wished he were dead. Louisa had contemptuously turned her back on him. She carried Jean–Christophe into the next room, and caressed him and tried to comfort him. The boy went on trembling, and did not answer his mother's questions; then he burst out sobbing. Louisa bathed his face with water. She kissed him, and used tender words, and wept with him. In the end they were both comforted. She knelt, and made him kneel by her side. They prayed to God to cure father of his disgusting habit, and make him the kind, good man that he used to be. Louisa put the child to bed. He wanted her to stay by his bedside and hold his hand. Louisa spent part of the night sitting on Jean–Christophe's bed. He was feverish. The drunken man snored on the floor.

Some time after that, one day at school, when Jean–Christophe was spending his time watching the flies on the ceiling, and thumping his neighbors, to make them fall off the form, the schoolmaster, who had taken a dislike to him, because he was always fidgeting and laughing, and would never learn anything, made an unhappy allusion. Jean–Christophe had fallen down himself, and the schoolmaster said he seemed to be like to follow brilliantly in the footsteps of a certain well–known person. All the boys burst out laughing, and some of them took upon themselves to point the allusion with comment both lucid and vigorous. Jean–Christophe got up, livid with shame, seized his ink–pot, and hurled it with all his strength at the nearest boy whom he saw laughing. The schoolmaster fell on him and beat him. He was thrashed, made to kneel, and set to do an enormous imposition.

He went home, pale and storming, though he said never a word. He declared frigidly that he would not go to school again. They paid no attention to what he said. Next morning, when his mother reminded him that it was time to go, he replied quietly that he had said that he was not going any more. In rain Louisa begged and screamed and threatened; it was no use. He stayed sitting in his corner, obstinate. Melchior thrashed him. He howled, but every time they bade him go after the thrashing was over he replied angrily, "No!" They asked him at least to say why. He clenched his teeth, and would not. Melchior took hold of him, carried him to school, and gave him into the master's charge. They set him on his form, and he began methodically to break everything within reach—his inkstand, his pen. He tore up his copy-book and lesson-book, all quite openly, with his eye on the schoolmaster, provocative. They shut him up in a dark room. A few moments later the schoolmaster found him with his handkerchief tied round his neck, tugging with all his strength at the two ends of it. He was trying to strangle himself.

They had to send him back.

* * * * *

Jean-Christophe was impervious to sickness. He had inherited from his father and grandfather their robust constitutions. They were not mollycoddles in that family; well or ill, they never worried, and nothing could bring about any change in the habits of the two Kraffts, father and son. They went out winter and summer, in all weathers, and stayed for hours together out in rain or sun, sometimes bareheaded and with their coats open, from carelessness or bravado, and walked for miles without being tired, and they looked with pity and disdain upon poor Louisa, who never said anything, but had to stop. She would go pale, and her legs would swell, and her heart would thump. Jean-Christophe was not far from sharing the scorn of his mother; he did not understand people being ill. When he fell, or knocked himself, or cut himself, or burned himself, he did not cry; but he was angry with the thing that had injured him. His father's brutalities and the roughness of his little playmates, the urchins of the street, with whom he used to fight, hardened him. He was not afraid of blows, and more than once he returned home with bleeding nose and bruised forehead. One day he had to be wrenched away, almost suffocated, from one of these fierce tussles in which he had bowled over his adversary, who was savagely banging his head on the ground. That seemed natural enough to him, for he was prepared to do unto others as they did unto himself.

And yet he was afraid of all sorts of things, and although no one knew it—for he was very proud—nothing brought him go much suffering during a part of his childhood as these same terrors. For two or three years especially they gnawed at him like a disease.

He was afraid of the mysterious something that lurks in darkness—evil powers that seemed to lie in wait for his life, the roaring of monsters which fearfully haunt the mind of every child and appear in everything that he sees, the relic perhaps of a form long dead, hallucinations of the first days after emerging from chaos, from the fearful slumber in his mother's womb, from the awakening of the larva from the depths of matter.

He was afraid of the garret door. It opened on to the stairs, and was almost always ajar. When he had to pass it he felt his heart heating; he would spring forward and jump by it without looking. It seemed to him that there was some one or something behind it. When it was closed he heard distinctly something moving behind it. That was not surprising, for there were large rats; but he imagined a monster, with rattling bones, and flesh hanging in rags, a horse's head, horrible and terrifying eyes, shapeless. He did not want to think of it, but did so in spite of himself. With trembling hand he would make sure that the door was locked; but that did not keep him from turning round ten times as he went downstairs.

He was afraid of the night outside. Sometimes he used to stay late with his grandfather, or was sent out in the evening on some errand. Old Krafft lived a little outside the town in the last house on the Cologne road. Between the house and the first lighted windows of the town there was a distance of two or three hundred yards, which seemed three times as long to Jean-Christophe. There were places where the road twisted and it was impossible to see anything. The country was deserted in the evening, the earth grew black, and the sky was awfully pale. When he came out from the hedges that lined the road, and climbed up the slope, he could still see a yellowish gleam on the horizon, but it gave no light, and was more oppressive than the night; it made the darkness only darker; it was a deathly light. The clouds came down almost to earth. The hedges grew enormous and moved. The gaunt trees were like grotesque old men. The sides of the wood were stark white. The darkness moved. There were dwarfs sitting in the ditches, lights in the grass, fearful flying things in the air, shrill cries of insects coming from nowhere. Jean-Christophe was always in anguish, expecting some fearsome or strange putting forth of Nature. He would run, with his heart leaping in his bosom.

When he saw the light in his grandfather's room he would gain confidence. But worst of all was when old Krafft was not at home. That was most terrifying. The old house, lost in the country, frightened the boy even in daylight. He forgot his fears when his grandfather was there, but sometimes the old man would leave him alone, and go out without warning him. Jean-Christophe did not mind that. The room was quiet. Everything in it was familiar and kindly. There was a great white wooden bedstead, by the bedside was a great Bible on a shelf, artificial flowers were on the mantelpiece, with photographs of the old man's two wives and eleven children—and at the bottom of each photograph he had written the date of birth and death—on the walls were framed texts and vile chromolithographs of Mozart and Beethoven. A little piano stood in one corner, a great violoncello in another; rows of books higgledy–piggledy, pipes, and in the window pots of geraniums. It was like being surrounded with friends. The old man could be heard moving about in the next room, and planing or hammering, and talking to himself, calling himself an idiot, or singing in a loud voice, improvising a *potpourri* of scraps of chants and sentimental *Lieder*, warlike marches, and drinking songs. Here was shelter and refuge. Jean–Christophe would sit in the great armchair by the window, with a book on his knees, bending over the pictures and losing himself in them. The day would die down, his eyes would grow weary, and then he would look no more, and fall into vague dreaming. The wheels of a cart would rumble by along the road, a cow would moo in the fields; the bells of the town, weary and sleepy, would ring the evening Angelus. Vague desires, happy presentiments, would awake in the heart of the dreaming child.

Suddenly Jean–Christophe would awake, filled with dull uneasiness. He would raise his eyes—night! He would listen—silence! His grandfather had just gone out. He shuddered. He leaned out of the window to try to see him. The road was deserted; things began to take on a threatening aspect. Oh God! If *that* should be coming! What? He could not tell. The fearful thing. The doors were not properly shut. The wooden stairs creaked as under a footstep. The boy leaped up, dragged the armchair, the two chairs and the table, to the most remote corner of the room; he made a barrier of them; the armchair against the wall, a chair to the right, a chair to the left, and the table in front of him. In the middle he planted a pair of steps, and, perched on top with his book and other books, like provisions against a siege, he breathed again, having decided in his childish imagination that the enemy could not pass the barrier—that was not to be allowed.

But the enemy would creep forth, even from his book. Among the old books which the old man had picked up were some with pictures which made a profound impression on the child: they attracted and yet terrified him. There were fantastic visions—temptations of St. Anthony—in which skeletons of birds hung in bottles, and thousands of eggs writhe like worms in disemboweled frogs, and heads walk on feet, and asses play trumpets, and household utensils and corpses of animals walk gravely, wrapped in great cloths, bowing like old ladies. Jean–Christophe was horrified by them, but always returned to them, drawn on by disgust. He would look at them for a long time, and every now and then look furtively about him to see what was stirring in the folds of the curtains. A picture of a flayed man in an anatomy book was still more horrible to him. He trembled as he turned the page when he came to the place where it was in the book. This shapeless medley was grimly etched for him. The creative power inherent in every child's mind filled out the meagerness of the setting of them. He saw no difference between the daubs and the reality. At night they had an even more powerful influence over his dreams than the living things that he saw during the day.

He was afraid to sleep. For several years nightmares poisoned his rest. He wandered in cellars, and through the manhole saw the grinning flayed man entering. He was alone in a room, and he heard a stealthy footstep in the corridor; he hurled himself against the door to close it, and was just in time to hold the handle; but it was turned from the outside; he could not turn the key, his strength left him, and he cried for help. He was with his family, and suddenly their faces changed; they did crazy things. He was reading quietly, and he felt that an invisible being was all *round* him. He tried to fly, but felt himself bound. He tried to cry out, but he was gagged. A loathsome grip was about his neck. He awoke, suffocating, and with his teeth chattering; and he went on trembling long after he was awake; he could not be rid of his agony.

The roam in which he slept was a hole without door or windows; an old curtain hung up by a curtain–rod over the entrance was all that separated it from the room of his father and mother. The thick air stifled him. His brother, who slept in the same bed, used to kick him. His head burned, and he was a prey to a sort of hallucination in which all the little troubles of the day reappeared infinitely magnified. In this state of nervous tension, bordering on delirium, the least shock was an agony to him. The creaking of a plank terrified him. His father's breathing took on fantastic proportions. It seemed to be no longer a human breathing, and the monstrous sound was horrible to him; it seemed to him that there must be a beast sleeping there. The night crushed him; it would never end; it must always be so; he was lying there for months and months. He gasped for breath; he half raised himself on his bed, sat up, dried his sweating face with his shirt–sleeve. Sometimes he nudged his brother Rodolphe to wake him up; but Rodolphe moaned, drew away from him the rest of the bedclothes, and went on sleeping.

So he stayed in feverish agony until a pale beam of light appeared on the floor below the curtain. This timorous paleness of the distant dawn suddenly brought him peace. He felt the light gliding into the room, when it was still impossible to distinguish it from darkness. Then his fever would die down, his blood would grow calm, like a flooded river returning to its bed; an even warmth would flow through all his body, and his eyes, burning from sleeplessness, would close in spite of himself.

47

In the evening it was terrible to him to see the approach of the hour of sleep. He vowed that he would not give way to it, to watch the whole night through, fearing his nightmares, But in the end weariness always overcame him, and it was always when he was least on his guard that the monsters returned.

Fearful night! So sweet to most children, so terrible to some!... He was afraid to sleep. He was afraid of not sleeping. Waking or sleeping, he was surrounded by monstrous shapes, the phantoms of his own brain, the larvae floating in the half–day and twilight of childhood, as in the dark chiaroscuro of sickness.

But these fancied terrors were soon to be blotted out in the great Fear—that which is in the hearts of all men; that Fear which Wisdom does in vain preen itself on forgetting or denying—Death.

* * * * *

One day when he was rummaging in a cupboard, he came upon several things that he did not know—a child's frock and a striped bonnet. He took them in triumph to his mother, who, instead of smiling at him, looked vexed, and bade him, take them back to the place where he had found them. When he hesitated to obey, and asked her why, she snatched them from him without reply, and put them on a shelf where he could not reach them. Roused to curiosity, he plied her with questions. At last she told him that there had been a little brother who had died before Jean–Christophe came into the world. He was taken aback—he had never heard tell of him. He was silent for a moment, and then tried to find out more. His mother seemed to be lost in thought; but she told him that the little brother was called Jean–Christophe like himself, but was more sensible. He put more questions to her, but she would not reply readily. She told him only that his brother was in Heaven, and was praying for them all. Jean–Christophe could get no more out of her; she bade him be quiet, and to let her go on with her work. She seemed to be absorbed in her sewing; she looked anxious, and did not raise her eyes. But after some time she looked at him where he was in the corner, whither he had retired to sulk, began to smile, and told him to go and play outside.

These scraps of conversation profoundly agitated Jean–Christophe. There had been a child, a little boy, belonging to his mother, like himself, bearing the same name, almost exactly the same, and he was dead! Dead! He did not exactly know what that was, but it was something terrible. And they never talked of this other Jean–Christophe; he was quite forgotten. It would be the same with him if he were to die? This thought was with him still in the evening at table with his family, when he saw them all laughing and talking of trifles. So, then, it was possible that they would be gay after he was dead! Oh! he never would have believed that his mother could be selfish enough to laugh after the death of her little boy! He hated them all. He wanted to weep for himself, for his own death, in advance. At the same time he wanted to ask a whole heap of questions, but he dared not; he remembered the voice in which his mother had bid him be quiet. At last he could contain himself no longer, and one night when he had gone to bed, and Louisa came to kiss him, he asked:

"Mother, did he sleep in my bed?"

The poor woman trembled, and, trying to take on an indifferent tone of voice, she asked:

"Who?"

"The little boy who is dead," said Jean–Christophe in a whisper.

His mother clutched him with her hands.

"Be quiet—quiet," she said.

Her voice trembled. Jean–Christophe, whose head was leaning against her bosom, heard her heart beating. There was a moment of silence, then she said:

"You must never talk of that, my dear.... Go to sleep.... No, it was not his bed."

She kissed him. He thought he felt her cheek wet against his. He wished he could have been sure of it. He was a little comforted. There was grief in her then! Then he doubted it again the next moment, when he heard her in the next room talking in a quiet, ordinary voice. Which was true—that or what had just been? He turned about for long in his bed without finding any answer. He wanted his mother to suffer; not that he also did not suffer in the knowledge that she was sad, but it would have done him so much good, in spite of everything! He would have felt himself less alone. He slept, and next day thought no more of it.

Some weeks afterwards one of the urchins with whom he played in the street did not come at the usual time. One of them said that he was ill, and they got used to not seeing him in their games. It was explained, it was quite simple. One evening Jean–Christophe had gone to bed; it was early, and from the recess in which his bed was, he saw the light in the room. There was a knock at the door. A neighbor had come to have a chat. He listened absently, telling himself stories as usual. The words of their talk did not reach him. Suddenly he heard the neighbor say: "He is dead." His blood stopped, for he had understood who was dead. He listened and held his breath. His parents cried out. Melchior's booming voice said:

"Jean–Christophe, do you hear? Poor Fritz is dead."

Jean–Christophe made an effort, and replied quietly:

"Yes, papa."

His bosom was drawn tight as in a vise.

Melchior went on:

"'Yes, papa.' Is that all you say? You are not grieved by it."

Louisa, who understood the child, said:

"'Ssh! Let him sleep!"

And they talked in whispers. But Jean–Christophe, pricking his ears, gathered all the details of illness—typhoid fever, cold baths, delirium, the parents' grief. He could not breathe, a lump in his throat choked him. He shuddered. All these horrible things took shape in his mind. Above all, he gleaned that the disease was contagious—that is, that he also might die in the same way—and terror froze him, for he remembered that he had shaken hands with Fritz the last time he had seen him, and that very day had gone past the house. But he made no sound, so as to avoid having to talk, and when his father, after the neighbor had gone, asked him: "Jean–Christophe, are you asleep?" he did not reply. He heard Melchior saying to Louisa:

"The boy has no heart."

Louisa did not reply, but a moment later she came and gently raised the curtain and looked at the little bed. Jean–Christophe only just had time to close his eyes and imitate the regular breathing which his brothers made when they were asleep. Louisa went away on tip–toe. And yet how he wanted to keep her! How he wanted to tell her that he was afraid, and to ask her to save him, or at least to comfort him! But he was afraid of their laughing at him, and treating him as a coward; and besides, he knew only too well that nothing that they might say would be any good. And for hours he lay there in agony, thinking that he felt the disease creeping over him, and pains in his head, a stricture of the heart, and thinking in terror: "It is the end. I am ill. I am going to die. I am going to die!"... Once he sat up in his bed and called to his mother in a low voice; but they were asleep, and he dared not wake them.

From that time on his childhood was poisoned by the idea of death. His nerves delivered him up to all sorts of little baseless sicknesses, to depression, to sudden transports, and fits of choking. His imagination ran riot with these troubles, and thought it saw in all of them the murderous beast which was to rob him of his life. How many times he suffered agonies, with his mother sitting only a few yards away from him, and she guessing nothing! For in his cowardice he was brave enough to conceal all his terror in a strange jumble of feeling—pride in not turning to others, shame of being afraid, and the scrupulousness of a tenderness which forbade him to trouble his mother. But he never ceased to think: "This time I am ill. I am seriously ill. It is diphtheria...." He had chanced on the word "diphtheria."... "Dear God! not this time!..."

He had religious ideas: he loved to believe what his mother had told, him, that after death the soul ascended to the Lord, and if it were pious entered into the garden of paradise. But the idea of this journey rather frightened than attracted him. He was not at all envious of the children whom God, as a recompense, according to his mother, took in their sleep and called to Him without having made them suffer. He trembled, as he went to sleep, for fear that God should indulge this whimsy at his expense. It must be terrible to be taken suddenly from the warmth of one's bed and dragged through the void into the presence of God. He imagined God as an enormous sun, with a voice of thunder. How it must hurt! It must barn the eyes, ears—all one's soul! Then, God could punish—you never know.... And besides, that did not prevent all the other horrors which he did not know very well, though he could guess them from what he had heard—your body in a box, all alone at the bottom of a hole, lost in the crowd of those revolting cemeteries to which he was taken to pray.... God! God! How sad! how sad!...

And yet it was not exactly joyous to live, and be hungry, and see your father drunk, and to be beaten, to suffer in so many ways from the wickedness of other children, from the insulting pity of grown–up persons, and to be understood by no one, not even by your mother. Everybody humiliates you, no one loves you. You are alone—alone, and matter so little! Yes; but it was just this that made him want to live. He felt in himself a surging power of wrath. A strange thing, that power! It could do nothing yet; it was as though it were afar off and gagged, swaddled, paralyzed; he had no idea what it wanted, what, later on, it would be. But it was in him; he was sure of it; he felt it stirring and crying out. To-morrow—to-morrow, what a voyage he would take! He had a savage desire to live, to punish the wicked, to do great things. "Oh! but how I will live when I am ..." he pondered a little—"when I am eighteen!" Sometimes he put it at twenty-one; that was the extreme limit. He thought that was enough for the domination of the world. He thought of the heroes dearest to him—of Napoleon, and of that other more remote hero, whom he preferred, Alexander the Great. Surely he would be like them if only he lived for another twelve—ten years. He never thought of pitying those who died at thirty. They were old; they had lived their lives; it was their fault if they hat failed. But to die now ... despair! Too terrible to pass while yet a little child, and forever to be in the minds of men a little boy whom everybody thinks he has the right to scold! He wept with rage at the thought, as though he were already dead.

This agony of death tortured his childish years—corrected only by disgust with all life and the sadness of his own.

    * * * * *

It was in the midst of these gloomy shadows, in the stifling night that every moment seemed to intensify about him, that there began to shine, like a star lost in the dark abysm of space, the light which was to illuminate his life: divine music....

His grandfather gave the children an old piano, which one of his clients, anxious to be rid of it, had asked him to take. His patient ingenuity had almost put it in order. The present had not been very well received. Louisa thought her room already too small, without filling it up any more; and Melchior said that Jean Michel had not ruined himself over it:

just firewood. Only Jean–Christophe was glad of it without exactly knowing why. It seemed to him a magic box, full of marvelous stories, just like the ones in the fairy–book—a volume of the "Thousand and One Nights"—which his grandfather read to him sometimes to their mutual delight. He had heard his father try the piano on the day of its arrival, and draw from it a little rain of arpeggios like the drops that a puff of wind shakes from the wet branches of a tree after a shower. He clapped his hands, and cried "Encore!" but Melchior scornfully closed the piano, saying that it was worthless. Jean–Christophe did not insist, but after that he was always hovering about the instrument. As soon as no one was near he would raise the lid, and softly press down a key, just as if he were moving with his finger the living shell of some great insect; he wanted to push out the creature that was locked up in it. Sometimes in his haste he would strike too hard, and then his mother would cry out, "Will you not be quiet? Don't go touching everything!" or else he would pinch himself cruelly in closing the piano, and make piteous faces as he sucked his bruised fingers....

Now his greatest joy is when his mother is gone out for a day's service, or to pay some visit in the town. He listens as she goes down the stairs, and into the street, and away. He is alone. He opens the piano, and brings up a chair, and perches on it. His shoulders just about reach the keyboard; it is enough for what he wants. Why does he wait until he is alone? No one would prevent his playing so long as he did not make too much noise. But he is ashamed before the others, and dare not. And then they talk and move about: that spoils his pleasure. It is so much more beautiful when he is alone! Jean–Christophe holds his breath so that the silence may be even greater, and also because he is a little excited, as though he were going to let off a gun. His heart beats as he lays his finger on the key; sometimes he lifts his finger after he has the key half pressed down, and lays it on another. Does he know what will come out of it, more than what will come out of the other? Suddenly a sound issues from it; there are deep sounds and high sounds, some tinkling, some roaring. The child listens to them one by one as they die away and finally cease to be; they hover in the air like bells heard far off, coming near in the wind, and then going away again; then when you listen you hear in the distance other voices, different, joining in and droning like flying insects; they seem to call to you, to draw you away farther—farther and farther into the mysterious regions, where they dive down and are lost.... They are gone!... No; still they murmur.... A little beating of wings.... How strange it all is! They are like spirits. How is it that they are so obedient? how is it that they are held captive in this old box? But best of all is when you lay two fingers on two keys at once. Then you never know exactly what will happen. Sometimes the two spirits are hostile; they are angry with each other, and fight; and hate each other, and buzz testily. Then voices are raised; they cry out, angrily, now sorrowfully. Jean–Christophe adores that; it is as though there were monsters chained up, biting at their fetters, beating against the bars of their prison; they are like to break them, and burst out like the monsters in the fairy–book—the genii imprisoned in the Arab bottles under the seal of Solomon. Others flatter you; they try to cajole you, but you feel that they only want to bite, that they are hot and fevered. Jean–Christophe does not know what they want, but they lure him and disturb him; they make him almost blush. And sometimes there are notes that love each other; sounds embrace, as people do with their arms when they kiss: they are gracious and sweet. These are the good spirits; their faces are smiling, and there are no lines in them; they love little Jean–Christophe, and little Jean–Christophe loves them. Tears come to his eyes as he hears them, and he is never weary of calling them up. They are his friends, his dear, tender friends....

So the child journeys through the forest of sounds, and round him he is conscious of thousands of forces lying in wait for him, and calling to him to caress or devour him....

One day Melchior came upon him thus. He made him jump with fear at the sound of his great voice. Jean–Christophe, thinking he was doing wrong, quickly put his hands up to his ears to ward off the blows he feared. But Melchior did not scold him, strange to say; he was in a good temper, and laughed.

"You like that, boy?" he asked, patting his head kindly. "Would you like me to teach you to play it?"

Would he like!... Delighted, he murmured: "Yes." The two of them sat down at the piano, Jean–Christophe perched this time on a pile of big books, and very attentively he took his first lesson. He learned first of all that the buzzing spirits have strange names, like Chinese names, of one syllable, or even of one letter. He was astonished; he imagined them to be different from that: beautiful, caressing names, like the princesses in the fairy stories. He did not like the familiarity with which his father talked of them. Again, when Melchior evoked them they were not the same; they seemed to become indifferent as they rolled out from under his fingers. But Jean–Christophe was glad to learn about the relationships between them, their hierarchy, the scales, which were like a King commanding an army, or like a band of negroes marching in single file. He was surprised to see that each soldier, or each negro, could become a monarch in his turn, or the head of a similar band, and that it was possible to summon whole battalions from one end to the other of the keyboard. It amused him to hold the thread which made them march. But it was a small thing compared with what he had seen at first; his enchanted forest was lost. However, he set himself to learn, for it was not tiresome, and he was surprised at his father's patience. Melchior did not weary of it either; he made him begin the same thing over again ten times. Jean-Christophe did not understand why he should take so much trouble; his father loved him, then? That was good! The boy worked away; his heart was filled with gratitude.

He would have been less docile had he known what thoughts were springing into being in his father's head.

* * * * *

From that day on Melchior took him to the house of a neighbor, where three times a week there was chamber music. Melchior played first violin, Jean Michel the violoncello. The other two were a bank-clerk and the old watchmaker of the *Schillerstrasse*. Every now and then the chemist joined them with his flute. They began at five, and went on till nine. Between each piece they drank beer. Neighbors used to come in and out, and listen without a word, leaning against the wall, and nodding their heads, and beating time with their feet, and filling the room with clouds of tobacco-smoke. Page followed page, piece followed piece, but the patience of the musicians was never exhausted. They did not speak; they were all attention; their brows were knit, and from time to time they grunted with pleasure, but for the rest they were perfectly incapable not only of expressing, but even of feeling, the beauty of what they played. They played neither very accurately nor in good time, but they never went off the rails, and followed faithfully the marked changes of tone. They had that musical facility which is easily satisfied, that mediocre perfection which, is so plentiful in the race which is said to be the most musical in the world. They had also that great appetite which does not stickle for the quality of its food, so only there be quantity—that healthy appetite to which all music is good, and the more substantial the better—it sees no difference between Brahms and Beethoven, or between the works of the same master, between an empty concerto and a moving sonata, because they are fashioned of the same stuff.

Jean-Christophe sat apart in a corner, which was his own, behind the piano. No one could disturb him there, for to reach it he had to go on all fours. It was half dark there, and the boy had just room to lie on the floor if he huddled up. The smoke of the tobacco filled his eyes and throat: dust, too; there were large flakes of it like sheepskin, but he did not mind that, and listened gravely, squatting there Turkish fashion, and widening the holes in the cloth of the piano with his dirty little fingers. He did not like everything that they played; but nothing that they played bored him, and he never tried to formulate his opinions, for he thought himself too small to know anything. Only some music sent him to sleep, some woke him up; it was never disagreeable to him. Without his knowing it, it was nearly always good music that excited him. Sure of not being seen, he made faces, he wrinkled his nose, ground his teeth, or stuck out his tongue; his eyes flashed with anger or drooped languidly; he moved his arms and legs with a defiant and valiant air; he wanted to march, to lunge out, to pulverize the world. He fidgeted so much that in the end a head would peer over the piano, and say: "Hullo, boy, are you mad? Leave the piano.... Take your hand away, or I'll pull your ears!" And that made him crestfallen and angry. Why did they want to spoil his pleasure? He was not doing any harm. Must he always be tormented! His father chimed in. They chid him for making a noise, and said that he did not like music. And in the end he believed it. These honest citizens grinding out concertos would have been astonished if they had been told that the only person in the company who really felt the music was the little boy.

If they wanted him to keep quiet, why did they play airs which make you march? In those pages were rearing horses, swords, war–cries, the pride of triumph; and they wanted him, like them, to do no more than wag his head and beat time with his feet! They had only to play placid dreams or some of those chattering pages which talk so much and say nothing. There are plenty of them, for example, like that piece of Goldmark's, of which the old watchmaker had just said with a delighted smile: "It is pretty. There is no harshness in it. All the corners are rounded off...." The boy was very quiet then. He became drowsy. He did not know what they were playing hardly heard it; but he was happy; his limbs were numbed, and he was dreaming.

His dreams were not a consecutive story; they had neither head nor tail. It was rarely that he saw a definite picture; his mother making a cake, and with a knife removing the paste that clung to her fingers; a water–rat that he had seen the night before swimming in the river; a whip that he wanted to make with a willow wand.... Heaven knows why these things should have cropped up in his memory at such a time! But most often he saw nothing at all, and yet he felt things innumerable and infinite. It was as though there were a number of very important things not to be spoken of, or not worth speaking of, because they were so well known, and because they had always been so. Some of them were sad, terribly sad; but there was nothing painful in them, as there is in the things that belong to real life; they were not ugly and debasing, like the blows that Jean–Christophe had from his father, or like the things that were in his head when, sick at heart with shame, he thought of some humiliation; they filled the mind with a melancholy calm. And some were bright and shining, shedding torrents of joy. And Jean–Christophe thought: "Yes, it is *thus*—thus that I will do by–and–by." He did not know exactly what *thus* was, nor why he said it, but he felt that he had to say it, and that it was clear as day. He heard the sound of a sea, and he was quite near to it, kept from it only by a wall of dunes. Jean–Christophe had no idea what sea it was, or what it wanted with him, but he was conscious that it would rise above the barrier of dunes. And then!... Then all would be well, and he would be quite happy. Nothing to do but to hear it, then, quite near, to sink to sleep to the sound of its great voice, soothing away all his little griefs and humiliations. They were sad still, but no longer shameful nor injurious; everything seemed natural and almost sweet.

Very often it was mediocre music that produced this intoxication in him. The writers of it were poor devils, with no thought in their heads but the gaining of money, or the hiding away of the emptiness of their lives by tagging notes together according to accepted formulae—or to be original, in defiance of formulae. But in the notes of music, even when handled by an idiot, there is such a power of life that they can let loose storms in a simple soul. Perhaps even the dreams suggested by the idiots are more mysterious and more free than those breathed by an imperious thought which drags you along by force; for aimless movement and empty chatter do not disturb the mind in its own pondering....

So, forgotten and forgetting, the child stayed in his corner behind the piano, until suddenly he felt ants climbing up his legs. And he remembered then that he was a little boy wife dirty nails, and that he was rubbing his nose against a white–washed wall, and holding his feet in his hands.

On the day when Melchior, stealing on tiptoe, had surprised the boy at the keyboard that was too high for him, he had stayed to watch him for a moment, and suddenly there had flashed upon him: "A little prodigy!... Why had he not thought of it?... What luck for the family!..." No doubt he had thought that the boy would be a little peasant like his mother. "It would cost nothing to try. What a great thing it would be! He would take him all over Germany, perhaps abroad. It would be a jolly life, and noble to boot." Melchior never failed to look for the nobility hidden in all he did, for it was not often that he failed to find it, after some reflection.

Strong in this assurance, immediately after supper, as soon as he had taken his last mouthful, he dumped the child once more in front of the piano, and made him go through the day's lesson until his eyes closed in weariness. Then three times the next day. Then the day after that. Then every day. Jean–Christophe soon tired of it; then he was sick to death of it; finally he could stand it no more, and tried to revolt against it. There was no point in what he was made to do: nothing but learning to run as fast as possible over the keys, by loosening the thumb, or exercising the fourth finger, which would cling awkwardly to the two next to it. It got on his nerves; there was nothing beautiful in it. There was an end of the magic sounds, and fascinating monsters, and the universe of dreams felt in one moment.... Nothing but scales and exercises—dry, monotonous, dull—duller than the conversation at meal–time, which was always the same—always about the dishes, and always the same dishes. At first the child listened absently to what his father said. When he was severely reprimanded he went on with a bad grace. He paid no attention to abuse; he met it with bad temper. The last straw was when one evening he heard Melchior unfold his plans in the next room. So it was in order to put him on show like a trick animal that he was so badgered and forced every day to move bits of ivory! He was not even given time to go and see his beloved river. What was it made them so set against him? He was angry, hurt in his pride, robbed of his liberty. He decided that he would play no more, or as badly as possible, and would discourage his father. It would be hard, but at all costs he must keep his independence.

The very next lesson he began to put his plan into execution. He set himself conscientiously to hit the notes awry, or to bungle every touch. Melchior cried out, then roared, and blows began to rain. He had a heavy ruler. At every false note he struck the boy's fingers, and at the same time shouted in his ears, so that he was like to deafen him. Jean–Christophe's face twitched tinder the pain of it; he bit his lips to keep himself from crying, and stoically went on hitting the notes all wrong, bobbing his head down whenever he felt a blow coming. But his system was not good, and it was not long before he began to see that it was so. Melchior was as obstinate as his son, and he swore that even if they were to stay there two days and two nights he would not let him off a single note until it had been properly played. Then Jean–Christophe tried too deliberately to play wrongly, and Melchior began to suspect the trick, as he saw that the boy's hand fell heavily to one side at every note with obvious intent. The blows became more frequent;

Jean–Christophe was no longer conscious of his fingers. He wept pitifully and silently, sniffing, and swallowing down his sobs and tears. He understood that he had nothing to gain by going on like that, and that he would have to resort to desperate measures. He stopped, and, trembling at the thought of the storm which was about to let loose, he said valiantly:

"Papa, I won't play any more."

Melchior choked.

"What! What!..." he cried.

He took and almost broke the boy's arm with shaking it. Jean–Christophe, trembling more and more, and raising his elbow to ward off the blows, said again:

"I won't play any more. First, because I don't like being beaten. And then...."

He could not finish. A terrific blow knocked the wind out of him, and Melchior roared:

"Ah! you don't like being beaten? You don't like it?..."

Blows rained. Jean–Christophe bawled through his sobs:

"And then ... I don't like music!... I don't like music!..."

He slipped down from his chair. Melchior roughly put him back, and knocked his knuckles against the keyboard. He cried:

"You shall play!"

And Jean–Christophe shouted:

"No! No! I won't play!"

Melchior had to surrender. He thrashed the boy, thrust him from the room, and said that he should have nothing to eat all day, or the whole month, until he had played all his exercises without a mistake. He kicked him out and slammed the door after him,

Jean–Christophe found himself on the stairs, the dark and dirty stairs, worm–eaten. A draught came through a broken pane in the skylight, and the walls were dripping. Jean–Christophe sat on one of the greasy steps; his heart was beating wildly with anger and emotion. In a low voice he cursed his father:

"Beast! That's what you are! A beast ... a gross creature ... a brute! Yes, a brute!... and I hate you, I hate you!... Oh, I wish you were dead! I wish you were dead!"

His bosom swelled. He looked desperately at the sticky staircase and the spider's web swinging in the wind above the broken pane. He felt alone, lost in his misery. He looked at the gap in the banisters.... What if he were to throw himself down?... or out of the window?... Yes, what if he were to kill himself to punish them? How remorseful they would be! He heard the noise of his fall from the stairs. The door upstairs opened suddenly. Agonized voices cried: "He has fallen!—He has fallen!" Footsteps clattered downstairs. His father and mother threw themselves weeping upon his body. His mother sobbed: "It is your fault! You have killed him!" His father waved his arms, threw himself on his knees, beat his head against the banisters, and cried: "What a wretch am I! What a wretch am I!" The sight of all this softened his misery. He was on the point of taking pity on their grief; but then he thought that it was well for them, Had he enjoyed his revenge....

When his story was ended, he found himself once more at the top of the stairs in the dark; he looked down once more, and his desire to throw himself down was gone. He even, shuddered a little, and moved away from the edge, thinking that he might fall. Then he felt that he was a prisoner, like a poor bird in a cage—a prisoner forever, with nothing to do but to break his head and hurt himself. He wept, wept, and he robbed his eyes with his dirty little hands, so that in a moment he was filthy. As he wept he never left off looking at the things about him, and he found some distraction in that. He stopped moaning for a moment to look at the spider which, had just begun to move. Then he began with less conviction. He listened to the sound of his own weeping, and went on, mechanically with his sobbing, without much knowing why he did so. Soon he got up; he was attracted by the window. He sat on the window–sill, retiring into the background, and watched the spider furtively. It interested while it revolted him.

Below the Rhine flowed, washing the walls of the house. In the staircase window it was like being suspended over the river in a moving sky. Jean–Christophe never limped down the stairs without taking a long look at it, but he had never yet seen it as it was to–day. Grief sharpens the senses; it is as though everything were more sharply graven on the vision after tears have washed away the dim traces of memory. The river was like a living thing to the child—a creature inexplicable, but how much more powerful than all the creatures that he knew! Jean–Christophe leaned forward to see it better; he pressed his mouth and flattened his nose against the pane. Where was *it* going? What did *it* want? *It* looked free, and sure of its road.... Nothing could stop *it*. At all hours of the day or night, rain or sun, whether there were joy or sorrow in the house, *it* went on going by, and it was as though nothing mattered to *it*, as though *it* never knew sorrow, and rejoiced in its strength. What joy to be like *it*, to run through the fields, and by willow–branches, and over little shining pebbles and crisping sand, and to care for nothing, to be cramped by nothing, to be free!...

The boy looked and listened greedily; it was as though he were borne along by the river, moving by with it.... When he closed his eyes he saw color—blue, green, yellow, red, and great chasing shadows and sunbeams.... What he sees takes shape. Now it is a large plain, reeds, corn waving under a breeze scented with new grass and mint. Flowers on every side—cornflowers, poppies, violets. How lovely it is! How sweet the air! How good it is to lie down in the thick, soft grass!... Jean–Christophe feels glad and a little bewildered, as he does when on feast–days his father pours into his glass a little Rhine wine.... The river goes by.... The country is changed.... Now there are trees leaning over the water; their delicate leaves, like little hands, dip, move, and turn about in the water. A village among the trees is mirrored in the river. There are cypress–trees, and the crosses of the cemetery showing above the white wall washed by the stream. Then there are rocks, a mountain gorge, vines on the slopes, a little pine–wood, and ruined castles.... And once more the plain, corn, birds, and the sun....

The great green mass of the river goes by smoothly, like a single thought; there are no waves, almost no ripples—smooth, oily patches. Jean–Christophe does not see it; he has closed his eyes to hear it better. The ceaseless roaring fills him, makes him giddy; he is exalted by this eternal, masterful dream which goes no man knows whither. Over the turmoil of its depths rush waters, in swift rhythm, eagerly, ardently. And from the rhythm ascends music, like a vine climbing a trellis—arpeggios from silver keys, sorrowful violins, velvety and smooth–sounding flutes.... The country has disappeared. The river has disappeared. There floats by only a strange, soft, and twilight atmosphere. Jean-Christophe's heart flutters with emotion. What does he see now? Oh! Charming faces!... A little girl with brown tresses calls to him, slowly, softly, and mockingly.... A pale boy's face looks at him with melancholy blue eyes.... Others smile; other eyes look at him—curious and provoking eyes, and their glances make him blush—eyes affectionate and mournful, like the eyes of a dog—eyes imperious, eyes suffering.... And the pale face of a woman, with black hair, and lips close pressed, and eyes so large that they obscure her other features, and they gaze upon Jean-Christophe with an ardor that hurts him.... And, dearest of all, that face which smiles upon him with clear gray eyes and lips a little open, showing gleaming white teeth.... Ah! how kind and tender is that smile! All his heart is tenderness from it! How good it is to love! Again! Smile upon me again! Do not go!... Alas! it is gone!... But it leaves in his heart sweetness ineffable. Evil, sorrow, are no more; nothing is left.... Nothing, only an airy dream, like serene music, floating down a sunbeam, like the gossamers on fine summer days.... What has happened? What are these visions that fill the child with sadness and sweet sorrow? Never had he seen them before, and yet he knew them and recognized them. Whence come they? From what obscure abysm of creation? Are they what has been ... *or what will be?*...

Now all is done, every haunting form is gone. Once more through a misty veil, as though he were soaring high above it, the river in flood appears, covering the fields, and rolling by, majestic, slow, almost still. And far, far away, like a steely light upon the horizon, a watery plain, a line of trembling waves—the sea. The river runs down to it. The sea seems to run up to the river. She fires him. He desires her. He must lose himself in her.... The music hovers; lovely dance rhythms swing out madly; all the world is rocked in their triumphant whirligig.... The soul, set free, cleaves space, like swallows' flight, like swallows drunk with the air, skimming across the sky with shrill cries.... Joy! Joy! There is nothing, nothing!... Oh, infinite happiness!...

Hours passed; it was evening; the staircase was in darkness. Drops of rain made rings upon the river's gown, and the current bore them dancing away. Sometimes the branch of a tree or pieces of black bark passed noiselessly and disappeared. The murderous spider had withdrawn to her darkest corner. And little Jean-Christophe was still leaning forward on the window-sill. His face was pale and dirty; happiness shone in him. He was asleep.

III

E la faccia del sol nascere ombrata.
Purgatorio, xxx.

He had to surrender. In spite of an obstinate and heroic resistance, blows triumphed over his ill–will. Every morning for three hours, and for three hours every evening, Jean–Christophe was set before the instrument of torture. All on edge with attention and weariness, with large tears rolling down his cheeks and nose, he moved his little red hands over the black and white keys—his hands were often stiff with cold—under the threatening ruler, which descended at every false note, and the harangues of his master, which were more odious to him than the blows. He thought that he hated music. And yet he applied himself to it with a zest which fear of Melchior did not altogether explain. Certain words of his grandfather had made an impression on him. The old man, seeing his grandson weeping, had told him, with that gravity which he always maintained for the boy, that it was worth while suffering a little for the most beautiful and noble art given to men for their consolation and glory. And Jean–Christophe, who was grateful to his grandfather for talking to him like a man, had been secretly touched by these simple words, which sorted well with his childish stoicism and growing pride. But, more than by argument, he was bound and enslaved by the memory of certain musical emotions, bound and enslaved to the detested art, against which he tried in vain to rebel.

There was in the town, as usual in Germany, a theater, where opera, opera–comique, operetta, drama, comedy, and vaudeville are presented—every sort of play of every style and fashion. There were performances three times a week from six to nine in the evening. Old Jean Michel never missed one, and was equally interested in everything. Once he took his grandson with him. Several days beforehand he told him at length what the piece was about. Jean–Christophe did not understand it, but he did gather that there would be terrible things in it, and while he was consumed with the desire to see them he was much afraid, though he dared not confess it. He knew that there was to be a storm, and he was fearful of being struck by lightning. He knew that there was to be a battle, and he was not at all sure that he would not be killed. On the night before, in bed, he went through real agony, and on the day of the performance he almost wished that his grandfather might be prevented from coming for him. But when the hour was near, and his grandfather did not come, he began to worry, and every other minute looked out of the window. At last the old man appeared, and they set out together. His heart leaped in his bosom; his tongue was dry, and he could not speak.

They arrived at the mysterious building which was so often talked about at home. At the door Jean Michel met some acquaintances, and the boy, who was holding his hand tight because he was afraid of being lost, could not understand how they could talk and laugh quietly at such a moment.

Jean Michel took his usual place in the first row behind the orchestra. He leaned on the balustrade, and began a long conversation with the contra–bass. He was at home there; there he was listened to because of his authority as a musician, and he made the most of it; it might almost be said that he abused it. Jean–Christophe could hear nothing. He was overwhelmed by his expectation of the play, by the appearance of the theater, which seemed magnificent to him, by the splendor of the audience, who frightened him terribly. He dared not turn his head, for he thought that all eyes were fixed on him. He hugged his little cap between his knees, and he stared at the magic curtain with round eyes.

At last three blows were struck. His grandfather blew his nose, and drew the *libretto* from his pocket. He always followed it scrupulously, so much so that sometimes he neglected what was happening on the stage. The orchestra began to play. With the opening chords Jean–Christophe felt more at ease. He was at home in this world of sound, and from that moment, however extravagant the play might be, it seemed natural to him.

The curtain was raised, to reveal pasteboard trees and creatures who were not much more real. The boy looked at it all, gaping with admiration, but he was not surprised. The piece set in a fantastic East, of which he could have had no idea. The poem was a web of ineptitudes, in which no human quality was perceptible. Jean–Christophe hardly grasped it at all; he made extraordinary mistakes, took one character for another, and pulled at his grandfather's sleeve to ask him absurd questions, which showed that he had understood nothing. He was not bored: passionately interested, on the contrary. Bound the idiotic *libretto* he built a romance of his own invention, which had no sort of relation to the one that was represented on the stage. Every moment some incident upset his romance, and he had to repair it, but that did not worry him. He had made his choice of the people who moved upon the stage, making all sorts of different sounds, and breathlessly he followed the fate of those upon whom he had fastened his sympathy. He was especially concerned with a fair lady, of uncertain age, who had long, brilliantly fair hair, eyes of an unnatural size, and bare feet. The monstrous improbabilities of the setting did not shock him. His keen, childish eyes did not perceive the grotesque ugliness of the actors, large and fleshy, and the deformed chorus of all sizes in two lines, nor the pointlessness of their gestures, nor their faces bloated by their shrieks, nor the full wigs, nor the high heels of the tenor, nor the make–up of his lady–love, whose face was streaked with variegated penciling. He was in the condition of a lover, whose passion blinds him to the actual aspect of the beloved object. The marvelous power of illusion, natural to children, stopped all unpleasant sensations on the way, and transformed them.

The music especially worked wonders. It bathed the whole scene in a misty atmosphere, in which everything became beautiful, noble, and desirable. It bred in the soul a desperate need of love, and at the same time showed phantoms of love on all sides, to fill the void that itself had created. Little Jean–Christophe was overwhelmed by his emotion. There were words, gestures, musical phrases which disturbed him; he dared not then raise his eyes; he knew not whether it were well or ill; he blushed and grew pale by turns; sometimes there came drops of sweat upon his brow, and he was fearful lest all the people there should see his distress. When the catastrophe came about which inevitably breaks upon lovers in the fourth act of an opera so as to provide the tenor and the *prima donna* with an opportunity for showing off their shrillest screams, the child thought he must choke; his throat hurt him as though he had caught cold; he clutched at his neck with his hands, and could not swallow his saliva; tears welled up in him; his hands and feet were frozen. Fortunately, his grandfather was not much less moved. He enjoyed the theater with a childish simplicity. During the dramatic passages he coughed carelessly to hide his distress, but Jean–Christophe saw it, and it delighted him. It was horribly hot; Jean–Christophe was dropping with sleep, and he was very uncomfortable. But he thought only: "Is there much longer? It cannot be finished!" Then suddenly it was finished, without his knowing why. The curtain fell; the audience rose; the enchantment was broken.

They went home through the night, the two children—the old man and the little boy. What a fine night! What a serene moonlight! They said nothing; they were turning over their memories. At last the old man said:

"Did you like it, boy?"

Jean–Christophe could not reply; he was still fearful from emotion, and he would not speak, so as not to break the spell; he had to make an effort to whisper, with a sigh:

"Oh yes."

The old man smiled. After a time he went on:

"It's a fine thing—a musician's trade! To create things like that, such marvelous spectacles—is there anything more glorious? It is to be God on earth!"

The boy's mind leaped to that. What! a man had made all that! That had not occurred to him. It had seemed that it must have made itself, must be the work of Nature. A man, a musician, such as he would be some day! Oh, to be that for one day, only one day! And then afterwards ... afterwards, whatever you like! Die, if necessary! He asked:

"What man made that, grandfather?"

The old man told him of Francois Marie Hassler, a young German artist who lived at Berlin. He had known him once. Jean–Christophe listened, all ears. Suddenly he said:

"And you, grandfather?"

The old man trembled.

"What?" he asked.

"Did you do things like that—you too?"

"Certainly," said the old man a little crossly.

He was silent, and after they had walked a little he sighed heavily. It was one of the sorrows of his life. He had always longed to write for the theater, and inspiration had always betrayed him. He had in his desk one or two acts written, but he had so little illusion as to their worth that he had never dared to submit them to an outside judgment.

They said no more until they reached home. Neither slept. The old man was troubled. He took his Bible for consolation. In bed Jean–Christophe turned over and over the events of the evening; he recollected the smallest details, and the girl with the bare feet reappeared before him. As he dozed off a musical phrase rang in his ears as distinctly as if the orchestra were there. All his body leaped; he sat up on his pillow, his head buzzing with music, and he thought: "Some day I also shall write. Oh, can I ever do it?"

From that moment he had only one desire, to go to the theater again, and he set himself to work more keenly, because they made a visit to the theater his reward. He thought of nothing but that; half the week he thought of the last performance, and the other half he thought of the next. He was fearful of being ill on a theater day, and this fear made him often, find in himself the symptoms of three or four illnesses. When the day came he did not eat; he fidgeted like a soul in agony; he looked at the clock fifty times, and thought that the evening would never come; finally, unable to contain himself, he would go out an hour before the office opened, for fear of not being able to procure a seat, and, as he was the first in the empty theater, he used to grow uneasy. His grandfather had told him that once or twice the audience had not been large enough, and so the players had preferred not to perform, and to give back the money. He watched the arrivals and counted them, thinking: "Twenty–three, twenty–four, twenty–five.... Oh, it is not enough ... there will never be enough!" 'And when he saw some important person enter the circle or the stalls, his heart was lighter, and he said to himself: "They will never dare to send him away. Surely they will play for him." But he was not convinced; he would not be reassured until the musicians took their places. And even then he would be afraid that the curtain would rise, and they would announce, as they had done one evening, a change of programme. With lynx eyes he watched the stand of the contra–bass to see if the title written on his music was that of the piece announced. And when he had seen it there, two minutes later he would look again to make quite sure that he had not been wrong. The conductor was not there. He must be ill. There was a stirring behind the curtain, and a sound of voices and hurried footsteps. Was there an accident, some untoward misfortune? Silence again. The conductor was at his post. Everything seemed ready at last.... They did not begin! What was happening? He boiled over with impatience. Then the bell rang. His heart thumped away. The orchestra began the overture, and for a few hours Jean–Christophe would swim in happiness, troubled only by the idea that it must soon come to an end.

* * * * *

Some time after that a musical event brought even more excitement into Jean–Christophe's thoughts. Francois Marie Hassler, the author of the first opera which had so bowled him over, was to visit the town. He was to conduct a concert consisting of his compositions. The town was excited. The young musician was the subject of violent discussion in Germany, and for a fortnight he was the only topic of conversation. It was a different matter when he arrived. The friends of Melchior and old Jean Michel continually came for news, and they went away with the most extravagant notions of the musician's habits and eccentricities. The child followed these narratives with eager attention. The idea that the great man was there in the town, breathing the same air as himself, treading the same stones, threw him into a state of dumb exaltation. He lived only in the hope of seeing him.

Hassler was staying at the Palace as the guest of the Grand Duke. He hardly went out, except to the theater for rehearsals, to which Jean–Christophe was not admitted, and as he was very lazy, he went to and fro in the Prince's carriage. Therefore, Jean–Christophe did not have many opportunities of seeing him, and he only succeeded once in catching sight of him as he drove in the carriage. He saw his fur coat, and wasted hours in waiting in the street, thrusting and jostling his way to right and left, and before and behind, to win and keep his place in front of the loungers. He consoled himself with spending half his days watching the windows of the Palace which had been pointed out as those of the master. Most often he only saw the shutters, for Hassler got up late, and the windows were closed almost all morning. This habit had made well–informed persons say that Hassler could not bear the light of day, and lived in eternal night.

At length Jean–Christophe was able to approach his hero. It was the day of the concert. All the town was there. The Grand Duke and his Court occupied the great royal box, surmounted with a crown supported by two chubby cherubim. The theater was in gala array. The stage was decorated with branches of oak and flowering laurel. All the musicians of any account made it a point of honor to take their places in the orchestra. Melchior was at his post, and Jean Michel was conducting the chorus.

When Hassler appeared there was loud applause from every part of the house, and the ladies rose to see him better. Jean–Christophe devoured him with his eyes. Hassler had a young, sensitive face, though it was already rather puffy and tired–looking; his temples were bald, and his hair was thin on the crown of his head; for the rest, fair, curly hair. His blue eyes looked vague. He had a little fair mustache and an expressive mouth, which was rarely still, but twitched with a thousand imperceptible movements. He was tall, and held himself badly—not from awkwardness, but from weariness or boredom. He conducted capriciously and lithely, with his whole awkward body swaying, like his music, with gestures, now caressing, now sharp and jerky. It was easy to see that he was very nervous, and his music was the exact reflection of himself. The quivering and jerky life of it broke through the usual apathy of the orchestra. Jean–Christophe breathed heavily; in spite of his fear of drawing attention to himself, he could not stand still in his place; he fidgeted, got up, and the music gave him such violent and unexpected shocks that he had to move his head, arms, and legs, to the great discomfort of his neighbors, who warded off his kicks as best they could. The whole audience was enthusiastic, fascinated by the success, rather than by the compositions. At the end there was a storm of applause and cries, in which the trumpets in the orchestra joined, German fashion, with their triumphant blare in salute of the conqueror, Jean–Christophe trembled with pride, as though these honors were for himself. He enjoyed seeing Hassler's face light up with childish pleasure. The ladies threw flowers, the men waved their hats, and the audience rushed for the platform. Every one wanted to shake the master's hand. Jean–Christophe saw one enthusiast raise the master's hand to his lips, another steal a handkerchief that Hassler had left on the corner of his desk. He wanted to reach the platform also, although he did not know why, for if at that moment he had found himself near Hassler, he would have fled at once in terror and emotion. But he butted with all his force, like a ram, among the skirts and legs that divided him from Hassler. He was too small; he could not break through.

Fortunately, when the concert was over, his grandfather came and took him to join in a party to serenade Hassler. It was night, and torches were lighted. All the musicians of the orchestra were there. They talked only of the marvelous compositions they had heard. They arrived outside the Palace, and took up their places without a sound under the master's windows. They took on an air of secrecy, although everybody, including Hassler, knew what was to come. In the silence of the night they began to play certain famous fragments of Hassler's compositions. He appeared at the window with the Prince, and they roared in their honor. Both bowed. A servant came from the Prince to invite the musicians to enter the Palace. They passed through great rooms, with frescoes representing naked men with helmets; they were of a reddish color, and were making gestures of defiance. The sky was covered with great clouds like sponges. There were also men and women of marble clad in waist–cloths made of iron. The guests walked on carpets so thick that their tread was inaudible, and they came at length to a room which was as light as day, and there were tables laden with drinks and good things.

The Grand Duke was there, but Jean-Christophe did not see him; he had eyes only for Hassler. Hassler came towards them; he thanked them. He picked his words carefully, stopped awkwardly in the middle of a sentence, and extricated himself with a quip which made everybody laugh. They began to eat. Hassler took four or five musicians aside. He singled out Jean-Christophe's grandfather, and addressed very flattering words to him: he recollected that Jean Michel had been one of the first to perform his works, and he said that he had often heard tell of his excellence from a friend of his who had been a pupil of the old man's. Jean-Christophe's grandfather expressed his gratitude profusely; he replied with such extraordinary eulogy that, in spite of his adoration of Hassler, the boy was ashamed. But to Hassler they seemed to be pleasant and in the rational order. Finally, the old man, who had lost himself in his rigmarole, took Jean-Christophe by the hand, and presented him to Hassler. Hassler smiled at Jean-Christophe, and carelessly patted his head, and when he learned that the boy liked his music, and had not slept for several nights in anticipation of seeing him, he took him in his arms and plied him with questions. Jean-Christophe, struck, dumb and blushing with pleasure, dared not look at him. Hassler took him by the chin and lifted his face up. Jean-Christophe ventured to look. Hassler's eyes were kind and smiling; he began to smile too. Then he felt so happy, so wonderfully happy in the great man's arms, that he burst into tears. Hassler was touched by this simple affection, and was more kind than ever. He kissed the boy and talked to him tenderly. At the same time he said funny things and tickled him to make him laugh; and Jean-Christophe could not help laughing through his tears. Soon he became at ease, and answered Hassler readily, and of his own accord he began to whisper in his ear all his small ambitions, as though he and Hassler were old friends; he told him how he wanted to be a musician like Hassler, and, like Hassler, to make beautiful things, and to be a great man. He, was always ashamed, talked confidently; he did not know what he was saying; he was in a sort of ecstasy, Hassler smiled at his prattling and said:

"When you are a man, and have become a good musician, you shall come and see me in Berlin. I shall make something of you."

Jean-Christophe was too delighted to reply.

Hassler teased him.

"You don't want to?"

Jean–Christophe nodded his head violently five or six times, meaning "Yes."

"It is a bargain, then?"

Jean–Christophe nodded again.

"Kiss me, then."

Jean–Christophe threw his arms round Hassler's neck and hugged him with all his strength.

"Oh, you are wetting me! Let go! Your nose wants wiping!"

Hassler laughed, and wiped the boy's nose himself, a little self–consciously, though he was quite jolly. He put him down, then took him by the hand and led him to a table, where he filled his pockets with cake, and left him, saying:

"Good–bye! Remember your promise."

Jean–Christophe swam in happiness. The rest of the world had ceased to exist for him. He could remember nothing of what had happened earlier in the evening; he followed lovingly Hassler's every expression and gesture. One thing that he said struck him. Hassler was holding a glass in his hand; he was talking, and his face suddenly hardened, and he said:

"The joy of such a day must not make us forget our enemies. We must never forget our enemies. It is not their fault that we are not crushed out of existence. It will not be our fault if that does not happen to them. That is why the toast I propose is that there are people whose health ... we will not drink!"

Everybody applauded and laughed at this original toast. Hassler had laughed with the others and his good–humored expression had returned. But Jean–Christophe was put off by it. Although he did not permit himself to criticise any action of his hero, it hurt him that he had thought ugly things, when on such a night there ought to be nothing but brilliant thoughts and fancies. But he did not examine what he felt, and the impression that it made was soon driven out by his great joy and the drop of champagne which he drank out of his grandfather's glass.

On the way back the old man never stopped talking; he was delighted with the praise that Hassler had given him; he cried out that Hassler was a genius such as had not been known for a century. Jean–Christophe said nothing, locking up in his heart his intoxication of love. *He* had kissed him. *He* had held him in his arms! How good *he* was! How great!

"Ah," he thought in bed, as he kissed his pillow passionately, "I would die for him—die for him!"

The brilliant meteor which had flashed across the sky of the little town that night had a decisive influence on Jean–Christophe's mind. All his childhood Hassler was the model on which his eyes were fixed, and to follow his example the little man of six decided that he also would write music. To tell the truth, he had been doing so for long enough without knowing it, and he had not waited to be conscious of composing before he composed.

Everything is music for the born musician. Everything that throbs, or moves, or stirs, or palpitates—sunlit summer days, nights when the wind howls, flickering light, the twinkling of the stars, storms, the song of birds, the buzzing of insects, the murmuring of trees, voices, loved or loathed, familiar fireside sounds, a creaking door, blood moving in the veins in the silence of the night—everything that is is music; all that is needed is that it should be heard. All the music of creation found its echo in Jean–Christophe. Everything that he saw, everything that he felt, was translated into music without his being conscious of it. He was like a buzzing hive of bees. But no one noticed it, himself least of all.

Like all children, he hummed perpetually at every hour of the day. Whatever he was doing—whether he were walking in the street, hopping on one foot, or lying on the floor at his grandfather's, with his head in his hands, absorbed in the pictures of a book, or sitting in his little chair in the darkest corner of the kitchen, dreaming aimlessly in the twilight—always the monotonous murmuring of his little trumpet was to be heard, played with lips closed and cheeks blown out. His mother seldom paid any heed to it, but, once in a while, she would protest.

When he was tired of this state of half–sleep he would have to move and make a noise. Then he made music, singing it at the top of his voice. He had made tunes for every occasion. He had a tune for splashing in his wash–basin in the morning, like a little duck. He had a tune for sitting on the piano–stool in front of the detested instrument, and another for getting off it, and this was a more brilliant affair than the other. He had one for his mother putting the soup on the table; he used to go before her then blowing a blare of trumpets. He played triumphal marches by which to go solemnly from the dining–room to the bedroom. Sometimes he would organize little processions with his two small brothers; all then would file out gravely, one after another, and each had a tune to march to. But, as was right and proper, Jean–Christophe kept the best for himself. Every one of his tunes was strictly appropriated to its special occasion, and Jean–Christophe never by any chance confused them. Anybody else would have made mistakes, but he knew the shades of difference between them exactly.

One day at his grandfather's house he was going round the room clicking his heels, head up and chest out; he went round and round and round, so that it was a wonder he did not turn sick, and played one of his compositions. The old man, who was shaving, stopped in the middle of it, and, with his face covered with lather, came to look at him, and said:

"What are you singing, boy?"

Jean–Christophe said he did not know.

"Sing it again!" said Jean Michel.

Jean–Christophe tried; he could not remember the tune. Proud of having attracted his grandfather's attention, he tried to make him admire his voice, and sang after his own fashion an air from some opera, but that was not what the old man wanted. Jean Michel said nothing, and seemed not to notice him any more. But he left the door of his room ajar while the boy was playing alone in the next room.

A few days later Jean–Christophe, with the chairs arranged about him, was playing a comedy in music, which he had made up of scraps that he remembered from the theater, and he was making steps and bows, as he had seen them done in a minuet, and addressing

73

himself to the portrait of Beethoven which hung above the table. As he turned with a pirouette he saw his grandfather watching him through the half–open door. He thought the old man was laughing at him; he was abashed, and stopped dead; he ran to the window, and pressed his face against the panes, pretending that he had been watching something of the greatest interest. But the old man said nothing; he came to him and kissed him, and Jean–Christophe saw that he was pleased. His vanity made the most of these signs; he was clever enough to see that he had been appreciated; but he did not know exactly which his grandfather had admired most—his talent as a dramatic author, or as a musician, or as a singer, or as a dancer. He inclined, to the latter, for he prided himself on this.

A week later, when he had forgotten the whole affair, his grandfather said mysteriously that he had something to show him. He opened his desk, took out a music–book, and put it on the rack of the piano, and told the boy to play. Jean–Christophe was very much interested, and deciphered it fairly well. The notes were written by hand in the old man's large handwriting, and he had taken especial pains with it. The headings were adorned with scrolls and flourishes. After some moments the old man, who was sitting beside Jean–Christophe turning the pages for him, asked him what the music was. Jean–Christophe had been too much absorbed in his playing to notice what he had played, and said that he did not know it.

"Listen!... You don't know it?"

Yes; he thought he knew it, but he did not know where he had heard it. The old man laughed.

"Think."

Jean–Christophe shook his head.

"I don't know."

A light was fast dawning in his mind; it seemed to him that the air.... But, no! He dared not.... He would not recognize it.

"I don't know, grandfather."

He blushed.

"What, you little fool, don't you see that it is your own?"

He was sure of it, but to hear it said made his heart thump.

"Oh! grandfather!..."

Beaming, the old man showed him the book.

"See: *Aria*. It is what you were singing on Tuesday when you were lying on the floor. *March*. That is what I asked you to sing again last week, and you could not remember it. *Minuet*. That is what you were dancing by the armchair. Look!"

On the cover was written in wonderful Gothic letters:

"*The Pleasures of Childhood: Aria, Minuetto, Valse, and Marcia, Op. 1, by Jean–Christophe Krafft.*"

Jean–Christophe was dazzled by it. To see his name, and that fine title, and that large book—his work!... He went on murmuring:

"Oh! grandfather! grandfather!..."

The old man drew him to him. Jean–Christophe threw himself on his knees, and hid his head in Jean Michel's bosom. He was covered with blushes from his happiness. The old man was even happier, and went on, in a voice which he tried to make indifferent, for he felt that he was on the point of breaking down:

"Of course, I added the accompaniment and the harmony to fit the song. And then"—he coughed—"and then, I added a *trio* to the minuet, because ... because it is usual ... and then.... I think it is not at all bad."

He played it. Jean–Christophe was very proud of collaborating with his grandfather.

"But, grandfather, you must put your name to it too."

"It is not worth while. It is not worth while others besides yourself knowing it. Only"—here his voice trembled—"only, later on, when I am no more, it will remind you of your old grandfather ... eh? You won't forget him?"

The poor old man did not say that he had been unable to resist the quite innocent pleasure of introducing one of his own unfortunate airs into his grandson's work, which he felt was destined to survive him; but his desire to share in this imaginary glory was very humble and very touching, since it was enough for him anonymously to transmit to posterity a scrap of his own thought, so as not altogether to perish. Jean–Christophe was touched by it, and covered his face with kisses, and the old man, growing more and more tender, kissed his hair.

"You will remember me? Later on, when you are a good musician, a great artist, who will bring honor to his family, to his art, and to his country, when you are famous, you will remember that it was your old grandfather who first perceived it, and foretold what you would be?"

There were tears in his eyes as he listened to his own words. He was reluctant to let such signs of weakness be seen. He had an attack of coughing, became moody, and sent the boy away hugging the precious manuscript.

Jean–Christophe went home bewildered by his happiness. The stones danced about him. The reception he had from his family sobered him a little. When he blurted out the splendor of his musical exploit they cried out upon him. His mother laughed at him. Melchior declared that the old man was mad, and that he would do better to take care of himself than to set about turning the boy's head. As for Jean–Christophe, he would oblige by putting such follies from his mind, and sitting down *illico* at the piano and playing exercises for four hours. He must first learn to play properly; and as for composing, there was plenty of time for that later on when he had nothing better to do.

Melchior was not, as these words of wisdom might indicate, trying to keep the boy from the dangerous exaltation of a too early pride. On the contrary, he proved immediately that this was not so. But never having himself had any idea to express in music, and never having had the least need to express an idea, he had come, as a *virtuoso*, to consider composing a secondary matter, which was only given value by the art of the executant. He was not insensible of the tremendous enthusiasm roused by great composers like

Hassler. For such ovations he had the respect which he always paid to success—mingled, perhaps, with a little secret jealousy—for it seemed to him that such applause was stolen from him. But he knew by experience that the successes of the great *virtuosi* are no less remarkable, and are more personal in character, and therefore more fruitful of agreeable and flattering consequences. He affected to pay profound homage to the genius of the master musicians; but he took a great delight in telling absurd anecdotes of them, presenting their intelligence and morals in a lamentable light. He placed the *virtuoso* at the top of the artistic ladder, for, he said, it is well known that the tongue is the noblest member of the body, and what would thought be without words? What would music be without the executant? But whatever may have been the reason for the scolding that he gave Jean–Christophe, it was not without its uses in restoring some common sense to the boy, who was almost beside himself with his grandfather's praises. It was not quite enough. Jean–Christophe, of course, decided that his grandfather was much cleverer than his father, and though he sat down at the piano without sulking, he did so not so much for the sake of obedience as to be able to dream in peace, as he always did while his fingers ran, mechanically over the keyboard. While he played his interminable exercises he heard a proud voice inside himself saying over and over again: "I am a composer—a great composer."

From that day on, since he was a composer, he set himself to composing. Before he had even learned to write, he continued to cipher crotchets and quavers on scraps of paper, which he tore from the household account–books. But in the effort to find out what he was thinking, and to set it down in black and white, he arrived at thinking nothing, except when he wanted to think something. But he did not for that give up making musical phrases, and as he was a born musician he made them somehow, even if they meant nothing at all. Then he would take them in triumph to his grandfather, who wept with joy over them—he wept easily now that he was growing old—and vowed that they were wonderful.

All this was like to spoil him altogether. Fortunately, his own good sense saved him, helped by the influence of a man who made no pretension of having any influence over anybody, and set nothing before the eyes of the world but a commonsense point of view. This man was Louisa's brother.

Like her, he was small, thin, puny, and rather round–shouldered. No one knew exactly how old he was; he could not be more than forty, but he looked more than fifty. He had a little wrinkled face, with a pink complexion, and kind pale blue eyes, like faded forget—me—nots. When he took off his cap, which he used fussily to wear everywhere from his fear of draughts, he exposed a little pink bald head, conical in shape, which was the great delight of Jean—Christophe and his brothers. They never left off teasing him about it, asking him what he had done with his hair, and, encouraged by Melchior's pleasantries, threatening to smack it. He was the first to laugh at them, and put up with their treatment of him patiently. He was a peddler; he used to go from village to village with a pack on his back, containing everything—groceries, stationery, confectionery, handkerchiefs, scarves, shoes, pickles, almanacs, songs, and drugs. Several attempts had been made to make him settle down, and to buy him a little business—a store or a drapery shop. But he could not do it. One night he would get up, push the key under the door, and set off again with his pack. Weeks and months went by before he was seen again. Then he would reappear. Some evening they would hear him fumbling at the door; it would half open, and the little bald head, politely uncovered, would appear with its kind eyes and timid smile. He would say, "Good—evening, everybody," carefully wipe his shoes before entering, salute everybody, beginning with the eldest, and go and sit in the most remote corner of the room. There he would light his pipe, and sit huddled up, waiting quietly until the usual storm of questions was over. The two Kraffts, Jean—Christophe's father and grandfather, had a jeering contempt for him. The little freak seemed ridiculous to them, and their pride was touched by the low degree of the peddler. They made him feel it, but he seemed to take no notice of it, and showed them a profound respect which disarmed them, especially the old man, who was very sensitive to what people thought of him. They used to crush him with heavy pleasantries, which often brought the blush to Louisa's cheeks. Accustomed to bow without dispute to the intellectual superiority of the Kraffts, she had no doubt that her husband and father—in—law were right; but she loved her brother, and her brother had for her a dumb adoration. They were the only members of their family, and they were both humble, crushed, and thrust aside by life; they were united in sadness and tenderness by a bond of mutual pity and common suffering, borne in secret. With the Kraffts—robust, noisy, brutal, solidly built for living, and living joyously—these two weak, kindly creatures, out of their setting, so to speak, outside life, understood and pitied each other without ever saying anything about it.

Jean—Christophe, with the cruel carelessness of childhood, shared the contempt of his father and grandfather for the little peddler. He made fun of him, and treated him as a comic figure; he worried him with stupid teasing, which his uncle bore with his unshakable phlegm. But Jean–Christophe loved him, without quite knowing why. He loved him first of all as a plaything with which he did what he liked. He loved him also because he always gave him something nice—a dainty, a picture, an amusing toy. The little man's return was a joy for the children, for he always had some surprise for them. Poor as he was, he always contrived to bring them each a present, and he never forgot the birthday of any one of the family. He always turned up on these august days, and brought out of his pocket some jolly present, lovingly chosen. They were so used to it that they hardly thought of thanking him; it seemed natural, and he appeared to be sufficiently repaid by the pleasure he had given. But Jean–Christophe, who did not sleep very well, and during the night used to turn over in his mind the events of the day, used sometimes to think that his uncle was very kind, and he used to be filled with floods of gratitude to the poor man. He never showed it when the day came, because he thought that the others would laugh at him. Besides, he was too little to see in kindness all the rare value that it has. In the language of children, kind and stupid are almost synonymous, and Uncle Gottfried seemed to be the living proof of it.

One evening when Melchior was dining out, Gottfried was left alone in the living–room, while Louisa put the children to bed. He went out, and sat by the river a few yards away from the house. Jean–Christophe, having nothing better to do, followed him, and, as usual, tormented him with his puppy tricks until he was out of breath, and dropped down on the grass at his feet. Lying on his belly, he buried his nose in the turf. When he had recovered his breath, he cast about for some new crazy thing to say. When he found it he shouted it out, and rolled about with laughing, with his face still buried in the earth. He received no answer. Surprised by the silence, he raised his head, and began to repeat his joke. He saw Gottfried's face lit up by the last beams of the setting sun cast through golden mists. He swallowed down his words. Gottfried smiled with his eyes half closed and his mouth half open, and in his sorrowful face was an expression of sadness and unutterable melancholy. Jean–Christophe, with his face in his hands, watched him. The night came; little by little Gottfried's face disappeared. Silence reigned. Jean–Christophe in his turn was filled with the mysterious impressions which had been reflected on Gottfried's face. He fell into a vague stupor. The earth was in darkness, the sky was bright; the stars peeped out. The little waves of the river chattered against the bank. The boy grew sleepy. Without seeing them, he bit off little blades of grass. A grasshopper chirped near him. It seemed to him that he was going to sleep.

Suddenly, in the dark, Gottfried began to sing. He sang in a weak, husky voice, as though to himself; he could not have been heard twenty yards away. But there was sincerity and emotion in his voice; it was as though he were thinking aloud, and that through the song, as through clear water, the very inmost heart of him was to be seen. Never had Jean–Christophe heard such singing, and never had he heard such a song. Slow, simple, childish, it moved gravely, sadly, a little monotonously, never hurrying—with long pauses—then setting out again on its way, careless where it arrived, and losing itself in the night. It seemed to come from far away, and it went no man knows whither. Its serenity was full of sorrow, and beneath its seeming peace there dwelt an agony of the ages. Jean–Christophe held his breath; he dared not move; he was cold with emotion. When it was done he crawled towards Gottfried, and in a choking voice said:

"Uncle!"

Gottfried did not reply.

"Uncle!" repeated the boy, placing his hands and chin on Gottfried's knees.

Gottfried said kindly:

"Well, boy..."

"What is it, uncle? Tell me! What were you singing?"

"I don't know."

"Tell me what it is!"

"I don't know. Just a song."

"A song that you made."

"No, not I! What an idea!... It is an old song."

"Who made it?"

"No one knows...."

"When?"

"No one knows...."

"When you were little?"

"Before I was born, before my father was born, and before his father, and before his father's father.... It has always been."

"How strange! No one has ever told me about it."

He thought for a moment.

"Uncle, do you know any other?"

"Yes."

"Sing another, please."

"Why should I sing another? One is enough. One sings when one wants to sing, when one has to sing. One must not sing for the fun of it."

"But what about when one makes music?"

"That is not music."

The boy was lost in thought. He did not quite understand. But he asked for no explanation. It was true, it was not music, not like all the rest. He went on:

"Uncle, have you ever made them?"

"Made what?"   .

"Songs!"

"Songs? Oh! How should I make them? They can't be made."

With his usual logic the boy insisted:

"But, uncle, it must have been made once...."

Gottfried shook his head obstinately.

"It has always been."

The boy returned to the attack:

"But, uncle, isn't it possible to make other songs, new songs?"

"Why make them? There are enough for everything. There are songs for when you are sad, and for when you are gay; for when you are weary, and for when you are thinking of home; for when you despise yourself, because you have been a vile sinner, a worm upon the earth; for when you want to weep, because people have not been kind to you; and for when your heart is glad because the world is beautiful, and you see God's heaven, which, like Him, is always kind, and seems to laugh at you.... There are songs for everything, everything. Why should I make them?"

"To be a great man!" said the boy, full of his grandfather's teaching and his simple dreams.

Gottfried laughed softly. Jean–Christophe, a little hurt, asked him:

"Why are you laughing?"

Gottfried said:

"Oh! I?... I am nobody."

He kissed the boy's head, and said:

"You want to be a great man?"

"Yes," said Jean–Christophe proudly. He thought Gottfried would admire him. But Gottfried replied:

"What for?"

Jean–Christophe was taken aback. He thought for a moment, and said:

"To make beautiful songs!"

Gottfried laughed again, and said:

"You want to make beautiful songs, so as to be a great man; and you want to be a great man, so as to make beautiful songs. You are like a dog chasing its own tail."

Jean–Christophe was dashed. At any other time he would not have borne his uncle laughing at him, he at whom he was used to laughing. And, at the same time, he would never have thought Gottfried clever enough to stump him with an argument. He cast about for some answer or some impertinence to throw at him, but could find none. Gottfried went on:

"When you are as great as from here to Coblentz, you will never make a single song."

Jean–Christophe revolted on that.

"And if I will!..."

"The more you want to, the less you can. To make songs, you have to be like those creatures. Listen...."

The moon had risen, round and gleaming, behind the fields. A silvery mist hovered above the ground and the shimmering waters. The frogs croaked, and in the meadows the melodious fluting of the toads arose. The shrill tremolo of the grasshoppers seemed to answer the twinkling of the stars. The wind rustled softly in the branches of the alders. From the hills above the river there came down the sweet light song of a nightingale.

"What need is there to sing?" sighed Gottfried, after a long silence. (It was not clear whether he were talking to himself or to Jean–Christophe.) "Don't they sing sweeter than anything that you could make?"

Jean–Christophe had often heard these sounds of the night, and he loved them. But never had he heard them as he heard them now. It was true: what need was there to sing?... His heart was full of tenderness and sorrow. He was fain to embrace the meadows, the river, the sky, the clear stars. He was filled with love for his uncle Gottfried, who seemed to him now the best, the cleverest, the most beautiful of men. He thought how he had misjudged him, and he thought that his uncle was sad because he, Jean–Christophe, had misjudged him. He was remorseful. He wanted to cry out: "Uncle, do not be sad! I will not be naughty again. Forgive me, I love you!" But he dared not. And suddenly he threw himself into Gottfried's arms, but the words would not come, only he repeated, "I love you!" and kissed him passionately. Gottfried was surprised and touched, and went on saying, "What? What?" and kissed him. Then he got up, took him by the hand, and said: "We must go in." Jean–Christophe was sad because his uncle had not understood him. But as they came to the house, Gottfried said: "If you like we'll go again to hear God's music, and I will sing you some more songs." And when Jean–Christophe kissed him gratefully as they said good–night, he saw that his uncle had understood.

Thereafter they often went for walks together in the evening, and they walked without a word along by the river, or through the fields. Gottfried slowly smoked his pipe, and Jean–Christophe, a little frightened by the darkness, would give him his hand. They would sit down on the grass, and after a few moments of silence Gottfried would talk to him about the stars and the clouds; he taught him to distinguish the breathing of the earth, air, and water, the songs, cries, and sounds of the little worlds of flying, creeping, hopping, and swimming things swarming in the darkness, and the signs of rain and fine weather, and the countless instruments of the symphony of the night. Sometimes Gottfried would sing tunes, sad or gay, but always of the same kind, and always in the end Jean–Christophe would be brought to the same sorrow. But he would never sing more than one song in an evening, and Jean–Christophe noticed that he did not sing gladly when he was asked to do so; it had to come of itself, just when he wanted to. Sometimes they had to wait for a long time without speaking, and just when Jean–Christophe was beginning to think, "He is not going to sing this evening," Gottfried would make up his mind.

One evening, when nothing would induce Gottfried to sing, Jean–Christophe thought of submitting to him one of his own small compositions, in the making of which he found so much trouble and pride. He wanted to show what an artist he was. Gottfried listened very quietly, and then said:

"That is very ugly, my poor dear Jean–Christophe!"

Jean–Christophe was so hurt that he could find nothing to say. Gottfried went on pityingly:

"Why did you do it? It is so ugly! No one forced you to do it."

Hot with anger, Jean–Christophe protested:

"My grandfather thinks my music fine."

"Ah!" said Gottfried, not turning a hair. "No doubt he is right. He is a learned man. He knows all about music. I know nothing about it...."

And after a moment:

"But I think that is very ugly."

He looked quietly at Jean–Christophe, and saw his angry face, and smiled, and said:

"Have you composed any others? Perhaps I shall like the others better than that."

Jean–Christophe thought that his other compositions might wipe out the impression of the first, and he sang them all. Gottfried said nothing; he waited until they were finished. Then he shook his head, and with profound conviction said:

"They are even more ugly."

Jean–Christophe shut his lips, and his chin trembled; he wanted to cry. Gottfried went on as though he himself were upset.

"How ugly they are!"

Jean–Christophe, with tears in his voice, cried out: "But why do you say they are ugly?"

Gottfried looked at him with his frank eyes.

"Why?... I don't know.... Wait.... They are ugly ... first, because they are stupid.... Yes, that's it.... They are stupid, they don't mean anything.... You see? When you wrote, you had nothing to say. Why did you write them?"

"I don't know," said Jean–Christophe, in a piteous voice. "I wanted to write something pretty."

"There you are! You wrote for the sake of writing. You wrote because you wanted to be a great musician, and to be admired. You have been proud; you have been a liar; you have been punished.... You see! A man is always punished when he is proud and a liar in music. Music must be modest and sincere—or else, what is it? Impious, a blasphemy of the Lord, who has given us song to tell the honest truth."

He saw the boy's distress, and tried to kiss him. But Jean–Christophe turned angrily away, and for several days he sulked. He hated Gottfried. But it was in vain that he said over and over to himself: "He is an ass! He knows nothing—nothing! My grandfather, who is much cleverer, likes my music." In his heart he knew that his uncle was right, and Gottfried's words were graven on his inmost soul; he was ashamed to have been a liar.

And, in spite of his resentment, he always thought of it when he was writing music, and often he tore up what he had written, being ashamed already of what Gottfried would have thought of it. When he got over it, and wrote a melody which he knew to be not quite sincere, he hid it carefully from his uncle; he was fearful of his judgment, and was quite happy when Gottfried just said of one of his pieces: "That is not so very ugly.... I like it...."

Sometimes, by way of revenge, he used to trick him by giving him as his own melodies from the great musicians, and he was delighted when it happened that Gottfried disliked them heartily. But that did not trouble Gottfried. He would laugh loudly when he saw Jean–Christophe clap his hands and dance about him delightedly, and he always returned to his usual argument: "It is well enough written, but it says nothing." He always refused to be present at one of the little concerts given in Melchior's house. However beautiful the music might be, he would begin to yawn and look sleepy with boredom. Very soon he would be unable to bear it any longer, and would steal away quietly. He used to say:

"You see, my boy, everything that you write in the house is not music. Music in a house is like sunshine in a room. Music is to be found outside where you breathe God's dear fresh air."

He was always talking of God, for he was very pious, unlike the two Kraffts, father and son, who were free–thinkers, and took care to eat meat on Fridays.

* * * * *

Suddenly, for no apparent reason, Melchior changed his opinion. Not only did he approve of his father having put together Jean–Christophe's inspirations, but, to the boy's great surprise, he spent several evenings in making two or three copies of his manuscript. To every question put to him on the subject, he replied impressively, "We shall see; ..." or he would rub his hands and laugh, smack the boy's head by way of a joke, or turn him up and blithely spank him. Jean–Christophe loathed these familiarities, but he saw that his father was pleased, and did not know why.

Then there were mysterious confabulations between Melchior and his father. And one evening Jean–Christophe, to his astonishment, learned that he, Jean–Christophe, had dedicated to H.S.H. the Grand Duke Leopold the *Pleasures of Childhood*. Melchior had sounded the disposition of the Prince, who had shown himself graciously inclined to accept the homage. Thereupon Melchior declared that without losing a moment they must, *primo*, draw up the official request to the Prince; *secondo*, publish the work; *tertio*, organize a concert to give it a hearing.

There were further long conferences between Melchior and Jean Michel. They argued heatedly for two or three evenings. It was forbidden to interrupt them. Melchior wrote, erased; erased, wrote. The old man talked loudly, as though he were reciting verses. Sometimes they squabbled or thumped on the table because they could not find a word.

Then Jean–Christophe was called, made to sit at the table with a pen in his hand, his father on his right, his grandfather on his left, and the old man began to dictate words which he did not understand, because he found it difficult to write every word in his enormous letters, because Melchior was shouting in his ear, and because the old man declaimed with such emphasis that Jean–Christophe, put out by the sound of the words, could not bother to listen to their meaning. The old man was no less in a state of emotion. He could not sit still, and he walked up and down the room, involuntarily illustrating the text of what he read with gestures, but he came every minute to look over what the boy had written, and Jean–Christophe, frightened by the two large faces looking over his shoulder, put out his tongue, and held his pen clumsily. A mist floated before his eyes; he made too many strokes, or smudged what he had written; and Melchior roared, and Jean Michel stormed; and he had to begin again, and then again, and when he thought that they had at last come to an end, a great blot fell on the immaculate page. Then they pulled his ears, and he burst into tears; but they forbade him to weep, because he was spoiling the paper, and they began to dictate, beginning all over again, and he thought it would go on like that to the end of his life.

At last it was finished, and Jean Michel leaned against the mantelpiece, and read over their handiwork in a voice trembling with pleasure, while Melchior sat straddled across a chair, and looked at the ceiling and wagged his chair and, as a connoisseur, rolled round his tongue the style of the following epistle:

"Most Noble and Sublime Highness! Most
Gracious Lord!

"From my fourth year Music has been the first occupation of my childish days. So soon as I allied myself to the noble Muse, who roused my soul to pure harmony, I loved her, and, as it seemed to me, she returned my love. Now I am in my sixth year, and for some time my Muse in hours of inspiration has whispered in my ears: 'Be bold! Be bold! Write down the harmonies of thy soul!' 'Six years old,' thought I, 'and how should I be bold? What would the learned in the art say of me?' I hesitated. I trembled. But my Muse insisted. I obeyed. I wrote.

"And now shall I,

"O Most Sublime Highness!

"—shall I have the temerity and audacity to place upon the steps of Thy Throne the first–fruits of my youthful labors?... Shall I make so bold as to hope that Thou wilt let fall upon them the august approbation of Thy paternal regard?...

"Oh, yes! For Science and the Arts have ever found in Thee their sage Maecenas, their generous champion, and talent puts forth its flowers under the aegis of Thy holy protection.

"In this profound and certain faith I dare, then, approach Thee with these youthful efforts. Receive them as a pure offering of my childish veneration, and of Thy goodness deign,

"*O Most Sublime Highness!*

"to glance at them, and at their young author, who bows at Thy feet deeply and in humility!

"*From the most submissive, faithful, and obedient servant of His Most Noble and Most Sublime Highness,*

"JEAN–CHRISTOPHE KRAFFT."

Jean–Christophe heard nothing. He was very happy to have finished, and, fearing that he would be made to begin again, he ran away to the fields. He had no idea of what he had written, and he cared not at all. But when the old man had finished his reading he began again to taste the full flavor of it, and when the second reading came to an end Melchior and he declared that it was a little masterpiece. That was also the opinion of the Grand Duke, to whom the letter was presented, with a copy of the musical work. He was kind enough to send word that he found both quite charming. He granted permission for the concert, and ordered that the hall of his Academy of Music should be put at Melchior's disposal, and deigned to promise that he would have the young artist presented to himself on the day of the performance.

Melchior set about organizing the concert as quickly as possible. He engaged the support of the *Hof Musik Verein*, and as the success of his first ventures had blown out his sense of proportion, he undertook at the same time to publish a magnificent edition of the *Pleasures of Childhood*. He wanted to have printed on the cover of it a portrait of

Jean-Christophe at the piano, with himself, Melchior, standing by his side, violin in hand. He had to abandon that, not on account of the cost—Melchior did not stop at any expense—but because there was not time enough. He fell back on an allegorical design representing a cradle, a trumpet, a drum, a wooden horse, grouped round a lyre which put forth rays like the sun. The title-page bore, together with a long dedication, in which the name of the Prince stood out in enormous letters, a notice to the effect that "Herr Jean-Christophe Krafft was six years old." He was, in fact, seven and a half. The printing of the design was very expensive. To meet the bill for it, Jean Michel had to sell an old eighteenth-century chest, carved with faces, which he had never consented to sell, in spite of the repeated offers of Wormser, the furniture-dealer. But Melchior had no doubt but the subscriptions would cover the cost, and beyond that the expenses of printing the composition.

One other question occupied his mind: how to dress Jean-Christophe on the day of the concert. There was a family council to decide the matter. Melchior would have liked the boy to appear in a short frock and bare legs, like a child of four. But Jean-Christophe was very large for his age, and everybody knew him. They could not hope to deceive any one. Melchior had a great idea. He decided that the boy should wear a dress-coat and white tie. In vain did Louisa protest that they would make her poor boy ridiculous. Melchior anticipated exactly the success and merriment that would be produced by such an unexpected appearance. It was decided on, and the tailor came and measured Jean-Christophe for his little coat. He had also to have fine linen and patent-leather pumps, and all that swallowed up their last penny. Jean-Christophe was very uncomfortable in his new clothes. To make him used to them they made him try on his various garments. For a whole month he hardly left the piano-stool. They taught him to bow. He had never a moment of liberty. He raged against it, but dared not rebel, for he thought that he was going to accomplish something startling. He was both proud and afraid of it. They pampered him; they were afraid he would catch cold; they swathed his neck in scarves; they warmed his boots in case they were wet; and at table he had the best of everything.

At last the great day arrived. The barber came to preside over his toilet and curl Jean-Christophe's rebellious hair. He did not leave it until he had made it look like a sheep-skin. All the family walked round Jean-Christophe and declared that he was superb. Melchior, after looking him up and down, and turning him about and about, was seized with an idea, and went off to fetch a large flower, which he put in his buttonhole.

But when Louisa saw him she raised her hands, and cried out distressfully that he looked like a monkey. That hurt him cruelly. He did not know whether to be ashamed or proud of his garb. Instinctively he felt humiliated, and he was more so at the concert. Humiliation was to be for him the outstanding emotion of that memorable day.

* * * * *

The concert was about to begin. The hall was half empty; the Grand Duke had not arrived. One of those kindly and well–informed friends who always appear on these occasions came and told them that there was a Council being held at the Palace, and that the Grand Duke would not come. He had it on good authority. Melchior was in despair. He fidgeted, paced up and down, and looked repeatedly out of the window. Old Jean Michel was also in torment, but he was concerned, for his grandson. He bombarded him with instructions. Jean–Christophe was infected by the nervousness of his family. He was not in the least anxious about his compositions, but he was troubled by the thought of the bows that he had to make to the audience, and thinking of them brought him to agony.

However, he had to begin; the audience was growing impatient. The orchestra of the *Hof Musik Verein* began the *Coriolan Overture*. The boy knew neither Coriolan nor Beethoven, for though he had often heard Beethoven's music, he had not known it. He never bothered about the names of the works he heard. He gave them names of his own invention, while he created little stories or pictures for them. He classified them usually in three categories: fire, water, and earth, with a thousand degrees between each. Mozart belonged almost always to water. He was a meadow by the side of a river, a transparent mist floating over the water, a spring shower, or a rainbow. Beethoven was fire—now a furnace with gigantic flames and vast columns of smoke; now a burning forest, a heavy and terrible cloud, flashing lightning; now a wide sky full of quivering stars, one of which breaks free, swoops, and; dies on a fine September night setting the heart beating. Now; the imperious ardor of that heroic soul burned him like fire. Everything else disappeared. What was it all to him?—Melchior in despair, Jean Michel agitated, all the busy world, the audience, the Grand Duke, little Jean–Christophe. What had.' he to do with all these? What lay between them and him? Was that he—he, himself?... He was given up to the furious will that carried him headlong. He followed it breathlessly, with tears in his eyes, and his legs numb, thrilling from the palms of his hands to the soles of his feet. His blood drummed! "Charge!" and he trembled in every limb. And as he listened so intensely, Hiding behind a curtain, his heart suddenly leaped violently. The orchestra had stopped short in the middle of a bar, and after a moment's silence, it broke into a crashing of brass and cymbals with a military march, officially strident. The transition from one sort of music to another was so brutal, so unexpected, that Jean–Christophe ground his teeth and stamped his foot with rage, and shook his fist at the wall. But Melchior rejoiced. The Grand Duke had come in, and the orchestra was saluting him with the National Anthem. And in a trembling voice Jean Michel gave his last instructions to his grandson.

The overture began again, and this time was finished. It was now Jean–Christophe's turn. Melchior had arranged the programme to show off at the same time the skill of both father and son. They were to play together a sonata of Mozart for violin and piano. For the sake of effect he had decided that Jean–Christophe should enter alone. He was led to the entrance of the stage and showed the piano at the front, and for the last time it was explained what he had to do, and then he was pushed on from the wings.

He was not much afraid, for he was used to the theater; but when he found himself alone on the platform, with hundreds of eyes staring at him, he became suddenly so frightened that instinctively he moved backwards and turned towards the wings to go back again. He saw his father there gesticulating and with his eyes blazing. He had to go on. Besides, the audience had seen him. As he advanced there arose a twittering of curiosity, followed soon by laughter, which grew louder and louder. Melchior had not been wrong, and the boy's garb had all the effect anticipated. The audience rocked with laughter at the sight of the child with his long hair and gipsy complexion timidly trotting across the platform in the evening dress of a man of the world. They got up to see him better. Soon the hilarity was general. There was nothing unkindly in it, but it would have made the most hardened musician lose his head. Jean–Christophe, terrified by the noise, and the eyes watching, and the glasses turned upon him, had only one idea: to reach the piano as quickly as possible, for it seemed to him a refuge, an island in the midst of the sea. With head down, looking neither to right nor left, he ran quickly across the platform, and when he reached the middle of it, instead of bowing to the audience, as had been arranged, he turned his back on it, and plunged straight for the piano. The chair was too high for him to sit down without his father's help, and in his distress, instead of waiting, he climbed up on to it on his knees. That increased the merriment of the audience, but now Jean–Christophe was safe. Sitting at his instrument, he was afraid of no one.

Melchior came at last. He gained by the good–humor of the audience, who welcomed him with warm applause. The sonata began. The boy played it with imperturbable certainty, with his lips pressed tight in concentration, his eyes fixed on the keys, his little legs hanging down from the chair. He became more at ease as the notes rolled out; he was among friends that he knew. A murmur of approbation reached him, and waves of pride and satisfaction surged through him as he thought that all these people were silent to listen to him and to admire him. But hardly had he finished when fear overcame him again, and the applause which greeted him gave him more shame than pleasure. His shame increased when Melchior took him by the hand, and advanced with him to the edge of the platform, and made him bow to the public. He obeyed, and bowed very low, with a funny awkwardness; but he was humiliated, and blushed for what he had done, as though it were a thing ridiculous and ugly.

He had to sit at the piano again, and he played the *Pleasures of Childhood*. Then the audience was enraptured. After each piece they shouted enthusiastically. They wanted him to begin again, and he was proud of his success and at the same time almost hurt by such applause, which was also a command. At the end the whole audience rose to acclaim him; the Grand Duke led the applause. But as Jean–Christophe was now alone on the platform he dared not budge from his seat. The applause redoubled. He bent his head lower and lower, blushing and hang–dog in expression, and he looked steadily away from the audience. Melchior came. He took him in his arms, and told him to blow kisses. He pointed out to him the Grand Duke's box. Jean–Christophe turned a deaf ear. Melchior took his arm, and threatened him in a low voice. Then he did as he was told passively, but he did not look at anybody, he did not raise his eyes, but went on turning his head away, and he was unhappy. He was suffering; how, he did not know. His vanity was suffering. He did not like the people who were there at all. It was no use their applauding; he could not forgive them for having laughed and for being amused by his humiliation; he could not forgive them for having seen him in such a ridiculous position—held in mid–air to blow kisses. He disliked them even for applauding, and when Melchior did at last put him down, he ran away to the wings. A lady threw a bunch of violets up at him as he went. It brushed his face. He was panic–stricken and ran as fast as he could, turning over a chair that was in his way. The faster he ran the more they laughed, and the more they laughed the faster he ran.

At last he reached the exit, which was filled with people looking at him. He forced his way through, butting, and ran and hid himself at the back of the anteroom. His grandfather was in high feather, and covered him with blessings. The musicians of the orchestra shouted with laughter, and congratulated the boy, who refused to look at them or to shake hands with them. Melchior listened intently, gaging the applause, which had not yet ceased, and wanted to take Jean–Christophe on to the stage again. But the boy refused angrily, clung to his grandfather's coat–tails, and kicked at everybody who came near him. At last he burst into tears, and they had to let him be.

Just at this moment an officer came to say that the Grand Duke wished the artists to go to his box. How could the child be presented in such a state? Melchior swore angrily, and his wrath only had the effect of making Jean–Christophe's tears flow faster. To stop them, his grandfather promised him a pound of chocolates if he would not cry any more, and Jean–Christophe, who was greedy, stopped dead, swallowed down his tears, and let them carry him off; but they had to swear at first most solemnly that they would not take him on to the platform again.

In the anteroom of the Grand Ducal box he was presented to a gentleman in a dress–coat, with a face like a pug–dog, bristling mustaches, and a short, pointed beard—a little red–faced man, inclined to stoutness, who addressed him with bantering familiarity, and called him "Mozart *redivivus!*" This was the Grand Duke. Then, he was presented in turn to the Grand Duchess and her daughter, and their suite. But as he did not dare raise his eyes, the only thing he could remember of this brilliant company was a series of gowns and uniforms from, the waist down to the feet. He sat on the lap of the young Princess, and dared not move or breathe. She asked him questions, which Melchior answered in an obsequious voice with formal replies, respectful and servile; but she did not listen to Melchior, and went on teasing the child. He grew redder and redder, and, thinking that everybody must have noticed it, he thought he must explain it away and said with a long sigh:

"My face is red. I am hot."

That made the girl shout with laughter. But Jean–Christophe did not mind it in her, as he had in his audience just before, for her laughter was pleasant, and she kissed him, and he did not dislike that.

Then he saw his grandfather in the passage at the door of the box, beaming and bashful. The old man was fain to show himself, and also to say a few words, but he dared not, because no one had spoken to him. He was enjoying his grandson's glory at a distance. Jean–Christophe became tender, and felt an irresistible impulse to procure justice also for the old man, so that they should know his worth. His tongue was loosed, and he reached up to the ear of his new friend and whispered to her:

"I will tell you a secret."

She laughed, and said:

"What?"

"You know," he went on—"you know the pretty *trio* in my *minuetto*, the *minuetto* I played?... You know it?..." (He hummed it gently.) "... Well, grandfather wrote it, not I. All the other airs are mine. But that is the best. Grandfather wrote it. Grandfather did not want me to say anything. You won't tell anybody?..." (He pointed out the old man.) "That is my grandfather. I love him; he is very kind to me."

At that the young Princess laughed again, said that he was a darling, covered him with kisses, and, to the consternation of Jean–Christophe and his grandfather, told everybody. Everybody laughed then, and the Grand Duke congratulated the old man, who was covered with confusion, tried in vain to explain himself, and stammered like a guilty criminal. But Jean–Christophe said not another word to the girl, and in spite of her wheedling he remained dumb and stiff. He despised her for having broken her promise. His idea of princes suffered considerably from this disloyalty. He was so angry about it that he did not hear anything that was said, or that the Prince had appointed him laughingly his pianist in ordinary, his *Hof Musicus.*

He went out with his relatives, and found himself surrounded in the corridors of the theater, and even in the street, with people congratulating him or kissing him. That displeased him greatly, for he did not like being kissed, and did not like people meddling with him without asking his permission.

At last they reached home, and then hardly was the door closed than Melchior began to call him a "little idiot" because he had said that the *trio* was not his own. As the boy was under the impression that he had done a fine thing, which deserved praise, and not blame, he rebelled, and was impertinent. Melchior lost his temper, and said that he would box his ears, although he had played his music well enough, because with his idiocy he had spoiled the whole effect of the concert. Jean–Christophe had a profound sense of justice. He went and sulked in a corner; he visited his contempt upon his father, the Princess, and the whole world. He was hurt also because the neighbors came and congratulated his parents and laughed with them, as if it were they who had played, and as if it were their affair.

At this moment a servant of the Court came with a beautiful gold watch from the Grand Duke and a box of lovely sweets from the young Princess. Both presents gave great pleasure to Jean–Christophe, and he did not know which gave him the more; but he was in such a bad temper that he would not admit it to himself, and he went on sulking, scowling at the sweets, and wondering whether he could properly accept a gift from a person who had betrayed his confidence. As he was on the point of giving in his father wanted to set him down at once at the table, and make him write at his dictation a letter of thanks. This was too much. Either from the nervous strain of the day, or from instinctive shame at beginning the letter, as Melchior wanted him to, with the words, "The little servant and musician—*Knecht und Musicus*—of Your Highness ..." he burst into tears, and was inconsolable. The servant waited and scoffed. Melchior had to write the letter. That did not make him exactly kindly disposed towards Jean–Christophe. As, a crowning misfortune, the boy let his watch fall and broke it, A storm of reproaches broke upon him. Melchior shouted that he would have to go without dessert. Jean–Christophe said angrily that that was what he wanted. To punish him, Louisa, said that she would begin by confiscating his sweets. Jean–Christophe was up in arms at that, and said that the box was his, and no one else's, and that no one should take it away from him! He was smacked, and in a fit of anger snatched the box from his mother's hands, hurled it on the floor, and stamped on it He was whipped, taken to his room, undressed, and put to bed.

In the evening he heard his parents dining with friends—a magnificent repast, prepared a week before in honor of the concert. He was like to die with wrath at such injustice. They laughed loudly, and touched glasses. They had told the guests that the boy was tired, and no one bothered about him. Only after dinner, when the party was breaking up, he heard a slow, shuffling step come into his room, and old Jean Michel bent over his bed and kissed him, and said: "Dear little Jean–Christophe!..." Then, as if he were ashamed, he went away without another word. He had slipped into his hand some sweetmeats which he had hidden in his pocket.

That softened Jean–Christophe; but he was so tired with all the day's emotions that he had not the strength to think about what his grandfather had done. He had not even the strength to reach out to the good things the old man had given him. He was worn out, and went to sleep almost at once.

His sleep was light. He had acute nervous attacks, like electric shocks, which shook his whole body. In his dreams he was haunted by wild music. He awoke in the night. The Beethoven overture that he had heard at the concert was roaring in his ears. It filled the room with its mighty beat. He sat, up in his bed, rubbed his eyes and ears, and asked himself if he were asleep. No; he was not asleep. He recognized the sound, he recognized those roars of anger, those savage cries; he heard the throbbing of that passionate heart leaping in his bosom, that tumult of the blood; he felt on his face the frantic heating of the wind; lashing and destroying, then stopping suddenly, cut off by an Herculean will. That Titanic soul entered his body, blew out his limbs and his soul, and seemed to give them colossal proportions. He strode over all the world. He was like a mountain, and storms raged within him—storms of wrath, storms of sorrow!... Ah, what sorrow!... But they were nothing! He felt so strong!... To suffer—still to suffer!... Ah, how good it is to be strong! How good it is to suffer when a man is strong!...

He laughed. His laughter rang out in the silence of the night. His father woke up and cried:

"Who is there?"

His mother whispered:

"Ssh! the boy is dreaming!"

All then were silent; round them all was silence. The music died away, and nothing sounded but the regular breathing of the human creatures asleep in the room, comrades in misery, thrown together by Fate in the same frail barque, bound onwards by a wild whirling force through the night.

(Jean–Christophe's letter to the Grand Duke Leopold is inspired by Beethoven's letter to the Prince Elector of Bonn, written when he was eleven.)

MORNING

I. THE DEATH OF JEAN MICHEL

Years have passed. Jean–Christophe is nearly eleven. His musical education is proceeding. He is learning harmony with Florian Holzer, the organist of St. Martin's, a friend of his grandfather's, a very learned man, who teaches him that the chords and series of chords that he most loves, and the harmonica which softly greet his heart and ear, those that he cannot hear without a little thrill running down his spine, are bad and forbidden. When he asks why, no reply is forthcoming but that it is so; the rules forbid them. As he is naturally in revolt against discipline, he loves them only the more. His delight is to find examples of them in the great and admired musicians, and to take them to his grandfather or his master. His grandfather replies that in the great musicians they are admirable, and that Beethoven and Bach can take any liberty. His master, less conciliatory, is angry, and says acidly that the masters did better things.

Jean–Christophe has a free pass for the concerts and the theater. He has learned to play every instrument a little. He is already quite skilful with the violin, and his father procured him a seat in the orchestra. He acquitted himself so well there that after a few months' probation he was officially appointed second violin in the *Hof Musik Verein*. He has begun to earn his living. Not too soon either, for affairs at home have gone from bad to worse. Melchior's intemperance has swamped him, and his grandfather is growing old.

Jean–Christophe has taken in the melancholy situation. He is already as grave and anxious as a man. He fulfils his task valiantly, though it does not interest him, and he is apt to fall asleep in the orchestra in the evenings, because it is late and he is tired. The theater no longer rouses in him the emotion it used to do when he was little. When he was little—four years ago—his greatest ambition had been to occupy the place that he now holds. But now he dislikes most of the music he is made to play. He dare not yet pronounce judgment upon it, but he does find it foolish; and if by chance they do play lovely things, he is displeased by the carelessness with which they are rendered, and his best-beloved works are made to appear like his neighbors and colleagues in the orchestra, who, as soon as the curtain has fallen, when they have done with blowing and scraping, mop their brows and smile and chatter quietly, as though they had just finished an hour's gymnastics. And he has been close to his former flame, the fair barefooted singer. He meets her quite often during the *entr'acte* in the saloon. She knows that he was once in love with her, and she kisses him often. That gives him no pleasure. He is disgusted by her paint and scent and her fat arms and her greediness. He hates her now.

The Grand Duke did not forget his pianist in ordinary. Not that the small pension, which was granted to him with this title was regularly paid—it had to be asked for—but from time to time Jean–Christophe used to receive orders to go to the Palace when there were distinguished guests, or simply when Their Highnesses took it into their heads that they wanted to hear him. It was almost always in the evening, at the time when Jean–Christophe wanted to be alone. He had to leave everything and hurry off. Sometimes he was made to wait in the anteroom, because dinner was not finished. The servants, accustomed to see him, used to address him familiarly. Then he would be led into a great room full of mirrors and lights, in which well–fed men and women used to stare at him with horrid curiosity. He had to cross the waxed floor to kiss Their Highnesses' hands, and the more he grew the more awkward he became, for he felt that he was in a ridiculous position, and his pride used to suffer.

When it was all done he used to sit at the piano and have to play for these idiots. He thought them idiots. There were moments when their indifference so oppressed him as he played that he was often on the point of stopping in the middle of a piece. There was no air about him; he was near suffocation, seemed losing his senses. When he finished he was overwhelmed with congratulations and laden with compliments; he was introduced all round. He thought they looked at him like some strange animal in the Prince's menagerie, and that the words of praise were addressed rather to his master than to himself. He thought himself brought low, and he developed a morbid sensibility from which he suffered the more as he dared not show it. He saw offense in the most simple actions. If any one laughed in a corner of the room, he imagined himself to be the cause of it, and he knew not whether it were his manners, or his clothes, or his person, or his hands, or his feet, that caused the laughter. He was humiliated by everything. He was humiliated if people did not talk to him, humiliated if they did, humiliated if they gave him sweets like a child, humiliated especially when the Grand Duke, as sometimes happened, in princely fashion dismissed him by pressing a piece of money into his hand. He was wretched at being poor and at being treated as a poor boy. One evening, as he was going home, the money that he had received weighed so heavily upon him that he threw it through a cellar window, and then immediately he would have done anything to get it back, for at home there was a month's old account with the butcher to pay.

His relatives never suspected these injuries to his pride. They were delighted at his favor with the Prince. Poor Louisa could conceive of nothing finer for her son than these evenings at the Palace in splendid society. As for Melchior, he used to brag of it continually to his boon–fellows. But Jean–Christophe's grandfather was happier than any. He pretended to be independent and democratic, and to despise greatness, but he had a simple admiration for money, power, honors, social distinction, and he took unbounded pride in seeing his grandson, moving among those who had these things. He delighted in them as though such glory was a reflection upon himself, and in spite of all his efforts to appear calm and indifferent, his face used to glow. On the evenings when Jean–Christophe went to the Palace, old Jean Michel used always to contrive to stay about the house on some pretext or another. He used to await his grandson's return with childish impatience, and when Jean–Christophe came in he would begin at once with a careless air to ply him with seeming idle questions, such as:

"Well, did things go well to–night?"

Or he would make little hints like:

"Here's our Jean–Christophe; he can tell us some news."

Or he would produce some ingenious compliment by way of flattery:

"Here's our young nobleman!"

But Jean–Christophe, out of sorts and out of temper, would reply with a curt "Good–evening!" and go and sulk in a corner. But the old man would persist, and ply him with more direct questions, to which the boy replied only "Yes," or "No." Then the others would join in and ask for details. Jean–Christophe would look more and more thunderous. They had to drag the words from his lips until Jean Michel would lose his temper and hurl insults at him. Then Jean–Christophe would reply with scant respect, and the end would be a rumpus. The old man would go out and slam the door. So Jean–Christophe spoiled the joy of these poor people, who had no inkling of the cause of his bad temper. It was not their fault if they had the souls of servants, and never dreamed that it is possible to be otherwise.

Jean–Christophe was turned into himself, and though he never judged his family, yet he felt a gulf between himself and them. No doubt he exaggerated what lay between them, and in spite of their different ways of thought it is quite probable that they could have understood each other if he had been able to talk intimately to them. But it is known that nothing is more difficult than absolute intimacy between children and parents, even when there is much love between them, for on the one side respect discourages confidence, and on the other the idea, often erroneous, of the superiority of age and experience prevents them taking seriously enough the child's feelings, which are often just as interesting as those of grown–up persons, and almost always more sincere.

But the people that Jean–Christophe saw at home and the conversation that he heard there widened the distance between himself and his family.

Melchior's friends used to frequent the house—mostly musicians of the orchestra, single men and hard drinkers. They were not bad fellows, but vulgar. They made the house shake with their footsteps and their laughter. They loved music, but they spoke of it with a stupidity that was revolting. The coarse indiscretion of their enthusiasm wounded the boy's modesty of feeling. When they praised a work that he loved it was as though they were insulting him personally. He would stiffen himself and grow pale, frozen, and pretend not to take any interest in music. He would have hated it had that been possible. Melchior used to say:

"The fellow has no heart. He feels nothing. I don't know where he gets it from."

Sometimes they used to sing German four–part songs—four–footed as well—and these were all exactly like themselves—slow–moving, solemn and broad, fashioned of dull melodies. Then Jean–Christophe used to fly to the most distant room and hurl insults at the wall.

His grandfather also had friends: the organist, the furniture–dealer, the watch–maker, the contra–bass—garrulous old men, who used always to pass round the same jokes and plunge into interminable discussions on art, politics, or the family trees of the countryside, much less interested in the subjects of which they talked than happy to talk and to find an audience.

As for Louisa, she used only to see some of her neighbors who brought her the gossip of the place, and at rare intervals a "kind lady," who, under pretext of taking an interest in her, used to come and engage her services for a dinner–party, and pretend to watch over the religious education of the children.

But of all who came to the house, none was more repugnant to Jean–Christophe than his Uncle Theodore, a stepson of his grandfather's, a son by a former marriage of his grandmother Clara, Jean Michel's first wife. He was a partner in a great commercial house which did business in Africa and the Far East. He was the exact type of one of those Germans of the new style, whose affectation it is scoffingly to repudiate the old idealism of the race, and, intoxicated by conquest, to maintain a cult of strength and success which shows that they are not accustomed to seeing them on their side. But as it is difficult at once to change the age–old nature of a people, the despised idealism sprang up again in him at every turn in language, manners, and moral habits and the quotations from Goethe to fit the smallest incidents of domestic life, for he was a singular compound of conscience and self–interest. There was in him a curious effort to reconcile the honest principles of the old German *bourgeoisie* with the cynicism of these new commercial *condottieri*—a compound which forever gave out a repulsive flavor of hypocrisy, forever striving to make of German strength, avarice, and self–interest the symbols of all right, justice, and truth.

Jean–Christophe's loyalty was deeply injured by all this. He could not tell whether his uncle were right or no, but he hated him, and marked him down for an enemy. His grandfather had no great love for him either, and was in revolt against his theories; but he was easily crushed in argument by Theodore's fluency, which was never hard put to it to turn into ridicule the old man's simple generosity. In the end Jean Michel came to be ashamed of his own good–heartedness, and by way of showing that he was not so much behind the times as they thought, he used to try to talk like Theodore; but the words came hollow from his lips, and he was ill at ease with them. Whatever he may have thought of him, Theodore did impress him. He felt respect for such practical skill, which he admired the more for knowing himself to be absolutely incapable of it. He used to dream of putting one of his grandsons to similar work. That was Melchior's idea also. He intended to make Rodolphe follow in his uncle's footsteps. And so the whole family set itself to flatter this rich relation of whom they expected help. He, seeing that he was necessary to them, took advantage of it to cut a fine masterful figure, He meddled in everything, gave advice upon everything, and made no attempt to conceal his contempt for art and artists.

Rather, he blazoned it abroad for the mere pleasure of humiliating his musicianly relations, and he used to indulge in stupid jokes at their expense, and the cowards used to laugh.

Jean–Christophe, especially, was singled out as a butt for his uncle's jests. He was not patient under them. He would say nothing, but he used to grind his teeth angrily, and his uncle used to laugh at his speechless rage. But one day, when Theodore went too far in his teasing, Jean–Christophe, losing control of himself, spat in his face. It was a fearful affair. The insult was so monstrous that his uncle was at first paralyzed by it; then words came back to him, and he broke out into a flood of abuse. Jean–Christophe sat petrified by the enormity of the thing that he had done, and did not even feel the blows that rained down upon him; but when they tried to force him down on his knees before his uncle, he broke away, jostled his mother aside, and ran out of the house. He did not stop until he could breathe no more, and then he was right out in the country. He heard voices calling him, and he debated within himself whether he had not better throw himself into the river, since he could not do so with his enemy. He spent the night in the fields. At dawn he went and knocked at his grandfather's door. The old man had been so upset by Jean–Christophe's disappearance—he had not slept for it—that he had not the heart to scold him. He took him home, and then nothing was said to him, because it was apparent that he was still in an excited condition, and they had to smooth him down, for he had to play at the Palace that evening. But for several weeks Melchior continued to overwhelm him with his complaints, addressed to nobody in particular, about the trouble that a man takes to give an example of an irreproachable life and good manners to unworthy creatures who dishonor him. And when his Uncle Theodore met him in the street, he turned his head and held his nose by way of showing his extreme disgust.

Finding so little sympathy at home, Jean–Christophe spent as little time there as possible. He chafed against the continual restraint which they strove to set upon him. There were too many things, too many people, that he had to respect, and he was never allowed to ask why, and Jean–Christophe did not possess the bump of respect. The more they tried to discipline him and to turn him into an honest little German *bourgeois*, the more he felt the need of breaking free from it all. It would have been his pleasure after the dull, tedious, formal performances which he had to attend in the orchestra or at the Palace to roll in the grass like a fowl, and to slide down the grassy slope on the seat of his new trousers, or to have a stone–fight with the urchins of the neighborhood. It was not because he was afraid of scoldings and thwackings that he did not do these things more often, but because he had no playmates. He could not get on with other children. Even the little guttersnipes did not like playing with him, because he took every game too seriously, and struck too lustily. He had grown used to being driven in on himself, and to living apart from children of his own age. He was ashamed of not being clever at games, and dared not take part in their sport. And he used to pretend to take no interest in it, although he was consumed by the desire to be asked to play with them. But they never said anything to him, and then he would go away hurt, but assuming indifference.

He found consolation in wandering with Uncle Gottfried when he was in the neighborhood. He became more and more friendly with him, and sympathized with his independent temper. He understood so well now Gottfried's delight in tramping the roads without a tie in the world! Often they used to go out together in the evening into the country, straight on, aimlessly, and as Gottfried always forgot the time, they used to come back very late, and then were scolded. Gottfried knew that it was wrong, but Jean–Christophe used to implore, and he could not himself resist the pleasure of it. About midnight he would stand in front of the house and whistle, an agreed signal. Jean–Christophe would be in his bed fully dressed. He would slip out with his shoes in his hand, and, holding his breath, creep with all the artful skill of a savage to the kitchen window, which opened on to the road. He would climb on to the table; Gottfried would take him on his shoulders, and then off they would go, happy as truants.

Sometimes they would go and seek out Jeremy the fisherman, a friend of Gottfried's, and then they would slip out in his boat under the moon. The water dropping from the oars gave out little arpeggios, then chromatic scales. A milky vapor hung tremulous over the surface of the waters. The stars quivered. The cocks called to each other from either bank, and sometimes in the depths of the sky they heard the trilling of larks ascending from earth, deceived by the light of the moon. They were silent. Gottfried hummed a tune. Jeremy told strange tales of the lives of the beasts—tales that gained in mystery from the curt and enigmatic manner of their telling. The moon hid herself behind the woods. They skirted the black mass of the hills. The darkness of the water and the sky mingled. There was never a ripple on the water. Sounds died down. The boat glided through the night. Was she gliding? Was she moving? Was she still?... The reeds parted with a sound like the rustling of silk. The boat grounded noiselessly. They climbed out on to the bank, and returned on foot. They would not return until dawn. They followed the river–bank. Clouds of silver ablets, green as ears of corn, or blue as jewels, teemed in the first light of day. They swarmed like the serpents of Medusa's head, and flung themselves greedily at the bread thrown to them; they plunged for it as it sank, and turned in spirals, and then darted away in a flash, like a ray of light. The river took on rosy and purple hues of reflection. The birds woke one after another. The truants hurried back. Just as carefully as when they had set out, they returned to the room, with its thick atmosphere, and Jean–Christophe, worn out, fell into bed, and slept at once, with his body sweet–smelling with the smell of the fields.

All was well, and nothing would have been known, but that one day Ernest, his younger brother, betrayed Jean–Christophe's midnight sallies. From that moment they were forbidden, and he was watched. But he contrived to escape, and he preferred the society of the little peddler and his friends to any other. His family was scandalized. Melchior said that he had the tastes of a laborer. Old Jean Michel was jealous of Jean–Christophe's affection for Gottfried, and used to lecture him about lowering himself so far as to like such vulgar company when he had the honor of mixing with the best people and of being the servant of princes. It was considered that Jean–Christophe was lacking in dignity and self–respect.

In spite of the penury which increased with Melchior's intemperance and folly, life was tolerable as long as Jean Michel was there. He was the only creature who had any influence over Melchior, and who could hold him back to a certain extent from his vice. The esteem in which he was generally held did serve to pass over the drunkard's freaks, and he used constantly to come to the aid of the household with money. Besides the modest pension which he enjoyed as retired *Kapellmeister*, he was still able to earn small sums by giving lessons and tuning pianos. He gave most of it to his daughter–in–law, for he perceived her difficulties, though she strove to hide them from him. Louisa hated the idea that he was denying himself for them, and it was all the more to the old man's credit in that he had always been accustomed to a large way of living and had great needs to satisfy. Sometimes even his ordinary sacrifices were not sufficient, and to meet some urgent debt Jean Michel would have secretly to sell a piece of furniture or books, or some relic that he set store by. Melchior knew that his father made presents to Louisa that were concealed from himself, and very often he would lay hands on them, in spite of protest. But when this came to the old man's ears—not from Louisa, who said nothing of her troubles to him, but from one of his grandchildren—he would fly into a terrible passion, and there were frightful scenes between the two men. They were both extraordinarily violent, and they would come to round oaths and threats—almost it seemed as though they would come to blows. But even in his most angry passion respect would hold

Melchior in check, and, however drunk he might be, in the end he would bow his head to the torrent of insults and humiliating reproach which his father poured out upon him. But for that he did not cease to watch for the first opportunity of breaking out again, and with his thoughts on the future, Jean Michel would be filled with melancholy and anxious fears.

"My poor children," he used to say to Louisa, "what will become, of you when I am no longer here?... Fortunately," he would add, fondling Jean–Christophe, "I can go on until this fellow pulls you out of the mire." But he was out in his reckoning; he was at the end of his road. No one would have suspected it. He was surprisingly strong. He was past eighty; he had a full head of hair, a white mane, still gray in patches, and in his thick beard were still black hairs. He had only about ten teeth left, but with these he could chew lustily. It was a pleasure to see him at table. He had a hearty appetite, and though, he reproached Melchior for drinking, he always emptied his bottle himself. He had a preference for white Moselle. For the rest—wine, beer, cider—he could do justice to all the good things that the Lord hath made. He was not so foolish as to lose his reason in his cups, and he kept to his allowance. It is true that it was a plentiful allowance, and that a feebler intelligence must have been made drunk by it. He was strong of foot and eye, and indefatigably active. He got up at six, and performed his ablutions scrupulously, for he cared for his appearance and respected his person. He lived alone in his house, of which he was sole occupant, and never let his daughter–in–law meddle with his affairs. He cleaned out his room, made his own coffee, sewed on his buttons, nailed, and glued, and altered; and going to and fro and up and down stairs in his shirt–sleeves, he never stopped singing in a sounding bass which he loved to let ring out as he accompanied himself with operatic gestures. And then he used to go out in all weathers. He went about his business, omitting none, but he was not often punctual. He was to be seen at every street corner arguing with some acquaintance or joking with some woman whose face he had remembered, for he loved pretty women and old friends. And so he was always late, and never knew the time. But he never let the dinner–hour slip by. He dined wherever he might be, inviting himself, and he would not go home until late—after nightfall, after a visit to his grandchildren. Then he would go to bed, and before he went to sleep read a page of his old Bible, and during the night—for he never slept for more than an hour or two together—he would get up to take down one of his old books, bought second–hand—history, theology, belles–lettres, or science. He used to read at random a few pages, which interested and bored him, and he did not rightly understand them, though he did not skip a word, until sleep came to him again. On Sunday he would go to church, walk with the children, and play bowls. He had never been ill, except for a little gout in his toes, which used to make him swear at night while he was reading his Bible. It seemed as though he might live to be a hundred, and he himself could see no reason why he should not live longer. When people said that he would die a centenarian, he used to think, like another illustrious old man, that no limit can be appointed to the goodness of Providence, The only sign that he was growing old was that he was more easily brought to tears, and was becoming every day more irritable. The smallest impatience with him could throw him into a violent fury. His red face and short neck would grow redder than ever. He would stutter angrily, and have to stop, choking. The family doctor, an old friend, had warned him to take care and to moderate both his anger and his appetite. But with an old man's obstinacy he plunged into acts of still greater recklessness out of bravado, and he laughed at medicine and doctors. He pretended to despise death, and did not mince his language when he declared that he was not afraid of it.

One summer day, when it was very hot, and he had drunk copiously, and argued in the market–place, he went home and began to work quietly in his garden. He loved digging. Bareheaded under the sun, still irritated by his argument, he dug angrily. Jean–Christophe was sitting in the arbor with a book in his hand, but he was not reading. He was dreaming and listening to the cheeping of the crickets, and mechanically following his grandfather's movements. The old man's back was towards him; he was bending and plucking out weeds. Suddenly Jean–Christophe saw him rise, beat against the air with his arms, and fall heavily with his face to the ground. For a moment he wanted to laugh; then he saw that the old man did not stir. He called to him, ran to him, and shook him with all his strength. Fear seized him. He knelt, and with his two hands tried to raise the great head from the ground. It was so heavy and he trembled so that he could hardly move it. But when he saw the eyes turned up, white and bloody, he was frozen with horror and, with a shrill cry, let the head fall. He got up in terror, ran away and out of the place. He cried and wept. A man passing by stopped the boy. Jean–Christophe could not speak, but he pointed to the house. The man went in, and Jean–Christophe followed him. Others had heard his cries, and they came from the neighboring houses. Soon the garden was full of people. They trampled the flowers, and bent down over the old man. They cried aloud. Two or three men lifted him up. Jean–Christophe stayed by the gate, turned to the wall, and hid his face in his hands. He was afraid to look, but he could not help himself, and when they passed him he saw through his fingers the old man's huge body, limp and flabby. One arm dragged along the ground, the head, leaning against the knee of one of the men carrying the body, bobbed at every step, and the face was scarred, covered with mud, bleeding. The mouth was open and the eyes were fearful. He howled again, and took to flight. He ran as though something were after him, and never stopped until he reached home. He burst into the kitchen with frightful cries. Louisa was cleaning vegetables. He hurled himself at her, and hugged her desperately, imploring her help. His face was distorted with his sobs; he could hardly speak. But at the first word she understood. She went white, let the things fall from her hands, and without a word rushed from the house.

Jean–Christophe was left alone, crouching against a cupboard. He went on weeping. His brothers were playing. He could not make out quite what had happened. He did not think of his grandfather; he was thinking only of the dreadful sights he had just seen, and he was in terror lest he should be made to return to see them again.

And as it turned out in the evening, when the other children, tired of doing every sort of mischief in the house, were beginning to feel wearied and hungry, Louisa rushed in again, took them by the hand, and led them to their grandfather's house. She walked very fast, and Ernest and Rodolphe tried to complain, as usual; but Louisa bade them be silent in such a tone of voice that they held their peace. An instinctive fear seized them, and when they entered the house they began to weep. It was not yet night. The last hours of the sunset cast strange lights over the inside of the house—on the door–handle, on the mirror, on the violin hung on the wall in the chief room, which was half in darkness. But in the old man's room a candle was alight, and the flickering flame, vying with the livid, dying day, made the heavy darkness of the room more oppressive. Melchior was sitting near the window, loudly weeping. The doctor, leaning over the bed, hid from sight what was lying there. Jean–Christophe's heart beat so that it was like to break. Louisa made the children kneel at the foot of the bed. Jean–Christophe stole a glance. He expected something so terrifying after what he had seen in the afternoon that at the first glimpse he was almost comforted. His grandfather lay motionless, and seemed to be asleep. For a moment the child believed that the old man was better, and that all was at an end. But when he heard his heavy breathing; when, as he looked closer, he saw the swollen face, on which the wound that he had come by in the fall had made a broad scar; when he understood that here was a man at point of death, he began to tremble; and while he repeated Louisa's prayer for the restoration of his grandfather, in his heart he prayed that if the old man could not get well he might be already dead. He was terrified at the prospect of what was going to happen.

The old man had not been conscious since the moment of his fall. He only returned to consciousness for a moment, enough to learn his condition, and that was lamentable. The priest was there, and recited the last prayers over him. They raised the old man on his pillow. He opened his eyes slowly, and they seemed no longer to obey his will. He breathed noisily, and with unseeing eyes looked at the faces and the lights, and suddenly he opened his mouth. A nameless terror showed on his features.

"But then ..." he gasped—"but I am going to die!"

The awful sound of his voice pierced Jean–Christophe's heart. Never, never was it to fade from his memory. The old man said no more. He moaned like a little child. The stupor took him once more, but his breathing became more and more difficult. He groaned, he fidgeted with his hands, he seemed to struggle against the mortal sleep. In his semi–consciousness he cried once:

"Mother!"

Oh, the biting impression that it made, this mumbling of the old man, calling in anguish on his mother, as Jean–Christophe would himself have done—his mother, of whom he was never known to talk in life, to whom he now turned instinctively, the last futile refuge in the last terror!... Then he seemed to be comforted for a moment. He had once more a flicker of consciousness. His heavy eyes, the pupils of which seemed to move aimlessly, met those of the boy frozen in his fear. They lit up. The old man tried to smile and speak. Louisa took Jean–Christophe and led him to the bedside. Jean Michel moved his lips, and tried to caress his head with his hand, but then he fell back into his torpor. It was the end.

They sent the children into the next room, but they had too much to do to worry about them, and Jean–Christophe, under the attraction of the horror of it, peeped through the half–open door at the tragic face on the pillow; the man strangled by the firm, clutch that had him by the neck; the face which grew ever more hollow as he watched; the sinking of the creature into the void, which seemed to suck it down like a pump; and the horrible death–rattle, the mechanical breathing, like a bubble of air bursting on the surface of waters; the last efforts of the body, which strives to live when the soul is no longer. Then the head fell on one side on the pillow. All, all was silence.

A few moments later, in the midst of the sobs and prayers and the confusion caused by the death, Louisa saw the child, pale, wide–eyed, with gaping mouth, clutching convulsively at the handle of the door. She ran to him. He had a seizure in her arms. She carried him away. He lost consciousness. He woke up to find himself in his bed. He howled in terror, because he had been left alone for a moment, had another seizure, and fainted again. For the rest of the night and the next day he was in a fever. Finally, he grew calm, and on the next night fell into a deep sleep, which lasted until the middle of the following day. He felt that some one was walking in his room, that his mother was leaning over his bed and kissing him. He thought he heard the sweet distant sound of bells. But he would not stir; he was in a dream.

When he opened his eyes again his Uncle Gottfried was sitting at the foot of his bed. Jean–Christophe was worn out, and could remember nothing. Then his memory returned, and: he began to weep. Gottfried got up and kissed him.

"Well, my boy—well?" he said gently.

"Oh, uncle, uncle!" sobbed the boy, clinging to him.

"Cry, then ..." said Gottfried. "Cry!"

He also was weeping.

When he was a little comforted Jean–Christophe dried his eyes and looked at Gottfried. Gottfried understood that he wanted to ask something.

"No," he said, putting a finger to his lips, "you must not talk. It is good to cry, bad to talk."

The boy insisted.

"It is no good."

"Only one thing—only one!..."

"What?"

Jean–Christophe hesitated.

"Oh, uncle!" he asked, "where is he now?"

Gottfried answered:

"He is with the Lord, my boy."

But that was not what Jean–Christophe had asked.

"No; you do not understand. Where is he—he *himself?*" (He meant the body.)

He went on in a trembling voice:

"Is *he* still in the house?"

"They buried the good man this morning," said Gottfried. "Did you not hear the bells?"

Jean–Christophe was comforted. Then, when he thought that he would never see his beloved grandfather again, he wept once more bitterly.

"Poor little beast!" said Gottfried, looking pityingly at the child.

Jean–Christophe expected Gottfried to console him, but Gottfried made no attempt to do so, knowing that it was useless.

"Uncle Gottfried," asked the boy, "are not you afraid of it, too?"

(Much did he wish that Gottfried should not have been afraid, and would tell him the secret of it!)

"'Ssh!" he said, in a troubled voice....

"And how is one not to be afraid?" he said, after a moment. "But what can one do? It is so. One must put up with it."

Jean–Christophe shook his head in protest.

"One has to put up with it, my boy," said Gottfried. "*He* ordered it up yonder. One has to love what *He* has ordered."

"I hate Him!" said Jean–Christophe, angrily shaking his fist at the sky.

Gottfried fearfully bade him be silent. Jean–Christophe himself was afraid of what he had just said, and he began to pray with Gottfried. But blood boiled, and as he repeated the words of servile humility and resignation there was in his inmost heart a feeling of passionate revolt and horror of the abominable thing and the monstrous Being who had been able to create it.

Days passed and nights of rain over the freshly–turned earth under which lay the remains of poor old Jean Michel. At the moment Melchior wept and cried and sobbed much, but the week was not out before Jean–Christophe heard him laughing heartily. When the name of the dead man was pronounced in his presence, his face grew longer and a lugubrious expression came into it, but in a moment he would begin to talk and gesticulate excitedly. He was sincerely afflicted, but it was impossible for him to remain sad for long.

Louisa, passive and resigned, accepted the misfortune as she accepted everything. She added a prayer to her daily prayers; she went regularly to the cemetery, and cared for the grass as if it were part of her household.

Gottfried paid touching attention to the little patch of ground where the old man slept. When he came to the neighborhood, he brought a little souvenir—a cross that he had made, or flowers that Jean Michel had loved. He never missed, even if he were only in the town for a few hours, and he did it by stealth.

Sometimes Louisa took Jean–Christophe with her on her visits to the cemetery. Jean–Christophe revolted in disgust against the fat patch of earth clad in its sinister adornment of flowers and trees, and against the heavy scent which mounts to the sun, mingling with the breath of the sonorous cypress. But he dared not confess his disgust, because he condemned it in himself as cowardly and impious. He was very unhappy. His grandfather's death haunted him incessantly, and yet he had long known what death was, and had thought about it and been afraid of it. But he had never before seen it, and he who sees it for the first time learns that he knew nothing, neither of death nor of life. One moment brings everything tottering. Reason is of no avail. You thought you were alive, you thought you had some experience of life; you see then that you knew nothing, that you have been living in a veil of illusions spun by your own mind to hide from your eyes the awful countenance of reality. There is no connection between the idea of suffering and the creature who bleeds and suffers. There is no connection between the idea of death and the convulsions of body and soul in combat and in death. Human language, human wisdom, are only a puppet–show of stiff mechanical dolls by the side of the grim charm of reality and the creatures of mind and blood, whose desperate and vain efforts are strained to the fixing of a life which crumbles away with every day.

Jean–Christophe thought of death day and night. Memories of the last agony pursued him. He heard that horrible breathing; every night, whatever he might be doing, he saw his grandfather again. All Nature was changed; it seemed as though there were an icy vapor drawn over her. Round him, everywhere, whichever way he turned, he felt upon his face the fatal breathing of the blind, all–powerful Beast; he felt himself in the grip of that fearful destructive Form, and he felt that there was nothing to be done. But, far from crushing him, the thought of it set him aflame with hate and indignation. He was never resigned to it. He butted head down against the impossible; it mattered nothing that he broke his head, and was forced to realize that he was not the stronger. He never ceased to revolt against suffering. From that time on his life was an unceasing struggle against the savagery of a Fate which he could not admit.

The very misery of his life afforded him relief from the obsession of his thoughts. The ruin of his family, which only Jean Michel had withheld, proceeded apace when he was removed. With him the Kraffts had lost their chief means of support, and misery entered the house.

Melchior increased it. Far from working more, he abandoned himself utterly to his vice when he was free of the only force that had held him in check. Almost every night he returned home drunk, and he never brought back his earnings. Besides, he had lost almost all his lessons. One day he had appeared at the house of one of his pupils in a state of complete intoxication, and, as a consequence of this scandal, all doors were closed to him. He was only tolerated in the orchestra out of regard for the memory of his father, but Louisa trembled lest he should he dismissed any day after a scene. He had already been threatened with it on several evenings when he had turned up in his place about the end of the performance.

Twice or thrice he had forgotten altogether to put in an appearance. And of what was he not capable in those moments of stupid excitement when he was taken with the itch to do and say idiotic things! Had he not taken it into his head one evening to try and play his great violin concerto in the middle of an act of the *Valkyrie*? They were hard put to it to stop him. Sometimes, too, he would shout with laughter in the middle of a performance at the amusing pictures that were presented on the stage or whirling in his own brain. He was a joy to his colleagues, and they passed over many things because he was so funny. But such indulgence was worse than severity, and Jean–Christophe could have died for shame.

The boy was now first violin in the orchestra. He sat so that he could watch over his father, and, when necessary, beseech him, and make him be silent. It was not easy, and the best thing was not to pay any attention to him, for if he did, as soon as the sot felt that eyes were upon him, he would take to making faces or launch out into a speech. Then Jean–Christophe would turn away, trembling with fear lest he should commit some outrageous prank. He would try to be absorbed in his work, but he could not help hearing Melchior's utterances and the laughter of his colleagues. Tears would come into his eyes. The musicians, good fellows that they were, had seen that, and were sorry for him. They would hush their laughter, and only talk about his father when Jean–Christophe was not by. But Jean–Christophe was conscious of their pity. He knew that as soon as he had gone their jokes would break out again, and that Melchior was the laughing–stock of the town. He could not stop him, and he was in torment. He used to bring his father home after the play. He would take his arm, put up with his pleasantries, and try to conceal the stumbling in his walk. But he deceived no one, and in spite of all his efforts it was very rarely that he could succeed in leading Melchior all the way home. At the corner of the street Melchior would declare that he had an urgent appointment with some friends, and no argument could dissuade him from keeping this engagement. Jean–Christophe took care not to insist too much, so as not to expose himself to a scene and paternal imprecations which might attract the neighbors to their windows.

All the household money slipped away in this fashion. Melchior was not satisfied with drinking away his earnings; he drank away all that his wife and son so hardly earned. Louisa used to weep, but she dared not resist, since her husband had harshly reminded her that nothing in the house belonged to her, and that he had married her without a sou. Jean–Christophe tried to resist. Melchior boxed his ears, treated him like a naughty child, and took the money out of his hands. The boy was twelve or thirteen. He was strong, and was beginning to kick against being beaten; but he was still afraid to rebel, and rather than expose himself to fresh humiliations of the kind he let himself be plundered. The only resource that Louisa and Jean–Christophe had was to hide their money; but Melchior was singularly ingenious in discovering their hiding–places when they were not there.

Soon that was not enough for him. He sold the things that he had inherited from his father. Jean–Christophe sadly saw the precious relics go—the books, the bed, the furniture, the portraits of musicians. He could say nothing. But one day, when Melchior had crashed into Jean Michel's old piano, he swore as he rubbed his knee, and said that there was no longer room to move about in his own house, and that he would rid the house of all such gimcrackery. Jean–Christophe cried aloud. It was true that the rooms were too full, since all Jean Michel's belongings were crowded into them, so as to be able to sell the house, that dear house in which Jean–Christophe had spent the happiest hours of his childhood. It was true also that the old piano was not worth much, that it was husky in tone, and that for a long time Jean–Christophe had not used it, since he played on the fine new piano due to the generosity of the Prince; but however old and useless it might be, it was Jean–Christophe's best friend. It had awakened the child to the boundless world of music; on its worn yellow keys he had discovered with his fingers the kingdom of sounds and its laws; it had been his grandfather's work (months had gone to repairing it for his grandson), and he was proud of it; it was in some sort a holy relic, and Jean–Christophe protested that his father had no right to sell it. Melchior bade him be silent. Jean–Christophe cried louder than ever that the piano was his, and that he forbade any one to touch it; but Melchior looked at him with an evil smile, and said nothing.

Next day Jean–Christophe had forgotten the affair. He came home tired, but in a fairly good temper. He was struck by the sly looks of his brothers. They pretended to be absorbed in their books, but they followed him with their eyes, and watched all his movements, and bent over their books again when he looked at them. He had no doubt that they had played some trick upon him, but he was used to that, and did not worry about it, but determined, when he had found it out, to give them a good thrashing, as he always did on such occasions. He scorned to look into the matter, and he began to talk to his father, who was sitting by the fire, and questioned him as to the doings of the day with an affectation of interest which suited him but ill; and while he talked he saw that Melchior was exchanging stealthy nods and winks with the two children. Something caught at his heart. He ran into his room. The place where the piano had stood was empty! He gave a cry of anguish. In the next room he heard the stifled laughter of his brothers. The blood rushed to his face. He rushed in to them, and cried:

"My piano!"

Melchior raised his head with an air of calm bewilderment which made the children roar with laughter. He could not contain himself when he saw Jean–Christophe's piteous look, and he turned aside to guffaw. Jean–Christophe no longer knew what he was doing. He hurled himself like a mad thing on his father. Melchior, lolling in his chair, had no time to protect himself. The boy seized him by the throat and cried:

"Thief! Thief!"

It was only for a moment. Melchior shook himself, and sent Jean–Christophe rolling down on to the tile floor, though in his fury he was clinging to him like grim death. The boy's head crashed against the tiles. Jean–Christophe got upon his knees. He was livid, and he went on saying in a choking voice:

"Thief, thief!... You are robbing us—mother and me.... Thief!... You are selling my grandfather!"

Melchior rose to his feet, and held his fist above Jean–Christophe's head. The boy stared at him with hate; in his eyes. He was trembling with rage. Melchior began to tremble, too.

He sat down, and hid his face in his hands. The two children had run away screaming. Silence followed the uproar. Melchior groaned and mumbled. Jean–Christophe, against the wall, never ceased glaring at him with clenched teeth, and he trembled in every limb. Melchior began to blame himself.

"I am a thief! I rob my family! My children despise me! It were better if I were dead!"

When he had finished whining, Jean–Christophe did not budge, but asked him harshly:

"Where is the piano?"

"At Wormser's," said Melchior, not daring to look at him.

Jean–Christophe took a step forward, and said:

"The money!"

Melchior, crushed, took the money from his pocket and gave it to his son. Jean–Christophe turned towards the door. Melchior called him:

"Jean–Christophe!"

Jean–Christophe stopped. Melchior went on in a quavering voice:

"Dear Jean–Christophe ... do not despise me!"

Jean–Christophe flung his arms round his neck and sobbed:

"No, father—dear father! I do not despise you! I am so unhappy!"

They wept loudly. Melchior lamented:

"It is not my fault. I am not bad. That's true, Jean–Christophe? I am not bad?"

He promised that he would drink no more. Jean–Christophe wagged his head doubtfully, and Melchior admitted that he could not resist it when he had money in his hands. Jean–Christophe thought for a moment and said:

"You see, father, we must..."

He stopped.

"What then?"

"I am ashamed..."

"Of whom?" asked Melchior naively.

"Of you."

Melchior made a face and said:

"That's nothing."

Jean–Christophe explained that they would have to put all the family money, even Melchior's contribution, into the hands of some one else, who would dole it out to Melchior day by day, or week by week, as he needed it. Melchior, who was in humble mood—he was not altogether starving—agreed to the proposition, and declared that he would then and there write a letter to the Grand Duke to ask that the pension which came to him should be regularly paid over in his name to Jean–Christophe. Jean–Christophe refused, blushing for his father's humiliation. But Melchior, thirsting for self–sacrifice, insisted on writing. He was much moved by his own magnanimity. Jean–Christophe refused to take the letter, and when Louisa came in and was acquainted with the turn of events, she declared that she would rather beg in the streets than expose her husband to such an insult. She added that she had every confidence in him, and that she was sure he would make amends out of love for the children and herself. In the end there was a scene of tender reconciliation and Melchior's letter was left on the table, and then fell under the cupboard, where it remained concealed.

But a few days later, when she was cleaning up, Louisa found it there, and as she was very unhappy about Melchior's fresh outbreaks—he had forgotten all about it—instead of tearing it up, she kept it. She kept it for several months, always rejecting the idea of making use of it, in spite of the suffering she had to endure. But one day, when she saw Melchior once more beating Jean–Christophe and robbing him of his money, she could bear it no longer, and when she was left alone with the boy, who was weeping, she went and fetched the letter, and gave it him, and said:

"Go!"

Jean–Christophe hesitated, but he understood that there was no other way if they wished to save from the wreck the little that was left to them. He went to the Palace. He took nearly an hour to walk a distance that ordinarily took twenty minutes. He was overwhelmed by the shame of what he was doing. His pride, which had grown great in the years of sorrow and isolation, bled at the thought of publicly confessing his father's vice. He knew perfectly well that it was known to everybody, but by a strange and natural inconsequence he would not admit it, and pretended to notice nothing, and he would rather have been hewn in pieces than agree. And now, of his own accord, he was going!... Twenty times he was on the point of turning back. He walked two or three times round the town, turning away just as he came near the Palace. He was not alone in his plight. His mother and brothers had also to be considered. Since his father had deserted them and betrayed them, it was his business as eldest son to take his place and come to their assistance. There was no room for hesitation or pride; he had to swallow down his shame. He entered the Palace. On the staircase he almost turned and fled. He knelt down on a step; he stayed for several minutes on the landing, with his hand on the door, until some one coming made him go in.

Every one in the offices knew him. He asked to see His Excellency the Director of the Theaters, Baron de Hammer Langbach. A young clerk, sleek, bald, pink-faced, with a white waistcoat and a pink tie, shook his hand familiarly, and began to talk about the opera of the night before. Jean-Christophe repeated his question. The clerk replied that His Excellency was busy for the moment, but that if Jean-Christophe had a request to make they could present it with other documents which were to be sent in for His Excellency's signature. Jean-Christophe held out his letter. The clerk read it, and gave a cry of surprise.

"Oh, indeed!" he said brightly. "That is a good idea. He ought to have thought of that long ago! He never did anything better in his life! Ah, the old sot! How the devil did he bring himself to do it?"

He stopped short. Jean-Christophe had snatched the paper out of his hands, and, white with rage, shouted:

"I forbid you!... I forbid you to insult me!"

The clerk was staggered.

"But, my dear Jean-Christophe," he began to say, "whoever thought of insulting you? I only said what everybody thinks, and what you think yourself."

"No!" cried Jean–Christophe angrily.

"What! you don't think so? You don't think that he drinks?"

"It is not true!" said Jean–Christophe.

He stamped his foot.

The clerk shrugged his shoulders.

"In that case, why did he write this letter?"

"Because," said Jean–Christophe (he did not know what to say)—"because, when I come for my wages every month, I prefer to take my father's at the same time. It is no good our both putting ourselves out.... My father is very busy."

He reddened at the absurdity of his explanation. The clerk looked at him with pity and irony in his eyes. Jean–Christophe crumpled the paper in his hands, and turned to go. The clerk got up and took him by the arm.

"Wait a moment," he said. "I'll go and fix it up for you."

He went into the Director's office. Jean–Christophe waited, with the eyes of the other clerks upon him. His blood boiled. He did not know what he was doing, what to do, or what he ought to do. He thought of going away before the answer was brought to him, and he had just made up his mind to that when the door opened.

"His Excellency will see you," said the too obliging clerk.

Jean–Christophe had to go in.

His Excellency Baron de Hammer Langbach, a little neat old man with whiskers, mustaches, and a shaven chin, looked at Jean–Christophe over his golden spectacles without stopping writing, nor did he give any response to the boy's awkward bow.

"So," he said, after a moment, "you are asking, Herr Krafft ...?"

"Your Excellency," said Jean–Christophe hurriedly, "I ask your pardon. I have thought better of it. I have nothing to ask."

The old man sought no explanation for this sudden reconsideration. He looked more closely at Jean–Christophe, coughed, and said:

"Herr Krafft, will you give me the letter that is in your hand?"

Jean–Christophe saw that the Director's gaze was fixed on the paper which he was still unconsciously holding crumpled up in his hand.

"It is no use, Your Excellency," he murmured. "It is not worth while now."

"Please give it me," said the old man quietly, as though he had not heard.

Mechanically Jean–Christophe gave him the crumpled letter, but he plunged into a torrent of stuttered words while he held out his hand for the letter. His Excellency carefully smoothed out the paper, read it, looked at Jean–Christophe, let him flounder about with his explanations, then checked him, and said with a malicious light in his eyes:

"Very well, Herr Krafft; the request is granted."

He dismissed him with a wave of his hand and went on with his writing.

Jean–Christophe went out, crushed.

"No offense, Jean–Christophe!" said the clerk kindly, when the boy came into the office again. Jean–Christophe let him shake his hand without daring to raise his eyes. He found himself outside the Palace. He was cold with shame. Everything that had been said to him recurred in his memory, and he imagined that there was an insulting irony in the pity of the people who honored and were sorry for him. He went home, and answered only with a few irritable words Louisa's questions, as though he bore a grudge against her for what he had just done. He was racked by remorse when he thought of his father. He wanted to confess everything to him, and to beg his pardon. Melchior was not there. Jean–Christophe kept awake far into the night, waiting for him. The more he thought of him the more his remorse quickened. He idealized him; he thought of him as weak, kind, unhappy, betrayed by his own family. As soon as he heard his step on the stairs he leaped from his bed to go and meet him, and throw himself in his arms; but Melchior was in such a disgusting state of intoxication that Jean–Christophe had not even the courage to go near him, and he went to bed again, laughing bitterly at his own illusions.

When Melchior learned a few days later of what had happened, he was in a towering passion, and, in spite of all Jean–Christophe's entreaties, he went and made a scene at the Palace. But he returned with his tail between his legs, and breathed not a word of what had happened. He had been very badly received. He had been told that he would have to take a very different tone about the matter, that the pension had only been continued out of consideration for the worth of his son, and that if in the future there came any scandal concerning him to their ears, it would be suppressed. And so Jean–Christophe was much surprised and comforted to see his father accept his living from day to day, and even boast about having taken, the initiative in the *sacrifice*.

But that did not keep Melchior from complaining outside that he had been robbed by his wife and children, that he had put himself out for them all his life, and that now they let him want for everything. He tried also to extract money from Jean–Christophe by all sorts of ingenious tricks and devices, which often used to make Jean–Christophe laugh, although he was hardly ever taken in by them. But as Jean–Christophe held firm, Melchior did not insist. He was curiously intimidated by the severity in the eyes of this boy of fourteen who judged him. He used to avenge himself by some stealthy, dirty trick. He used to go to the cabaret and eat and drink as much as he pleased, and then pay nothing, pretending that his son would pay his debts. Jean–Christophe did not protest, for fear of increasing the scandal, and he and Louisa exhausted their resources in discharging Melchior's debts. In the end Melchior more and more lost interest in his work as violinist, since he no longer received his wages, and his absence from the theater became so frequent that, in spite of Jean–Christophe's entreaties, they had to dismiss him. The boy was left to support his father, his brothers, and the whole household.

So at fourteen Jean–Christophe became the head of the family.

* * * * *

He stoutly faced his formidable task. His pride would not allow him to resort to the charity of others. He vowed that he would pull through alone. From his earliest days he had suffered too much from seeing his mother accept and even ask for humiliating charitable offerings. He used to argue the matter with her when she returned home triumphant with some present that she had obtained from one of her patronesses. She saw no harm in it, and was glad to be able, thanks to the money, to spare Jean–Christophe a little, and to bring another meager dish forth for supper. But Jean–Christophe would become gloomy, and would not talk all evening, and would even refuse, without giving any reason, to touch food gained in this way. Louisa was vexed, and clumsily urged her son to eat. He was not to be budged, and in the end she would lose her temper, and say unkind things to him, and he would retort. Then he would fling his napkin on the table and go out. His father would shrug his shoulders and call him a *poseur*; his brothers would laugh at him and eat his portion.

But he had somehow to find a livelihood. His earnings from the orchestra were not enough. He gave lessons. His talents as an instrumentalist, his good reputation, and, above all, the Prince's patronage, brought him a numerous *clientele* among the middle classes. Every morning from nine o'clock on he taught the piano to little girls, many of them older than himself, who frightened him horribly with their coquetry and maddened him with the clumsiness of their playing. They were absolutely stupid as far as music went, but, on the other hand, they had all, more or less, a keen sense of ridicule, and their mocking looks spared none of Jean–Christophe's awkwardnesses. It was torture for him. Sitting by their side on the edge of his chair, stiff, and red in the face; bursting with anger, and not daring to stir; controlling himself so as not to say stupid things, and afraid of the sound of his own voice, so that he could hardly speak a word; trying to look severe, and feeling that his pupil was looking at him out of the corner of her eye, he would lose countenance, grow confused in the middle of a remark; fearing to make himself ridiculous, he would become so, and break out into violent reproach. But it was very easy for his pupils to avenge themselves, and they did not fail to do so, and upset him by a certain way of looking at him, and by asking him the simplest questions, which made him blush up to the roots of his hair; or they would ask him to do them some small service, such as fetching something they had forgotten from a piece of furniture, and that was for him a most painful ordeal, for he had to cross the room under fire of malicious looks, which pitilessly remarked the least awkwardness in his movements and his clumsy legs, his stiff arms, his body cramped by his shyness.

From these lessons he had to hasten to rehearsal at the theater. Often he had no time for lunch, and he used to carry a piece of bread and some cold meat in his pocket to eat during the interval. Sometimes he had to take the place of Tobias Pfeiffer, the *Musik Direktor*, who was interested in him, and sometimes had him to conduct the orchestra rehearsals instead of himself. And he had also to go on with his own musical education. Other piano lessons filled his day until the hour of the performance, and very often in the evening after the play he was sent for to play at the Palace. There he had to play for an hour or two. The Princess laid claim to a knowledge of music. She was very fond of it, but had never been able to perceive the difference between good and bad. She used to make Jean–Christophe play through strange programmes, in which dull rhapsodies stood side by side with masterpieces. But her greatest pleasure was to make him improvise, and she used to provide him with heartbreakingly sentimental themes.

Jean–Christophe used to leave about midnight, worn out, with his hands burning, his head aching, his stomach empty. He was in a sweat, and outside snow would be falling, or there would be an icy fog. He had to walk across half the town to reach home. He went on foot, his teeth chattering, longing to sleep and to cry, and he had to take care not to splash his only evening dress–suit in the puddles.

He would go up to his room, which he still shared with his brothers, and never was he so overwhelmed by disgust and despair with his life as at the moment when in his attic, with its stifling smell, he was at last permitted to take off the halter of his misery. He had hardly the heart to undress himself. Happily, no sooner did his head touch the pillow than he would sink into a heavy sleep which deprived him of all consciousness of his troubles.

But he had to get up by dawn in summer, and before dawn in winter. He wished to do his own work. It was all the free time that he had between five o'clock and eight. Even then he had to waste some of it by work to command, for his title of *Hof Musicus* and his favor with the Grand Duke exacted from him official compositions for the Court festivals.

So the very source of his life was poisoned. Even his dreams were not free, but, as usual, this restraint made them only the stronger. When nothing hampers action, the soul has fewer reasons for action, and the closer the walls of Jean–Christophe's prison of care and banal tasks were drawn about him, the more his heart in its revolt felt its independence. In a life without obstacles he would doubtless have abandoned himself to chance and to the voluptuous sauntering of adolescence. As he could be free only for an hour or two a day,

124

his strength flowed into that space of time like a river between walls of rock. It is a good discipline for art for a man to confine his efforts between unshakable bounds. In that sense it may be said that misery is a master, not only of thought, but of style; it teaches sobriety to the mind as to the body. When time is doled out and thoughts measured, a man says no word too much, and grows accustomed to thinking only what is essential; so he lives at double pressure, having less time for living.

This had happened in Jean–Christophe's case. Under his yoke he took full stock of the value of liberty and he never frittered away the precious minutes with useless words or actions. His natural tendency to write diffusely, given up to all the caprice of a mind sincere but indiscriminating, found correction in being forced to think and do as much as possible in the least possible time. Nothing had so much influence on his artistic and moral development—not the lessons of his masters, nor the example of the masterpieces. During the years when the character is formed he came to consider music as an exact language, in which every sound has a meaning, and at the same time he came to loathe those musicians who talk without saying anything.

And yet the compositions which he wrote at this time were still far from expressing himself completely, because he was still very far from having completely discovered himself. He was seeking himself through the mass of acquired feelings which education imposes on a child as second nature. He had only intuitions of his true being, until he should feel the passions of adolescence, which strip the personality of its borrowed garments as a thunder–clap purges the sky of the mists that hang over it. Vague and great forebodings were mingled in him with strange memories, of which he could not rid himself. He raged against these lies; he was wretched to see how inferior what he wrote was to what he thought; he had bitter doubts of himself. But he could not resign himself to such a stupid defeat. He longed passionately to do better, to write great things, and always he missed fire. After a moment of illusion as he wrote, he saw that what he had done was worthless. He tore it up; he burned everything that he did; and, to crown his humiliation, he had to see his official works, the most mediocre of all, preserved, and he could not destroy them—the concerto, *The Royal Eagle*, for the Prince's birthday and the cantata, *The Marriage of Pallas*, written on the occasion of the marriage of Princess Adelaide—published at great expense in *editions de luxe*, which perpetuated his imbecilities for posterity; for he believed in posterity. He wept in his humiliation.

Fevered years! No respite, no release—nothing to create a diversion from such maddening toil; no games, no friends. How should he have them? In the afternoon, when other children played, young Jean–Christophe, with his brows knit in attention, was at his place in the orchestra in the dusty and ill–lighted theater; and in the evening, when other children were abed, he was still there, sitting in his chair, bowed with weariness.

No intimacy with his brothers. The younger, Ernest, was twelve. He was a little ragamuffin, vicious and impudent, who spent his days with other rapscallions like himself, and from their company had caught not only deplorable manners, but shameful habits which good Jean–Christophe, who had never so much as suspected their existence, was horrified to see one day. The other, Rodolphe, the favorite of Uncle Theodore, was to go into business. He was steady, quiet, but sly. He thought himself much superior to Jean–Christophe, and did not admit his authority in the house, although it seemed natural to him to eat the food that he provided. He had espoused the cause of Theodore and Melchior's ill–feeling against Jean–Christophe and used to repeat their absurd gossip. Neither of the brothers cared for music, and Rodolphe, in imitation of his uncle, affected to despise it. Chafing against Jean–Christophe's authority and lectures—for he took himself very seriously as the head of the family—the two boys had tried to rebel; but Jean–Christophe, who had lusty fists and the consciousness of right, sent them packing. Still they did not for that cease to do with him as they liked. They abused his credulity, and laid traps for him, into which he invariably fell. They used to extort money from him with barefaced lies, and laughed at him behind his back. Jean–Christophe was always taken in. He had so much need of being loved that an affectionate word was enough to disarm his rancor. He would have forgiven them everything for a little love. But his confidence was cruelly shaken when he heard them laughing at his stupidity after a scene of hypocritical embracing which had moved him to tears, and they had taken advantage of it to rob him of a gold watch, a present from the Prince, which they coveted. He despised them, and yet went on letting himself be taken in from his unconquerable tendency to trust and to love. He knew it. He raged against himself, and he used to thrash his brothers soundly when he discovered once more that they had tricked him. That did not keep him from swallowing almost immediately the fresh hook which it pleased them to bait for him.

A more bitter cause of suffering was in store for him. He learned from officious neighbors that his father was speaking ill of him. After having been proud of his son's successes, and having boasted of them everywhere, Melchior was weak and shameful enough to be jealous of them. He tried to decry them. It was stupid to weep; Jean–Christophe could only shrug his shoulders in contempt. It was no use being angry about it, for his father did not know what he was doing, and was embittered by his own downfall. The boy said nothing. He was afraid, if he said anything, of being too hard; but he was cut to the heart.

They were melancholy gatherings at the family evening meal round the lamp, with a spotted cloth, with all the stupid chatter and the sound of the jaws of these people whom he despised and pitied, and yet loved in spite of everything. Only between himself and his brave mother did Jean–Christophe feel a bond of affection. But Louisa, like himself, exhausted herself during the day, and in the evening she was worn out and hardly spoke, and after dinner used to sleep in her chair over her darning. And she was so good that she seemed to make no difference in her love between her husband and her three sons. She loved them all equally. Jean–Christophe did not find in her the trusted friend that he so much needed.

So he was driven in upon himself. For days together he would not speak, fulfilling his tiresome and wearing task with a sort of silent rage. Such a mode of living was dangerous, especially for a child at a critical age, when he is most sensitive, and is exposed to every agent of destruction and the risk of being deformed for the rest of his life. Jean–Christophe's health suffered seriously. He had been endowed by his parents with a healthy constitution and a sound and healthy body; but his very healthiness only served to feed his suffering when the weight of weariness and too early cares had opened up a gap by which it might enter. Quite early in life there were signs of grave nervous disorders. When he was a small boy he was subject to fainting–fits and convulsions and vomiting whenever he encountered opposition. When he was seven or eight, about the time of the concert, his sleep had been troubled. He used to talk, cry, laugh and weep in his sleep, and this habit returned to him whenever he had too much to think of. Then he had cruel headaches, sometimes shooting pains at the base of his skull or the top of his head, sometimes a leaden heaviness. His eyes troubled him. Sometimes it was as though red–hot needles were piercing his eyeballs. He was subject to fits of dizziness, when he could not see to read, and had to stop for a minute or two. Insufficient and unsound food and irregular meals ruined the health of his stomach. He was racked by internal pains or exhausted by diarrhea. But nothing brought him more suffering than his heart. It beat with a crazy irregularity. Sometimes it would leap in his bosom, and seem like to break; sometimes it would hardly beat at all, and seem like to stop. At night his temperature would vary alarmingly; it would change suddenly from fever–point to next to nothing. He would burn, then shiver with cold, pass through agony. His throat would go dry; a lump in it would prevent his breathing. Naturally his imagination took fire. He dared not say anything to his family of what he was going through, but he was continually dissecting it with a minuteness which either enlarged his sufferings or created new ones. He decided that he had every known illness one after the other. He believed that he was going blind, and as he sometimes used to turn giddy as he walked, he thought that he was going to fall down dead. Always that dreadful fear of being stopped on his road, of dying before his time, obsessed him, overwhelmed him, and pursued him. Ah, if he had to die, at least let it not be now, not before he had tasted victory!...

Victory ... the fixed idea which never ceases to burn within him without his being fully aware of it—the idea which bears him up through all his disgust and fatigues and the stagnant morass of such a life! A dim and great foreknowledge of what he will be some day, of what he is already!... What is he? A sick, nervous child, who plays the violin in the orchestra and writes mediocre concertos? No; far more than such a child. That is no more than the wrapping, the seeming of a day; that is not his Being. There is no connection between his Being and the existing shape of his face and thought. He knows that well. When he looks at himself in the mirror he does not know himself. That broad red face, those prominent eyebrows, those little sunken eyes, that short thick nose, that sullen mouth—the whole mask, ugly and vulgar, is foreign to himself. Neither does he know himself in his writings. He judges, he knows that what he does and what he is are nothing; and yet he is sure of what he will be and do. Sometimes he falls foul of such certainty as a vain lie. He takes pleasure in humiliating himself and bitterly mortifying himself by way of punishment. But his certainty endures; nothing can alter it. Whatever he does, whatever he thinks, none of his thoughts, actions, or writings contain him or express him, He knows, he has this strange presentiment, that the more that he is, is not contained in the present but is what he *will be*, what he *will be to–morrow. He will be!*... He is fired by that faith, he is intoxicated by that light! Ah, if only *To–day* does not block the way! If only he does not fall into one of the cunning traps which *To–day* is forever laying for him!

So he steers his bark across the sea of days, turning his eyes neither to right nor left, motionless at the helm, with his gaze fixed on the bourne, the refuge, the end that he has in sight. In the orchestra, among the talkative musicians, at table with his own family, at the Palace, while he is playing without a thought of what he is playing, for the entertainment of Royal folk—it is in that future, that future which a speck may bring toppling to earth—no matter, it is in that that he lives.

* * * * *

He is at his old piano, in his garret, alone. Night falls. The dying light of day is cast upon his music. He strains his eyes to read the notes until the last ray of light is dead. The tenderness of hearts that are dead breathed forth from the dumb page fills him with love. His eyes are filled with tears. It seems to him that a beloved creature is standing behind him, that soft breathing caresses his cheek, that two arms are about his neck. He turns, trembling. He feels, he knows, that he is not alone. A soul that loves and is loved is there, near him. He groans aloud because he cannot perceive it, and yet that shadow of bitterness falling upon his ecstasy has sweetness, too. Even sadness has its light. He thinks of his beloved masters, of the genius that is gone, though its soul lives on in the music which it had lived in its life. His heart is overflowing with love; he dreams of the superhuman happiness which must have been the lot of these glorious men, since the reflection only of their happiness is still so much aflame. He dreams of being like them, of giving out such love as this, with lost rays to lighten his misery with a godlike smile. In his turn to be a god, to give out the warmth of joy, to be a sun of life!...

Alas! if one day he does become the equal of those whom he loves, if he does achieve that brilliant happiness for which he longs, he will see the illusion that was upon him....

II. OTTO

One Sunday when Jean–Christophe had been invited by his *Musik Direktor* to dine at the little country house which Tobias Pfeiffer owned an hour's journey from the town, he took the Rhine steamboat. On deck he sat next to a boy about his own age, who eagerly made room for him. Jean–Christophe paid no attention, but after a moment, feeling that his neighbor had never taken his eyes off him, he turned and looked at him. He was a fair boy, with round pink cheeks, with his hair parted on one side, and a shade of down on his lip. He looked frankly what he was—a hobbledehoy—though he made great efforts to seem grown up. He was dressed with ostentatious care—flannel suit, light gloves, white shoes, and a pale blue tie—and he carried a little stick in his hand. He looked at Jean–Christophe out of the corner of his eye without turning his head, with his neck stiff, like a hen; and when Jean–Christophe looked at him he blushed up to his ears, took a newspaper from his pocket, and pretended to be absorbed in it, and to look important over it. But a few minutes later he dashed to pick up Jean–Christophe's hat, which had fallen. Jean–Christophe, surprised at such politeness, looked once more at the boy, and once more he blushed. Jean–Christophe thanked him curtly, for he did not like such obsequious eagerness, and he hated to be fussed with. All the same, he was flattered by it.

Soon it passed from his thoughts; his attention was occupied by the view. It was long since he had been able to escape from the town, and so he had keen pleasure in the wind that beat against his face, in the sound of the water against the boat, in the great stretch of water and the changing spectacle presented by the banks—bluffs gray and dull, willow–trees half under water, pale vines, legendary rocks, towns crowned with Gothic towers and factory chimneys belching black smoke. And as he was in ecstasy over it all, his neighbor in a choking voice timidly imparted a few historic facts concerning the ruins that they saw, cleverly restored and covered with ivy. He seemed to be lecturing to himself. Jean–Christophe, roused to interest, plied him with questions. The other replied eagerly, glad to display his knowledge, and with every sentence he addressed himself directly to Jean–Christophe, calling him *"Herr Hof Violinist."*

"You know me, then?" said Jean–Christophe.

"Oh yes," said the boy, with a simple admiration that tickled Jean–Christophe's vanity.

They talked. The boy had often seen Jean–Christophe at concerts, and his imagination had been touched by everything that he had heard about him. He did not say so to Jean–Christophe, but Jean–Christophe felt it, and was pleasantly surprised by it. He was not used to being spoken to in this tone of eager respect. He went on questioning his neighbor about the history of the country through which they were passing. The other set out all the knowledge that he had, and Jean–Christophe admired his learning. But that was only the peg on which their conversation hung. What interested them was the making of each other's acquaintance. They dared not frankly approach the subject; they returned to it again and again with awkward questions. Finally they plunged, and Jean–Christophe learned that his new friend was called Otto Diener, and was the son of a rich merchant in the town. It appeared, naturally, that they had friends in common, and little by little their tongues were loosed. They were talking eagerly when the boat arrived at the town at which Jean–Christophe was to get out. Otto got out, too. That surprised them, and

Jean–Christophe proposed that they should take a walk together until dinner–time. They struck out across the fields. Jean–Christophe had taken Otto's arm familiarly, and was telling him his plans as if he had known him from his birth. He had been so much deprived of the society of children of his own age that he found an inexpressible joy in being with this boy, so learned and well brought up, who was in sympathy with him.

Time passed, and Jean–Christophe took no count of it. Diener, proud of the confidence which the young musician showed him, dared not point out that the dinner–hour had rung. At last he thought that he must remind him of it, but Jean–Christophe, who had begun the ascent of a hill in the woods, declared that they most go to the top, and when they reached it he lay down on the grass as though he meant to spend the day there. After a quarter of an hour Diener, seeing that he seemed to have no intention of moving, hazarded again:

"And your dinner?"

Jean–Christophe, lying at full length, with his hands behind his head, said quietly:

"Tssh!"

Then he looked at Otto, saw his scared look, and began to laugh.

"It is too good here," he explained. "I shan't go. Let them wait for me!"

He half rose.

"Are you in a hurry? No? Do you know what we'll do? We'll dine together. I know of an inn."

Diener would have had many objections to make—not that any one was waiting for him, but because it was hard for him to come to any sudden decision, whatever it might be. He was methodical, and needed to be prepared beforehand. But Jean–Christophe's question was put in such a tone as allowed of no refusal. He let himself be dragged off, and they began to talk again.

At the inn their eagerness died down. Both were occupied with the question as to who should give the dinner, and each within himself made it a point of honor to give it—Diener because he was the richer, Jean–Christophe because he was the poorer. They made no direct reference to the matter, but Diener made great efforts to assert his right by the tone of authority which he tried to take as he asked for the menu. Jean–Christophe understood what he was at and turned the tables on him by ordering other dishes of a rare kind. He wanted to show that he was as much at his ease as anybody, and when Diener tried again by endeavoring to take upon himself the choice of wine, Jean–Christophe crushed him with a look, and ordered a bottle of one of the most expensive vintages they had in the inn.

When they found themselves seated before a considerable repast, they were abashed by it. They could find nothing to say, ate mincingly, and were awkward and constrained in their movements. They became conscious suddenly that they were strangers, and they watched each other. They made vain efforts to revive the conversation; it dropped immediately. Their first half–hour was a time of fearful boredom. Fortunately, the meat and drink soon had an effect on them, and they looked at each other more confidently. Jean–Christophe especially, who was not used to such good things, became extraordinarily loquacious. He told of the difficulties of his life, and Otto, breaking through his reserve, confessed that he also was not happy. He was weak and timid, and his schoolfellows put upon him. They laughed at him, and could not forgive him for despising their vulgar manners. They played all sorts of tricks on him. Jean–Christophe clenched his fists, and said they had better not try it in his presence. Otto also was misunderstood by his family. Jean–Christophe knew the unhappiness of that, and they commiserated each other on their common misfortunes. Diener's parents wanted him to become a merchant, and to step into his father's place, but he wanted to be a poet. He would be a poet, even though he had to fly the town, like Schiller, and brave poverty! (His father's fortune would all come to him, and it was considerable.) He confessed blushingly that he had already written verses on the sadness of life, but he could not bring himself to recite them, in spite of Jean–Christophe's entreaties. But in the end he did give two or three of them, dithering with emotion. Jean–Christophe thought them admirable. They exchanged plans. Later on they would work together; they would write dramas and song–cycles. They admired each other. Besides his reputation as a musician, Jean–Christophe's strength and bold ways made an impression on Otto, and Jean–Christophe was sensible of Otto's elegance and distinguished manners—everything in this world is relative—and of his ease of manner—that ease of manner which he looked and longed for.

Made drowsy by their meal, with their elbows on the table, they talked and listened to each other with softness in their eyes. The afternoon drew on; they had to go. Otto made a last attempt to procure the bill, but Jean–Christophe nailed him to his seat with an angry look which made it impossible for him to insist. Jean–Christophe was only uneasy on one point—that he might be asked for more than he had. He would have given his watch and everything that he had about him rather than admit it to Otto. But he was not called on to go so far. He had to spend on the dinner almost the whole of his month's money.

They went down the hill again. The shades of evening were beginning to fall over the pine–woods. Their tops were still bathed in rosy light; they swung slowly with a surging sound. The carpet of purple pine–needles deadened the sound of their footsteps. They said no word. Jean–Christophe felt a strange sweet sadness welling through his heart. He was happy; he wished to talk, but was weighed down with his sweet sorrow. He stopped for a moment, and so did Otto. All was silence. Flies buzzed high above them in a ray of sunlight; a rotten branch fell. Jean–Christophe took Otto's hand, and in a trembling voice said:

"Will you be my friend?"

Otto murmured:

"Yes."

They shook hands; their hearts beat; they dared hardly look at each other.

After a moment they walked on. They were a few paces away from each other, and they dared say no more until they were out of the woods. They were fearful of each other, and of their strange emotion. They walked very fast, and never stopped until they had issued from the shadow of the trees; then they took courage again, and joined hands. They marveled at the limpid evening falling, and they talked disconnectedly.

On the boat, sitting at the bows in the brilliant twilight, they tried to talk of trivial matters, but they gave no heed to what they were saying. They were lost in their own happiness and weariness. They felt no need to talk, or to hold hands, or even to look at each other;

they were near each other.

When they were near their journey's end they agreed to meet again on the following Sunday, Jean–Christophe took Otto to his door. Under the light of the gas they timidly smiled and murmured *au revoir*. They were glad to part, so wearied were they by the tension at which they had been living for those hours and by the pain it cost them to break the silence with a single word.

Jean–Christophe returned alone in the night. His heart was singing: "I have a friend! I have a friend!" He saw nothing, he heard nothing, he thought of nothing else.

He was very sleepy, and fell asleep as soon as he reached his room; but he was awakened twice or thrice during the night, as by some fixed idea. He repeated, "I have a friend," and went to sleep again at once.

Next morning it seemed to be all a dream. To test the reality of it, he tried to recall the smallest details of the day. He was absorbed by this occupation while he was giving his lessons, and even during the afternoon he was so absent during the orchestra rehearsal that when he left he could hardly remember what he had been playing.

When he returned home he found a letter waiting for him. He had no need to ask himself whence it came. He ran and shut himself up in his room to read it. It was written on pale blue paper in a labored, long, uncertain hand, with very correct flourishes:

DEAR HERR JEAN–CHRISTOPHE—dare I say HONORED FRIEND?—

I am thinking much of our doings yesterday, and I do thank you tremendously for your kindness to me. I am so grateful for all that you have done, and for your kind words, and the delightful walk and the excellent dinner! I am only worried that you should have spent so much money on it. What a lovely day! Do you not think there was something providential in that strange meeting? It seems to me that it was Fate decreed that we should meet. How glad I shall be to see you again on Sunday! I hope you will not have had too much unpleasantness for having missed the *Hof Musik Direktor's* dinner. I should be so sorry if you had any trouble because of me.

Dear Herr Jean–Christophe, I am always

Your very devoted servant and friend,

OTTO DIENER.

P.S.—On Sunday please do not call for me at home. It would be better, if you will, for us to meet at the *Schloss Garten.*

Jean–Christophe read the letter with tears in his eyes. He kissed it; he laughed aloud; he jumped about on his bed. Then he ran to the table and took pen in hand to reply at once. He could not wait a moment. But he was not used to writing. He could not express what was swelling in his heart; he dug into the paper with his pen, and blackened his fingers with ink; he stamped impatiently. At last, by dint of putting out his tongue and making five or six drafts, he succeeded in writing in malformed letters, which flew out in all directions, and with terrific mistakes in spelling:

"MY SOUL,—

"How dare you speak of gratitude, because I love you? Have I not told you how sad I was and lonely before I knew you? Your friendship is the greatest of blessings. Yesterday I was happy, happy!—for the first time in my life. I weep for joy as I read your letter. Yes, my beloved, there is no doubt that it was Fate brought us together. Fate wishes that we should be friends to do great things. Friends! The lovely word! Can it be that at last I have a friend? Oh! you will never leave me? You will be faithful to me? Always! always!... How beautiful it will be to grow up together, to work together, to bring together—I my musical whimsies, and all the crazy things that go chasing through my mind; you your intelligence and amazing learning! How much you know! I have never met a man so clever as you. There are moments when I am uneasy. I seem to be unworthy of your friendship. You are so noble and so accomplished, and I am so grateful to you for loving so coarse a creature as myself!... But no! I have just said, let there be no talk of gratitude. In friendship there is no obligation nor benefaction. I would not accept any benefaction! We are equal, since we love. How impatient I am to see you! I will not call for you at home, since you do not wish it—although, to tell the truth, I do not understand all these precautions—but you are the wiser; you are surely right....

"One word only! No more talk of money. I hate money—the word and the thing itself. If I am not rich, I am yet rich enough to give to my friend, and it is my joy to give all I can for him. Would not you do the same? And if I needed it, would you not be the first to give me all your fortune? But that shall never be! I have sound fists and a sound head, and I shall always be able to earn the bread that I eat. Till Sunday! Dear God, a whole week without seeing you! And for two days I have not seen you! How have I been able to live so long without you?

"The conductor tried to grumble, but do not bother about it any more than I do. What are others to me? I care nothing what they think or what they may ever think of me. Only you matter. Love me well, my soul; love me as I love you! I cannot tell you how much I love you. I am yours, yours, yours, from the tips of my fingers to the apple of my eye.

"Yours always,

"JEAN–CHRISTOPHE."

Jean–Christophe was devoured with impatience for the rest of the week. He would go out of his way, and make long turns to pass by Otto's house. Not that he counted on seeing him, but the sight of the house was enough to make him grow pale and red with emotion. On the Thursday he could bear it no longer, and sent a second letter even more high–flown than the first. Otto answered it sentimentally.

Sunday came at length, and Otto was punctually at the meeting–place. But Jean–Christophe had been there for an hour, waiting impatiently for the walk. He began to imagine dreadfully that Otto would not come. He trembled lest Otto should be ill, for he did not suppose for a moment that Otto might break his word. He whispered over and over again, "Dear God, let him come—let him come!" and he struck at the pebbles in the avenue with his stick, saying to himself that if he missed three times Otto would not come, but if he hit them Otto would appear at once. In spite of his care and the easiness of the test, he had just missed three times when he saw Otto coming at his easy, deliberate pace; for Otto was above all things correct, even when he was most moved. Jean–Christophe ran to him, and with his throat dry wished him "Good–day!" Otto replied, "Good–day!" and they found that they had nothing more to say to each other, except that the weather was fine and that it was five or six minutes past ten, or it might be ten past, because the castle clock was always slow.

They went to the station, and went by rail to a neighboring place which was a favorite excursion from the town. On the way they exchanged not more than ten words. They tried to make up for it by eloquent looks, but they were no more successful. In vain did they try to tell each other what friends they were; their eyes would say nothing at all. They were just playacting. Jean–Christophe saw that, and was humiliated. He did not understand how he could not express or even feel all that had filled his heart an hour before. Otto did not, perhaps, so exactly take stock of their failure, because he was less sincere, and examined himself with more circumspection, but he was just as disappointed. The truth is that the boys had, during their week of separation, blown out their feelings to such a diapason that it was impossible for them to keep them actually at that pitch, and when they met again their first impression must of necessity be false. They had to break away from it, but they could not bring themselves to agree to it.

All day they wandered in the country without ever breaking through the awkwardness and constraint that were upon them. It was a holiday. The inns and woods were filled with a rabble of excursionists—little *bourgeois* families who made a great noise and ate everywhere. That added to their ill–humor. They attributed to the poor people the impossibility of again finding the carelessness of their first walk. But they talked, they took great pains to find subjects of conversation; they were afraid of finding that they had nothing to say to each other. Otto displayed his school–learning; Jean–Christophe entered into technical explanations of musical compositions and violin–playing. They oppressed each other; they crushed each other by talking; and they never stopped talking, trembling lest they should, for then there opened before them abysses of silence which horrified them. Otto came near to weeping, and Jean–Christophe was near leaving him and running away as hard as he could, he was so bored and ashamed.

Only an hour before they had to take the train again did they thaw. In the depths of the woods a dog was barking; he was hunting on his own account. Jean–Christophe proposed that they should hide by his path to try and see his quarry. They ran into the midst of the thicket. The dog came near them, and then went away again. They went to right and left, went forward and doubled. The barking grew louder: the dog was choking with impatience in his lust for slaughter. He came near once more. Jean–Christophe and Otto, lying on the dead leaves in the rut of a path, waited and held their breath. The barking stopped; the dog had lost the scent. They heard his yap once again in the distance; then silence came upon the woods. Not a sound, only the mysterious hum of millions of creatures, insects, and creeping things, moving unceasingly, destroying the forest—the measured breathing of death, which never stops. The boys listened, they did not stir. Just when they got up, disappointed, and said, "It is all over; he will not come!" a little hare plunged out of the thicket. He came straight upon them. They saw him at the same moment, and gave a cry of joy. The hare turned in his tracks and jumped aside. They saw him dash into the brushwood head over heels. The stirring of the rumpled leaves vanished away like a ripple on the face of waters. Although they were sorry for having cried out, the adventure filled them with joy. They rocked with laughter as they thought of the hare's terrified leap, and Jean–Christophe imitated it grotesquely. Otto did the same. Then they chased each other. Otto was the hare, Jean–Christophe the dog. They plunged through woods and meadows, dashing through hedges and leaping ditches. A peasant shouted at them, because they had rushed over a field of rye. They did not stop to hear him. Jean–Christophe imitated the hoarse barking of the dog to such perfection that Otto laughed until he cried. At last they rolled down a slope, shouting like mad things. When they could not utter another sound they sat up and looked at each other, with tears of laughter in their eyes. They were quite happy and pleased with themselves. They were no longer trying to play the heroic friend; they were frankly what they were—two boys.

They came back arm–in–arm, singing senseless songs, and yet, when they were on the point of returning to the town, they thought they had better resume their pose, and under the last tree of the woods they carved their initials intertwined. But then good temper had the better of their sentimentality, and in the train they shouted with laughter whenever they looked at each other. They parted assuring each other that they had had a "hugely delightful" (*kolossal entzueckend*) day, and that conviction gained with them when they were alone once more.

* * * * *

They resumed their work of construction more patient and ingenious even than that of the bees, for of a few mediocre scraps of memory they fashioned a marvelous image of themselves and their friendship. After having idealized each other during the week, they met again on the Sunday, and in spite of the discrepancy between the truth and their illusion, they got used to not noticing it and to twisting things to fit in with their desires.

They were proud of being friends. The very contrast of their natures brought them together. Jean–Christophe knew nothing so beautiful as Otto. His fine hands, his lovely hair, his fresh complexion, his shy speech, the politeness of his manners, and his scrupulous care of his appearance delighted him. Otto was subjugated by Jean–Christophe's brimming strength and independence. Accustomed by age–old inheritance to religious respect for all authority, he took a fearful joy in the company of a comrade in whose nature was so little reverence for the established order of things. He had a little voluptuous thrill of terror whenever he heard him decry every reputation in the town, and even mimic the Grand Duke himself. Jean–Christophe knew the fascination that he exercised over his friend, and used to exaggerate his aggressive temper. Like some old revolutionary, he hewed away at social conventions and the laws of the State. Otto would listen, scandalized and delighted. He used timidly to try and join in, but he was always careful to look round to see if any one could hear.

Jean–Christophe never failed, when they walked together, to leap the fences of a field whenever he saw a board forbidding it, or he would pick fruit over the walls of private grounds. Otto was in terror lest they should be discovered. But such feelings had for him an exquisite savor, and in the evening, when he had returned, he would think himself a hero. He admired Jean–Christophe fearfully. His instinct of obedience found a satisfying quality in a friendship in which he had only to acquiesce in the will of his friend. Jean–Christophe never put him to the trouble of coming to a decision. He decided everything, decreed the doings of the day, decreed even the ordering of life, making plans, which admitted of no discussion, for Otto's future, just as he did for his own family. Otto fell in with them, though he was a little put aback by hearing Jean–Christophe dispose of his fortune for the building later on of a theater of his own contriving. But, intimidated by his friend's imperious tones, he did not protest, being convinced also by his friend's conviction that the money amassed by *Commerzienrath* Oscar Diener could be put to no nobler use. Jean–Christophe never for a moment had any idea that he might be violating Otto's will. He was instinctively a despot, and never imagined that his friend's wishes might be different from his own. Had Otto expressed a desire different from his own, he would not have hesitated to sacrifice his own personal preference. He would have sacrificed even more for him. He was consumed by the desire to run some risk for him. He wished passionately that there might appear some opportunity of putting his friendship to the test. When they were out walking he used to hope that they might meet some danger, so that he might fling himself forward to face it. He would have loved to die for Otto. Meanwhile, he watched over him with a restless solicitude, gave him his hand in awkward places, as though he were a girl. He was afraid that he might be tired, afraid that he might be hot, afraid that he might be cold. When they sat down under a tree he took off his coat to put it about his friend's shoulders; when they walked he carried his cloak. He would have carried Otto himself. He used to devour him with his eyes like a lover, and, to tell the truth, he was in love.

He did not know it, not knowing yet what love was. But sometimes, when they were together, he was overtaken by a strange unease—the same that had choked him on that first day of their friendship in the pine–woods—and the blood would rush to his face and set his cheeks aflame. He was afraid. By an instinctive unanimity the two boys used furtively to separate and run away from each other, and one would lag behind on the road. They would pretend to be busy looking for blackberries in the hedges, and they did not know what it was that so perturbed them.

But it was in their letters especially that their feelings flew high. They were not then in any danger of being contradicted by facts, and nothing could check their illusions or intimidate them. They wrote to each other two or three times a week in a passionately lyric style. They hardly ever spoke of real happenings or common things; they raised great problems in an apocalyptic manner, which passed imperceptibly from enthusiasm to despair. They called each other, "My blessing, my hope, my beloved, my Self." They made a fearful hash of the word "Soul." They painted in tragic colors the sadness of their lot, and were desolate at having brought into the existence of their friend the sorrows of their existence.

"I am sorry, my love," wrote Jean–Christophe, "for the pain which I bring you. I cannot bear that you should suffer. It must not be. *I will not have it.*" (He underlined the words with a stroke of the pen that dug into the paper.) "If you suffer, where shall I find strength to live? I have no happiness but in you. Oh, be happy! I will gladly take all the burden of sorrow upon myself! Think of me! Love me! I have such great need of being loved. From your love there comes to me a warmth which gives me life. If you knew how I shiver! There is winter and a biting wind in my heart. I embrace your soul."

"My thought kisses yours," replied Otto.

"I take your face in my hands," was Jean–Christophe's answer, "and what I have not done and will not do with my lips I do with all my being. I kiss you as I love you, Prudence!",

Otto pretended to doubt him.

"Do you love me as much as I love you?"

"O God," wrote Jean–Christophe, "not as much, but ten a hundred, a thousand times more! What! Do you not feel it? What would you have me do to stir your heart?"

"What a lovely friendship is ours!" sighed Otto. "Was, there ever its like in history? It is sweet and fresh as a dream. If only it does not pass away! If you were to cease to love me!"

"How stupid you are, my beloved!" replied Jean–Christophe. "Forgive me, but your weakling fear enrages me. How can you ask whether I shall cease to love you! For me to live is to love you. Death is powerless against my love. You yourself could do nothing if you wished to destroy it. Even if you betrayed me, even if you rent my heart, I should die with a blessing upon you for the love with which you fill me. Once for all, then, do not be uneasy, and vex me no more with these cowardly doubts!"

But a week later it was he who wrote:

"It is three days now since I heard a word fall from your lips. I tremble. Would you forget me? My blood freezes at the thought.... Yes, doubtless.... The other day only I saw your coldness towards me. You love me no longer! You are thinking of leaving me!... Listen! If you forget me, if you ever betray me, I will kill you like a dog!"

"You do me wrong, my dear heart," groaned Otto. "You draw tears from me. I do not deserve this. But you can do as you will. You have such rights over me that, if you were to break my soul, there would always be a spark left to live and love you always!"

"Heavenly powers!" cried Jean–Christophe. "I have made my friend weep!... Heap insults on me, beat me, trample me underfoot! I am a wretch! I do not deserve your love!"

They had special ways of writing the address on their letters, of placing the stamp—upside down, askew, at bottom in a corner of the envelope—to distinguish their letters from those which they wrote to persons who did not matter. These childish secrets had the charm of the sweet mysteries of love.

* * * * *

One day, as he was returning from a lesson, Jean–Christophe saw Otto in the street with a boy of his own age. They were laughing and talking familiarly. Jean–Christophe went pale, and followed them with his eyes until they had disappeared round the corner of the street. They had not seen him. He went home. It was as though a cloud had passed over the sun; all was dark.

When they met on the following Sunday, Jean–Christophe said nothing at first; but after they had been walking for half an hour he said in a choking voice:

"I saw you on Wednesday in the *Koeniggasse*."

"Ah!" said Otto.

And he blushed.

Jean–Christophe went on:

"You were not alone."

"No," said Otto; "I was with some one."

Jean–Christophe swallowed down his spittle and asked in a voice which he strove to make careless:

"Who was it?"

"My cousin Franz."

"Ah!" said Jean–Christophe; and after a moment: "You have never said anything about him to me."

"He lives at Rheinbach."

"Do you see him often?"

"He comes here sometimes."

"And you, do you go and stay with him?"

"Sometimes."

"Ah!" said Jean–Christophe again.

Otto, who was not sorry to turn the conversation, pointed out a bird who was pecking at a tree. They talked of other things. Ten minutes later Jean–Christophe broke out again:

"Are you friends with him?"

"With whom?" asked Otto.

(He knew perfectly who was meant.)

"With your cousin."

"Yes. Why?"

"Oh, nothing!"

Otto did not like his cousin much, for he used to bother him with bad jokes; but a strange malign instinct made him add a few moments later:

"He is very nice."

"Who?" asked Jean–Christophe.

(He knew quite well who was meant.)

"Franz."

Otto waited for Jean–Christophe to say something, but he seemed not to have heard. He was cutting a switch from a hazel–tree. Otto went on:

"He is amusing. He has all sorts of stories."

Jean–Christophe whistled carelessly.

Otto renewed the attack:

"And he is so clever ... and distinguished!..."

Jean–Christophe shrugged his shoulders as though to say:

"What interest can this person have for me?"

And as Otto, piqued, began to go on, he brutally cut him short, and pointed out a spot to which to run.

They did not touch on the subject again the whole afternoon, but they were frigid, affecting an exaggerated politeness which was unusual for them, especially for Jean–Christophe. The words stuck in his throat. At last he could contain himself no longer, and in the middle of the road he turned to Otto, who was lagging five yards behind. He took him fiercely by the hands, and let loose upon him:

"Listen, Otto! I will not—I will not let you be so friendly with Franz, because ... because you are my friend, and I will not let you love any one more than me! I will not! You see, you are everything to me! You cannot ... you must not!... If I lost you, there would be nothing left but death. I do not know what I should do. I should kill myself; I should kill you! No, forgive me!..."

Tears fell from his eyes.

Otto, moved and frightened by the sincerity of such grief, growling out threats, made haste to swear that he did not and never would love anybody so much as Jean–Christophe, that Franz was nothing to him, and that he would not see him again if Jean–Christophe wished it. Jean–Christophe drank in his words, and his heart took new life. He laughed and breathed heavily; he thanked Otto effusively. He was ashamed of having made such a scene, but he was relieved of a great weight. They stood face to face and looked at each other, not moving, and holding hands. They were very happy and very much embarrassed. They became silent; then they began to talk again, and found their old gaiety. They felt more at one than ever.

But it was not the last scene of the kind. Now that Otto felt his power over Jean-Christophe, he was tempted to abuse it. He knew his sore spot, and was irresistibly tempted to place his finger on it. Not that he had any pleasure in Jean-Christophe's anger; on the contrary, it made him unhappy—but he felt his power by making Jean-Christophe suffer. He was not bad; he had the soul of a girl.

In spite of his promises, he continued to appear arm in arm with Franz or some other comrade. They made a great noise between them, and he used to laugh in an affected way. When Jean-Christophe reproached him with it, he used to titter and pretend not to take him seriously, until, seeing Jean-Christophe's eyes change and his lips tremble with anger, he would change his tone, and fearfully promise not to do it again, and the next day he would do it. Jean-Christophe would write him furious letters, in which he called him:

"Scoundrel! Let me never hear of you again! I do not know you! May the devil take you and all dogs of your kidney!"

But a tearful word from Otto, or, as he ever did, the sending of a flower as a token of his eternal constancy, was enough for Jean-Christophe to be plunged in remorse, and to write:

"My angel, I am mad! Forget my idiocy. You are the best of men. Your little finger alone is worth more than all stupid Jean-Christophe. You have the treasures of an ingenuous and delicate tenderness. I kiss your flower with tears in my eyes. It is there on my heart. I thrust it into my skin with blows of my fist. I would that it could make me bleed, so that I might the more feel your exquisite goodness and my own infamous folly!..."

But they began to weary of each other. It is false to pretend that little quarrels feed friendship. Jean-Christophe was sore against Otto for the injustice that Otto made him be guilty of. He tried to argue with himself; he laid the blame upon his own despotic temper. His loyal and eager nature, brought for the first time to the test of love, gave itself utterly, and demanded a gift as utter without the reservation of one particle of the heart. He admitted no sharing in friendship. Being ready to sacrifice all for his friend, he thought it right and even necessary that his friend should wholly sacrifice himself and everything for him. But he was beginning to feel that the world was not built on the model of his own inflexible character, and that he was asking things which others could not give. Then he tried to submit. He blamed himself, he regarded himself as an egoist, who had no right to encroach upon the liberty of his friend, and to monopolize his affection. He did sincerely endeavor to leave him free, whatever it might cost himself. In a spirit of humiliation he did set himself to pledge Otto not to neglect Franz; he tried to persuade himself that he was glad to see him finding pleasure in society other than his own. But when Otto, who was not deceived, maliciously obeyed him, he could not help lowering at him, and then he broke out again.

If necessary, he would have forgiven Otto for preferring other friends to himself; but what he could not stomach was the lie. Otto was neither liar nor hypocrite, but it was as difficult for him to tell the truth as for a stutterer to pronounce words. What he said was never altogether true nor altogether false. Either from timidity or from uncertainty of his own feelings he rarely spoke definitely. His answers were equivocal, and, above all, upon every occasion he made mystery and was secret in a way that set Jean-Christophe beside himself. When he was caught tripping, or was caught in what, according to the conventions of their friendship, was a fault, instead of admitting it he would go on denying it and telling absurd stories. One day Jean-Christophe, exasperated, struck him. He thought it must be the end of their friendship and that Otto would never forgive him; but after sulking for a few hours Otto came back as though nothing had happened. He had no resentment for Jean-Christophe's violence—perhaps even it was not unpleasing to him, and had a certain charm for him—and yet he resented Jean-Christophe letting himself be tricked, gulping down all his mendacities. He despised him a little, and thought himself superior. Jean-Christophe, for his part, resented Otto's receiving blows without revolting.

They no longer saw each other with the eyes of those first days. Their failings showed up in full light. Otto found Jean-Christophe's independence less charming. Jean-Christophe was a tiresome companion when they went walking. He had no sort of concern for correctness. He used to dress as he liked, take off his coat, open his waistcoat, walk with open collar, roll up his shirt-sleeves, put his hat on the end of his stick, and fling out his chest in the air. He used to swing his arms as he walked, whistle, and sing at the top of his voice. He used to be red in the face, sweaty, and dusty. He looked like a peasant returning from a fair. The aristocratic Otto used to be mortified at being seen in his company. When he saw a carriage coming he used to contrive to lag some ten paces behind, and to look as though he were walking alone.

Jean–Christophe was no less embarrassing company when he began to talk at an inn or in a railway–carriage when they were returning home. He used to talk loudly, and say anything that came into his head, and treat Otto with a disgusting familiarity. He used to express opinions quite recklessly concerning people known to everybody, or even about the appearance of people sitting only a few yards away from him, or he would enter into intimate details concerning his health and domestic affairs. It was useless for Otto to roll his eyes and to make signals of alarm. Jean–Christophe seemed not to notice them, and no more controlled himself than if he had been alone. Otto would see smiles on the faces of his neighbors, and would gladly have sunk into the ground. He thought Jean–Christophe coarse, and could not understand how he could ever have found delight in him.

What was most serious was that Jean–Christophe was just as reckless and indifferent concerning all the hedges, fences, inclosures, walls, prohibitions of entry, threats of fines, *Verbot* of all sorts, and everything that sought to confine his liberty and protect the sacred rights of property against it. Otto lived in fear from moment to moment, and all his protests were useless. Jean–Christophe grew worse out of bravado.

One day, when Jean–Christophe, with Otto at his heels, was walking perfectly at home across a private wood, in spite of, or because of, the walls fortified with broken bottles which they had had to clear, they found themselves suddenly face to face with a gamekeeper, who let fire a volley of oaths at them, and after keeping them for some time under a threat of legal proceedings, packed them off in the most ignominious fashion. Otto did not shine under this ordeal. He thought that he was already in jail, and wept, stupidly protesting that he had gone in by accident, and that he had followed Jean–Christophe without knowing whither he was going. When he saw that he was safe, instead of being glad, he bitterly reproached Jean–Christophe. He complained that Jean–Christophe had brought him into trouble. Jean–Christophe quelled him with a look, and called him "Lily–liver!" There was a quick passage of words. Otto would have left Jean–Christophe if he had known how to find the way home. He was forced to follow him, but they affected to pretend that they were not together.

A storm was brewing. In their anger they had not seen it coming. The baking countryside resounded with the cries of insects. Suddenly all was still. They only grew aware of the silence after a few minutes. Their ears buzzed. They raised their eyes; the sky was black; huge, heavy, livid clouds overcast it. They came up from every side like a cavalry−charge. They seemed all to be hastening towards an invisible point, drawn by a gap in the sky. Otto, in terror, dare not tell his fears, and Jean−Christophe took a malignant pleasure in pretending not to notice anything. But without saying a word they drew nearer together. They were alone in the wide country. Silence. Not a wind stirred,—hardly a fevered tremor that made the little leaves of the trees shiver now and then. Suddenly a whirling wind raised the dust, twisted the trees and lashed them furiously. And the silence came again, more terrible than before. Otto, in a trembling voice, spoke at last.

"It is a storm. We must go home."

Jean−Christophe said:

"Let us go home."

But it was too late. A blinding, savage light flashed, the heavens roared, the vault of clouds rumbled. In a moment they were wrapped about by the hurricane, maddened by the lightning, deafened by the thunder, drenched from head to foot. They were in deserted country, half an hour from the nearest house. In the lashing rain, in the dim light, came the great red flashes of the storm. They tried to run but, their wet clothes clinging, they could hardly walk. Their shoes slipped on their feet, the water trickled down their bodies. It was difficult to breathe. Otto's teeth were chattering, and he was mad with rage. He said biting things to Jean−Christophe. He wanted to stop; he declared that it was dangerous to walk; he threatened to sit down on the road, to sleep on the soil in the middle of the plowed fields. Jean−Christophe made no reply. He went on walking, blinded by the wind, the rain, and the lightning; deafened by the noise; a little uneasy, but unwilling to admit it.

And suddenly it was all over. The storm had passed, as it had come. But they were both in a pitiful condition. In truth, Jean−Christophe was, as usual, so disheveled that a little more disorder made hardly any difference to him. But Otto, so neat, so careful of his appearance, cut a sorry figure. It was as though he had just taken a bath in his clothes, and Jean–Christophe, turning and seeing him, could not help roaring with laughter. Otto was so exhausted that he could not even be angry. Jean–Christophe took pity and talked gaily to him. Otto replied with a look of fury. Jean–Christophe made him stop at a farm. They dried themselves before a great fire, and drank hot wine. Jean–Christophe thought the adventure funny, and tried to laugh at it; but that was not at all to Otto's taste, and he was morose and silent for the rest of their walk. They came back sulking and did not shake hands when they parted.

As a result of this prank they did not see each other for more than a week. They were severe in their judgment of each other. But after inflicting punishment on themselves by depriving themselves of one of their Sunday walks, they got so bored that their rancor died away. Jean–Christophe made the first advances as usual. Otto condescended to meet them, and they made peace.

In spite of their disagreement it was impossible for them to do without each other. They had many faults; they were both egoists. But their egoism was naive; it knew not the self–seeking of maturity which makes it so repulsive; it knew not itself even; it was almost lovable, and did not prevent them from sincerely loving each other! Young Otto used to weep on his pillow as he told himself stories of romantic devotion of which he was the hero; lie used to invent pathetic adventures, in which he was strong, valiant, intrepid, and protected Jean–Christophe, whom he used to imagine that he adored. Jean–Christophe never saw or heard anything beautiful or strange without thinking: "If only Otto were here!" He carried the image of his friend into his whole life, and that image used to be transfigured, and become so gentle that, in spite of all that he knew about Otto, it used to intoxicate him. Certain words of Otto's which he used to remember long after they were spoken, and to embellish by the way, used to make him tremble with emotion. They imitated each other. Otto aped Jean–Christophe's manners, gestures, and writing. Jean–Christophe was sometimes irritated by the shadow which repeated every word that he said and dished up his thoughts as though they were its own. But he did not see that he himself was imitating Otto, and copying his way of dressing, walking, and pronouncing certain words. They were under a fascination. They were infused one in the other; their hearts were overflowing with tenderness. They trickled over with it on every side like a fountain. Each imagined that his friend was the cause of it. They did not know that it was the waking of their adolescence.

* * * * *

Jean–Christophe, who never distrusted any one, used to leave his papers lying about. But an instinctive modesty made him keep together the drafts of the letters which he scrawled to Otto, and the replies. But he did not lock them up; he just placed them between the leaves of one of his music–books, where he felt certain that no one would look for them. He reckoned without his brothers' malice.

He had seen them for some time laughing and whispering and looking at him; they were declaiming to each other fragments of speech which threw them into wild laughter. Jean–Christophe could not catch the words, and, following his usual tactics with them, he feigned utter indifference to everything they might do or say. A few words roused his attention; he thought he recognized them. Soon he was left without doubt that they had read his letters. But when he challenged Ernest and Rodolphe, who were calling each other "My dear soul," with pretended earnestness, he could get nothing from them. The little wretches pretended not to understand, and said that they had the right to call each other whatever they liked. Jean–Christophe, who had found all the letters in their places, did not insist farther.

Shortly afterwards he caught Ernest in the act of thieving; the little beast was rummaging in the drawer of the chest in which Louisa kept her money. Jean–Christophe shook him, and took advantage of the opportunity to tell him everything that he had stored up against him. He enumerated, in terms of scant courtesy, the misdeeds of Ernest, and it was not a short catalogue. Ernest took the lecture in bad part; he replied impudently that Jean–Christophe had nothing to reproach him with, and he hinted at unmentionable things in his brother's friendship with Otto. Jean–Christophe did not understand; but when he grasped that Otto was being dragged into the quarrel he demanded an explanation of Ernest. The boy tittered; then, when he saw Jean–Christophe white with anger, he refused to say any more. Jean–Christophe saw that he would obtain nothing in that way; he sat down, shrugged his shoulders, and affected a profound contempt for Ernest. Ernest, piqued by this, was impudent again; he set himself to hurt his brother, and set forth a litany of things each more cruel and more vile than the last. Jean–Christophe kept a tight hand on himself. When at last he did understand, he saw red; he leaped from his chair. Ernest had no time to cry out. Jean–Christophe had hurled himself on him, and rolled with him into the middle of the room, and beat his head against the tiles. On the frightful cries of the victim, Louisa, Melchior, everybody, came running. They rescued Ernest in a parlous state. Jean–Christophe would not loose his prey; they had to beat and beat him. They called him a savage beast, and he looked it. His eyes were bursting from his head, he was grinding his teeth, and his only thought was to hurl himself again on Ernest. When they asked him what had happened, his fury increased, and he cried out that he would kill him. Ernest also refused to tell.

Jean–Christophe could not eat nor sleep. He was shaking with fever, and wept in his bed. It was not only for Otto that he was suffering. A revolution was taking place in him. Ernest had no idea of the hurt that he had been able to do his brother. Jean–Christophe was at heart of a puritanical intolerance, which could not admit the dark ways of life, and was discovering them one by one with horror. At fifteen, with his free life and strong instincts, he remained strangely simple. His natural purity and ceaseless toil had protected him. His brother's words had opened up abyss on abyss before him. Never would he have conceived such infamies, and now that the idea of it had come to him, all his joy in loving and being loved was spoiled. Not only his friendship with Otto, but friendship itself was poisoned.

It was much worse when certain sarcastic allusions made him think, perhaps wrongly, that he was the object of the unwholesome curiosity of the town, and especially, when, some time afterwards, Melchior made a remark about his walks with Otto. Probably there was no malice in Melchior, but Jean–Christophe, on the watch, read hidden meanings into every word, and almost he thought himself guilty. At the same time Otto was passing through a similar crisis.

They tried still to see each other in secret. But it was impossible for them to regain the carelessness of their old relation. Their frankness was spoiled. The two boys who loved each other with a tenderness so fearful that they had never dared exchange a fraternal kiss, and had imagined that there could be no greater happiness than in seeing each other, and in being friends, and sharing each other's dreams, now felt that they were stained and spotted by the suspicion of evil minds. They came to see evil even in the most innocent acts: a look, a hand–clasp—they blushed, they had evil thoughts. Their relation became intolerable.

Without saying anything they saw each other less often. They tried writing to each other, but they set a watch upon their expressions. Their letters became cold and insipid. They grew disheartened. Jean–Christophe excused himself on the ground of his work, Otto on the ground of being too busy, and their correspondence ceased. Soon afterwards Otto left for the University, and the friendship which had lightened a few months of their lives died down and out.

And also, a new love, of which this had been only the forerunner, took possession of Jean–Christophe's heart, and made every other light seem pale by its side.

III. MINNA

Four or five months before these events Frau Josephs von Kerich, widow of Councilor Stephan von Kerich, had left Berlin, where her husband's duties had hitherto detained them, and settled down with her daughter in the little Rhine town, in her native country. She had an old house with a large garden, almost a park, which sloped down to the river, not far from Jean–Christophe's home. From his attic Jean–Christophe could see the heavy branches of the trees hanging over the walls, and the high peak of the red roof with its mossy tiles. A little sloping alley, with hardly room to pass, ran alongside the park to the right; from there, by climbing a post, you could look over the wall. Jean–Christophe did not fail to make use of it. He could then see the grassy avenues, the lawns like open meadows, the trees interlacing and growing wild, and the white front of the house with its shutters obstinately closed. Once or twice a year a gardener made the rounds, and aired the house. But soon Nature resumed her sway over the garden, and silence reigned over all.

That silence impressed Jean–Christophe. He used often stealthily to climb up to his watch–tower, and as he grew taller, his eyes, then his nose, then his mouth reached up to the top of the wall; now he could put his arms over it if he stood on tiptoe, and, in spite of the discomfort of that position, he used to stay so, with his chin on the wall, looking, listening, while the evening unfolded over the lawns its soft waves of gold, which lit up with bluish rays the shade of the pines. There he could forget himself until he heard footsteps approaching in the street. The night scattered its scents over the garden: lilac in spring, acacia in summer, dead leaves in the autumn. When Jean–Christophe, was on his way home in the evening from the Palace, however weary he might be, he used to stand by the door to drink in the delicious scent, and it was hard for him to go back to the smells of his room. And often he had played—when he used to play—in the little square with its tufts of grass between the stones, before the gateway of the house of the Kerichs. On each side of the gate grew a chestnut–tree a hundred years old; his grandfather used to come and sit beneath them, and smoke his pipe, and the children used to use the nuts for missiles, and toys.

One morning, as he went up the alley, he climbed up the post as usual. He was thinking of other things, and looked absently. He was just going to climb down when he felt that there was something unusual about it. He looked towards the house. The windows were open; the sun was shining into them and, although no one was to be seen, the old place seemed to have been roused from its fifteen years' sleep, and to be smiling in its awakening. Jean–Christophe went home uneasy in his mind.

At dinner his father talked of what was the topic of the neighborhood: the arrival of Frau Kerich and her daughter with an incredible quantity of luggage. The chestnut square was filled with rascals who had turned up to help unload the carts. Jean–Christophe was excited by the news, which, in his limited life, was an important event, and he returned to his work, trying to imagine the inhabitants of the enchanted house from his father's story, as usual hyperbolical. Then he became absorbed in his work, and had forgotten the whole affair when, just as he was about to go home in the evening, he remembered it all, and he was impelled by curiosity to climb his watch–tower to spy out what might be toward within the walls. He saw nothing but the quiet avenue, in which the motionless trees seemed to be sleeping in the last rays of the sun. In a few moments he had forgotten why he was looking, and abandoned himself as he always did to the sweetness of the silence. That strange place—standing erect, perilously balanced on the top of a post—was meet for dreams. Coming from the ugly alley, stuffy and dark, the sunny gardens were of a magical radiance. His spirit wandered freely through these regions of harmony, and music sang in him; they lulled him and he forgot time and material things, and was only concerned to miss none of the whisperings of his heart.

So he dreamed open–eyed and open–mouthed, and he could not have told how long he had been dreaming, for he saw nothing. Suddenly his heart leaped. In front of him, at a bend in an avenue, were two women's faces looking at him. One, a young lady in black, with fine irregular features and fair hair, tail, elegant, with carelessness and indifference in the poise of her head, was looking at him with kind, laughing eyes. The other, a girl of fifteen, also in deep mourning, looked as though she were going to burst out into a fit of wild laughter; she was standing a little behind her mother, who, without looking at her, signed to her to be quiet. She covered her lips with her hands, as if she were hard put to it not to burst out laughing. She was a little creature with a fresh face, white, pink, and round–cheeked; she had a plump little nose, a plump little mouth, a plump little chin, firm eyebrows, bright eyes, and a mass of fair hair plaited and wound round her head in a crown to show her rounded neck and her smooth white forehead—a Cranach face.

Jean–Christophe was turned to stone by this apparition. He could not go away, but stayed, glued to his post, with his mouth wide open. It was only when he saw the young lady coming towards him with her kindly mocking smile that he wrenched himself away, and jumped—tumbled—down into the alley, dragging with him pieces of plaster from the wall. He heard a kind voice calling him, "Little boy!" and a shout of childish laughter, clear and liquid as the song of a bird. He found himself in the alley on hands and knees, and, after a moment's bewilderment, he ran away as hard as he could go, as though he was afraid of being pursued. He was ashamed, and his shame kept bursting upon him again when he was alone in his room at home. After that he dared not go down the alley, fearing oddly that they might be lying in wait for him. When he had to go by the house, he kept close to the walls, lowered his head, and almost ran without ever looking back. At the same time he never ceased to think of the two faces that he had seen; he used to go up to the attic, taking off his shoes so as not to be heard, and to look his hardest out through the skylight in the direction of the Kerichs' house and park, although he knew perfectly well that it was impossible to see anything but the tops of the trees and the topmost chimneys.

About a month later, at one of the weekly concerts of the *Hof Musik Verein*, he was playing a concerto for piano and orchestra of his own composition. He had reached the last movement when he chanced to see in the box facing him Frau and Fraeulein Kerich looking at him. He so little expected to see them that he was astounded, and almost missed out his reply to the orchestra. He went on playing mechanically to the end of the piece. When it was finished he saw, although he was not looking in their direction, that Frau and Fraeulein Kerich were applauding a little exaggeratedly, as though they wished him to see that they were applauding. He hurried away from the stage. As he was leaving the theater he saw Frau Kerich in the lobby, separated from him by several rows of people, and she seemed to be waiting for him to pass. It was impossible for him not to see her, but he pretended not to do so, and, brushing his way through, he left hurriedly by the stage–door of the theater. Then he was angry with himself, for he knew quite well that Frau Kerich meant no harm. But he knew that in the same situation he would do the same again. He was in terror of meeting her in the street. Whenever he saw at a distance a figure that resembled her, he used to turn aside and take another road.

* * * * *

It was she who came to him. She sought him out at home.

One morning when he came back to dinner Louisa proudly told him that a lackey in breeches and livery had left a letter for him, and she gave him a large black–edged envelope, on the back of which was engraved the Kerich arms. Jean–Christophe opened it, and trembled as he read these words:

"Frau Josepha von Kerich requests the pleasure of *Hof Musicus* Jean–Christophe Krafft's company at tea to–day at half–past five."

"I shall not go," declared Jean–Christophe.

"What!" cried Louisa. "I said that you would go."

Jean–Christophe made a scene, and reproached his mother with meddling in affairs that were no concern of hers.

"The servant waited for a reply. I said that you were free to–day. You have nothing to do then."

In vain did Jean–Christophe lose his temper, and swear that he would not go; he could not get out of it now. When the appointed time came, he got ready fuming; in his heart of hearts he was not sorry that chance had so done violence to his whims.

Frau von Kerich had had no difficulty in recognizing in the pianist at the concert the little savage whose shaggy head had appeared over her garden wall on the day of her arrival. She had made inquiries about him of her neighbors, and what she learned about Jean–Christophe's family and the boy's brave and difficult life had roused interest in him, and a desire to talk to him.

Jean–Christophe, trussed up in an absurd coat, which made him look like a country parson, arrived at the house quite ill with shyness. He tried to persuade himself that Frau and Fraeulein Kerich had had no time to remark his features on the day when they had first seen him. A servant led him down a long corridor, thickly carpeted, so that his footsteps made no sound, to a room with a glass–paneled door which opened on to the garden. It was raining a little, and cold; a good fire was burning in the fireplace. Near the window, through which he had a peep of the wet trees in the mist, the two ladies were sitting. Frau Kerich was working and her daughter was reading a book when Jean–Christophe entered. When they saw him they exchanged a sly look.

"They know me again," thought Jean–Christophe, abashed.

He bobbed awkwardly, and went on bobbing.

Frau von Kerich smiled cheerfully, and held out her hand.

"Good–day, my dear neighbor," she said. "I am glad to see you. Since I heard you at the concert I have been wanting to tell you how much pleasure you gave me. And as the only way of telling you was to invite you here, I hope you will forgive me for having done so."

In the kindly, conventional words of welcome there was so much cordiality, in spite of a hidden sting of irony, that Jean–Christophe grew more at his ease.

"They do not know me again," he thought, comforted.

Frau von Kerich presented her daughter, who had closed her book and was looking interestedly at Jean–Christophe.

"My daughter Minna," she said, "She wanted so much to see you."

"But, mamma," said Minna, "it is not the first time that we have seen each other."

And she laughed aloud.

"They do know me again," thought Jean–Christophe, crestfallen.

"True," said Frau von Kerich, laughing too, "you paid us a visit the day we came."

At these words the girl laughed again, and Jean–Christophe looked so pitiful that when Minna looked at him she laughed more than ever. She could not control herself, and she laughed until she cried. Frau von Kerich tried to stop her, but she, too, could not help laughing, and Jean–Christophe, in spite of his constraint, fell victim to the contagiousness of it. Their merriment was irresistible; it was impossible to take offense at it. But Jean–Christophe lost countenance altogether when Minna caught her breath again, and asked him whatever he could be doing on the wall. She was tickled by his uneasiness. He murmured, altogether at a loss. Frau von Kerich came to his aid, and turned the conversation by pouring out tea.

She questioned him amiably about his life. But he did not gain confidence. He could not sit down; he could not hold his cup, which threatened to upset; and whenever they offered him water, milk, sugar or cakes, he thought that he had to get up hurriedly and bow his thanks, stiff, trussed up in his frock–coat, collar, and tie, like a tortoise in its shell, not daring and not being able to turn his head to right or left, and overwhelmed by Frau von Kerich's innumerable questions, and the warmth of her manner, frozen by Minna's looks, which he felt were taking in his features, his hands, his movements, his clothes. They made him even more uncomfortable by trying to put him at his ease—Frau von Kerich, by her flow of words, Minna by the coquettish eyes which instinctively she made at him to amuse herself.

Finally they gave up trying to get anything more from him than bows and monosyllables, and Frau von Kerich, who had the whole burden of the conversation, asked him, when she was worn out, to play the piano. Much more shy of them than of a concert audience, he played an adagio of Mozart. But his very shyness, the uneasiness which was beginning to fill his heart from the company of the two women, the ingenuous emotion with which his bosom swelled, which made him happy and unhappy, were in tune with the tenderness and youthful modesty of the music, and gave it the charm of spring. Frau von Kerich was moved by it; she said so with the exaggerated words of praise customary among men and women of the world; she was none the less sincere for that, and the very excess of the flattery was sweet coming from such charming lips. Naughty Minna said nothing, and looked astonished at the boy who was so stupid when he talked, but was so eloquent with his fingers. Jean–Christophe felt their sympathy, and grew bold under it. He went on playing; then, half turning towards Minna, with an awkward smile and without raising his eyes, he said timidly:

"This is what I was doing on the wall."

He played a little piece in which he had, in fact, developed the musical ideas which had come to him in his favorite spot as he looked into the garden, not, be it said, on the evening when he had seen Minna and Frau von Kerich—for some obscure reason, known only to his heart, he was trying to persuade himself that it was so—but long before, and in the calm rhythm of the *andante con moto*, there were to be found the serene impression of the singing of birds, mutterings of beasts, and the majestic slumber of the great trees in the peace of the sunset.

The two hearers listened delightedly. When he had finished Frau von Kerich rose, took his hands with her usual vivacity, and thanked him effusively. Minna clapped her hands, and cried that it was "admirable," and that to make him compose other works as "sublime" as that, she would have a ladder placed against the wall, so that he might work there at his case. Frau von Kerich told Jean–Christophe not to listen to silly Minna; she begged him to come as often as he liked to her garden, since he loved it, and she added that he need never bother to call on them if he found it tiresome.

"You need never bother to come and see us," added Minna. "Only if you do not come, beware!"

She wagged her finger in menace.

Minna was possessed by no imperious desire that Jean–Christophe should come to see her, or should even follow the rules of politeness with regard to herself, but it pleased her to produce a little effect which instinctively she felt to be charming.

Jean–Christophe blushed delightedly. Frau von Kerich won him completely by the tact with which she spoke of his mother and grandfather, whom she had known. The warmth and kindness of the two ladies touched his heart; he exaggerated their easy urbanity, their worldly graciousness, in his desire to think it heartfelt and deep. He began to tell them, with his naive trustfulness, of his plans and his wretchedness. He did not notice that more than an hour had passed, and he jumped with surprise when a servant came and announced dinner. But his confusion turned to happiness when Frau von Kerich told him to stay and dine with them, like the good friends that they were going to be, and were already. A place was laid for him between the mother and daughter, and at table his talents did not show to such advantage as at the piano. That part of his education had been much neglected; it was his impression that eating and drinking were the essential things at table, and not the manner of them. And so tidy Minna looked at him, pouting and a little horrified.

They thought that he would go immediately after supper. But he followed them into the little room, and sat with them, and had no idea of going. Minna stifled her yawns, and made signs to her mother. He did not notice them, because he was dumb with his happiness, and thought they were like himself—because Minna, when she looked at him, made eyes at him from habit—and finally, once he was seated, he did not quite know how to get up and take his leave. He would have stayed all night had not Frau von Kerich sent him away herself, without ceremony, but kindly.

He went, carrying in his heart the soft light of the brown eyes of Frau von Kerich and the blue eyes of Minna; on his hands he felt the sweet contact of soft fingers, soft as flowers, and a subtle perfume, which he had never before breathed, enveloped him, bewildered him, brought him almost to swooning.

* * * * *

He went again two days later, as was arranged, to give Minna a music–lesson. Thereafter, under this arrangement, he went regularly twice a week in the morning, and very often he went again in the evening to play and talk.

Frau von Kerich was glad to see him. She was a clever and a kind woman. She was thirty–five when she lost her husband, and although young in body and at heart, she was not sorry to withdraw from the world in which she had gone far since her marriage. Perhaps she left it the more easily because she had found it very amusing, and thought wisely that she could not both eat her cake and have it. She was devoted to the memory of Herr von Kerich, not that she had felt anything like love for him when they married; but good–fellowship was enough for her; she was of an easy temper and an affectionate disposition.

She had given herself up to her daughter's education; but the same moderation which she had had in her love, held in check the impulsive and morbid quality which is sometimes in motherhood, when the child is the only creature upon whom the woman can expend her jealous need of loving and being loved. She loved Minna much, but was clear in her judgment of her, and did not conceal any of her imperfections any more than she tried to deceive herself about herself. Witty and clever, she had a keen eye for discovering at a glance the weakness, and ridiculous side, of any person; she took great pleasure in it, without ever being the least malicious, for she was as indulgent as she was scoffing, and while she laughed at people she loved to be of use to them.

Young Jean–Christophe gave food both to her kindness and to her critical mind. During the first days of her sojourn in the little town, when her mourning kept her out of society, Jean–Christophe was a distraction for her—primarily by his talent. She loved music, although she was no musician; she found in it a physical and moral well–being in which thoughts could idly sink into a pleasant melancholy. Sitting by the fire—while Jean–Christophe played—a book in her hands, and smiling vaguely, she took a silent delight in the mechanical movements of his fingers, and the purposeless wanderings of her reverie, hovering among the sad, sweet images of the past.

But more even than the music, the musician interested her. She was clever enough to be conscious of Jean–Christophe's rare gifts, although she was not capable of perceiving his really original quality. It gave her a curious pleasure to watch the waking of those mysterious fires which she saw kindling in him. She had quickly appreciated his moral qualities, his uprightness, his courage, the sort of Stoicism in him, so touching in a child. But for all that she did mot view him the less with the usual perspicacity of her sharp, mocking eyes. His awkwardness, his ugliness, his little ridiculous qualities amused her; she did not take him altogether seriously; she did not take many things seriously. Jean–Christophe's antic outbursts, his violence, his fantastic humor, made her think sometimes that he was a little unbalanced; she saw in him one of the Kraffts, honest men and good musicians, but always a little wrong in the head. Her light irony escaped Jean–Christophe; he was conscious only of Frau von Kerich's kindness. He was so unused to any one being kind to him! Although his duties at the Palace brought him into daily contact with the world, poor Jean–Christophe had remained a little savage, untutored and uneducated. The selfishness of the Court was only concerned in turning him to its profit and not in helping him in any way. He went to the Palace, sat at the piano, played, and went away again, and nobody ever took the trouble to talk to him, except absently to pay him some banal compliment. Since his grandfather's death, no one, either at home or outside, had ever thought of helping him to learn the conduct of life, or to be a man. He suffered cruelly from his ignorance and the roughness of his manners. He went through an agony and bloody sweat to shape himself alone, but he did not succeed. Books, conversation, example—all were lacking. He would fain have confessed his

160

distress to a friend, but could not bring himself to do so. Even with Otto he had not dared, because at the first words he had uttered, Otto had assumed a tone of disdainful superiority which had burned into him like hot iron.

And now with Frau von Kerich it all became easy. Of her own accord, without his having to ask anything—it cost Jean–Christophe's pride so much!—she showed him gently what he should not do, told him what he ought to do, advised him how to dress, eat, walk, talk, and never passed over any fault of manners, taste, or language; and he could not be hurt by it, so light and careful was her touch in the handling of the boy's easily injured vanity. She took in hand also his literary education without seeming to be concerned with it; she never showed surprise at his strange ignorance, but never let slip an opportunity of correcting his mistakes simply, easily, as if it were natural for him to have been in error; and, instead of alarming him with pedantic lessons, she conceived the idea of employing their evening meetings by making Minna or Jean–Christophe read passages of history, or of the poets, German and foreign. She treated him as a son of the house, with a few fine shades of patronizing familiarity which he never saw. She was even concerned with his clothes, gave him new ones, knitted him a woolen comforter, presented him with little toilet things, and all so gently that he never was put about by her care or her presents. In short, she gave him all the little attentions and the quasi–maternal care which come to every good woman instinctively for a child who is intrusted to her, or trusts himself to her, without her having any deep feeling for it. But Jean–Christophe thought that all the tenderness was given to him personally, and he was filled with gratitude; he would break out into little awkward, passionate speeches, which seemed a little ridiculous to Frau von Kerich, though they did not fail to give her pleasure.

With Minna his relation was very different. When Jean–Christophe met her again at her first lesson, he was still intoxicated by his memories of the preceding evening and of the girl's soft looks, and he was greatly surprised to find her an altogether different person from the girl he had seen only a few hours before. She hardly looked at him, and did not listen to what he said, and when she raised her eyes to him, he saw in them so icy a coldness that he was chilled by it. He tortured himself for a long time to discover wherein lay his offense. He had given none, and Minna's feelings were neither more nor less favorable than on the preceding day; just as she had been then, Minna was completely indifferent to him. If on the first occasion she had smiled upon him in welcome, it was from a girl's instinctive coquetry, who delights to try the power of her eyes on the first comer, be it only a trimmed poodle who turns up to fill her idle hours. But since the preceding day the too–easy conquest had already lost interest for her. She had subjected Jean–Christophe to a severe scrutiny and she thought him an ugly boy, poor, ill–bred, who played the piano well, though he had ugly hands, held his fork at table abominably, and ate his fish with a knife. Then he seemed to her very uninteresting. She wanted to have music–lessons from him; she wanted, even, to amuse herself with him, because for the moment she had no other companion, and because in spite of her pretensions of being no longer a child, she had still in gusts a crazy longing to play, a need of expending her superfluous gaiety, which was, in her as in her mother, still further roused by the constraint imposed by their mourning. But she took no more account of Jean–Christophe than of a domestic animal, and if it still happened occasionally during the days of her greatest coldness that she made eyes at him, it was purely out of forgetfulness, and because she was thinking of something else, or simply so as not to get out of practice. And when she looked at him like that, Jean–Christophe's heart used to leap. It is doubtful if she saw it; she was telling herself stories. For she was at the age when we delight the senses with sweet fluttering dreams. She was forever absorbed in thoughts of love, filled with a curiosity which was only innocent from ignorance. And she only thought of love, as a well–taught young lady should, in terms of marriage. Her ideal was far from having taken definite shape. Sometimes she dreamed of marrying a lieutenant, sometimes of marrying a poet, properly sublime, *a la* Schiller. One project devoured another and the last was always welcomed with the same gravity and just the same amount of conviction. For the rest, all of them were quite ready to give way before a profitable reality, for it is wonderful to see how easily romantic girls forget their dreams, when something less ideal, but more certain, appears before them.

As it was, sentimental Minna was, in spite of all, calm and cold. In spite of her aristocratic name, and the pride with which the ennobling particle filled her, she had the soul of a little German housewife in the exquisite days of adolescence.

* * * * *

Naturally Jean–Christophe did not in the least understand the complicated mechanism—more complicated in appearance than in reality—of the feminine heart. He was often baffled by the ways of his friends, but he was so happy in loving them that he credited them with all that disturbed and made him sad with them, so as to persuade himself that he was as much loved by them as he loved them himself. A word or an affectionate look plunged him in delight. Sometimes he was so bowled over by it that he would burst into tears.

Sitting by the table in the quiet little room, with Frau von Kerich a few yards away sewing by the light of the lamp—Minna reading on the other side of the table, and no one talking, he looking through the half–open garden–door at the gravel of the avenue glistening under the moon, a soft murmur coming from the tops of the trees—his heart would be so full of happiness that suddenly, for no reason, he would leap from his chair, throw himself at Frau von Kerich's feet, seize her hand, needle or no needle, cover it with kisses, press it to his lips, his cheeks, his eyes, and sob. Minna would raise her eyes, lightly shrug her shoulders, and make a face. Frau von Kerich would smile down at the big boy groveling at her feet, and pat his head with her free hand, and say to him in her pretty voice, affectionately and ironically:

"Well, well, old fellow! What is it?"

Oh, the sweetness of that voice, that peace, that silence, that soft air in which were no shouts, no roughness, no violence, that oasis in the harsh desert of life, and—heroic light gilding with its rays people and things—the light of the enchanted world conjured up by the reading of the divine poets! Goethe, Schiller, Shakespeare, springs of strength, of sorrow, and of love!...

Minna, with her head down over the book, and her face faintly colored by her animated delivery, would read in her fresh voice, with its slight lisp, and try to sound important when she spoke in the characters of warriors and kings. Sometimes Frau von Kerich herself would take the book; then she would lend to tragic histories the spiritual and tender graciousness of her own nature, but most often she would listen, lying back in her chair, her never–ending needlework in her lap; she would smile at her own thoughts, for always she would come back to them through every book.

Jean–Christophe also had tried to read, but he had had to give it up; he stammered, stumbled over the words, skipped the punctuation, seemed to understand nothing, and would be so moved that he would have to stop in the middle of the pathetic passages, feeling tears coming. Then in a tantrum he would throw the book down on the table, and his two friends would burst out laughing.... How he loved them! He carried the image of them everywhere with him, and they were mingled with the persons in Shakespeare and Goethe. He could hardly distinguish between them. Some fragrant word of the poets which called up from the depths of his being passionate emotions could not in him be severed from the beloved lips that had made him hear it for the first time. Even twenty years later he could never read Egmont or Romeo, or see them played, without there leaping up in him at certain lines the memory of those quiet evenings, those dreams of happiness, and the beloved faces of Frau von Kerich and Minna.

He would spend hours looking at them in the evening when they were reading; in the night when he was dreaming in his bed, awake, with his eyes closed; during the day, when he was dreaming at his place in the orchestra, playing mechanically with his eyes half closed. He had the most innocent tenderness for them, and, knowing nothing of love, he thought he was in love. But he did not quite know whether it was with the mother or the daughter. He went into the matter gravely, and did not know which to choose. And yet, as it seemed to him he must at all costs make his choice, he inclined towards Frau von Kerich. And he did in fact discover, as soon as he had made up his mind to it, that it was she that he loved. He loved her quick eyes, the absent smile upon her half–open lips, her pretty forehead, so young in seeming, and the parting to one side in her fine, soft hair, her rather husky voice, with its little cough, her motherly hands, the elegance of her movements, and her mysterious soul. He would thrill with happiness when, sitting by his side, she would kindly explain to him the meaning of some passage in a book which he did not understand; she would lay her hand on Jean–Christophe's shoulder; he would feel the warmth of her fingers, her breath on his cheek, the sweet perfume of her body; he would listen in ecstasy, lose all thought of the book, and understand nothing at all. She would see that and ask him to repeat what she had said; then he would say nothing, and she would laughingly be angry, and tap his nose with her book, telling him that he would always be a little donkey. To that he would reply that he did not care so long as he was *her* little donkey, and she did not drive him out of her house. She would pretend to make objections; then she would say that although he was an ugly little donkey, and very stupid, she would agree to keep him—and perhaps even to love him—although he was good for nothing, if at the least he would be just *good*. Then they would both laugh, and he would go swimming in his joy.

* * * * *

When he discovered that he loved Frau von Kerich, Jean–Christophe broke away from Minna. He was beginning to be irritated by her coldness and disdain, and as, by dint of seeing her often, he had been emboldened little by little to resume his freedom of manner with her, he did not conceal his exasperation from her. She loved to sting him, and he would reply sharply. They were always saying unkind things to each other, and Frau von Kerich only laughed at them. Jean–Christophe, who never got the better in such passages of words, used sometimes to issue from them so infuriated that he thought he detested Minna; and he persuaded himself that he only went to her house again because of Frau von Kerich.

He went on giving her music lessons. Twice a week, from nine to ten in the morning, he superintended the girl's scales and exercises. The room in which they did this was Minna's studio—an odd workroom, which, with an amusing fidelity, reflected the singular disorder of her little feminine mind.

On the table were little figures of musical cats—a whole orchestra—one playing a violin, another the violoncello—a little pocket–mirror, toilet things and writing things, tidily arranged. On the shelves were tiny busts of musicians—Beethoven frowning, Wagner with his velvet cap, and the Apollo Belvedere. On the mantelpiece, by a frog smoking a red pipe, a paper fan on which was painted the Bayreuth Theater. On the two bookshelves were a few books—Luebke, Mommsen, Schiller, "Sans Famille," Jules Verne, Montaigne. On the walls large photographs of the Sistine Madonna, and pictures by Herkomer, edged with blue and green ribbons. There was also a view of a Swiss hotel in a frame of silver thistles; and above all, everywhere in profusion, in every corner of the room, photographs of officers, tenors, conductors, girl–friends, all with inscriptions, almost all with verse—or at least what is accepted as verse in Germany. In the center of the room, on a marble pillar, was enthroned a bust of Brahms, with a beard; and, above the piano, little plush monkeys and cotillion trophies hung by threads.

Minna would arrive late, her eyes still puffy with sleep, sulky; she would hardly reach out her hand to Jean–Christophe, coldly bid him good–day, and, without a word, gravely and with dignity sit down at the piano. When she was alone, it pleased her to play interminable scales, for that allowed her agreeably to prolong her half–somnolent condition and the dreams which she was spinning for herself. But Jean–Christophe would compel her to fix her attention on difficult exercises, and so sometimes she would avenge herself by playing them as badly as she could. She was a fair musician, but she did not like music—like many German women. But, like them, she thought she ought to like it, and she took her lessons conscientiously enough, except for certain moments of diabolical malice indulged in to enrage her master. She could enrage him much more by the icy indifference with which she set herself to her task. But the worst was when she took it into her head that it was her duty to throw her soul into an expressive passage: then she would become sentimental and feel nothing.

Young Jean–Christophe, sitting by her side, was not very polite. He never paid her compliments—far from it. She resented that, and never let any remark pass without answering it. She would argue about everything that he said, and when she made a mistake she would insist that she was playing what was written. He would get cross, and they would go on exchanging ungracious words and impertinences. With her eyes on the keys, she never ceased to watch Jean–Christophe and enjoy his fury. As a relief from boredom she would invent stupid little tricks, with no other object than to interrupt the lesson and to annoy Jean–Christophe. She would pretend to choke, so as to make herself interesting; she would have a fit of coughing, or she would have something very important to say to the maid. Jean–Christophe knew that she was play–acting; and Minna knew that Jean–Christophe knew that she was play–acting; and it amused her, for Jean–Christophe could not tell her what he was thinking.

One day, when she was indulging in this amusement and was coughing languidly, hiding her mouth in her handkerchief, as if she were on the point of choking, but in reality watching Jean–Christophe's exasperation out of the corner of her eye, she conceived the ingenious idea of letting the handkerchief fall, so as to make Jean–Christophe pick it up, which he did with the worst grace in the world. She rewarded him with a "Thank you!" in her grand manner, which nearly made him explode.

She thought the game too good not to be repeated. Next day she did it again. Jean–Christophe did not budge; he was boiling with rage. She waited a moment, and then said in an injured tone:

"Will you please pick up my handkerchief?"

Jean–Christophe could not contain himself.

"I am not your servant!" he cried roughly. "Pick it up yourself!"

Minna choked with rage. She got up suddenly from her stool, which fell over.

"Oh, this is too much!" she said, and angrily thumped the piano; and she left the room in a fury.

Jean–Christophe waited. She did not come back. He was ashamed of what he had done; he felt that he had behaved like a little cad. And he was at the end of his tether; she made fun of him too impudently! He was afraid lest Minna should complain to her mother, and he should be forever banished from Frau von Kerich's thoughts. He knew not what to do; for if he was sorry for his brutality, no power on earth would have made him ask pardon.

He came again on the chance the next day, although he thought that Minna would refuse to take her lesson. But Minna, who was too proud to complain to anybody—Minna, whose conscience was not shielded against reproach—appeared again, after making him wait five minutes more than usual; and she sat down at the piano, stiff, upright, without turning her head or saying a word, as though Jean–Christophe no longer existed for her. But she did not fail to take her lesson, and all the subsequent lessons, because she knew very well that Jean–Christophe was a fine musician, and that she ought to learn to play the piano properly if she wished to be—what she wished to be—a well–bred young lady of finished education.

But how bored she was! How they bored each other!

* * * * *

One misty morning in March, when little flakes of snow were flying, like feathers, in the gray air, they were in the studio. It was hardly daylight. Minna was arguing, as usual, about a false note that she had struck, and pretending that it "was written so." Although he knew perfectly well that she was lying, Jean–Christophe bent over the book to look at the passage in question closely. Her hand was on the rack, and she did not move it. His lips were near her hand. He tried to read and could not; he was looking at something else—a thing soft, transparent, like the petals of a flower. Suddenly—he did not know what he was thinking of—he pressed his lips as hard as he could on the little hand.

They were both dumfounded by it. He flung backwards; she withdrew her hand—both blushing. They said no word; they did not look at each other. After a moment of confused silence she began to play again; she was very uneasy: her bosom rose and fell as though she were under some weight; she struck wrong note after wrong note. He did not notice

167

it; he was more uneasy than she. His temples throbbed; he heard nothing; he knew not what she was playing; and, to break the silence, he made a few random remarks in a choking voice. He thought that he was forever lost in Minna's opinion. He was confounded by what he had done, thought it stupid and rude. The lesson–hour over, he left Minna without looking at her, and even forgot to say good–bye. She did not mind. She had no thought now of deeming Jean–Christophe ill–mannered; and if she made so many mistakes in playing, it was because all the time she was watching him out of the corner of her eye with astonishment and curiosity, and—for the first time—sympathy.

When she was left alone, instead of going to look for her mother as usual, she shut herself up in her room and examined this extraordinary event. She sat with her face in her hands in front of the mirror. Her eyes seemed to her soft and gleaming. She bit gently at her lip in the effort of thinking. And as she looked complacently at her pretty face, she visualized the scene, and blushed and smiled. At dinner she was animated and merry. She refused to go out at once, and stayed in the drawing–room for part of the afternoon; she had some work in her hand, and did not make ten stitches without a mistake, but what did that matter! In a corner of the room, with her back turned to her mother, she smiled; or, under a sudden impulse to let herself go, she pranced about the room and sang at the top of her voice. Frau von Kerich started and called her mad. Minna flung her arms round her neck, shaking with laughter, and hugged and kissed her.

In the evening, when she went to her room, it was a long time before she went to bed. She went on looking at herself in the mirror, trying to remember, and having thought all through the day of the same thing—thinking of nothing. She undressed slowly; she stopped every moment, sitting on the bed, trying to remember what Jean–Christophe was like. It was a Jean–Christophe of fantasy who appeared, and now he did not seem nearly so uncouth to her. She went to bed and put out the light. Ten minutes later the scene of the morning rushed back into her mind, and she burst out laughing. Her mother got up softly and opened the door, thinking that, against orders, she was reading in bed. She found Minna lying quietly in her bed, with her eyes wide open in the dim candlelight.

"What is it?" she asked. "What is amusing you?"

"Nothing," said Minna gravely. "I was thinking."

"You are very lucky to find your own company so amusing. But go to sleep."

"Yes, mamma," replied Minna meekly. Inside herself she was grumbling; "Go away! Do go away!" until the door was closed, and she could go on enjoying her dreams. She fell into a sweet drowsiness. When she was nearly asleep, she leaped for joy:

"He loves me.... What happiness! How good of him to love me!... How I love him!"

She kissed her pillow and went fast asleep.

* * * * *

When next they were together Jean–Christophe was surprised at Minna's amiability. She gave him "Good–day," and asked him how he was in a very soft voice; she sat at the piano, looking wise and modest; she was an angel of docility. There were none of her naughty schoolgirl's tricks, but she listened religiously to Jean–Christophe's remarks, acknowledged that they were right, gave little timid cries herself when she made a mistake and set herself to be more accurate. Jean–Christophe could not understand it. In a very short time she made astounding progress. Not only did she play better, but with musical feeling. Little as he was given to flattery, he had to pay her a compliment. She blushed with pleasure, and thanked him for it with a look tearful with gratitude. She took pains with her toilet for him; she wore ribbons of an exquisite shade; she gave Jean–Christophe little smiles and soft glances, which he disliked, for they irritated him, and moved him to the depths of his soul. And now it was she who made conversation, but there was nothing childish in what she said; she talked gravely, and quoted the poets in a pedantic and pretentious way. He hardly ever replied; he was ill at ease. This new Minna that he did not know astonished and disquieted him.

Always she watched him. She was waiting.... For what?... Did she know herself?... She was waiting for him to do it again. He took good care not to; for he was convinced that he had behaved like a clod; he seemed never to give a thought to it. She grew restless, and one day when he was sitting quietly at a respectful distance from her dangerous little paws, she was seized with impatience: with a movement so quick that she had no time to think of it, she herself thrust her little hand against his lips. He was staggered by it, then furious and ashamed. But none the less he kissed it very passionately. Her naive effrontery enraged him; he was on the point of leaving her there and then.

But he could not. He was entrapped. Whirling thoughts rushed in his mind; he could make nothing of them. Like mists ascending from a valley they rose from the depths of his heart. He wandered hither and thither at random through this mist of love, and whatever he did, he did but turn round and round an obscure fixed idea, a Desire unknown, terrible and fascinating as a flame to an insect. It was the sudden eruption of the blind forces of Nature.

* * * * *

They passed through a period of waiting. They watched each other, desired each other, were fearful of each other. They were uneasy. But they did not for that desist from their little hostilities and sulkinesses; only there were no more familiarities between them; they were silent. Each was busy constructing their love in silence.

Love has curious retroactive effects. As soon as Jean–Christophe discovered that he loved Minna, he discovered at the same time that he had always loved her. For three months they had been seeing each other almost every day without ever suspecting the existence of their love. But from the day when he did actually love her, he was absolutely convinced that he had loved her from all eternity.

It was a good thing for him to have discovered at last *whom* he loved. He had loved for so long without knowing whom! It was a sort of relief to him, like a sick man, who, suffering from a general illness, vague and enervating, sees it become definite in sharp pain in some portion of his body. Nothing is more wearing than love without a definite object; it eats away and saps the strength like a fever. A known passion leads the mind to excess; that is exhausting, but at least one knows why. It is an excess; it is not a wasting away. Anything rather than emptiness.

Although Minna had given Jean–Christophe good reason to believe that she was not indifferent to him, he did not fail to torture himself with the idea that she despised him. They had never had any very clear idea of each other, but this idea had never been more confused and false than it was now; it consisted of a series of strange fantasies which could never be made to agree, for they passed from one extreme to the other, endowing each other in turn with faults and charms which they did not possess—charms when they were parted, faults when they were together. In either case they were wide of the mark.

They did not know themselves what they desired. For Jean-Christophe his love took shape as that thirst for tenderness, imperious, absolute, demanding reciprocation, which had burned in him since childhood, which he demanded from others, and wished to impose on them by will or force. Sometimes this despotic desire of full sacrifice of himself and others—especially others, perhaps—was mingled with gusts of a brutal and obscure desire, which set him whirling, and he did not understand it. Minna, curious above all things, and delighted to have a romance, tried to extract as much pleasure as possible from it for her vanity and sentimentality; she tricked herself whole-heartedly as to what she was feeling. A great part of their love was purely literary. They fed on the books they had read, and were forever ascribing to themselves feelings which they did not possess.

But the moment was to come when all these little lies and small egoisms were to vanish away before the divine light of love. A day, an hour, a few seconds of eternity.... And it was so unexpected!...

* * * * *

One evening they were alone and talking. The room was growing dark. Their conversation took a serious turn. They talked of the infinite, of Life, and Death. It made a larger frame for their little passion. Minna complained of her loneliness, which led naturally to Jean-Christophe's answer that she was not so lonely as she thought.

"No," she said, shaking her head. "That is only words. Every one lives for himself; no one is interested in you; nobody loves you."

Silence.

"And I?" said Jean-Christophe suddenly, pale with emotion.

Impulsive Minna jumped to her feet, and took his hands.

The door opened. They flung apart. Frau von Kerich entered. Jean-Christophe buried himself in a book, which he held upside down. Minna bent over her work, and pricked her finger with her needle.

They were not alone together for the rest of the evening, and they were afraid of being left. When Frau von Kerich got up to look for something in the next room, Minna, not usually obliging, ran to fetch it for her, and Jean–Christophe took advantage of her absence to take his leave without saying goodnight to her.

Next day they met again, impatient to resume their interrupted conversation. They did not succeed. Yet circumstances were favorable to them. They went a walk with Frau von Kerich, and had plenty of opportunity for talking as much as they liked. But Jean–Christophe could not speak, and he was so unhappy that he stayed as far away as possible from Minna. And she pretended not to notice his discourtesy; but she was piqued by it, and showed it. When Jean–Christophe did at last contrive to utter a few words, she listened icily; he had hardly the courage to finish his sentence. They were coming to the end of the walk. Time was flying. And he was wretched at not having been able to make use of it.

A week passed. They thought they had mistaken their feeling for each other. They were not sure but that they had dreamed the scene of that evening. Minna was resentful against Jean–Christophe. Jean–Christophe was afraid of meeting her alone. They were colder to each other than ever.

A day came when it had rained all morning and part of the afternoon. They had stayed in the house without speaking, reading, yawning, looking out of the window; they were bored and cross. About four o'clock the sky cleared. They ran into the garden. They leaned their elbows on the terrace wall, and looked down at the lawns sloping to the river. The earth was steaming; a soft mist was ascending to the sun; little rain–drops glittered on the grass; the smell of the damp earth and the perfume of the flowers intermingled; around them buzzed a golden swarm of bees. They were side by side, not looking at each other; they could not bring themselves to break the silence. A bee came up and clung awkwardly to a clump of wistaria heavy with rain, and sent a shower of water down on them. They both laughed, and at once they felt that they were no longer cross with each other, and were friends again. But still they did not look at each other. Suddenly, without turning her head, she took his hand, and said:

"Come!"

She led him quickly to the little labyrinth with its box–bordered paths, which was in the middle of the grove. They climbed up the slope, slipping on the soaking ground, and the wet trees shook out their branches over them. Near the top she stopped to breathe.

"Wait ... wait ..." she said in a low voice, trying to take breath.

He looked at her. She was looking away; she was smiling, breathing hard, with her lips parted; her hand was trembling in Jean–Christophe's. They felt the blood throbbing in their linked hands and their trembling fingers. Around them all was silent. The pale shoots of the trees were quivering in the sun; a gentle rain dropped from the leaves with silvery sounds, and in the sky were the shrill cries of swallows.

She turned her head towards him; it was a lightning flash. She flung her arms about his neck; he flung himself into her arms.

"Minna! Minna! My darling!..."

"I love you, Jean Christophe! I love you!"

They sat on a wet wooden seat. They were filled with love, sweet, profound, absurd. Everything else had vanished. No more egoism, no more vanity, no more reservation. Love, love—that is what their laughing, tearful eyes were saying. The cold coquette of a girl, the proud boy, were devoured with the need of self–sacrifice, of giving, of suffering, of dying for each other. They did not know each other; they were not the same; everything was changed; their hearts, their faces, their eyes, gave out a radiance of the most touching kindness and tenderness. Moments of purity, of self–denial, of absolute giving of themselves, which through life will never return!

After a desperate murmuring of words and passionate promises to belong to each other forever, after kisses and incoherent words of delight, they saw that it was late, and they ran back hand in hand, almost falling in the narrow paths, bumping into trees, feeling nothing, blind and drunk with the joy of it.

When he left her he did not go home; he could not have gone to sleep. He left the town, and walked over the fields; he walked blindly through the night. The air was fresh, the country dark and deserted. A screech–owl hooted shrilly. Jean–Christophe went on like a sleep–walker. The little lights of the town quivered on the plain, and the stars in the dark sky. He sat on a wall by the road and suddenly burst into tears. He did not know why. He was too happy, and the excess of his joy was compounded of sadness and delight; there was in it thankfulness for his happiness, pity for those who were not happy, a melancholy and sweet feeling of the frailty of things, the mad joy of living. He wept for delight, and slept in the midst of his tears. When he awoke dawn was peeping. White mists floated over the river, and veiled the town, where Minna, worn out; was sleeping, while in her heart was the light of her smile of happiness.

* * * * *

They contrived to meet again in the garden next morning and told their love once more, but now the divine unconsciousness of it all was gone. She was a little playing the part of the girl in love, and he, though more sincere, was also playing a part. They talked of what their life should be. He regretted his poverty and humble estate. She affected to be generous, and enjoyed her generosity. She said that she cared nothing for money. That was true, for she knew nothing about it, having never known the lack of it. He promised that he would become a great artist; that she thought fine and amusing, like a novel. She thought it her duty to behave really like a woman in love. She read poetry; she was sentimental. He was touched by the infection. He took pains with his dress; he was absurd; he set a guard upon his speech; he was pretentious. Frau von Kerich watched him and laughed, and asked herself what could have made him so stupid.

But they had moments of marvelous poetry, and these would suddenly burst upon them out of dull days, like sunshine through a mist. A look, a gesture, a meaningless word, and they were bathed in happiness; they had their good–byes in the evening on the dimly–lighted stairs, and their eyes would seek each other, divine each other through the half darkness, and the thrill of their hands as they touched, the trembling in their voices, all those little nothings that fed their memory at night, as they slept so lightly that the chiming of each hour would awake them, and their hearts would sing "I am loved," like the murmuring of a stream.

They discovered the charm of things. Spring smiled with a marvelous sweetness. The heavens were brilliant, the air was soft, as they had never been before. All the town—the red roofs, the old walls, the cobbled streets—showed with a kindly charm that moved Jean–Christophe. At night, when everybody was asleep, Minna would get up from her bed, and stand by the window, drowsy and feverish. And in the afternoon, when he was not there, she would sit in a swing, and dream, with a book on her knees, her eyes half closed, sleepy and lazily happy, mind and body hovering in the spring air. She would spend hours at the piano, with a patience exasperating to others, going over and over again scales and passages which made her turn pale and cold with emotion. She would weep when she heard Schumann's music. She felt full of pity and kindness for all creatures, and so did he. They would give money stealthily to poor people whom they met in the street, and would then exchange glances of compassion; they were happy in their kindness.

To tell the truth, they were kind only by fits and starts. Minna suddenly discovered how sad was the humble life of devotion of old Frida, who had been a servant in the house since her mother's childhood, and at once she ran and hugged her, to the great astonishment of the good old creature, who was busy mending the linen in the kitchen. But that did not keep her from speaking harshly to her a few hours later, when Frida did not come at once on the sound of the bell. And Jean–Christophe, who was consumed with love for all humanity, and would turn aside so as not to crush an insect, was entirely indifferent to his own family. By a strange reaction he was colder and more curt with them the more affectionate he was to all other creatures; he hardly gave thought to them; he spoke abruptly to them, and found no interest in seeing them. Both in Jean–Christophe and Minna their kindness was only a surfeit of tenderness which overflowed at intervals to the benefit of the first comer. Except for these overflowings they were more egoistic than ever, for their minds were filled only with the one thought, and everything was brought back to that.

How much of Jean–Christophe's life was filled with the girl's face! What emotion was in him when he saw her white frock in the distance, when he was looking for her in the garden; when at the theater, sitting a few yards away from their empty places, he heard the door of their box open, and the mocking voice that he knew so well; when in some outside conversation the dear name of Kerich cropped up! He would go pale and blush; for a moment or two he would see and hear nothing. And then there would be a rush of blood over all his body, the assault of unknown forces.

The little German girl, naive and sensual, had odd little tricks. She would place her ring on a little pile of flour, and he would have to get it again and again with his teeth without whitening his nose. Or she would pass a thread through a biscuit, and put one end of it in her mouth and one in his, and then they had to nibble the thread to see who could get to the biscuit first. Their faces would come together; they would feel each other's breathing; their lips would touch, and they would laugh forcedly, while their hands would turn to ice. Jean–Christophe would feel a desire to bite, to hurt; he would fling back, and she would go on laughing forcedly. They would turn away, pretend indifference, and steal glances at each other.

These disturbing games had a disquieting attraction for them; they wanted to play them, and yet avoided them. Jean–Christophe was fearful of them, and preferred even the constraint of the meetings when Frau von Kerich or some one else was present. So outside presence could break in upon the converse of their loving hearts; constraint only made their love sweeter and more intense. Everything gained infinitely in value; a word, a movement of the lips, a glance were enough to make the rich new treasure of their inner life shine through the dull veil of ordinary existence. They alone could see it, or so they thought, and smiled, happy in their little mysteries. Their words were no more than those of a drawing–room conversation about trivial matters; to them they were an unending song of love. They read the most fleeting changes in their faces and voices as in an open book; they could have read as well with their eyes closed, for they had only to listen to their hearts to hear in them the echo of the heart of the beloved. They were full of confidence in life, in happiness, in themselves. Their hopes were boundless. They loved, they were loved, happy, without a shadow, without a doubt, without a fear of the future. Wonderful serenity of those days of spring! Not a cloud in the sky. A faith so fresh that it seems that nothing can ever tarnish it. A joy so abounding that nothing can ever exhaust it. Are they living? Are they dreaming? Doubtless they are dreaming. There is nothing in common between life and their dream—nothing, except in that moment of magic: they are but a dream themselves; their being has melted away at the touch of love.

* * * * *

It was not long before Frau von Kerich perceived their little intrigue, which they thought very subtly managed, though it was very clumsy. Minna had suspected it from the moment when her mother had entered suddenly one day when she was talking to Jean–Christophe, and standing as near to him as she could, and on the click of the door they had darted apart as quickly as possible, covered with confusion. Frau von Kerich had pretended to see nothing. Minna was almost sorry. She would have liked a tussle with her mother; it would have been more romantic.

Her mother took care to give her no opportunity for it; she was too clever to be anxious, or to make any remark about it. But to Minna she talked ironically about Jean–Christophe, and made merciless fun of his foibles; she demolished him in a few words. She did not do it deliberately; she acted upon instinct, with the treachery natural to a woman who is defending her own. It was useless for Minna to resist, and sulk, and be impertinent, and go on denying the truth of her remarks; there was only too much justification for them, and Frau von Kerich had a cruel skill in flicking the raw spot. The largeness of Jean–Christophe's boots, the ugliness of his clothes, his ill–brushed hat, his provincial accent, his ridiculous way of bowing, the vulgarity of his loud–voicedness, nothing was forgotten which might sting Minna's vanity. Such remarks were always simple and made by the way; they never took the form of a set speech, and when Minna, irritated, got upon her high horse to reply, Frau von Kerich would innocently be off on another subject. But the blow struck home, and Minna was sore under it.

She began to look at Jean–Christophe with a less indulgent eye. He was vaguely conscious of it, and uneasily asked her:

"Why do you look at me like that?"

And she answered:

"Oh, nothing!"

But a moment after, when he was merry, she would harshly reproach him for laughing so loudly. He was abashed; he never would have thought that he would have to take care not to laugh too loudly with her: all his gaiety was spoiled. Or when he was talking absolutely at his ease, she would absently interrupt him to make some unpleasant remark about his clothes, or she would take exception to his common expressions with pedantic aggressiveness. Then he would lose all desire to talk, and sometimes would be cross. Then he would persuade himself that these ways which so irritated him were a proof of Minna's interest in him, and she would persuade herself also that it was so. He would try humbly to do better. But she was never much pleased with him, for he hardly ever succeeded.

But he had no time—nor had Minna—to perceive the change that was taking place in her. Easter came, and Minna had to go with her mother to stay with some relations near

Weimar.

During the last week before the separation they returned to the intimacy of the first days. Except for little outbursts of impatience Minna was more affectionate than ever. On the eve of her departure they went for a long walk in the park; she led Jean–Christophe mysteriously to the arbor, and put about his neck a little scented bag, in which she had placed a lock of her hair; they renewed their eternal vows, and swore to write to each other every day; and they chose a star out of the sky, and arranged to look at it every evening at the same time.

The fatal day arrived. Ten times during the night he had asked himself, "Where will she be to-morrow?" and now he thought, "It is to-day. This morning she is still here; to-night she will be here no longer." He went to her house before eight o'clock. She was not up; he set out to walk in the park; he could not; he returned. The passages were full of boxes and parcels; he sat down in a corner of the room listening for the creaking of doors and floors, and recognizing the footsteps on the floor above him. Frau von Kerich passed, smiled as she saw him and, without stopping, threw him a mocking good-day. Minna came at last; she was pale, her eyelids were swollen; she had not slept any more than he during the night. She gave orders busily to the servants; she held out her hand to Jean–Christophe, and went on talking to old Frida. She was ready to go. Frau von Kerich came back. They argued about a hat-box. Minna seemed to pay no attention to Jean–Christophe, who was standing, forgotten and unhappy, by the piano. She went out with her mother, then came back; from the door she called out to Frau von Kerich. She closed the door. They were alone. She ran to him, took his hand, and dragged him into the little room next door; its shutters were closed. Then she put her face up to Jean–Christophe's and kissed him wildly. With tears in her eyes she said:

"You promise—you promise that you will love me always?"

They sobbed quietly, and made convulsive efforts to choke their sobs down so as not to be heard. They broke apart as they heard footsteps approaching. Minna dried her eyes, and resumed her busy air with the servants, but her voice trembled.

He succeeded in snatching her handkerchief, which she had let fall—her little dirty handkerchief, crumpled and wet with her tears.

He went to the station with his friends in their carriage. Sitting opposite each other Jean–Christophe and Minna hardly dared look at each other for fear of bursting into tears. Their hands sought each other, and clasped until they hurt. Frau von Kerich watched them with quizzical good–humor, and seemed not to see anything. The time arrived. Jean–Christophe was standing by the door of the train when it began to move, and he ran alongside the carriage, not looking where he was going, jostling against porters, his eyes fixed on Minna's eyes, until the train was gone. He went on running until it was lost from sight. Then he stopped, out of breath, and found himself on the station platform among people of no importance. He went home, and, fortunately, his family were all out, and all through the morning he wept.

* * * * *

For the first time he knew the frightful sorrow of parting, an intolerable torture for all loving hearts. The world is empty; life is empty; all is empty. The heart is choked; it is impossible to breathe; there is mortal agony; it is difficult, impossible, to live—especially when all around you there are the traces of the departed loved one, when everything about you is forever calling up her image, when you remain in the surroundings in which you lived together, she and you, when it is a torment to try to live again in the same places the happiness that is gone. Then it is as though an abyss were opened at your feet; you lean over it; you turn giddy; you almost fall. You fall. You think you are face to face with Death. And so you are; parting is one of his faces. You watch the beloved of your heart pass away; life is effaced; only a black hole is left—nothingness.

Jean–Christophe went and visited all the beloved spots, so as to suffer more. Frau von Kerich had left him the key of the garden, so that he could go there while they were away. He went there that very day, and was like to choke with sorrow. It seemed to him as he entered that he might find there a little of her who was gone; he found only too much of her; her image hovered over all the lawns; he expected to see her appear at all the corners of the paths; he knew well that she would not appear, but he tormented himself with pretending that she might, and he went over the tracks of his memories of love—the path to the labyrinth, the terrace carpeted with wistaria, the seat in the arbor, and he inflicted torture on himself by saying: "A week ago ... three days ago ... yesterday, it was so. Yesterday she was here ... this very morning...." He racked his heart with these thoughts until he had to stop, choking, and like to die. In his sorrow was mingled anger with himself for having wasted all that time, and not having made use of it. So many minutes, so many hours, when he had enjoyed the infinite happiness of seeing her, breathing her, and feeding upon her. And he had not appreciated it! He had let the time go by without having tasted to the full every tiny moment! And now!... Now it was too late.... Irreparable! Irreparable!

He went home. His family seemed odious to him. He could not bear their faces, their gestures, their fatuous conversation, the same as that of the preceding day, the same as that of all the preceding days—always the same. They went on living their usual life, as though no such misfortune had come to pass in their midst. And the town had no more idea of it than they. The people were all going about their affairs, laughing, noisy, busy; the crickets were chirping; the sky was bright. He hated them all; he felt himself crushed by this universal egoism. But he himself was more egoistic than the whole universe. Nothing was worth while to him. He had no kindness. He loved nobody.

He passed several lamentable days. His work absorbed him again automatically: but he had no heart for living.

One evening when he was at supper with his family, silent and depressed, the postman knocked at the door and left a letter for him. His heart knew the sender of it before he had seen the handwriting. Four pairs of eyes, fixed on him with undisguised curiosity, waited for him to read it, clutching at the hope that this interruption might take them out of their usual boredom. He placed the letter by his plate, and would not open it, pretending carelessly that he knew what it was about. But his brothers, annoyed, would not believe it, and went on prying at it; and so he was in tortures until the meal was ended. Then he was free to lock himself up in his room. His heart was beating so that he almost tore the letter as he opened it. He trembled to think what might be in it; but as soon as he had glanced over the first words he was filled with joy.

A few very affectionate words. Minna was writing to him by stealth. She called him "Dear *Christlein*" and told him that she had wept much, had looked at the star every evening, that she had been to Frankfort, which was a splendid town, where there were wonderful shops, but that she had never bothered about anything because she was thinking of him. She reminded him that he had sworn to be faithful to her, and not to see anybody while she was away, so that he might think only of her. She wanted him to work all the time while she was gone, so as to make himself famous, and her too. She ended by asking him if he remembered the little room where they had said good–bye on the morning when she had left him: she assured him that she would be there still in thought, and that she would still say good–bye to him in the same way. She signed herself, "Eternally yours! Eternally!..." and she had added a postscript bidding him buy a straw hat instead of his ugly felt—all the distinguished people there were wearing them—a coarse straw hat, with a broad blue ribbon.

Jean–Christophe read the letter four times before he could quite take it all in. He was so overwhelmed that he could not even be happy; and suddenly he felt so tired that he lay down and read and re–read the letter and kissed it again and again. He put it under his pillow, and his hand was forever making sure that it was there. An ineffable sense of well–being permeated his whole soul. He slept all through the night.

His life became more tolerable. He had ever sweet, soaring thoughts of Minna. He set about answering her; but he could not write freely to her; he had to hide his feelings: that was painful and difficult for him. He continued clumsily to conceal his love beneath formulae of ceremonious politeness, which he always used in an absurd fashion.

When he had sent it he awaited Minna's reply, and only lived in expectation of it. To win patience he tried to go for walks and to read. But his thoughts were only of Minna: he went on crazily repeating her name over and over again; he was so abject in his love and worship of her name that he carried everywhere with him a volume of Lessing, because the name of Minna occurred in it, and every day when he left the theater he went a long distance out of his way so as to pass a mercery shop, on whose signboard the five adored letters were written.

He reproached himself for wasting time when she had bid him so urgently to work, so as to make her famous. The naive vanity of her request touched him, as a mark of her confidence in him. He resolved, by way of fulfilling it, to write a work which should be not only dedicated, but consecrated, to her. He could not have written any other at that time. Hardly had the scheme occurred to him than musical ideas rushed in upon him. It was like a flood of water accumulated in a reservoir for several months, until it should suddenly rush down, breaking all its dams. He did not leave his room for a week. Louisa left his dinner at the door; for he did not allow even her to enter.

He wrote a quintette for clarionet and strings. The first movement was a poem of youthful hope and desire; the last a lover's joke, in which Jean–Christophe's wild humor peeped out. But the whole work was written for the sake of the second movement, the *larghetto*, in which Jean–Christophe had depicted an ardent and ingenuous little soul, which was, or was meant to be, a portrait of Minna. No one would have recognized it, least of all herself; but the great thing was that it was perfectly recognizable to himself; and he had a thrill of pleasure in the illusion of feeling that he had caught the essence of his beloved. No work had ever been so easily or happily written; it was an outlet for the excess of love which the parting had stored up in him; and at the same time his care for the work of art, the effort necessary to dominate and concentrate his passion into a beautiful and clear form, gave him a healthiness of mind, a balance in his faculties, which gave him a sort of physical delight—a sovereign enjoyment known to every creative artist. While he is creating he escapes altogether from the slavery of desire and sorrow; he becomes then master in his turn; and all that gave him joy or suffering seems then to him to be only the fine play of his will. Such moments are too short; for when they are done he finds about him, more heavy than ever, the chains of reality.

While Jean–Christophe was busy with his work he hardly had time to think of his parting from Minna; he was living with her. Minna was no longer in Minna; she was in himself. But when he had finished he found that he was alone, more alone than before, more weary, exhausted by the effort; he remembered that it was a fortnight since he had written to Minna and that she had not replied.

He wrote to her again, and this time he could not bring himself altogether to exercise the constraint which he had imposed on himself for the first letter. He reproached Minna jocularly—for he did not believe it himself—with having forgotten him. He scolded her for her laziness and teased her affectionately. He spoke of his work with much mystery, so as to rouse her curiosity, and because he wished to keep it as a surprise for her when she returned. He described minutely the hat that he had bought; and he told how, to carry out the little despot's orders—for he had taken all her commands literally—he did not go out at all, and said that he was ill as an excuse for refusing invitations. He did not add that he was even on bad terms with the Grand Duke, because, in excess of zeal, he had refused to go to a party at the Palace to which he had been invited. The whole letter was full of a careless joy, and conveyed those little secrets so dear to lovers. He imagined that Minna alone had the key to them, and thought himself very clever, because he had carefully replaced every word of love with words of friendship.

After he had written he felt comforted for a moment; first, because the letter had given him the illusion of conversation with his absent fair, but chiefly because he had no doubt but that Minna would reply to it at once. He was very patient for the three days which he had allowed for the post to take his letter to Minna and bring back her answer; but when the fourth day had passed he began once more to find life difficult. He had no energy or interest in things, except during the hour before the post's arrival. Then he was trembling with impatience. He became superstitious, and looked for the smallest sign—the crackling of the fire, a chance word—to give him an assurance that the letter would come. Once that hour was passed he would collapse again. No more work, no more walks; the only object of his existence was to wait for the next post, and all his energy was expended in finding strength to wait for so long. But when evening came, and all hope was gone for the day, then he was crushed; it seemed to him that he could never live until the morrow, and he would stay for hours, sitting at his table, without speaking or thinking, without even the power to go to bed, until some remnant of his will would take him off to it; and he would sleep heavily, haunted by stupid dreams, which made him think that the night would never end.

This continual expectation became at length a physical torture, an actual illness. Jean–Christophe went so far as to suspect his father, his brother, even the postman, of having taken the letter and hidden it from him. He was racked with uneasiness. He never doubted Minna's fidelity for an instant. If she did not write, it must be because she was ill, dying, perhaps dead. Then he rushed to his pen and wrote a third letter, a few heartrending lines, in which he had no more thought of guarding his feelings than of taking care with his spelling. The time for the post to go was drawing near; he had crossed out and smudged the sheet as he turned it over, dirtied the envelope as he closed it. No matter! He could not wait until the next post. He ran and hurled his letter into the box and waited in mortal agony. On the next night but one he had a clear vision of Minna, ill, calling to him; he got up, and was on the point of setting out on foot to go to her. But where? Where should he find her?

On the fourth morning Minna's letter came at last—hardly a half–sheet—cold and stiff. Minna said that she did not understand what could have filled him with such stupid fears, that she was quite well, that she had no time to write, and begged him not to get so excited in future, and not to write any more.

Jean–Christophe was stunned. He never doubted Minna's sincerity. He blamed himself; he thought that Minna was justly annoyed by the impudent and absurd letters that he had written. He thought himself an idiot, and beat at his head with his fist. But it was all in vain; he was forced to feel that Minna did not love him as much as he loved her.

The days that followed were so mournful that it is impossible to describe them. Nothingness cannot be described. Deprived of the only boon that made living worth while for him—his letters to Minna—Jean–Christophe now only lived mechanically, and the only thing which interested him at all was when in the evening, as he was going to bed, he ticked off on the calendar, like a schoolboy, one of the interminable days which lay between himself and Minna's return. The day of the return was past. They ought to have been at home a week. Feverish excitement had succeeded Jean–Christophe's prostration. Minna had promised when she left to advise him of the day and hour of their arrival. He waited from moment to moment to go and meet them; and he tied himself up in a web of guesses as to the reasons for their delay.

One evening one of their neighbors, a friend of his grandfather, Fischer, the furniture dealer, came in to smoke and chat with Melchior after dinner as he often did. Jean–Christophe, in torment, was going up to his room after waiting for the postman to pass when a word made him tremble. Fischer said that next day he had to go early in the morning to the Kerichs' to hang up the curtains. Jean–Christophe stopped dead, and asked:

"Have they returned?"

"You wag! You know that as well as I do," said old Fischer roguishly. "Fine weather! They came back the day before yesterday."

Jean–Christophe heard no more; he left the room, and got ready to go out. His mother, who for some time had secretly been watching him without his knowing it, followed him into the lobby, and asked him timidly where he was going. He made no answer, and went out. He was hurt.

He ran to the Kerichs' house. It was nine o'clock in the evening. They were both in the drawing–room and did not appear to be surprised to see him. They said "Good–evening" quietly. Minna was busy writing, and held out her hand over the table and went on with her letter, vaguely asking him for his news. She asked him to forgive her discourtesy, and pretended to be listening to what he said, but she interrupted him to ask something of her mother. He had prepared touching words concerning all that he had suffered during her absence; he could hardly summon a few words; no one was interested in them, and he had not the heart to go on—it all rang so false.

When Minna had finished her letter she took up some work, and, sitting a little away from him, began to tell him about her travels. She talked about the pleasant weeks she had spent—riding on horseback, country–house life, interesting society; she got excited gradually, and made allusions to events and people whom Jean–Christophe did not know, and the memory of them made her mother and herself laugh. Jean–Christophe felt that he was a stranger during the story; he did not know how to take it, and laughed awkwardly. He never took his eyes from Minna's face, beseeching her to look at him, imploring her to throw him a glance for alms. But when she did look at him—which was not often, for she addressed herself more to her mother than to him—her eyes, like her voice, were cold and indifferent. Was she so constrained because of her mother, or was it that he did not understand? He wished to speak to her alone, but Frau von Kerich never left them for a moment. He tried to bring the conversation round to some subject interesting to himself; he spoke of his work and his plans; he was dimly conscious that Minna was evading him, and instinctively he tried to interest her in himself. Indeed, she seemed to listen attentively enough; she broke in upon his narrative with various interjections, which were never very apt, but always seemed to be full of interest. But just as he was beginning to hope once more, carried off his feet by one of her charming smiles, he saw Minna put her little hand to her lips and yawn. He broke off short. She saw that, and asked his pardon amiably, saying that she was tired. He got up, thinking that they would persuade him to stay, but they said nothing. He spun out his "Good–bye," and waited for a word to ask him to come again next day; there was no suggestion of it. He had to go. Minna did not take him to the door. She held out her hand to him—an indifferent hand that drooped limply in his—and he took his leave of them in the middle of the room.

He went home with terror in his heart. Of the Minna of two months before, of his beloved Minna, nothing was left. What had happened? What had become of her? For a poor boy who has never yet experienced the continual change, the complete disappearance, and the absolute renovation of living souls, of which the majority are not so much souls as collections of souls in succession changing and dying away continually, the simple truth was too cruel for him to be able to believe it. He rejected the idea of it in terror, and tried to persuade himself that he had not been able to see properly, and that Minna was just the same. He decided to go again to the house next morning, and to talk to her at all costs.

He did not sleep. Through the night he counted one after another the chimes of the clock. From one o'clock on he was rambling round the Kerichs' house; he entered it as soon as he could. He did not see Minna, but Frau von Kerich. Always busy and an early riser, she was watering the pots of flowers on the veranda. She gave a mocking cry when she saw Jean–Christophe.

"Ah!" she said. "It is you!... I am glad you have come. I have something to talk to you about. Wait a moment...."

She went in for a moment to put down her watering can and to dry her hands, and came back with a little smile as she saw Jean–Christophe's discomfiture; he was conscious of the approach of disaster.

"Come into the garden," she said; "we shall be quieter."

In the garden that was full still of his love he followed Frau von Kerich. She did not hasten to speak, and enjoyed the boy's uneasiness.

"Let us sit here," she said at last. They were sitting on the seat in the place where Minna had held up her lips to him on the eve of her departure.

"I think you know what is the matter," said Frau von Kerich, looking serious so as to complete his confusion. "I should never have thought it of you, Jean–Christophe. I thought you a serious boy. I had every confidence in you. I should never have thought that you would abuse it to try and turn my daughter's head. She was in your keeping. You ought to have shown respect for her, respect for me, respect for yourself."

There was a light irony in her accents. Frau von Kerich attached not the least importance to this childish love affair; but Jean–Christophe was not conscious of it, and her reproaches, which he took, as he took everything, tragically, went to his heart.

"But, Madam ... but, Madam ..." he stammered, with tears in his eyes, "I have never abused your confidence.... Please do not think that.... I am not a bad man, that I swear!... I love Fraeulein Minna. I love her with all my Soul, and I wish to marry her."

Frau von Kerich smiled.

"No, my poor boy," she said, with that kindly smile in which was so much disdain, as at last he was to understand, "no, it is impossible; it is just a childish folly."

"Why? Why?" he asked.

He took her hands, not believing that she could be speaking seriously, and almost reassured by the new softness in her voice. She smiled still, and said:

"Because...."

He insisted. With ironical deliberation—she did not take him altogether seriously—she told him that he had no fortune, that Minna had different tastes. He protested that that made no difference; that he would be rich, famous; that he would win honors, money, all that Minna could desire. Frau von Kerich looked skeptical; she was amused by his self–confidence, and only shook her head by way of saying no. But he stuck to it.

"No, Jean–Christophe," she said firmly, "no. It is not worth arguing. It is impossible. It is not only a question of money. So many things! The position...."

She had no need to finish. That was a needle that pierced to his very marrow. His eyes were opened. He saw the irony of the friendly smile, he saw the coldness of the kindly look, he understood suddenly what it was that separated him from this woman whom he loved as a son, this woman who seemed to treat him like a mother; he was conscious of all that was patronizing and disdainful in her affection. He got up. He was pale. Frau von Kerich went on talking to him in her caressing voice, but it was the end; he heard no more the music of the words; he perceived under every word the falseness of that elegant soul. He could not answer a word. He went. Everything about him was going round and round.

When he regained his room he flung himself on his bed, and gave way to a fit of anger and injured pride, just as he used to do when he was a little boy. He bit his pillow; he crammed his handkerchief into his mouth, so that no one should hear him crying. He hated Frau von Kerich. He hated Minna. He despised them mightily. It seemed to him that he had been insulted, and he trembled with shame and rage. He had to reply, to take immediate action. If he could not avenge himself he would die.

He got up, and wrote an idiotically violent letter:

"MADAM,—

"I do not know if, as you say, you have been deceived in me. But I do know that I have been cruelly deceived in you. I thought that you were my friends. You said so. You pretended to be so, and I loved you more than my life. I see now that it was all a lie, that your affection for me was only a sham; you made use of me. I amused you, provided you with entertainment, made music for you. I was your servant. Your servant: that I am not! I am no man's servant!

"You have made me feel cruelly that I had no right to love your daughter. Nothing in the world can prevent my heart from loving where it loves, and if I am not your equal in rank, I am as noble as you. It is the heart that ennobles a man. If I am not a Count, I have perhaps more honor than many Counts. Lackey or Count, when a man insults me, I despise him. I despise as much any one who pretends to be noble, and is not noble of soul.

"Farewell! You have mistaken me. You have deceived me. I detest you!

"He who, in spite of you, loves, and will love till death, Fraeulein Minna, *because she is his*, and nothing can take her from him."

Hardly had he thrown his letter into the box than he was filled with terror at what he had done. He tried not to think of it, but certain phrases cropped up in his memory; he was in a cold sweat as he thought of Frau von Kerich reading those enormities. At first he was upheld by his very despair, but next day he saw that his letter could only bring about a final separation from Minna, and that seemed to him the direst of misfortunes. He still hoped that Frau von Kerich, who knew his violent fits, would not take it seriously, that she would only reprimand him severely, and—who knows?—that she would be touched perhaps by the sincerity of his passion. One word, and he would have thrown himself at her feet. He waited for five days. Then came, a letter. She said:

"DEAR SIR,—

"Since, as you say, there has been a misunderstanding between us, it would be wise not any further to prolong it. I should be very sorry to force upon you a relationship which has become painful to you. You will think it natural, therefore, that we should break it off. I hope that you will in time to come have no lack of other friends who will be able to appreciate you as you wish to be appreciated. I have no doubt as to your future, and from a distance shall, with sympathy, follow your progress in your musical career. Kind regards.

"JOSEPHA VON KERICH."

The most bitter reproaches would have been less cruel. Jean–Christophe saw that he was lost. It is possible to reply to an unjust accusation. But what is to be done against the negativeness of such polite indifference? He raged against it. He thought that he would never see Minna again, and he could not bear it. He felt how little all the pride in the world weighs against a little love. He forgot his dignity; he became cowardly; he wrote more letters, in which he implored forgiveness. They were no less stupid than the letter in which he had railed against her. They evoked no response. And everything was said.

* * * * *

He nearly died of it. He thought of killing himself. He thought of murder. At least, he imagined that he thought of it. He was possessed by incendiary and murderous desires. People have little idea of the paroxysm of love or hate which sometimes devours the hearts of children. It was the most terrible crisis of his childhood. It ended his childhood. It stiffened his will. But it came near to breaking it forever.

He found life impossible. He would sit for hours with his elbows on the window–sill looking down into the courtyard, and dreaming, as he used to when he was a little boy, of some means of escaping from the torture of life when it became too great. The remedy was there, under his eyes. Immediate ... immediate? How could one know?... Perhaps after hours—centuries—horrible sufferings!... But so utter was his childish despair that he let himself be carried away by the giddy round of such thoughts.

Louisa saw that he was suffering. She could not gauge exactly what was happening to him, but her instinct gave her a dim warning of danger. She tried to approach her son, to discover his sorrow, so as to console him. But the poor woman had lost the habit of talking intimately to Jean–Christophe. For many years he had kept his thoughts to himself, and she had been too much taken up by the material cares of life to find time to discover them or divine them. Now that she would so gladly have come to his aid she knew not what to do. She hovered about him like a soul in torment; she would gladly have found words to bring him comfort, and she dared not speak for fear of irritating him. And in spite of all her care she did irritate him by her every gesture and by her very presence, for she was not very adroit, and he was not very indulgent. And yet he loved her; they loved each other. But so little is needed to part two creatures who are dear to each other, and love each other with all their hearts! A too violent expression, an awkward gesture, a harmless twitching of an eye or a nose, a trick of eating, walking, or laughing, a physical constraint which is beyond analysis.... You say that these things are nothing, and yet they are all the world. Often they are enough to keep a mother and a son, a brother and a brother, a friend and a friend, who live in proximity to each other, forever strangers to each other.

Jean–Christophe did not find in his mother's grief a sufficient prop in the crisis through which he was passing. Besides, what is the affection of others to the egoism of passion preoccupied with itself?

One night when his family were sleeping, and he was sitting by his desk, not thinking or moving, he was engulfed in his perilous ideas, when a sound of footsteps resounded down the little silent street, and a knock on the door brought him from his stupor. There was a murmuring of thick voices. He remembered that his father had not come in, and he thought angrily that they were bringing him back drunk, as they had done a week or two before, when they had found him lying in the street. For Melchior had abandoned all restraint, and was more and more the victim of his vice, though his athletic health seemed not in the least to suffer from an excess and a recklessness which would have killed any other man. He ate enough for four, drank until he dropped, passed whole nights out of doors in icy rain, was knocked down and stunned in brawls, and would get up again next day, with his rowdy gaiety, wanting everybody about him to be gay too.

Louisa, hurrying up, rushed to open the door. Jean–Christophe, who had not budged, stopped his ears so as not to hear Melchior's vicious voice and the tittering comments of the neighbors....

... Suddenly a strange terror seized him; for no reason he began to tremble, with his face hidden in his hands. And on the instant a piercing cry made him raise his head. He rushed to the door....

In the midst of a group of men talking in low voices, in the dark passage, lit only by the flickering light of a lantern, lying, just as his grandfather had done, on a stretcher, was a body dripping with water, motionless. Louisa was clinging to it and sobbing. They had just found Melchior drowned in the mill–race.

Jean–Christophe gave a cry. Everything else vanished; all his other sorrows were swept aside. He threw himself on his fathers body by Louisa's side, and they wept together.

Seated by the bedside, watching Melchior's last sleep, on whose face was now a severe and solemn expression, he felt the dark peace of death enter into his soul. His childish passion was gone from him like a fit of fever; the icy breath of the grave had taken it all away. Minna, his pride, his love, and himself.... Alas! What misery! How small everything showed by the side of this reality, the only reality—death! Was it worth while to suffer so much, to desire so much, to be so much put about to come in the end to that!...

He watched his father's sleep, and he was filled with an infinite pity. He remembered the smallest of his acts of kindness and tenderness. For with all his faults Melchior was not bad; there was much good in him. He loved his family. He was honest. He had a little of the uncompromising probity of the Kraffts, which, in all questions of morality and honor, suffered no discussion, and never would admit the least of those small moral impurities which so many people in society regard not altogether as faults. He was brave, and whenever there was any danger faced it with a sort of enjoyment. If he was extravagant himself, he was so for others too; he could not bear anybody to be sad, and very gladly gave away all that belonged to him—and did not belong to him—to the poor devils he met by the wayside. All his qualities appeared to Jean–Christophe now, and he invented some of them, or exaggerated them. It seemed to him that he had misunderstood his father. He reproached himself with not having loved him enough. He saw him as broken by Life; he thought he heard that unhappy soul, drifting, too weak to struggle, crying out for the life so uselessly lost. He heard that lamentable entreaty that had so cut him to the

191

heart one day:

"Jean–Christophe! Do not despise me!"

And he was overwhelmed by remorse. He threw himself on the bed, and kissed the dead face and wept. And as he had done that day, he said again:

"Dear father, I do not despise you. I love you. Forgive me!"

But that piteous entreaty was not appeased, and went on:

"De not despise me! Do not despise me!" And suddenly Jean–Christophe saw himself lying in the place of the dead man; he heard the terrible words coming from his own lips; he felt weighing on his heart the despair of a useless life, irreparably lost. And he thought in terror: "Ah! everything, all the suffering, all the misery in the world, rather than come to that!..." How near he had been to it! Had he not all but yielded to the temptation to snap off his life himself, cowardly to escape his sorrow? As if all the sorrows, all betrayals, were not childish griefs beside the torture and the crime of self–betrayal, denial of faith, of self–contempt in death!

He saw that life was a battle without armistice, without mercy, in which he who wishes to be a man worthy of the name of a man must forever fight against whole armies of invisible enemies; against the murderous forces of Nature, uneasy desires, dark thoughts, treacherously leading him to degradation and destruction. He saw that he had been on the point of falling into the trap. He saw that happiness and love were only the friends of a moment to lead the heart to disarm and abdicate. And the little puritan of fifteen heard the voice of his God:

"Go, go, and never rest."

"But whither, Lord, shall I go? Whatsoever I do, whithersoever I go, is not the end always the same? Is not the end of all things in that?"

"Go on to Death, you who must die! Go and suffer, you who must suffer! You do not live to be happy. You live to fulfil my Law. Suffer; die. But be what you must be—a Man."

YOUTH

Christofori faciem die quaeunque tueris, Illa nempe die non morte mala morieris.

I. THE HOUSE OF EULER

The house was plunged in silence. Since Melchior's death everything seemed dead. Now that his loud voice was stilled, from morning to night nothing was heard but the wearisome murmuring of the river.

Christophe hurled himself into his work. He took a fiercely angry pleasure in self–castigation for having wished to be happy. To expressions of sympathy and kind words he made no reply, but was proud and stiff. Without a word he went about his daily task, and gave his lessons with icy politeness. His pupils who knew of his misfortune were shocked by his insensibility. But, those who were older and had some experience of sorrow knew that this apparent coldness might, in a child, be used only to conceal suffering: and they pitied him. He was not grateful for their sympathy. Even music could bring him no comfort. He played without pleasure, and as a duty. It was as though he found a cruel joy in no longer taking pleasure in anything, or in persuading himself that he did not: in depriving himself of every reason for living, and yet going on.

His two brothers, terrified by the silence of the house of death, ran away from it as quickly as possible. Rodolphe went into the office of his uncle Theodore, and lived with him, and Ernest, after trying two or three trades, found work on one of the Rhine steamers plying between Mainz and Cologne, and he used to come back only when he wanted money. Christophe was left alone with his mother in the house, which was too large for them; and the meagerness of their resources, and the payment of certain debts which had been discovered after his father's death, forced them, whatever pain it might cost, to seek another more lowly and less expensive dwelling.

They found a little flat,—two or three rooms on the second floor of a house in the Market Street. It was a noisy district in the middle of the town, far from the river, far from the trees, far from the country and all the familiar places. But they had to consult reason, not sentiment, and Christophe found in it a fine opportunity for gratifying his bitter creed of self–mortification. Besides, the owner of the house, old registrar Euler, was a friend of his grandfather, and knew the family: that was enough for Louisa, who was lost in her empty house, and was irresistibly drawn towards those who had known the creatures whom she had loved.

They got ready to leave. They took long draughts of the bitter melancholy of the last days passed by the sad, beloved fireside that was to be left forever. They dared hardly tell their sorrow: they were ashamed of it, or afraid. Each thought that they ought not to show their weakness to the other. At table, sitting alone in a dark room with half–closed shutters, they dared not raise their voices: they ate hurriedly and did not look at each other for fear of not being able to conceal their trouble. They parted as soon as they had finished. Christophe went back to his work; but as soon as he was free for a moment, he would come back, go stealthily home, and creep on tiptoe to his room or to the attic. Then he would shut the door, sit down in a corner on an old trunk or on the window–ledge, or stay there without thinking, letting the indefinable buzzing and humming of the old house, which trembled with the lightest tread, thrill through him. His heart would tremble with it. He would listen anxiously for the faintest breath in or out of doors, for the creaking of floors, for all the imperceptible familiar noises: he knew them all. He would lose consciousness, his thoughts would be filled with the images of the past, and he would issue from his stupor only at the sound of St. Martin's clock, reminding him that it was time to go.

In the room below him he could hear Louisa's footsteps passing softly to and fro, then for hours she could not be heard; she made no noise. Christophe would listen intently. He would go down, a little uneasy, as one is for a long time after a great misfortune. He would push the door ajar; Louisa would turn her back on him; she would be sitting in front of a cupboard in the midst of a heap of things—rags, old belongings, odd garments, treasures, which she had brought out intending to sort them. But she had no strength for it; everything reminded her of something; she would turn and turn it in her hands and begin to dream; it would drop from her hands; she would stay for hours together with her arms hanging down, lying back exhausted in a chair, given up to a stupor of sorrow.

Poor Louisa was now spending most of her life in the past—that sad past, which had been very niggardly of joy for her; but she was so used to suffering that she was still grateful for the least tenderness shown to her, and the pale lights which had shone here and there in the drab days of her life, were still enough to make them bright. All the evil that Melchior had done her was forgotten; she remembered only the good. Her marriage had been the great romance of her life. If Melchior had been drawn into it by a caprice, of which he had quickly repented, she had given herself with her whole heart; she thought that she was loved as much as she had loved; and to Melchior she was ever most tenderly grateful. She did not try to understand what he had become in the sequel. Incapable of seeing reality as it is, she only knew how to bear it as it is, humbly and honestly, as a woman who has no need of understanding life in order to be able to live. What she could not explain, she left to God for explanation. In her singular piety, she put upon God the responsibility for all the injustice that she had suffered at the hands of Melchior and the others, and only visited them with the good that they had given her. And so her life of misery had left her with no bitter memory. She only felt worn out—weak as she was—by those years of privation and fatigue. And now that Melchior was no longer there, now that two of her sons were gone from their home, and the third seemed to be able to do without her, she had lost all heart for action; she was tired, sleepy; her will was stupefied. She was going through one of those crises of neurasthenia which often come upon active and industrious people in the decline of life, when some unforeseen event deprives them of every reason for living. She had not the heart even to finish the stocking she was knitting, to tidy the drawer in which she was looking, to get up to shut the window; she would sit there, without a thought, without strength—save for recollection. She was conscious of her collapse, and was ashamed of it or blushed for it; she tried to hide it from her son; and Christophe, wrapped up in the egoism of his own grief, never noticed it. No doubt he was often secretly impatient with his mother's slowness in speaking, and acting, and doing the smallest thing; but different though her ways were from her usual activity, he never gave a thought to the matter until then.

Suddenly on that day it came home to him for the first time when he surprised her in the midst of her rags, turned out on the floor, heaped up at her feet, in her arms, and in her lap. Her neck was drawn out, her head was bowed, her face was stiff and rigid. When she heard him come in she started; her white cheeks were suffused with red; with an instinctive movement she tried to hide the things she was holding, and muttered with an awkward smile:

"You see, I was sorting...."

The sight of the poor soul stranded among the relics of the past cut to his heart, and he was filled with pity. But he spoke with a bitter asperity and seemed to scold, to drag her from her apathy:

"Come, come, mother; you must not stay there, in the middle of all that dust, with the room all shut up! It is not good for you. You must pull yourself together, and have done with all this."

"Yes," said she meekly.

She tried to get up to put the things back in the drawer. But she sat down again at once and listlessly let them fall from her hands.

"Oh! I can't ... I can't," she moaned. "I shall never finish!"

He was frightened. He leaned over her. He caressed her forehead with his hands.

"Come, mother, what is it?" he said. "Shall I help you? Are you ill?"

She did not answer. She gave a sort of stifled sob. He took her hands, and knelt down by her side, the better to see her in the dusky room.

"Mother!" he said anxiously.

Louisa laid her head on his shoulder and burst into tears.

"My boy, my boy," she cried, holding close to him. "My boy!... You will not leave me? Promise me that you will not leave me?"

His heart was torn with pity.

"No, mother, no. I will not leave you. What made you think of such a thing?"

"I am so unhappy! They have all left me, all...."

She pointed to the things all about her, and he did not know whether she was speaking of them or of her sons and the dead.

"You will stay with me? You will not leave me?... What should I do, if you went too?"

"I will not go, I tell you; we will stay together. Don't cry. I promise."

She went on weeping. She could not stop herself. He dried her eyes with his handkerchief.

"What is it, mother dear? Are you in pain?"

"I don't know; I don't know what it is." She tried to calm herself and to smile.

"I do try to be sensible. I do. But just nothing at all makes me cry.... You see, I'm doing it again.... Forgive me. I am so stupid. I am old. I have no strength left. I have no taste for anything any more. I am no good for anything. I wish I were buried with all the rest...."

He held her to him, close, like a child.

"Don't worry, mother; be calm; don't think about it...."

Gradually she grew quiet.

"It is foolish. I am ashamed.... But what is it? What is it?"

She who had always worked so hard could not understand why her strength had suddenly snapped, and she was humiliated to the very depths of her being. He pretended not to see it.

"A little weariness, mother," he said, trying to speak carelessly. "It is nothing; you will see; it is nothing."

But he too was anxious. From his childhood he had been accustomed to see her brave, resigned, in silence withstanding every test. And he was astonished to see her suddenly broken: he was afraid.

He helped her to sort the things scattered on the floor. Every now and then she would linger over something, but he would gently take it from her hands, and she suffered him.

From that time on he took pains to be more with her. As soon as he had finished his work, instead of shutting himself up in his room, as he loved to do, he would return to her. He felt her loneliness and that she was not strong enough to be left alone: there was danger in leaving her alone.

He would sit by her side in the evening near the open window looking on to the road. The view would slowly disappear. The people were returning home. Little lights appeared in the houses far off. They had seen it all a thousand times. But soon they would see it no more. They would talk disjointedly. They would point out to each other the smallest of the familiar incidents and expectations of the evening, always with fresh interest. They would have long intimate silences, or Louisa, for no apparent reason, would tell some reminiscence, some disconnected story that passed through her mind. Her tongue was loosed a little now that she felt that she was with one who loved her. She tried hard to talk. It was difficult for her, for she had grown used to living apart from her family; she looked upon her sons and her husband as too clever to talk to her, and she had never dared to join in their conversation. Christophe's tender care was a new thing to her and infinitely sweet, though it made her afraid. She deliberated over her words; she found it difficult to express herself; her sentences were left unfinished and obscure. Sometimes she was ashamed of what she was saying; she would look at her son, and stop in the middle of her narrative. But he would press her hand, and she would be reassured. He was filled with love and pity for the childish, motherly creature, to whom he had turned when he was a child, and now she turned to him for support. And he took a melancholy pleasure in her prattle, that had no interest for anybody but himself, in her trivial memories of a life that had always been joyless and mediocre, though it seemed to Louisa to be of infinite worth. Sometimes he would try to interrupt her; he was afraid that her memories would make her sadder than ever, and he would urge her to sleep. She would understand what he was at, and would say with gratitude in her eyes:

"No. I assure you, it does one good; let us stay a little longer."

They would stay until the night was far gone and the neighbors were abed. Then they would say good–night, she a little comforted by being rid of some of her trouble, he with a heavy heart under this new burden added to that which already he had to bear.

The day came for their departure. On the night before they stayed longer than usual in the unlighted room. They did not speak. Every now and then Louisa moaned: "Fear God!

198

Fear God!" Christophe tried to keep her attention fixed on the thousand details of the morrow's removal. She would not go to bed until he gently compelled her. But he went up to his room and did not go to bed for a long time. When leaning out of the window he tried to gaze through the darkness to see for the last time the moving shadows of the river beneath the house. He heard the wind in the tall trees in Minna's garden. The sky was black. There was no one in the street. A cold rain was just falling. The weathercocks creaked. In a house near by a child was crying. The night weighed with an overwhelming heaviness upon the earth and upon his soul. The dull chiming of the hours, the cracked note of the halves and quarters, dropped one after another into the grim silence, broken only by the sound of the rain on the roofs and the cobbles.

When Christophe at last made up his mind to go to bed, chilled in body and soul, he heard the window below him shut. And, as he lay, he thought sadly that it is cruel for the poor to dwell on the past, for they have no right to have a past, like the rich: they have no home, no corner of the earth wherein to house their memories: their joys, their sorrows, all their days, are scattered in the wind.

Next day in beating rain they moved their scanty furniture to their new dwelling. Fischer, the old furniture dealer, lent them a cart and a pony; he came and helped them himself. But they could not take everything, for the rooms to which they were going were much smaller than the old. Christophe had to make his mother leave the oldest and most useless of their belongings. It was not altogether easy; the least thing had its worth for her: a shaky table, a broken chair, she wished to leave nothing behind. Fischer, fortified by the authority of his old friendship with Jean Michel, had to join Christophe in complaining, and, good–fellow that he was and understanding her grief, had even to promise to keep some of her precious rubbish for her against the day when she should want it again. Then she agreed to tear herself away.

The two brothers had been told of the removal, but Ernest came on the night before to say that he could not be there, and Rodolphe appeared for a moment about noon; he watched them load the furniture, gave some advice, and went away again looking mightily busy.

The procession set out through the muddy streets. Christophe led the horse, which slipped on the greasy cobbles. Louisa walked by her son's side, and tried to shelter him from the rain. And so they had a melancholy homecoming in the damp rooms, that were made darker than ever by the dull light coming from the lowering sky. They could not have fought against the depression that was upon them had it not been for the attentions of their landlord and his family. But, when the cart had driven away, as night fell, leaving the furniture heaped up in the room; and Christophe and Louisa were sitting, worn out, one on a box, the other on a sack; they heard a little dry cough on the staircase; there was a knock at the door. Old Euler came in. He begged pardon elaborately for disturbing his guests, and said that by way of celebrating their first evening he hoped that they would be kind enough to sup with himself and his family. Louisa, stunned by her sorrow, wished to refuse. Christophe was not much more tempted than she by this friendly gathering, but the old man insisted and Christophe, thinking that it would be better for his mother not to spend their first evening in their new home alone with her thoughts, made her accept.

They went down to the floor below, where they found the whole family collected: the old man, his daughter, his son–in–law, Vogel, and his grandchildren, a boy and a girl, both a little younger than Christophe. They clustered around their guests, bade them welcome, asked if they were tired, if they were pleased with their rooms, if they needed anything; putting so many questions that Christophe in bewilderment could make nothing of them, for everybody spoke at once. The soup was placed on the table; they sat down. But the noise went on. Amalia, Euler's daughter, had set herself at once to acquaint Louisa with local details: with the topography of the district, the habits and advantages of the house, the time when the milkman called, the time when she got up, the various tradespeople and the prices that she paid. She did not stop until she had explained everything. Louisa, half–asleep, tried hard to take an interest in the information, but the remarks which she ventured showed that she had understood not a word, and provoked Amalia to indignant exclamations and repetition of every detail. Old Euler, a clerk, tried to explain to Christophe the difficulties of a musical career. Christophe's other neighbor, Rosa, Amalia's daughter, never stopped talking from the moment when they sat down,—so volubly that she had no time to breathe; she lost her breath in the middle of a sentence, but at once she was off again. Vogel was gloomy and complained of the food, and there were embittered arguments on the subject. Amalia, Euler, the girl, left off talking to take part in the discussion; and there were endless controversies as to whether there was too much salt in the stew or not enough; they called each other to witness, and, naturally, no two opinions were the same. Each despised his neighbor's taste, and thought only his own healthy and reasonable. They might have gone on arguing until the Last Judgment.

But, in the end, they all joined in crying out upon the bad weather. They all commiserated Louisa and Christophe upon their troubles, and in terms which moved him greatly they praised him for his courageous conduct. They took great pleasure in recalling not only the misfortunes of their guests, but also their own, and those of their friends and all their acquaintance, and they all agreed that the good are always unhappy, and that there is joy only for the selfish and dishonest. They decided that life is sad, that it is quite useless, and that they were all better dead, were it not the indubitable will of God that they should go on living so as to suffer. All these ideas came very near to Christophe's actual pessimism, he thought the better of his landlord, and closed his eyes to their little oddities.

When he went upstairs again with his mother to the disordered rooms, they were weary and sad, but they felt a little less lonely; and while Christophe lay awake through the night, for he could not sleep because of his weariness and the noise of the neighborhood, and listened to the heavy carts shaking the walls, and the breathing of the family sleeping below, he tried to persuade himself that he would be, if not happy, at least less unhappy here, with these good people—a little tiresome, if the truth be told—who suffered from like misfortunes, who seemed to understand him, and whom, he thought, he understood.

But when at last he did fall asleep, he was roused unpleasantly at dawn by the voices of his neighbors arguing, and the creaking of a pump worked furiously by some one who was in a hurry to swill the yard and the stairs.

* * * * *

Justus Euler was a little bent old man, with uneasy, gloomy eyes, a red face, all lines and pimples, gap–toothed, with an unkempt beard, with which he was forever fidgeting with his hands. Very honest, quite able, profoundly moral, he had been on quite good terms with Christophe's grandfather. He was said to be like him. And, in truth, he was of the same generation and brought up with the same principles; but he lacked Jean Michel's strong physique, that is, while he was of the same opinion on many points, fundamentally he was hardly at all like him, for it is temperament far more than ideas that makes a man, and whatever the divisions, fictitious or real, marked between men by intellect, the great divisions between men and men are into those who are healthy and those who are not. Old Euler was not a healthy man. He talked morality, like Jean Michel, but his morals were not the same as Jean Michel's; he had not his sound stomach, his lungs, or his jovial strength. Everything in Euler and his family was built on a more parsimonious and niggardly plan. He had been an official for forty years, was now retired, and suffered from that melancholy that comes from inactivity and weighs so heavily upon old men,

201

who have not made provision in their inner life for their last years. All his habits, natural and acquired, all the habits of his trade had given him a meticulous and peevish quality, which was reproduced to a certain extent in each of his children.

His son–in–law, Vogel, a clerk at the Chancery Court, was fifty years old. Tall, strong, almost bald, with gold spectacles, fairly good–looking, he considered himself ill, and no doubt was so, although obviously he did not have the diseases which he thought he had, but only a mind soured by the stupidity of his calling and a body ruined to a certain extent by his sedentary life. Very industrious, not without merit, even cultured up to a point; he was a victim of our ridiculous modern life, or like so many clerks, locked up in their offices, he had succumbed to the demon of hypochondria. One of those unfortunates whom Goethe called *"ein trauriger, ungriechischer Hypochondrist"*—"a gloomy and un–Greek hypochondriac,"—and pitied, though he took good care to avoid them.

Amalia was neither the one nor the other. Strong, loud, and active, she wasted no sympathy on her husband's jeremiads; she used to shake him roughly. But no human strength can bear up against living together, and when in a household one or other is neurasthenic, the chances are that in time they will both be so. In vain did Amalia cry out upon Vogel, in vain did she go on protesting either from habit or because it was necessary; next moment she herself was lamenting her condition more loudly even than he, and, passing imperceptibly from scolding to lamentation, she did him no good; she increased his ills tenfold by loudly singing chorus to his follies. In the end not only did she crush the unhappy Vogel, terrified by the proportions assumed by his own outcries sent sounding back by this echo, but she crushed everybody, even herself. In her turn she caught the trick of unwarrantably bemoaning her health, and her father's, and her daughter's, and her son's. It became a mania; by constant repetition she came to believe what she said. She took the least chill tragically; she was uneasy and worried about everybody. More than that, when they were well, she still worried, because of the sickness that was bound to come. So life was passed in perpetual fear. Outside that they were all in fairly good health, and it seemed as though their state of continual moaning and groaning did serve to keep them well. They all ate and slept and worked as usual, and the life of this household was not relaxed for it all. Amalia's activity was not satisfied with working from morning to night up and down the house; they all had to toil with her, and there was forever a moving of furniture, a washing of floors, a polishing of wood, a sound of voices, footsteps, quivering, movement.

The two children, crushed by such loud authority, leaving nobody alone, seemed to find it natural enough to submit to it. The boy, Leonard, was good looking, though insignificant of feature, and stiff in manner. The girl, Rosa, fair–haired, with pretty blue eyes, gentle and affectionate, would have been pleasing especially with the freshness of her delicate complexion, and her kind manner, had her nose not been quite so large or so awkwardly placed; it made her face heavy and gave her a foolish expression. She was like a girl of Holbein, in the gallery at Basle—the daughter of burgomaster Meier—sitting, with eyes cast down, her hands on her knees, her fair hair falling down to her shoulders, looking embarrassed and ashamed of her uncomely nose. But so far Rosa had not been troubled by it, and it never had broken in upon her inexhaustible chatter. Always her shrill voice was heard in the house telling stories, always breathless, as though she had no time to say everything, always excited and animated, in spite of the protests which she drew from her mother, her father, and even her grandfather, exasperated, not so much because she was forever talking as because she prevented them talking themselves. For these good people, kind, loyal, devoted—the very cream of good people—had almost all the virtues, but they lacked one virtue which is capital, and is the charm of life: the virtue of silence.

Christophe was in tolerant mood. His sorrow had softened his intolerant and emphatic temper. His experience of the cruel indifference of the elegant made him more conscious of the worth of these honest folk, graceless and devilish tiresome, who had yet an austere conception of life, and because they lived joylessly, seemed to him to live without weakness. Having decided that they were excellent, and that he ought to like them, like the German that he was, he tried to persuade himself that he did in fact like them. But he did not succeed; he lacked that easy Germanic idealism, which does not wish to see, and does not see, what would be displeasing to its sight, for fear of disturbing the very proper tranquillity of its judgment and the pleasantness of its existence. On the contrary, he never was so conscious of the defects of these people as when he loved them, when he wanted to love them absolutely without reservation; it was a sort of unconscious loyalty, and an inexorable demand for truth, which, in spite of himself, made him more clear–sighted, and more exacting, with what was dearest to him. And it was not long before he began to be irritated by the oddities of the family. They made no attempt to conceal them. Contrary to the usual habit they displayed every intolerable quality they possessed, and all the good in them was hidden. So Christophe told himself, for he judged himself to have been unjust, and tried to surmount his first impressions, and to discover in them the excellent qualities which they so carefully concealed.

He tried to converse with old Justus Euler, who asked nothing better. He had a secret sympathy with him, remembering that his grandfather had liked to praise him. But good old Jean Michel had more of the pleasant faculty of deceiving himself about his friends than Christophe, and Christophe soon saw that. In vain did he try to accept Euler's memories of his grandfather. He could only get from him a discolored caricature of Jean Michel, and scraps of talk that were utterly uninteresting. Euler's stories used invariably to begin with: "As I used to say to your poor grandfather..." He could remember nothing else. He had heard only what he had said himself.

Perhaps Jean Michel used only to listen in the same way. Most friendships are little more than arrangements for mutual satisfaction, so that each party may talk about himself to the other. But at least Jean Michel, however naively he used to give himself up to the delight of talking, had sympathy which he was always ready to lavish on all sides. He was interested in everything; he always regretted that he was no longer fifteen, so as to be able to see the marvelous inventions of the new generations, and to share their thoughts. He had the quality, perhaps the most precious in life, a curiosity always fresh, sever changing with the years, born anew every morning. He had not the talent to turn this gift to account; but how many men of talent might envy him! Most men die at twenty or thirty; thereafter they are only reflections of themselves: for the rest of their lives they are aping themselves, repeating from day to day more and more mechanically and affectedly what they said and did and thought and loved when they were alive.

It was so long since old Euler had been alive, and he had been such a small thing then, that what was left of him now was very poor and rather ridiculous. Outside his former trade and his family life he knew nothing, and wished to know nothing. On every subject he had ideas ready–made, dating from his youth. He pretended to some knowledge of the arts, but he clung to certain hallowed names of men, about whom he was forever reiterating his emphatic formulae: everything else was naught and had never been. When modern interests were mentioned he would not listen, and talked of something else. He declared that he loved music passionately, and he would ask Christophe to play. But as soon as Christophe, who had been caught once or twice, began to play, the old fellow would begin to talk loudly to his daughter, as though the music only increased his interest in everything but music. Christophe would get up exasperated in the middle of his piece, so one would notice it. There were only a few old airs—three or four—some very beautiful, others very ugly, but all equally sacred, which were privileged to gain comparative silence and absolute approval. With the very first notes the old man would go into ecstasies, tears would come to his eyes, not so much for the pleasure he was enjoying as for the pleasure which once he had enjoyed. In the end Christophe had a horror of these airs, though some of them, like the *Adelaide* of Beethoven, were very dear to him; the old man was always humming the first bars of them, and never failed to declare, "There, that is music," contemptuously comparing it with "all the blessed modern music, in which there is no melody." Truth to tell, he knew nothing whatever about it.

His son–in–law was better educated and kept in touch with artistic movements; but that was even worse, for in his judgment there was always a disparaging tinge. He was lacking neither in taste nor intelligence; but he could not bring himself to admire anything modern. He would have disparaged Mozart and Beethoven, if they had been contemporary, just as he would have acknowledged the merits of Wagner and Richard Strauss had they been dead for a century. His discontented temper refused to allow that there might be great men living during his own lifetime; the idea was distasteful to him. He was so embittered by his wasted life that he insisted on pretending that every life was wasted, that it could not be otherwise, and that those who thought the opposite, or pretended to think so, were one of two things: fools or humbugs.

And so he never spoke of any new celebrity except in a tone of bitter irony, and as he was not stupid he never failed to discover at the first glance the weak or ridiculous sides of them. Any new name roused him to distrust; before he knew anything about the man he was inclined to criticise him—because he knew nothing about him. If he was sympathetic towards Christophe it was because he thought that the misanthropic boy found life as evil as he did himself, and that he was not a genius. Nothing so unites the small of soul in their suffering and discontent as the statement of their common impotence. Nothing so much restores the desire for health or life to those who are healthy and made for the joy of life as contact with the stupid pessimism of the mediocre and the sick, who, because they are not happy, deny the happiness of others. Christophe felt this. And yet these gloomy thoughts were familiar to him; but he was surprised to find them on Vogel's lips, where they were unrecognizable; more than that, they were repugnant to him; they offended him.

He was even more in revolt against Amalia's ways. The good creature did no more than practise Christophe's theories of duty. The word was upon her lips at every turn. She worked unceasingly, and wanted everybody to work as she did. Her work was never directed towards making herself and others happier; on the contrary. It almost seemed as though it Was mainly intended to incommode everybody and to make life as disagreeable as possible so as to sanctify it. Nothing would induce her for a moment to relinquish her holy duties in the household, that sacro–sanct institution which in so many women takes the place of all other duties, social and moral. She would have thought herself lost had she not on the same day, at the same time, polished the wooden floors, washed the tiles, cleaned the door–handles, beaten the carpets, moved the chairs, the cupboards, the tables. She was ostentatious about it. It was as though it was a point of honor with her. And after all, is it not in much the same spirit that many women conceive and defend their honor? It is a sort of piece of furniture which they have to keep polished, a well waxed floor, cold, hard—and slippery.

The accomplishment of her task did not make Frau Vogel more amicable. She sacrificed herself to the trivialities of the household, as to a duty imposed by God. And she despised those who did not do as she did, those who rested, and were able to enjoy life a little in the intervals of work. She would go and rouse Louisa in her room when from time to time she sat down in the middle of her work to dream. Louisa would sigh, but she submitted to it with a half–shamed smile. Fortunately, Christophe knew nothing about it; Amalia used to wait until he had gone out before she made these irruptions into their rooms, and so far she had not directly attacked him; he would not have put up with it. When he was with her he was conscious of a latent hostility within himself. What he could least forgive her was the noise she made. He was maddened by it. When he was locked in his room—a little low room looking out on the yard—with the window hermetically sealed, in spite of the want of air, so as not to hear the clatter in the house, he could not escape from it. Involuntarily he was forced to listen attentively for the least sound coming up from below, and when the terrible voice which penetrated all the walls broke out again after a moment of silence he was filled with rage; he would shout, stamp with his foot, and roar insults at her through the wall. In the general uproars no one ever noticed it; they thought he was composing. He would consign Frau Vogel to the depths of hell. He had no respect for her, nor esteem to check him. At such times it seemed to him that he would have preferred the loosest and most stupid of women, if only she did not talk, to cleverness, honesty, all the virtues, when they make too much noise.

His hatred of noise brought him in touch with Leonard. In the midst of the general excitement the boy was the only one to keep calm, and never to raise his voice more at one moment than another. He always expressed himself correctly and deliberately, choosing his words, and never hurrying. Amalia, simmering, never had patience to wait until he had finished; the whole family cried out upon his slowness. He did not worry about it. Nothing could upset his calm, respectful deference. Christophe was the more attracted to him when he learned that Leonard intended to devote his life to the Church, and his curiosity was roused.

With regard to religion, Christophe was in a queer position; he did not know himself how he stood towards it. He had never had time to think seriously about it. He was not well enough educated, and he was too much absorbed by the difficulties of existence to be able to analyze himself and to set his ideas in order. His violence led him from one extreme to the other, from absolute facts to complete negation, without troubling to find out whether in either case he agreed with himself. When he was happy he hardly thought of God at all, but he was quite ready to believe in Him. When he was unhappy he thought of Him, but did not believe; it seemed to him impossible that a God could authorize unhappiness and, injustice. But these difficulties did not greatly exercise him. He was too fundamentally religious to think much about God. He lived in God; he had no need to believe in Him. That is well enough for the weak and worn, for those whose lives are anaemic. They aspire to God, as a plant does to the sun. The dying cling to life. But he who bears in his soul the sun and life, what need has he to seek them outside himself?

Christophe would probably never have bothered about these questions had he lived alone. But the obligations of social life forced him to bring his thoughts to bear on these puerile and useless problems, which occupy a place out of all proportion in the world; it is impossible not to take them into account since at every step they are in the way. As if a healthy, generous creature, overflowing with strength and love, had not a thousand more worthy things to do than to worry as to whether God exists or no!... If it were only a question of believing in God! But it is needful to believe in *a* God, of whatever shape or size and color and race. So far Christophe never gave a thought to the matter. Jesus hardly occupied his thoughts at all. It was not that he did not love him: he loved him when he thought of him: but he never thought of him. Sometimes he reproached himself for it, was angry with himself, could not understand why he did not take more interest in him. And yet he professed, all his family professed; his grandfather was forever reading the Bible; he went regularly to Mass; he served it in a sort of way, for he was an organist; and he set about his task conscientiously and in an exemplary manner. But when he left the church he would have been hard put to it to say what he had been thinking about. He set himself to read the Holy Books in order to fix his ideas, and he found amusement and even pleasure in them, just as in any beautiful strange books, not essentially different from other books, which no one ever thinks of calling sacred. In truth, if Jesus appealed to him, Beethoven did no less. And at his organ in Saint Florian's Church, where he accompanied on Sundays, he was more taken up with his organ than with Mass, and he was more religious when he played Bach than when he played Mendelssohn, Some of the ritual brought him to a fervor of exaltation. But did he then love God, or was it only the music, as an impudent priest said to him one day in jest, without thinking of the unhappiness which his quip might cause in him? Anybody else would not have paid any attention to it, and would not have changed his mode of living—(so many people put up with not knowing what they think!) But Christophe was cursed with an awkward need for sincerity, which filled him with scruples at every turn. And when scruples came to him they possessed him forever. He tortured himself; he thought that he had acted with duplicity. Did he believe or did he not?... He had no means, material or intellectual—(knowledge and leisure are necessary)—of solving the problem by himself. And yet it had to be solved, or he was either indifferent or a hypocrite. Now, he was incapable of being either one or the other.

He tried timidly to sound those about him. They all seemed to be sure of themselves. Christophe burned to know their reasons. He could not discover them. Hardly did he receive a definite answer; they always talked obliquely. Some thought him arrogant, and said that there is no arguing these things, that thousands of men cleverer and better than himself had believed without argument, and that he needed only to do as they had done. There were some who were a little hurt, as though it were a personal affront to ask them such a question, and yet they were of all perhaps the least certain of their facts. Others shrugged their shoulders and said with a smile: "Bah! it can't do any harm." And their smile said: "And it is so useful!..." Christophe despised them with all his heart.

He had tried to lay his uncertainties before a priest, but he was discouraged by the experiment. He could not discuss the matter seriously with him. Though his interlocution was quite pleasant, he made Christophe feel, quite politely, that there was no real equality between them; he seemed to assume in advance that his superiority was beyond dispute, and that the discussion could not exceed the limits which he laid down for it, without a kind of impropriety; it was just a fencing bout, and was quite inoffensive. When Christophe wished to exceed the limits and to ask questions which the worthy man was pleased not to answer, he stepped back with a patronizing smile, and a few Latin quotations, and a fatherly objurgation to pray, pray that God would enlighten him.

Christophe issued from the interview humiliated and wounded by his love of polite superiority. Wrong or right, he would never again for anything in the world have recourse to a priest. He admitted that these men were his superiors in intelligence or by reason of their sacred calling; but in argument there is neither superiority, nor inferiority, nor title, nor age, nor name; nothing is of worth but truth, before which all men are equal.

So he was glad to find a boy of his own age who believed. He asked no more than belief, and he hoped that Leonard would give him good reason for believing. He made advances to him. Leonard replied with his usual gentleness, but without eagerness; he was never eager about anything. As they could not carry on a long conversation in the house without being interrupted every moment by Amalia or the old man, Christophe proposed that they should go for a walk one evening after dinner. Leonard was too polite to refuse, although he would gladly have got out of it, for his indolent nature disliked walking, talking, and anything that cost him an effort.

Christophe had some difficulty in opening up the conversation. After two or three awkward sentences about trivialities he plunged with a brusqueness that was almost brutal. He asked Leonard if he were really going to be a priest, and if he liked the idea. Leonard was nonplussed, and looked at him uneasily, but when he saw that Christophe was not hostilely disposed he was reassured.

"Yes," he replied. "How could it be otherwise?"

"Ah!" said Christophe. "You are very happy." Leonard was conscious of a shade of envy in Christophe's voice and was agreeably flattered by it. He altered his manner, became expansive, his face brightened.

"Yes," he said, "I am happy." He beamed.

"What do you do to be so?" asked Christophe.

Before replying Leonard proposed that they should sit down, on a quiet seat in the cloisters of St. Martin's. From there they could see a corner of the little square, planted with acacias, and beyond it the town, the country, bathed in the evening mists. The Rhine flowed at the foot of the hill. An old deserted cemetery, with graves lost under the rich grass, lay in slumber beside them behind the closed gates.

Leonard began to talk. He said, with his eyes shining with contentment, how happy he was to escape from life, to have found a refuge, where a man is, and forever will be, in shelter. Christophe, still sore from his wounds, felt passionately the desire for rest and forgetfulness; but it was mingled with regret. He asked with a sigh:

"And yet, does it cost you nothing to renounce life altogether?"

"Oh!" said Leonard quietly. "What is there to regret? Isn't life sad and ugly?"

"There are lovely things too," said Christophe, looking at the beautiful evening.

"There are some beautiful things, but very few."

"The few that there are are yet many to me."

"Oh, well! it is simply a matter of common sense. On the one hand a little good and much evil; on the other neither good nor evil on earth, and after, infinite happiness—how can one hesitate?"

Christophe was not very pleased with this sort of arithmetic. So economic a life seemed to him very poor. But he tried to persuade himself that it was wisdom.

"So," he asked a little ironically, "there is no risk of your being seduced by an hour's pleasure?"

"How foolish! When you know that it is only an hour, and that after it there is all eternity!"

"You are quite certain of eternity?"

"Of course."

Christophe questioned him. He was thrilled with hope and desire. Perhaps Leonard would at last give him impregnable reasons for believing. With what a passion he would himself renounce all the world to follow him to God.

At first Leonard, proud of his role of apostle, and convinced that Christophe's doubts were only a matter of form, and that they would of course give way before his first arguments, relied upon the Holy Books, the authority of the Gospel, the miracles, and traditions. But he began to grow gloomy when, after Christophe had listened for a few minutes, he stopped him and said that he was answering questions with questions, and that he had not asked him to tell exactly what it was that he was doubting, but to give some means of resolving his doubts. Leonard then had to realize that Christophe was much more ill than he seemed, and that he would only allow himself to be convinced by the light of reason. But he still thought that Christophe was playing the free thinker—(it never occurred to him that he might be so sincerely).—He was not discouraged, and, strong in his recently acquired knowledge, he turned back to his school learning: he unfolded higgledy, piggledy, with more authority than order, his metaphysical proofs of the existence of God and the immortality of the soul. Christophe, with his mind at stretch, and his brow knit in the effort, labored in silence, and made him say it all over again; tried hard to gather the meaning, and to take it to himself, and to follow the reasoning. Then suddenly he burst out, vowed that Leonard was laughing at him, that it was all tricks, jests of the fine talkers who forged words and then amused themselves with pretending that these words were things. Leonard was nettled, and guaranteed the good faith of his authors. Christophe shrugged his shoulders, and said with an oath that they were only humbugs, infernal writers; and he demanded fresh proof.

Leonard perceived to his horror that Christophe was incurably attainted, and took no more interest in him. He remembered that he had been told not to waste his time in arguing with skeptics,—at least when they stubbornly refuse to believe. There was the risk of being shaken himself, without profiting the other. It was better to leave the unfortunate fellow to the will of God, who, if He so designs, would see to it that the skeptic was enlightened: or if not, who would dare to go against the will of God? Leonard did not insist then on carrying on the discussion. He only said gently that for the time being there was nothing to be done, that no reasoning could show the way to a man who was determined not to see it, and that Jean–Christophe must pray and appeal to Grace: nothing is possible without that: he must desire grace and the will to believe.

"The will," thought Christophe bitterly. "So then, God will exist because I will Him to exist? So then, death will not exist, because it pleases me to deny it!... Alas! How easy life is to those who have no need to see the truth, to those who can see what they wish to see, and are forever forging pleasant dreams in which softly to sleep!" In such a bed,

Christophe knew well that be would never sleep....

Leonard went on talking. He had fallen back on his favorite subject, the sweets of the contemplative life, and once on this neutral ground, he was inexhaustible. In his monotonous voice, that shook with the pleasure in him, he told of the joys of the life in God, outside, above the world, far from noise, of which he spoke in a sudden tone of hatred (he detested it almost as much as Christophe), far from violence, far from frivolity, far from the little miseries that one has to suffer every day, in the warm, secure nest of faith, from which you can contemplate in peace the wretchedness of a strange and distant world. And as Christophe listened, he perceived the egoism of that faith. Leonard saw that. He hurriedly explained: the contemplative life was not a lazy life. On the contrary, a man is more active in prayer than in action. What would the world be without prayer? You expiate the sins of others, you bear the burden of their misdeeds, you offer up your talents, you intercede between the world and God.

Christophe listened in silence with increasing hostility. He was conscious of the hypocrisy of such renunciation in Leonard. He was not unjust enough to assume hypocrisy in all those who believe. He knew well that with a few, such abdication of life comes from the impossibility of living, from a bitter despair, an appeal to death,—that with still fewer, it is an ecstasy of passion.... (How long does it last?).... But with the majority of men is it not too often the cold reasoning of souls more busied with their own ease and peace than with the happiness of others, or with truth? And if sincere men are conscious of it, how much they must suffer by such profanation of their ideal!...

Leonard was quite happy, and now set forth the beauty and harmony of the world, seen from the loftiness of the divine roost: below all was dark, unjust, sorrowful; seen from on high, it all became clear, luminous, ordered: the world was like the works of a clock, perfectly ordered....

Now Christophe only listened absently. He was asking himself: "Does he believe, or does he believe that he believes?" And yet his own faith, his own passionate desire for faith was not shaken. Not the mediocrity of soul, and the poverty of argument of a fool like Leonard could touch that....

Night came down over the town. The seat on which they were sitting was in darkness: the stars shone out, a white mist came up from the river, the crickets chirped under the trees in the cemetery. The bells began to ring: first the highest of them, alone, like a plaintive bird, challenging the sky: then the second, a third lower, joined in its plaint: at last came the, deepest, on the fifth, and seemed to answer them. The three voices were merged in each other. At the bottom of the towers there was a buzzing, as of a gigantic hive of bees. The air and the boy's heart quivered. Christophe held his breath, and thought how poor was the music of musicians compared with such an ocean of music, with all the sounds of thousands of creatures: the former, the free world of sounds, compared with the world tamed, catalogued, coldly labeled by human intelligence. He sank and sank into that sonorous and immense world without continents or bounds....

And when the great murmuring had died away, when the air had ceased at last to quiver, Christophe woke up. He looked about him startled.... He knew nothing. Around him and in him everything was changed. There was no God....

As with faith, so the loss of faith is often equally a flood of grace, a sudden light. Reason counts for nothing: the smallest thing is enough—a word, silence, the sound of bells. A man walks, dreams, expects nothing. Suddenly the world crumbles away. All about him is in ruins. He is alone. He no longer believes.

Christophe was terrified, and could not understand how it had come about. It was like the flooding of a river in the spring....

Leonard's voice was still sounding, more monotonous than the voice of a cricket. Christophe did not hear it: he heard nothing. Night was fully come. Leonard stopped. Surprised to find Christophe motionless, uneasy because of the lateness of the hour, he suggested that they should go home. Christophe did not reply. Leonard took his arm. Christophe trembled, and looked at Leonard with wild eyes.

"Christophe, we must go home," said Leonard.

"Go to hell!" cried Christophe furiously.

"Oh! Christophe! What have I done?" asked Leonard tremulously. He was dumfounded.

Christophe came to himself.

"Yes. You are right," he said more gently. "I do not know what I'm saying. Go to God! Go to God!"

He was alone. He was in bitter distress.

"Ah! my God! my God!" he cried, wringing his hands, passionately raising his face to the dark sky. "Why do I no longer believe? Why can I believe no more? What has happened to me?..."

The disproportion between the wreck of his faith and the conversation that he had just had with Leonard was too great: it was obvious that the conversation had no more brought it about than that the boisterousness of Amalia's gabble and the pettiness of the people with whom he lived were not the cause of the upheaval which for some days had been taking place in his moral resolutions. These were only pretexts. The uneasiness had not come from without. It was within himself. He felt stirring in his heart monstrous and unknown things, and he dared not rely on his thoughts to face the evil. The evil? Was it evil? A languor, an intoxication, a voluptuous agony filled all his being. He was no longer master of himself. In vain he sought to fortify himself with his former stoicism. His whole being crashed down. He had a sudden consciousness of the vast world, burning, wild, a world immeasurable.... How it swallows up God!

Only for a moment. But the whole balance of his old life was in that moment destroyed.

* * * * *

There was only one person in the family to whom Christophe paid no attention: this was little Rosa. She was not beautiful: and Christophe, who was far from beautiful himself, was very exacting of beauty in others. He had that calm, cruelty of youth, for which a woman does not exist if she be ugly,—unless she has passed the age for inspiring tenderness, and there is then no need to feel for her anything but grave, peaceful, and quasi–religious sentiments. Rosa also was not distinguished by any especial gift, although she was not without intelligence: and she was cursed with a chattering tongue which drove Christophe from her. And he had never taken the trouble to know her, thinking that there was in her nothing to know; and the most he ever did was to glance at her.

But she was of better stuff than most girls: she was certainly better than Minna, whom he had so loved. She was a good girl, no coquette, not at all vain, and until Christophe came it had never occurred to her that she was plain, or if it had, it had not worried her: for none of her family bothered about it. Whenever her grandfather or her mother told her so out of a desire to grumble, she only laughed: she did not believe it, or she attached no importance to it; nor did they. So many others, just as plain, and more, had found some one to love them! The Germans are very mildly indulgent to physical imperfections: they cannot see them: they are even able to embellish them, by virtue of an easy imagination which finds unexpected qualities in the face of their desire to make them like the most illustrious examples of human beauty. Old Euler would not have needed much urging to make him declare that his granddaughter had the nose of the Juno Ludovisi. Happily he was too grumpy to pay compliments: and Rosa, unconcerned about the shape of her nose, had no vanity except in the accomplishment, with all the ritual, of the famous household duties. She had accepted as Gospel all that she had been taught. She hardly ever went out, and she had very little standard of comparison; she admired her family naively, and believed what they said. She was of an expansive and confiding nature, easily satisfied, and tried to fall in with the mournfulness of her home, and docilely used to repeat the pessimistic ideas which she heard. She was a creature of devotion—always thinking of others, trying to please, sharing anxieties, guessing at what others wanted; she had a great need of loving without demanding anything in return. Naturally her family took advantage of her, although they were kind and loved her: but there is always a temptation to take advantage of the love of those who are absolutely delivered into your hands. Her family were so sure of her attentions that they were not at all grateful for them: whatever she did, they expected more. And then, she was clumsy; she was awkward and hasty; her movements were jerky and boyish; she had outbursts of tenderness which used to end in disaster: a broken glass, a jug upset, a door slammed to: things which let loose upon her the wrath of everybody in the house. She was always being snubbed and would go and weep in a corner. Her tears did not last long. She would soon smile again, and begin to chatter without a suspicion of rancor against anybody.

Christophe's advent was an important event in her life. She had often heard of him. Christophe had some place in the gossip of the town: he was a sort of little local celebrity: his name used often to recur in the family conversation, especially when old Jean Michel was alive, who, proud of his grandson, used to sing his praises to all of his acquaintance. Rosa had seen the young musician once or twice at concerts. When she heard that he was coming to live with them, she clapped her hands. She was sternly rebuked for her breach of manners and became confused. She saw no harm in it. In a life so monotonous as hers, a new lodger was a great distraction. She spent the last few days before his arrival in a fever of expectancy. She was fearful lest he should not like the house, and she tried hard to make every room as attractive as possible. On the morning of his arrival, she even put a little bunch of flowers on the mantelpiece to bid him welcome. As to herself, she took no care at all to look her best; and one glance was enough to make Christophe decide that she was plain, and slovenly dressed. She did not think the same of him, though she had good reason to do so: for Christophe, busy, exhausted, ill–kempt, was even more ugly than usual. But Rosa, who was incapable of thinking the least ill of anybody, Rosa, who thought her grandfather, her father, and her mother, all perfectly beautiful, saw Christophe exactly as she had expected to see him, and admired him with all her heart. She was frightened at sitting next to him at table; and unfortunately her shyness took the shape of a flood of words, which at once alienated Christophe's sympathies. She did not see this, and that first evening remained a shining memory in her life. When she was alone in her room, after, they had all gone upstairs, she heard the tread of the new lodgers as they walked over her head; and the sound of it ran joyously through her; the house seemed to her to taken new life.

The next morning for the first time in her life she looked at herself in the mirror carefully and: uneasily, and without exactly knowing the extent of her misfortune she began to be conscious of it. She tried to decide about her features, one by one; but she could not. She was filled with sadness and apprehension. She sighed deeply, and thought of introducing certain changes in her toilet, but she only made herself look still more plain. She conceived the unlucky idea of overwhelming Christophe with her kindness. In her naive desire to be always seeing her new friends, and doing them service, she was forever going up and down the stairs, bringing them some utterly useless thing, insisting on helping them, and always laughing and talking and shouting. Her zeal and her stream of talk could only be interrupted by her mother's impatient voice calling her. Christophe looked grim; but for his good resolutions he must have lost his temper quite twenty times. He restrained himself for two days; on the third, he locked his door. Rosa knocked, called, understood, went downstairs in dismay, and did not try again. When he saw her he explained that he was very busy and could not be disturbed. She humbly begged his pardon. She could not deceive herself as to the failure of her innocent advances: they had accomplished the opposite of her intention: they had alienated Christophe. He no longer took the trouble to conceal his ill–humor; he did not listen when she talked, and did not disguise his impatience. She felt that her chatter irritated him, and by force of will she succeeded in keeping silent for a part of the evening: but the thing was stronger than herself: suddenly she would break out again and her words would tumble over each other more tumultuously than ever. Christophe would leave her in the middle of a sentence. She was not angry with him. She was angry with herself. She thought herself stupid, tiresome, ridiculous: all her faults assumed enormous proportions and she tried to wrestle with them: but she was discouraged by the check upon her first attempts, and said to herself that she could not do it, that she was not strong enough. But she would try again.

But there were other faults against which she was powerless: what could she do against her plainness? There was no doubt about it. The certainty of her misfortune had suddenly been revealed to her one day when she was looking at herself in the mirror; it came like a thunderclap. Of course she exaggerated the evil, and saw her nose as ten times larger than it was; it seemed to her to fill all her face; she dared not show herself; she wished to die. But there is in youth such a power of hope that these fits of discouragement never lasted long: she would end by pretending that she had been mistaken; she would try to believe it, and for a moment or two would actually succeed in thinking her nose quite ordinary and almost shapely. Her instinct made her attempt, though very clumsily, certain childish tricks, a way of doing her hair so as not so much to show her forehead and so accentuate the disproportion of her face. And yet, there was no coquetry in her; no thought of love had crossed her mind, or she was unconscious of it. She asked little: nothing but a little friendship: but Christophe did not show any inclination to give her that little. It seemed to Rosa that she would have been perfectly happy had he only condescended to say good–day when they met. A friendly good–evening with a little kindness. But Christophe usually looked so hard and so cold! It chilled her. He never said anything disagreeable to her, but she would rather have had cruel reproaches than such cruel silence.

One evening Christophe was playing his piano. He had taken up his quarters in a little attic at the top of the house so as not to be so much disturbed by the noise. Downstairs Rosa was listening to him, deeply moved. She loved music though her taste was bad and unformed. While her mother was there, she stayed in a corner of the room and bent over her sewing, apparently absorbed in her work; but her heart was with the sounds coming from upstairs, and she wished to miss nothing. As soon as Amalia went out for a walk in the neighborhood, Rosa leaped to her feet, threw down her sewing, and went upstairs with her heart beating until she came to the attic door. She held her breath and laid her ear against the door. She stayed like that until Amalia returned. She went on tiptoe, taking care to make no noise, but as she was not very sure–footed, and was always in a hurry, she was always tripping upon the stairs; and once while she was listening, leaning forward with her cheek glued to the keyhole, she lost her balance, and banged her forehead against the door. She was so alarmed that she lost her breath. The piano stopped dead: she could not escape. She was getting up when the door opened. Christophe saw her, glared at her furiously, and then without a word, brushed her aside, walked angrily downstairs, and went out. He did not return until dinner time, paid no heed to the despairing looks with which she asked his pardon, ignored her existence, and for several weeks he never played at all. Rosa secretly shed many tears; no one noticed it, no one paid any attention to her. Ardently she prayed to God ... for what? She did not know. She had to confide her grief in some one. She was sure that Christophe detested her.

And, in spite of all, she hoped. It was enough for her if Christophe seemed to show any sign of interest in her, if he appeared to listen to what she said, if he pressed her hand with a little more friendliness than usual....

A few imprudent words from her relations set her imagination off upon a false road.

＊ ＊ ＊ ＊ ＊

The whole family was filled with sympathy for Christophe. The big boy of sixteen, serious and solitary, who had such lofty ideas of his duty, inspired a sort of respect in them all. His fits of ill–temper, his obstinate silences, his gloomy air, his brusque manner, were not surprising in such a house as that. Frau Vogel, herself, who regarded every artist as a loafer, dared not reproach him aggressively, as she would have liked to do, with the hours that he spent in star–gazing in the evening, leaning, motionless, out of the attic window overlooking the yard, until night fell; for she knew that during the rest of the day he was hard at work with his lessons; and she humored him—like the rest—for an ulterior motive which no one expressed though everybody knew it.

Rosa had seen her parents exchanging looks and mysterious whisperings when she was talking to Christophe. At first she took no notice of it. Then she was puzzled and roused by it; she longed to know what they were saying, but dared not ask.

One evening when she had climbed on to a garden seat to untie the clothes–line hung between two trees, she leaned on Christophe's shoulder to jump down. Just at that moment her eyes met her grandfather's and her father's; they were sitting smoking their pipes, and leaning against the wall of the house. The two men winked at each other, and Justus Euler said to Vogel:

"They will make a fine couple."

Vogel nudged him, seeing that the girl was listening, and he covered his remark very cleverly—(or so he thought)—with a loud "Hm! hm!" that could have been heard twenty yards away. Christophe, whose back was turned, saw nothing, but Rosa was so bowled over by it that she forgot that she was jumping down, and sprained her foot. She would have fallen had not Christophe caught her, muttering curses on her clumsiness. She had hurt herself badly, but she did not show it; she hardly thought of it; she thought only of what she had just heard. She walked to her room; every step was agony to her; she stiffened herself against it so as not to let it be seen. A delicious, vague uneasiness surged through her. She fell into a chair at the foot of her bed and hid her face in the coverlet. Her cheeks were burning; there were tears in her eyes, and she laughed. She was ashamed, she wished to sink into the depths of the earth, she could not fix her ideas; her blood beat in her temples, there were sharp pains in her ankle; she was in a feverish stupor. Vaguely she heard sounds outside, children crying and playing in the street, and her grandfather's words were ringing in her ears; she was thrilled, she laughed softly, she blushed, with her face buried in the eiderdown: she prayed, gave thanks, desired, feared—she loved.

Her mother called her. She tried to get up. At the first step she felt a pain so unbearable that she almost fainted; her head swam. She thought she was going to die, she wished to die, and at the same time she wished to live with all the forces of her being, to live for the promised happiness. Her mother came at last, and the whole household was soon excited. She was scolded as usual, her ankle was dressed, she was put to bed, and sank into the sweet bewilderment of her physical pain and her inward joy. The night was sweet.... The smallest memory of that dear evening was hallowed for her. She did not think of Christophe, she knew not what she thought. She was happy.

The next day, Christophe, who thought himself in some measure responsible for the accident, came to make inquiries, and for the first time he made some show of affection for her. She was filled with gratitude, and blessed her sprained ankle. She would gladly have suffered all her life, if, all her life, she might have such joy.—She had to lie down for several days and never move; she spent them in turning over and over her grandfather's words, and considering them. Had he said:

"They will...."

Or:

"They would ...?"

But it was possible that he had never said anything of this kind?—Yes. He had said it; she was certain of it.... What! Did they not see that she was ugly, and that Christophe could not bear her?... But it was so good to hope! She came to believe that perhaps she had been wrong, that she was not as ugly as she thought; she would sit up on her sofa to try and see herself in the mirror on the wall opposite, above the mantelpiece; she did not know what to think. After all, her father and her grandfather were better judges than herself; people cannot tell about themselves.... Oh! Heaven, if it were possible!... If it could be ... if, she never dared think it, if ... if she were pretty!... Perhaps, also, she had exaggerated Christophe's antipathy. No doubt he was indifferent, and after the interest he had shown in her the day after the accident did not bother about her any more; he forgot to inquire; but Rosa made excuses for him, he was so busy! How should he think of her? An artist cannot be judged like other men....

And yet, resigned though she was, she could not help expecting with beating heart a word of sympathy from him when he came near her. A word only, a look ... her imagination did the rest. In the beginning love needs so little food! It is enough to see, to touch as you pass; such a power of dreams flows from the soul in such moments, that almost of itself it can create its love: a trifle can plunge it into ecstasy that later, when it is more satisfied, and in proportion more exacting, it will hardly find again when at last it does possess the object of its desire.—Rosa lived absolutely, though no one knew it, in a romance of her own fashioning, pieced together by herself: Christophe loved her secretly, and was too shy to confess his love, or there was some stupid reason, fantastic or romantic, delightful to the imagination of the sentimental little ninny. She fashioned endless stories, and all perfectly absurd; she knew it herself, but tried not to know it; she lied to herself voluptuously for days and days as she bent over her sewing. It made her forget to talk: her flood of words was turned inward, like a river which suddenly disappears underground. But then the river took its revenge. What a debauch of speeches, of unuttered conversations which no one heard but herself! Sometimes her lips would move as they do with people who have to spell out the syllables to themselves as they read so as to understand them.

When her dreams left her she was happy and sad. She knew that things were not as she had just told herself: but she was left with a reflected happiness, and had greater confidence for her life. She did not despair of winning Christophe.

She did not admit it to herself, but she set about doing it. With the sureness of instinct that great affection brings, the awkward, ignorant girl contrived immediately to find the road by which she might reach her beloved's heart. She did not turn directly to him. But as soon as she was better and could once more walk about the house she approached Louisa. The smallest excuse served. She found a thousand little services to render her. When she went out she never failed to undertake various errands: she spared her going to the market, arguments with tradespeople, she would fetch water for her from the pump in the yard; she cleaned the windows and polished the floors in spite of Louisa's protestations, who was confused when she did not do her work alone; but she was so weary that she had not the strength to oppose anybody who came to help her. Christophe was out all day. Louisa felt that she was deserted, and the companionship of the affectionate, chattering girl was pleasant to her. Rosa took up her quarters in her room. She brought her sewing, and talked all the time. By clumsy devices she tried to bring conversation round to Christophe. Just to hear of him, even to hear his name, made her happy; her hands would tremble; she would sit with downcast eyes. Louisa was delighted to talk of her beloved Christophe, and would tell little tales of his childhood, trivial and just a little ridiculous; but there was no fear of Rosa thinking them so: she took a great joy, and there was a dear emotion for her in imagining Christophe as a child, and doing all the tricks and having all the darling ways of children: in her the motherly tenderness which lies in the hearts of all women was mingled deliciously with that other tenderness: she would laugh heartily and tears would come to her eyes. Louisa was touched by the interest that Rosa took in her. She guessed dimly what was in the girl's heart, but she never let it appear that she did so; but she was glad of it; for of all in the house she only knew the worth of the girl's heart. Sometimes she would stop talking to look at her. Rosa, surprised by her silence, would raise her eyes from her work. Louisa would smile at her. Rosa would throw herself into her arms, suddenly, passionately, and would hide her face in Louisa's bosom. Then they would go on working and talking, as if nothing had happened.

In the evening when Christophe came home, Louisa, grateful for Rosa's attentions, and in pursuance of the little plan she had made, always praised the girl to the skies. Christophe was touched by Rosa's kindness. He saw how much good she was doing his mother, in whose face there was more serenity: and he would thank her effusively. Rosa would murmur, and escape to conceal her embarrassment: so she appeared a thousand times more intelligent and sympathetic to Christophe than if she had spoken. He looked at her less with a prejudiced eye, and did not conceal his surprise at finding unsuspected qualities in her. Rosa saw that; she marked the progress that she made in his sympathy and thought that his sympathy would lead to love. She gave herself up more than ever to her dreams. She came near to believing with the beautiful presumption of youth that what you desire with all your being is always accomplished in the end. Besides, how was her desire unreasonable? Should not Christophe have been more sensible than any other of her goodness and her affectionate need of self–devotion?

But Christophe gave no thought to her. He esteemed her; but she filled no room in his thoughts. He was busied with far other things at the moment. Christophe was no longer Christophe. He did not know himself. He was in a mighty travail that was like to sweep everything away, a complete upheaval.

     * * * * *

Christophe was conscious of extreme weariness and great uneasiness. He was for no reason worn out; his head was heavy, his eyes, his ears, all his senses were dumb and throbbing. He could not give his attention to anything. His mind leaped from one subject to another, and was in a fever that sucked him dry. The perpetual fluttering of images in his mind made him giddy. At first he attributed it to fatigue and the enervation of the first days of spring. But spring passed and his sickness only grew worse.

It was what the poets who only touch lightly on things call the unease of adolescence, the trouble of the cherubim, the waking of the desire of love in the young body and soul. As if the fearful crisis of all a man's being, breaking up, dying, and coming to full rebirth, as if the cataclysm in which everything, faith, thought, action, all life, seems like to be blotted out, and then to be new–forged in the convulsions of sorrow and joy, can be reduced to terms of a child's folly!

All his body and soul were in a ferment. He watched them, having no strength to struggle, with a mixture of curiosity and disgust. He did not understand what was happening in himself. His whole being was disintegrated. He spent days together in absolute torpor. Work was torture to him. At night he slept heavily and in snatches, dreaming monstrously, with gusts of desire; the soul of a beast was racing madly in him. Burning, bathed in sweat, he watched himself in horror; he tried to break free of the crazy and unclean thoughts that possessed him, and he wondered if he were going mad.

The day gave him no shelter from his brutish thoughts. In the depths of his soul he felt that he was slipping down and down; there was no stay to clutch at; no barrier to keep back chaos. All his defenses, all his citadels, with the quadruple rampart that hemmed him in so proudly—his God, his art, his pride, his moral faith, all was crumbling away, falling piece by piece from him. He saw himself naked, bound, lying unable to move, like a corpse on which vermin swarm. He had spasms of revolt: where was his will, of which he was so proud? He called to it in vain: it was like the efforts that one makes in sleep, knowing that one is dreaming, and trying to awake. Then one succeeds only in falling from one dream to another like a lump of lead, and in being more and more choked by the suffocation of the soul in bondage. At last he found that it was less painful not to struggle. He decided not to do so, with, fatalistic apathy and despair.

The even tenor of his life seemed to be broken up. Now he slipped down a subterranean crevasse and was like to disappear; now he bounded up again with a violent jerk. The chain of his days was snapped. In the midst of the even plain of the hours great gaping holes would open to engulf his soul. Christophe looked on at the spectacle as though it did not concern him. Everything, everybody,—and himself—were strange to him. He went about his business, did his work, automatically: it seemed to him that the machinery of his life might stop at any moment: the wheels were out of gear. At dinner with his mother and the others, in the orchestra with the musicians and the audience, suddenly there would be a void and emptiness in his brain; he would look stupidly at the grinning faces about him; and he could not understand. He would ask himself:

"What is there between these creatures and ...?"

He dared not even say:

"... and me."

For he knew not whether he existed. He would speak and his voice would seem to issue from another body. He would move, and he saw his movements from afar, from above—from the top of a tower. He would pass his hand over his face, and his eyes would wander. He was often near doing crazy things.

It was especially when he was most in public that he had to keep guard on himself. For example, on the evenings when he went to the Palace or was playing in public. Then he would suddenly be seized by a terrific desire to make a face, or say something outrageous, to pull the Grand Duke's nose, or to take a running kick at one of the ladies. One whole evening while he was conducting the orchestra, he struggled against an insensate desire to undress himself in public; and he was haunted by the idea from the moment when he tried to check it; he had to exert all his strength not to give way to it. When he issued from the brute struggle he was dripping with sweat and his mind was blank. He was really mad. It was enough for him to think that he must not do a thing for it to fasten on him with the maddening tenacity of a fixed idea.

So his life was spent in a series of unbridled outbreaks and of endless falls into emptiness. A furious wind in the desert. Whence came this wind? From what abyss came these desires that wrenched his body and mind? He was like a bow stretched to breaking point by a strong hand,—to what end unknown?—which then springs back like a piece of dead wood. Of what force was he the prey? He dared not probe for it. He felt that he was beaten, humiliated, and he would not face his defeat. He was weary and broken in spirit. He understood now the people whom formerly he had despised: those who will not seek awkward truth. In the empty hours, when he remembered that time was passing, his work neglected, the future lost, he was frozen with terror. But there was no reaction: and his cowardice found excuses in desperate affirmation of the void in which he lived: he took a bitter delight in abandoning himself to it like a wreck on the waters. What was the good of fighting? There was nothing beautiful, nor good; neither God, nor life, nor being of any sort. In the street as he walked, suddenly the earth would sink away from him: there was neither ground, nor air, nor light, nor himself: there was nothing. He would fall, his head would drag him down, face forwards: he could hardly hold himself up; he was on the point of collapse. He thought he was going to die, suddenly, struck down. He thought he was dead....

Christophe was growing a new skin. Christophe was growing a new soul. And seeing the worn out and rotten soul of his childhood falling away he never dreamed that he was taking on a new one, young and stronger. As through life we change our bodies, so also do we change our souls: and the metamorphosis does not always take place slowly over many days; there are times of crisis when the whole is suddenly renewed. The adult changes his soul. The old soul that is cast off dies. In those hours of anguish we think that all is at an end. And the whole thing begins again. A life dies. Another life has already come into being.

One night he was alone in his room, with his elbow on his desk under the light of a candle. His back was turned to the window. He was not working. He had not been able to work for weeks. Everything was twisting and turning in his head. He had brought everything under scrutiny at once: religion, morals, art, the whole of life. And in the general dissolution of his thoughts was no method, no order: he had plunged into the reading of books taken haphazard from his grandfather's heterogeneous library or from Vogel's collection of books: books of theology, science, philosophy, an odd lot, of which he understood nothing, having everything to learn: he could not finish any of them, and in the middle of them went off on divagations, endless whimsies, which left him weary, empty, and in mortal sorrow.

So, that evening, he was sunk in an exhausted torpor. The whole house was asleep. His window was open. Not a breath came up from the yard. Thick clouds filled the sky. Christophe mechanically watched the candle burn away at the bottom of the candlestick. He could not go to bed. He had no thought of anything. He felt the void growing, growing from moment to moment. He tried not to see the abyss that drew him to its brink: and in spite of himself he leaned over and his eyes gazed into the depths of the night. In the void, chaos was stirring, and faint sounds came from the darkness. Agony filled him: a shiver ran down his spine: his skin tingled: he clutched the table so as not to fall. Convulsively he awaited nameless things, a miracle, a God....

Suddenly, like an opened sluice, in the yard behind him, a deluge of water, a heavy rain, large drops, down pouring, fell. The still air quivered. The dry, hard soil rang out like a bell. And the vast scent of the earth, burning, warm as that of an animal, the smell of the flowers, fruit, and amorous flesh rose in a spasm of fury and pleasure. Christophe, under illusion, at fullest stretch, shook. He trembled.... The veil was rent. He was blinded. By a flash of lightning, he saw, in the depths of the night, he saw—he was God. God was in himself; He burst the ceiling of the room, the walls of the house; He cracked the very bounds of existence. He filled the sky, the universe, space. The world coursed through

Him, like a cataract. In the horror and ecstasy of that cataclysm, Christophe fell too, swept along by the whirlwind which brushed away and crushed like straws the laws of nature. He was breathless: he was drunk with the swift hurtling down into God ... God–abyss! God–gulf! Fire of Being! Hurricane of life! Madness of living,—aimless, uncontrolled, beyond reason,—for the fury of living!

* * * * *

When the crisis was over, he fell into a deep sleep and slept as he had not done for long enough. Next day when he awoke his head swam: he was as broken as though he had been drunk. But in his inmost heart he had still a beam of that somber and great light that had struck him down the night before. He tried to relight it. In vain. The more he pursued it, the more it eluded him. From that time on, all his energy was directed towards recalling the vision of a moment. The endeavor was futile. Ecstasy does not answer the bidding of the will.

But that mystic exaltation was not the only experience that he had of it: it recurred several times, but never with the intensity of the first. It came always at moments when Christophe was least expecting it, for a second only, a time so short, so sudden,—no longer than a wink of an eye or a raising of a hand—that the vision was gone before he could discover that it was: and then he would wonder whether he had not dreamed it. After that fiery bolt that had set the night aflame, it was a gleaming dust, shedding fleeting sparks, which the eye could hardly see as they sped by. But they reappeared more and more often: and in the end they surrounded Christophe with a halo of perpetual misty dreams, in which his spirit melted. Everything that distracted him in his state of semi–hallucination was an irritation to him. It was impossible to work; he gave up thinking about it. Society was odious to him; and more than any, that of his intimates, even that of his mother, because they arrogated to themselves more rights over his soul.

He left the house: he took to spending his days abroad, and never returned until nightfall. He sought the solitude of the fields, and delivered himself up to it, drank his fill of it, like a maniac who wishes not to be disturbed by anything in the obsession of his fixed ideas.—But in the great sweet air, in contact with the earth, his obsession relaxed, his ideas ceased to appear like specters. His exaltation was no less: rather it was heightened, but it was no longer a dangerous delirium of the mind but a healthy intoxication of his whole being: body; and soul crazy in their strength.

He rediscovered the world, as though he had never seen it. It was a new childhood. It was as though a magic word had been uttered. An "Open Sesame!"—Nature flamed with gladness. The sun boiled. The liquid sky ran like a clear river. The earth steamed and cried aloud in delight. The plants, the trees, the insects, all the innumerable creatures were like dazzling tongues of flame in the fire of life writhing upwards. Everything sang aloud in joy.

And that joy was his own. That strength was his own. He was no longer cut off from the rest of the world. Till then, even in the happy days of childhood, when he saw nature with ardent and delightful curiosity, all creatures had seemed to him to be little worlds shut up, terrifying and grotesque, unrelated to himself, and incomprehensible. He was not even sure that they had feeling and life. They were strange machines. And sometimes Christophe had even, with the unconscious cruelty of a child, dismembered wretched insects without dreaming that they might suffer—for the pleasure of watching their queer contortions. His uncle Gottfried, usually so calm, had one day indignantly to snatch from his hands an unhappy fly that he was torturing. The boy had tried to laugh at first: then he had burst into tears, moved by his uncle's emotion: he began to understand that his victim did really exist, as well as himself, and that he had committed a crime. But if thereafter nothing would have induced him to do harm to the beasts, he never felt any sympathy for them: he used to pass them by without ever trying to feel what it was that worked their machinery: rather he was afraid to think of it: it was something like a bad dream.—And now everything was made plaint These humble, obscure creatures became in their turn centers of light.

Lying on his belly in the grass where creatures swarmed, in the shade of the trees that buzzed with insects, Christophe would watch the fevered movements of the ants, the long–legged spiders, that seemed to dance as they walked, the bounding grasshoppers, that leap aside, the heavy, bustling beetles, and the naked worms, pink and glabrous, mottled with white, or with his hands under his head and his eyes dosed he would listen to the invisible orchestra, the roundelay of the frenzied insects circling in a sunbeam about the scented pines, the trumpeting of the mosquitoes, the organ, notes of the wasps, the brass of the wild bees humming like bells in the tops of the trees, and the godlike whispering of the swaying trees, the sweet moaning of the wind in the branches, the soft whispering of the waving grass, like a breath of wind rippling the limpid surface of a lake, like the rustling of a light dress and lovers footsteps coming near, and passing, then lost upon the air.

He heard all these sounds and cries within himself. Through all these creatures from the smallest to the greatest flowed the same river of life: and in it he too swam. So, he was one of them, he was of their blood, and, brotherly, he heard the echo of their sorrows and their joys: their strength was merged is his like a river fed with thousands of streams. He sank into them. His lungs were like to burst with the wind, too freely blowing, too strong, that burst the windows and forced its way, into the closed house of his suffocating heart. The change was too abrupt: after finding everywhere a void, when he had been buried only in his own existence, and had felt it slipping from him and dissolving like rain, now everywhere he found infinite and unmeasured Being, now that he longed to forget himself, to find rebirth in the universe. He seemed to have issued from the grave. He swam voluptuously in life flowing free and full: and borne on by its current he thought that he was free. He did not know that he was less free than ever, that no creature is ever free, that even the law that governs the universe is not free, that only death—perhaps—can bring deliverance.

But the chrysalis issuing from its stifling sheath, joyously, stretched its limbs in its new shape, and had no time as yet to mark the bounds of its new prison.

* * * * *

There began a new cycle of days. Days of gold and fever, mysterious, enchanted, like those of his childhood, when by one he discovered things for the first time. From dawn to set of sun he lived in one long mirage. He deserted all his business. The conscientious boy, who for years had never missed a lesson, or an orchestra rehearsal, even when he was ill, was forever finding paltry excuses for neglecting his work. He was not afraid to lie. He had no remorse about it. The stoic principles of life, to which he had hitherto delighted to bend his will, morality, duty, now seemed to him to have no truth, nor reason. Their jealous despotism was smashed against Nature. Human nature, healthy, strong, free, that alone was virtue: to hell with all the rest! It provoked pitying laughter to see the little peddling rules of prudence and policy which the world adorns with the name of morality, while it pretends to inclose all life within them. A preposterous mole–hill, an ant–like people! Life sees to it that they are brought to reason. Life does but pass, and all is swept away....

Bursting with energy Christophe had moments when he was consumed with a desire to destroy, to burn, to smash, to glut with actions blind and uncontrolled the force which choked him. These outbursts usually ended in a sharp reaction: he would weep, and fling himself down on the ground, and kiss the earth, and try to dig into it with his teeth and hands, to feed himself with it, to merge into it: he trembled then with fever and desire.

One evening he was walking in the outskirts of a wood. His eyes were swimming with the light, his head was whirling: he was in that state of exaltation when all creatures and things were transfigured. To that was added the magic of the soft warm light of evening. Bays of purple and gold hovered in the trees. From the meadows seemed to come a phosphorescent glimmer. In a field near by a girl was making hay. In her blouse and short skirt, with her arms and neck bare, she was raking the hay and heaping it up. She had a short nose, wide cheeks, a round face, a handkerchief thrown over her hair. The setting sun touched with red her sunburned skin, which, like a piece of pottery, seemed to absorb the last beams of the day.

She fascinated Christophe. Leaning against a beech–tree he watched her come towards the verge of the woods, eagerly, passionately. Everything else had disappeared. She took no notice of him. For a moment she looked at him cautiously: he saw her eyes blue and hard in her brown face. She passed so near to him that, when she leaned down to gather up the hay, through her open blouse he saw a soft down on her shoulders and back. Suddenly the vague desire which was in him leaped forth. He hurled himself at her from behind, seized her neck and waist, threw back her head and fastened his lips upon hers. He kissed her dry, cracked lips until he came against her teeth that bit him angrily. His hands ran over her rough arms, over her blouse wet with her sweat. She struggled. He held her tighter, he wished to strangle her. She broke loose, cried out, spat, wiped her lips with her hand, and hurled insults at him. He let her go and fled across the fields. She threw stones at him and went on discharging after him a litany of filthy epithets. He blushed, less for anything that she might say or think, but for what he was thinking himself. The sudden unconscious act filled him with terror. What had he done? What should he do? What he was able to understand of it all only filled him with disgust. And he was tempted by his disgust. He fought against himself and knew not on which side was the real Christophe. A blind force beset him: in vain did he fly from it: it was only to fly from himself. What would she do about him? What should he do to–morrow ... in an hour ... the time it took to cross the plowed field to reach the road?... Would he ever reach it? Should he not stop, and go back, and run back to the girl? And then?... He remembered that delirious moment when he had held her by the throat. Everything was possible. All things were worth while. A crime even.... Yes, even a crime.... The turmoil in his heart made him breathless. When he reached the road he stopped to breathe. Over there the girl was talking to another girl who had been attracted by her cries: and with arms akimbo, they were looking at each other and shouting with laughter.

II. SABINE

He went home. He shut himself up in his room and never stirred for several days. He only went out even into the town, when he was compelled. He was fearful of ever going out beyond the gates and venturing forth into the fields: he was afraid of once more falling in with the soft, maddening breath that had blown upon him like a rushing wind during a calm in a storm. He thought that the walls of the town might preserve him from it. He never dreamed that for the enemy to slip within there needed be only the smallest crack in the closed shutters, no more than is needed for a peep out.

In a wing of the house, on the other side of the yard, there lodged on the ground floor a young woman of twenty, some months a widow, with a little girl. Frau Sabine Froehlich was also a tenant of old Euler's. She occupied the shop which opened on to the street, and she had as well two rooms looking on to the yard, together with a little patch of garden, marked off from the Eulers' by a wire fence up which ivy climbed. They did not often see her: the child used to play down in the garden from morning to night making mud pies: and the garden was left to itself, to the great distress of old Justus, who loved tidy paths and neatness in the beds. He had tried to bring the matter to the attention of his tenant: but that was probably why she did not appear: and the garden was not improved by it.

Frau Froehlich kept a little draper's shop which might have had customers enough, thanks to its position in a street of shops in the center of the town: but she did not bother about it any more than about her garden. Instead of doing her housework herself, as, according to Frau Vogel, every self–respecting woman ought to do—especially when she is in circumstances which do not permit much less excuse idleness—she had hired a little servant, a girl of fifteen, who came in for a few hours in the morning to clean the rooms and look after the shop, while the young woman lay in bed or dawdled over her toilet.

Christophe used to see her sometimes, through his windows, walking about her room, with bare feet, in her long nightgown, or sitting for hours together before her mirror: for she was so careless that she used to forget to draw her curtains: and when she saw him, she was so lazy that she could not take the trouble, to go and lower them. Christophe, more modest than she, would leave the window so as not to incommode her: but the temptation was great. He would blush a little and steal a glance at her bare arms, which were rather thin, as she drew them languidly around her flowing hair, and with her hands, clasped behind her head, lost herself in a dream, until they were numbed, and then she would let them fall. Christophe would pretend that he only saw these pleasant sights inadvertently as he happened to pass the window, and that they did not disturb him in his musical thoughts; but he liked it, and in the end he wasted as much time in watching Frau Sabine, as she did over her toilet. Not that she was a coquette: she was rather careless, generally, and did not take anything like the meticulous care with her appearance that Amalia or Rosa did. If she dawdled in front of her dressing table it was from pure laziness; every time she put in a pin she had to rest from the effort of it, while she made little piteous faces at herself in the mirrors. She was never quite properly dressed at the end of the day.

Often her servant used to go before Sabine was ready: and a customer would ring the shop–bell. She would let him ring and call once or twice before she could make up her mind to get up from her chair. She would go down, smiling, and never hurrying,—never hurrying would look for the article required,—and if she could not find it after looking for some time, or even (as happened sometimes) if she had to take too much trouble to reach it, as for instance, taking the ladder from one end of the shop to the other,—she would say calmly that she did not have it in stock: and as she never bothered to put her stock in order, or to order more of the articles of which she had run out, her customers used to lose patience and go elsewhere. But she never minded. How could you be angry with such a pleasant creature who spoke so sweetly, and was never excited about anything! She did not mind what anybody said to her: and she made this so plain that those who began to complain never had the courage to go on: they used to go, answering her charming smile with a smile: but they never came back. She never bothered about it. She went on smiling.

She was like a little Florentine figure. Her well marked eyebrows were arched: her gray eyes were half open behind the curtain of her lashes. The lower eyelid was a little swollen, with a little crease below it. Her little, finely drawn nose turned up slightly at the end. Another little curve lay between it and her upper lip, which curled up above her half–open mouth, pouting in a weary smile. Her lower lip was a little thick: the lower part of her face was rounded, and had the serious expression of the little virgins of

Filippo Lippi. Her complexion was a little muddy, her hair was light brown, always untidy, and done up in a slovenly chignon. She was slight of figure, small–boned. And her movements were lazy. Dressed carelessly—a gaping bodice, buttons missing, ugly, worn shoes, always looking a little slovenly—she charmed by her grace and youth, her gentleness, her instinctively coaxing ways. When she appeared to take the air at the door of her shop, the young men who passed used to look at her with pleasure: and although she did not bother about them, she noticed it none the less. Always then she wore that grateful and glad expression which is in the eyes of all women when they know that they have been seen with sympathetic eyes. It seemed to say:

"Thank you!... Again! Look at me again!" But though it gave her pleasure to please, her indifference would never let her make the smallest effort to please.

She was an object of scandal to the Euler–Vogels. Everything about her offended them: her indolence, the untidiness of her house, the carelessness of her dress, her polite indifference to their remarks, her perpetual smile, the impertinent serenity with which she had accepted her husband's death, her child's illnesses, her straitened circumstances, the great and annoyances of her daily life, while nothing could change one jot of her favorite habits, or her eternal longing,—everything about her offended them: and the worst of all was that, as she was, she did give pleasure. Frau Vogel could not forgive her that. It was almost as though Sabine did it on purpose, on purpose, ironically, to set at naught by her conduct the great traditions, the true principles, the savorless duty, the pleasureless labor, the restlessness, the noise, the quarrels, the mooning ways, the healthy pessimism which was the motive power of the Euler family, as it is that of all respectable persons, and made their life a foretaste of purgatory. That a woman who did nothing but dawdle about all the blessed day should take upon herself to defy them with her calm insolence, while they bore their suffering in silence like galley–slaves,—and that people should approve of her into the bargain—that was beyond the limit, that was enough to turn you against respectability!... Fortunately, thank God, there were still a few sensible people left in the world. Frau Vogel consoled herself with them. They exchanged remarks about the little widow, and spied on her through her shutters. Such gossip was the joy of the family when they met at supper. Christophe would listen absently. He was so used to hearing the Vogels set themselves up as censors of their neighbors that he never took any notice of it. Besides he knew nothing of Frau Sabine except her bare neck and arms, and though they were pleasing enough, they did not justify his coming to a definite opinion about her. However, he was conscious; of a kindly feeling towards her: and in a contradictory spirit he was especially grateful to her for displeasing Frau Vogel.

* * * * *

After dinner in the evening when it was very hot it was impossible to stay in the stifling yard, where the sun shone the whole afternoon. The only place in the house where it was possible to breathe was the rooms looking into the street, Euler and his son–in–law used sometimes to go and sit on the doorstep with Louisa. Frau Vogel and Rosa would only appear for a moment: they were kept by their housework: Frau Vogel took a pride in showing that she had no time for dawdling: and she used to say, loudly enough to be overheard, that all the people sitting there and yawning on their doorsteps, without doing a stitch of work, got on her nerves. As she could not—(to her sorrow)—compel them to work, she would pretend not to see them, and would go in and work furiously. Rosa thought she must do likewise. Euler and Vogel would discover draughts everywhere, and fearful of catching cold, would go up to their rooms: they used to go to bed early, and would have thought themselves ruined had they changed the least of their habits. After nine o'clock only Louisa and Christophe would be left. Louisa spent the day in her room: and, In the evening, Christophe used to take pains to be with her, whenever he could, to make her take the air. If she were left alone she would never go out: the noise of the street frightened her. Children were always chasing each other with shrill cries. All the dogs of the neighborhood took it up and barked. The sound of a piano came up, a little farther off a clarinet, and in the next street a cornet a piston. Voices chattered. People came and went and stood in groups in front of their houses. Louisa would have lost her head if she had been left alone in all the uproar. But when her son was with her it gave her pleasure. The noise would gradually die down. The children and the dogs would go to bed first. The groups of people would break up. The air would become more pure. Silence would descend upon the street. Louisa would tell in her thin voice the little scraps of news that she had heard from Amalia or Rosa. She was not greatly interested in them. But she never knew what to talk about to her son, and she felt the need of keeping in touch with him, of saying something to him. And Christophe, who felt her need, would pretend to be interested in everything she said: but he did not listen. He was off in vague dreams, turning over in his mind the doings of the day. One evening when they were sitting there—while his mother Was talking he saw the door of the draper's shop open. A woman came out silently and sat in the street. Her chair was only a few yards from Louisa. She was sitting in the darkest shadow. Christophe could not see her face: but he recognized her. His dreams vanished. The air seemed sweeter to him. Louisa had not noticed Sabine's presence, and went on with her chatter in a low voice. Christophe paid more attention to her, and, he felt impelled to throw out a remark here and there, to talk, perhaps to be heard. The slight figure sat there without stirring, a little limp, with her legs lightly crossed and her hands lying crossed in her lap. She was looking straight in front of her, and seemed to hear nothing. Louisa was overcome with drowsiness. She went in. Christophe said he would stay a little longer.

It was nearly ten. The street was empty. The people were going indoors. The sound of the shops being shut was heard. The lighted windows winked and then were dark again. One or two were still lit: then they were blotted out. Silence.... They were alone, they did not look at each other, they held their breath, they seemed not to be aware of each other. From the distant fields came the smell of the new–mown hay, and from a balcony in a house near by the scent of a pot of cloves. No wind stirred. Above their heads was the Milky Way. To their right red Jupiter. Above a chimney Charles' Wain bent its axles: in the pale green sky its stars flowered like daisies. From the bells of the parish church eleven o'clock rang out and was caught up by all the other churches, with their voices clear or muffled, and, from the houses, by the dim chiming of the clock or husky cuckoos.

They awoke suddenly from their dreams, and got up at the same moment. And just as they were going indoors they both bowed without speaking. Christophe went up to his room. He lighted his candle, and sat down by his desk with his head in his hands, and stayed so for a long time without a thought. Then he sighed and went to bed.

Next day when he got up, mechanically he went to his window to look down into Sabine's room. But the curtains were drawn. They were drawn the whole morning. They were drawn ever after.

＊ ＊ ＊ ＊ ＊

Next evening Christophe proposed to his mother that they should go again to sit by the door. He did so regularly. Louisa was glad of it: she did not like his shutting himself up in his room immediately after dinner with the window and shutters closed.—The little silent shadow never failed to come and sit in its usual place. They gave each other a quick nod, which Louisa never noticed. Christophe would talk to his mother. Sabine would smile at her little girl, playing in the street: about nine she would go and put her to bed and would then return noiselessly. If she stayed a little Christophe would begin to be afraid that she would not come back. He would listen for sounds in the house, the laughter of the little girl who would not go to sleep: he would hear the rustling of Sabine's dress before she appeared on the threshold of the shop. Then he would look away and talk to his mother more eagerly. Sometimes he would feel that Sabine was looking at him. In turn he would furtively look at her. But their eyes would never meet.

The child was a bond between them. She would run about in the street with other children. They would find amusement in teasing a good–tempered dog sleeping there with his nose in his paws: he would cock a red eye and at last would emit a growl of boredom: then they would fly this way and that screaming in terror and happiness. The little girl would give piercing shrieks, and look behind her as though she were being pursued; she would throw herself into Louisa's lap, and Louisa would smile fondly. She would keep the child and question her: and so she would enter into conversation with Sabine. Christophe never joined in. He never spoke to Sabine. Sabine never spoke to him. By tacit agreement they pretended to ignore each other. But he never lost a word of what they said as they talked over him. His silence seemed unfriendly to Louisa. Sabine never thought it so: but it would make her shy, and she would grow confused in her remarks. Then she would find some excuse for going in.

For a whole week Louisa kept indoors for a cold. Christophe and Sabine were left alone. The first time they were frightened by it. Sabine, to seem at her ease, took her little girl on her knees and loaded her with caresses. Christophe was embarrassed and did not know whether he ought to go on ignoring what was happening at his side. It became difficult: although they had not spoken a single word to each other, they did know each other, thanks to Louisa. He tried to begin several times: but the words stuck in his throat. Once more the little girl extricated them from their difficulty. She played hide–and–seek, and went round Christophe's chair. He caught her as she passed and kissed her. He was not very fond of children: but it was curiously pleasant to him to kiss the little girl. She struggled to be free, for she was busy with her game. He teased her, she bit his hands: he let her fall. Sabine laughed. They looked at the child and exchanged a few trivial words. Then Christophe tried—(he thought he must)—to enter into conversation: but he had nothing very much to go upon: and Sabine did not make his task any the easier: she only repeated what he said:

"It is a fine evening."

"Yes. It is a very fine evening."

"Impossible to breathe in the yard."

"Yes. The yard was stifling."

Conversation became very difficult. Sabine discovered that it was time to take the little girl in, and went in herself: and she did not appear again.

Christophe was afraid she would do the same on the evenings that followed and that she would avoid being left alone with him, as long as Louisa was not there. But on the contrary, the next evening Sabine tried to resume their conversation. She did so deliberately rather than for pleasure: she was obviously taking a great deal of trouble to find subjects of conversation, and bored with the questions she put: questions and answers came between heartbreaking silences. Christophe remembered his first interviews with Otto: but with Sabine their subjects were even more limited than then, and she had not Otto's patience. When she saw the small success of her endeavors she did not try any more: she had to give herself too much trouble, and she lost interest in it. She said no more, and he followed her lead.

And then there was sweet peace again. The night was calm once more, and they returned to their inward thoughts. Sabine rocked slowly in her chair, dreaming. Christophe also was dreaming. They said nothing. After half an hour Christophe began to talk to himself, and in a low voice cried out with pleasure in the delicious scent brought by the soft wind that came from a cart of strawberries. Sabine said a word or two in reply. Again they were silent. They were enjoying the charm of these indefinite silences, and trivial words. Their dreams were the same, they had but one thought: they did not know what it was: they did not admit it to themselves. At eleven they smiled and parted.

Next day they did not even try to talk: they resumed their sweet silence. At long intervals a word or two let them know that they were thinking of the same things.

Sabine began to laugh.

"How much better it is," she said, "not to try to talk! One thinks one must, and it is so tiresome!"

"Ah!" said Christophe with conviction, "if only everybody thought the same."

They both laughed. They were thinking of Frau Vogel.

"Poor woman!" said Sabine; "how exhausting she is!"

"She is never exhausted," replied Christophe gloomily.

She was tickled by his manner and his jest.

"You think it amusing?" he asked. "That is easy for you. You are sheltered."

"So I am," said Sabine. "I lock myself in." She had a little soft laugh that hardly sounded. Christophe heard it with delight in the calm of the evening. He snuffed the fresh air luxuriously.

"Ah! It is good to be silent!" he said, stretching his limbs.

"And talking is no use!" said she.

"Yes," returned Christophe, "we understand each other so well!"

They relapsed into silence. In the darkness they could not see each other. They were both smiling.

And yet, though they felt the same, when they were together—or imagined that they did—in reality they knew nothing of each other. Sabine did not bother about it. Christophe was more curious. One evening he asked her:

"Do you like music?"

"No," she said simply. "It bores me, I don't understand it."

Her frankness charmed him. He was sick of the lies of people who said that they were mad about music, and were bored to death when they heard it: and it seemed to him almost a virtue not to like it and to say so. He asked if Sabine read.

"So. She had no books."

He offered to lend her his.

"Serious books?" she asked uneasily.

"Not serious books if she did not want them. Poetry."

"But those are serious books."

"Novels, then."

She pouted.

"They don't interest you?"

"Yes. She was interested in them: but they were always too long: she never had the patience to finish them. She forgot the beginning: skipped chapters and then lost the thread. And then she threw the book away."

"Fine interest you take!"

"Bah! Enough for a story that is not true. She kept her interest for better things than books."

"For the theater, then?"

"No.... No."

"Didn't she go to the theater?"

"No. It was too hot. There were too many people. So much better at home. The lights tired her eyes. And the actors were so ugly!"

He agreed with her in that. But there were other things in the theater: the play, for instance.

"Yes," she said absently. "But I have no time."

"What do you do all day?"

She smiled.

"There is so much to do."

"True," said he. "There is your shop."

"Oh!" she said calmly. "That does not take much time."

"Your little girl takes up your time then?"

"Oh! no, poor child! She is very good and plays by herself."

"Then?"

He begged pardon for his indiscretion. But she was amused by it.

"There are so many things."

"What things?"

"She could not say. All sorts of things. Getting up, dressing, thinking of dinner, cooking dinner, eating dinner, thinking of supper, cleaning her room.... And then the day was over.... And besides you must have a little time for doing nothing!"

"And you are not bored?"

"Never."

"Even when you are doing nothing?"

"Especially when I am doing nothing. It is much worse doing something: that bores me."

They looked at each other and laughed.

"You are very happy!" said Christophe. "I can't do nothing."

"It seems to me that you know how."

"I have been learning lately."

"Ah! well, you'll learn."

When he left off talking to her he was at his ease and comfortable. It was enough for him to see her. He was rid of his anxieties, and irritations, and the nervous trouble that made him sick at heart. When he was talking to her he was beyond care: and so when he thought of her. He dared not admit it to himself: but as soon as he was in her presence, he was filled with a delicious soft emotion that brought him almost to unconsciousness. At night he slept as he had never done.

* * * * *

When he came back from his work he would look into this shop. It was not often that he did not see Sabine. They bowed and smiled. Sometimes she was at the door and then they would exchange a few words: and he would open the door and call the little girl and hand her a packet of sweets.

One day he decided to go in. He pretended that he wanted some waistcoat buttons. She began to look for them: but she could not find them. All the buttons were mixed up: it was impossible to pick them out. She was a little put out that he should see her untidiness. He laughed at it and bent over the better to see it.

"No," she said, trying to hide the drawers with her hands. "Don't look! It is a dreadful muddle...."

She went on looking. But Christophe embarrassed her. She was cross, and as she pushed the drawer back she said:

"I can't find any. Go to Lisi, in the next street. She is sure to have them. She has everything that people want."

He laughed at her way of doing business.

"Do you send all your customers away like that?"

"Well. You are not the first," said Sabine warmly.

And yet she was a little ashamed:

"It is too much trouble to tidy up," she said. "I put off doing it from day to day.... But I shall certainly do it to–morrow."

"Shall I help you?" asked Christophe.

She refused. She would gladly have accepted: but she dared not, for fear of gossip. And besides it humiliated her.

They went on talking.

"And your buttons?" she said to Christophe a moment later. "Aren't you going to Lisi?"

"Never," said Christophe. "I shall wait until you have tidied up."

"Oh!" said Sabine, who had already forgotten what she had just said, "don't wait all that time!"

Her frankness delighted them both.

Christophe went to the drawer that she had shut.

"Let me look."

She ran to prevent his doing so.

"No, now please. I am sure I haven't any."

"I bet you have."

At once he found the button he wanted, and was triumphant. He wanted others. He wanted to go on rummaging; but she snatched the box from his hands, and, hurt in her vanity, she began to look herself.

The light was fading. She went to the window. Christophe sat a little away from her: the little girl clambered on to his knees. He pretended to listen to her chatter and answered her absently. He was looking at Sabine and she knew that he was looking at her. She bent over the box. He could see her neck and a little of her cheek.—And as he looked he saw that she was blushing. And he blushed too.

The child went on talking. No one answered her. Sabine did not move. Christophe could not see what she was doing, he was sure she was doing nothing: she was not even looking at the box in her hands. The silence went on and on. The little girl grew uneasy and slipped down from Christophe's knees.

"Why don't you say anything?"

Sabine turned sharply and took her in her arms. The box was spilled on the floor: the little girl shouted with glee and ran on hands and knees after the buttons rolling under the furniture. Sabine went to the window again and laid her cheek against the pane. She seemed to be absorbed in what she saw outside.

"Good–night!" said Christophe, ill at ease. She did not turn her head, and said in a low voice:

"Good–night."

* * * * *

On Sundays the house was empty during the afternoon. The whole family went to church for Vespers. Sabine did not go. Christophe jokingly reproached her with it once when he saw her sitting at her door in the little garden, while the lovely bells were bawling themselves hoarse summoning her. She replied in the same tone that only Mass was compulsory: not Vespers: it was then no use, and perhaps a little indiscreet to be too zealous: and she liked to think that God would be rather pleased than angry with her.

"You have made God in your own image," said Christophe.

"I should be so bored if I were in His place," replied she with conviction.

"You would not bother much about the world if you were in His place."

"All that I should ask of it would be that it should not bother itself about me."

"Perhaps it would be none the worse for that," said Christophe.

"Tssh!" cried Sabine, "we are being irreligious."

"I don't see anything irreligious in saying that God is like you. I am sure He is flattered."

"Will you be silent!" said Sabine, half laughing, half angry. She was beginning to be afraid that God would be scandalized. She quickly turned the conversation.

"Besides," she said, "it is the only time in the week when one can enjoy the garden in peace."

"Yes," said Christophe. "They are gone." They looked at each other.

"How silent it is," muttered Sabine. "We are not used to it. One hardly knows where one is...."

"Oh!" cried Christophe suddenly and angrily.

"There are days when I would like to strangle her!" There was no need to ask of whom he was speaking.

"And the others?" asked Sabine gaily.

"True," said Christophe, a little abashed. "There is Rosa."

"Poor child!" said Sabine.

They were silent.

"If only it were always as it is now!" sighed Christophe.

She raised her laughing eyes to his, and then dropped them. He saw that she was working.

"What are you doing?" he asked.

(The fence of ivy that separated the two gardens was between them.)

"Look!" she said, lifting a basin that she was holding in heir lap. "I am shelling peas."

She sighed.

"But that is not unpleasant," he raid, laughing.

"Oh!" she replied, "it is disgusting, always having to think of dinner."

"I bet that if it were possible," he said, "you would go without your dinner rather than haw the trouble of cooking it."

"That's true," cried she.

"Wait! I'll come and help you."

He climbed over the fence and came to her.

She was sitting in a chair in the door. He sat on a step at her feet. He dipped into her lap for handfuls of green pods; and he poured the little round peas into the basin that Sabine held between her knees. He looked down. He saw Sabine's black stockings clinging to her ankles and feet—one of her feet was half out of its shoe. He dared not raise his eyes to look at her.

The air was heavy. The sky was dull and clouds hung low: There was no wind. No leaf stirred. The garden was inclosed within high walls: there was no world beyond them.

The child had gone out with one of the neighbors. They were alone. They said nothing. They could say nothing. Without looking he went on taking handfuls of peas from Sabine's lap: his fingers trembled as he touched her: among the fresh smooth pods they met Sabine's fingers, and they trembled too. They could not go on. They sat still, not looking at each other: she leaned back in her chair with her lips half–open and her arms hanging: he sat at her feet leaning against her: along his shoulder and arm he could feel the warmth of Sabine's leg. They were breathless. Christophe laid his hands against the stones to cool them: one of his hands touched Sabine's foot, that she had thrust out of her shoe, and he left it there, could not move it. They shivered. Almost they lost control. Christophe's hand closed on the slender toes of Sabine's little foot. Sabine turned cold, the sweat broke out on her brow, she leaned towards Christophe....

Familiar voices broke the spell. They trembled. Christophe leaped to his feet and crossed the fence again. Sabine picked up the shells in her lap and went in. In the yard he turned. She was at her door. They looked at each other. Drops of rain were beginning to patter on the leaves of the trees.... She closed her door. Frau Vogel and Rosa came in.... He went up to his room....

In the yellow light of the waning day drowned in the torrents of rain, he got up from his desk in response to an irresistible impulse: he ran to his window and held out his arms to the opposite window. At the same moment through the opposite window in the half–darkness of the room he saw—he thought he saw—Sabine holding out her arms to him.

He rushed from his room. He went downstairs. He ran to the garden fence. At the risk of being seen he was about to clear it. But when he looked at the window at which she had appeared, he saw that the shutters were closed. The house seemed to be asleep. He stopped. Old Euler, going to his cellar, saw him and called him. He retraced his footsteps. He thought he must have been dreaming.

It was not long before Rosa began to see what was happening. She had no diffidence and she did not yet know what jealousy was. She was ready to give wholly and to ask nothing in return. But if she was sorrowfully resigned to not being loved by Christophe, she had never considered the possibility of Christophe loving another.

One evening, after dinner, she had just finished a piece of embroidery at which she had been working for months. She was happy, and wanted for once in a way to leave her work and go and talk to Christophe. She waited until her mother's back was turned and then slipped from the room. She crept from the house like a truant. She wanted to go and confound Christophe, who had vowed scornfully that she would never finish her work. She thought it would be a good joke to go and take them by surprise in the street. It was no use the poor child knowing how Christophe felt towards her: she was always inclined to measure the pleasure which others should have at seeing her by that which she had herself in meeting them.

She went out. Christophe and Sabine were sitting as usual in front of the house. There was a catch at Rosa's heart. And yet she did not stop for the irrational idea that was in her: and she chaffed Christophe warmly. The sound of her shrill voice in the silence of the night struck on Christophe like a false note. He started in his chair, and frowned angrily. Rosa waved her embroidery in his face triumphantly. Christophe snubbed her impatiently.

"It is finished—finished!" insisted Rosa.

"Oh! well—go and begin another," said Christophe curtly.

Rosa was crestfallen. All her delight vanished. Christophe went on crossly:

"And when you have done thirty, when you are very old, you will at least be able to say to yourself that your life has not been wasted!"

Rosa was near weeping.

"How cross you are, Christophe!" she said.

Christophe was ashamed and spoke kindly to her. She was satisfied with so little that she regained confidence: and she began once more to chatter noisily: she could not speak low, she shouted deafeningly, like everybody in the house. In spite of himself Christophe could not conceal his ill–humor. At first he answered her with a few irritated monosyllables: then he said nothing at all, turned his back on her, fidgeted in his chair, and ground his teeth as she rattled on. Rosa saw that he was losing his temper and knew that she ought to stop: but she went on louder than ever. Sabine, a few yards away, in the dark, said nothing, watched the scene with ironic impassivity. Then she was weary and, feeling that the evening was wasted, she got up and went in. Christophe only noticed her departure after she had gone. He got up at once and without ceremony went away with a curt "Good–evening."

Rosa was left alone in the street, and looked in bewilderment at the door by which he had just gone in. Tears came to her eyes. She rushed in, went up to her room without a sound, so as not to have to talk to her mother, undressed hurriedly, and when she was in her bed, buried under the clothes, sobbed and sobbed. She made no attempt to think over what had passed: she did not ask herself whether Christophe loved Sabine, or whether Christophe and Sabine could not bear her: she knew only that all was lost, that life was useless, that there was nothing left to her but death.

Next morning thought came to her once more with eternal illusive hope. She recalled the events of the evening and told herself that she was wrong to attach so much importance to them. No doubt Christophe did not love her: she was resigned to that, though in her heart she thought, though she did not admit the thought, that in the end she would win his love by her love for him. But what reason had she for thinking that there was anything between Sabine and him? How could he, so clever as he was, love a little creature whose insignificance and mediocrity were patent? She was reassured,—but for that she did not watch Christophe any the less closely. She saw nothing all day, because there was nothing to see: but Christophe seeing her prowling about him all day long without any sort of explanation was peculiarly irritated by it. She set the crown on her efforts in the evening when she appeared again and sat with them in the street. The scene of the previous evening was repeated. Rosa talked alone. But Sabine did not wait so long before she went indoors: and Christophe followed her example. Rosa could no longer pretend that her presence was not unwelcome: but the unhappy girl tried to deceive herself. She did not perceive that she could have done nothing worse than to try so to impose on herself: and with her usual clumsiness she went on through the succeeding days.

Next day with Rosa sitting by his side Christophe waited is vain for Sabine to appear.

The day after Rosa was alone. They had given up the struggle. But she gained nothing by it save resentment from Christophe, who was furious at being robbed of his beloved evenings, his only happiness. He was the less inclined to forgive her, for being absorbed with his own feelings, he had no suspicion of Rosa's.

Sabine had known them for some time: she knew that Rosa was jealous even before she knew that she herself was in love: but she said nothing about it: and, with the natural cruelty of a pretty woman, who is certain of her victory, in quizzical silence she watched the futile efforts of her awkward rival.

     * * * * *

Left mistress of the field of battle Rosa gazed piteously upon the results of her tactics. The best thing she could have done would have been not to persist, and to leave Christophe alone, at least for the time being: but that was not what she did: and as the worst thing she could have done was to talk to him; about Sabine, that was precisely what she did.

With a fluttering at her heart, by way of sounding him, she said timidly that Sabine was pretty. Christophe replied curtly; that she was very pretty. And although Rosa might have foreseen the reply she would provoke, her heart thumped when she heard him. She knew that Sabine was pretty: but she had never particularly remarked it: now she saw her for the first time with the eyes of Christophe: she saw her delicate features, her short nose, her fine mouth, her slender figure, her graceful movements.... Ah! how sad!... What would not she have given to possess Sabine's body, and live in it! She did not go closely into why it should be preferred to her own!... Her own!... What had she done to possess such a body? What a burden it was upon her. How ugly it seemed to her! It was odious to her. And to think that nothing but death could ever free her from it!... She was at once too proud and too humble to complain that she was not loved: she had no right to do so: and she tried even more to humble herself. But her instinct revolted.... No. It was not just!... Why should she have such a body, she, and not Sabine?... And why should Sabine be loved? What had she done to be loved?... Rosa saw her with no kindly eye, lazy, careless, egoistic, indifferent towards everybody, not looking after her house, or her child, or anybody, loving only herself, living only for sleeping, dawdling, and doing nothing....

And it was such a woman who pleased ... who pleased Christophe.... Christophe who was so severe, Christophe who was so discerning, Christophe whom she esteemed and admired more than anybody!... How could Christophe be blind to it?—She could not help from time to time dropping an unkind remark about Sabine in his hearing. She did not wish to do so: but the impulse was stronger than herself. She was always sorry for it, for she was a kind creature and disliked speaking ill of anybody. But she was the more sorry because she drew down on herself such cruel replies as showed how much Christophe was in love. He did not mince matters. Hurt in his love, he tried to hurt in return: and succeeded. Rosa would make no reply and go out with her head bowed, and her lips tight pressed to keep from crying. She thought that it was her own fault, that she deserved it for having hurt Christophe by attacking the object of his love.

Her mother was less patient. Frau Vogel, who saw everything, and old Euler, also, had not been slow to notice Christophe's interviews with their young neighbor: it was not difficult to guess their romance. Their secret projects of one day marrying Rosa to Christophe were set at naught by it: and that seemed to them a personal affront of Christophe, although he was not supposed to know that they had disposed of him without consulting his wishes. But Amalia's despotism did not admit of ideas contrary to her own: and it seemed scandalous to her that Christophe should have disregarded the contemptuous opinion she had often expressed of Sabine.

She did not hesitate to repeat it for his benefit. Whenever he was present she found some excuse for talking about her neighbor: she cast about for the most injurious things to say of her, things which might sting Christophe most cruelly: and with the crudity of her point of view and language she had no difficulty in finding them. The ferocious instinct of a woman, so superior to that of a man in the art of doing evil, as well as of doing good, made her insist less on Sabine's laziness and moral failings than on her uncleanliness. Her indiscreet and prying eye had watched through the window for proofs of it in the secret processes of Sabine's toilet: and she exposed them with coarse complacency. When from decency she could not say everything she left the more to be understood.

Christophe would go pale with shame and anger: he would go white as a sheet and his lips would quiver. Rosa, foreseeing what must happen, would implore her mother to have done: she would even try to defend Sabine. But she only succeeded in making Amalia more aggressive.

And suddenly Christophe would leap from his chair. He would thump on the table and begin to shout that it was monstrous to speak of a woman, to spy upon her, to expose her misfortunes; only an evil mind could so persecute a creature who was good, charming, quiet, keeping herself to herself, and doing no harm to anybody, and speaking no ill of anybody. But they were making a great mistake if they thought they could do her harm; they only made him more sympathetic and made her kindness shine forth only the more clearly.

Amalia would feel then that she had gone too far: but she was hurt by feeling it; and, shifting her ground, she would say that it was only too easy to talk of kindness: that the word was called in as an excuse for everything. Heavens! It was easy enough to be thought kind when you never bothered about anything or anybody, and never did your duty!

To which Christophe would reply that the first duty of all was to make life pleasant for others, but that there were people for whom duty meant only ugliness, unpleasantness, tiresomeness, and everything that interferes with the liberty of others and annoys and injures their neighbors, their servants, their families, and themselves. God save us from such people, and such a notion of duty, as from the plague!...

They would grow venomous. Amalia would be very bitter. Christophe would not budge an inch.—And the result of it all was that henceforth Christophe made a point of being seen continually with Sabine. He would go and knock at her door. He would talk gaily and laugh with her. He would choose moments when Amalia and Rosa could see him. Amalia would avenge herself with angry words. But the innocent Rosa's heart was rent and torn by this refinement of cruelty: she felt that he detested them and wished to avenge himself: and she wept bitterly.

* * * * *

So, Christophe, who had suffered so much from injustice, learned unjustly to inflict suffering.

Some time after that Sabine's brother, a miller at Landegg, a little town a few miles away, was to celebrate the christening of a child. Sabine was to be godmother. She invited Christophe. He had no liking for these functions: but for the pleasure of annoying the

Vogels and of being with Sabine he accepted eagerly.

Sabine gave herself the malicious satisfaction of inviting Amalia and Rosa also, being quite sure that they would refuse. They did. Rosa was longing to accept. She did not dislike Sabine: sometimes even her heart was filled with tenderness for her because Christophe loved her: sometimes she longed to tell her so and to throw her arms about her neck. But there was her mother and her mother's example. She stiffened herself in her pride and refused. Then, when they had gone, and she thought of them together, happy together, driving in the country on the lovely July day, while she was left shut up in her room, with a pile of linen to mend, with her mother grumbling by her side, she thought she must choke: and she cursed her pride. Oh! if there were still time!... Alas! if it were all to do again, she would have done the same....

The miller had sent his wagonette to fetch Christophe and Sabine. They took up several guests from the town and the farms on the road.. It was fresh dry weather. The bright sun made the red berries of the brown trees by the road and the wild cherry trees in the fields shine. Sabine was smiling. Her pale face was rosy under the keen wind. Christophe had her little girl on his knees. They did not try to talk to each other: they talked to their neighbors without caring to whom or of what: they were glad to hear each other's voices: they were glad to be driving in the same carriage. They looked at each other in childish glee as they pointed out to each other a house, a tree, a passerby. Sabine loved the country: but she hardly ever went into it: her incurable laziness made excursions impossible: it was almost a year since she had been outside the town: and so she delighted in the smallest things she saw. They were not new to Christophe: but he loved Sabine, and like all lovers he saw everything through her eyes, and felt all her thrills of pleasure, and all and more than the emotion that was in her: for, merging himself with his beloved, he endowed her with all that he was himself.

When they came to the mill they found in the yard all the people of the farm and the other guests, who received them with a deafening noise. The fowls, the ducks, and the dogs joined in. The miller, Bertold, a great fair–haired fellow, square of head and shoulders, as big and tall as Sabine was slight, took his little sister in his arms and put her down gently as though he were afraid of breaking her. It was not long before Christophe saw that the little sister, as usual, did just as she liked with the giant, and that while he made heavy fun of her whims, and her laziness, and her thousand and one failings, he was at her feet, her slave. She was used to it, and thought it natural. She did nothing to win love: it seemed to her right that she should be loved: and if she were not, did not care: that is why everybody loved her.

Christophe made another discovery not so pleasing. For a christening a godfather is necessary as well as a godmother, and the godfather has certain rights over the godmother, rights which he does not often renounce, especially when she is young and pretty. He learned this suddenly when he saw a farmer, with fair curly hair, and rings in his ears, go up to Sabine laughing and kiss her on both cheeks. Instead of telling himself that he was an ass to have forgotten this privilege, and more than an ass to be huffy about it, he was cross with Sabine, as though she had deliberately drawn him into the snare. His crossness grew worse when he found himself separated from her during the ceremony. Sabine turned round every now and then as the procession wound across the fields and threw him a friendly glance. He pretended not to see it. She felt that he was annoyed, and guessed why: but it did not trouble her: it amused her. If she had had a real squabble with some one she loved, in spite of all the pain it might have caused her, she would never have made the least effort to break down any misunderstanding: it would have been too much trouble. Everything would come right if it were only left alone.

At dinner, sitting between the miller's wife and a fat girl with red cheeks whom he had escorted to the service without ever paying any attention to her, it occurred to Christophe to turn and look at his neighbor: and, finding her comely, out of revenge, he flirted desperately with her with the idea of catching Sabine's attention. He succeeded: but Sabine was not the sort of woman to be jealous of anybody or anything: so long as she was loved, she did not care whether her lover did or did not pay court to others: and instead of being angry, she was delighted to see Christophe amusing himself. From the other end of the table she gave him her most charming smile. Christophe was disgruntled: there was no doubt then that Sabine was indifferent to him: and he relapsed into his sulky mood from which nothing could draw him, neither the soft eyes of his neighbor, nor the wine that he drank. Finally, when he was half asleep, he asked himself angrily what on earth he was doing at such an interminable orgy, and did not hear the miller propose a trip on the water to take certain of the guests home. Nor did he see Sabine beckoning him to come with her so that they should be in the same boat. When it occurred to him, there was no room for him: and he had to go in another boat. This fresh mishap was not likely to make him more amiable until he discovered that he was to be rid of almost all his companions on the way. Then he relaxed and was pleasant. Besides the pleasant afternoon on the water, the pleasure of rowing, the merriment of these good people, rid him of his ill–humor. As Sabine was no longer there he lost his self–consciousness, and had no scruple about being frankly amused like the others.

They were in their boats. They followed each other closely, and tried to pass each other. They threw laughing insults at each other. When the boats bumped Christophe saw Sabine's smiling face: and he could not help smiling too: they felt that peace was made. He knew that very soon they would return together.

They began to sing part songs. Each voice took up a line in time and the refrain was taken up in chorus. The people in the different boats, some way from each other, now echoed each other. The notes skimmed over the water like birds. From time to time a boat would go in to the bank: a few peasants would climb out: they would stand there and wave to the boats as they went further and further away. Little by little they were disbanded. One by one voices left the chorus. At last they were alone, Christophe, Sabine, and the miller.

They came back in the same boat, floating down the river. Christophe and Bertold held the oars, but they did not row. Sabine sat in the stern facing Christophe, and talked to her brother and looked at Christophe. Talking so, they were able to look at each other undisturbedly. They could never have done so had the words ceased to flow. The deceitful words seemed to say: "It is not you that I see." But their eyes said to each other: "Who are you? Who are you? You that I love!... You that I love, whoever you be!..."

The sky was clouded, mists rose from the fields, the river steamed, the sun went down behind the clouds. Sabine shivered and wrapped her little black shawl round her head and shoulders. She seemed to be tired. As the boat, hugging the bank, passed under the spreading branches of the willows, she closed her eyes: her thin face was pale: her lips were sorrowful: she did not stir, she seemed to suffer,—to have suffered,—to be dead. Christophe's heart ached. He leaned over to her. She opened her eyes again and saw Christophe's uneasy eyes upon her and she smiled into them. It was like a ray of sunlight to him. He asked in a whisper:

"Are you ill?"

She shook her head and said:

"I am cold."

The two men put their overcoats about her, wrapped up her feet, her legs, her knees, like a child being tucked up in bed. She suffered it arid thanked them with her eyes. A fine, cold rain was beginning to fall. They took the oars and went quietly home. Heavy clouds hung in the sky. The river was inky black. Lights showed in the windows of the houses here and there in the fields. When they reached the mill the rain was pouring down and Sabine was numbed.

They lit a large fire in the kitchen and waited until the deluge should he over. But it only grew worse, and the wind rose. They had to drive three miles to get back to the town. The miller declared that he would not let Sabine go in such weather: and he proposed that they should both spend the night in the farmhouse. Christophe was reluctant to accept: he looked at Sabine for counsel: but her eyes were fixed on the fire on the hearth: it was as though they were afraid of influencing Christophe's decision. But when Christophe had said "Yes," she turned to him and she was blushing—(or was it the reflection of the fire?)—and he saw that she was pleased.

A jolly evening.... The rain stormed outside. In the black chimney the fire darted jets of golden sparks. They spun round and round. Their fantastic shapes were marked against the wall. The miller showed Sabine's little girl how to make shadows with her hands. The child laughed and was not altogether at her ease. Sabine leaned over the fire and poked it mechanically with a heavy pair of tongs: she was a little weary, and smiled dreamily, while, without listening, she nodded to her sister–in–law's chatter of her domestic affairs. Christophe sat in the shadow by the miller's side and watched Sabine smiling. He knew that she was smiling at him. They never had an opportunity of being alone all evening, or of looking at each other: they sought none.

  * * * * *

They parted early. Their rooms were adjoining, and communicated by a door. Christophe examined the door and found that the lock was on Sabine's side. He went to bed and tried to sleep. The rain was pattering against the windows. The wind howled in the chimney. On the floor above him a door was banging. Outside the window a poplar bent and groaned under the tempest. Christophe could not close his eyes. He was thinking that he was under the same roof, near her. A wall only divided them. He heard no sound in Sabine's room. But he thought he could see her. He sat up in his bed and called to her in a low voice through the wall: tender, passionate words he said: he held out his arms to her.

And it seemed to him that she was holding out her arms to him. In his heart he heard the beloved voice answering him, repeating his words, calling low to him: and he did not know whether it was he who asked and answered all the questions, or whether it was really she who spoke. The voice came louder, the call to him: he could not resist: he leaped from his bed: he groped his way to the door: he did not wish to open it: he was reassured by the closed door. And when he laid his hand once more on the handle he found that the door was opening....

He stopped dead. He closed it softly: he opened it once more: he closed it again. Was it not closed just now? Yes. He was sure it was. Who had opened it?... His heart beat so that he choked. He leaned over his bed, and sat down to breathe again. He was overwhelmed by his passion. It robbed him of the power to see or hear or move: his whole body shook. He was in terror of this unknown joy for which for months he had been craving, which was with him now, near him, so that nothing could keep it from him. Suddenly the violent boy filled with love was afraid of these desires newly realized and revolted from them. He was ashamed of them, ashamed of what he wished to do. He was too much in love to dare to enjoy what he loved: he was afraid: he would have done anything to escape his happiness. Is it only possible to love, to love, at the cost of the profanation of the beloved?...

He went to the door again: and trembling with love and fear, with his hand on the latch he could not bring himself to open it.

And on the other side of the door, standing barefooted on the tiled floor, shivering with cold, was Sabine.

So they stayed ... for how long? Minutes? Hours?... They did not know that they were there: and yet they did know. They held out their arms to each other,—he was overwhelmed by a love so great that he had not the courage to enter,—she called to him, waited for him, trembled lest he should enter.... And when at last he made up his mind to enter, she had just made up her mind to turn the lock again.

Then he cursed himself for a fool. He leaned against the door with all his strength. With his lips to the lock he implored her:

"Open."

He called to Sabine in a whisper: she could hear his heated breathing. She stayed motionless near the door: she was frozen: her teeth were chattering: she had no strength either to open the door or to go to bed again....

The storm made the trees crack and the doors in the house bang.... They turned away and went to their beds, worn out, sad and sick at heart. The cocks crowed huskily. The first light of dawn crept through the wet windows, a wretched, pale dawn, drowned in the persistent rain....

Christophe got up as soon as he could: he went down to the kitchen and talked to the people there. He was in a hurry to be gone and was afraid of being left alone with Sabine again. He was almost relieved when the miller's wife said that Sabine was unwell, and had caught cold during the drive and would not be going that morning.

His journey home was melancholy. He refused to drive, and walked through the soaking fields, in the yellow mist that covered the earth, the trees, the houses, with a shroud. Like the light, life seemed to be blotted out. Everything loomed like a specter. He was like a specter himself.

     * * * * *

At home he found angry faces. They were all scandalized at his having passed the night God knows where with Sabine. He shut himself up in his room and applied himself to his work. Sabine returned the next day and shut herself up also. They avoided meeting each other. The weather was still wet and cold: neither of them went out. They saw each other through their closed windows. Sabine was wrapped up by her fire, dreaming. Christophe was buried in his papers. They bowed to each other a little coldly and reservedly and then pretended to be absorbed again. They did not take stock of what they were feeling: they were angry with each other, with themselves, with things generally. The night at the farmhouse had been thrust aside in their memories: they were ashamed of it, and did not know whether they were more ashamed of their folly or of not having yielded to it. It was painful to them to see each other: for that made them remember things from which they wished to escape: and by joint agreement they retired into the depths of their rooms so as utterly to forget each other. But that was impossible, and they suffered keenly under the secret hostility which they felt was between them. Christophe was haunted by the expression of dumb rancor which he had once seen in Sabine's cold eyes. From such thoughts her suffering was not less: in vain did she struggle against them, and even deny them: she could not rid herself of them. They were augmented by her shame that Christophe should have guessed what was happening within her: and the shame of having offered herself ... the shame of having offered herself without having given.

Christophe gladly accepted an opportunity which cropped up to go to Cologne and Duesseldorf for some concerts. He was glad to spend two or three weeks away from home. Preparation for the concerts and the composition of a new work that he wished to play at them took up all his time and he succeeded in forgetting his obstinate memories. They disappeared from Sabine's mind too, and she fell back into the torpor of her usual life. They came to think of each other with indifference. Had they really loved each other? They doubted it. Christophe was on the point of leaving for Cologne without saying good–bye to Sabine.

On the evening before his departure they were brought together again by some imperceptible influence. It was one of the Sunday afternoons when everybody was at church. Christophe had gone out too to make his final preparations for the journey. Sabine was sitting in her tiny garden warming herself in the last rays of the sun. Christophe came home: he was in a hurry and his first inclination when he saw her was; to bow and pass on. But something held him back as he was passing: was it Sabine's paleness, or some indefinable feeling: remorse, fear, tenderness?... He stopped, turned to Sabine, and, leaning over the fence, he bade her good–evening. Without replying she held out her hand. Her smile was all kindness,—such kindness as he had never seen in her. Her gesture seemed to say: "Peace between us...." He took her hand over the fence, bent over it, and kissed it. She made no attempt to withdraw it. He longed to go down on his knees and say, "I love you.".... They looked at each other in silence. But they offered no explanation. After a moment she removed her hand and turned her head. He turned too to hide his emotion. Then they looked at each other again with untroubled eyes. The sun was setting. Subtle shades of color, violet, orange, and mauve, chased across the cold clear sky. She shivered and drew her shawl closer about her shoulders with a movement that he knew well. He asked:

"How are you?"

She made a little grimace, as if the question were not worth answering. They went on looking at each other and were happy. It was as though they had lost, and had just found each other again....

At last he broke the silence and said:

"I am going away to–morrow."

There was alarm in Sabine's eyes.

"Going away?" she said.

He added quickly:

"Oh! only for two or three weeks."

"Two or three weeks," she said in dismay.

He explained that he was engaged for the concerts, but that when he came back he would not stir all winter.

"Winter," she said. "That is a long time off...."

"Oh! no. It will soon be here."

She saddened and did not look at him.

"When shall we meet again?" she asked a moment later.

He did not understand the question: he had already answered it.

"As soon as I come back: in a fortnight, or three weeks at most."

She still looked dismayed. He tried to tease her:

"It won't be long for you," he said. "You will sleep."

"Yes," said Sabine.

She looked down, she tried to smile: but her eyes trembled.

"Christophe!..." she said suddenly, turning towards him.

There was a note of distress in her voice. She seemed to say:

"Stay! Don't go!..."

He took her hand, looked at her, did not understand the importance she attached to his fortnight's absence: but he was only waiting for a word from her to say:

"I will stay...."

And just as she was going to speak, the front door was opened and Rosa appeared. Sabine withdrew her hand from Christophe's and went hurriedly into her house. At the door she turned and looked at him once more—and disappeared.

* * * * *

Christophe thought he should see her again in the evening. But he was watched by the Vogels, and followed everywhere by his mother: as usual, he was behindhand with his preparations for his journey and could not find time to leave the house for a moment.

Next day he left very early. As he passed Sabine's door he longed to go in, to tap at the window: it hurt him to leave her without saying good–bye: for he had been interrupted by Rosa before he had had time to do so. But he thought she must be asleep and would be cross with him if he woke her up. And then, what could he say to her? It was too late now to abandon his journey: and what if she were to ask him to do so?... He did not admit to himself that he was not averse to exercising his power over her,—if need be, causing her a little pain.... He did not take seriously the grief that his departure brought Sabine: and he thought that his short absence would increase the tenderness which, perhaps, she had for him.

He ran to the station. In spite of everything he was a little remorseful. But as soon as the train had started it was all forgotten. There was youth in his heart. Gaily he saluted the old town with its roofs and towers rosy under the sun: and with the carelessness of those who are departing he said good–bye to those whom he was leaving, and thought no more of them.

The whole time that he was at Duesseldorf and Cologne Sabine never once recurred to his mind. Taken up from morning till night with rehearsals and concerts, dinners and talk, busied with a thousand and one new things and the pride and satisfaction of his success he had no time for recollection. Once only, on the fifth night after he left home, he woke suddenly after a dream and knew that he had been thinking of *her* in his sleep and that the thought of *her* had wakened him up: but he could not remember how he had been thinking of her. He was unhappy and feverish. It was not surprising: he had been playing at a concert that evening, and when he left the hall he had been dragged off to a supper at which he had drunk several glasses of champagne. He could not sleep and got up. He was obsessed by a musical idea. He pretended that it was that which had broken in upon his sleep and he wrote it down. As he read through it he was astonished to see how sad it was. There was no sadness in him when he wrote: at least, so he thought. But he remembered that on other occasions when he had been sad he had only been able to write joyous music, so gay that it offended his mood. He gave no more thought to it. He was used to the surprises of his mind world without ever being able to understand them. He went to sleep at once, and knew no more until the next morning.

He extended his stay by three or four days. It pleased him to prolong it, knowing he could return whenever he liked: he was in no hurry to go home. It was only when he was on the way, in the train, that the thought of Sabine came back to him. He had not written to her. He was even careless enough never to have taken the trouble to ask at the post–office for any letters that might have been written to him. He took a secret delight in his silence: he knew that at home he was expected, that he was loved.... Loved? She had never told him so: he had never told her so. No doubt they knew it and had no need to tell it. And yet there was nothing so precious as the certainty of such an avowal. Why had they waited so long to make it? When they had been on the point of speaking always something—some mischance, shyness, embarrassment,—had hindered them. Why? Why? How much time they had lost!... He longed to hear the dear words from the lips of the beloved. He longed to say them to her: he said them aloud in the empty carriage. As he neared the town he was torn with impatience, a sort of agony.... Faster! Faster! Oh! To think that in an hour he would see her again!...

* * * * *

It was half–past six in the morning when he reached home. Nobody was up yet. Sabine's windows were closed. He went into the yard on tiptoe so that she should not hear him. He chuckled at the thought of taking her by surprise. He went up to his room. His mother was asleep. He washed and brushed his hair without making any noise. He was hungry: but he was afraid of waking Louisa by rummaging in the pantry. He heard footsteps in the yard: he opened his window softly and saw Rosa, first up as usual, beginning to sweep. He called her gently. She started in glad surprise when she saw him: then she looked solemn. He thought she was still offended with him: but for the moment he was in a very good temper. He went down to her.

"Rosa, Rosa," he said gaily, "give me something to eat or I shall eat you! I am dying of hunger!"

Rosa smiled and took him to the kitchen on the ground floor. She poured him out a bowl of milk and then could not refrain from plying him with a string of questions about his travels and his concerts. But although he was quite ready to answer them,—(in the happiness of his return he was almost glad to hear Rosa's chatter once more)—Rosa stopped suddenly in the middle of her cross–examination, her face fell, her eyes turned away, and she became sorrowful. Then her chatter broke out again: but soon it seemed that she thought it out of place and once more she stopped short. And he noticed it then and said:

"What is the matter, Rosa? Are you cross with me?"

She shook her head violently in denial, and turning towards him with her usual suddenness took his arm with both hands:

"Oh! Christophe!..." she said.

He was alarmed. He let his piece of bread fall from his hands.

"What! What is the matter?" he stammered.

She said again:

"Oh! Christophe!... Such an awful thing has happened!"

He thrust away from the table. He stuttered:

"H—here?"

She pointed to the house on the other side of the yard.

He cried:

"Sabine!"

She wept:

"She is dead."

Christophe saw nothing. He got up: he almost fell: he clung to the table, upset the things on it: he wished to cry out. He suffered fearful agony. He turned sick.

Rosa hastened to his side: she was frightened: she held his head and wept.

As soon as he could speak he said;

"It is not true!"

He knew that it was true. But he wanted to deny it, he wanted to pretend that it could not be. When he saw Rosa's face wet with tears he could doubt no more and he sobbed aloud.

Rosa raised her head:

"Christophe!" she said.

He hid his face in his hands. She leaned towards him.

"Christophe!... Mamma is coming!..."

Christophe got up.

"No, no," he said. "She must not see me."

She took his hand and led him, stumbling and blinded by his tears, to a little woodshed which opened on to the yard. She closed the door. They were in darkness. He sat on a block of wood used for chopping sticks. She sat on the fagots. Sounds from without were deadened and distant. There he could weep without fear of being heard. He let himself go and sobbed furiously. Rosa had never seen him weep: she had even thought that he could not weep: she knew only her own girlish tears and such despair in a man filled her with terror and pity. She was filled with a passionate love for Christophe. It was an absolutely unselfish love: an immense need of sacrifice, a maternal self–denial, a hunger to suffer for him, to take his sorrow upon herself. She put her arm round his shoulders.

"Dear Christophe," she said, "do not cry!"

Christophe turned from her.

"I wish to die!"

Rosa clasped her hands.

"Don't say that, Christophe!"

"I wish to die. I cannot ... cannot live now.... What is the good of living?"

"Christophe, dear Christophe! You are not alone. You are loved...."

"What is that to me? I love nothing now. It is nothing to me whether everything else live or die. I love nothing: I loved only her. I loved only her!"

He sobbed louder than ever with his face buried in his hands. Rosa could find nothing to say. The egoism of Christophe's passion stabbed her to the heart. Now when she thought herself most near to him, she felt more isolated and more miserable than ever. Grief instead of bringing them together thrust them only the more widely apart. She wept bitterly.

After some time, Christophe stopped weeping and asked:

"How?... How?..."

Rosa understood.

"She fell ill of influenza on the evening you left. And she was taken suddenly...."

He groaned.

"Dear God!... Why did you not write to me?"

She said:

"I did write. I did not know your address: you did not give us any. I went and asked at the theater. Nobody knew it."

He knew how timid she was, and how much it must have cost her. He asked:

"Did she ... did she tell you to do that?"

She shook her head:

"No. But I thought ..."

He thanked her with a look. Rosa's heart melted.

"My poor ... poor Christophe!" she said.

She flung her arms round his neck and wept. Christophe felt the worth of such pure tenderness. He had so much need of consolation! He kissed her:

"How kind you are," he said. "You loved her too?"

She broke away from him, she threw him a passionate look, did not reply, and began to weep again.

That look was a revelation to him. It meant:

"It was not she whom I loved...."

Christophe saw at last what he had not known—what for months he had not wished to see. He saw that she loved him.

"'Ssh," she said. "They are calling me." They heard Amalia's voice.

Rosa asked:

"Do you want to go back to your room?"

He said:

"No. I could not yet: I could not bear to talk to my mother.... Later on...."

She said:

"Stay here. I will come back soon."

He stayed in the dark woodshed to which only a thread of light penetrated through a small airhole filled with cobwebs. From the street there came up the cry of a hawker, against the wall a horse in a stable next door was snorting and kicking. The revelation that had just come to Christophe gave him no pleasure; but it held his attention for a moment. It made plain many things that he had not understood. A multitude of little things that he had disregarded occurred to him and were explained. He was surprised to find himself thinking of it; he was ashamed to be turned aside even for a moment from his misery. But that misery was so frightful, so irrepressible that the mistrust of self–preservation, stronger than his will, than his courage, than his love, forced him to turn away from it, seized on this new idea, as the suicide drowning seizes in spite of himself on the first object which can help him, not to save himself, but to keep himself for a moment longer above the water. And it was because he was suffering that he was able to feel what another was suffering—suffering through him. He understood the tears that he had brought to her eyes. He was filled with pity for Rosa. He thought how cruel he had been to her—how cruel he must still be. For he did not love her. What good was it for her to love him? Poor girl!... In vain did he tell himself that she was good (she had just proved it). What was her goodness to him? What was her life to him?...

He thought:

"Why is it not she who is dead, and the other who is alive?"

He thought:

"She is alive: she loves me: she can tell me that to–day, to–morrow, all my life: and the other, the woman I love, she is dead and never told me that she loved me: I never have told her that I loved her: I shall never hear her say it: she will never know it...."

And suddenly he remembered that last evening: he remembered that they were just going to talk when Rosa came and prevented it. And he hated Rosa....

The door of the woodshed was opened. Rosa called Christophe softly, and groped towards him. She took his hand. He felt an aversion in her near presence: in vain did he reproach himself for it: it was stronger than himself.

Rosa was silent: her great pity had taught her silence. Christophe was grateful to her for not breaking in upon his grief with useless words. And yet he wished to know ... she was the only creature who could talk to him of *her*. He asked in a whisper:

"When did she..."

(He dared not say: die.)

She replied:

"Last Saturday week."

Dimly he remembered. He said:

"At night?"

Rosa looked at him in astonishment and said:

"Yes. At night. Between two and three."

The sorrowful melody came back to him. He asked, trembling:

"Did she suffer much?"

"No, no. God be thanked, dear Christophe: she hardly suffered at all. She was so weak. She did not struggle against it. Suddenly they saw that she was lost...."

"And she ... did she know it?"

"I don't know. I think ..."

"Did she say anything?"

"No. Nothing. She was sorry for herself like a child."

"You were there?"

"Yes. For the first two days I was there alone, before her brother came."

He pressed her hand in gratitude.

"Thank you."

She felt the blood rush to her heart.

After a silence he said, he murmured the question which was choking him:

"Did she say anything ... for me?"

Rosa shook her head sadly. She would have given much to be able to let him have the answer he expected: she was almost sorry that she could not lie about it. She tried to console him:

"She was not conscious."

"But she did speak?"

"One could not make out what she said. It was in a very low voice."

"Where is the child?"

"Her brother took her away with him to the country."

"And *she*?"

"She is there too. She was taken away last Monday week."

They began to weep again.

Frau Vogel's voice called Rosa once more. Christophe, left alone again, lived through those days of death. A week, already a week ago.... O God! What had become of her? How it had rained that week!... And all that time he was laughing, he was happy!

In his pocket he felt a little parcel wrapped up in soft paper: they were silver buckles that he had brought her for her shoes. He remembered the evening when he had placed his hand on the little stockinged foot. Her little feet: where were they now? How cold they must be!... He thought the memory of that warm contact was the only one that he had of the beloved creature. He had never dared to touch her, to take her in his arms, to hold her to his breast. She was gone forever, and he had never known her. He knew nothing of her, neither soul nor body. He had no memory of her body, of her life, of her love.... Her love?... What proof had he of that?... He had not even a letter, a token,—nothing. Where could he seek to hold her, in himself, or outside himself?... Oh! Nothing! There was nothing left him but the love he had for her, nothing left him but himself.—And in spite of all, his desperate desire to snatch her from destruction, his need of denying death, made him cling to the last piece of wreckage, in an act of blind faith:

"... *he son gia morto: e ben, c'albergo cangi resto in te vivo. C'or mi vedi e piangi, se l'un nell' altro amante si trasforma.*"

"... I am not dead: I have changed my dwelling. I live still in thee who art faithful to me. The soul of the beloved is merged in the soul of the lover."

He had never read these sublime words: but they were in him. Each one of us in turn climbs the Calvary of the age. Each one of us finds anew the agony, each one of us finds anew the desperate hope and folly of the ages. Each one of us follows in the footsteps of those who were, of those before us who struggled with death, denied death—and are dead.

* * * * *

He shut himself up in his room. His shutters were closed all day so as not to see the windows of the house opposite. He avoided the Vogels: they were odious to his sight. He had nothing to reproach them with: they were too honest, and too pious not to have thrust back their feelings in the face of death. They knew Christophe's grief and respected it, whatever they might think of it: they never uttered Sabine's name in his presence. But they had been her enemies when she was alive: that was enough to make him their enemy now that she was dead.

Besides they had not altered their noisy habits: and in spite of the sincere though passing pity that they had felt, it was obvious that at bottom they were untouched by the misfortune—(it was too natural)—perhaps even they were secretly relieved by it. Christophe imagined so at least. Now that the Vogels' intentions with regard to himself were made plain he exaggerated them in his own mind. In reality they attached little importance to him: he set too great store by himself. But he had no doubt that the death of Sabine, by removing the greatest obstacle in the way of his landlords' plans, did seem to them to leave the field clear for Rosa. So he detested her. That they—(the Vogels, Louisa, and even Rosa)—should have tacitly disposed of him, without consulting him, was enough in any case to make him lose all affection for the person whom he was destined to love. He shied whenever he thought an attempt was made upon his umbrageous sense of liberty. But now it was not only a question of himself. The rights which these others had assumed over him did not only infringe upon his own rights but upon those of the dead woman to whom his heart was given. So he defended them doggedly, although no one was for attacking them. He suspected Rosa's goodness. She suffered in seeing him suffer and would often come and knock at his door to console him and talk to him about the other. He did not drive her away: he needed to talk of Sabine with some one who had known her: he wanted to know the smallest of what had happened during her illness. But he was not grateful to Rosa: he attributed ulterior motives to her. Was it not plain that her family, even Amalia, permitted these visits and long colloquies which she would never have allowed if they had not fallen in with her wishes? Was not Rosa in league with her family? He could not believe that her pity was absolutely sincere and free of personal thoughts.

And, no doubt, it was not. Rosa pitied Christophe with all her heart. She tried hard to see Sabine through Christophe's eyes, and through him to love her: she was angry with herself for all the unkind feelings that she had ever had towards her, and asked her pardon in her prayers at night. But could she forget that she was alive, that she was seeing Christophe every moment of the day, that she loved him, that she was no longer afraid of the other, that the other was gone, that her memory would also fade away in its turn, that she was left alone, that one day perhaps ...? In the midst of her sorrow, and the sorrow of her friend more hers than her own, could she repress a glad impulse, an unreasoning hope? For that too she was angry with herself. It was only a flash. It was enough. He saw it. He threw her a glance which froze her heart: she read in it hateful thoughts: he hated her for being alive while the other was dead.

The miller brought his cart for Sabine's little furniture. Coming back from a lesson Christophe saw heaped up before the door in the street the bed, the cupboard, the mattress, the linen, all that she had possessed, all that was left of her. It was a dreadful sight to him. He rushed past it. In the doorway he bumped into Bertold, who stopped him.

"Ah! my dear sir," he said, shaking his hand effusively. "Ah! who would have thought it when we were together? How happy we were! And yet it was because of that day, because of that cursed row on the water, that she fell ill. Oh well. It is no use complaining! She is dead. It will be our turn next. That is life.... And how are you? I'm very well, thank God!"

He was red in the face, sweating, and smelled of wine. The idea that he was her brother, that he had rights in her memory, hurt Christophe. It offended him to hear this man talking of his beloved. The miller on the contrary was glad, to find a friend with whom he could talk of Sabine: he did not understand Christophe's coldness. He had no idea of all the sorrow that his presence, the sudden calling to mind of the day at his farm, the happy memories that he recalled so blunderingly, the poor relics of Sabine, heaped upon the ground, which he kicked as he talked, set stirring in Christophe's soul. He made some excuse for stopping Bertold's tongue. He went up the steps: but the other clung to him, stopped him, and went on with his harangue. At last when the miller took to telling him of Sabine's illness, with that strange pleasure which certain people, and especially the common people, take in talking of illness, with a plethora of painful details, Christophe could bear it no longer—(he took a tight hold of himself so as not to cry out in his sorrow). He cut him short:

"Pardon," he said curtly and icily. "I must leave you."

He left him without another word.

His insensibility revolted the miller. He had guessed the secret affection of his sister and Christophe. And that Christophe should now show such indifference seemed monstrous to him: he thought he had no heart.

Christophe had fled to his room: he was choking. Until the removal was over he never left his room. He vowed that he would never look out of the window, but he could not help doing so: and hiding in a corner behind the curtain he followed the departure of the goods and chattels of the beloved eagerly and with profound sorrow. When he saw them disappearing forever he all but ran down to the street to cry: "No! no! Leave them to me! Do not take them from me!" He longed to beg at least for some little thing, only one little thing, so that she should not be altogether taken from him. But how could he ask such a thing of the miller? It was nothing to him. She herself had not known his love: how dared he then reveal it to another? And besides, if he had tried to say a word he would have burst out crying.... No. No. He had to say nothing, to watch all go, without being able—without daring to save one fragment from the wreck....

And when it was all over, when the house was empty, when the yard gate was closed after the miller, when the wheels of his cart moved on, shaking the windows, when they were out of hearing, he threw himself on the floor—not a tear left in him, not a thought of suffering, of struggling, frozen, and like one dead.

There was a knock at the door. He did not move. Another knock. He had forgotten to lock the door. Rosa came in. She cried out on seeing him stretched on the floor and stopped in terror. He raised his head angrily:

"What? What do you want? Leave me!"

She did not go: she stayed, hesitating, leaning against the floor, and said again:

"Christophe...."

He got up in silence: he was ashamed of having been seen so. He dusted himself with his hand and asked harshly:

"Well. What do you want?"

Rosa said shyly:

"Forgive me ... Christophe ... I came in ... I was bringing you...."

He saw that she had something in her hand.

"See," she said, holding it out to him. "I asked Bertold to give me a little token of her. I thought you would like it...."

It was a little silver mirror, the pocket mirror in which she used to look at herself for hours, not so much from coquetry as from want of occupation. Christophe took it, took also the hand which held it.

"Oh! Rosa!..." he said.

He was filled with her kindness and the knowledge of his own injustice. On a passionate impulse he knelt to her and kissed her hand.

"Forgive ... Forgive ..." he said.

Rosa did not understand at first: then she understood only too well: she blushed, she trembled, she began to weep. She understood that he meant:

"Forgive me if I am unjust.... Forgive me if I do not love you.... Forgive me if I cannot ... if I cannot love you, if I can never love you!..."

She did not withdraw her hand from him: she knew that it was not herself that he was kissing. And with his cheek against Rosa's hand, he wept hot tears, knowing that she was reading through him: there was sorrow and bitterness in being unable to love her and making her suffer.

They stayed so, both weeping, in the dim light of the room.

At last she withdrew her hand. He went on murmuring;

"Forgive!..."

She laid her hand gently on his hand. He rose to his feet. They kissed in silence: they felt on their lips the bitter savor of their tears.

"We shall always be friends," he said softly. She bowed her head and left him, too sad to speak.

They thought that the world is ill made. The lover is unloved. The beloved does not love. The lover who is loved is sooner or later torn from his love.... There is suffering. There is the bringing of suffering. And the most wretched is not always the one who suffers.

* * * * *

Once more Christophe took to avoiding the house. He could not bear it. He could not bear to see the curtainless windows, the empty rooms.

A worse sorrow awaited him. Old Euler lost no time in reletting the ground floor. One day Christophe saw strange faces in Sabine's room. New lives blotted out the traces of the life that was gone.

It became impossible for him to stay in his rooms. He passed whole days outside, not coming back until nightfall, when it was too dark to see anything. Once more he took to making expeditions in the country. Irresistibly he was drawn to Bertold's farm. But he never went in, dared not go near it, wandered about it at a distance. He discovered a place on a hill from which he could see the house, the plain, the river: it was thither that his steps usually turned. From thence he could follow with his eyes the meanderings of the water down to the willow clump under which he had seen the shadow of death pass across Sabine's face. From thence he could pick out the two windows of the rooms in which they had waited, side by side, so near, so far, separated by a door—the door to eternity. From thence he could survey the cemetery. He had never been able to bring himself to enter it: from childhood he had had a horror of those fields of decay and corruption, and refused to think of those whom he loved in connection with them. But from a distance and seen from above, the little graveyard never looked grim, it was calm, it slept with the sun.... Sleep!... She loved to sleep! Nothing would disturb her there. The crowing cocks answered each other across the plains. From the homestead rose the roaring of the mill, the clucking of the poultry yard, the cries of children playing. He could make out Sabine's little girl, he could see her running, he could mark her laughter. Once he lay in wait for her near the gate of the farmyard, in a turn of the sunk road made by the walls: he seized her as she passed and kissed her. The child was afraid and began, to cry. She had almost forgotten him already. He asked her:

"Are you happy here?"

"Yes. It is fun...."

"You don't want to come back?"

"No!"

He let her go. The child's indifference plunged him in sorrow. Poor Sabine!... And yet it was she, something of her.... So little! The child was hardly at all like her mother: had lived in her, but was not she: in that mysterious passage through her being the child had hardly retained more than the faintest perfume of the creature who was gone: inflections of her voice, a pursing of the lips, a trick of bending the head. The rest of her was another being altogether: and that being mingled with the being of Sabine was repulsive to Christophe though he never admitted it to himself.

It was only in himself that Christophe could find the image of Sabine. It followed him everywhere, hovering above him; but he only felt himself really to be with her when he was alone. Nowhere was she nearer to him than in this refuge, on the hill, far from strange eyes, in the midst of the country that was so full of the memory of her. He would go miles to it, climbing at a run, his heart beating as though he were going to a meeting with her: and so it was indeed. When he reached it he would lie on the ground—the same earth in which *her* body was laid: he would close his eyes: and *she* would come to him. He could not see her face: he could not hear her voice; he had no need: she entered into him, held him, he possessed her utterly. In this state of passionate hallucination he would lose the power of thought, he would be unconscious of what was happening: he was unconscious of everything save that he was with her.

That state of things did not last long.—To tell the truth he was only once altogether sincere. From the day following, his will had its share in the proceedings. And from that time on Christophe tried in vain to bring it back to life. It was only then that he thought of evoking in himself the face and form of Sabine: until then he had never thought of it. He succeeded spasmodically and he was fired by it. But it was only at the cost of hours of waiting and of darkness.

"Poor Sabine!" he would think. "They have all forgotten you. There is only I who love you, who keep your memory alive forever. Oh, my treasure, my precious! I have you, I hold you, I will never let you go!..."

He spoke these words because already she was escaping him: she was slipping from his thoughts like water through his fingers. He would return again and again, faithful to the tryst. He wished to think of her and he would close his eyes. But after half an hour, or an hour, or sometimes two hours, he would begin to see that he had been thinking of nothing. The sounds of the valley, the roar of the wind, the little bells of the two goats browsing on the hill, the noise of the wind in the little slender trees under which he lay, were sucked up by his thoughts soft and porous like a sponge. He was angry with his thoughts: they tried to obey him, and to fix the vanished image to which he was striving to attach his life: but his thoughts fell back weary and chastened and once more with a sigh of comfort abandoned themselves to the listless stream of sensations.

He shook off his torpor. He strode through the country hither and thither seeking Sabine. He sought her in the mirror that once had held her smile. He sought her by the river bank where her hands had dipped in the water. But the mirror and the water gave him only the reflection of himself. The excitement of walking, the fresh air, the beating of his own healthy blood awoke music in him once more. He wished to find change.

"Oh! Sabine!..." he sighed.

He dedicated his songs to her: he strove to call her to life in his music, his love, and his sorrow.... In vain: love and sorrow came to life surely: but poor Sabine had no share in them. Love and sorrow looked towards the future, not towards the past. Christophe was powerless against his youth. The sap of life swelled up again in him with new vigor. His grief, his regrets, his chaste and ardent love, his baffled desires, heightened the fever that was in him. In spite of his sorrow, his heart beat in lively, sturdy rhythm: wild songs leaped forth in mad, intoxicated strains: everything in him hymned life and even sadness took on a festival shape. Christophe was too frank to persist in self–deception: and he despised himself. But life swept him headlong: and in his sadness, with death in his heart, and life in all his limbs, he abandoned himself to the forces newborn in him, to the absurd, delicious joy of living, which grief, pity, despair, the aching wound of an irreparable loss, all the torment of death, can only sharpen and kindle into being in the strong, as they rowel their sides with furious spur.

And Christophe knew that, in himself, in the secret hidden depths of his soul, he had an inaccessible and inviolable sanctuary where lay the shadow of Sabine. That the flood of life could not bear away.... Each of us bears in his soul as it were a little graveyard of those whom he has loved. They sleep there, through the years, untroubled. But a day cometh,—this we know,—when the graves shall reopen. The dead issue from the tomb and smile with their pale lips—loving, always—on the beloved, and the lover, in whose breast their memory dwells, like the child sleeping in the mother's womb.

III. ADA

After the wet summer the autumn was radiant. In the orchards the trees were weighed down with fruit The red apples shone like billiard balls. Already some of the trees were taking on their brilliant garb of the falling year: flame color, fruit color, color of ripe melon, of oranges and lemons, of good cooking, and fried dishes. Misty lights glowed through the woods: and from the meadows there rose the little pink flames of the saffron.

He was going down a hill. It was a Sunday afternoon. He was striding, almost running, gaining speed down the slope. He was singing a phrase, the rhythm of which had been obsessing him all through his walk. He was red, disheveled: he was walking, swinging his arms, and rolling his eyes like a madman, when as he turned a bend in the road he came suddenly on a fair girl perched on a wall tugging with all her might at a branch of a tree from which she was greedily plucking and eating purple plums. Their astonishment was mutual. She looked at him, stared, with her mouth full. Then she burst out laughing. So did he. She was good to see, with her round face framed in fair curly hair, which was like a sunlit cloud about her, her full pink cheeks, her wide blue eyes, her rather large nose, impertinently turned up, her little red mouth showing white teeth—the canine little, strong, and projecting—her plump chin, and her full figure, large and plump, well built, solidly put together. He called out:

"Good eating!" And was for going on his road. But she called to him:

"Sir! Sir! Will you be very nice? Help me to get down. I can't...."

He returned and asked her how she had climbed up.

"With my hands and feet.... It is easy enough to get up...."

"Especially when there are tempting plums hanging above your head...."

"Yes.... But when you have eaten your courage goes. You can't find the way to get down."

He looked at her on her perch. He said:

"You are all right there. Stay there quietly. I'll come and see you to–morrow. Good–night!"

But he did not budge, and stood beneath her. She pretended to be afraid, and begged him with little glances not to leave her. They stayed looking at each other and laughing. She showed him the branch to which she was clinging and asked:

"Would you like some?"

Respect for property had not developed in Christophe since the days of his expeditions with Otto: he accepted without hesitation. She amused herself with pelting him with plums. When he had eaten she said:

"Now!..."

He took a wicked pleasure in keeping her waiting. She grew impatient on her wall. At last he said:

"Come, then!" and held his hand up to her.

But just as she was about to jump down she thought a moment.

"Wait! We must make provision first!"

She gathered the finest plums within reach and filled the front of her blouse with them.

"Carefully! Don't crush them!"

He felt almost inclined to do so.

She lowered herself from the wall and jumped into his arms. Although he was sturdy he bent under her weight and all but dragged her down. They were of the same height. Their faces came together. He kissed her lips, moist and sweet with the juice of the plums: and she returned his kiss without more ceremony.

"Where are you going?" he asked.

"I don't know."

"Are you out alone?"

"No. I am with friends. But I have lost them.... Hi! Hi!" she called suddenly as loudly as she could.

No answer.

She did not bother about it any more. They began to walk, at random, following their noses.

"And you ... where are you going?" said she.

"I don't know, either."

"Good. We'll go together."

She took some plums from her gaping blouse and began to munch them.

"You'll make yourself sick," he said.

"Not I! I've been eating them all day."

Through the gap in her blouse he saw the white of her chemise.

"They are all warm now," she said.

"Let me see!"

She held him one and laughed. He ate it. She watched him out of the corner of her eye as she sucked at the fruit like a child. He did not know how the adventure would end. It is probable that she at least had some suspicion. She waited.

"Hi! Hi!" Voices in the woods.

"Hi! Hi!" she answered. "Ah! There they are!" she said to Christophe. "Not a bad thing, either!"

But on the contrary she was thinking that it was rather a pity. But speech was not given to woman for her to say what she is thinking.... Thank God! for there would be an end of morality on earth....

The voices came near. Her friends were near the road. She leaped the ditch, climbed the hedge, and hid behind the trees. He watched her in amazement. She signed to him imperiously to come to her. He followed her. She plunged into the depths of the wood.

"Hi! Hi!" she called once more when they had gone some distance. "You see, they must look for me!" she explained to Christophe.

Her friends had stopped on the road and were listening for her voice to mark where it came from. They answered her and in their turn entered the woods. But she did not wait for them. She turned about on right and on left. They bawled loudly after her. She let them, and then went and called in the opposite direction. At last they wearied of it, and, making sure that the best way of making her come was to give up seeking her, they called:

"Good–bye!" and went off singing.

She was furious that they should not have bothered about her any more than that. She had tried to be rid of them: but she had not counted on their going off so easily. Christophe looked rather foolish: this game of hide–and–seek with a girl whom he did not know did not exactly enthrall him: and he had no thought of taking advantage of their solitude. Nor did she think of it: in her annoyance she forgot Christophe.

"Oh! It's too much," she said, thumping her hands together. "They have left me."

"But," said Christophe, "you wanted them to."

"Not at all."

"You ran away."

"If I ran away from them that is my affair, not theirs. They ought to look for me. What if I were lost?..."

Already she was beginning to be sorry for herself because if what might have happened if ... if the opposite of what actually had occurred had come about.

"Oh!" she said. "I'll shake them!" She turned back and strode off.

As she went she remembered Christophe and looked at him once more.—But it was too late. She began to laugh. The little demon which had been in her the moment before was

280

gone. While she was waiting for another to come she saw Christophe with the eyes of indifference. And then, she was hungry. Her stomach was reminding her that it was supper–time: she was in a hurry to rejoin her friends at the inn. She took Christophe's arm, leaned on it with all her weight, groaned, and said that she was exhausted. That did not keep her from dragging Christophe down a slope, running, and shouting, and laughing like a mad thing.

They talked. She learned who he was: she did not know his name, and seemed not to be greatly impressed by his title of musician. He learned that she was a shop–girl from a dress–maker's in the *Kaiserstrasse* (the most fashionable street in the town): her name was Adelheid—to friends, Ada. Her companions on the excursion were one of her friends, who worked at the same place as herself, and two nice young men, a clerk at Weiller's bank, and a clerk from a big linen–draper's. They were turning their Sunday to account: they had decided to dine at the Brochet inn, from which there is a fine view over the Rhine, and then to return by boat.

The others had already established themselves at the inn when they arrived. Ada made a scene with her friends: she complained of their cowardly desertion and presented Christophe as her savior. They did not listen to her complaints: but they knew Christophe, the bank–clerk by reputation, the clerk from having heard some of his compositions—(he thought it a good idea to hum an air from one of them immediately afterwards)—and the respect which they showed him made an impression on Ada, the more so as Myrrha, the other young woman—(her real name was Hansi or Johanna)—a brunette with blinking eyes, bumpy forehead, hair screwed back, Chinese face, a little too animated, but clever and not without charm, in spite of her goat–like head and her oily golden–yellow complexion,—at once began to make advances to their *Hof Musicus*. They begged him to be so good as to honor their repast with his presence.

Never had he been in such high feather: for he was overwhelmed with attentions, and the two women, like good friends as they were, tried each to rob the other of him. Both courted him: Myrrha with ceremonious manners, sly looks, as she rubbed her leg against his under the table—Ada, openly making play with her fine eyes, her pretty mouth, and all the seductive resources at her command. Such coquetry in its almost coarseness incommoded and distressed Christophe. These two bold young women were a change from the unkindly faces he was accustomed to at home. Myrrha interested him, he guessed her to be more intelligent than Ada: but her obsequious manners and her ambiguous smile were curiously attractive and repulsive to him at the same time. She could do nothing against Ada's radiance of life and pleasure: and she was aware of it. When she saw that she had lost the bout, she abandoned the effort, turned in upon herself, went on smiling, and patiently waited for her day to come. Ada, seeing herself mistress of the field, did not seek to push forward the advantage she had gained: what she had done had been mainly to despite her friend: she had succeeded, she was satisfied. But she had been caught in her own game. She felt as she looked into Christophe's eyes the passion that she had kindled in him: and that same passion began to awake in her. She was silent: she left her vulgar teasing: they looked at each other in silence: on their lips they had the savor of their kiss. From time to time by fits and starts they joined vociferously in the jokes of the others: then they relapsed into silence, stealing glances at each other. At last they did not even look at each other, as though they were afraid of betraying themselves. Absorbed in themselves they brooded over their desire.

When the meal was over they got ready to go. They had to go a mile and a half through the woods to reach the pier. Ada got up first: Christophe followed her. They waited on the steps until the others were ready: without speaking, side by side, in the thick mist that was hardly at all lit up by the single lamp hanging by the inn door.—Myrrha was dawdling by the mirror.

Ada took Christophe's hand and led him along the house towards the garden into the darkness. Under a balcony from which hung a curtain of vines they hid. All about them was dense darkness. They could not even see each other. The wind stirred the tops of the pines. He felt Ada's warm fingers entwined in his and the sweet scent of a heliotrope flower that she had at her breast.

Suddenly she dragged him to her: Christophe's lips found Ada's hair, wet with the mist, and kissed her eyes, her eyebrows, her nose, her cheeks, the corners of her mouth, seeking her lips, and finding them, staying pressed to them.

The others had gone. They called:

"Ada!..."

They did not stir, they hardly breathed, pressed close to each other, lips and bodies.

They heard Myrrha:

"They have gone on."

The footsteps of their companions died away in the night. They held each other closer, in silence, stifling on their lips a passionate murmuring.

In the distance a village clock rang out. They broke apart. They had to run to the pier. Without a word they set out, arms and hands entwined, keeping step—a little quick, firm step, like hers. The road was deserted: no creature was abroad: they could not see ten yards ahead of them: they went, serene and sure, into the beloved night. They never stumbled over the pebbles on the road. As they were late they took a short cut. The path led for some way down through vines and then began to ascend and wind up the side of the hill. Through the mist they could hear the roar of the river and the heavy paddles of the steamer approaching. They left the road and ran across the fields. At last they found themselves on the bank of the Rhine but still far from the pier. Their serenity was not disturbed. Ada had forgotten her fatigue of the evening. It seemed to them that they could have walked all night like that, on the silent grass, in the hovering mists, that grew wetter and more dense along the river that was wrapped in a whiteness as of the moon. The steamer's siren hooted: the invisible monster plunged heavily away and away. They said, laughing:

"We will take the next."

By the edge of the river soft lapping waves broke at their feet. At the landing stage they were told:

"The last boat has just gone."

Christophe's heart thumped. Ada's hand grasped his arm more tightly.

"But," she said, "there will be another one to–morrow."

A few yards away in a halo of mist was the flickering light of a lamp hung on a post on a terrace by the river. A little farther on were a few lighted windows—a little inn.

They went into the tiny garden. The sand ground under their feet. They groped their way to the steps. When they entered, the lights were being put out. Ada, on Christophe's arm, asked for a room. The room to which they were led opened on to the little garden. Christophe leaned out of the window and saw the phosphorescent flow of the river, and the shade of the lamp on the glass of which were crushed mosquitoes with large wings. The door was closed. Ada was standing by the bed and smiling. He dared not look at her. She did not look at him: but through her lashes she followed Christophe's every movement. The floor creaked with every step. They could hear the least noise in the house. They sat on the bed and embraced in silence.

* * * * *

The flickering light of the garden is dead. All is dead.... Night.... The abyss.... Neither light nor consciousness.... Being. The obscure, devouring forces of Being. Joy all–powerful. Joy rending. Joy which sucks down the human creature as the void a stone. The sprout of desire sucking up thought. The absurd delicious law of the blind intoxicated worlds which roll at night....

... A night which is many nights, hours that are centuries, records which are death.... Dreams shared, words spoken with eyes closed, tears and laughter, the happiness of loving in the voice, of sharing the nothingness of sleep, the swiftly passing images flouting in the brain, the hallucinations of the roaring night.... The Rhine laps in a little creek by the house; in the distance his waters over the dams and breakwaters make a sound as of a gentle rain falling on sand. The hull of the boat cracks and groans under the weight of water. The chain by which it is tied sags and grows taut with a rusty clattering. The voice of the river rises: it fills the room. The bed is like a boat. They are swept along side by side by a giddy current—hung in mid–air like a soaring bird. The night grows ever more dark, the void more empty. Ada weeps, Christophe loses consciousness: both are swept down under the flowing waters of the night....

Night.... Death.... Why wake to life again?...

The light of the dawning day peeps through the dripping panes. The spark of life glows once more in their languorous bodies. He awakes, Ada's eyes are looking at him. A whole life passes in a few moments: days of sin, greatness, and peace....

284

"Where am I? And am I two? Do I still exist? I am no longer conscious of being. All about me is the infinite: I have the soul of a statue, with large tranquil eyes, filled with Olympian peace...."

They fall back into the world of sleep. And the familiar sounds of the dawn, the distant bells, a passing boat, oars dripping water, footsteps on the road, all caress without disturbing their happy sleep, reminding them that they are alive, and making them delight in the savor of their happiness....

* * * * *

The puffing of the steamer outside the window brought Christophe from his torpor. They had agreed to leave at seven so as to return to the town in time for their usual occupations. He whispered:

"Do you hear?"

She did not open her eyes; she smiled, she put out her lips, she tried to kiss him and then let her head fall back on his shoulder.... Through the window panes he saw the funnel of the steamer slip by against the sky, he saw the empty deck, and clouds of smoke. Once more he slipped into dreaminess....

An hour passed without his knowing it. He heard it strike and started in astonishment.

"Ada!..." he whispered to the girl. "Ada!" he said again. "It's eight o'clock."

Her eyes were still closed: she frowned and pouted pettishly.

"Oh! let me sleep!" she said.

She sighed wearily and turned her back on him and went to sleep once more.

He began to dream. His blood ran bravely, calmly through him. His limpid senses received the smallest impressions simply and freshly. He rejoiced in his strength and youth. Unwittingly he was proud of being a man. He smiled in his happiness, and felt himself alone: alone as he had always been, more lonely even but without sadness, in a divine solitude. No more fever. "No more shadows. Nature could freely cast her reflection upon his soul in its serenity. Lying on his back, facing the window, his eyes gazing deep into the dazzling air with its luminous mists, he smiled:

"How good it is to live!..."

To live!... A boat passed.... The thought suddenly of those who were no longer alive, of a boat gone by on which they were together: he—she.... She?... Not that one, sleeping by his side.—She, the only she, the beloved, the poor little woman who was dead.—But is it that one? How came she there? How did they come to this room? He looks at her, he does not know her: she is a stranger to him: yesterday morning she did not exist for him. What does he know of her?—He knows that she is not clever. He knows that she is not good. He knows that she is not even beautiful with her face spiritless and bloated with sleep, her low forehead, her mouth open in breathing, her swollen dried lips pouting like a fish. He knows that he does not love her. And he is filled with a bitter sorrow when he thinks that he kissed those strange lips, in the first moment with her, that he has taken this beautiful body for which he cares nothing on the first night of their meeting,—and that she whom he loved, he watched her live and die by his side and never dared touch her hair with his lips, that he will never know the perfume of her being. Nothing more. All is crumbled away. The earth has taken all from him. And he never defended what was his....

And while he leaned over the innocent sleeper and scanned her face, and looked at her with eyes of unkindness, she felt his eyes upon her. Uneasy under his scrutiny she made a great effort to raise her heavy lids and to smile: and she said, stammering a little like a waking child:

"Don't look at me. I'm ugly...."

She fell back at once, weighed down with sleep, smiled once more, murmured.

"Oh! I'm so ... so sleepy!..." and went off again into her dreams.

He could not help laughing: he kissed her childish lips more tenderly. He watched the girl sleeping for a moment longer, and got up quietly. She gave a comfortable sigh when he was gone. He tried not to wake her as he dressed, though there was no danger of that: and when he had done he sat in the chair near the window and watched the steaming smoking river which looked as though it were covered with ice: and he fell into a brown study in which there hovered music, pastoral, melancholy.

From time to time she half opened her eyes and looked at him vaguely, took a second or two, smiled at him, and passed from one sleep to another. She asked him the time.

"A quarter to nine."

Half asleep she pondered:

"What! Can it be a quarter to nine?"

At half–past nine she stretched, sighed, and said that she was going to get up.

It was ten o'clock before she stirred. She was petulant.

"Striking again!... The clock is fast!..." He laughed and went and sat on the bed by her side. She put her arms round his neck and told him her dreams. He did not listen very attentively and interrupted her with little love words. But she made him be silent and went on very seriously, as though she were telling something of the highest importance:

"She was at dinner: the Grand Duke was there: Myrrha was a Newfoundland dog.... No, a frizzy sheep who waited at table.... Ada had discovered a method of rising from the earth, of walking, dancing, and lying down in the air. You see it was quite simple: you had only to do ... thus ... thus ... and it was done...."

Christophe laughed at her. She laughed too, though a little ruffled at his laughing. She shrugged her shoulders.

"Ah! you don't understand!..."

They breakfasted on the bed from the same cup, with the same spoon.

At last she got up: she threw off the bedclothes and slipped down from the bed. Then she sat down to recover her breath and looked at her feet. Finally she clapped her hands and told him to go out: and as he was in no hurry about it she took him by the shoulders and thrust him out of the door and then locked it.

After she had dawdled, looked over and stretched each of her handsome limbs, she sang, as she washed, a sentimental *Lied* in fourteen couplets, threw water at Christophe's face—he was outside drumming on the window—and as they left she plucked the last rose in the garden and then they took the steamer. The mist was not yet gone: but the sun shone through it: they floated through a creamy light. Ada sat at the stern with Christophe: she was sleepy and a little sulky: she grumbled about the light in her eyes, and said that she would have a headache all day. And as Christophe did not take her complaints seriously enough she returned into morose silence. Her eyes were hardly opened and in them was the funny gravity of children who have just woke up. But at the next landing–stage an elegant lady came and sat not far from her, and she grew lively at once: she talked eagerly to Christophe about things sentimental and distinguished. She had resumed with him the ceremonious *Sie*.

Christophe was thinking about what she could say to her employer by way of excuse for her lateness. She was hardly at all concerned about it.

"Bah! It's not the first time."

"The first time that ... what?"

"That I have been late," she said, put out by the question.

He dared not ask her what had caused her lateness.

"What will you tell her?"

"That my mother is ill, dead ... how do I know?"

He was hurt by her talking so lightly.

"I don't want you to lie."

She took offense:

"First of all, I never lie.... And then, I cannot very well tell her...."

He asked her half in jest, half in earnest:

"Why not?"

She laughed, shrugged, and said that he was coarse and ill–bred, and that she had already asked him not to use the *Du* to her.

"Haven't I the right?"

"Certainly not."

"After what has happened?"

"Nothing has happened."

She looked at him a little defiantly and laughed: and although she was joking, he felt most strongly that it would not have cost her much to say it seriously and almost to believe it. But some pleasant memory tickled her: for she burst out laughing and looked at Christophe and kissed him loudly without any concern for the people about, who did not seem to be in the least surprised by it.

＊ ＊ ＊ ＊ ＊

Now on all his excursions he was accompanied by shop–girls and clerks: he did not like their vulgarity, and used to try to lose them: but Ada out of contrariness was no longer disposed for wandering in the woods. When it rained or for some other reason they did not leave the town he would take her to the theater, or the museum, or the *Thiergarten*: for she insisted on being seen with him. She even wanted him to go to church with her; but he was so absurdly sincere that he would not set foot inside a church since he had lost his belief—(on some other excuse he had resigned his position as organist)—and at the same time, unknown to himself, remained much too religious not to think Ada's proposal sacrilegious.

He used to go to her rooms in the evening. Myrrha would be there, for she lived in the same house. Myrrha was not at all resentful against him: she would hold out her soft hand, caressingly, and talk of trivial and improper things and then dip away discreetly. The two women had never seemed to be such friends as since they had had small reason for being so: they were always together. Ada had no secrets from Myrrha: she told her everything: Myrrha listened to everything: they seemed to be equally pleased with it all.

Christophe was ill at ease in the company of the two women. Their friendship, their strange conversations, their freedom of manner, the crude way in which Myrrha especially viewed and spoke of things—(not so much in his presence, however, as when he was not there, but Ada used to repeat her sayings to him)—their indiscreet and impertinent curiosity, which was forever turned upon subjects that were silly or basely sensual, the whole equivocal and rather animal atmosphere oppressed him terribly, though it interested him: for he knew nothing like it. He was at sea in the conversations of the two little beasts, who talked of dress, and made silly jokes, and laughed in an inept way with their eyes shining with delight when they were off on the track of some spicy story. He was more at ease when Myrrha left them. When the two women were together it was like being in a foreign country without knowing the language. It was impossible to make himself understood: they did not even listen: they poked fun at the foreigner.

When he was alone with Ada they went on speaking different languages: but at least they did make some attempt to understand each other. To tell the truth, the more he understood her, the less he understood her. She was the first woman he had known. For if poor Sabine was a woman he had known, he had known nothing of her: she had always remained for him a phantom of his heart. Ada took upon herself to make him make up for lost time. In his turn he tried to solve the riddle of woman; an enigma which perhaps is no enigma except for those who seek some meaning in it.

Ada was without intelligence: that was the least of her faults. Christophe would have commended her for it, if she had approved it herself. But although she was occupied only with stupidities, she claimed to have some knowledge of the things of the spirit: and she judged everything with complete assurance. She would talk about music, and explain to Christophe things which he knew perfectly, and would pronounce absolute judgment and sentence. It was useless to try to convince her she had pretensions and susceptibilities in everything; she gave herself airs, she was obstinate, vain: she would not—she could not understand anything. Why would she not accept that she could understand nothing? He loved her so much better when she was content with being just what she was, simply, with her own qualities and failings, instead of trying to impose on others and herself!

In fact, she was little concerned with thought. She was concerned with eating, drinking, singing, dancing, crying, laughing, sleeping: she wanted to be happy: and that would have been all right if she had succeeded. But although she had every gift for it: she was greedy, lazy, sensual, and frankly egoistic in a way that revolted and amused Christophe: although she had almost all the vices which make life pleasant for their fortunate possessor, if not for their friends—(and even then does not a happy face, at least if it be pretty, shed happiness on all those who come near it?)—in spite of so many reasons for being satisfied with life and herself Ada was not even clever enough for that. The pretty, robust girl, fresh, hearty, healthy–looking, endowed with abundant spirits and fierce appetites, was anxious about her health. She bemoaned her weakness, while she ate enough for four. She was always sorry for herself: she could not drag herself along, she could not breathe, she had a headache, feet–ache, her eyes ached, her stomach ached, her soul ached. She was afraid of everything, and madly superstitious, and saw omens everywhere: at meals the crossing of knives and forks, the number of the guests, the upsetting of a salt–cellar: then there must be a whole ritual to turn aside misfortune. Out walking she would count the crows, and never failed to watch which side they flew to: she would anxiously watch the road at her feet, and when a spider crossed her path in the morning she would cry out aloud: then she would wish to go home and there would be no other means of not interrupting the walk than to persuade her that it was after twelve, and so the omen was one of hope rather than of evil. She was afraid of her dreams: she would recount them at length to Christophe; for hours she would try to recollect some detail that she had forgotten; she never spared him one; absurdities piled one on the other, strange marriages, deaths, dressmakers' prices, burlesque, and sometimes, obscene things. He had to listen to her and give her his advice. Often she would be for a whole day under the obsession of her inept fancies. She would find life ill–ordered, she would see things and people rawly and overwhelm Christophe with her jeremiads; and it seemed hardly worth while to have broken away from the gloomy middle–class people with whom he lived to find once more the eternal enemy: the *"trauriger ungriechischer Hypochondrist."*

But suddenly in the midst of her sulks and grumblings, she would become gay, noisy, exaggerated: there was no more dealing with her gaiety than with her moroseness: she would burst out laughing for no reason and seem as though she were never going to stop: she would rush across the fields, play mad tricks and childish pranks, take a delight in doing silly things, in mixing with the earth, and dirty things, and the beasts, and the spiders, and worms, in teasing them, and hurting them, and making them eat each other: the cats eat the birds, the fowls the worms, the ants the spiders, not from any wickedness, or perhaps from an altogether unconscious instinct for evil, from curiosity, or from having nothing better to do. She seemed to be driven always to say stupid things, to repeat senseless words again and again, to irritate Christophe, to exasperate him, set his nerves on edge, and make him almost beside himself. And her coquetry as soon as anybody—no matter who—appeared on the road!... Then she would talk excitedly, laugh noisily, make faces, draw attention to herself: she would assume an affected mincing gait. Christophe would have a horrible presentiment that she was going to plunge into serious discussion.—And, indeed, she would do so. She would become sentimental, uncontrolledly, just as she did everything: she would unbosom herself in a loud voice. Christophe would suffer and long to beat her. Least of all could he forgive her her lack of sincerity. He did not yet know that sincerity is a gift as rare as intelligence or beauty and that it cannot justly be expected of everybody. He could not bear a lie: and Ada gave him lies in full measure. She was always lying, quite calmly, in spite of evidence to the contrary. She had that astounding faculty for forgetting what is displeasing to them—or even what has been pleasing to them—which those women possess who live from moment to moment.

And, in spite of everything, they loved each other with all their hearts. Ada was as sincere as Christophe in her love. Their love was none the less true for not being based on intellectual sympathy: it had nothing in common with base passion. It was the beautiful love of youth: it was sensual, but not vulgar, because it was altogether youthful: it was naive, almost chaste, purged by the ingenuous ardor of pleasure. Although Ada was not, by a long way, so ignorant as Christophe, yet she had still the divine privilege of youth of soul and body, that freshness of the senses, limpid and vivid as a running stream, which almost gives the illusion of purity and through life is never replaced. Egoistic, commonplace, insincere in her ordinary life,—love made her simple, true, almost good: she understood in love the joy that is to be found in self–forgetfulness. Christophe saw this with delight: and he would gladly have died for her. Who can tell all the absurd and touching illusions that a loving heart brings to its love! And the natural illusion of the lover was magnified an hundredfold in Christophe by the power of illusion which is born in the artist. Ada's smile held profound meanings for him: an affectionate word was the proof of the goodness of her heart. He loved in her all that is good and beautiful in the universe. He called her his own, his soul, his life. They wept together over their love.

Pleasure was not the only bond between them: there was an indefinable poetry of memories and dreams,—their own? or those of the men and women who had loved before them, who had been before them,—in them?... Without a word, perhaps without knowing it, they preserved the fascination of the first moments of their meeting in the woods, the first days, the first nights together: those hours of sleep in each other's arms, still, unthinking, sinking down into a flood of love and silent joy. Swift fancies, visions, dumb thoughts, titillating, and making them go pale, and their hearts sink under their desire, bringing all about them a buzzing as of bees. A fine light, and tender.... Their hearts sink and beat no more, borne down in excess of sweetness. Silence, languor, and fever, the mysterious weary smile of the earth quivering under the first sunlight of spring.... So fresh a love in two young creatures is like an April morning. Like April it must pass. Youth of the heart is like an early feast of sunshine.

* * * * *

Nothing could have brought Christophe closer to Ada in his love than the way in which he was judged by others.

The day after their first meeting it was known all over the town. Ada made no attempt to cover up the adventure, and rather plumed herself on her conquest. Christophe would have liked more discretion: but he felt that the curiosity of the people was upon him: and as he did not wish to seem to fly from it, he threw in his lot with Ada. The little town buzzed with tattle. Christophe's colleagues in the orchestra paid him sly compliments to which he did not reply, because he would not allow any meddling with his affairs. The respectable people of the town judged his conduct very severely. He lost his music lessons with certain families. With others, the mothers thought that they must now be present at the daughters' lessons, watching with suspicious eyes, as though Christophe were intending to carry off the precious darlings. The young ladies were supposed to know nothing. Naturally they knew everything: and while they were cold towards Christophe for his lack of taste, they were longing to have further details. It was only among the small tradespeople, and the shop people, that Christophe was popular: but not for long: he was just as annoyed by their approval as by the condemnation of the rest: and being unable to do anything against that condemnation, he took steps not to keep their approval: there was no difficulty about that. He was furious with the general indiscretion.

The most indignant of all with him were Justus Euler and the Vogels. They took Christophe's misconduct as a personal outrage. They had not made any serious plans concerning him: they distrusted—especially Frau Vogel—these artistic temperaments. But as they were naturally discontented and always inclined to think themselves persecuted by fate, they persuaded themselves that they had counted on the marriage of Christophe and Rosa; as soon as they were quite certain that such a marriage would never come to pass, they saw in it the mark of the usual ill luck. Logically, if fate were responsible for their miscalculation, Christophe could not be: but the Vogels' logic was that which gave them the greatest opportunity for finding reasons for being sorry for themselves. So they decided that if Christophe had misconducted himself it was not so much for his own pleasure as to give offense to them. They were scandalized. Very religious, moral, and oozing domestic virtue, they were of those to whom the sins of the flesh are the most shameful, the most serious, almost the only sins, because they are the only dreadful sins—(it is obvious that respectable people are never likely to be tempted to steal or murder).—And so Christophe seemed to them absolutely wicked, and they changed their demeanor towards him. They were icy towards him and turned away as they passed him. Christophe, who was in no particular need of their conversation, shrugged his shoulders at all the fuss. He pretended not to notice Amalia's insolence: who, while she affected contemptuously to avoid him, did all that she could to make him fall in with her so that she might tell him all that was rankling in her.

Christophe was only touched by Rosa's attitude. The girl condemned him more harshly even than his family. Not that this new love of Christophe's seemed to her to destroy her last chances of being loved by him: she knew that she had no chance left—(although perhaps she went on hoping: she always hoped).—But she had made an idol of Christophe: and that idol had crumbled away. It was the worst sorrow for her ... yes, a sorrow more cruel to the innocence and honesty of her heart, than being disdained and forgotten by him. Brought up puritanically, with a narrow code of morality, in which she believed passionately, what she had heard about Christophe had not only brought her to despair but had broken her heart. She had suffered already when he was in love with Sabine: she had begun then to lose some of her illusions about her hero. That Christophe could love so commonplace a creature seemed to her inexplicable and inglorious. But at least that love was pure, and Sabine was not unworthy of it. And in the end death had passed over it and sanctified it.... But that at once Christophe should love another woman,—and such a woman!—was base, and odious! She took upon herself the defense of the dead woman against him. She could not forgive him for having forgotten her....

Alas! He was thinking of her more than she: but she never thought that in a passionate heart there might be room for two sentiments at once: she thought it impossible to be faithful to the past without sacrifice of the present. Pure and cold, she had no idea of life or of Christophe: everything in her eyes was pure, narrow, submissive to duty, like herself. Modest of soul, modest of herself, she had only one source of pride: purity: she demanded it of herself and of others. She could not forgive Christophe for having so lowered himself, and she would never forgive him.

Christophe tried to talk to her, though not to explain himself—(what could he say to her? what could he say to a little puritanical and naive girl?).—He would have liked to assure her that he was her friend, that he wished for her esteem, and had still the right to it He wished to prevent her absurdly estranging herself from him.—But Rosa avoided him in stern silence: he felt that she despised him.

He was both sorry and angry. He felt that he did not deserve such contempt; and yet in the end he was bowled over by it: and thought himself guilty. Of all the reproaches cast against him the most bitter came from himself when he thought of Sabine. He tormented himself.

"Oh! God, how is it possible? What sort of creature am I?..."

But he could not resist the stream that bore him on. He thought that life is criminal: and he closed his eyes so as to live without seeing it. He had so great a need to live, and be happy, and love, and believe!... No: there was nothing despicable in his love! He knew that it was impossible to be very wise, or intelligent, or even very happy in his love for Ada: but what was there in it that could be called vile? Suppose—(he forced the idea on himself)—that Ada were not a woman of any great moral worth, how was the love that he had for her the less pure for that? Love is in the lover, not in the beloved. Everything is worthy of the lover, everything is worthy of love. To the pure all is pure. All is pure in the strong and the healthy of mind. Love, which adorns certain birds with their loveliest colors, calls forth from the souls that are true all that is most noble in them. The desire to show to the beloved only what is worthy makes the lover take pleasure only in those thoughts and actions which are in harmony with the beautiful image fashioned by love. And the waters of youth in which the soul is bathed, the blessed radiance of strength and joy, are beautiful and health–giving, making the heart great.

That his friends misunderstood him filled him with bitterness. But the worst trial of all was that his mother was beginning to be unhappy about it.

The good creature was far from sharing the narrow views of the Vogels. She had seen real sorrows too near ever to try to invent others. Humble, broken by life, having received little joy from it, and having asked even less, resigned to everything that happened, without even trying to understand it, she was careful not to judge or censure others: she thought she had no right. She thought herself too stupid to pretend that they were wrong when they did not think as she did: it would have seemed ridiculous to try to impose on others the inflexible rules of her morality and belief. Besides that, her morality and her belief were purely instinctive: pious and pure in herself she closed her eyes to the conduct of others, with the indulgence of her class for certain faults and certain weaknesses. That had been one of the complaints that her father–in–law, Jean Michel, had lodged against her: she did not sufficiently distinguish between those who were honorable and those who were not: she was not afraid of stopping in the street or the market–place to shake hands and talk with young women, notorious in the neighborhood, whom a respectable woman ought to pretend to ignore. She left it to God to distinguish between good and evil, to punish or to forgive. From others she asked only a little of that affectionate sympathy which is so necessary to soften the ways of life. If people were only kind she asked no more.

But since she had lived with the Vogels a change had come about in her. The disparaging temper of the family had found her an easier prey because she was crushed and had no strength to resist. Amalia had taken her in hand: and from morning to night when they were working together alone, and Amalia did all the talking, Louisa, broken and passive, unconsciously assumed the habit of judging and criticising everything. Frau Vogel did not fail to tell her what she thought of Christophe's conduct. Louisa's calmness irritated her. She thought it indecent of Louisa to be so little concerned about what put him beyond the pale: she was not satisfied until she had upset her altogether. Christophe saw it. Louisa dared not reproach him: but every day she made little timid remarks, uneasy, insistent: and when he lost patience and replied sharply, she said no more: but still he could see the trouble in her eyes: and when he came home sometimes he could see that she had been weeping. He knew his mother too well not to be absolutely certain that her uneasiness did not come from herself.—And he knew well whence it came.

He determined to make an end of it. One evening when Louisa was unable to hold back her tears and had got up from the table in the middle of supper without Christophe being able to discover what was the matter, he rushed downstairs four steps at a time and knocked at the Vogels' door. He was boiling with rage. He was not only angry about Frau Vogel's treatment of his mother: he had to avenge himself for her having turned Rosa against him, for her bickering against Sabine, for all that he had had to put up with at her hands for months. For months he had borne his pent–up feelings against her and now made haste to let them loose.

He burst in on Frau Vogel and in a voice that he tried to keep calm, though it was trembling with fury, he asked her what she had told his mother to bring her to such a state.

Amalia took it very badly: she replied that she would say what she pleased, and was responsible to no one for her actions—to him least of all. And seizing the opportunity to deliver the speech which she had prepared, she added that if Louisa was unhappy he had to go no further for the cause of it than his own conduct, which was a shame to himself and a scandal to everybody else.

Christophe was only waiting for her onslaught to strike out, He shouted angrily that his conduct was his own affair, that he did not care a rap whether it pleased Frau Vogel or not, that if she wished to complain of it she must do so to him, and that she could say to him whatever she liked: that rested with her, but he *forbade* her—(did she hear?)—*forbade* her to say anything to his mother: it was cowardly and mean so to attack a poor sick old woman.

Frau Vogel cried loudly. Never had any one dared to speak to her in such a manner. She said that she was not to be lectured fey a rapscallion,—and in her own house, too!—And she treated him with abuse.

The others came running up on the noise of the quarrel,—except Vogel, who fled from anything that might upset, his health. Old Euler was called to witness by the indignant Amalia and sternly bade Christophe in future to refrain from speaking to or visiting them. He said that they did not need him to tell them what they ought to do, that they did their duty and would always do it.

Christophe declared that he would go and would never again set foot in their house. However, he did not go until he had relieved his feelings by telling them what he had still to say about their famous Duty, which had become to him a personal enemy. He said that their Duty was the sort of thing to make him love vice. It was people like them who discouraged good, by insisting on making it unpleasant. It was their fault that so many find delight by contrast among those who are dishonest, but amiable and laughter-loving. It was a profanation of the name of duty to apply it to everything, to the most stupid tasks, to trivial things, with a stiff and arrogant severity which ends by darkening and poisoning life. Duty, he said, was exceptional: it should be kept for moments of real sacrifice, and not used to lend the lover of its name to ill-humor and the desire to be disagreeable to others. There was no reason, because they were stupid enough or ungracious enough to be sad, to want everybody else to be so too and to impose on everybody their decrepit way of living.... The first of all virtues is joy. Virtue must be happy, free, and unconstrained. He who does good must give pleasure to himself. But this perpetual upstart Duty, this pedagogic tyranny, this peevishness, this futile discussion, this acrid, puerile quibbling, this ungraciousness, this charmless life, without politeness, without silence, this mean-spirited pessimism, which lets slip nothing that can make existence poorer than it is, this vainglorious unintelligence, which finds it easier to despise others than to understand them, all this middle-class morality, without greatness, without largeness, without happiness, without beauty, all these things are odious and hurtful: they make vice appear more human than virtue.

So thought Christophe: and in his desire to hurt those who had wounded him, he did not see that he was being as unjust as those of whom he spoke.

No doubt these unfortunate people were, almost as he saw them. But it was not their fault: it was the fault of their ungracious life, which had made their faces, their doings, and their thoughts ungracious. They had suffered the deformation of misery—not that great misery which swoops down and slays or forges anew—but the misery of ever recurring ill-fortune, that small misery which trickles down drop by drop from the first day to the last.... Sad, indeed! For beneath these rough exteriors what treasures in reserve are there, of uprightness, of kindness, of silent heroism!... The whole strength of a people, all the sap of the future.

Christophe was not wrong in thinking duty exceptional. But love is so no less. Everything is exceptional. Everything that is of worth has no worse enemy—not the evil (the vices are of worth)—but the habitual. The mortal enemy of the soul is the daily wear and tear.

Ada was beginning to weary of it. She was not clever enough to find new food for her love in an abundant nature like that of Christophe. Her senses and her vanity had extracted from it all the pleasure they could find in it. There was left her only the pleasure of destroying it. She had that secret instinct common to so many women, even good women, to so many men, even clever men, who are not creative either of art, or of children, or of pure action,—no matter what: of life—and yet have too much life in apathy and resignation to bear with their uselessness. They desire others to be as useless as themselves and do their best to make them so. Sometimes they do so in spite of themselves: and when they become aware of their criminal desire they hotly thrust it back. But often they hug it to themselves: and they set themselves according to their strength—some modestly in their own intimate circle—others largely with vast audiences—to destroy everything that has life, everything that loves life, everything that deserves life. The critic who takes upon himself to diminish the stature of great men and great thoughts—and the girl who amuses herself with dragging down her lovers, are both mischievous beasts of the same kind.—But the second is the pleasanter of the two.

Ada then would have liked to corrupt Christophe a little, to humiliate him. In truth, she was not strong enough. More intelligence was needed, even in corruption. She felt that: and it was not the least of her rankling feelings against Christophe that her love could do him no harm. She did not admit the desire that was in her to do him harm: perhaps she would have done him none if she had been able. But it annoyed her that she could not do it. It is to fail in love for a woman not to leave her the illusion of her power for good or evil over her lover: to do that must inevitably be to impel her irresistibly to the test of it. Christophe paid no attention to it. When Ada asked him jokingly:

"Would you leave your music for me?"

(Although she had no wish for him to do so.)

He replied frankly:

"No, my dear: neither you nor anybody else can do anything against that. I shall always make music."

"And you say you love?" cried she, put out.

She hated his music—the more so because she did not understand it, and it was impossible for her to find a means of coming to grips with this invisible enemy and so to wound Christophe in his passion. If she tried to talk of it contemptuously, or scornfully to judge Christophe's compositions, he would shout with laughter; and in spite of her exasperation Ada would relapse into silence: for she saw that she was being ridiculous.

But if there was nothing to be done in that direction, she had discovered another weak spot in Christophe, one more easy of access: his moral faith. In spite of his squabble with the Vogels, and in spite of the intoxication of his adolescence, Christophe had preserved an instinctive modesty, a need of purity, of which he was entirely unconscious. At first it struck Ada, attracted and charmed her, then made her impatient and irritable, and finally, being the woman she was, she detested it. She did not make a frontal attack. She would ask insidiously:

"Do you love me?"

"Of course!"

"How much do you love me?"

"As much as it is possible to love."

"That is not much ... after all!... What would you do for me?"

"Whatever you like."

"Would you do something dishonest."

"That would be a queer way of loving."

"That is not what I asked. Would you?"

"It is not necessary."

"But if I wished it?"

"You would be wrong."

"Perhaps.... Would you do it?"

He tried to kiss her. But she thrust him away.

"Would you do it? Yes or no?"

"No, my dear."

She turned her back on him and was furious.

"You do not love me. You do not know what love is."

"That is quite possible," he said good–humoredly. He knew that, like anybody else, he was capable in a moment of passion of committing some folly, perhaps something dishonest, and—who knows?—even more: but he would have thought shame of himself if he had boasted of it in cold blood, and certainly it would be dangerous to confess it to Ada. Some instinct warmed him that the beloved foe was lying in ambush, and taking stock of his smallest remark; he would not give her any weapon against him.

She would return to the charge again, and ask him:

"Do you love me because you love me, or because I love you?"

"Because I love you."

"Then if I did not love you, you would still love me?"

"Yes."

"And if I loved some one else you would still love me?"

"Ah! I don't know about that.... I don't think so.... In any case you would be the last person to whom I should say so."

"How would it be changed?"

"Many things would be changed. Myself, perhaps. You, certainly."

"And if I changed, what would it matter?"

"All the difference in the world. I love you as you are. If you become another creature I can't promise to love you."

"You do not love, you do not love! What is the use of all this quibbling? You love or you do not love. If you love me you ought to love me just as I am, whatever I do, always."

"That would be to love you like an animal."

"I want to be loved like that."

"Then you have made a mistake," said he jokingly. "I am not the sort of man you want. I would like to be, but I cannot. And I will not."

"You are very proud of your intelligence! You love your intelligence more than you do me."

"But I love you, you wretch, more than you love yourself. The more beautiful and the more good you are, the more I love you."

"You are a schoolmaster," she said with asperity.

"What would you? I love what is beautiful. Anything ugly disgusts me."

"Even in me?"

"Especially in you."

She drummed angrily with her foot.

"I will not be judged."

"Then complain of what I judge you to be, and of what I love in you," said he tenderly to appease her.

She let him take her in his arms, and deigned to smile, and let him kiss her. But in a moment when he thought she had forgotten she asked uneasily:

"What do you think ugly in me?"

He would not tell her: he replied cowardly:

"I don't think anything ugly in you."

She thought for a moment, smiled, and said:

"Just a moment, Christli: you say that you do not like lying?"

"I despise it."

"You are right," she said. "I despise it too. I am of a good conscience. I never lie."

He stared at her: she was sincere. Her unconsciousness disarmed him.

"Then," she went on, putting her arms about his neck, "why would you be cross with me if I loved some one else and told you so?"

"Don't tease me."

"I'm not teasing: I am not saying that I do love some one else: I am saying that I do not.... But if I did love some one later on...."

"Well, don't let us think of it."

"But I want to think of it.... You would not be angry, with me? You could not be angry with me?"

"I should not be angry with you. I should leave you. That is all."

"Leave me? Why? If I still loved you ...?"

"While you loved some one else?"

"Of course. It happens sometimes."

"Well, it will not happen with us."

"Why?"

"Because as soon as you love some one else, I shall love you no longer, my dear, never, never again."

"But just now you said perhaps.... Ah! you see you do not love me!"

"Well then: all the better for you."

"Because ...?"

"Because if I loved you when you loved some one else it might turn out badly for you, me, and him."

"Then!... Now you are mad. Then I am condemned to stay with you all my life?"

"Be calm. You are free. You shall leave me when you like. Only it will not be *au revoir*: it will be good–bye."

"But if I still love you?"

"When people love, they sacrifice themselves to each other."

"Well, then ... sacrifice yourself!"

He could not help laughing at her egoism: and she laughed too.

"The sacrifice of one only," he said, "means the love of one only."

"Not at all. It means the love of both. I shall not love you much longer if you do not sacrifice yourself for me. And think, Christli, how much you will love me, when you have sacrificed yourself, and how happy you will be."

They laughed and were glad to have a change from the seriousness of the disagreement.

He laughed and looked at her. At heart, as she said, she had no desire to leave Christophe at present: if he irritated her and often bored her she knew the worth of such devotion as his: and she loved no one else. She talked so for fun, partly because she knew he disliked it, partly because she took pleasure in playing with equivocal and unclean thoughts like a child which delights to mess about with dirty water. He knew this. He did not mind. But he was tired of these unwholesome discussions, of the silent struggle against this uncertain and uneasy creature whom he loved, who perhaps loved him: he was tired from the effort that he had to make to deceive himself about her, sometimes tired almost to tears. He would think: "Why, why is she like this? Why are people like this? How second–rate life is!"... At the same time he would smile as he saw her pretty face above him, her blue eyes, her flower–like complexion, her laughing, chattering lips, foolish a little, half open to reveal the brilliance of her tongue and her white teeth. Their lips would almost touch: and he would look at her as from a distance, a great distance, as from another world: he would see her going farther and farther from him, vanishing in a mist.... And then he would lose sight of her. He could hear her no more. He would fall into a sort of smiling oblivion, in which he thought of his music, his dreams, a thousand things foreign, to Ada.... Ah! beautiful music!... so sad, so mortally sad! and yet kind, loving.... Ah! how good it is!... It is that, it is that.... Nothing else is true....

She would shake his arm. A voice would cry:

"Eh, what's the matter with you? You are mad, quite mad. Why do you look at me like that? Why don't you answer?"

Once more he would see the eyes looking at him. Who was it?... Ah! yes.... He would sigh.

She would watch him. She would try to discover what he was thinking of. She did not understand: but she felt that it was useless: that she could not keep hold of him, that there was always a door by which he could escape. She would conceal her irritation.

"Why are you crying?" she asked him once as he returned from one of his strange journeys into another life.

He drew his hands across his eyes. He felt that they were wet.

"I do not know," he said.

"Why don't you answer? Three times you have said the same thing."

"What do you want?" he asked gently.

She went back to her absurd discussions. He waved his hand wearily.

"Yes," she said. "I've done. Only a word more!" And off she started again.

Christophe shook himself angrily.

"Will you keep your dirtiness to yourself!"

"I was only joking."

"Find cleaner subjects, then!"

"Tell me why, then. Tell me why you don't like it."

"Why? You can't argue as to why a dump–heap smells. It does smell, and that is all! I hold my nose and go away."

He went away, furious: and he strode along taking in great breaths of the cold air.

But she would begin again, once, twice, ten times. She would bring forward every possible subject that could shock him and offend his conscience.

He thought it was only a morbid jest of a neurasthenic girl, amusing herself by annoying him. He would shrug his shoulders or pretend not to hear her: he would not take her seriously. But sometimes he would long to throw her out of the window: for neurasthenia and the neurasthenics were very little to his taste....

But ten minutes away from her were enough to make him forget everything that had annoyed him. He would return to Ada with a fresh store of hopes and new illusions. He loved her. Love is a perpetual act of faith. Whether God exist or no is a small matter: we believe, because we believe. We love because we love; there is no need of reasons!...

* * * * *

After Christophe's quarrel with the Vogels it became impossible for them to stay in the house, and Louisa had to seek another lodging for herself and her son.

One day Christophe's younger brother Ernest, of whom they had not heard for a long time, suddenly turned up. He was out of work, having been dismissed in turn from all the situations he had procured; his purse was empty and his health ruined; and so he had thought it would be as well to re–establish himself in his mother's house.

Ernest was not on bad terms with either of his brothers: they thought very little of him and he knew it: but he did not bear any grudge against them, for he did not care. They had no ill–feeling against him. It was not worth the trouble. Everything they said to him slipped off his back without leaving a mark. He just smiled with his sly eyes, tried to look contrite, thought of something else, agreed, thanked them, and in the end always managed to extort money from one or other of them. In spite of himself Christophe was fond of the pleasant mortal who, like himself, and more than himself, resembled their father Melchior in feature. Tall and strong like Christophe, he had regular features, a frank expression, a straight nose, a laughing mouth, fine teeth, and endearing manners. When even Christophe saw him he was disarmed and could not deliver half the reproaches that he had prepared: in his heart he had a sort of motherly indulgence for the handsome boy who was of his blood, and physically at all events did him credit. He did not believe him to be bad: and Ernest was not a fool. Without culture, he was not without

307

brains: he was even not incapable of taking an interest in the things of the mind. He enjoyed listening to music: and without understanding his brother's compositions he would listen to them with interest. Christophe, who did not receive too much sympathy from his family, had been glad to see him at some of his concerts.

But Ernest's chief talent was the knowledge that he possessed of the character of his two brothers, and his skill in making use of his knowledge. It was no use Christophe knowing Ernest's egoism and indifference: it was no use his seeing that Ernest never thought of his mother or himself except when he had need of them: he was always taken in by his affectionate ways and very rarely did he refuse him anything. He much preferred him to his other brother Rodolphe, who was orderly and correct, assiduous in his business, strictly moral, never asked for money, and never gave any either, visited his mother regularly every Sunday, stayed an hour, and only talked about himself, boasting about himself, his firm, and everything that concerned him, never asking about the others, and taking mo interest in them, and going away when the hour was up, quite satisfied with having done his duty. Christophe could not bear him. He always arranged to be out when Rodolphe came. Rodolphe was jealous of him: he despised artists, and Christophe's success really hurt him, though he did not fail to turn his small fame to account in the commercial circles in which he moved: but he never said a word about it either to his mother or to Christophe: he pretended to ignore it. On the other hand, he never ignored the least of the unpleasant things that happened to Christophe. Christophe despised such pettiness, and pretended not to notice it: but it would really have hurt him to know, though he never thought about it, that much of the unpleasant information that Rodolphe had about him came from Ernest. The young rascal fed the differences between Christophe and Rodolphe: no doubt he recognized Christophe's superiority and perhaps even sympathized a little ironically with his candor. But he took good care to turn it to account: and while he despised Rodolphe's ill–feeling he exploited it shamefully. He flattered his vanity and jealousy, accepted his rebukes deferentially and kept him primed with the scandalous gossip of the town, especially with everything concerning Christophe,—of which he was always marvelously informed. So he attained his ends, and Rodolphe, in spite of his avarice, allowed Ernest to despoil him just as Christophe did.

So Ernest made use and a mock of them both, impartially. And so both of them loved him.

In spite of his tricks Ernest was in a pitiful condition when he turned up at his mother's house. He had come from Munich, where he had found and, as usual, almost immediately lost a situation. He had had to travel the best part of the way on foot, through storms of rain, sleeping God knows where. He was covered with mud, ragged, looking like a beggar, and coughing miserably. Louisa was upset and Christophe ran to him in alarm when they saw him come in. Ernest, whose tears flowed easily, did not fail to make use of the effect he had produced: and there was a general reconciliation: all three wept in each other's arms.

Christophe gave up his room: they warmed the bed, and laid the invalid in it, who seemed to be on the point of death. Louisa and Christophe sat by his bedside and took it in turns to watch by him. They called in a doctor, procured medicines, made a good fire in the room, and gave him special food.

Then they had to clothe him from head to foot: linen, shoes, clothes, everything new. Ernest left himself in their hands. Louisa and Christophe sweated to squeeze the money from their expenditure. They were very straitened at the moment: the removal, the new lodgings, which were dearer though just as uncomfortable, fewer lessons for Christophe and more expenses. They could just make both ends meet. They managed somehow. No doubt Christophe could have applied to Rodolphe, who was more in a position to help Ernest, but he would not: he made it a point of honor to help his brother alone. He thought himself obliged to do so as the eldest,—and because he was Christophe. Hot with shame he had to accept, to declare his willingness to accept an offer which he had indignantly rejected a fortnight before,—a proposal from an agent of an unknown wealthy amateur who wanted to buy a musical composition for publication under his own name. Louisa took work out, mending linen. They hid their sacrifice from each other: they lied about the money they brought home.

When Ernest was convalescent and sitting huddled up by the fire, he confessed one day between his fits of coughing that he had a few debts.—They were paid. No one reproached him. That would not have been kind to an invalid and a prodigal son who had repented and returned home. For Ernest seemed to have been changed by adversity and sickness. With tears in his eyes he spoke of his past misdeeds: and Louisa kissed him and told him to think no more of them. He was fond: he had always been able to get round his mother by his demonstrations of affection: Christophe had once been a little jealous of him. Now he thought it natural that the youngest and the weakest son should be the most loved. In spite of the small difference in their ages he regarded him almost as a son rather than as a brother. Ernest showed great respect for him: sometimes he would allude to the burdens that Christophe was taking upon himself, and to his sacrifice of money: but Christophe would not let him go on, and Ernest would content himself with showing his gratitude in his eyes humbly and affectionately. He would argue with the advice that Christophe gave him: and he would seem disposed to change his way of living and to work seriously as soon as he was well again.

He recovered: but had a long convalescence. The doctor declared that his health, which he had abused, needed to be fostered. So he stayed on in his mother's house, sharing Christophe's bed, eating heartily the bread that his brother earned, and the little dainty dishes that Louisa prepared, for him. He never spoke of going. Louisa and Christophe never mentioned it either. They were too happy to have found again the son and the brother they loved.

Little by little in the long evenings that he spent with Ernest Christophe began to talk intimately to him. He needed to confide in somebody. Ernest was clever: he had a quick mind and understood—or seemed to understand—on a hint only. There was pleasure in talking to him. And yet Christophe dared not tell him about what lay nearest to his heart: his love. He was kept back by a sort of modesty. Ernest, who knew all about it, never let it appear that he knew.

One day when Ernest was quite well again he went in the sunny afternoon and lounged along the Rhine. As he passed a noisy inn a little way out of the town, where there were drinking and dancing on Sundays, he saw Christophe sitting with Ada and Myrrha, who were making a great noise. Christophe saw him too, and blushed. Ernest was discreet and passed on without acknowledging him.

Christophe was much embarrassed by the encounter: it made him more keenly conscious of the company in which he was: it hurt him that his brother should have seen him then: not only because it made him lose the right of judging Ernest's conduct, but because he had a very lofty, very naive, and rather archaic notion of his duties as an elder brother which would have seemed absurd to many people: he thought that in failing in that duty, as he was doing, he was lowered in his own eyes.

In the evening when they were together in their room, he waited for Ernest to allude to what had happened. But Ernest prudently said nothing and waited also. Then while they were undressing Christophe decided to speak about his love. He was so ill at ease that he dared not look at Ernest: and in his shyness he assumed a gruff way of speaking. Ernest did not help him out: he was silent and did not look at him, though he watched him all the same: and he missed none of the humor of Christophe's awkwardness and clumsy words. Christophe hardly dared pronounce Ada's name: and the portrait that he drew of her would have done just as well for any woman who was loved. But he spoke of his love: little by little he was carried away by the flood of tenderness that filled his heart: he said how good it was to love, how wretched he had been before he had found that light in the darkness, and that life was nothing without a dear, deep–seated love. His brother listened gravely: he replied tactfully, and asked no questions: but a warm handshake showed that he was of Christophe's way of thinking. They exchanged ideas concerning love and life. Christophe was happy at being so well understood. They exchanged a brotherly embrace before they went to sleep.

Christophe grew accustomed to confiding his love to Ernest, though always shyly and reservedly. Ernest's discretion reassured him. He let him know his uneasiness about Ada: but he never blamed her: he blamed himself: and with tears in his eyes he would declare that he could not live if he were to lose her.

He did not forget to tell Ada about Ernest: he praised his wit and his good looks.

Ernest never approached Christophe with a request to be introduced to Ada: but he would shut himself up in his room and sadly refuse to go out, saying that he did not know anybody. Christophe would think ill of himself on Sundays for going on his excursions with Ada, while his brother stayed at home. And yet he hated not to be alone with his beloved: he accused himself of selfishness and proposed that Ernest should come with them.

The introduction took place at Ada's door, on the landing. Ernest and Ada bowed politely. Ada came out, followed by her inseparable Myrrha, who when she saw Ernest gave a little cry of surprise. Ernest smiled, went up to Myrrha, and kissed her: she seemed to take it as a matter of course.

"What! You know each other?" asked Christophe in astonishment.

"Why, yes!" said Myrrha, laughing.

"Since when?"

"Oh, a long time!"

"And you knew?" asked Christophe, turning to Ada. "Why, did you not tell me?"

"Do you think I know all Myrrha's lovers?" said Ada, shrugging her shoulders.

Myrrha took up the word and pretended in fun to be angry. Christophe could not find out any more about it. He was depressed. It seemed to him that Ernest and Myrrha and Ada had been lacking in honesty, although indeed he could not have brought any lie up against them: but it was difficult to believe that Myrrha, who had no secrets from Ada, had made a mystery of this, and that Ernest and Ada were not already acquainted with each other. He watched them. But they only exchanged a few trivial words and Ernest only paid attention to Myrrha all the rest of the day. Ada only spoke to Christophe: and she was much more amiable to him than usual.

From that time on Ernest always joined them. Christophe could have done without him: but he dared not say so. He had no other motive for wanting to leave his brother out than his shame in having him for boon companion. He had no suspicion of him. Ernest gave him no cause for it: he seemed to be in love with Myrrha and was always reserved and polite with Ada, and even affected to avoid her in a way that was a little out of place: it was as though he wished to show his brother's mistress a little of the respect he showed to himself. Ada was not surprised by it and was none the less careful.

They went on long excursions together. The two brothers would walk on in front. Ada and Myrrha, laughing and whispering, would follow a few yards behind. They would stop in the middle of the road and talk. Christophe and Ernest would stop and wait for them. Christophe would lose patience and go on: but soon he would turn back annoyed and irritated, by hearing Ernest talking and laughing with the two young women. He would want to know what they were saying: but when they came up with him their conversation would stop.

"What are you three always plotting together?" he would ask.

They would reply with some joke. They had a secret understanding like thieves at a fair.

* * * * *

Christophe had a sharp quarrel with Ada. They had been cross with each other all day. Strange to say, Ada had not assumed her air of offended dignity, to which she usually resorted in such cases, so as to avenge herself, by making herself as intolerably tiresome as usual. Now she simply pretended to ignore Christophe's existence and she was in excellent spirits with the other two. It was as though in her heart she was not put out at all by the quarrel.

Christophe, on the other hand, longed to make peace: he was more in love than ever. His tenderness was now mingled with a feeling of gratitude for all the good things love had brought him, and regret for the hours he had wasted in stupid argument and angry thoughts—and the unreasoning fear, the mysterious idea that their love was nearing its end. Sadly he looked at Ada's pretty face and she pretended not to see him while she was laughing with the others: and the sight of her woke in him so many dear memories, of great love, of sincere intimacy.—Her face had sometimes—it had now—so much goodness in it, a smile so pure, that Christophe asked himself why things were not better between them, why they spoiled their happiness with their whimsies, why she would insist on forgetting their bright hours, and denying and combating all that was good and honest in her—what strange satisfaction she could find in spoiling, and smudging, if only in thought, the purity of their love. He was conscious of an immense need of believing in the object of his love, and he tried once more to bring back his illusions. He accused himself of injustice: he was remorseful for the thoughts that he attributed to her, and of his lack of charity.

He went to, her and tried to talk to her; she answered him with a few curt words: she had no desire for a reconciliation with him. He insisted: he begged her to listen to him for a moment away from the others. She followed him ungraciously. When they were a few yards away so that neither Myrrha nor Ernest could see them, he took her hands and begged her pardon, and knelt at her feet in the dead leaves of the wood. He told her that he could not go on living so at loggerheads with her: that he found no pleasure in the walk, or the fine day: that he could enjoy nothing, and could not even breathe, knowing that she detested him: he needed her love. Yes: he was often unjust, violent, disagreeable: he begged her to forgive him: it was the fault of his love, he could not bear anything

313

second–rate in her, nothing that was altogether unworthy of her and their memories of their dear past. He reminded her of it all, of their first meeting, their first days together: he said that he loved her just as much, that he would always love her, that she should not go away from him! She was everything to him....

Ada listened to him, smiling, uneasy, almost softened. She looked at him with kind eyes, eyes that said that they loved each other, and that she was no longer angry. They kissed, and holding each other close they went into the leafless woods. She thought Christophe good and gentle, and was grateful to him for his tender words: but she did not relinquish the naughty whims that were in her mind. But she hesitated, she did not cling to them so tightly: and yet she did not abandon what she had planned to do. Why? Who can say?... Because she had vowed what she would do?—Who knows? Perhaps she thought it more entertaining to deceive her lover that day, to prove to him, to prove to herself her freedom. She had no thought of losing him: she did not wish for that. She thought herself more sure of him than ever.

They reached a clearing in the forest. There were two paths. Christophe took one. Ernest declared that the other led more quickly to the top of the hill whither they were going. Ada agreed with him. Christophe, who knew the way, having often been there, maintained that they were wrong. They did not yield. Then they agreed to try it: and each wagered that he would arrive first. Ada went with Ernest. Myrrha accompanied Christophe: she pretended that she was sure that he was right: and she added, "As usual." Christophe had taken the game seriously: and as he never liked to lose, he walked quickly, too quickly for Myrrha's liking, for she was in much less of a hurry than he.

"Don't be in a hurry, my friend," she said, in her quiet, ironic voice, "we shall get there first."

He was a little sorry.

"True," he said, "I am going a little too fast: there is no need."

He slackened his pace.

"But I know them," he went on. "I am sure they will run so as to be there before us."

Myrrha burst out laughing.

"Oh! no," she said. "Oh! no: don't you worry about that."

She hung on his arm and pressed close to him. She was a little shorter than Christophe, and as they walked she raised her soft eyes to his. She was really pretty and alluring. He hardly recognized her: the change was extraordinary. Usually her face was rather pale and puffy: but the smallest excitement, a merry thought, or the desire to please, was enough to make her worn expression vanish, and her cheeks go pink, and the little wrinkles in her eyelids round and below her eyes disappear, and her eyes flash, and her whole face take on a youth, a life, a spiritual quality that never was in Ada's. Christophe was surprised by this metamorphosis, and turned his eyes away from hers: he was a little uneasy at being alone with her. She embarrassed him and prevented him from dreaming as he pleased: he did not listen to what she said, he did not answer her, or if he did it was only at random: he was thinking—he wished to think only of Ada. He thought of the kindness in her eyes, her smile, her kiss: and his heart was filled with love. Myrrha wanted to make him admire the beauty of the trees with their little branches against the clear sky.... Yes: it was all beautiful: the clouds were gone, Ada had returned to him, he had succeeded in breaking the ice that lay between them: they loved once more: near or far, they were one. He sighed with relief: how light the air was! Ada had come back to him ... Everything brought her to mind.... It was a little damp: would she not be cold?... The lovely trees were powdered with hoar–frost: what a pity she should not see them!... But he remembered the wager, and hurried on: he was concerned only with not losing the way. He shouted joyfully as they reached the goal:

"We are first!"

He waved his hat gleefully. Myrrha watched him and smiled.

The place where they stood was a high, steep rock in the middle of the woods. From this flat summit with its fringe of nut–trees and little stunted oaks they could see, over the wooded slopes, the tops of the pines bathed in a purple mist, and the long ribbon of the Rhine in the blue valley. Not a bird called. Not a voice. Not a breath of air. A still, calm winter's day, its chilliness faintly warmed by the pale beams of a misty sun. Now and then in the distance there came the sharp whistle of a train in the valley. Christophe stood at the edge of the rock and looked down at the countryside. Myrrha watched Christophe.

He turned to her amiably:

"Well! The lazy things. I told them so!... Well: we must wait for them...."

He lay stretched out in the sun on the cracked earth.

"Yes. Let us wait...." said Myrrha, taking off her hat.

In her voice there was something so quizzical that he raised his head and looked at her.

"What is it?" she asked quietly.

"What did you say?"

"I said: Let us wait. It was no use making me run so fast."

"True."

They waited lying on the rough ground. Myrrha hummed a tune. Christophe took it up for a few phrases. But he stopped every now and then to listen.

"I think I can hear them."

Myrrha went on singing.

"Do stop for a moment."

Myrrha stopped.

"No. It is nothing."

She went on with her song.

Christophe could not stay still.

"Perhaps they have lost their way."

"Lost? They could not. Ernest knows all the paths."

A fantastic idea passed through Christophe's mind.

"Perhaps they arrived first, and went away before we came!"

Myrrha was lying on her back and looking at the sun. She was seized with a wild burst of laughter in the middle of her song and all but choked. Christophe insisted. He wanted to go down to the station, saying that their friends would be there already. Myrrha at last made up her mind to move.

"You would be certain to lose them!... There was never any talk about the station. We were to meet here."

He sat down by her side. She was amused by his eagerness. He was conscious of the irony in her gaze as she looked at him. He began to be seriously troubled—to be anxious about them: he did not suspect them. He got up once more. He spoke of going down into the woods again and looking for them, calling to them. Myrrha gave a little chuckle: she took from her pocket a needle, scissors, and thread: and she calmly undid and sewed in again the feathers in her hat: she seemed to have established herself for the day.

"No, no, silly," she said. "If they wanted to come do you think they would not come of their own accord?"

There was a catch at his heart. He turned towards her: she did not look at him: she was busy with her work. He went up to her.

"Myrrha!" he said.

"Eh?" she replied without stopping. He knelt now to look more nearly at her.

"Myrrha!" he repeated.

"Well?" she asked, raising her eyes from her work and looking at him with a smile. "What is it?"

She had a mocking expression as she saw his downcast face.

"Myrrha!" he asked, choking, "tell me what you think...."

She shrugged her shoulders, smiled, and went on working.

He caught her hands and took away the hat at which she was sewing.

"Leave off, leave off, and tell me...."

She looked squarely at him and waited. She saw that Christophe's lips were trembling.

"You think," he said in a low voice, "that Ernest and Ada ...?"

She smiled.

"Oh! well!"

He started back angrily.

"No! No! It is impossible! You don't think that!... No! No!"

She put her hands on his shoulders and rocked with laughter.

"How dense you are, how dense, my dear!"

He shook her violently.

"Don't laugh! Why do you laugh? You would not laugh if it were true. You love Ernest...."

She went on laughing and drew him to her and kissed him. In spite of himself he returned her kiss. But when he felt her lips on his, her lips, still warm with his brother's kisses, he flung her away from him and held her face away from his own: he asked:

"You knew it? It was arranged between you?"

She said "Yes," and laughed.

Christophe did not cry out, he made no movement of anger. He opened his mouth as though he could not breathe: he closed his eyes and clutched at his breast with his hands: his heart was bursting. Then he lay down on the ground with his face buried in his hands and he was shaken by a crisis of disgust and despair like a child.

Myrrha, who was not very soft–hearted, was sorry for him: involuntarily she was filled with motherly compassion, and leaned over him, and spoke affectionately to him, and tried to make him sniff at her smelling–bottle. But he thrust her away in horror and got up so sharply that she was afraid. He had neither strength nor desire for revenge. He looked at her with his face twisted with grief.

"You drab," he said in despair. "You do not know the harm you have done...."

She tried to hold him back. He fled through the woods, spitting out his disgust with such ignominy, with such muddy hearts, with such incestuous sharing as that to which they had tried to bring him. He wept, he trembled: he sobbed with disgust. He was filled with horror, of them all, of himself, of his body and soul. A storm of contempt broke loose in him: it had long been brewing: sooner or later there had to come the reaction against the base thoughts, the degrading compromises, the stale and pestilential atmosphere in which he had been living for months: but the need of loving, of deceiving himself about the woman he loved, had postponed the crisis as long as possible. Suddenly it burst upon him: and it was better so. There was a great gust of wind of a biting purity, an icy breeze which swept away the miasma. Disgust in one swoop had killed his love for Ada.

If Ada thought more firmly to establish her domination over Christophe by such an act, that proved once more her gross inappreciation of her lover. Jealousy which binds souls that are besmirched could only revolt a nature like Christophe's, young, proud, and pure. But what he could not forgive, what he never would forgive, was that the betrayal was not the outcome of passion in Ada, hardly even of one of those absurd and degrading though often irresistible caprices to which the reason of a woman is sometimes hard put to it not to surrender. No—he understood now,—it was in her a secret desire to degrade him, to humiliate him, to punish him for his moral resistance, for his inimical faith, to lower him to the common level, to bring him to her feet, to prove to herself her own power for evil. And he asked himself with horror: what is this impulse towards dirtiness, which is in the majority of human beings—this desire to besmirch the purity of themselves and others,—these swinish souls, who take a delight in rolling in filth, and are happy when not one inch of their skins is left clean!...

Ada waited two days for Christophe to return to her. Then she began to be anxious, and sent him a tender note in which she made no allusion to what had happened. Christophe did not even reply. He hated Ada so profoundly that no words could express his hatred. He had cut her out of his life. She no longer existed for him.

* * * * *

Christophe was free of Ada, but he was not free of himself. In vain did he try to return into illusion and to take up again the calm and chaste strength of the past. We cannot return to the past. We have to go onward: it is useless to turn back, save only to see the places by which we have passed, the distant smoke from the roofs under which we have slept, dying away on the horizon in the mists of memory. But nothing so distances us from the soul that we had as a few months of passion. The road takes a sudden turn: the country is changed: it is as though we were saying good–bye for the last time to all that we are leaving behind.

Christophe could not yield to it. He held out his arms to the past: he strove desperately to bring to life again the soul that had been his, lonely and resigned. But it was gone. Passion itself is not so dangerous as the ruins that it heaps up and leaves behind. In vain did Christophe not love, in vain—for a moment—did he despise love: he bore the marks of its talons: his whole being was steeped in it: there was in his heart a void which must be filled. With that terrible need of tenderness and pleasure which devours men and women when they have once tasted it, some other passion was needed, were it only the contrary passion, the passion of contempt, of proud purity, of faith in virtue.—They were not enough, they were not enough to stay his hunger: they were only the food of a moment. His life consisted of a succession of violent reactions—leaps from one extreme to the other. Sometimes he would bend his passion to rules inhumanly ascetic: not eating, drinking water, wearing himself out with walking, heavy tasks, and so not sleeping, denying himself every sort of pleasure. Sometimes he would persuade himself that strength is the true morality for people like himself: and he would plunge into the quest of joy. In either case he was unhappy. He could no longer be alone. He could no longer not be alone.

The only thing that could have saved him would have been to find a true friendship,—Rosa's perhaps: he could have taken refuge in that. But the rupture was complete between the two families. They no longer met. Only once had Christophe seen Rosa. She was just coming out from Mass. He had hesitated to bow to her: and when she saw him she had made a movement towards him: but when he had tried to go to her through the stream of the devout walking down the steps, she had turned her eyes away: and when he approached her she bowed coldly and passed on. In the girl's heart he felt intense, icy contempt. And he did not feel that she still loved him and would have liked to tell him so: but she had come to think of her love as a fault and foolishness: she thought Christophe bad and corrupt, and further from her than ever. So they were lost to each other forever. And perhaps it was as well for both of them. In spite of her goodness, she was not near enough to life to be able to understand him. In spite of his need of affection and respect he would have stifled in a commonplace and confined existence, without joy, without sorrow, without air. They would both have suffered. The unfortunate occurrence which cut them apart was, when all was told, perhaps, fortunate as often happens—as always happens—to those who are strong and endure.

But at the moment it was a great sorrow and a great misfortune for them. Especially for Christophe. Such virtuous intolerance, such narrowness of soul, which sometimes seems to deprive those who have the most of them of all intelligence, and those who are most good of kindness, irritated him, hurt him, and flung him back in protest into a freer life.

During his loafing with Ada in the beer gardens of the neighborhood he had made acquaintance with several good fellows—Bohemians, whose carelessness and freedom of manners had not been altogether distasteful to him. One of them, Friedemann, a musician like himself, an organist, a man of thirty, was not without intelligence, and was good at his work, but he was incurably lazy and rather than make the slightest effort to be more than mediocre, he would have died of hunger, though not, perhaps, of thirst. He comforted himself in his indolence by speaking ill of those who lived energetically, God knows why; and his sallies, rather heavy for the most part, generally made people laugh. Having more liberty than his companions, he was not afraid,—though timidly, and with winks and nods and suggestive remarks,—to sneer at those who held positions: he was even capable of not having ready–made opinions about music, and of having a sly fling at the forged reputations of the great men of the day. He had no mercy upon women either: when he was making his jokes he loved to repeat the old saying of some misogynist monk about them, and Christophe enjoyed its bitterness just then more than anybody:

"Femina mors animae."

In his state of upheaval Christophe found some distraction in talking to Friedemann. He judged him, he could not long take pleasure in this vulgar bantering wit: his mockery and perpetual denial became irritating before long and he felt the impotence of it all: but it did soothe his exasperation with the self–sufficient stupidity of the Philistines. While he heartily despised his companion, Christophe could not do without him. They were continually seen together sitting with the unclassed and doubtful people of Friedemann's acquaintance, who were even more worthless than himself. They used to play, and harangue, and drink the whole evening. Christophe would suddenly wake up in the midst of the dreadful smell of food and tobacco: he would look at the people about him with strange eyes: he would not recognize them: he would think in agony:

"Where am I? Who are these people? What have I to do with them?"

Their remarks and their laughter would make him sick. But he could not bring himself to leave them: he was afraid of going home and of being left alone face to face with his soul, his desires, and remorse. He was going to the dogs: he knew it: he was doing it deliberately,—with cruel clarity he saw in Friedemann the degraded image of what he was—of what he would be one day: and he was passing through a phase of such disheartenedness and disgust that instead of being brought to himself by such a menace, it actually brought him low.

He would have gone to the dogs, if he could. Fortunately, like all creatures of his kind, he had a spring, a succor against destruction which others do not possess: his strength, his instinct for life, his instinct against letting himself perish, an instinct more intelligent than his intelligence, and stronger than his will. And also, unknown to himself, he had the strange curiosity of the artist, that passionate, impersonal quality, which is in every creature really endowed with creative power. In vain did he love, suffer, give himself utterly to all his passions: he saw them. They were in him but they were not himself. A myriad of little souls moved obscurely in him towards a fixed point unknown, yet certain, just like the planetary worlds which are drawn through space into a mysterious abyss. That perpetual state of unconscious action and reaction was shown especially in those giddy moments when sleep came over his daily life, and from the depths of sleep and the night rose the multiform face of Being with its sphinx–like gaze. For a year Christophe had been obsessed with dreams in which in a second of time he felt clearly with perfect illusion that he *was* at one and the same time several different creatures, often far removed from each other by countries, worlds, centuries. In his waking state Christophe was still under his hallucination and uneasiness, though he could not remember what had caused it. It was like the weariness left by some fixed idea that is gone, though traces of it are left and there is no understanding it. But while his soul was so troublously struggling through the network of the days, another soul, eager and serene, was watching all his desperate efforts. He did not see it: but it cast over him the reflection of its hidden light. That soul was joyously greedy to feel everything, to suffer everything, to observe and understand men, women, the earth, life, desires, passions, thoughts, even those that were torturing, even those that were mediocre, even those that were vile: and it was enough to lend them a little of its light, to save Christophe from destruction. It made him feel—he did not know how—that he was not altogether alone. That love of being and of knowing everything, that second soul, raised a rampart against his destroying passions.

But if it was enough to keep his head above water, it did not allow him to climb out of it unaided. He could not succeed in seeing clearly into himself, and mastering himself, and regaining possession of himself. Work was impossible for him. He was passing through an intellectual crisis: the most fruitful of his life: all his future life was germinating in it: but that inner wealth for the time being only showed itself in extravagance: and the immediate effect of such superabundance was not different from that of the flattest sterility. Christophe was submerged by his life. All his powers had shot up and grown too fast, all at once, suddenly. Only his will had not grown with them: and it was dismayed by such a throng of monsters. His personality was cracking in every part. Of this earthquake, this inner cataclysm, others saw nothing. Christophe himself could see only his impotence to will, to create, to be. Desires, instincts, thoughts issued one after another like clouds of sulphur from the fissures of a volcano: and he was forever asking himself: "And now, what will come out? What will become of me? Will it always be so? or is this the end of all? Shall I be nothing, always?"

And now there sprang up in him his hereditary fires, the vices of those who had gone before him.—He got drunk. He would return home smelling of wine, laughing, in a state of collapse.

Poor Louisa would look at him, sigh, say nothing, and pray.

But one evening when he was coming out of an inn by the gates of the town he saw, a few yards in front of him on the road, the droll shadow of his uncle Gottfried, with his pack on his back. The little man had not been home for months, and his periods of absence were growing longer and longer. Christophe hailed him gleefully. Gottfried, bending under his load, turned round: he looked at Christophe, who was making extravagant gestures, and sat down on a milestone to wait for him. Christophe came up to him with a beaming face, skipping along, and shook his uncle's hand with great demonstrations of affection. Gottfried took a long look at him and then he said:

"Good–day, Melchior."

Christophe thought his uncle had made a mistake, and burst out laughing.

"The poor man is breaking up," he thought; "he is losing his memory."

Indeed, Gottfried did look old, shriveled, shrunken, and dried: his breathing came short and painfully. Christophe went on talking. Gottfried took his pack on his shoulders again and went on in silence. They went home together, Christophe gesticulating and talking at the top of his voice, Gottfried coughing and saying nothing. And when Christophe questioned him, Gottfried still called him Melchior. And then Christophe asked him:

"What do you mean by calling me Melchior? My name is Christophe, you know. Have you forgotten my name?"

Gottfried did not stop. He raised his eyes toward Christophe and looked at him, shook his head, and said coldly:

"No. You are Melchior: I know you."

Christophe stopped dumfounded. Gottfried trotted along: Christophe followed him without a word. He was sobered. As they passed the door of a cafe he went up to the dark panes of glass, in which the gas–jets of the entrance and the empty streets were reflected, and he looked at himself: he recognized Melchior. He went home crushed.

He spent the night—a night of anguish—in examining himself, in soul–searching. He understood now. Yes: he recognized the instincts and vices that had come to light in him:

they horrified him. He thought of that dark watching by the body of Melchior, of all that he had sworn to do, and, surveying his life since then, he knew that he had failed to keep his vows. What had he done in the year? What had he done for his God, for his art, for his soul? What had he done for eternity? There was not a day that had not been wasted, botched, besmirched. Not a single piece of work, not a thought, not an effort of enduring quality. A chaos of desires destructive of each other. Wind, dust, nothing.... What did his intentions avail him? He had fulfilled none of them. He had done exactly the opposite of what he had intended. He had become what he had no wish to be: that was the balance–sheet of his life.

He did not go to bed. About six in the morning it was still dark,—he heard Gottfried getting ready to depart.—For Gottfried had had no intentions of staying on. As he was passing the town he had come as usual to embrace his sister and nephew: but he had announced that he would go on next morning.

Christophe went downstairs. Gottfried saw his pale face and his eyes hollow with a night of torment. He smiled fondly at him and asked him to go a little of the way with him. They set out together before dawn. They had no need to talk: they understood each other. As they passed the cemetery Gottfried said:

"Shall we go in?"

When he came to the place he never failed to pay a visit to Jean Michel and Melchior. Christophe had not been there for a year. Gottfried knelt by Melchior's grave and said:

"Let us pray that they may sleep well and not come to torment us."

His thought was a mixture of strange superstitions and sound sense: sometimes it surprised Christophe: but now it was only too dear to him. They said no more until they left the cemetery.

When they had closed the creaking gate, and were walking along the wall through the cold fields, waking from slumber, by the little path which led them under the cypress trees from which the snow was dropping, Christophe began to weep.

"Oh! uncle," he said, "how wretched I am!"

He dared not speak of his experience in love, from an odd fear of embarrassing or hurting Gottfried: but he spoke of his shame, his mediocrity, his cowardice, his broken vows.

"What am I to do, uncle? I have tried, I have struggled: and after a year I am no further on than before. Worse: I have gone back. I am good for nothing. I am good for nothing! I have ruined my life. I am perjured!..."

They were walking up the hill above the town. Gottfried said kindly:

"Not for the last time, my boy. We do not do what we will to do. We will and we live: two things. You must be comforted. The great thing is, you see, never to give up willing and living. The rest does not depend on us."

Christophe repeated desperately:

"I have perjured myself."

"Do you hear?" said Gottfried.

(The cocks were crowing in all the countryside.)

"They, too, are crowing for another who is perjured. They crow for every one of us, every morning."

"A day will come," said Christophe bitterly, "when, they will no longer crow for me ... A day to which there is no to–morrow. And what shall I have made of my life?"

"There is always a to–morrow," said Gottfried.

"But what can one do, if willing is no use?"

"Watch and pray."

"I do not believe."

Gottfried smiled.

"You would not be alive if you did not believe. Every one believes. Pray."

"Pray to what?"

Gottfried pointed to the sun appearing on the horizon, red and frozen.

"Be reverent before the dawning day. Do not think of what will be in a year, or in ten years. Think of to–day. Leave your theories. All theories, you see, even those of virtue, are bad, foolish, mischievous. Do not abuse life. Live in to–day. Be reverent towards each day. Love it, respect it, do not sully it, do not hinder it from coming to flower. Love it even when it is gray and sad like to–day. Do not be anxious. See. It is winter now. Everything is asleep. The good earth will awake again. You have only to be good and patient like the earth. Be reverent. Wait. If you are good, all will go well. If you are not, if you are weak, if you do not succeed, well, you must be happy in that. No doubt it is the best you can do. So, then, why *will*? Why be angry because of what you cannot do? We all have to do what we can.... *Als ich kann.*"

"It is not enough," said Christophe, making a face.

Gottfried laughed pleasantly.

"It is more than anybody does. You are a vain fellow. You want to be a hero. That is why you do such silly things.... A hero!... I don't quite know what that is: but, you see, I imagine that a hero is a man who does what he can. The others do not do it."

"Oh!" sighed Christophe. "Then what is the good of living? It is not worth while. And yet there are people who say: 'He who wills can!'"...

Gottfried laughed again softly.

"Yes?... Oh! well, they are liars, my friend. Or they do not will anything much...."

They had reached the top of the hill. They embraced affectionately. The little peddler went on, treading wearily. Christophe stayed there, lost in thought, and watched him go. He repeated his uncle's saying:

"*Als ich kann* (The best I can)."

And he smiled, thinking:

"Yes.... All the same.... It is enough."

He returned to the town. The frozen snow crackled under his feet. The bitter winter wind made the bare branches of the stunted trees on the hill shiver. It reddened his cheeks, and made his skin tingle, and set his blood racing. The red roofs of the town below were smiling under the brilliant, cold sun. The air was strong and harsh. The frozen earth seemed to rejoice in bitter gladness. And Christophe's heart was like that. He thought:

"I, too, shall wake again."

There were still tears in his eyes. He dried them with the back of his hand, and laughed to see the sun dipping down behind a veil of mist. The clouds, heavy with snow, were floating over the town, lashed by the squall. He laughed at them. The wind blew icily....

"Blow, blow!... Do what you will with me. Bear me with you!... I know now where I am going."

REVOLT

I. SHIFTING SANDS

Free! He felt that he was free!... Free of others and of himself! The network of passion in which he had been enmeshed for more than a year had suddenly been burst asunder. How? He did not know. The filaments had given before the growth of his being. It was one of those crises of growth in which robust natures tear away the dead casing of the year that is past, the old soul in which they are cramped and stifled.

Christophe breathed deeply, without understanding what had happened. An icy whirlwind was rushing through the great gate of the town as he returned from taking Gottfried on his way. The people were walking with heads lowered against the storm. Girls going to their work were struggling against the wind that blew against their skirts: they stopped every now and then to breathe, with their nose and cheeks red, and they looked exasperated, and as though they wanted to cry. He thought of that other torment through which he had passed. He looked at the wintry sky, the town covered with snow, the people struggling along past him: he looked about him, into himself: he was no longer bound. He was alone!... Alone! How happy to be alone, to be his own! What joy to have escaped from his bonds, from his torturing memories, from the hallucinations of faces that he loved or detested! What joy at last to live, without being the prey of life, to have become his own master!...

He went home white with snow. He shook himself gaily like a dog. As he passed his mother, who was sweeping the passage, he lifted her up, giving little inarticulate cries of affection such as one makes to a tiny child. Poor old Louisa struggled in her son's arms: she was wet with the melting snow: and she called him, with a jolly laugh, a great gaby.

He went up to his room three steps at a time.—He could hardly see himself in his little mirror it was so dark. But his heart was glad. His room was low and narrow and it was difficult to move in it, but it was like a kingdom to him. He locked the door and laughed with pleasure. At last he was finding himself! How long he had been gone astray! He was eager to plunge into thought like a bather into water. It was like a great lake afar off melting into the mists of blue and gold. After a night of fever and oppressive heat he stood by the edge of it, with his legs bathed in the freshness of the water, his body kissed by the wind of a summer morning. He plunged in and swam: he knew not whither he was going, and did not care: it was joy to swim whithersoever he listed. He was silent, then he laughed, and listened for the thousand thousand sounds of his soul: it swarmed with life. He could make out nothing: his head was swimming: he felt only a bewildering happiness. He was glad to feel in himself such unknown forces: and indolently postponing putting his powers to the test he sank back into the intoxication of pride in the inward flowering, which, held back for months, now burst forth like a sudden spring.

His mother called him to breakfast. He went down: he was giddy and light–headed as though he had spent a day in the open air: but there was such a radiance of joy in him that Louisa asked what was the matter. He made no reply: he seized her by the waist and forced her to dance with him round the table on which the tureen was steaming. Out of breath Louisa cried that he was mad: then she clasped her hands.

"Dear God!" she said anxiously. "Sure, he is in love again!"

Christophe roared with laughter. He hurled his napkin into the air.

"In love?..." he cried. "Oh! Lord!... but no! I've had enough! You can be easy on that score. That is done, done, forever!... Ouf!"

He drank a glassful of water.

Louisa looked at him, reassured, wagged her head, and smiled.

"That's a drunkard's pledge," she said. "It won't last until to–night."

"Then the day is clear gain," he replied good–humoredly.

"Oh, yes!" she said. "But what has made you so happy?"

"I am happy. That is all."

Sitting opposite her with his elbows on the table he tried to tell her all that he was going to do. She listened with kindly skepticism and gently pointed out that his soup was going cold. He knew that she did not hear what he was saying: but he did not care: he was talking for his own satisfaction.

They looked at each other smiling: he talking: she hardly listening. Although she was proud of her son she attached no great importance to his artistic projects: she was thinking: "He is happy: that matters most."—While he was growing more and more excited with his discourse he watched his mother's dear face, with her black shawl tightly tied round her head, her white hair, her young eyes that devoured him lovingly, her sweet and tranquil kindliness. He knew exactly what she was thinking. He said to her jokingly:

"It is all one to you, eh? You don't care about what I'm telling you?"

She protested weakly:

"Oh, no! Oh, no!"

He kissed her.

"Oh, yes! Oh, yes! You need not defend yourself. You are right. Only love me. There is no need to understand me—either for you or for anybody else. I do not need anybody or anything now: I have everything in myself...."

"Oh!" said Louisa. "Another maggot in his brain!... But if he must have one I prefer this to the other."

* * * * *

What sweet happiness to float on the surface of the lake of his thoughts!... Lying in the bottom of a boat with his body bathed in sun, his face kissed by the light fresh wind that skims over the face of the waters, he goes to sleep: he is swung by threads from the sky. Under his body lying at full length, under the rocking boat he feels the deep, swelling water: his hand dips into it. He rises: and with his chin on the edge of the boat he watches the water flowing by as he did when he was a child. He sees the reflection of strange creatures darting by like lightning.... More, and yet more.... They are never the same. He laughs at the fantastic spectacle that is unfolded within him: he laughs at his own thoughts: he has no need to catch and hold them. Select? Why select among So many thousands of dreams? There is plenty of time!... Later on!... He has only to throw out a line at will to draw in the monsters whom he sees gleaming in the water. He lets them pass.... Later on!...

The boat floats on at the whim of the warm wind and the insentient stream. All is soft, sun, and silence.

* * * * *

At last languidly he throws out his line. Leaning out over the lapping water he follows it with his eyes until it disappears. After a few moments of torpor he draws it in slowly: as he draws it in it becomes heavier: just as he is about to fish it out of the water he stops to take breath. He knows that he has his prey: he does not know what it is: he prolongs the pleasure of expectancy.

At last he makes up his mind: fish with gleaming, many–colored scales appear from the water: they writhe like a nest of snakes. He looks at them curiously, he stirs them with his finger: but hardly has he drawn them from the water than their colors fade and they slip between his fingers. He throws them back into the water and begins to fish for others. He is more eager to see one after another all the dreams stirring in him than to catch at any one of them: they all seem more beautiful to him when they are freely swimming in the transparent lake....

He caught all kinds of them, each more extravagant than the last. Ideas had been heaped up in him for months and he had not drawn upon them, so that he was bursting with riches. But it was all higgledy–piggledy: his mind was a Babel, an old Jew's curiosity shop in which there were piled up in the one room rare treasures, precious stuffs, scrap–iron, and rags. He could not distinguish their values: everything amused him. There were thrilling chords, colors which rang like bells, harmonies which buzzed like bees, melodies smiling like lovers' lips. There were visions of the country, faces, passions, souls, characters, literary ideas, metaphysical ideas. There were great projects, vast and impossible, tetralogies, decalogies, pretending to depict everything in music, covering whole worlds. And, most often there were obscure, flashing sensations, called forth by a trifle, the sound of a voice, a man or a woman passing in the street, the pattering of rain. An inward rhythm.—Many of these projects advanced no further than their title: most of them were never more than a note or two: it was enough. Like all very young people, he thought he had created what he dreamed of creating.

* * * * *

But he was too keenly alive to be satisfied for long with such fantasies. He wearied of an illusory possession: he wished to seize his dreams.—How to begin? They seemed to him all equally important. He turned and turned them: he rejected them, he took them up again.... No, he never took them up again: they were no longer the same, they were never to be caught twice: they were always changing: they changed in his hands, under his eyes, while he was watching them. He must make haste: he could not: he was appalled by the slowness with which he worked. He would have liked to do everything in one day, and he found it horribly difficult to complete the smallest thing. His dreams were passing and he was passing himself: while he was doing one thing it worried him not to be doing another. It was as though it was enough to have chosen one of his fine subjects for it to lose all interest for him. And so all his riches availed him nothing. His thoughts had life only on condition that he did not tamper with them: everything that he succeeded in doing was still–born. It was the torment of Tantalus: within reach were fruits that became stones as soon as he plucked them: near his lips was a clear stream which sank away whenever he bent down, to drink.

To slake his thirst lie tried to sip at the springs that he had conquered, his old compositions.... Loathsome in taste! At the first gulp, he spat it out again, cursing. What! That tepid water, that insipid music, was that his music?—He read through all his compositions: he was horrified: he understood not a note of them, he could not even understand how he had come to write them. He blushed. Once after reading through a page more foolish than the rest he turned round to make sure that there was nobody in the room, and then he went and hid his face in his pillow like a child ashamed. Sometimes they seemed to him so preposterously silly that they were quite funny, and he forgot that they were his own....

"What an idiot!" he would cry, rocking with laughter.

But nothing touched him more than those compositions in which he had set out to express his own passionate feelings: the sorrows and joys of love. Then he would bound in his chair as though a fly had stung him: he would thump on the table, beat his head, and roar angrily: he would coarsely apostrophize himself: he would vow himself to be a swine, trebly a scoundrel, a clod, and a clown—a whole litany of denunciation. In the end he would go and stand before his mirror, red with shouting, and then he would take hold of his chin and say:

"Look, look, you scurvy knave, look at the ass–face that is yours! I'll teach you to lie, you blackguard! Water, sir, water."

He would plunge his face into his basin, and hold it under water until he was like to choke. When he drew himself up, scarlet, with his eyes starting from his head, snorting like a seal, he would rush to his table, without bothering to sponge away the water trickling down him: he would seize the unhappy compositions, angrily tear them in pieces, growling:

"There, you beast!... There, there, there!..."

Then he would recover.

What exasperated him most in his compositions was their untruth. Not a spark of feeling in them. A phraseology got by heart, a schoolboy's rhetoric: he spoke of love like a blind man of color: he spoke of it from hearsay, only repeating the current platitudes. And it was not only love: it was the same with all the passions, which had been used for themes and declamations.—And yet he had always tried to be sincere.—But it is not enough to wish to be sincere: it is necessary to have the power to be so: and how can a man be so when as yet he knows nothing of life? What had revealed the falseness of his work, what had suddenly digged a pit between himself and his past was the experience which he had had during the last six months of life. He had left fantasy: there was now in him a real standard to which he could bring all the thoughts for judgment as to their truth or untruth.

The disgust which his old work, written without passion, roused in him, made him decide with his usual exaggeration that he would write no more until he was forced to write by some passionate need: and leaving the pursuit of his ideas at that, he swore that he would renounce music forever, unless creation were imposed upon him in a thunderclap.

* * * * *

He made this resolve because he knew quite well that the storm was coming.

Thunder falls when it will, and where it will. But there are peaks which attract it. Certain places—certain souls—breed storms: they create them, or draw them from all points of the horizon: and certain ages of life, like certain months of the year, are so saturated with electricity, that thunderstorms are produced in them,—if not at will—at any rate when they are expected.

The whole being of a man is taut for it. Often the storm lies brooding for days and days. The pale sky is hung with burning, fleecy clouds. No wind stirs. The still air ferments, and seems to boil. The earth lies in a stupor: no sound comes from it. The brain hums feverishly: all nature awaits the explosion of the gathering forces, the thud of the hammer which is slowly rising to fall back suddenly on the anvil of the clouds. Dark, warm shadows pass: a fiery wind rises through the body, the nerves quiver like leaves.... Then silence falls again. The sky goes on gathering thunder.

In such expectancy there is voluptuous anguish. In spite of the discomfort that weighs so heavily upon you, you feel in your veins the fire which is consuming the universe. The

334

soul surfeited boils in the furnace, like wine in a vat. Thousands of germs of life and death are in labor in it. What will issue from it? The soul knows not. Like a woman with child, it is silent: it gazes in upon itself: it listens anxiously for the stirring in its womb, and thinks: "What will be born of me?"...

Sometimes such waiting is in vain. The storm passes without breaking: but you wake heavy, cheated, enervated, disheartened. But it is only postponed: the storm will break: if not to–day, then to–morrow: the longer it is delayed, the more violent will it be....

Now it comes!... The clouds have come up from all corners of the soul. Thick masses, blue and black, torn by the frantic darting of the lightning: they advance heavily, drunkenly, darkening the soul's horizon, blotting out light. An hour of madness!... The exasperated Elements, let loose from the cage in which they are held bound by the Laws which hold the balance between the mind and the existence of things, reign, formless and colossal, in the night of consciousness. The soul is in agony. There is no longer the will to live. There is only longing for the end, for the deliverance of death....

And suddenly there is lightning!

Christophe shouted for joy.

* * * * *

Joy, furious joy, the sun that lights up all that is and will be, the godlike joy of creation! There is no joy but in creation. There are no living beings but those who create. All the rest are shadows, hovering over the earth, strangers to life. All the joys of life are the joys of creation: love, genius, action,—quickened by flames issuing from one and the same fire. Even those who cannot find a place by the great fireside: the ambitious, the egoists, the sterile sensualists,—try to gain warmth in the pale reflections of its light.

To create in the region of the body, or in the region of the mind, is to issue from the prison of the body: it is to ride upon the storm of life: it is to be He who Is. To create is to triumph over death.

Wretched is the sterile creature, that man or that woman who remains alone and lost upon the earth, scanning their withered bodies, and the sight of themselves from which no flame of life will ever leap! Wretched is the soul that does not feel its own fruitfulness, and know itself to be big with life and love, as a tree with blossom in the spring! The world may heap honors and benefits upon such a soul: it does but crown a corpse.

* * * * *

When Christophe was struck by the flash of lightning, an electric fluid coursed through his body: he trembled under the shock. It was as though on the high seas, in the dark night, he had suddenly sighted land. Or it was as though in a crowd he had gazed into two eyes saluting him. Often it would happen to him after hours of prostration when his mind was leaping desperately through the void. But more often still it came in moments when he was thinking of something else, talking to his mother, or walking through the streets. If he were in the street a certain human respect kept him from too loudly demonstrating his joy. But if he were at home nothing could keep him back. He would stamp. He would sound a blare of triumph: his mother knew that well, and she had come to know what it meant. She used to tell Christophe that he was like a hen that has laid an egg.

He was permeated with his musical imagination. Sometimes it took shape in an isolated phrase complete in itself: more often it would appear as a nebula enveloping a whole work: the structure of the work, its general lines, could be perceived through a veil, torn asunder here and there by dazzling phrases which stood out from the darkness with the clarity of sculpture. It was only a flash: sometimes others would come in quick succession: each lit up other corners of the night. But usually, the capricious force having once shown itself unexpectedly, would disappear again for several days into its mysterious retreats, leaving behind it a luminous ray.

This delight in inspiration was so vivid that Christophe was disgusted by everything else. The experienced artist knows that inspiration is rare and that intelligence is left to complete the work of intuition: he puts his ideas under the press and squeezes out of them the last drop of the divine juices that are in them—(and if need be sometimes he does not shrink from diluting them with clear water)—Christophe was too young and too sure of himself not to despise such contemptible practices. He dreamed impossibly of producing nothing that was not absolutely spontaneous. If he had not been deliberately blind he would certainly have seen the absurdity of his aims. Ho doubt he was at that time in a period of inward abundance in which there was no gap, no chink, through which boredom or emptiness could creep. Everything served as an excuse to his inexhaustible fecundity:

everything that his eyes saw or his ears heard, everything with which he came in contact in his daily life: every look, every word, brought forth a crop of dreams. In the boundless heaven of his thoughts he saw circling millions of milky stars, rivers of living light.—And yet, even then, there were moments when everything was suddenly blotted out. And although the night could not endure, although he had hardly time to suffer from these long silences of his soul, he did not escape a secret terror of that unknown power which came upon him, left him, came again, and disappeared.... How long, this time? Would it ever come again?—His pride rejected that thought and said: "This force is myself. When it ceases to be, I shall cease to be: I shall kill myself."—He never ceased to tremble: but it was only another delight.

But, if, for the moment, there was no danger of the spring running dry, Christophe was able already to perceive that it was never enough to fertilize a complete work. Ideas almost always appeared rawly: he had painfully to dig them out of the ore. And always they appeared without any sort of sequence, and by fits and starts: to unite them he had to bring to bear on them an element of reflection and deliberation and cold will, which fashioned them into new form. Christophe was too much of an artist not to do so: but he would not accept it: he forced himself to believe that he did no more than transcribe what was within himself, while he was always compelled more or less to transform it so as to make it intelligible.—More than that: sometimes he would absolutely forge a meaning for it. However violently the musical idea might come upon him it would often have been impossible for him to say what it meant. It would come surging up from the depths of life, from far beyond the limits of consciousness: and in that absolutely pure Force, which eluded common rhythms, consciousness could never recognize in it any of the motives which stirred in it, none of the human feelings which it defines and classifies: joys, sorrows, they were all merged in one single passion which was unintelligible, because it was above the intelligence. And yet, whether it understood or no, the intelligence needed to give a name to this form, to bind it down to one or other of the structures of logic, which man is forever building indefatigably in the hive of his brain.

So Christophe convinced himself—he wished to do so—that the obscure power that moved him had an exact meaning, and that its meaning was in accordance with his will. His free instinct, risen from the unconscious depths, was willy–nilly forced to plod on under the yoke of reason with perfectly clear ideas which had nothing at all in common with it. And work so produced was no more than a lying juxtaposition of one of those great subjects that Christophe's mind had marked out for itself, and those wild forces which had an altogether different meaning unknown to himself.

* * * * *

He groped his way, head down, borne on by the contradictory forces warring in him, and hurling into his incoherent works a fiery and strong quality of life which he could not express, though he was joyously and proudly conscious of it.

The consciousness of his new vigor made him able for the first time to envisage squarely everything about him, everything that he had been taught to honor, everything that he had respected without question: and he judged it all with insolent freedom. The veil was rent: he saw the German lie.

Every race, every art has its hypocrisy. The world is fed with a little truth and many lies. The human mind is feeble: pure truth agrees with it but ill: its religion, its morality, its states, its poets, its artists, must all be presented to it swathed in lies. These lies are adapted to the mind of each race: they vary from one to the other: it is they that make it so difficult for nations to understand each other, and so easy for them to despise each other. Truth is the same for all of us: but every nation has its own lie, which it calls its idealism: every creature therein breathes it from birth to death: it has become a condition of life: there are only a few men of genius who can break free from it through heroic moments of crisis, when they are alone in the free world of their thoughts.

It was a trivial thing which suddenly revealed to Christophe the lie of German art. It was not because it had not always been visible that he had not seen it: he was not near it, he had not recoiled from it. Now the mountain appeared to his gaze because he had moved away from it.

He was at a concert of the *Staedtische Townhalle*. The concert was given in a large hall occupied by ten or twelve rows of little tables—about two or three hundred of them. At the end of the room was a stage where the orchestra was sitting. All round Christophe were officers dressed up in their long, dark coats,—with broad, shaven faces, red, serious, and commonplace: women talking and laughing noisily, ostentatiously at their ease: jolly little girls smiling and showing all their teeth: and large men hidden behind their beards and spectacles, looking like kindly spiders with round eyes. They got up with every fresh glass to drink a toast: they did this almost religiously: their faces, their voices changed: it was as though they were saying Mass: they offered each other the libations, they drank of the chalice with a mixture of solemnity and buffoonery. The music was drowned under the conversation and the clinking of glasses. And yet everybody was trying to talk and eat quietly. The *Herr Konzertmeister*, a tall, bent old man, with a white beard hanging like a tail from his chin, and a long aquiline nose, with spectacles, looked like a philologist.—All these types were familiar to Christophe. But on that day he had an inclination—he did not know why—to see them as caricatures. There are days like that when, for no apparent reason, the grotesque in people and things which in ordinary life passes unnoticed, suddenly leaps into view.

The programme of the music included the *Egmont* overture, a valse of Waldteufel, *Tannhaeuser's Pilgrimage to Rome*, the overture to the *Merry Wives* of Nicolai, the religious march of *Athalie*, and a fantasy on the *North Star*. The orchestra played the Beethoven overture correctly, and the valse deliciously. During the *Pilgrimage of Tannhaeuser*, the uncorking of bottles was heard. A big man sitting at the table next to Christophe beat time to the *Merry Wives* by imitating Falstaff. A stout old lady, in a pale blue dress, with a white belt, golden pince–nez on her flat nose, red arms, and an enormous waist, sang in a loud voice *Lieder* of Schumann and Brahms. She raised her eyebrows, made eyes at the wings, smiled with a smile that seemed to curdle on her moon–face, made exaggerated gestures which must certainly have called to mind the *cafe–concert* but for the majestic honesty which shone in her: this mother of a family played the part of the giddy girl, youth, passion: and Schumann's poetry had a faint smack of the nursery. The audience was in ecstasies.—But they grew solemn and attentive when there appeared the Choral Society of the Germans of the South (*Sueddeutschen Maenner Liedertafel*), who alternately cooed and roared part songs full of feeling. There were forty and they sang four parts: it seemed as though they had set themselves to free their execution of every trace of style that could properly be called choral: a hotch–potch of little melodious effects, little timid puling shades of sound, dying *pianissimos*, with sudden swelling, roaring *crescendos*, like some one heating on an empty box: no breadth or balance, a mawkish style: it was like Bottom:

"Let me play the lion. I will roar you as gently as any sucking dove. I will roar you as it were a nightingale."

Christophe listened: foam the beginning with growing amazement. There was nothing new in it all to him. He knew these concerts, the orchestra, the audience. But suddenly it all seemed to him false. All of it: even to what he most loved, the *Egmont* overture, in which the pompous disorder and correct agitation hurt him in that hour like a want of frankness. No doubt it was not Beethoven or Schumann that he heard, but their absurd interpreters, their cud–chewing audience whose crass stupidity was spread about their works like a heavy mist.—No matter, there was in the works, even the most beautiful of them, a disturbing quality which Christophe had never before felt.—What was it? He dared not analyze it, deeming it a sacrilege to question his beloved masters. But in vain did he shut his eyes to it: he had seen it. And, in spite of himself, he went on seeing it: like the *Vergognosa* at Pisa he looked: between his fingers.

He saw German art stripped. All of them—the great and the idiots—laid bare their souls with a complacent tenderness. Emotion overflowed, moral nobility trickled down, their hearts melted in distracted effusions: the sluice gates were opened to the fearful German tender–heartedness: it weakened the energy of the stronger, it drowned the weaker under its grayish waters: it was a flood: in the depths of it slept German thought. And, what thoughts were those of a Mendelssohn, a Brahms, a Schumann, and, following them, the whole legion of little writers of affected and tearful *Lieder*! Built on sand. Never rock. Wet and shapeless clay.—It was all so foolish, so childish often, that Christophe could not believe that it never occurred to the audience. He looked about him: but he saw only gaping faces, convinced in advance of the beauties they were hearing and the pleasure that they ought to find in it. How could they admit their own right to judge for themselves? They were filled with respect for these hallowed names. What did they not respect? They were respectful before their programmes, before their glasses, before themselves. It was clear that mentally they dubbed everything excellent that remotely or nearly concerned them.

Christophe passed in review the audience and the music alternately: the music reflected the audience, the audience reflected the music. Christophe felt laughter overcoming him and he made faces. However, he controlled himself. But when the Germans of the South came and solemnly sang the *Confession* that reminded him of the blushes of a girl in love, Christophe could not contain himself. He shouted with laughter. Indignant cries of "Ssh!" were raised. His neighbors looked at him, scared: their honest, scandalized faces filled him with joy: he laughed louder than ever, he laughed, he laughed until he cried. Suddenly the audience grew angry. They cried: "Put him out!" He got up, and went, shrugging his shoulders, shaking with suppressed laughter. His departure caused a scandal. It was the beginning of hostilities between Christophe and his birthplace.

* * * * *

After that experience Christophe shut himself up and set himself to read once more the works of the "hallowed" musicians. He was appalled to find that certain of the masters whom he loved most had *lied*. He tried hard to doubt it at first, to believe that he was mistaken.—But no, there was no way out of it. He was staggered by the conglomeration of mediocrity and untruth which constitutes the artistic treasure of a great people. How many pages could bear examination!

From that time on he could begin to read other works, other masters, who were dear to him, only with a fluttering heart.... Alas! There was some spell cast upon him: always there was the same discomfiture. With some of them his heart was rent: it was as though he had lost a dear friend, as if he had suddenly seen that a friend in whom he had reposed entire confidence had been deceiving him for years. He wept for it. He did not sleep at night: he could not escape his torment. He blamed himself: perhaps he had lost his judgment? Perhaps he had become altogether an idiot?—No, no. More than ever he saw the radiant beauty of the day and with more freshness and love than ever he felt the generous abundance of life: his heart was not deceiving him....

But for a long time he dared not approach those who were the best for him, the purest, the Holy of Holies. He trembled at the thought of bringing his faith in them to the test. But how resist the pitiless instinct of a brave and truthful soul, which will go on to the end, and see things as they are, whatever suffering may be got in doing so?—So he opened the sacred works, he called upon the last reserve, the imperial guard.... At the first glance he saw that they were no more immaculate than the others. He had not the courage to go on. Every now and then he stopped and closed the book: like the son of Noah, he threw his cloak about his father's nakedness....

Then he was prostrate in the midst of all these ruins. He would rather have lost an arm, than have tampered with his blessed illusions. In his heart he mourned. But there was so much sap in him, so much reserve of life, that his confidence in art was not shaken. With a young man's naive presumption he began life again as though no one had ever lived it before him. Intoxicated by his new strength, he felt—not without reason, perhaps—that with a very few exceptions there is almost no relation between living passion and the expression which art has striven to give to it. But he was mistaken in thinking himself more happy or more true when he expressed it. As he was filled with passion it was easy for him to discover it at the back of what he had written: but no one else would have recognized it through the imperfect vocabulary with which he designated its variations. Many artists whom he condemned were in the same case. They had had, and had translated profound emotions: but the secret of their language had died with them.

Christophe was no psychologist: he was not bothered with all these arguments: what was dead for him had always been so. He revised his judgment of the past with all the confident and fierce injustice of youth. He stripped the noblest souls, and had no pity for their foibles. There were the rich melancholy, the distinguished fantasy, the kindly thinking emptiness of Mendelssohn. There were the bead–stringing and the affectation of Weber, his dryness of heart, his cerebral emotion. There was Liszt, the noble priest, the circus rider, neo–classical and vagabond, a mixture in equal doses of real and false nobility, of serene idealism and disgusting virtuosity. Schubert, swallowed up by his sentimentality, drowned at the bottom of leagues of stale, transparent water. The men of the heroic ages, the demi–gods, the Prophets, the Fathers of the Church, were not spared. Even the great Sebastian, the man of ages, who bore in himself the past and the future,—Bach,—was not free of untruth, of fashionable folly, of school–chattering. The man who had seen God, the man who lived in God, seemed sometimes to Christophe to have had an insipid and sugared religion, a Jesuitical style, rococo. In his cantatas there were languorous and devout airs—(dialogues of the Soul coquetting with Jesus)—which sickened Christophe: then he seemed to see chubby cherubim with round limbs, and flying draperies. And also he had a feeling that the genial *Cantor* always wrote in a closed room: his work smacked of stuffiness: there was not in his music that brave outdoor air that was breathed in others, not such great musicians, perhaps, but greater men—more human—than he. Like Beethoven or Haendel. What hurt him in all of them, especially in the classics, was their lack of freedom: almost all their works were "constructed." Sometimes an emotion was filled out with all the commonplaces of musical rhetoric, sometimes with a simple rhythm, an ornamental design, repeated, turned upside down, combined in every conceivable way in a mechanical fashion. These symmetrical and twaddling constructions—classical, and neo–classical sonatas and symphonies—exasperated Christophe, who, at that time, was not very sensible of the beauty of order, and vast and well–conceived plans. That seemed to him to be rather masons' work than musicians'.

But he was no less severe with the romantics. It was a strange thing, and he was more surprised by it than anybody,—but no musicians irritated him more than those who had pretended to be—and had actually been—the most free, the most spontaneous, the least constructive,—those, who, like Schumann, had poured drop by drop, minute by minute, into their innumerable little works, their whole life. He was the more indignantly in revolt against them as he recognized in them his adolescent soul and all the follies that he had vowed to pluck out of it. In truth, the candid Schumann could not be taxed with falsity: he hardly ever said anything that he had not felt. But that was just it: his example made Christophe understand that the worst falsity in German art came into it not when the artists tried to express something which they had not felt, but rather when they tried to express the feelings which they did in fact feel—*feelings which were false*. Music is an implacable mirror of the soul. The more a German musician is naive and in good faith, the more he displays the weaknesses of the German soul, its uncertain depths, its soft tenderness, its want of frankness, its rather sly idealism, its incapacity for seeing itself, for daring to come face to face with itself. That false idealism is the secret sore even of the greatest—of Wagner. As he read his works Christophe ground his teeth. *Lohengrin* seemed to him a blatant lie. He loathed the huxtering chivalry, the hypocritical mummery, the hero without fear and without a heart, the incarnation of cold and selfish virtue admiring itself and most patently self–satisfied. He knew it too well, he had seen it in reality, the type of German Pharisee, foppish, impeccable, and hard, bowing down before its own image, the divinity to which it has no scruple about sacrificing others. The *Flying Dutchman* overwhelmed him with its massive sentimentality and its gloomy boredom. The loves of the barbarous decadents of the *Tetralogy* were of a sickening staleness. Siegmund carrying off his sister sang a tenor drawing–room song. Siegfried and Bruennhilde, like respectable German married people, in the *Goetterdaemmerung* laid bare before each other, especially for the benefit of the audience, their pompous and voluble conjugal passion. Every sort of lie had arranged to meet in that work: false idealism, false Christianity, false Gothicism, false legend, false gods, false humans. Never did more monstrous convention appear than in that theater which was to upset all the conventions. Neither eyes, nor mind, nor heart could be deceived by it for a moment: if they were, then they must wish to be so.—They did wish to be so. Germany was delighted with that doting, childish art, an art of brutes let loose, and mystic, namby–pamby little girls.

And Christophe could do nothing: as soon as he heard the music he was caught up like the others, more than the others, by the flood, and the diabolical will of the man who had let it loose. He laughed, and he trembled, and his cheeks burned, and he felt galloping armies rushing through him! And he thought that those who bore such storms within themselves might have all allowances made for them. What cries of joy he uttered when in the hallowed works which he could not read without trembling he felt once more his old emotion, ardent still, with nothing to tarnish the purity of what he loved! These were glorious relics that he saved from the wreck. What happiness they gave him! It seemed to him that he had saved a part of himself. And was it not himself? These great Germans, against whom he revolted, were they not his blood, his flesh, his most precious life? He was only severe with them because he was severe with himself. Who loved them better than he? Who felt more than he the goodness of Schubert, the innocence of Haydn, the tenderness of Mozart, the great heroic heart of Beethoven? Who more often than he took refuge in the murmuring of the forests of Weber, and the cool shade of the cathedrals of John Sebastian, raising against the gray sky of the North, above the plains of Germany, their pile of stone, and their gigantic towers with their sun–tipped spires?—But he suffered from their lies, and he could not forget them. He attributed them to the race, their greatness to themselves. He was wrong. Greatness and weaknesses belong equally to the race whose great, shifting thought flows like the greatest river of music and poetry at which Europe comes to drink.—And in what other people would he have found the simple purity which now made it possible for him to condemn it so harshly?

He had no notion of that. With the ingratitude of a spoiled child he turned against his mother the weapons which he had received from her. Later, later, he was to feel all that he owed to her, and how dear she was to him....

But he was in a phase of blind reaction against all the idols of his childhood. He was angry with himself and with them because he had believed in them absolutely and passionately—and it was well that it was so. There is an age in life when we must dare to be unjust, when we must make a clean sweep of all admiration and respect got at second–hand, and deny everything—truth and untruth—everything which we have not of ourselves known for truth. Through education, and through everything that he sees and hears about him, a child absorbs so many lies and blind follies mixed with the essential verities of life, that the first duty of the adolescent who wishes to grow into a healthy man is to sacrifice everything.

* * * * *

Christophe was passing through that crisis of healthy disgust. His instinct was impelling him to eliminate from his life all the undigested elements which encumbered it.

First of all to go was that sickening sweet tenderness which sucked away the soul of Germany like a damp and moldy riverbed. Light! Light! A rough, dry wind which should sweep away the miasmas of the swamp, the misty staleness of the *Lieder, Liedchen, Liedlein*, as numerous as drops of rain in which inexhaustibly the Germanic *Gemuet* is poured forth: the countless things like *Sehnsucht* (Desire), *Heimweh* (Homesickness), *Aufschwung* (Soaring), *Trage* (A question), *Warum?* (Why?), *an den Mond* (To the Moon), *an die Sterne* (To the Stars), *an die Nachtigall* (To the Nightingale), *an den Fruehling* (To Spring), *an den Sonnenschein* (To Sunshine): like *Fruehlingslied* (Spring Song), *Fruehlingslust* (Delights of Spring), *Fruehlingsgruss* (Hail to the Spring), *Fruelingsfahrt* (A Spring Journey), *Fruelingsnacht* (A Spring Night), *Fruehlingsbotschaft* (The Message of Spring): like *Stimme der Liebe* (The Voice of Love), *Sprache der Liebe* (The Language of Love), *Trauer der Liebe* (Love's Sorrow), *Geist der Liebe* (The Spirit of Love), *Fuelle der Liebe* (The Fullness of Love): like *Blumenlied* (The Song of the Flowers), *Blumenbrief* (The Letter of the Flowers), *Blumengruss* (Flowers' Greeting): like *Herzeleid* (Heart Pangs), *Mein Herz ist schwer* (My Heart is Heavy), *Mein Herz ist betruebt* (My Heart is Troubled), *Mein Aug' ist trueb* (My Eye is Heavy): like the candid and silly dialogues with the *Roeselein* (The Little Rose), with the brook, with the turtle dove, with the lark: like those idiotic questions: *"If the briar could have no thorns?"*—*"Is an old husband like a lark who has built a nest?"*—*"Is she newly plighted?"*: the whole deluge of stale tenderness, stale emotion, stale melancholy, stale poetry.... How many lovely things profaned, rare things, used in season or out! For the worst of it was that it was all useless: a habit of undressing their hearts in public, a fond and foolish propensity of the honest people of Germany for plunging loudly into confidences. With nothing to say they were always talking! Would their chatter never cease?—As well bid frogs in a pond be silent.

It was in the expression of love that Christophe was most rawly conscious of untruth: for he was in a position to compare it with the reality. The conventional love songs, lacrymose and proper, contained nothing like the desires of man or the heart of woman. And yet the people who had written them must have loved at least once in their lives! Was it possible that they could have loved like that? No, no, they had lied, as they always did, they had lied to themselves: they had tried to idealize themselves.... Idealism! That meant that they were afraid of looking at life squarely, were incapable of seeing things like a man, as they are.—Everywhere the same timidity, the same lack of manly frankness. Everywhere the same chilly enthusiasm, the same pompous lying solemnity, in their patriotism, in their drinking, in their religion. The *Trinklieder* (Drinking Songs) were prosopopeia to wine and the bowl: *"Du, herrlich Glas ..."* ("Thou, noble glass ..."). Faith—the one thing in the world which should be spontaneous, springing from the soul like an unexpected sudden stream—was a manufactured article, a commodity of trade. Their patriotic songs were made for docile flocks of sheep basking in unison.... Shout, then!—What! Must you go on lying—*"idealizing "*—till you are surfeited, till it brings you to slaughter and madness!...

Christophe ended by hating all idealism. He preferred frank brutality to such lying. But at heart he was more of an idealist than the rest, and he had not—he could not have—any more real enemies than the brutal realists whom he thought he preferred.

He was blinded by passion. He was frozen by the mist, the anaemic lying, "the sunless phantom Ideas." With his whole being he reached upwards to the sun. In his youthful contempt for the hypocrisy with which he was surrounded, or for what he took to be hypocrisy, he did not see the high, practical wisdom of the race which little by little had built up for itself its grandiose idealism in order to suppress its savage instincts, or to turn them to account. Not arbitrary reasons, not moral and religious codes, not legislators and statesmen, priests and philosophers, transform the souls of peoples and often impose upon them a new nature: but centuries of misfortune and experience, which forge the life of peoples who have the will to live.

    * * * * *

And yet Christophe went on composing: and his compositions were not examples of the faults which he found in others. In him creation was an irresistible necessity which would not submit to the rules which his intelligence laid down for it. No man creates from reason, but from necessity.—It is not enough to have recognized the untruth and affectation inherent in the majority of the feelings to avoid falling into them: long and painful endeavor is necessary: nothing is more difficult than to be absolutely true in modern society with its crushing heritage of indolent habits handed down through generations. It is especially difficult for those people, those nations who are possessed by an indiscreet mania for letting their hearts speak—for making them speak—unceasingly, when most generally it had much better have been silent.

Christophe's heart was very German in that: it had not yet learned the virtue of silence: and that virtue did not belong to his age. He had inherited from his father a need for talking, and talking loudly. He knew it and struggled against it: bat the conflict paralyzed part of his forces.—And he had another gift of heredity, no less burdensome, which had come to him from his grandfather: an extraordinary difficulty—in expressing himself exactly.—He was the son of a *virtuoso*. He was conscious of the dangerous attraction of virtuosity: a physical pleasure, the pleasure of skill, of agility, of satisfied muscular activity, the pleasure of conquering, of dazzling, of enthralling in his own person the many–headed audience: an excusable pleasure, in a young man almost an innocent pleasure, though none the less destructive of art and soul: Christophe knew it: it was in his blood: he despised it, but all the same he yielded to it.

And so, torn between the instincts of his race and those of his genius, weighed down by the burden of a parasitical past, which covered him with a crust that he could not break through, he floundered along, and was much nearer than he thought to all that he shunned and banned. All his compositions were a mixture of truth and turgidness, of lucid strength and faltering stupidity. It was only in rare moments that his personality could pierce the casing of the dead personality which hampered his movements.

He was alone. He had no guide to help him out of the mire. When he thought he was out of it he slipped back again. He went blindly on, wasting his time and strength in futile efforts. He was spared no trial: and in the disorder of his creative striving he never knew what was of greatest worth in what he created. He tied himself up in absurd projects, symphonic poems, which pretended to philosophy and were of monstrous dimensions. He was too sincere to be able to hold to them for long together: and he would discard them in disgust before he had stretched out a single movement. Or he would set out to translate into overtures the most inaccessible works of poetry. Then he would flounder about in a domain which was not his own. When he drew up scenarios for himself—(for he stuck at nothing)—they were idiotic: and when he attacked the great works of Goethe, Hebbel, Kleist, or Shakespeare, he understood them all wrong. It was not want of intelligence but want of the critical spirit: he could not yet understand others, he was too much taken up with himself: he found himself everywhere with his naive and turgid soul.

But besides these monsters who were not really begotten, he wrote a quantity of small pieces, which were the immediate expression of passing emotions—the most eternal of all: musical thoughts, *Lieder*. In this as in other things he was in passionate reaction against current practices. He would take up the most famous poems, already set to music, and was impertinent enough to try to treat them differently and with greater truth than

Schumann and Schubert. Sometimes he would try to give to the poetic figures of Goethe—to Mignon, the Harpist in *Wilhelm Meister*, their individual character, exact and changing. Sometimes he would tackle certain love songs which the weakness of the artists and the dullness of the audience in tacit agreement had clothed about with sickly sentimentality: and he would unclothe them: he would restore to them their rough, crude sensuality. In a word, he set out to make passions and people live for themselves and not to serve as toys for German families seeking an easy emotionalism on Sundays when they sat about in some *Biergarten*.

But generally he would find the poets, even the greatest of them, too literary: and he would select the simplest texts for preference: texts of old *Lieder*, jolly old songs, which he had read perhaps in some improving work: he would take care not to preserve their choral character: he would treat them with a fine, lively, and altogether lay audacity. Or he would take words from the Gospel, or proverbs, sometimes even words heard by chance, scraps of dialogues of the people, children's thoughts: words often awkward and prosaic in which there was only pure feeling. With them he was at his ease, and he would reach a depth with them which was not in his other compositions, a depth which he himself never suspected.

Good or bad, more often bad than good, his works as a whole had abounding vitality. They were not altogether new: far from it. Christophe was often banal, through his very sincerity: he repeated sometimes forms already used because they exactly rendered his thought, because he also felt in that way and not otherwise. Nothing would have induced him to try to be original: it seemed to him that a man must be very commonplace to burden himself with such an idea. He tried to be himself, to say what he felt, without worrying as to whether what he said had been said before him or not. He took a pride in believing that it was the best way of being original and that Christophe had only been and only would be alive once. With the magnificent impudence of youth, nothing seemed to him to have been done before: and everything seemed to him to be left for doing—or for doing again. And the feeling of this inward fullness of life, of a life stretching endless before him, brought him to a state of exuberant and rather indiscreet happiness. He was perpetually in a state of jubilation, which had no need of joy: it could adapt itself to sorrow: its source overflowed with life, was, in its strength, mother of all happiness and virtue. To live, to live too much!... A man who does not feel within himself this intoxication of strength, this jubilation in living—even in the depths of misery,—is not an artist. That is the touchstone. True greatness is shown in this power of rejoicing through joy and sorrow. A Mendelssohn or a Brahms, gods of the mists of October, and of fine rain, have never known the divine power.

Christophe was conscious of it: and he showed his joy simply, impudently. He saw no harm in it, he only asked to share it with others. He did not see how such joy hurts the majority of men, who never can possess it and are always envious of it. For the rest he never bothered about pleasing or displeasing: he was sure of himself, and nothing seemed to him simpler than to communicate his conviction to others,—to conquer. Instinctively he compared his riches with the general poverty of the makers of music: and he thought that it would be very easy to make his superiority recognized. Too easy, even. He had only to show himself.

He showed himself.

* * * * *

They were waiting for him.

Christophe had made no secret of his feelings. Since he had become aware of German Pharisaism, which refuses to see things as they are, he had made it a law for himself that he should be absolutely, continually, uncompromisingly sincere in everything without regard for anything or anybody or himself. And as he could do nothing without going to extremes, he was extravagant in his sincerity: he would say outrageous things and scandalize people a thousand times less naive than himself. He never dreamed that it might annoy them. When he realized the idiocy of some hallowed composition he would make haste to impart his discovery to everybody he encountered: musicians of the orchestra, or amateurs of his acquaintance. He would pronounce the most absurd judgments with a beaming face. At first no one took him seriously: they laughed at his freaks. But it was not long before they found that he was always reverting to them, insisting on them in a way that was really bad taste. It became evident that Christophe believed in his paradoxes: and they became less amusing. He was a nuisance: at concerts he would make ironic remarks in a loud voice, or would express his scorn for the glorious masters in no veiled fashion wherever he might be.

Everything passed from mouth to mouth in the little town: not a word was lost. People were already affronted by his conduct during the past year. They had not forgotten the scandalous fashion in which he had shown himself abroad with Ada and the troublous times of the sequel. He had forgotten, it himself: one day wiped out another, and he was very different from what he had been two months before. But others had not forgotten: those who, in all small towns, take upon themselves scrupulously to note down all the faults, all the imperfections, all the sad, ugly, and unpleasant happenings concerning their neighbors, so that nothing is ever forgotten. Christophe's new extravagances were naturally set, side by side with his former indiscretions, in the scroll. The former explained the latter. The outraged feelings of offended morality were now bolstered up by those of scandalized good taste. The kindliest of them said:

"He is trying to be particular."

But most alleged:

"Total verrueckt!" (Absolutely mad.)

An opinion no less severe and even more dangerous was beginning to find currency—an opinion assured of success by reason of its illustrious origin: it was said that, at the Palace, whither Christophe still went upon his official duties, he had had the bad taste in conversation with the Grand Duke himself, with revolting lack of decency, to give vent to his ideas concerning the illustrious masters: it was said that he had called Mendelssohn's *Elijah* "a clerical humbug's paternoster," and he had called certain *Lieder* of Schumann "*Backfisch Musik*": and that in the face of the declared preference of the august Princess for those works! The Grand Duke had cut short his impertinences by saying dryly:

"To hear you, sir, one would doubt your being a German." This vengeful utterance, coming from so lofty an eminence, reached the lowest depths: and everybody who thought he had reason to be annoyed with Christophe, either for his success, or for some more personal if not more cogent reason, did not fail to call to mind that he was not in fact pure German. His father's family, it was remembered, came originally from Belgium. It was not surprising, therefore, that this immigrant should decry the national glories. That explained everything and German vanity found reasons therein for greater self-esteem, and at the same time for despising its adversary.

Christophe himself most substantially fed this Platonic vengeance. It is very imprudent to criticise others when you are yourself on the point of challenging criticism. A cleverer or less frank artist would have shown more modesty and more respect for his predecessors. But Christophe could see no reason for hiding his contempt for mediocrity or his joy in his own strength, and his joy was shown in no temperate fashion. Although from childhood Christophe had been turned in upon himself for want of any creature to confide in, of late he had come by a need of expansiveness. He had too much joy for himself: his breast was too small to contain it: he would have burst if he had not shared his delight. Failing a friend, he had confided in his colleague in the orchestra, the second *Kapellmeister*, Siegmund Ochs, a young Wurtemberger, a good fellow, though crafty, who showed him an effusive deference. Christophe did not distrust him: and, even if he had, how could it have occurred to him that it might be harmful to confide his joy to one who did not care, or even to an enemy? Ought they not rather to be grateful to him? Was it not for them also that he was working? He brought happiness for all, friends and enemies alike.—He had no idea that there is nothing more difficult than to make men accept a new happiness: they almost prefer their old misery: they need food that has been masticated for ages. But what is most intolerable to them is the thought that they owe such happiness to another. They cannot forgive that offense until there is no way of evading it: and in any case, they do contrive to make the giver pay dearly for it.

There were, then, a thousand reasons why Christophe's confidences should not be kindly received by anybody. But there were a thousand and one reasons why they should not be acceptable to Siegmund Ochs. The first *Kapellmeister*, Tobias Pfeiffer, was on the point of retiring: and, in spite of his youth, Christophe had every chance of succeeding him. Ochs was too good a German not to recognize that Christophe was worthy of the position, since the Court was on his side. But he had too good an opinion of himself not to believe that he would have been more worthy had the Court known him better. And so he received Christophe's effusions with a strange smile when, he arrived at the theater in the morning with a face that he tried hard to make serious, though it beamed in spite of himself.

"Well?" he would say slyly as he came up to him, "another masterpiece?"

Christophe would take his arm.

"Ah! my friend. It is the best of all ... If you could hear it!... Devil take me, it is too beautiful! There has never been anything like it. God help the poor audience! They will only long for one thing when they have heard it: to die."

His words did not fall upon deaf ears. Instead of smiling, or of chaffing Christophe about his childish enthusiasm—he would have been the first to laugh at it and beg pardon if he had been made to feel the absurdity of it—Ochs went into ironic ecstasies: he drew Christophe on to further enormities: and when he left him made haste to repeat them all, making them even more grotesque. The little circle of musicians chuckled over them: and every one was impatient for the opportunity of judging the unhappy compositions.—They were all judged beforehand.

At last they appeared—Christophe had chosen from the better of his works an overture to the *Judith* of Hebbel, the savage energy of which had attracted him, in his reaction against German atony, although he was beginning to lose his taste for it, knowing intuitively the unnaturalness of such assumption of genius, always and at all costs. He had added a symphony which bore the bombastic title of the Basle Boecklin, "*The Dream of Life*," and the motto: "*Vita somnium breve*." A song–cycle completed the programme, with a few classical works, and a *Festmarsch* by Ochs, which Christophe had kindly offered to include in his concert, though he knew it to be mediocre.

Nothing much happened during the rehearsals. Although the orchestra understood absolutely nothing of the composition it was playing and everybody was privately disconcerted by the oddities of the new music, they had no time to form an opinion: they were not capable of doing so until the public had pronounced on it. Besides, Christophe's confidence imposed on the artists, who, like every good German orchestra, were docile and disciplined. His only difficulties were with the singer. She was the blue lady of the *Townhalle* concert. She was famous through Germany: the domestic creature sang Bruennhilde Kundry at Dresden and Bayreuth with undoubted lung–power. But if in the Wagnerian school she had learned the art of which that school is justly proud, the art of good articulation, of projecting the consonants through space, and of battering the gaping audience with the vowels as with a club, she had not learned—designedly—the art of being natural. She provided for every word: everything was accentuated: the syllables moved with leaden feet, and there was a tragedy in every sentence. Christophe implored her to moderate her dramatic power a little. She tried at first graciously enough: but her natural heaviness and her need for letting her voice go carried her away. Christophe became nervous. He told the respectable lady that he had tried to make human beings speak with his speaking–trumpet and not the dragon Fafner. She took his insolence in bad part—naturally. She said that, thank Heaven! she knew what singing was, and that she had had the honor of interpreting the *Lieder* of Maestro Brahms, in the presence of that great man, and that he had never tired of hearing her.

"So much the worse! So much the worse!" cried Christophe.

She asked him with a haughty smile to be kind enough to explain the meaning of his energetic remark. He replied that never in his life had Brahms known what it was to be natural, that his eulogies were the worst possible censure, and that although he—Christophe—was not very polite, as she had justly observed, never would he have gone so far as to say anything so unpleasant.

The argument went on in this fashion: and the lady insisted on singing in her own way, with heavy pathos and melodramatic effects—until one day when Christophe declared coldly that he saw the truth: it was her nature and nothing could change it: but since the *Lieder* could not be sung properly, they should not be sung at all: he withdrew them from the programme.—It was on the eve of the concert and they were counting on the *Lieder*: she had talked about them: she was musician enough to appreciate certain of their qualities: Christophe insulted her: and as she was not sure that the morrow's concert would not set the seal on the young man's fame, she did not wish to quarrel with a rising star. She gave way suddenly: and during the last rehearsal she submitted docilely to all Christophe's wishes. But she had made up her mind—at the concert—to have her own way.

* * * * *

The day came. Christophe had no anxiety. He was too full of his music to be able to judge it. He realized that some of his works in certain places bordered on the ridiculous. But what did that matter? Nothing great can be written without touching the ridiculous. To reach the heart of things it is necessary to dare human respect, politeness, modesty, the timidity of social lies under which the heart is stifled. If nobody is to be affronted and success attained, a man must be resigned all his life to remain bound by convention and to give to second–rate people the second–rate truth, mitigated, diluted, which they are capable of receiving: he must dwell in prison all his life. A man is great only when he has set his foot on such anxieties. Christophe trampled them underfoot. Let them hiss him: he was sure of not leaving them indifferent. He conjured up the faces that certain people of his acquaintance would make as they heard certain rather bold passages. He expected bitter criticism: he smiled at it already. In any case they would have to be blind—or deaf—to deny that there was force in it—pleasant or otherwise, what did it matter?—Pleasant! Pleasant!... Force! That is enough. Let it go its way, and bear all before it, like the Rhine!...

He had one setback. The Grand Duke did not come. The royal box was only occupied by Court people, a few ladies–in–waiting. Christophe was irritated by it. He thought: "The fool is cross with me. He does not know what to think of my work: he is afraid of compromising himself." He shrugged his shoulders, pretending not to be put out by such idiocy. Others paid more attention to it: it was the first lesson for him, a menace of his future.

The public had not shown much more interest than the Grand Duke: quite a third of the hall was empty. Christophe could not help thinking bitterly of the crowded halls at his concerts when he was a child. He would not have been surprised by the change if he had had more experience: it would have seemed natural to him that there were fewer people come to hear him when he made good music than when he made bad: for it is not music but the musician in which the greater part of the public is interested: and it is obvious that a musician who is a man and like everybody else is much less interesting than a musician in a child's little trowsers or short frock, who tickles sentimentality or amuses idleness.

After waiting in vain for the hall to fill, Christophe decided to begin. He tried to pretend that it was better so, saying, "A few friends but good."—His optimism did not last long.

His pieces were played in silence.—There is a silence in an audience which seems big and overflowing with love. But there was nothing in this. Nothing. Utter sleep. Blankness. Every phrase seemed to drop into depths of indifference. With his back turned to the audience, busy with his orchestra, Christophe was fully aware of everything that was happening in the hall, with those inner antennae which every true musician is endowed, so that he knows whether what he is playing is waking an echo in the hearts about him. He went on conducting and growing excited while he was frozen by the cold mist of boredom rising from the stalls and the boxes behind him.

At last the overture was ended: and the audience applauded. It applauded coldly, politely, and was then silent. Christophe would rather have had them hoot.... A hiss! One hiss! Anything to give a sign of life, or at least of reaction against his work!... Nothing.—He looked at the audience. The people were looking at each other, each trying to find out what the other thought. They did not succeed and relapsed into indifference.

The music went on. The symphony was played.—Christophe found it hard to go on to the end. Several times he was on the point of throwing down his baton and running away. Their apathy overtook him: at last he could not understand what he was conducting: he could not breathe: he felt that he was falling into fathomless boredom. There was not even the whispered ironic comment which he had anticipated at certain passages: the audience were reading their programmes. Christophe heard the pages turned all together with a dry rustling: and then, once more there was silence until the last chord, when the same polite applause showed that they had not understood that the symphony was finished.—And yet there were four pairs of hands went on clapping when the others had finished: but they awoke no echo, and stopped ashamed: that made the emptiness seem more empty, and the little incident served to show the audience how bored it had been.

Christophe took a seat in the middle of the orchestra: he dared not look to right or left. He wanted to cry: and at the same time he was quivering with rage. He was fain to get up and shout at them: "You bore me! Ah! How you bore me! I cannot bear it!... Go away! Go away, all of you!..."

The audience woke up a little: they were expecting the singer,—they were accustomed to applauding her. In that ocean of new music in which they were drifting without a compass, she at least was sure, a known land, and a solid, in which there was no danger of being lost. Christophe divined their thoughts exactly, and he laughed bitterly. The singer was no less conscious of the expectancy of the audience: Christophe saw that in her regal airs when he came and told her that it was her turn to appear. They looked at each other inimically. Instead of offering her his arm, Christophe thrust his hands into his pockets and let her go on alone. Furious and out of countenance she passed him. He followed her with a bored expression. As soon as she appeared the audience gave her an ovation: that made everybody happier: every face brightened, the audience grew interested, and glasses were brought into play. Certain of her power she tackled the *Lieder*, in her own way, of course, and absolutely disregarded Christophe's remarks of the evening before. Christophe, who was accompanying her, went pale. He had foreseen her rebellion. At the first change that she made he tapped on the piano and said angrily:

"No!"

She went on. He whispered behind her back in a low voice of fury:

"No! No! Not like that!... Not that!"

Unnerved by his fierce growls, which the audience could not hear, though the orchestra caught every syllable, she stuck to it, dragging her notes, making pauses like organ stops. He paid no heed to them and went ahead: in the end they got out of time. The audience did not notice it: for some time they had been saying that Christophe's music was not made to seem pleasant or right to the ear: but Christophe, who was not of that opinion, was making lunatic grimaces: and at last he exploded. He stopped short in the middle of a bar:

"Stop," he shouted.

She was carried on by her own impetus for half a bar and then stopped:

"That's enough," he said dryly.

There was a moment of amazement in the audience. After a few seconds he said icily:

"Begin again!"

She looked at him in stupefaction: her hands trembled: she thought for a moment of throwing his book at his head: afterwards she did not understand how it was that she did not do so. But she was overwhelmed by Christophe's authority and his unanswerable tone of voice: she began again. She sang the song–cycle, without changing one shade of meaning, or a single movement: for she felt that he would spare her nothing: and she shuddered at the thought of a fresh insult.

When she had finished the audience recalled her frantically. They were not applauding the *Lieder*—(they would have applauded just the same if she had sung any others)—but the famous singer who had grown old in harness: they knew that they could safely admire her. Besides, they wanted to make up to her for the insult she had just received. They were not quite sure, but they did vaguely understand that the singer had made a mistake: and they thought it indecent of Christophe to call their attention to it. They encored the songs. But Christophe shut the piano firmly.

The singer did not notice his insolence: she was too much upset to think of singing again. She left the stage hurriedly and shut herself up in her box: and then for a quarter of an hour she relieved her heart of the flood of wrath and rage that was pent up in it: a nervous attack, a deluge of tears, indignant outcries and imprecations against Christophe,—she omitted nothing. Her cries of anger could be heard through the closed door. Those of her friends who had made their way there told everybody when they left that Christophe had behaved like a cad. Opinion travels quickly in a concert hall. And so when Christophe went to his desk for the last piece of music the audience was stormy. But it was not his composition: it was the *Festmarsch* by Ochs, which Christophe had kindly included in his programme. The audience—who were quite at their ease with the dull music—found a very simple method of displaying their disapproval of Christophe without going so far as to hiss him: they acclaimed Ochs ostentatiously, recalled the composer two or three times, and he appeared readily. And that was the end of the concert.

The Grand Duke and everybody at the Court—the bored, gossiping little provincial town—lost no detail of what had happened. The papers which were friendly towards the singer made no allusion to the incident: but they all agreed in exalting her art while they only mentioned the titles of the *Lieder* which she had sung. They published only a few lines about Christophe's other compositions, and they all said almost the same things: "... Knowledge of counterpoint. Complicated writing. Lack of inspiration. No melody. Written with the head, not with the heart. Want of sincerity. Trying to be original...." Followed a paragraph on true originality, that of the masters who are dead and buried, Mozart, Beethoven, Loewe, Schubert, Brahms, "those who are original without thinking of it."—Then by a natural transition they passed to the revival at the Grand Ducal Theater of the *Nachtlager von Granada* of Konradin Kreutzer: a long account was given of "the delicious music, as fresh and jolly as when it was first written."

Christophe's compositions met with absolute and astonished lack of comprehension from the most kindly disposed critics: veiled hostility from those who did not like him, and were arming themselves for later ventures: and from the general public, guided by neither friendly nor hostile critics, silence. Left to its own thoughts the general public does not think at all: that goes without saying.

* * * * *

Christophe was bowled over.

And yet there was nothing surprising in his defeat. There were reasons, three to one, why his compositions should not please. They were immature. They were, secondly, too advanced to be understood at once. And, lastly, people were only too glad to give a lesson to the impertinent youngster.—But Christophe was not cool–headed enough to admit that his reverse was legitimate. He had none of that serenity which the true artist gains from the mournful experience of long misunderstanding at the hands of men and their incurable stupidity. His naive confidence in the public and in success which he thought he could easily gain because he deserved it, crumbled away. He would have thought it natural to have enemies. But what staggered him was to find that he had not a single friend. Those on whom he had counted, those who hitherto had seemed to be interested in everything that he wrote, had not given him a single word of encouragement since the concert. He tried to probe them: they took refuge behind vague words. He insisted, he wanted to know what they really thought: the most sincere of them referred back to his former works, his foolish early efforts.—More than once in his life he was to hear his new works condemned by comparison, with the older ones,—and that by the same people who, a few years before, had condemned his older works when they were new: that is the usual ordering of these things. Christophe did not like it: he exclaimed loudly. If people did not like him, well and good: he accepted that: it even pleased him since he could not be friends with everybody. But that people should pretend to be fond of him and not allow him to grow up, that they should try to force him all his life to remain a child, was beyond the pale! What is good at twelve is not good at twenty: and he hoped not to stay at that, but to change and to go on changing always.... These idiots who tried to stop life!... What was interesting in his childish compositions was not their childishness and silliness, but the force in them hungering for the future. And they were trying to kill his future!... No, they had never understood what he was, they had never loved him, never then or now: they only loved the weakness and vulgarity in him, everything that he had in common with others, and not *himself*, not what he really was: their friendship was a misunderstanding....

He was exaggerating, perhaps. It often happens with quite nice people who are incapable of liking new work which they sincerely love when it is twenty years old. New life smacks too strong for their weak senses—the scent of it must evaporate in the winds of Time. A work of art only becomes intelligible to them when it is crusted over with the dust of years.

But Christophe could not admit of not being understood when he was *present* and of being understood when he was *past*. He preferred to think that he was not understood at all, in any case, even. And he raged against it. He was foolish enough to want to make himself understood, to explain himself, to argue. Although no good purpose was served thereby: he would have had to reform the taste of his time. But he was afraid of nothing. He was determined by hook or by crook to clean up German taste. But it was utterly impossible: he could not convince anybody by means of conversation, in which he found it difficult to find words, and expressed himself with an excess of violence about the great musicians and even about the men to whom he was talking: he only succeeded in making a few more enemies. He would have had to prepare his ideas beforehand, and then to force the public to hear him....

And just then, at the appointed hour, his star—his evil star—gave him the means of doing so.

* * * * *

He was sitting in the restaurant of the theater in a group of musicians belonging to the orchestra whom he was scandalizing by his artistic judgments. They were not all of the same opinion: but they were all ruffled by the freedom of his language. Old Krause, the alto, a good fellow and a good musician, who sincerely loved Christophe, tried to turn the conversation: he coughed, then looked out for an opportunity of making a pun. But Christophe did not hear him: he went on: and Krause mourned and thought:

"What makes him say such things? God bless him! You can think these things: but you must not say them."

The odd thing was that he also thought "these things": at least, he had a glimmering of them, and Christophe's words roused many doubts in him: but he had not the courage to confess it, or openly to agree—half from fear of compromising himself, half from modesty and distrust of himself.

Weigl, the cornet–player, did not want to know anything: he was ready to admire anything, or anybody, good or bad, star or gas–jet: everything was the same to him: there were no degrees in his admiration: he admired, admired, admired. It was a vital necessity to him: it hurt him when anybody tried to curb him.

Old Kuh, the violoncellist, suffered even more. He loved bad music with all his heart. Everything that Christophe hounded down with his sarcasm and invective was infinitely dear to him: instinctively his choice pitched on the most conventional works: his soul was a reservoir of tearful and high–flown emotion. Indeed, he was not dishonest in his tender regard for all the sham great men. It was when he tried to pretend that he liked the real great men that he was lying to himself—in perfect innocence. There are "Brahmins" who think to find in their God the breath of old men of genius: they love Beethoven in Brahms. Kuh went one better: he loved Brahms in Beethoven.

But the most enraged of all with. Christophe's paradoxes was Spitz, the bassoon. It was not so much his musical instinct that was wounded as his natural servility. One of the Roman Emperors wished to die standing. Spitz wished to die, as he had lived, crawling: that was his natural position: it was delightful to him to grovel at the feet of everything that was official, hallowed, "arrived": and he was beside himself when anybody tried to keep him from playing the lackey, comfortably.

So, Kuh groaned, Weigl threw up his hands in despair, Krause made jokes, and Spitz shouted in a shrill voice. But Christophe went on imperturbably shouting louder than the rest: and saying monstrous things about Germany and the Germans.

At the next table a young man was listening to him and rocking with laughter. He had black curly hair, fine, intelligent eyes, a large nose, which at its end could not make up its mind to go either to right or left, and rather than go straight on, went to both sides at once, thick lips, and a clever, mobile face: he was following everything that Christophe said, hanging on his lips, reflecting every word with a sympathetic and yet mocking attention, wrinkling up his forehead, his temples, the corners of his eyes, round his nostrils and cheeks, grimacing with laughter, and every now and then shaking all over convulsively. He did not join in the conversation, but he did not miss a word of it. He showed his joy especially when he saw Christophe, involved in some argument and heckled by Spitz, flounder about, stammer, and stutter with anger, until he had found the word he was seeking,—a rock with which to crush his adversary. And his delight knew no bounds when Christophe, swept along by his passions far beyond the capacity of his thought, enunciated monstrous paradoxes which made his hearers snort.

At last they broke up, each of them tired out with feeling and alleging his own superiority. As Christophe, the last to go, was leaving the room he was accosted by the young man who had listened to his words with such pleasure. He had not yet noticed him. The other politely removed his hat, smiled, and asked permission to introduce himself:

"Franz Mannheim."

He begged pardon for his indiscretion in listening to the argument, and congratulated Christophe on the *maestria* with which he had pulverized his opponents. He was still laughing at the thought of it. Christophe was glad to hear it, and looked at him a little distrustfully:

"Seriously?" he asked. "You are not laughing at me?"

The other swore by the gods. Christophe's face lit up.

"Then you think I am right? You are of my opinion?"

"Well," said Mannheim, "I am not a musician. I know nothing of music. The only music I like—(if it is not too flattering to say so)—is yours.... That may show you that my taste is not so bad...."

"Oh!" said Christophe skeptically, though he was flattered all the same, "that proves nothing."

"You are difficult to please.... Good!... I think as you do: that proves nothing. And I don't venture to judge what you say of German musicians. But, anyhow, it is so true of the Germans in general, the old Germans, all the romantic idiots with their rancid thought, their sloppy emotion, their senile reiteration which we are asked to admire, '*the eternal Yesterday, which has always been, and always will be, and will be law to–morrow because it is law to–day.*' ...!"

He recited a few lines of the famous passage in Schiller:

> "*... Das ewig Gestrige,
> Das immer war imd immer wiederkehrt....*"

"Himself, first of all!" He stopped in the middle of his recitation.

"Who?" asked Christophe.

"The pump–maker who wrote that!"

Christophe did not understand. But Mannheim went on:

"I should like to have a general cleaning up of art and thought every fifty years—nothing to be left standing."

"A little drastic," said Christophe, smiling.

"No, I assure you. Fifty years is too much: I should say thirty.... And even less!... It is a hygienic measure. One does not keep one's ancestors in one's house. One gets rid of them, when they are dead, and sends, them elsewhere,—there politely to rot, and one places stones on them to be quite sure that they will not come back. Nice people put flowers on them, too. I don't mind if they like it. All I ask is to be left in peace. I leave them alone! Each for his own side, say I: the dead and the living."

"There are some dead who are more alive than the living."

"No, no! It would be more true to say that there are some living who are more dead than the dead."

"Maybe. In any case, there are old things which are still young."

"Then if they are still young we can find them for ourselves.... But I don't believe it. What has been good once never is good again. Nothing is good but change. Before all we have to rid ourselves of the old men and things. There are too many of them in Germany. Death to them, say I!"

Christophe listened to these squibs attentively and labored to discuss them: he was in part in sympathy with them, he recognized certain of his own thoughts in them: and at the same time he felt a little embarrassed at having them so blown out to the point of caricature. But as he assumed that everybody else was as serious as himself, he thought that perhaps Mannheim, who seemed to be more learned than himself and spoke more easily, was right, and was drawing the logical conclusions from his principles. Vain

362

Christophe, whom so many people could not forgive for his faith in himself, was really most naively modest often tricked by his modesty when he was with those who were better educated than himself,—especially, when they consented not to plume themselves on it to avoid an awkward discussion. Mannheim, who was amusing himself with his own paradoxes, and from one sally to another had reached extravagant quips and cranks, at which he was laughing immensely, was not accustomed to being taken seriously: he was delighted with the trouble that Christophe was taking to discuss his nonsense, and even to understand it: and while he laughed, he was grateful for the importance which Christophe gave him: he thought him absurd and charming.

They parted very good friends: and Christophe was not a little surprised three hours later at rehearsal to see Mannheim's head poked through the little door leading to the orchestra, smiling and grimacing, and making mysterious signs at him. When the rehearsal was over Christophe went to him. Mannheim took his arm familiarly.

"You can spare a moment?... Listen. I have an idea. Perhaps you will think it absurd.... Would not you like for once in a way to write what you think of music and the musicos? Instead of wasting your breath in haranguing four dirty knaves of your band who are good for nothing but scraping and blowing into bits of wood, would it not be better to address the general public?"

"Not better? Would I like?... My word! And when do you want me to write? It is good of you!..."

"I've a proposal for you.... Some friends and I: Adalbert von Waldhaus, Raphael Goldenring, Adolf Mai, and Lucien Ehrenfeld,—have started a Review, the only intelligent Review in the town: the *Dionysos*.—(You must know it....)—We all admire each other and should be glad if you would join us. Will you take over our musical criticism?"

Christophe was abashed by such an honor: he was longing to accept: he was only afraid of not being worthy: he could not write.

"Oh! come," said Mannheim, "I am sure you can. And besides, as soon as you are a critic you can do anything you like. You've no need to be afraid of the public. The public is incredibly stupid. It is nothing to be an artist: an artist is only a sort of comedian: an artist

363

can be hissed. But a critic has the right to say: 'Hiss me that man!' The whole audience lets him do its thinking. Think whatever you like. Only look as if you were thinking something. Provided you give the fools their food, it does not much matter what, they will gulp down anything."

In the end Christophe consented, with effusive thanks. He only made it a condition that he should be allowed to say what he liked.

"Of course, of course," said Mannheim. "Absolute freedom! We are all free."

He looked him up at the theater once more after the performance to introduce him to Adalbert von Waldhaus and his friends. They welcomed him warmly.

With the exception of Waldhaus, who belonged to one of the noble families of the neighborhood, they were all Jews and all very rich: Mannheim was the son of a banker: Mai the son of the manager of a metallurgical establishment: and Ehrenfeld's father was a great jeweler. Their fathers belonged to the older generation of Jews, industrious and acquisitive, attached to the spirit of their race, building their fortunes with keen energy, and enjoying their energy much more than their fortunes. Their sons seemed to be made to destroy what their fathers had builded: they laughed at family prejudice and their ant–like mania for economy and delving: they posed as artists, affected to despise money and to fling it out of window. But in reality they hardly ever let it slip through their fingers: and in vain did they do all sorts of foolish things: they never could altogether lead astray their lucidity of mind and practical sense. For the rest, their parents kept an eye on them, and reined them in. The most prodigal of them, Mannheim, would sincerely have given away all that he had: but he never had anything: and although he was always loudly inveighing against his father's niggardliness, in his heart he laughed at it and thought that he was right. In fine, there was only Waldhaus really who was in control of his fortune, and went into it wholeheartedly and reckless of cost, and bore that of the Review. He was a poet. He wrote "*Polymetres*" in the manner of Arno Holz and Walt Whitman, with lines alternately very long and very short, in which stops, double and triple stops, dashes, silences, commas, italics and italics, played a great part. And so did alliteration and repetition—of a word—of a line—of a whole phrase. He interpolated words of every language. He wanted—(no one has ever known why)—to render the *Cezanne* into verse. In truth, he was poetic enough and had a distinguished taste for stale things. He was sentimental and dry, naive and foppish: his labored verses affected a cavalier carelessness. He would have been a good poet for men of the world. But there are too many of the kind in the Reviews and artistic circles: and he wished to be alone. He had taken it into his head to play the great gentleman who is above the prejudices of his caste. He had more prejudices than anybody. He did not admit their existence. He took a delight in surrounding himself with Jews in the Review which he edited, to rouse the indignation of his family, who were very anti–Semite, and to prove his own freedom of mind to himself. With his colleagues, he assumed a tone of courteous equality. But in his heart he had a calm and boundless contempt for them. He was not unaware that they were very glad to make use of his name and money: and he let them do so because it pleased him to despise them.

And they despised him for letting them do so: for they knew very well that it served his turn. A fair exchange, Waldhaus lent them his name and fortune: and they brought him their talents, their eye for business and subscribers. They were much more intelligent than he. Not that they had more personality. They had perhaps even less. But in the little town they were, as the Jews are everywhere and always,—by the mere fact of their difference of race which for centuries has isolated them and sharpened their faculty for making observation—they were the most advanced in mind, the most sensible of the absurdity of its moldy institutions and decrepit thought. Only, as their character was less free than their intelligence, it did not help them, while they mocked, from trying rather to turn those institutions and ideas to account than to reform them. In spite of their independent professions of faith, they were like the noble Adalbert, little provincial snobs, rich, idle young men of family, who dabbled and flirted with letters for the fun of it. They were very glad to swagger about as giant–killers: but they were kindly enough and never slew anybody but a few inoffensive people or those whom they thought could never harm them. They cared nothing for setting by the ears a society to which they knew very well they would one day return and embrace all the prejudices which they had combated. And when they did venture to make a stir on a little scandal, or loudly to declare war on some idol of the day,—who was beginning to totter,—they took care never to burn their boats: in case of danger they re–embarked. Whatever then might be the issue of the campaign,—when it was finished it was a long time before war would break out again: the Philistines could sleep in peace. All that these new *Davidsbuendler* wanted to do was to make it appear that they could have been terrible if they had so desired: but they did not desire. They preferred to be on friendly terms with artists and to give suppers to actresses.

Christophe was not happy in such a set. They were always talking of women and horses: and their talk was not refined. They were stiff and formal. Adalbert spoke in a mincing, slow voice, with exaggerated, bored, and boring politeness. Adolf Mai, the secretary of the Review, a heavy, thick–set, bull–necked, brutal–looking young man, always pretended to be in the right: he laid down the law, never listened to what anybody said, seemed to despise the opinion of the person he was talking to, and also that person. Goldenring, the art critic, who had a twitch, and eyes perpetually winking behind his large spectacles,—no doubt in imitation of the painters whose society he cultivated, wore long hair, smoked in silence, mumbled scraps of sentences which he never finished, and made vague gestures in the air with his thumb. Ehrenfeld was little, bald, and smiling, had a fair beard and a sensitive, weary–looking face, a hooked nose, and he wrote the fashions and the society notes in the Review. In a silky voice he used to talk obscurely: he had a wit, though of a malignant and often ignoble kind.—All these young millionaires were anarchists, of course: when a man possesses everything it is the supreme luxury for him to deny society: for in that way he can evade his responsibilities. So might a robber, who has just fleeced a traveler, say to him: "What are you staying for? Get along! I have no more use for you."

Of the whole bunch Christophe was only in sympathy with Mannheim: he was certainly the most lively of the five: he was amused by everything that he said and everything that was said to him: stuttering, stammering, blundering, sniggering, talking nonsense, he was incapable of following an argument, or of knowing exactly what he thought himself: but he was quite kindly, bearing no malice, having not a spark of ambition. In truth, he was not very frank: he was always playing a part: but quite innocently, and he never did anybody any harm.

He espoused all sorts of strange Utopias—most often generous. He was too subtle and too skeptical to keep his head even in his enthusiasms, and he never compromised himself by applying his theories. But he had to have some hobby: it was a game to him, and he was always changing from one to another. For the time being his craze was for kindness. It was not enough for him to be kind naturally: he wished to be thought kind: he professed kindness, and acted it. Out of reaction against the hard, dry activity of his kinsfolk, and against German austerity, militarism, and Philistinism, he was a Tolstoyan, a Nirvanian, an evangelist, a Buddhist,—he was not quite sure what,—an apostle of a new morality that was soft, boneless, indulgent, placid, easy–living, effusively forgiving every sin, especially the sins of the flesh, a morality which did not conceal its predilection for those sins and much less readily forgave the virtues—a morality which was only a compact of pleasure, a libertine association of mutual accommodations, which amused itself by donning the halo of sanctity. There was in it a spice of hypocrisy which was a little offensive to delicate palates, and would have even been frankly nauseating if it had taken itself seriously. But it made no pretensions towards that: it merely amused itself. His blackguardly Christianity was only meant to serve until some other hobby came along to take its place—no matter what: brute force, imperialism, "laughing lions."—Mannheim was always playing a part, playing with his whole heart: he was trying on all the feelings that he did not possess before becoming a good Jew like the rest and with all the spirit of his race. He was very sympathetic, and extremely irritating. For some time Christophe was one of his hobbies. Mannheim swore by him. He blew his trumpet everywhere. He dinned his praises into the ears of his family. According to him Christophe was a genius, an extraordinary man, who made strange music and talked about it in an astonishing fashion, a witty man—and a handsome: fine lips, magnificent teeth. He added that Christophe admired him.—One evening he took him home to dinner. Christophe found himself talking to his new friend's father, Lothair Mannheim, the banker, and Franz's sister, Judith.

It was the first time that he had been in a Jew's house. Although there were many Jews in the little town, and although they played an important part in its life by reason of their wealth, cohesion, and intelligence, they lived a little apart. There were always rooted prejudices in the minds of the people and a secret hostility that was credulous and injurious against them. Christophe's family shared these prejudices. His grandfather did not love Jews: but the irony of fate had decreed that his two best pupils should be of the race—(one had become a composer, the other a famous *virtuoso*): for there had been moments when he was fain to embrace these two good musicians: and then he would remember sadly that they had crucified the Lord: and he did not know how to reconcile his two incompatible currents of feeling. But in the end he did embrace them. He was inclined to think that the Lord would forgive them because of their love for music.—Christophe's father, Melchior, who pretended to be broad-minded, had had fewer scruples about taking money from the Jews: and he even thought it good to do so: but he ridiculed them, and despised them.—As for his mother, she was not sure that she was not committing a sin when she went to cook for them. Those whom she had had to do with were disdainful enough with her: but she had no grudge against them, she bore nobody any ill-will: she was filled with pity for these unhappy people whom God had damned: sometimes she would be filled with compassion when she saw the daughter of

1ea!!

one of them go by or heard the merry laughter of their children.

"So pretty she is!... Such pretty children!... How dreadful!..." she would think.

She dared not say anything to Christophe, when he told her that he was going to dine with the Mannheims: but her heart sank. She thought that it was unnecessary to believe everything bad that was said about the Jews—(people speak ill of everybody)—and that there are honest people everywhere, but that it was better and more proper to keep themselves to themselves, the Jews on their side, the Christians on theirs.

Christophe shared none of these prejudices. In his perpetual reaction against his surroundings he was rather attracted towards the different race. But he hardly knew them. He had only come in contact with the more vulgar of the Jews: little shopkeepers, the populace swarming in certain streets between the Rhine and the cathedral, forming, with the gregarious instinct of all human beings, a sort of little ghetto. He had often strolled through the neighborhood, catching sight of and feeling a sort of sympathy with certain types of women with hollow cheeks, and full lips, and wide cheek–bones, a da Vinci smile, rather depraved, while the coarse language and shrill laughter destroyed this harmony that was in their faces when in repose. Even in the dregs of the people, in those large–headed, beady–eyed creatures with their bestial faces, their thick–set, squat bodies, those degenerate descendants of the most noble of all peoples, even in that thick, fetid muddiness there were strange phosphorescent gleams, like will–o'–the–wisps dancing over a swamp: marvelous glances, minds subtle and brilliant, a subtle electricity emanating from the ooze which fascinated and disturbed Christophe. He thought that hidden deep were fine souls struggling, great hearts striving to break free from the dung: and he would have liked to meet them, and to aid them: without knowing them, he loved them, while he was a little fearful of them. And he had never had any opportunity of meeting the best of the Jews.

His dinner at the Mannheims' had for him the attraction of novelty and something of that of forbidden fruit. The Eve who gave him the fruit sweetened its flavor. From the first moment Christophe had eyes only for Judith Mannheim. She was utterly different from all the women he had known. Tall and slender, rather thin, though solidly built, with her face framed in her black hair, not long, but thick and curled low on her head, covering her temples and her broad, golden brow; rather short–sighted, with large pupils, and slightly prominent eyes: with a largish nose and wide nostrils, thin cheeks, a heavy chin, strong coloring, she had a fine profile showing much energy and alertness: full face, her expression was more changing, uncertain, complex: her eyes and her cheeks were irregular. She seemed to give revelation of a strong race, and in the mold of that race, roughly thrown together, were manifold incongruous elements, of doubtful and unequal quality, beautiful and vulgar at the same time. Her beauty lay especially in her silent lips, and in her eyes, in which there seemed to be greater depth by reason of their short–sightedness, and darker by reason of the bluish markings round them.

It needed to be more used than Christophe was to those eyes, which are more those of a race than of an individual, to be able to read through the limpidity that unveiled them with such vivid quality, the real soul of the woman whom he thus encountered. It was the soul of the people of Israel that he saw in her sad and burning eyes, the soul that, unknown to them, shone forth from them. He lost himself as he gazed into them. It was only after some time that he was able, after losing his way again and again, to strike the track again on that oriental sea.

She looked at him: and nothing could disturb the clearness of her gaze: nothing in his Christian soul seemed to escape her. He felt that. Under the seduction of the woman's eyes upon him he was conscious of a virile desire, clear and cold, Which stirred in him brutally, indiscreetly. There was no evil in the brutality of it. She took possession of him: not like a coquette, whose desire is to seduce without caring whom she seduces. Had she been a coquette she would have gone to greatest lengths: but she knew her power, and she left it to her natural instinct to make use of it in its own way,—especially when she had so easy a prey as Christophe.—What interested her more was to know her adversary—(any man, any stranger, was an adversary for her,—an adversary with whom later on, if occasion served, she could sign a compact of alliance).—She wished to know his quality. Life being a game, in which the cleverest wins, it was a matter of reading her opponent's cards and of not showing her own. When she succeeded she tasted the sweets of victory. It mattered little whether she could turn it to any account. It was purely for her pleasure. She had a passion for intelligence: not abstract intelligence, although she had brains enough, if she had liked, to have succeeded in any, branch of knowledge and would have made a much better successor to Lothair Mannheim, the banker, than her brother. But she preferred intelligence in the quick, the sort of intelligence which studies men. She loved to pierce through to the soul and to weigh its value—(she gave as scrupulous an attention to it as the Jewess of Matsys to the weighing of her gold)—with marvelous divination she could find the weak spot in the armor, the imperfections and foibles which are the key to the soul,—she could lay her hands on its secrets: it was her way of feeling her sway over it. But she never dallied with her victory: she never did anything with her prize. Once her curiosity and her vanity were satisfied she lost her interest and passed on to another specimen. All her power was sterile. There was something of death in her living soul. She had the genius of curiosity and boredom.

* * * * *

And so she looked at Christophe and he looked at her. She hardly spoke. An imperceptible smile was enough, a little movement of the corners of her mouth: Christophe was hypnotized by her. Every now and then her smile would fade away, her face would become cold, her eyes indifferent: she would attend to the meal or speak coldly to the servants: it was as though she were no longer listening. Then her eyes would light up again: and a few words coming pat would show that she had heard and understood everything.

She coldly examined her brother's judgment of Christophe: she knew Franz's crazes: her irony had had fine sport when she saw Christophe appear, whose looks and distinction had been vaunted by her brother—(it seemed to her that Franz had a special gift for seeing facts as they are not: or perhaps he only thought it a paradoxical joke).—But when she looked at Christophe more closely she recognized that what Franz had said was not altogether false: and as she went on with her scrutiny she discovered in Christophe a vague, unbalanced, though robust and bold power: that gave her pleasure, for she knew, better than any, the rarity of power. She was able to make Christophe talk about whatever she liked, and reveal his thoughts, and display the limitations and defects of his mind: she made him play the piano: she did not love music but she understood it: and she saw Christophe's musical originality, although his music had roused no sort of emotion in her. Without the least change in the coldness of her manner, with a few short, apt, and certainly not flattering, remarks she showed her growing interest in Christophe.

Christophe saw it: and he was proud of it: for he felt the worth of such judgment and the rarity of her approbation. He made no secret of his desire to win it: and he set about it so naively as to make the three of them smile: he talked only to Judith and for Judith: he was as unconcerned with the others as though they did not exist.

Franz watched him as he talked: he followed his every word, with his lips and eyes, with a mixture of admiration and amusement: and he laughed aloud as he glanced at his father and his sister, who listened impassively and pretended not to notice him.

Lothair Mannheim,—a tall old man, heavily built, stooping a little, red–faced, with gray hair standing straight up on end, very black mustache and eyebrows, a heavy though energetic and jovial face, which gave the impression of great vitality—had also studied Christophe during the first part of the dinner, slyly but good–naturedly: and he too had recognized at once that there was "something" in the boy. But he was not interested in music or musicians: it was not in his line: he knew nothing about it and made no secret of his ignorance: he even boasted of it—(when a man of that sort confesses his ignorance of anything he does so to feed his vanity).—As Christophe had clearly shown at once, with a rudeness in which there was no shade of malice, that, he could without regret dispense with the society of the banker, and that the society of Fraeulein Judith Mannheim would serve perfectly to fill his evening, old Lothair in some amusement had taken his seat by the fire: he read his paper, listening vaguely and ironically to Christophe's crotchets and his queer music, which sometimes made him laugh inwardly at the idea that there could be people who understood it and found pleasure in it. He did not trouble to follow the conversation: he relied on his daughter's cleverness to tell him exactly what the newcomer was worth. She discharged her duty conscientiously.

When Christophe had gone Lothair asked Judith:

"Well, you probed him enough: what do you think of the artist?"

She laughed, thought for a moment, reckoned up, and said:

"He is a little cracked: but he is not stupid."

"Good," said Lothair. "I thought so too. He will succeed, then?"

"Yes, I think so. He has power,"

"Very good," said Lothair with the magnificent logic of the strong who are only interested in the strong, "we must help him."

* * * * *

Christophe went away filled with admiration for Judith Mannheim. He was not in love with her as Judith thought. They were both—she with her subtlety, he with his instinct which took the place of mind in him,—mistaken about each other. Christophe was fascinated by the enigma and the intense activity of her mind: but he did not love her. His eyes and his intelligence were ensnared: his heart escaped.—Why?—It were difficult to tell. Because he had caught a glimpse of some doubtful, disturbing quality in her?—In other circumstances that would have been a reason the more for loving: love is never stronger than when it goes out to one who will make it suffer.—If Christophe did not love Judith it was not the fault of either of them. The real reason, humiliating enough for both, was that he was still too near his last love. Experience had not made him wiser. But he had loved Ada so much, he had consumed so much faith, force, and illusion in that passion that there was not enough left for a new passion. Before another flame could be kindled he would have to build a new pyre in his heart: short of that there could only be a few flickerings, remnants of the conflagration that had escaped by chance, which asked only to be allowed to burn, cast a brief and brilliant light and then died down for want of food. Six months later, perhaps, he might have loved Judith blindly. Now he saw in her only a friend,—a rather disturbing friend in truth—but he tried to drive his uneasiness back: it reminded him of Ada: there was no attraction in that memory: he preferred not to think of it. What attracted him in Judith was everything in her which was different from other women, not that which she had in common with them. She was the first intelligent woman he had met. She was intelligent from head to foot. Even her beauty—her gestures, her movements, her features, the fold of her lips, her eyes, her hands, her slender elegance—was the reflection of her intelligence: her body was molded by her intelligence: without her intelligence she would have passed unnoticed: and no doubt she would even have been thought plain by most people. Her intelligence delighted Christophe. He thought it larger and more free than it was: he could not yet know how deceptive it was. He longed ardently to confide in her and to impart his ideas to her. He had never found anybody to take an interest in his dreams: he was turned in upon, himself: what joy then to find a woman to be his friend! That he had not a sister had been one of the sorrows of his childhood: it seemed to him that a sister would have understood him more than a brother could have done. And when he met Judith he felt that childish and illusory hope of having a brotherly love spring up in him. Not being in love, love seemed to him a poor thing compared with friendship.

Judith felt this little shade of feeling and was hurt by it. She was not in love with Christophe, and as she had excited other passions in other young men of the town, rich young men of better position, she could not feel any great satisfaction in knowing Christophe to be in love with her. But it piqued her to know that he was not in love. No doubt she was pleased with him for confiding his plans: she was not surprised by it: but it was a little mortifying for her to know that she could only exercise an intellectual influence over him—(an unreasoning influence is much more precious to a woman).—She did not even exercise her influence: Christophe only courted her mind. Judith's intellect was imperious. She was used to molding to her will the soft thoughts of the young men of her acquaintance. As she knew their mediocrity she found no pleasure in holding sway over them. With Christophe the pursuit was more interesting because more difficult. She was not interested in his projects: but she would have liked to direct his originality of thought, his ill–grown power, and to make them good,—in her own way, of course, and not in Christophe's, which she did not take the trouble to understand. She saw at once that she could not succeed without a struggle: she had marked down in Christophe all sorts of notions and ideas which she thought childish and extravagant: they were weeds to her: she tried hard to eradicate them. She did not get rid of a single one. She did not gain the least satisfaction for her vanity. Christophe was intractable. Not being in love he had no reason for surrendering his ideas to her.

She grew keen on the game and instinctively tried for some time to overcome him. Christophe was very nearly taken in again in spite of his lucidity of mind at that time. Men are easily taken in by any flattery of their vanity or their desires: and an artist is twice as easy to trick as any other man because he has more imagination. Judith had only to draw Christophe into a dangerous flirtation to bowl him over once more more thoroughly than ever. But as usual she soon wearied of the game: she found that such a conquest was hardly worth while: Christophe was already boring her: she did not understand him.

She did not understand him beyond a certain point. Up to that she understood everything. Her admirable intelligence could not take her beyond it: she needed a heart, or in default of that the thing which could give the illusion of one for a time: love. She understood Christophe's criticism of people and things: it amused her and seemed to her true enough: she had thought much the same herself. But what she did not understand was that such ideas might have an influence on practical life when it might be dangerous or awkward to apply them. The attitude of revolt against everybody and everything which Christophe

373

had taken up led to nothing: he could not imagine that he was going to reform the world.... And then?... It was waste of time to knock one's head against a wall. A clever man judges men, laughs at them in secret, despises them a little: but he does as they do—only a little better: it is the only way of mastering them. Thought is one world: action is another. What boots it for a man to be the victim of his thoughts? Since men are so stupid as not to be able to bear the truth, why force it on them? To accept their weakness, to seem to bow to it, and to feel free to despise them in his heart, is there not a secret joy in that? The joy of a clever slave? Certainly. But all the world is a slave: there is no getting away from that: it is useless to protest against it: better to be a slave deliberately of one's own free will and to avoid ridiculous and futile conflict. Besides, the worst slavery of all is to be the slave of one's own thoughts and to sacrifice everything to them. There is no need to deceive one's self.—She saw clearly that if Christophe went on, as he seemed determined to do, with his aggressive refusal to compromise with the prejudices of German art and German mind, he would turn everybody against him, even his patrons: he was courting inevitable ruin. She did not understand why he so obstinately held out against himself, and so took pleasure in digging his own ruin.

To have understood him she would have had to be able to understand that his aim was not success but his own faith. He believed in art: he believed in *his* art: he believed in himself, as realities not only superior to interest, but also to his own life. When he was a little out of patience with her remarks and told her so in his naive arrogance, she just shrugged her shoulders: she did not take him seriously. She thought he was using big words such as she was accustomed to hearing from her brother when he announced periodically his absurd and ridiculous resolutions, which he never by any chance put into practice. And then when she saw that Christophe really believed in what he said, she thought him mad and lost interest in him.

After that she took no trouble to appear to advantage, and she showed herself as she was: much more German, and average German, than she seemed to be at first, more perhaps than she thought.—The Jews are quite erroneously reproached with not belonging to any nation and with forming from one end of Europe to the other a homogeneous people impervious to the influence of the different races with which they have pitched their tents. In reality there is no race which more easily takes on the impress of the country through which it passes: and if there are many characteristics in common between a French Jew and a German Jew, there are many more different characteristics derived from their new country, of which with incredible rapidity they assimilate the habits of mind: more the habits than the mind, indeed. But habit, which is a second nature to all men, is in most of them all the nature that they have, and the result is that the majority of the autochthonous citizens of any country have very little right to reproach the Jews with the lack of a profound and reasonable national feeling of which they themselves possess nothing at all.

The women, always more sensible to external influences, more easily adaptable to the conditions of life and to change with them—Jewish women throughout Europe assume the physical and moral customs, often exaggerating them, of the country in which they live,—without losing the shadow and the strange fluid, solid, and haunting quality of their race.—This idea came to Christophe. At the Mannheims' he met Judith's aunts, cousins, and friends. Though there was little of the German in their eyes, ardent and too close together, their noses going down to their lips, their strong features, their red blood coursing under their coarse brown skins: though almost all of them seemed hardly at all fashioned to be German—they were all extraordinarily German: they had the same way of talking, of dressing,—of overdressing.—Judith was much the best of them all: and comparison with them made all that was exceptional in her intelligence, all that she had made of herself, shine forth. But she had most of their faults just as much as they. She was much more free than they morally—almost absolutely free—but socially she was no more free: or at least her practical sense usurped the place of her freedom of mind. She believed in society, in class, in prejudice, because when all was told she found them to her advantage. It was idle for her to laugh at the German spirit: she followed it like any German. Her intelligence made her see the mediocrity of some artist of reputation: but she respected him none the less because of his reputation: and if she met him personally she would admire him: for her vanity was flattered. She had no love for the works of Brahms and she suspected him of being an artist of the second rank: but his fame impressed her: and as she had received five or six letters from him the result was that she thought him the greatest musician of the day. She had no doubt as to Christophe's real worth, or as to the stupidity of Lieutenant Detlev von Fleischer: but she was more flattered by the homage the lieutenant deigned to pay to her millions than by Christophe's friendship: for a dull officer is a man of another caste: it is more difficult for a German Jewess to enter that caste than for any other woman. Although she was not deceived by these feudal follies, and although she knew quite well that if she did marry Lieutenant Detlev von Fleischer she would be doing him a great honor, she set herself to the conquest: she stooped so low as to make eyes at the fool and to flatter his vanity. The proud Jewess, who had a thousand reasons for her pride—the clever, disdainful daughter of Mannheim the banker lowered herself, and acted like any of the little middle–class German women whom she despised.

* * * * *

That experience was short. Christophe lost his illusions about Judith as quickly as he had found them. It is only just to say that Judith did nothing to preserve them. As soon as a woman of that stamp has judged a man she is done with him: he ceases to exist for her: she will not see him again. And she no more hesitates to reveal her soul to him, with calm impudence, that to appear naked before her dog, her cat, or any other domestic animal. Christophe saw Judith's egoism and coldness, and the mediocrity of her character. He had not had time to be absolutely caught. But he had been enough caught to make him suffer and to bring him to a sort of fever. He did not so much love Judith as what she might have been—what she ought to have been. Her fine eyes exercised a melancholy fascination over him: he could not forget them: although he knew now the drab soul that slumbered in their depths he went on seeing them as he wished to see them, as he had first seen them. It was one of those loveless hallucinations of love which take up so much of the hearts of artists when they are not entirely absorbed by their work. A passing face is enough to create it: they see in it all the beauty that is in it, unknown to its indifferent possessor. And they love it the more for its indifference. They love it as a beautiful thing that must die without any man having known its worth or that it even had life.

Perhaps he was deceiving himself, and Judith Mannheim could not have been anything more than she was. But for a moment Christophe had believed in her: and her charm endured: he could not judge her impartially. All her beauty seemed to him to be hers, to be herself. All that was vulgar in her he cast back upon her twofold race, Jew and German, and perhaps he was more indignant with the German than with the Jew, for it had made him suffer more. As he did not yet know any other nation, the German spirit was for him a sort of scapegoat: he put upon it all the sins of the world. That Judith had deceived him was a reason the more for combating it: he could not forgive it for having crushed the life out of such a soul.

Such was his first encounter with Israel. He had hoped much from it. He had hoped to find in that strong race living apart from the rest an ally for his fight. He lost that hope. With the flexibility of his passionate intuition, which made him leap from one extreme to another, he persuaded himself that the Jewish race was much weaker than it was said to be, and much more open—much too open—to outside influence. It had all its own weaknesses augmented by those of the rest of the world picked up on its way. It was not in them that he could find assistance in working the lever of his art. Rather he was in danger of being swallowed with them in the sands of the desert.

Having seen the danger, and not feeling sure enough of himself to brave it, he suddenly gave up going to the Mannheims'. He was invited several times and begged to be excused without giving any reason. As up till then he had shown an excessive eagerness to accept, such a sudden change was remarked: it was attributed to his "originality": but the Mannheims had no doubt that the fair Judith had something to do with it: Lothair and Franz joked about it at dinner. Judith shrugged her shoulders and said it was a fine conquest, and she asked her brother frigidly not to make such a fuss about it. But she left no stone unturned in her effort to bring Christophe back. She wrote to him for some musical information which no one else could supply: and at the end of her letter she made a friendly allusion to the rarity of his visits and the pleasure it would give them to see him. Christophe replied, giving the desired information, said that he was very busy, and did not go. They met sometimes at the theater. Christophe obstinately looked away from the Mannheims' box: and he would pretend not to see Judith, who held herself in readiness to give him her most charming smile. She did not persist. As she did not count on him for anything she was annoyed that the little artist should let her do all the labor of their friendship, and pure waste at that. If he wanted to come, he would. If not—oh, well, they could do without him....

They did without him: and his absence left no very great gap in the Mannheims' evenings. But in spite of herself Judith was really annoyed with Christophe. It seemed natural enough not to bother about him when he was there: and she could allow him to show his displeasure at being neglected: but that his displeasure should go so far as to break off their relationship altogether seemed to her to show a stupid pride and a heart more egoistic than in love.—Judith could not tolerate her own faults in others.

She followed the more attentively everything that Christophe did and wrote. Without seeming to do so, she would lead her brother to the subject of Christophe: she would make him tell her of his intercourse with him: and she would punctuate the narrative with clever ironic comment, which never let any ridiculous feature escape, and gradually destroyed Franz's enthusiasm without his knowing it.

At first all went well with the Review. Christophe had not yet perceived the mediocrity of his colleagues: and, since he was one of them, they hailed him as a genius. Mannheim, who had discovered him, went everywhere repeating that Christophe was an admirable critic, though he had never read anything he had written, that he had mistaken his vocation, and that he, Mannheim, had revealed it to him. They advertised his articles in mysterious terms which roused curiosity: and his first effort was in fact like a stone falling into a duck–pond in the atony of the little town. It was called: *Too much music.*

"Too much music, too much drinking, too much eating," wrote Christophe. "Eating, drinking, hearing, without hunger, thirst, or need, from sheer habitual gormandizing. Living like Strasburg geese. These people are sick from a diseased appetite. It matters little what you give them: *Tristram* or the *Trompeter von Saekkingen*, Beethoven or Mascagni, a fugue or a two–step, Adam, Bach, Puccini, Mozart, or Marschner: they do not know what they are eating: the great thing is to eat. They find no pleasure in it. Look at them at a concert. Talk of German gaiety! These people do not know what gaiety means: they are always gay! Their gaiety, like their sorrow, drops like rain: their joy is dust: there is neither life nor force in it. They would stay for hours smilingly and vaguely drinking in sounds, sounds, sounds. They think of nothing: they feel nothing: they are sponges. True joy, or true sorrow—strength—is not drawn out over hours like beer from a cask. They take you by the throat and have you down: after they are gone there is no desire left in a man to drink in anything: he is full!...

"Too much music! You are slaying each other and it. If you choose to murder each other that is your affair: I can't help it. But where music is concerned,—hands off! I will not suffer you to debase the loveliness of the world by heaping up in the same basket things holy and things shameful, by giving, as you do at present, the prelude to *Parsifal* between a fantasia on the *Daughter of the Regiment* and a saxophone quartette, or an adagio of Beethoven between a cakewalk and the rubbish of Leoncavallo. You boast of being a musical people. You pretend to love music. What sort of music do you love? Good or bad? You applaud both equally. Well, then, choose! What exactly do you want? You do not know yourselves. You do not want to know: you are too fearful of taking sides and compromising yourselves.... To the devil with your prudence!—You are above party, do you say?—Above? You mean below...."

And he quoted the lines of old Gottfried Keller, the rude citizen of Zurich—one of the German writers who was most dear to him by reason of his vigorous loyalty and his keen savor of the soil:

"Wer ueber den Parlein sich waehnt mit stolzen Mienen Der steht zumeist vielmehr betraechtlich unter ihnen."

("He who proudly preens himself on being above parties is rather immeasurably beneath them.")

"Have courage and be true," he went on. "Have courage and be ugly. If you like bad music, then say so frankly. Show yourselves, see yourselves as you are. Kid your souls of the loathsome burden of all your compromise and equivocation. Wash it in pure water. How long is it since you have seen. yourselves in a mirror? I will show you yourselves. Composers, *virtuosi*, conductors, singers, and you, dear public. You shall for once know yourselves.... Be what you like: but, for any sake, be true! Be true even though art and artists—and I myself—have to suffer for it! If art and truth cannot live together, then let art disappear. Truth is life. Lies are death."

Naturally, this youthful, wild outburst, which was all of a piece, and in very bad taste, produced an outcry. And yet, as everybody was attacked and nobody in particular, its pertinency was not recognized. Every one is, or believes himself to be, or says that he is the best friend of truth: there was therefore no danger of the conclusions of the article being attacked. Only people were shocked by its general tone: everybody agreed that it was hardly proper, especially from an artist in a semi–official position. A few musicians began to be uneasy and protested bitterly: they saw that Christophe would not stop at that. Others thought themselves more clever and congratulated Christophe on his courage: they were no less uneasy about his next articles.

Both tactics produced the same result. Christophe had plunged: nothing could stop him: and as he had promised, everybody was passed in survey, composers and interpreters alike.

The first victims were the *Kapellmeisters*. Christophe did not confine himself to general remarks on the art of conducting an orchestra. He mentioned his colleagues of his own town and the neighboring towns by name: or if he did not name them his allusions were so transparent that nobody could be mistaken. Everybody recognized the apathetic conductor of the Court, Alois von Werner, a cautious old man, laden with honors, who was afraid of everything, dodged everything, was too timid to make a remark to his musicians and meekly followed whatever they chose to do,—who never risked anything on his programme that had not been consecrated by twenty years of success, or, at least, guaranteed by the official stamp of some academic dignity. Christophe ironically applauded his boldness: he congratulated him on having discovered Gade, Dvorak, or Tschaikowsky: he waxed enthusiastic over his unfailing correctness, his metronomic equality, the always *fein–nuanciert* (finely shaded) playing of his orchestra: he proposed to orchestrate the *Ecole de la Velocite* of Czerny for his next concert, and implored him not to try himself so much, not to give rein to his passions, to look after his precious health.—Or he cried out indignantly upon the way in which he had conducted the *Eroica* of Beethoven:

"A cannon! A cannon! Mow me down these people!... But have you then no idea of the conflict, the fight between human stupidity and human ferocity,—and the strength which tramples them underfoot with a glad shout of laughter?—How could you know it? It is you against whom it fights! You expend all the heroism that is in you in listening or in playing the *Eroica* of Beethoven without a yawn—(for it bores you.... Confess that it bores you to death!)—or in risking a draught as you stand with bare head and bowed back to let some Serene Highness pass."

He could not be sarcastic enough about the pontiffs of the Conservatories who interpreted the great men of the past as "classics."

"Classical! That word expresses everything. Free passion, arranged and expurgated for the use of schools! Life, that vast plain swept by the winds,—inclosed within the four walls of a school playground! The fierce, proud beat of a heart in anguish, reduced to the tic–tacs of a four–tune pendulum, which goes its jolly way, hobbling and imperturbably leaning on the crutch of time!... To enjoy the Ocean you need to put it in a bowl with goldfish. You only understand life when you have killed it."

If he was not kind to the "bird–stuffers" as he called them, he was even less kind to the ringmen of the orchestra, the illustrious *Kapellmeisters* who toured the country to show off their flourishes and their dainty hands, those who exercised their virtuosity at the expense of the masters, tried hard to make the most familiar works unrecognizable, and turned somersaults through the hoop of the *Symphony in C minor*. He made them appear as old coquettes, *prima donnas* of the orchestra, gipsies, and rope–dancers.

The *virtuosi* naturally provided him with splendid material. He declared himself incompetent when he had to criticise their conjuring performances. He said that such mechanical exercises belonged to the School of Arts and Crafts, and that not musical criticism but charts registering the duration, and number of the notes, and the energy expended, could decide the merit of such labors. Sometimes he would set at naught some famous piano *virtuoso* who during a two hours' concert had surmounted the formidable difficulties, with a smile on his lips and his hair hanging down into his eyes—of executing a childish *andante* of Mozart.—He did not ignore the pleasure of overcoming difficulties. He had tasted it himself: it was one of the joys of life to him. But only to see the most material aspect of it, and to reduce all the heroism of art to that, seemed to him grotesque and degrading. He could not forgive the "lions" or "panthers" of the piano.—But he was not very indulgent either towards the town pedants, famous in Germany, who, while they are rightly anxious not to alter the text of the masters, carefully suppress every flight of thought, and, like E. d'Albert and H. von Buelow, seem to be giving a lesson in diction when they are rendering a passionate sonata.

The singers had their turn. Christophe was full to the brim of things to say about their barbarous heaviness and their provincial affectations. It was not only because of his recent misadventures with the enraged lady, but because of all the torture he had suffered during so many performances. It was difficult to know which had suffered most, ears or eyes. And Christophe had not enough standards of comparison to be able to have any idea of the ugliness of the setting, the hideous costumes, the screaming colors. He was only shocked by the vulgarity of the people, their gestures and attitudes, their unnatural playing, the inability of the actors to take on other souls than their own, and by the stupefying indifference with which they passed from one role to another, provided they were written more or less in the same register. Matrons of opulent flesh, hearty and buxom, appeared alternately as Ysolde and Carmen. Amfortas played Figaro.—But what most offended Christophe was the ugliness of the singing, especially in the classical works in which the beauty of melody is essential. No one in Germany could sing the perfect music of the eighteenth century: no one would take the trouble. The clear, pure style of Gluck and Mozart which, like that of Goethe, seems to be bathed in the light of Italy—the style which begins to change and to become vibrant and dazzling with Weber—the style ridiculed by the ponderous caricatures of the author of *Crociato*—had been killed by the triumph of Wagner. The wild flight of the Valkyries with their strident cries had passed over the Grecian sky. The heavy clouds of Odin dimmed the light. No one now thought of singing music: they sang poems. Ugliness and carelessness of detail, even false notes were let pass under pretext that only the whole, only the thought behind it mattered....

"Thought! Let us talk of that. As if you understood it!... But whether or no you do understand it, I pray you respect the form that thought has chosen for itself. Above all, let music be and remain music!"

And the great concern of German artists with expression and profundity of thought was, according to Christophe, a good joke. Expression? Thought? Yes, they introduced them into everything—everything impartially. They would have found thought in a skein of wool just as much—neither more nor less—as in a statue of Michael Angelo. They played anything, anybody's music with exactly the same energy. For most of them the great thing in music—so he declared—was the volume of sound, just a musical noise. The pleasure of singing so potent in Germany was in some sort a pleasure of vocal gymnastics. It was just a matter of being inflated with air and then letting it go vigorously, powerfully, for a long time together and rhythmically.—And by way of compliment he accorded a certain great singer a certificate of good health. He was not content with flaying the artists. He strode over the footlights and trounced the public for coming, gaping, to such performances. The public was staggered and did not know whether it ought to laugh or be angry. They had every right to cry out upon his injustice: they had taken care not to be mixed up in any artistic conflict: they stood aside prudently from any burning question: and to avoid making any mistake they applauded everything! And now Christophe declared that it was a crime to applaud!... To applaud bad works?—That would have been enough! But Christophe went further: he stormed at them for applauding great works:

"Humbugs!" he said. "You would have us believe that you have as much enthusiasm as that?... Oh! Come! Spare yourselves the trouble! You only prove exactly the opposite of what you are trying to prove. Applaud if you like those works and passages which in some measure deserve applause. Applaud those loud final movements which are written, as Mozart said, 'for long ears.' Applaud as much as you like, then: your braying is anticipated: it is part of the concert.—But after the *Missa Solemnis* of Beethoven!... Poor wretches!... It is the Last Judgment. You have just seen the maddening *Gloria* pass like a storm over the ocean. You have seen the waterspout of an athletic and tremendous well, which stops, breaks, reaches up to the clouds clinging by its two hands above the abyss, then plunging once more into space in full swing. The squall shrieks and whirls along.

And when the hurricane is at its height there is a sudden modulation, a radiance of sound which cleaves the darkness of the sky and falls upon the livid sea like a patch of light. It is the end: the furious flight of the destroying angel stops short, its wings transfixed by these flashes of lightning. Around you all is buzzing and quivering. The eye gazes fixedly forward in stupor. The heart beats, breathing stops, the limbs are paralyzed.... And hardly has the last note sounded than already you are gay and merry. You shout, you laugh, you criticise, you applaud.... But you have seen nothing, heard nothing, felt nothing, understood nothing, nothing, nothing, absolutely nothing! The sufferings of an artist are a show to you. You think the tears of agony of a Beethoven are finely painted. You would cry 'Encore' to the Crucifixion. A great soul struggles all its life long in sorrow to divert your idleness for an hour!..."

So, without knowing it, he confirmed Goethe's great words: but he had not yet attained his lofty serenity:

"The people make a sport of the sublime. If they could see it as it is, they would be unable to bear its aspect."

If he had only stopped at that!—But, whirled along by his enthusiasm, he swept past the public and plunged like a cannon ball into the sanctuary, the tabernacle, the inviolable refuge of mediocrity: Criticism. He bombarded his colleagues. One of them had taken upon himself to attack the most gifted of living composers, the most advanced representative of the new school, Hassler, the writer of programme symphonies, extravagant in truth, but full of genius. Christophe who—as perhaps will be remembered—had been presented to him when he was a child, had always had a secret tenderness for him in his gratitude for the enthusiasm and emotion that he had had then. To see a stupid critic, whose ignorance he knew, instructing a man of that caliber, calling him to order, and reminding him of set principles, infuriated him:

"Order! Order!" he cried. "You do not know any order but that of the police. Genius is not to be dragged along the beaten track. It creates order, and makes its will a law."

After this arrogant declaration he took the unlucky critic, considered all the idiocies he had written for some time past, and administered correction.

All the critics felt the affront. Up to that time they had stood aside from the conflict. They did not care to risk a rebuff: they knew Christophe, they knew his efficiency, and they knew also that he was not long–suffering. Certain of them had discreetly expressed their regret that so gifted a composer should dabble in a profession not his own. Whatever might be their opinion (when they had one), and however hurt they might be by Christophe, they respected in him their own privilege of being able to criticise everything without being criticised themselves. But when they saw Christophe rudely break the tacit convention which bound them, they saw in him an enemy of public order. With one consent it seemed revolting to them that a very young man should take upon himself to show scant respect for the national glories: and they began a furious campaign against him. They did not write long articles or consecutive arguments—(they were unwilling to venture upon such ground with an adversary better armed than themselves: although a journalist has the special faculty of being able to discuss without taking his adversary's arguments into consideration, and even without having read them)—but long experience had taught them that, as the reader of a paper always agrees with it, even to appear to argue was to weaken its credit with him: it was necessary to affirm, or better still, to deny—(negation is twice as powerful as affirmation: it is a direct consequence of the law of gravity: it is much easier to drop a stone than to throw it up).—They adopted, therefore, a system of little notes, perfidious, ironic, injurious, which were repeated day by day, in an easily accessible position, with unwearying assiduity. They held the insolent Christophe up to ridicule, though they never mentioned him by name, but always transparently alluded to him. They twisted his words to make them look absurd: they told anecdotes about him, true for the most part, though the rest were a tissue of lies, nicely calculated to set him at loggerheads with the whole town, and, worse still, with the Court: even his physical appearance, his features, his manner of dressing, were attacked and caricatured in a way that by dint of repetition came to be like him.

* * * * *

It would have mattered little to Christophe's friends if their Review had not also come in for blows in the battle. In truth, it served rather as an advertisement: there was no desire to commit the Review to the quarrel: rather the attempt was made to cut Christophe off from it: there was astonishment that it should so compromise its good name, and they were given to understand that if they did not take care steps would be taken, however unpleasant it might be, to make the whole editorial staff responsible. There were signs of attack, gentle enough, upon Adolf Mai and Mannheim, which stirred up the wasps' nest.

Mannheim only laughed at it: he thought that it would infuriate his father, his uncles, cousins, and his innumerable family, who took upon themselves to watch everything he did and to be scandalized by it. But Adolf Mai took it very seriously and blamed Christophe for compromising the Review. Christophe sent him packing. The others who had not been attacked found it rather amusing that Mai, who was apt to pontificate over them, should be their scapegoat. Waldhaus was secretly delighted: he said that there was never a fight without a few heads being broken. Naturally he took good care that it should not be his own: he thought he was sheltered from onslaught by the position of his family; and his relatives: and he saw no harm in the Jews, his allies, being mauled a little. Ehrenfeld and Goldenring, who were so far untouched, would not have been worried by attack: they could reply. But what did touch them on the raw was that Christophe should go on persistently putting them in the wrong with their friends, and especially their women friends. They had laughed loudly at the first articles and thought them good fun: they admired Christophe's vigorous window–smashing: they thought they had only to give the word to check his combativeness, or at least to turn his attack from men and women whom they might mention.—But no. Christophe would listen to nothing: he paid no heed to any remark and went on like a madman. If they let him go on there would be no living in the place. Already their young women friends, furious and in tears, had come and made scenes at the offices of the Review. They brought all their diplomacy to bear on Christophe to persuade him at least to moderate certain of his criticisms: Christophe changed nothing. They lost their tempers: Christophe lost his, but he changed nothing. Waldhaus was amused by the unhappiness of his friends, which in no wise touched him, and took Christophe's part to annoy them. Perhaps also he was more capable than they of appreciating Christophe's extravagance, who with head down hurled himself upon everything without keeping any line of retreat, or preparing any refuge for the future. As for Mannheim he was royally amused by the farce: it seemed to him a good joke to have introduced this madman among these correct people, and he rocked with laughter both at the blows which Christophe dealt and at those which he received. Although under his sister's influence he was beginning to think that Christophe was decidedly a little cracked, he only liked him the more for it—(it was necessary for him to find those who were in sympathy with him a little absurd).—And so he joined Waldhaus in supporting Christophe against the others.

As he was not wanting in practical sense, in spite of all his efforts to pretend to the contrary, he thought very justly that it would be to his friend's advantage to ally himself with the cause of the most advanced musical party in the country.

As in most German towns, there was in the town a *Wagner–Verein*, which represented new ideas against the conservative element.—In truth, there was no great risk in defending Wagner when his fame was acknowledged everywhere and his works included in the repertory of every Opera House in Germany. And yet his victory was rather won by force than by universal accord, and at heart the majority were obstinately conservative, especially in the small towns such as this which have been rather left outside the great modern movements and are rather proud of their ancient fame. More than anywhere else there reigned the distrust, so innate in the German people, of anything new, the sort of laziness in feeling anything true or powerful which has not been pondered and digested by several generations. It was apparent in the reluctance with which—if not the works of Wagner which are beyond discussion—every new work inspired by the Wagnerian spirit was accepted. And so the *Wagner–Vereine* would have had a useful task to fulfil if they had set themselves to defend all the young and original forces in art. Sometimes they did so, and Bruckner or Hugo Wolf found in some of them their best allies. But too often the egoism of the master weighed upon his disciples: and just as Bayreuth serves only monstrously to glorify one man, the *offshoots* of Bayreuth were little churches in which Mass was eternally sung in honor of the one God. At the most the faithful disciples were admitted to the side chapels, the disciples who applied the hallowed doctrines to the letter, and, prostrate in the dust, adored the only Divinity with His many faces: music, poetry, drama, and metaphysics.

The *Wagner–Verein* of the town was in exactly this case.—However, they went through the form of activity: they were always trying to enroll young men of talent who looked as though they might be useful to it: and they had long had their eyes on Christophe. They had discreetly made advances to him, of which Christophe had not taken any notice, because he felt no need of being associated with anybody: he could not understand the necessity which drove his compatriots always to be banding themselves together in groups, being unable to do anything alone: neither to sing, nor to walk, nor to drink. He was averse to all *Vereinswesen*. But on the whole he was more kindly disposed to the *Wagner–Verein* than to any other *Verein*: at least they did provide an excuse for fine concerts: and although he did not share all the Wagnerian ideas on art, he was much nearer them than to those of any other group in music. He could he thought find common ground with a party which was as unjust as himself towards Brahms and the "Brahmins." So he let himself be put up for it. Mannheim introduced him: he knew everybody. Without being a musician he was a member of the *Wagner–Verein*.—The managing committee had followed the campaign which Christophe was conducting in the Review.

His slaughter in the opposing camp had seemed to them to give signs of a strong grip which it would be as well to have in their service. Christophe had also let fly certain disrespectful remarks about the sacred fetish: but they had preferred to close their eyes to that: and perhaps his attacks, not yet very offensive, had not been without their influence, unconsciously, in making them so eager to enroll Christophe before he had time to deliver himself manfully. They came and very amiably asked his permission to play some of his compositions at one of the approaching concerts of the Association. Christophe was flattered, and accepted: he went to the *Wagner–Verein*, and, urged by Mannheim, he was made a member.

At that time there were at the head of the *Wagner–Verein* two men, of whom one enjoyed a certain notoriety as a writer, and the other as a conductor. Both had a Mohammedan belief in Wagner. The first, Josias Kling, had compiled a Wagner Dictionary—*Wagner Lexikon* —which made it possible in a moment to know the master's thoughts *de omni re scibili*: it had been his life's work. He was capable of reciting whole chapters of it at table, as the French provincials used to troll the songs of the Maid. He used also to publish in the *Bayreuther Blaetter* articles on Wagner and the Aryan Spirit. Of course, Wagner was to him the type of the pure Aryan, of whom the German race had remained the last inviolable refuge against the corrupting influences of Latin Semitism, especially the French. He declared that the impure French spirit was finally destroyed, though he did not desist from attacking it bitterly day by day as though the eternal enemy were still a menace. He would only acknowledge one great man in France: the Count of Gobineau. Kling was a little man, very little, and he used to blush like a girl.—The other pillar of the *Wagner–Verein*, Erich Lauber, had been manager of a chemical works until four years before: then he had given up everything to become a conductor. He had succeeded by force of will, and because he was very rich. He was a Bayreuth fanatic: it was said that he had gone there on foot, from Munich, wearing pilgrim's sandals. It was a strange thing that a man who had read much, traveled much, practised divers professions, and in everything displayed an energetic personality, should have become in music a sheep of Panurge: all his originality was expended in his being a little more stupid than the others. He was not sure enough of himself in music to trust to his own personal feelings, and so he slavishly followed the interpretations of Wagner given by the *Kapellmeisters*, and the licensees of Bayreuth. He desired to reproduce even to the smallest detail the setting and the variegated costumes which delighted the puerile and barbarous taste of the little Court of Wahnfried. He was like the fanatical admirer of Michael Angelo who used to reproduce in his copies even the cracks in the wall of the moldy patches which had themselves been hallowed by their appearance in the hallowed pictures.

Christophe was not likely to approve greatly of the two men. But they were men of the world, pleasant, and both well–read: and Lauber's conversation was always interesting on any other subject than music. He was a bit of a crank: and Christophe did not dislike cranks: they were a change from the horrible banality of reasonable people. He did not yet know that there is nothing more devastating than an irrational man, and that originality is even more rare among those who are called "originals" than among the rest. For these "originals" are simply maniacs whose thoughts are reduced to clockwork.

Josias Kling and Lauber, being desirous of winning Christophe's support, were at first very keenly interested in him. Kling wrote a eulogistic article about him and Lauber followed all his directions when he conducted his compositions at one of the concerts of the Society. Christophe was touched by it all. Unfortunately all their attentions were spoiled by the stupidity of those who paid them. He had not the facility of pretending about people because they admired him. He was exacting. He demanded that no one should admire him for the opposite of what he was: and he was always prone to regard as enemies those who were his friends, by mistake. And so he was not at all pleased with Kling for seeing in him a disciple of Wagner, and trying to see connections between passages of his *Lieder* and passages of the *Tetralogy*, which had nothing in common but certain notes of the scale. And he had no pleasure in hearing one of his works sandwiched—together with a worthless imitation by a Wagnerian student—between two enormous blocks of Wagnerian drama.

It was not long before he was stifled in the little chapel. It was just another Conservatoire, as narrow as the old Conservatoires, and more intolerant because it was the latest comer in art. Christophe began to lose his illusions about the absolute value of a form of art or of thought. Hitherto he had always believed that great ideas bear their own light within themselves. Now he saw that ideas may change, but that men remain the same: and, in fine, nothing counted but men: ideas were what they were. If they were born mediocre and servile, even genius became mediocre in its passage through their souls, and the shout of freedom of the hero breaking his bonds became the act of slavery of succeeding generations.—Christophe could mot refrain from expressing his feelings. He let no opportunity slip of jeering at fetishism in art. He declared that there was no need of idols, or classics of any sort, and that he only had the right to call himself the heir of the spirit of Wagner who was capable of trampling Wagner underfoot and so walking on and keeping himself in close communion with life. Kling's stupidity made Christophe aggressive. He set out all the faults and absurdities he could see in Wagner. The Wagnerians at once credited him with a grotesque jealousy of their God. Christophe for his part had no doubt that these same people who exalted Wagner since he was dead would have been the first to strangle him in his life: and he did them an injustice. The Klings and the Laubers also had had their hour of illumination: they had been advanced twenty years ago: and then like most people they had stopped short at that. Man has so little force that he is out of breath after the first ascent: very few are long–winded enough to go on.

Christophe's attitude quickly alienated him from his new friends. Their sympathy was a bargain: he had to side with them if they were to side with him: and it was quite evident that Christophe would not yield an inch: he would not join them. They lost their enthusiasm for him. The eulogies which he refused to accord to the gods and demi–gods who were approved by the cult, were withheld from him. They showed less eagerness to welcome his compositions: and some of the members began to protest against his name being too often on the programmes. They laughed at him behind his back, and criticism went on: Kling and Lauber by not protesting seemed to take part in it. They would have avoided a breach with Christophe if possible: first because the minds of the Germans of the Rhine like mixed solutions, solutions which are not solutions, and have the privilege of prolonging indefinitely an ambiguous situation: and secondly, because they hoped in spite of everything to be able to make use of him, by wearing him down, if not by persuasion.

Christophe gave them no time for it. Whenever he thought he felt that at heart any man disliked him, but would not admit it and tried to cover it up so as to remain on good terms with him, he would never rest until he had succeeded in proving to him that he was his enemy. One evening at the *Wagner–Verein* when he had come up against a wall of hypocritical hostility, he could bear it no longer and sent in his resignation to Lauber without wasting words. Lauber could not understand it: and Mannheim hastened to Christophe to try and pacify him. At his first words Christophe burst out:

"No, no, no,—no! Don't talk to me about these people. I will not see them again.... I cannot. I cannot.... I am disgusted, horribly, with men: I can hardly bear to look at one."

Mannheim laughed heartily. He was thinking much less of smoothing Christophe down than of having the fun of it.

"I know that they are not beautiful," he said; "but that is nothing new: what new thing has happened?"

"Nothing. I have had enough, that is all.... Yes, laugh, laugh at me: everybody knows I am mad. Prudent people act in accordance with the laws of logic and reason and sanity. I am not like that: I am a man who acts only on his own impulse. When a certain quantity of electricity is accumulated in me it has to expend itself, at all costs: and so much the worse for the others if it touches them! And so much the worse for them! I am not made for living in society. Henceforth I shall belong only to myself."

"You think you can do without everybody else?" said Mannheim. "You cannot play your music all by yourself. You need singers, an orchestra, a conductor, an audience, a claque...."

Christophe shouted.

"No! no! no!"

But the last word made him jump.

"A claque! Are you not ashamed?"

"I am not talking of a paid claque—(although, indeed, it is the only means yet discovered of revealing the merit of a composition to the audience).—But you must have a claque: the author's coterie is a claque, properly drilled by him: every author has his claque: that is what friends are for."

"I don't want any friends!"

"Then you will be hissed."

"I want to be hissed!"

Mannheim was in the seventh heaven.

"You won't have even that pleasure for long. They won't play you."

"So be it, then! Do you think I care about being a famous man?... Yes. I was making for that with all my might.... Nonsense! Folly! Idiocy!... As if the satisfaction of the vulgarest sort of pride could compensate for all the sacrifices—weariness, suffering, infamy, insults, degradation, ignoble concessions—which are the price of fame! Devil take me if I ever bother my head about such things again! Never again! Publicity is a vulgar infamy. I will be a private citizen and live for myself and those whom I love...."

"Good," said Mannheim ironically. "You must choose a profession. Why shouldn't you make shoes?"

"Ah! if I were a cobbler like the incomparable Sachs!" cried Christophe. "How happy my life would be! A cobbler all through the week,—and a musician on Sunday, privately, intimately, for my own pleasure and that of my friends! What a life that would be!... Am I mad, to waste my time and trouble for the magnificent pleasure of being a prey to the judgment of idiots? Is it not much better and finer to be loved and understood by a few honest men than to be heard, criticised, and toadied by thousands of fools?... The devil of pride and thirst for fame shall never again take me: trust me for that!"

"Certainly," said Mannheim. He thought:

"In an hour he will say just the opposite." He remarked quietly:

"Then I am to go and smooth things down with the *Wagner–Verein* ?"

Christophe waved his arms.

"What is the good of my shouting myself hoarse with telling you 'No', for the last hour?... I tell you that I will never set foot inside it again! I loathe all these *Wagner–Vereine*, all these *Vereine*, all these flocks of sheep who have to huddle together to be able to baa in unison. Go and tell those sheep from me that I am a wolf, that I have teeth, and am not made far the pasture!"

"Good, good, I will tell them," said Mannheim, as he went. He was delighted with his morning's entertainment. He thought:

"He is mad, mad, mad as a hatter...."

His sister, to whom he reported the interview, at once shrugged her shoulders and said:

"Mad? He would like us to think so!... He is stupid, and absurdly vain...."

* * * * *

Christophe went on with his fierce campaign in Waldhaus's Review. It was not that it gave him pleasure: criticism disgusted him, and he was always wishing it at the bottom of the sea. But he stuck to it because people were trying to stop him: he did not wish to appear to have given in.

Waldhaus was beginning to be uneasy. As long as he was out of reach he had looked on at the affray with the calmness of an Olympian god. But for some weeks past the other papers had seemed to be beginning to disregard his inviolability: they had begun to attack his vanity as a writer with a rare malevolence in which, had Waldhaus been more subtle, he might have recognized the hand of a friend. As a matter of fact, the attacks were cunningly instigated by Ehrenfeld and Goldenring: they could see no other way of inducing him to stop Christophe's polemics. Their perception was justified. Waldhaus at once declared that Christophe was beginning to weary him: and he withdrew his support. All the staff of the Review then tried hard to silence Christophe! But it were as easy to muzzle a dog who is about to devour his prey! Everything they said to him only excited him more. He called them poltroons and declared that he would say everything—everything that he ought to say. If they wished to get rid of him, they were free to do so! The whole town would know that they were as cowardly as the rest: but he would not go of his own accord.

They looked at each other in consternation, bitterly blaming Mannheim for the trick he had played them in bringing such a madman among them. Mannheim laughed and tried hard to curb Christophe himself: and he vowed that with the next article Christophe would water his wine. They were incredulous: but the event proved that Mannheim had not boasted vainly. Christophe's next article, though not a model of courtesy, did not contain a single offensive remark about anybody. Mannheim's method was very simple: they were all amazed at not having thought of it before: Christophe never read what he wrote in the Review, and he hardly read the proofs of his articles, only very quickly and carelessly. Adolf Mai had more than once passed caustic remarks on the subject: he said that a printer's error was a disgrace to a Review: and Christophe, who did not regard criticism altogether as an art, replied that those who were upbraided in it would understand well enough. Mannheim turned this to account: he said that Christophe was right and that correcting proofs was printers' work: and he offered to take it over. Christophe was overwhelmed with gratitude: but they told him that such an arrangement would be of service to them and a saving of time for the Review. So Christophe left his proofs to Mannheim and asked him to correct them carefully. Mannheim did: it was sport for him. At first he only ventured to tone down certain phrases and to delete here and there certain ungracious epithets. Emboldened by success, he went further with his experiments: he began to alter sentences and their meaning: and he was really skilful in it. The whole art of it consisted in preserving the general appearance of the sentence and its characteristic form while making it say exactly the opposite of what Christophe had meant. Mannheim took far more trouble to disfigure Christophe's articles than he would have done to write them himself: never had he worked so hard. But he enjoyed the result: certain musicians whom Christophe had hitherto pursued with his sarcasms were astounded to see him grow gradually gentle and at last sing their praises. The staff of the Review were delighted. Mannheim used to read aloud his lucubrations to them. They roared with laughter. Ehrenfeld and Goldenring would say to Mannheim occasionally:

"Be careful! You are going too far."

"There's no danger," Mannheim would say. And he would go on with it.

Christophe never noticed anything. He used to go to the office of the Review, leave his copy, and not bother about it any more. Sometimes he would take Mannheim aside and say:

"This time I really have done for the swine. Just read...."

Mannheim would read.

"Well, what do you think of it?"

"Terrible, my dear fellow, there's nothing left of them!"

"What do you think they will say?"

"Oh! there will be a fine row."

But there never was a row. On the contrary, everybody beamed at Christophe: people whom he detested would bow to him in the street. One day he came to the office uneasy and scowling: and, throwing a visiting card on the table, he asked:

"What does this mean?"

It was the card of a musician whom he slaughtered.

"*A thousand thanks.*"

Mannheim replied with a laugh:

"It is ironical."

Christophe was set at rest.

"Oh!" he said. "I was afraid my article had pleased him."

"He is furious," said Ehrenfeld: "but he does not wish to seem so: he is posing as the strong man, and is just laughing."

"Laughing?... Swine!" said Christophe, furious once more. "I shall write another article about him. He laughs best who laughs last."

"No, no," said Waldhaus anxiously. "I don't think he is laughing at you. It is humility: he is a good Christian. He is holding out the other cheek to the smiter."

"So much the better!" said Christophe. "Ah! Coward! He has asked for it: he shall have his flogging."

Waldhaus tried to intervene. But the others laughed.

"Let him be...." said Mannheim.

"After all ..." replied Waldhaus, suddenly reassured, "a little more or less makes no matter!..."

Christophe went away. His colleagues rocked and roared with laughter. When they had had their fill of it Waldhaus said to Mannheim:

"All the same, it was a narrow squeak.... Please be careful. We shall be caught yet."

"Bah!" said Mannheim. "We have plenty of time.... And besides, I am making friends for him."

II. ENGULFED

Christophe had got so far with his clumsy efforts towards the reform of German art when there happened to pass through the town a troupe of French actors. It would be more exact to say, a band; for, as usual, they were a collection of poor devils, picked up goodness knows where, and young unknown players too happy to learn their art, provided they were allowed to act. They were all harnessed to the chariot of a famous and elderly actress who was making tour of Germany, and passing through the little princely town, gave their performances there.

Waldhaus' review made a great fuss over them. Mannheim and his friends knew or pretended to know about the literary and social life of Paris: they used to repeat gossip picked up in the boulevard newspapers and more or less understood; they represented the French spirit in Germany. That robbed Christophe of any desire to know more about it. Mannheim used to overwhelm him with praises of Paris. He had been there several times; certain members of his family were there. He had relations in every country in Europe, and they had everywhere assumed the nationality and aspect of the country: this tribe of the seed of Abraham included an English baronet, a Belgian senator, a French minister, a deputy in the *Reichstag*, and a Papal Count; and all of them, although they were united and filled with respect for the stock from which they sprang, were sincerely English,

Belgian, French, German, or Papal, for their pride never allowed of doubt that the country of their adoption was the greatest of all. Mannheim was paradoxically the only one of them who was pleased to prefer all the countries to which he did not belong. He used often to talk of Paris enthusiastically, but as he was always extravagant in his talk, and, by way of praising the Parisians, used to represent them as a species of scatterbrains, lewd and rowdy, who spent their time in love–making and revolutions without ever taking themselves seriously, Christophe was not greatly attracted by the "Byzantine and decadent republic beyond the Vosges." He used rather to imagine Paris as it was presented in a naive engraving which he had seen as a frontispiece to a book that had recently appeared in a German art publication; the Devil of Notre Dame appeared huddled up above the roofs of the town with the legend:

"Eternal luxury like an insatiable Vampire devours its prey above the great city."

Like a good German he despised the debauched Volcae and their literature, of which he only knew lively buffooneries like *L'Aiglon, Madame Sans Gene*, and a few cafe songs. The snobbishness of the little town, where those people who were most notoriously incapable of being interested in art flocked noisily to take places at the box office, brought him to an affectation of scornful indifference towards the great actress. He vowed that he would not go one yard to hear her. It was the easier for him to keep his promise as seats had reached an exorbitant price which he could not afford.

The repertory which the French actors had brought included a few classical pieces; but for the most part it was composed of those idiotic pieces which are expressly manufactured in Paris for exportation, for nothing is more international than mediocrity. Christophe knew *La Tosca*, which was to be the first production of the touring actors; he had seen it in translation adorned with all those easy graces which the company of a little Rhenish theater can give to a French play: and he laughed scornfully and declared that he was very glad, when he saw his friends go off to the theater, not to have to see it again. But next day he listened none the less eagerly, without seeming to listen, to the enthusiastic tales of the delightful evening they had had: he was angry at having lost the right to contradict them by having refused to see what everybody was talking about.

The second production announced was a French translation of *Hamlet*. Christophe had never missed an opportunity of seeing a play of Shakespeare's. Shakespeare was to him of the same order as Beethoven, an inexhaustible spring of life. *Hamlet* had been specially dear to him during the period of stress and tumultuous doubts through which he had just passed. In spite of his fear of seeing himself reflected in that magic mirror he was fascinated by it: and he prowled about the theater notices, though he did not admit that he was longing to book a seat. But he was so obstinate that after what he had said to his friends he would not eat his words: and he would have stayed at home that evening if chance had not brought him in contact with Mannheim just as he was sadly going home.

Mannheim took his arm and told him angrily, though he never ceased his banter, that an old beast of a relation, his father's sister, had just come down upon them with all her retinue and that they had all to stay at home to welcome her. He had time to get out of it: but his father would brook no trifling with questions of family etiquette and the respect due to elderly relatives: and as he had to handle his father carefully because he wanted presently to get money out of him, he had had to give in and not go to the play.

"You had tickets?" asked Christophe.

"An excellent box: and I have to go and give it—(I am just going now)—to that old pig, Gruenebaum, papa's partner, so that he can swagger there with the she Gruenebaum and their turkey hen of a daughter. Jolly!... I want to find something very disagreeable to say to them. They won't mind so long as I give them the tickets—although they would much rather they were banknotes."

He stopped short with his month open and looked at Christophe:

"Oh! but—but just the man I want!" He chuckled:

"Christophe, are you going to the theater?"

"No."

"Good. You shall go. I ask it as a favor. Yon cannot refuse."

Christophe did not understand.

"But I have no seat."

"Here you are!" said Mannheim triumphantly, thrusting the ticket into his hand.

"You are mad," said Christophe. "What about your father's orders?"

Mannheim laughed:

"He will be furious!" he said.

He dried his eyes and went on:

"I shall tap him to–morrow morning as soon as he is up before he knows anything."

"I cannot accept," said Christophe, "knowing that he would not like it."

"It does not concern you: you know nothing about it."

Christophe had unfolded the ticket:

"And what would I do with a box for four?"

"Whatever you like. You can sleep in it, dance if you like. Take some women. You must know some? If need be we can lend you some."

Christophe held out the ticket to Mannheim:

"Certainly not. Take it back."

"Not I," said Mannheim, stepping back a pace. "I can't force you to go if it bores you, but I shan't take it back. You can throw it in the fire or even take it virtuously to the Gruenebaums. I don't care. Good–night!"

He left Christophe in the middle of the street, ticket in hand, and went away.

Christophe was unhappy about it. He said to himself that he ought to take it to the Gruenebaums: but he was not keen about the idea. He went home still pondering, and when later he looked at the clock he saw that he had only just time enough to dress for the theater. It would be too silly to waste the ticket. He asked his mother to go with him. But Louisa declared that she would rather go to bed. He went. At heart he was filled with childish glee at the thought of his evening. Only one thing worried him: the thought of having to be alone in such a pleasure. He had no remorse about Mannheim's father or the Gruenebaums, whose box he was taking: but he was remorseful about those whom he might have taken with him. He thought of the joy it could give to other young people like himself: and it hurt him not to be able to give it them. He cast about but could find nobody to whom he could offer his ticket. Besides, it was late and he must hurry.

As he entered the theater he passed by the closed window on which a poster announced that there was not a single seat left in the office. Among the people who were turning away from it disappointedly he noticed a girl who could not make up her mind to leave and was enviously watching the people going in. She was dressed very simply in black; she was not very tall; her face was thin and she looked delicate; and at the moment he did not notice whether she were pretty or plain. He passed her: then he stopped, turned, and without stopping to think:

"You can't get a seat, Fraeulein?" he asked point–blank.

She blushed and said with a foreign accent:

"No, sir."

"I have a box which I don't know what to do with. Will you make use of it with me?"

She blushed again and thanked him and said she could not accept. Christophe was embarrassed by her refusal, begged her pardon and tried to insist, but he could not persuade her, although it was obvious that she was dying to accept. He was very perplexed. He made up his mind suddenly.

"There is a way out of the difficulty," he said. "You take the ticket. I don't want it. I have seen the play." (He was boasting). "It will give you more pleasure than me. Take it, please."

The girl was so touched by his proposal and the cordial manner in which it was made that tears all but came to her eyes. She murmured gratefully that she could not think of depriving him of it.

"Then, come," he said, smiling.

He looked so kind and honest that she was ashamed of having refused, and she said in some confusion:

"Thank you. I will come."

    * * * * *

They went in. The Mannheims' box was wide, big, and faced the stage: it was impossible not to be seen in it if they had wished. It is useless to say that their entry passed unnoticed. Christophe made the girl sit at the front, while he stayed a little behind so as not to embarrass her. She sat stiffly upright, not daring to turn her head: she was horribly shy: she would have given much not to have accepted. To give her time to recover her composure and not knowing what to talk to her about, Christophe pretended to look the other way. Whichever way he looked it was easily seen that his presence with an unknown companion among the brilliant people of the boxes was exciting much curiosity and comment. He darted furious glances at those who were looking at him: he was angry that people should go on being interested in him when he took no interest in them. It did not occur to him that their indiscreet curiosity was more busied with his companion than with himself and that there was more offense in it. By way of showing his utter indifference to anything they might say or think he leaned towards the girl and began to talk to her. She looked so scared by his talking and so unhappy at having to reply, and it seemed to be so difficult for her to wrench out a "Yes" or a "No" without ever daring to look at him, that he took pity on her shyness, and drew back to a corner. Fortunately the play began.

Christophe had not seen the play bill and he hardly cared to know what part the great actress was playing: he was one of those simple people who go to the theater to see the play and not the actors. He had never wondered whether the famous player would be Ophelia or the Queen; if he had wondered about it he would have inclined towards the Queen, bearing in naiad the ages of the two ladies. But it could never have occurred to him that she would play Hamlet. When he saw Hamlet, and heard his mechanical dolly squeak, it was some time before he could believe it; he wondered if he were not dreaming.

"But who? Who is it?" he asked half aloud. "It can't be...."

And when he had to accept that it *was* Hamlet, he rapped out an oath, which fortunately his companion did not hear, because she was a foreigner, though it was heard perfectly in the next box: for he was at once indignantly bidden to be silent. He withdrew to the back of the box to swear his fill. He could not recover his temper. If he had been just he would have given homage to the elegance of the travesty and the *tour de force* of nature and art, which made it possible for a woman of sixty to appear in a youth's costume and even to seem beautiful in it—at least to kindly eyes. But he hated all *tours de force*, everything which violates and falsifies Nature, He liked a woman to be a woman, and a man a man. (It does not often happen nowadays.) The childish and absurd travesty of the Leonora of Beethoven did not please him much. But this travesty of Hamlet was beyond all dreams of the preposterous. To make of the robust Dane, fat and pale, choleric, cunning, intellectual, subject to hallucinations, a woman,—not even a woman: for a woman playing the man can only be a monster,—to make of Hamlet a eunuch or an androgynous betwixt and between,—the times must be flabby indeed, criticism must be idiotic, to let such disgusting folly be tolerated for a single day and not hissed off the boards! The actress's voice infuriated Christophe. She had that singing, labored diction, that monotonous melopoeia which seems to have been dear to the least poetic people in the world since the days of the *Champmesle* and the *Hotel de Bourgogne*. Christophe was so exasperated by it that he wanted to go away. He turned his back on the scene, and he made hideous faces against the wall of the box like a child put in the corner. Fortunately his companion dared not look at him: for if she had seen him she would have thought him mad.

Suddenly Christophe stopped making faces. He stopped still and made no sound. A lovely musical voice, a young woman's voice, grave and sweet, was heard. Christophe pricked his ears. As she went on with her words he turned again, keenly interested to see what bird could warble so. He saw Ophelia. In truth she was nothing like the Ophelia of Shakespeare. She was a beautiful girl, tall, big and fine like a young fresh statue—Electra or Cassandra. She was brimming with life. In spite of her efforts to keep within her part, the force of youth and joy that was in her shone forth from her body, her movements, her gestures, her brown eyes that laughed in spite of herself. Such is the power of physical beauty that Christophe who a moment before had been merciless in judging the interpretation of Hamlet never for a moment thought of regretting that Ophelia was hardly at all like his image of her: and he sacrificed his image to the present vision of her remorselessly. With the unconscious faithlessness of people of passion he even found a profound truth in the youthful ardor brimming in the depths of the chaste and unhappy virgin heart. But the magic of the voice, pure, warm, and velvety, worked the spell: every word sounded like a lovely chord: about every syllable there hovered like the scent of thyme or wild mint the laughing accent of the Midi with its full rhythm. Strange was this vision of an Ophelia from Arles! In it was something of that golden sun and its wild northwest wind, its *mistral.*

Christophe forgot his companion and came and sat by her side at the front of the box: he never took his eyes off the beautiful actress whose name he did not know. But the audience who had not come to see an unknown player paid no attention to her, and only applauded when the female Hamlet spoke. That made Christophe growl and call them: "Idiots!" in a low voice which could be heard ten yards away.

It was not until the curtain was lowered upon the first act that he remembered the existence of his companion, and seeing that she was still shy he thought with a smile of how he must have scared her with his extravagances. He was not far wrong: the girl whom chance had thrown in his company for a few hours was almost morbidly shy; she must have been in an abnormal state of excitement to have accepted Christophe's invitation. She had hardly accepted it than she had wished at any cost to get out of it, to make some excuse and to escape. It had been much worse for her when she had seen that she was an object of general curiosity, and her unhappiness had been increased almost past endurance when she heard behind her back—(she dared not turn round)—her companion's low growls and imprecations. She expected anything now, and when he came and sat by her she was frozen with terror: what eccentricity would he commit next? She would gladly have sunk into the ground fathoms down. She drew back instinctively: she was afraid of touching him.

But all her fears vanished when the interval came and she heard him say quite kindly:

"I am an unpleasant companion, eh? I beg your pardon."

Then she looked at him and saw his kind smile which had induced her to come with him.

He went on:

"I cannot hide what I think.... But you know it is too much!... That woman, that old woman!..."

He made a face of disgust.

She smiled and said in a low voice:

"It is fine in spite of everything."

He noticed her accent and asked:

"You are a foreigner?"

"Yes," said she.

He looked at her modest gown.

"A governess?" he said.

"Yes."

"What nationality?"

She said:

"I am French."

He made a gesture of surprise:

"French? I should not have thought it."

"Why?" she asked timidly.

"You are so ... serious!" said he.

(She thought it was not altogether a compliment from him.)

"There are serious people also in France," said she confusedly. He looked at her honest little face, with its broad forehead, little straight nose, delicate chin, and thin cheeks framed in her chestnut hair. It was not she that he saw: he was thinking of the beautiful actress. He repeated:

"It is strange that you should be French!... Are you really of the same nationality as Ophelia? One would never think it"

After a moment's silence he went on:

"How beautiful she is!" without noticing that he seemed to be making a comparison between the actress and his companion that was not at all flattering to her. But she felt it: but she did not mind: for she was of the same opinion. He tried to find out about the actress from her: but she knew nothing: it was plain that she did not know much about the theater.

"You must be glad to hear French?" he asked. He meant it in jest, but he touched her.

"Ah!" she said with an accent of sincerity which struck him, "it does me so much good! I am stifled here."

He looked at her more closely: she clasped her hands, and seemed to be oppressed. But at once she thought of how her words might hurt him:

"Forgive me," she said. "I don't know what I am saying."

He laughed:

"Don't beg pardon! You are quite right. You don't need to be French to be stifled here. Ouf!"

He threw back his shoulders and took a long breath.

But she was ashamed of having been so free and relapsed into silence. Besides she had just seen that the people in the boxes next to them were listening to what they were saying: he noticed it too and was wrathful. They broke off: and until the end of the interval he went out into the corridor. The girl's words were ringing in his ears, but he was lost in dreams: the image of Ophelia filled his thoughts. During the succeeding acts she took hold of him completely, and when the beautiful actress came to the mad scene and the melancholy songs of love and death, her voice gave forth notes so moving that he was bowled over: he felt that he was going to burst into tears. Angry with himself for what he took to be a sign of weakness—(for he would not admit that a true artist can weep)—and not wishing to make an object of himself, he left the box abruptly. The corridors and the foyer were empty. In his agitation he went down the stairs of the theater and went out without knowing it. He had to breathe the cold night air, and to go striding through the dark, half–empty streets. He came to himself by the edge of a canal, and leaned on the parapet of the bank and watched the silent water whereon the reflections of the street lamps danced in the darkness. His soul was like that: it was dark and heaving: he could see nothing in it but great joy dancing on the surface. The clocks rang the hour. It was impossible for him to go back to the theater and hear the end of the play. To see the triumph of Fortinbras? No, that did not tempt him. A fine triumph that! Who thinks of envying the conqueror? Who would be he after being gorged with all the wild and absurd savagery of life? The whole play is a formidable indictment of life. But there is such a power of life in it that sadness becomes joy, and bitterness intoxicates....

Christophe went home without a thought for the unknown girl, whose name even he had not ascertained.

* * * * *

Next morning he went to see the actress at the little third–rate hotel in which the impresario had quartered her with her comrades while the great actress had put up at the best hotel in the town. He was conducted to a very untidy room where the remains of breakfast were left on an open piano, together with hairpins and torn and dirty sheets of music. In the next room Ophelia was singing at the top of her voice, like a child, for the pleasure of making a noise. She stopped for a moment when her visitor was announced to ask merrily in a loud voice without ever caring whether she were heard through the wall:

405

"What does he want? What is his name? Christophe? Christophe what? Christophe Krafft? What a name!"

(She repeated it two or three times, rolling her *r*'s terribly.)

"It is like a swear—"

(She swore.)

"Is he young or old? Pleasant? Very well. I'll come."

She began to sing again:

"*Nothing is sweeter than my love....*" while she rushed about her room cursing a tortoise–shell pin which had got lost in all the rubbish. She lost patience, began to grumble, and roared. Although he could not see her Christophe followed all her movements on the other side of the wall in imagination and laughed to himself. At last he heard steps approaching, the door was flung open, and Ophelia appeared.

She was half dressed, in a loose gown which she was holding about her waist: her bare arms showed in her wide sleeves: her hair was carelessly done, and locks of it fell down into her eyes and over her cheeks. Her fine brown eyes smiled, her lips smiled, her cheeks smiled, and a charming dimple in her chin smiled. In her beautiful grave melodious voice she asked him to excuse her appearance. She knew that there was nothing to excuse and that he could only be very grateful to her for it. She thought he was a journalist come to interview her. Instead of being annoyed when he told her that he had come to her entirely of his own accord and because he admired her, she was delighted. She was a good girl, affectionate, delighted to please, and making no effort to conceal her delight. Christophe's visit and his enthusiasm made her very happy—(she was not yet spoiled by flattery). She was so natural in all her movements and ways, even in her little vanities and her naive delight in giving pleasure, that he was not embarrassed for a single moment. They became old friends at once. He could jabber a few words of French: and she could jabber a few words of German: after an hour they told each other all their secrets. She never thought of sending him away. The splendid gay southern creature, intelligent and warm–hearted, who would have been bored to tears with her stupid companions and in a country whose language she did not know, a country without the natural joy that was in herself, was glad to find some one to talk to. As for Christophe it was an untold blessing for him to meet the free–hearted girl of the Midi filled with the life of the people, in the midst of his narrow and insincere fellow citizens. He did not yet know the workings of such natures which, unlike the Germans, have no more in their minds and hearts than they show, and often not even as much. But at the least she was young, she was alive, she said frankly, rawly, what she thought: she judged everything freely from a new and a fresh point of view: in her it was possible to breathe a little of the northwest wind that sweeps away mists. She was gifted. Uneducated and unthinking, she could at once feel with her whole heart and be sincerely moved by things which were beautiful and good; and then, a moment later, she would burst out laughing. She was a coquette and made eyes; she did not mind showing her bare arms and neck under her half open gown; she would have liked to turn Christophe's head, but it was all purely instinctive. There was no thought of gaining her own ends in her, and she much preferred to laugh, and talk blithely, to be a good fellow, a good chum, without ceremony or awkwardness. She told him about the underworld of the theater, her little sorrows, the silly susceptibilities of her comrades, the bickerings of Jezebel—(so she called the great actress)—who took good care not to let her shine. He confided his sufferings at the hands of the Germans: she clapped her hands and played chords to him. She was kind and would not speak ill of anybody; but that did not keep her from doing so, and while she blamed herself for her malice, when she laughed at anybody, she had a fund of mocking humor and that realistic and witty gift of observation which belongs to the people of the South; she could not resist it and drew cuttingly satirical portraits. With her pale lips she laughed merrily to show her teeth, like those of a puppy, and dark eyes shone in her pale face, which was a little discolored by grease paint.

They noticed suddenly that they had been talking for more than an hour. Christophe proposed to come for Corinne—(that was her stage name)—in the afternoon and show her over the town. She was delighted with the idea, and they arranged to meet immediately after dinner.

At the appointed hour, he turned up. Corinne was sitting in the little drawing–room of the hotel, with a book in her hand, which she was reading aloud. She greeted him with smiling eyes but did not stop reading until she had finished her sentence. Then she signed to him to sit down on the sofa by her side:

"Sit there," she said, "and don't talk. I am going over my part. I shall have finished in a quarter of an hour."

She followed the script with her finger nail and read quickly and carelessly like a little girl in a hurry. He offered to hear her her words. She passed him the book and got up to repeat what she had learned. She floundered and would repeat the end of one sentence four times before going on to the next. She shook her head as she recited her part; her hair–pins fell down and all over the room. When she could not recollect sometimes some word she was as impatient as a naughty child; sometimes she swore comically or she would use big words;—one word with which she apostrophized herself was very big and very short. Christophe was astonished by the mixture of talent and childishness in her. She would produce moving tones of voice quite aptly, but in the middle of a speech into which she seemed to be throwing her whole heart she would say a whole string of words that had absolutely no meaning. She recited her lesson like a parrot, without troubling about its meaning, and then she produced burlesque nonsense. She did not worry about it. When she saw it she would shout with laughter. At last she said: "Zut!", snatched the book from him, flung it into a corner of the room, and said:

"Holidays! The hour has struck!... Now let us go out."

He was a little anxious about her part and asked:

"You think you will know it?"

She replied confidently:

"Certainly. What is the prompter for?" She went into her room to put on her hat. Christophe sat at the piano while he was waiting for her and struck a few chords. From the next room she called:

"Oh! What is that? Play some more! How pretty it is!"

She ran in, pinning on her hat. He went on. When he had finished she wanted him to play more. She went into ecstasies with all the little arch exclamations habitual to Frenchwomen which they make about *Tristan* and a cup of chocolate equally. It made Christophe laugh; it was a change from the tremendous affected, clumsy exclamations of the Germans; they were both exaggerated in different directions; one made a mountain out of a mole–hill, the other made a mole–hill out of a mountain; the French was not less ridiculous than the German, but for the moment it seemed more pleasant because he loved the lips from which it came. Corinne wanted to know what he was playing, and when she learned that he had composed it she gave a shout. He had told her during their conversation in the morning that he was a composer, but she had hardly listened to him. She sat by him and insisted on his playing everything that he had composed. Their walk was forgotten. It was not mere politeness on her part; she adored music and had an admirable instinct for it which supplied the deficiencies of her education. At first he did not take her seriously and played his easiest melodies. But when he had played a passage by which he set more store and saw that she preferred it too, although he had not said anything about it, he was joyfully surprised. With the naive astonishment of the Germans when they meet a Frenchman who is a good musician he said:

"Odd. How good your taste is! I should never have thought it...."

Corinne laughed in his face.

He amused himself then by selecting compositions more and more difficult to understand, to see how far she would go with him. But she did not seem to be put out by his boldness, and after a particularly new melody which Christophe himself had almost come to doubt because he had never succeeded in having it accepted in Germany, he was greatly astonished when Corinne begged him to play it again, and she got up and began to sing the notes from memory almost without a mistake! He turned towards her and took her hands warmly:

"But you are a musician!" he cried.

She began to laugh and explained that she had made her debut as a singer in provincial opera houses, but that an impresario of touring companies had recognized her disposition towards the poetic theater and had enrolled her in its services. He exclaimed:

"What a pity!"

"Why?" said she. "Poetry also is a sort of music."

She made him explain to her the meaning of his *Lieder*; he told her the German words, and she repeated them with easy mimicry, copying even the movements of his lips and eyes as he pronounced the words. When she had these to sing from memory, then she made grotesque mistakes, and when she forgot, she invented words, guttural and barbarously sonorous, which made them both laugh. She did not tire of making him play, nor he of playing for her and hearing her pretty voice; she did not know the tricks of the trade and sang a little from the throat like little girls, and there was a curious fragile quality in her voice that was very touching. She told him frankly what she thought. Although she could not explain why she liked or disliked anything there was always some grain of sense hidden in her judgment. The odd thing was that she found least pleasure in the most classical passages which were most appreciated in Germany; she paid him a few compliments out of politeness; but they obviously meant nothing. As she had no musical culture she had not the pleasure which amateurs and even artists find in what is *already heard*, a pleasure which often makes them unconsciously reproduce, or, in a new composition, like forms or formulae which they have already used in old compositions. Nor did she have the German taste for melodious sentimentality (or, at least, her sentimentality was different; Christophe did not yet know its failings)—she did not go into ecstasies over the soft insipid music preferred in Germany; she did not single out the most melodious of his *Lieder*,—a melody which he would have liked to destroy because his friends, only too glad to be able to compliment him on something, were always talking about it. Corinne's dramatic instinct made her prefer the melodies which frankly reproduced a certain passion; he also set most store by them. And yet she did not hesitate to show her lack of sympathy with certain rude harmonies which seemed quite natural to Christophe; they gave her a sort of shock when she came upon them; she would stop then and ask "if it was really so." When he said "Yes," then she would rush at the difficulty; but she would make a little grimace which did not escape Christophe. Sometimes even she would prefer to skip the bar. Then he would play it again on the piano.

"You don't like that?" he would ask.

She would screw up her nose.

"It is wrong," she would say.

"Not at all," he would reply with a laugh. "It is quite right. Think of its meaning. It is rhythmic, isn't it?"

(He pointed to her heart.)

But she would shake her head:

"May be; but it is wrong here." (She pulled her ear.)

And she would be a little shocked by the sudden outbursts of German declamation.

"Why should he talk so loud?" she would ask. "He is all alone. Aren't you afraid of his neighbors overhearing him? It is as though—(Forgive me! You won't be angry?)—he were hailing a boat."

He was not angry; he laughed heartily, he recognized that there was some truth in what she said. Her remarks amused him; nobody had ever said such things before. They agreed that declamation in singing generally deforms the natural word like a magnifying glass. Corinne asked Christophe to write music for a piece in which she would speak to the accompaniment of the orchestra, singing a few sentences every now and then. He was fired by the idea in spite of the difficulties of the stage setting which, he thought, Corinne's musical voice would easily overcome, and they made plans for the future. It was not far short of five o'clock when they thought of going out. Night fell early. They could not think of going for a walk. Corinne had a rehearsal at the theater in the evening; nobody was allowed to be present. She made him promise to come and fetch her during the next afternoon to take the walk they had planned.

* * * * *

Next day they did almost the same again. He found Corinne in front of her mirror, perched on a high stool, swinging her legs; she was trying on a wig. Her dresser was there and a hair dresser of the town to whom she was giving instructions about a curl which she wished to have higher up. As she looked in the glass she saw Christophe smiling behind her back; she put out her tongue at him. The hair dresser went away with the wig and she turned gaily to Christophe:

"Good–day, my friend!" she said.

She held up her cheek to be kissed. He had not expected such intimacy, but he took advantage of it all the same. She did not attach so much importance to the favor; it was to her a greeting like any other.

"Oh! I am happy!" said she. "It will do very well to–night." (She was talking of her wig.) "I was so wretched! If you had come this morning you would have found me absolutely miserable."

He asked why.

It was because the Parisian hair dresser had made a mistake in packing and had sent a wig which was not suitable to the part.

"Quite flat," she said, "and falling straight down. When I saw it I wept like a Magdalen. Didn't I, Desiree?"

"When I came in," said Desiree, "I was afraid for Madame. Madame was quite white. Madame looked like death."

Christophe laughed. Corinne saw him in her mirror:

"Heartless wretch; it makes you laugh," she said indignantly.

She began to laugh too.

He asked her how the rehearsal had gone. Everything had gone off well. She would have liked the other parts to be cut more and her own less. They talked so much that they wasted part of the afternoon. She dressed slowly; she amused herself by asking Christophe's opinion about her dresses. Christophe praised her elegance and told her naively in his Franco–German jargon, that he had never seen anybody so "luxurious." She looked at him for a moment and then burst out laughing.

"What have I said?" he asked. "Have I said anything wrong?"

"Yes, yes," she cried, rocking with laughter. "You have indeed."

At last they went out. Her striking costume and her exuberant chatter attracted attention. She looked at everything with her mocking eyes and made no effort to conceal her impressions. She chuckled at the dressmakers' shops, and at the picture post–card shops in which sentimental scenes, comic and obscene drawings, the town prostitutes, the imperial family, the Emperor as a sea–dog holding the wheel of the *Germania* and defying the heavens, were all thrown together higgledy–piggledy. She giggled at a dinner–service decoration with Wagner's cross–grained face, or at a hair dresser's shop–window in which there was the wax head of a man. She made no attempt to modify her hilarity over the patriotic monument representing the old Emperor in a traveling coat and a peaked cap, together with Prussia, the German States, and a nude Genius of War. She made remarks about anything in the faces of the people or their way of speaking that struck her as funny. Her victims were left in no doubt about it as she maliciously picked out their absurdities. Her instinctive mimicry made her sometimes imitate with her mouth and nose their broad grimaces and frowns, without thinking; and she would blow out her cheeks as she repeated fragments of sentences and words that struck her as grotesque in sound as she caught them. He laughed heartily and was not at all embarrassed by her impertinence, for he was no longer easily embarrassed. Fortunately he had no great reputation to lose, or his walk would have ruined it for ever.

They visited the cathedral. Corinne wanted to go to the top of the spire, in spite of her high heels, and long dress which swept the stairs or was caught in a corner of the staircase; she did not worry about it, but pulled the stuff which split, and went on climbing, holding it up. She wanted very much to ring the bells. From the top of the tower she declaimed Victor Hugo (he did not understand it), and sang a popular French song. After that she played the muezzin. Dusk was falling. They went down into the cathedral where the dark shadows were creeping along the gigantic walls in which the magic eyes of the windows were shining. Kneeling in one of the side chapels, Christophe saw the girl who had shared his box at *Hamlet*. She was so absorbed in her prayers that she did not see him: he saw that she was looking sad and strained. He would have liked to speak to her, just to say, "How do you do?" but Corinne dragged him off like a whirlwind.

They parted soon afterwards. She had to get ready for the performance, which began early, as usual in Germany. He had hardly reached home when there was a ring at the door and a letter from Corinne was handed in:

"Luck! Jezebel ill! No performance! No school! Come! Let us dine together! Your friend,

"CORINETTE.

"P.S. Bring plenty of music!"

It was some time before he understood. When he did understand he was as happy as Corinne, and went to the hotel at once. He was afraid of finding the whole company assembled at dinner; but he saw nobody. Corinne herself was not there. At last he heard her laughing voice at the back of the house: he went to look for her and found her in the kitchen. She had taken it into her head to cook a dish in her own way, one of those southern dishes which fills the whole neighborhood with its aroma and would awaken a stone. She was on excellent terms with the large proprietress of the hotel, and they were jabbering in a horrible jargon that was a mixture of German, French, and negro, though there is no word to describe it in any language. They were laughing loudly and making each other taste their cooking. Christophe's appearance made them noisier than ever. They tried to push him out; but he struggled and succeeded in tasting the famous dish. He made a face. She said he was a barbarous Teuton and that it was no use putting herself out for him.

They went up to the little sitting–room when the table was laid; there were only two places, for himself and Corinne. He could not help asking her where her companions were. Corinne waved her hands carelessly:

"I don't know."

"Don't you sup together?"

"Never! We see enough of each other at the theater!... And it would be awful if we had to meet at meals!..."

It was so different from German custom that he was surprised and charmed by it.

"I thought," he said, "you were a sociable people!"

"Well," said she, "am I not sociable?"

"Sociable means living in society. We have to see each other! Men, women, children, we all belong to societies from birth to death. We are always making societies: we eat, sing, think in societies. When the societies sneeze, we sneeze too: we don't have a drink except with our societies."

"That must be amusing," said she. "Why not out of the same glass?"

"Brotherly, isn't it?"

"That for fraternity! I like being 'brotherly' with people I like: not with the others ... Pooh! That's not society: that is an ant heap."

"Well, you can imagine how happy I am here, for I think as you do."

"Come to us, then!"

He asked nothing better. He questioned her about Paris and the French. She told him much that was not perfectly accurate. Her southern propensity for boasting was mixed with an instinctive desire to shine before him. According to her, everybody in Paris was free: and as everybody in Paris was intelligent, everybody made good use of their liberty, and no one abused it. Everybody did what they liked: thought, believed, loved or did not love, as they liked; nobody had anything to say about it. There nobody meddled with other people's beliefs, or spied on their consciences or tried to regulate their thoughts. There politicians never dabbled in literature or the arts, and never gave orders, jobs, and money to their friends or clients. There little cliques never disposed of reputation or success, journalists were never bought; there men of letters never entered into controversies with the church, that could lead to nothing. There criticism never stifled unknown talent, or exhausted its praises upon recognized talent. There success, success at all costs, did not justify the means, and command the adoration of the public. There were only gentle manners, kindly and sweet. There was never any bitterness, never any scandal. Everybody helped everybody else. Every worthy newcomer was certain to find hands held out to him and the way made smooth for him. Pure love, of beauty filled the chivalrous and disinterested souls of the French, and they were only absurd in their idealism, which, in spite of their acknowledged wit, made them the dupes of other nations. Christophe listened open–mouthed. It was certainly marvelous. Corinne marveled herself as she heard her words. She had forgotten what she had told Christophe the day before about the difficulties of her past life. He gave no more thought to it than she.

And yet Corinne was not only concerned with making the Germans love her country: she wanted to make herself loved, too. A whole evening without flirtation would have seemed austere and rather absurd to her. She made eyes at Christophe; but it was trouble wasted: he did not notice it. Christophe did not know what it was to flirt. He loved or did not love. When he did not love he was miles from any thought of love. He liked Corinne enormously. He felt the attraction of her southern nature; it was so new to him. And her sweetness and good humor, her quick and lively intelligence: many more reasons than he needed for loving. But the spirit blows where it listeth. It did not blow in that direction, and as for playing at love, in love's absence, the idea had never occurred to him.

Corinne was amused by his coldness. She sat by his side at the piano while he played the music he had brought with him, and put her arm round his neck, and to follow the music she leaned towards the keyboard, almost pressing her cheek against his. He felt her hair touch his face, and quite close to him saw the corner of her mocking eye, her pretty little mouth, and the light down on her tip–tilted nose. She waited, smiling—she waited. Christophe did not understand the invitation. Corinne was in his way: that was all he thought of. Mechanically he broke free from her and moved his chair. And when, a moment later, he turned to speak to Corinne, he saw that she was choking with laughter: her cheeks were dimpled, her lips were pressed together, and she seemed to be holding herself in.

"What is the matter?" he said, in his astonishment.

She looked at him and laughed aloud.

He did not understand.

"Why are you laughing?" he asked. "Did I say anything funny?"

The more he insisted, the more she laughed. When she had almost finished she had only to look at his crestfallen appearance to break out again. She got up, ran to the sofa at the other end of the room, and buried her face in the cushions to laugh her fill; her whole body shook with it. He began to laugh too, came towards her, and slapped her on the back. When she had done laughing she raised her head, dried the tears in her eyes, and held out her hands to him.

"What a good boy you are!" she said.

"No worse than another."

She went on, shaking occasionally with laughter, still holding his hands.

"Frenchwomen are not serious?" she asked. (She pronounced it: " *Francouese.*")

"You are making fun of me," he said good–humoredly.

She looked at him kindly, shook his hands vigorously, and said:

"Friends?"

"Friends!" said he, shaking her hand.

"You will think of Corinette when she is gone? You won't be angry with the Frenchwoman for not being serious?"

"And Corinette won't be angry with the barbarous Teuton for being so stupid?"

"That is why she loves him ... You will come and see her in Paris?"

"It is a promise ... And she—she will write to him?"

"I swear it ... You say: 'I swear.'"

"I swear."

"No, not like that. You must hold up your hand." She recited the oath of the Horatii. She made him promise to write a play for her, a melodrama, which could be translated into

French and played in Paris by her. She was going away next day with her company. He promised to go and see her again the day after at Frankfort, where they were giving a performance.

They stayed talking for some time. She presented Christophe with a photograph in which she was much decolletee, draped only in a garment fastening below her shoulders. They parted gaily, and kissed like brother and sister. And, indeed, once Corinne had seen that Christophe was fond of her, but not at all in love, she began to be fond of him, too, without love, as a good friend.

Their sleep was not troubled by it. He could not see her off next day, because he was occupied by a rehearsal. But on the day following he managed to go to Frankfort as he had promised. It was a few hours' journey by rail. Corinne hardly believed Christophe's promise. But he had taken it seriously, and when the performance began he was there. When he knocked at her dressing–room door during the interval, she gave a cry of glad surprise and threw her arms round his neck with her usual exuberance. She was sincerely grateful to him for having come. Unfortunately for Christophe, she was much more sought after in the city of rich, intelligent Jews, who could appreciate her actual beauty and her future success. Almost every minute there was a knock at the door, and it opened to reveal men with heavy faces and quick eyes, who said the conventional things with a thick accent. Corinne naturally made eyes, and then she would go on talking to Christophe in the same affected, provoking voice, and that irritated him. And he found no pleasure in the calm lack of modesty with which she went on dressing in his presence, and the paint and grease with which she larded her arms, throat, and face filled him with profound disgust. He was on the point of going away without seeing her again after the performance; but when he said good–bye and begged to be excused from going to the supper that was to be given to her after the play, she was so hurt by it and so affectionate, too, that he could not hold out against her. She had a time–table brought, so as to prove that he could and must stay an hour with her. He only needed to be convinced, and he was at the supper. He was even able to control his annoyance with the follies that were indulged in and his irritation at Corinne's coquetries with all and sundry. It was impossible to be angry with her. She was an honest girl, without any moral principles, lazy, sensual, pleasure–loving, childishly coquettish; but at the same time so loyal, so kind, and all her faults were so spontaneous and so healthy that it was only possible to smile at them and even to love them. Christophe, who was sitting opposite her, watched her animation, her radiant eyes, her sticky lips, with their Italian smile—that smile in which there is kindness, subtlety, and a sort of heavy greediness. He saw her more clearly than he had yet done. Some of her features reminded him of Ada: certain gestures, certain looks, certain sensual and rather coarse tricks—the eternal feminine. But what he loved in her was her southern nature, that generous nature which is not niggardly with its gifts, which never troubles to fashion drawing–room beauties and literary cleverness, but harmonious creatures who are made body and mind to grow in the air and the sun. When he left she got up from the table to say good–bye to him away from the others. They kissed and renewed their promises to write and meet again.

He took the last train home. At a station the train coming from the opposite direction was waiting. In the carriage opposite his—a third–class compartment—Christophe saw the young Frenchwoman who had been with him to the performance of *Hamlet*. She saw Christophe and recognized him. They were both astonished. They bowed and did not move, and dared not look again. And yet he had seen at once that she was wearing a little traveling toque and had an old valise by her side. It did not occur to him that she was leaving the country. He thought she must be going away for a few days. He did not know whether he ought to speak to her. He stopped, turned over in his mind what to say, and was just about to lower the window of the carriage to address a few words to her, when the signal was given. He gave up the idea. A few seconds passed before the train moved. They looked straight at each other. Each was alone, and their faces were pressed against the windows and they looked into each other's eyes through the night. They were separated by two windows. If they had reached out their hands they could have touched each other. So near. So far. The carriages shook heavily. She was still looking at him, shy no longer, now that they were parting. They were so absorbed in looking at each other that they never even thought of bowing for the last time. She was slowly borne away. He saw her disappear, and the train which bore her plunged into the night. Like two circling worlds, they had passed close to each other in infinite space, and now they sped apart perhaps for eternity.

When she had disappeared he felt the emptiness that her strange eyes had left in him, and he did not understand why; but the emptiness was there. Sleepy, with eyes half–closed, lying in a corner of the carriage, he felt her eyes looking into his, and all other thoughts ceased, to let him feel them more keenly. The image of Corinne fluttered outside his heart like an insect breaking its wings against a window; but he did not let it in.

He found it again when he got out of the train on his arrival, when the keen night air and his walk through the streets of the sleeping town had shaken off his drowsiness. He scowled at the thought of the pretty actress, with a mixture of pleasure and irritation, according as he recalled her affectionate ways or her vulgar coquetries.

"Oh! these French people," he growled, laughing softly, while he was undressing quietly, so as not to waken his mother, who was asleep in the next room.

A remark that he had heard the other evening in the box occurred to him:

"There are others also."

At his first encounter with France she laid before him the enigma of her double nature. But, like all Germans, he did not trouble to solve it, and as he thought of the girl in the train he said quietly:

"She does not look like a Frenchwoman."

As if a German could say what is French and what is not.

* * * * *

French or not, she filled his thoughts; for he woke in the middle of the night with a pang: he had just remembered the valise on the seat by the girl's side; and suddenly the idea that she had gone forever crossed his mind. The idea must have come to him at the time, but he had not thought of it. It filled him with a strange sadness. He shrugged his shoulders.

"What does it matter to me?" he said. "It is not my affair."

He went to sleep.

But next day the first person he met when he went out was Mannheim, who called him "Bluecher," and asked him if he had made up his mind to conquer all France. From the garrulous newsmonger he learned that the story of the box had had a success exceeding all Mannheim's expectations.

"Thanks to you! Thanks to you!" cried Mannheim. "You are a great man. I am nothing compared with you."

"What have I done?" said Christophe.

"You are wonderful!" Mannheim replied. "I am jealous of you. To shut the box in the Gruenebaums' faces, and then to ask the French governess instead of them—no, that takes the cake! I should never have thought of that!"

"She was the Gruenebaums' governess?" said Christophe in amazement.

"Yes. Pretend you don't know, pretend to be innocent. You'd better!... My father is beside himself. The Gruenebaums are in a rage!... It was not for long: they have sacked the girl."

"What!" cried Christophe. "They have dismissed her? Dismissed her because of me?"

"Didn't you know?" said Mannheim. "Didn't she tell you?"

Christophe was in despair.

"You mustn't be angry, old man," said Mannheim. "It does not matter. Besides, one had only to expect that the Gruenebaums would find out..."

"What?" cried Christophe. "Find out what?"

"That she was your mistress, of course!"

"But I do not even know her. I don't know who she is."

Mannheim smiled, as if to say:

"You take me for a fool."

Christophe lost his temper and bade Mannheim do him the honor of believing what he said. Mannheim said:

"Then it is even more humorous."

Christophe worried about it, and talked of going to the Gruenebaums and telling them the facts and justifying the girl. Mannheim dissuaded him.

"My dear fellow," he said, "anything you may say will only convince them of the contrary. Besides, it is too late. The girl has gone away."

Christophe was utterly sick at heart and tried to trace the young Frenchwoman. He wanted to write to her to beg her pardon. But nothing was known of her. He applied to the Gruenebaums, but they snubbed him. They did not know themselves where she had gone, and they did not care. The idea of the harm he had done in trying to do good tortured Christophe: he was remorseful. But added to his remorse was a mysterious attraction, which shone upon him from the eyes of the woman who was gone. Attraction and remorse both seemed to be blotted out, engulfed in the flood of the day's new thoughts. But they endured in the depths of his heart. Christophe did not forget the woman whom he called his victim. He had sworn to meet her again. He knew how small were the chances of his ever seeing her again: and he was sure that he would see her again.

As for Corinne, she never answered his letters. But three months later, when he had given up expecting to hear from her, he received a telegram of forty words of utter nonsense, in which she addressed him in little familiar terms, and asked "if they were still fond of each other." Then, after nearly a year's silence, there came a scrappy letter scrawled in her enormous childish zigzag writing, in which she tried to play the lady,—a few affectionate, droll words. And there she left it. She did not forget him, but she had no time to think of him.

* * * * *

Still under the spell of Corinne and full of the ideas they had exchanged about art, Christophe dreamed of writing the music for a play in which Corinne should act and sing a few airs—a sort of poetic melodrama. That form of art once so much in favor in Germany, passionately admired by Mozart, and practised by Beethoven, Weber, Mendelssohn and Schumann, and all the great classics, had fallen into discredit since the triumph of Wagnerism, which claimed to have realized the definite formula of the theater and music. The Wagnerian pedants, not content with proscribing every new melodrama, busied themselves with dressing up the old melodramas and operas. They carefully effaced every trace of spoken dialogue and wrote for Mozart, Beethoven, or Weber, recitations in their own manner; they were convinced that they were doing a service to the fame of the masters and filling out their thoughts by the pious deposit of their dung upon masterpieces.

Christophe, who had been made more sensible of the heaviness, and often the ugliness, of Wagnerian declamation by Corinne, had for some time been debating whether it was not nonsense and an offense against nature to harness and yoke together the spoken word and the word sung in the theater: it was like harnessing a horse and a bird to a cart. Speech and singing each had its rhythm. It was comprehensible that an artist should sacrifice one of the two arts to the triumph of that which he preferred. But to try to find a compromise between them was to sacrifice both: it was to want speech no longer to be speech, and singing no longer to be singing; to want singing to let its vast flood be confined between the banks of monotonous canals, to want speech to cloak its lovely naked limbs with rich, heavy stuffs which must paralyze its gestures and movements. Why not leave both with their spontaneity and freedom of movement? Like a beautiful girl walking tranquilly, lithely along a stream, dreaming as she goes: the gay murmur of the water lulls her dreams, and unconsciously she brings her steps and her thoughts in tune with the song of the stream. So being both free, music and poesy would go side by side, dreaming, their dreams mingling. Assuredly all music was not good for such a union, nor all poetry. The opponents of melodrama had good ground for attack in the coarseness of the attempts which had been made in that form, and of the interpreters. Christophe had for long shared their dislike: the stupidity of the actors who delivered these recitations spoken to an instrumental accompaniment, without bothering about the accompaniment, without trying to merge their voices in it, rather, on the contrary, trying to prevent anything being heard but themselves, was calculated to revolt any musical ear. But since he had tasted the beauty of Corinne's harmonious voice—that liquid and pure voice which played upon music like a ray of light on water, which wedded every turn of a melody, which was like the most fluid and most free singing,—he had caught a glimpse of the beauty of a new art.

Perhaps he was right, but he was still too inexperienced to venture without peril upon a form which—if it is meant to be beautiful and really artistic—is the most difficult of all. That art especially demands one essential condition, the perfect harmony of the combined efforts of the poet, the musicians, and the actors. Christophe had no tremors about it: he hurled himself blindly at an unknown art of which the laws were only known to himself.

His first idea had been to clothe in music a fairy fantasy of Shakespeare or an act of the second part of *Faust*. But the theaters showed little disposition to make the experiment. It would be too costly and appeared absurd. They were quite willing to admit Christophe's efficiency in music, but that he should take upon himself to have ideas about poetry and the theater made them smile. They did not take him seriously. The world of music and the world of poesy were like two foreign and secretly hostile states. Christophe had to accept the collaboration of a poet to be able to set foot upon poetic territory, and he was not allowed to choose his own poet. He would not have dared to choose himself. He did not trust his taste in poetry. He had been told that he knew nothing about it; and, indeed, he could not understand the poetry which was admired by those about him. With his usual honesty and stubbornness, he had tried hard sometimes to feel the beauty of some of these works, but he had always been bewildered and a little ashamed of himself. No, decidedly he was not a poet. In truth, he loved passionately certain old poets, and that consoled him a little. But no doubt he did not love them as they should be loved. Had he not once expressed, the ridiculous idea that those poets only are great who remain great even when they are translated into prose, and even into the prose of a foreign language, and that words have no value apart from the soul which they express? His friends had laughed at him. Mannheim had called him a goose. He did not try to defend himself. As every day he saw, through the example of writers who talk of music, the absurdity of artists who attempt to image any art other than their own, he resigned himself—though a little incredulous at heart—to his incompetence in poetry, and he shut his eyes and accepted the judgments of those whom he thought were better informed than himself. So he let his friends of the Review impose one of their number on him, a great man of a decadent coterie, Stephen von Hellmuth, who brought him an *Iphigenia*. It was at the time when German poets (like their colleagues in France) were recasting all the Greek tragedies. Stephen von Hellmuth's work was one of those astounding Graeco–German plays in which Ibsen, Homer, and Oscar Wilde are compounded—and, of course, a few manuals of archeology. Agamemnon was neurasthenic and Achilles impotent: they lamented their condition at length, and naturally their outcries produced no change. The energy of the drama was concentrated in the role of Iphigenia—a nervous, hysterical, and pedantic Iphigenia, who lectured the hero, declaimed furiously, laid bare for the audience her Nietzschian pessimism and, glutted with death, cut her throat, shrieking with laughter.

Nothing could be more contrary to Christophe's mind than such pretentious, degenerate, Ostrogothic stuff, in Greek dress. It was hailed as a masterpiece by everybody about him. He was cowardly and was overpersuaded. In truth, he was bursting with music and thinking much more of his music than of the text. The text was a new bed into which to let loose the flood of his passions. He was as far as possible from the state of abnegation and intelligent impersonality proper to musical translation of a poetic work. He was thinking only of himself and not at all of the work. He never thought of adapting himself to it. He was under an illusion: he saw in the poem something absolutely different from what was actually in it—just as when he was a child he used to compose in his mind a play entirely different from that which was upon the stage.

It was not until it came to rehearsal that he saw the real play. One day he was listening to a scene, and he thought it so stupid that he fancied the actors must be spoiling it, and went so far as to explain it to them in the poet's presence; but also to explain it to the poet himself, who was defending his interpretation. The author refused bluntly to hear him, and said with some asperity that he thought he knew what he had meant to write. Christophe would not give in, and maintained that Hellmuth knew nothing about it. The general merriment told him that he was making himself ridiculous. He said no more, agreeing that after all it was not he who had written the poem. Then he saw the appalling emptiness of the play and was overwhelmed by it: he wondered how he could ever have been persuaded to try it. He called himself an idiot and tore his hair. He tried in vain to reassure himself by saying: "You know nothing about it; it is not your business. Keep to your music." He was so much ashamed of certain idiotic things in it, of the pretentious pathos, the crying falsity of the words, the gestures and attitudes, that sometimes, when he was conducting the orchestra, he hardly had the strength to raise his baton. He wanted to go and hide in the prompter's box. He was too frank and too little politic to conceal what he thought. Every one noticed it: his friends, the actors, and the author. Hellmuth said to him with a frigid smile:

"Is it not fortunate enough to please you?"

Christophe replied honestly:

"Truth to tell, no. I don't understand it,"

"Then you did not read it when you set it to music?"

"Yes," said Christophe naively, "but I made a mistake. I understood it differently."

"It is a pity you did not write what you understood yourself."

"Oh! If only I could have done so!" said Christophe.

The poet was vexed, and in his turn criticised the music. He complained that it was in the way and prevented his words being heard.

If the poet did not understand the musician, or the musician the poet, the actors understood neither the one nor the other, and did not care. They were only asking for sentences in their parts on which to bring in their usual effects. They had no idea of adapting their declamation to the formality of the piece and the musical rhythm. They went one way, the music another. It was as though they were constantly singing out of tune. Christophe ground his teeth and shouted the note at them until he was hoarse. They let him shout and went on imperturbably, not even understanding what he wanted them to do.

Christophe would have flung the whole thing up if the rehearsals had not been so far advanced, and he had not been bound to go on by fear of legal proceedings. Mannheim, to whom he confided his discouragement, laughed at him:

"What is it?" he asked. "It is all going well. You don't understand each other? What does that matter? Who has ever understood his work but the author? It is a toss–up whether he understands it himself!"

Christophe was worried about the stupidity of the poem, which, he said, would ruin the music. Mannheim made no difficulty about admitting that there was no common sense in the poem and that Hellmuth was "a muff," but he would not worry about him: Hellmuth gave good dinners and had a pretty wife. What more did criticism want?

Christophe shrugged his shoulders and said that he had no time to listen to nonsense.

"It is not nonsense!" said Mannheim, laughing. "How serious people are! They have no idea of what matters in life."

And he advised Christophe not to bother so much about Hellmuth's business, but to attend to his own. He wanted him to advertise a little. Christophe refused indignantly. To a reporter who came and asked for a history of his life, he replied furiously:

"It is not your affair!"

And when they asked for his photograph for a review, he stamped with rage and shouted that he was not, thank God! an emperor, to have his face passed from hand to hand. It was impossible to bring him into touch with influential people. He never replied to invitations, and when he had been forced by any chance to accept, he would forget to go or would go with such a bad grace that he seemed to have set himself to be disagreeable to everybody.

But the climax came when he quarreled with his review, two days before the performance.

＊ ＊ ＊ ＊

The thing was bound to happen. Mannheim had gone on revising Christophe's articles, and he no longer scrupled about deleting whole lines of criticism and replacing them with compliments.

One day, out visiting, Christophe met a certain virtuoso—a foppish pianist whom he had slaughtered. The man came and thanked him with a smile that showed all his white teeth. He replied brutally that there was no reason for it. The other insisted and poured forth expressions of gratitude. Christophe cut him short by saying, that if he was satisfied with the article that was his affair, but that the article had certainly not been written with a view to pleasing him. And he turned his back on him. The virtuoso thought him a kindly boor and went away laughing. But Christophe remembered having received a card of thanks from another of his victims, and a suspicion flashed upon him. He went out, bought the last number of the Review at a news–stand, turned to his article, and read... At first he wondered if he were going mad. Then he understood, and, mad with rage, he ran to the office of the *Dionysos*.

Waldhaus and Mannheim were there, talking to an actress whom they knew. They had no need to ask Christophe what brought him. Throwing a number of the Review on the table,

Christophe let fly at them without stopping to take breath, with extraordinary violence, shouting, calling them rogues, rascals, forgers, thumping on the floor with a chair. Mannheim began to laugh. Christophe tried to kick him. Mannheim took refuge behind the table and rolled with laughter. But Waldhaus took it very loftily. With dignity, formally, he tried to make himself heard through the row, and said that he would not allow any one to talk to him in such a tone, that Christophe should hear from him, and he held out his card. Christophe flung it in his face.

"Mischief–maker!—I don't need your card to know what you are.... You are a rascal and a forger!... And you think I would fight with you ... a thrashing is all you deserve!..."

His voice could be heard in the street. People stopped to listen. Mannheim closed the windows. The actress tried to escape, but Christophe was blocking the way. Waldhaus was pale and choking. Mannheim was stuttering and stammering and trying to reply. Christophe did not let them speak. He let loose upon them every expression he could think of, and never stopped until he was out of breath and had come to an end of his insults. Waldhaus and Mannheim only found their tongues after he had gone. Mannheim quickly recovered himself: insults slipped from him like water from a duck's back. But Waldhaus was still sore: his dignity had been outraged, and what made the affront more mortifying was that there had been witnesses. He would never forgive it. His colleagues joined chorus with him. Mannheim only of the staff of the Review was not angry with Christophe. He had had his fill of entertainment out of him: it did not seem to him a heavy price to pay for his pound of flesh, to suffer a few violent words. It had been a good joke. If he had been the butt of it he would have been the first to laugh. And so he was quite ready to shake hands with Christophe as though nothing had happened. But Christophe was more rancorous and rejected all advances. Mannheim did not care. Christophe was a toy from which he had extracted all the amusement possible. He was beginning to want a new puppet. From that very day all was over between them. But that did not prevent Mannheim still saying, whenever Christophe was mentioned in his presence, that they were intimate friends. And perhaps he thought they were.

Two days after the quarrel the first performance of *Iphigenia* took place. It was an utter failure. Waldhaus' review praised the poem and made no mention of the music. The other papers and reviews made merry over it. They laughed and hissed. The piece was withdrawn after the third performance, but the jokes at its expense did not disappear so quickly. People were only too glad of the opportunity of having a fling at Christophe, and for several weeks the *Iphigenia* remained an unfailing subject for joking. They knew that Christophe had no weapon of defense, and they took advantage of it. The only thing which held them back a little was his position at the Court. Although his relation with the Grand Duke had become quite cold, for the Prince had several times made remarks to which he had paid no attention whatever, he still went to the Palace at intervals, and still enjoyed, in the eye of the public, a sort of official protection, though it was more visionary than real. He took upon himself to destroy even that last support.

He suffered from the criticisms. They were concerned not only with his music, but also with his idea of a new form of art, which the writers did not take the trouble to understand. It was very easy to travesty it and make fun of it. Christophe was not yet wise enough to know that the best reply to dishonest critics is to make none and to go on working. For some months past he had fallen into the bad habit of not letting any unjust attack go unanswered. He wrote an article in which he did not spare certain of his adversaries. The two papers to which he took it returned it with ironically polite excuses for being unable to publish it. Christophe stuck to his guns. He remembered that the socialist paper in the town had made advances to him. He knew one of the editors. They used to meet and talk occasionally. Christophe was glad to find some one who would talk freely about power, the army and oppression and archaic prejudices. But they could not go far with each other, for the socialist always came back to Karl Marx, about whom Christophe cared not a rap. Moreover, Christophe used to find in his speeches about the free man—besides a materialism which was not much to his taste—a pedantic severity and a despotism of thought, a secret cult of force, an inverse militarism, all of which did not sound very different from what he heard every day in German.

However, he thought of this man and his paper when he saw all other doors in journalism closed to him. He knew that his doing so would cause a scandal. The paper was violent, malignant, and always being condemned. But as Christophe never read it, he only thought of the boldness of its ideas, of which he was not afraid, and not of the baseness of its tone, which would have repelled him. Besides, he was so angry at seeing the other papers in alliance to suppress him that perhaps he would have gone on even if he had been warned. He wanted to show people that he was not so easily got rid of. So he took his article to the socialist paper, which received it with open arms. The next day the article appeared, and the paper announced in large letters that it had engaged the support of the young and talented maestro, Jean–Christophe Krafft, whose keen sympathy with the demands of the working classes was well known.

Christophe read neither the note nor the article, for he had gone out before dawn for a walk in the country, it being Sunday. He was in fine fettle. As he saw the sun rise he shouted, laughed, yodeled, leaped, and danced. No more review, no more criticisms to do! It was spring and there was once more the music of the heavens and the earth, the most beautiful of all. No more dark concert rooms, stuffy and smelly, unpleasant people, dull performers. Now the marvelous song of the murmuring forests was to be heard, and over the fields like waves there passed the intoxicating scents of life, breaking through the crust of the earth and issuing from the grave.

He went home with his head buzzing with light and music, and his mother gave him a letter which had been brought from the Palace while he was away. The letter was in an impersonal form, and told Herr Krafft that he was to go to the Palace that morning. The morning was past, it was nearly one o'clock. Christophe was not put about.

"It is too late now," he said. "It will do to–morrow."

But his mother said anxiously:

"No, no. You cannot put off an appointment with His Highness like that: you must go at once. Perhaps it is a matter of importance."

Christophe shrugged his shoulders.

"Important! As if those people could have anything important to say!... He wants to tell me his ideas about music. That will be funny!... If only he has not taken it into his head to rival Siegfried Meyer [Footnote: A nickname given by German pamphleteers to H.M. (His Majesty) the Emperor.] and wants to show me a *Hymn to Aegis*! I vow that I will not spare him. I shall say: 'Stick to politics. You are master there. You will always be right. But beware of art! In art you are seen without your plumes, your helmet, your uniform, your money, your titles, your ancestors, your policemen—and just think for a moment what will be left of you then!'"

Poor Louisa took him quite seriously and raised her hands in horror.

"You won't say that!... You are mad! Mad!"

It amused him to make her uneasy by playing upon her credulity until he became so extravagant that Louisa began to see that he was making fun of her.

"You are stupid, my boy!"

He laughed and kissed her. He was in a wonderfully good humor. On his walk he had found a beautiful musical theme, and he felt it frolicking in him like a fish in water. He refused to go to the Palace until he had had something to eat. He was as hungry as an ape. Louisa then supervised his dressing, for he was beginning to tease her again, pretending that he was quite all right as he was with his old clothes and dusty boots. But he changed them all the same, and cleaned his boots, whistling like a blackbird and imitating all the instruments in an orchestra. When he had finished his mother inspected him and gravely tied his tie for him again. For once in a way he was very patient, because he was pleased with himself—which was not very usual. He went off saying that he was going to elope with Princess Adelaide—the Grand Duke's daughter, quite a pretty woman, who was married to a German princeling and had come to stay with her parents for a few weeks. She had shown sympathy for Christophe when he was a child, and he had a soft side for her. Louisa used to declare that he was in love with her, and he would pretend to be so in fun.

He did not hurry; he dawdled and looked into the shops, and stopped to pat some dog that he knew as it lay on its side and yawned in the sun. He jumped over the harmless railings which inclosed the Palace square—a great empty square, surrounded with houses, with two little fountains, two symmetrical bare flower-beds, divided, as by a parting, by a gravel path, carefully raked and bordered by orange trees in tubs. In the middle was the bronze statue of some unknown Grand Duke in the costume of Louis Philippe, on a pediment adorned at the four corners by allegorical figures representing the Virtues. On a seat one solitary man was dozing over his paper. Behind the silly moat of the earthworks of the Palace two sleepy cannon yawned upon the sleepy town. Christophe laughed at the whole thing.

He entered the Palace without troubling to take on a more official manner. At most he stopped humming, but his thoughts went dancing on inside him. He threw his hat on the table in the hall and familiarly greeted the old usher, whom he had known since he was a child. (The old man had been there on the day when Christophe had first entered the Palace, on the evening when he had seen Hassler.) But to-day the old man, who always used to reply good–humoredly to Christophe's disrespectful sallies, now seemed a little haughty. Christophe paid no heed to it. A little farther on, in the ante–chamber, he met a clerk of the chancery, who was usually full of conversation and very friendly. He was surprised to see him hurry past him to avoid having to talk. However, he did not attach any significance to it, and went on and asked to be shown in.

He went in. They had just finished dinner. His Highness was in one of the drawing–rooms. He was leaning against the mantelpiece, smoking, and talking to his guests, among whom Christophe saw *his* princess, who was also smoking. She was lying back in an armchair and talking in a loud voice to some officers who made a circle about her. The gathering was lively. They were all very merry, and when Christophe entered he heard the Grand Duke's thick laugh. But he stopped dead when he saw Christophe. He growled and pounced on him.

"Ah! There you are!" he said. "You have condescended to come at last? Do you think you can go on making fun of me any longer? You're a blackguard, sir!"

Christophe was so staggered by this brutal attack that it was some time before he could utter a word. He was thinking that he was only late, and that that could not have provoked such violence. He murmured:

"What have I done, Your Highness?"

His Highness did not listen and went on angrily:

"Be silent! I will not be insulted by a blackguard!" Christophe turned pale, and gulped so as to try to speak, for he was choking. He made an effort, and said:

"Your Highness, you have no right—you have no right to insult me without telling me what I have done."

The Grand Duke turned to his secretary, who produced a paper from his pocket and held it out to him. He was in such a state of exasperation as could not be explained only by his anger: the fumes of good wine had their share in it, too. He came and stood in front of Christophe, and like a toreador with his cape, furiously waved the crumpled newspaper in his face and shouted:

"Your muck, sir!... You deserve to have your nose rubbed in it!"

Christophe recognized the socialist paper.

"I don't see what harm there is in it," he said.

"What! What!" screamed the Grand Duke. "You are impudent!... This rascally paper, which insults me from day to day, and spews out filthy insults upon me!..."

"Sire," said Christophe, "I have not read it."

"You lie!" shouted the Grand Duke.

"You shall not call me a liar," said Christophe. "I have not read it. I am only concerned with reviews, and besides, I have the right to write in whatever paper I like."

"You have no right but to hold your tongue. I have been too kind to you. I have heaped kindness upon you, you and yours, in spite of your misconduct and your father's, which would have justified me in cutting you off. I forbid you to go on writing in a paper which is hostile to me. And further: I forbid you altogether to write anything in future without my authority. I have had enough of your musical polemics. I will not allow any one who enjoys my patronage to spend his time in attacking everything which is dear to people of taste and feeling, to all true Germans. You would do better to write better music, or if that is impossible, to practise your scales and exercises. I don't want to have anything to do with a musical Bebel who amuses himself by decrying all our national glories and upsetting the minds of the people. We know what is good, thank God. We do not need to wait for you to tell us. Go to your piano, sir, or leave us in peace!"

Standing face to face with Christophe the fat man glared at him insultingly. Christophe was livid, and tried to speak. His lips moved; he stammered:

"I am not your slave. I shall say what I like and write what I like ..."

He choked. He was almost weeping with shame and rage. His legs were trembling. He jerked his elbow and upset an ornament on a table by his side. He felt that he was in a ridiculous position. He heard people laughing. He looked down the room, and as through a mist saw the princess watching the scene and exchanging ironically commiserating remarks with her neighbors. He lost count of what exactly happened. The Grand Duke shouted. Christophe shouted louder than he without knowing what he said. The Prince's secretary and another official came towards him and tried to stop him. He pushed them away, and while he talked he waved an ash–tray which he had mechanically picked up from the table against which he was leaning. He heard the secretary say:

"Put it down! Put it down!"

And he heard himself shouting inarticulately and knocking on the edge of the table with the ash–tray.

"Go!" roared the Grand Duke, beside himself with rage. "Go! Go! I'll have you thrown out!"

The officers had come up to the Prince and were trying to calm him. The Grand Duke looked apoplectic. His eyes were starting from his head, he shouted to them to throw the rascal out. Christophe saw red. He longed to thrust his fist in the Grand Duke's face; but he was crushed under a weight of conflicting feelings: shame, fury, a remnant of shyness, of German loyalty, traditional respect, habits of humility in the Prince's presence. He tried to speak; he could not. He tried to move; he could not. He could not see or hear. He suffered them to push him along and left the room.

He passed through the impassive servants who had come up to the door, and had missed nothing of the quarrel. He had to go thirty yards to cross the ante–chamber, and it seemed a lifetime. The corridor grew longer and longer as he walked up it. He would never get out!... The light of day which he saw shining downstairs through the glass door was his haven. He went stumbling down the stairs. He forgot that he was bareheaded. The old usher reminded him to take his hat. He had to gather all his forces to leave the castle, cross the court, reach his home. His teeth were chattering when he opened the door. His mother was terrified by his face and his trembling. He avoided her and refused to answer her questions. He went up to his room, shut himself in, and lay down. He was shaking so that he could not undress. His breathing came in jerks and his whole body seemed shattered.... Oh! If only he could see no more, feel no more, no longer have to bear with his wretched body, no longer have to struggle against ignoble life, and fall, fall, breathless, without thought, and no longer be anywhere!... With frightful difficulty he tore off his clothes and left them on the ground, and then flung himself into his bed and drew the coverings over him. There was no sound in the room save that of the little iron bed rattling on the tiled floor.

Louisa listened at the door. She knocked in vain. She called softly. There was no reply. She waited, anxiously listening through the silence. Then she went away. Once or twice during the day she came and listened, and again at night, before she went to bed. Day passed, and the night. The house was still. Christophe was shaking with fever. Every now and then he wept, and in the night he got up several times and shook his fist at the wall. About two o'clock, in an access of madness, he got up from his bed, sweating and half naked. He wanted to go and kill the Grand Duke, He was devoured by hate and shame. His body and his heart writhed in the fire of it. Nothing of all the storm in him could be heard outside; not a word, not a sound. With clenched teeth he fought it down and forced it back into himself.

    * * * * *

Next morning he came down as usual. He was a wreck. He said nothing and his mother dared not question him. She knew, from the gossip of the neighborhood. All day he stayed sitting by the fire, silent, feverish, and with bent head, like a little old man. And when he was alone he wept in silence.

In the evening the editor of the socialist paper came to see him. Naturally he had heard and wished to have details. Christophe was touched by his coming, and interpreted it naively as a mark of sympathy and a desire for forgiveness on the part of those who had compromised him. He made a point of seeming to regret nothing and he let himself go and said everything that was rankling in him. It was some solace for him to talk freely to a man who shared his hatred of oppression. The other urged him on. He saw a good chance for his journal in the event, and an opportunity for a scandalous article, for which he expected Christophe to provide him with material if he did not write it himself; for he thought that after such an explosion the Court musician would put his very considerable political talents and his no less considerable little tit–bits of secret information about the Court at the service of "the cause." As he did not plume himself on his subtlety he presented the thing rawly in the crudest light. Christophe started. He declared that he would write nothing and said that any attack on the Grand Duke that he might make would be interpreted as an act of personal vengeance, and that he would be more reserved now that he was free than when, not being free, he ran some risk in saying what he thought. The journalist could not understand his scruples. He thought Christophe narrow and clerical at heart, but he also decided that Christophe was afraid. He said:

"Oh, well! Leave it to us. I will write it myself. You need not bother about it."

Christophe begged him to say nothing, but he had no means of restraining him. Besides, the journalist declared that the affair was not his concern only: the insult touched the paper, which had the right to avenge itself. There was nothing to be said to that. All that Christophe could do was to ask him on his word of honor not to abuse certain of his confidences which had been made to his friend and not to the journalist. The other made no difficulty about that. Christophe was not reassured by it. He knew too well how imprudent he had been. When he was left alone he turned over everything that he had said, and shuddered. Without hesitating for a moment, he wrote to the journalist imploring him once more not to repeat what he had confided to him. (The poor wretch repeated it in part himself in the letter.)

Next day, as he opened the paper with feverish haste, the first thing he read was his story at great length on the front page. Everything that he had said on the evening before was immeasurably enlarged, having suffered that peculiar deformation which everything has to suffer in its passage through the mind of a journalist. The article attacked the Grand Duke and the Court with low invective. Certain details which it gave were too personal to Christophe, too obviously known only to him, for the article not to be attributed to him in its entirety.

Christophe was crushed by this fresh blow. As he read a cold sweat came out on his face. When he had finished he was dumfounded. He wanted to rush to the office of the paper, but his mother withheld him, not unreasonably being fearful of his violence. He was afraid of it himself. He felt that if he went there he would do something foolish; and he stayed—and did a very foolish thing. He wrote an indignant letter to the journalist in which he reproached him for his conduct in insulting terms, disclaimed the article, and broke with the party. The disclaimer did not appear.

Christophe wrote again to the paper, demanding that his letter should be published. They sent him a copy of his first letter, written on the night of the interview and confirming it. They asked if they were to publish that, too. He felt that he was in their hands. Thereupon he unfortunately met the indiscreet interviewer in the street. He could not help telling him of his contempt for him. Next day the paper, without a spark of shame, published an insulting paragraph about the servants of the Court, who even when they are dismissed remain servants and are incapable of being free. A few allusions to recent events left no room for doubt that Christophe was meant.

* * * * *

When it became evident to everybody that Christophe had no single support, there suddenly cropped up a host of enemies whose existence he had never suspected. All those whom he had offended, directly or indirectly, either by personal criticism or by attacking their ideas and taste, now took the offensive and avenged themselves with interest. The general public whom Christophe had tried to shake out of their apathy were quite pleased to see the insolent young man, who had presumed to reform opinion and disturb the rest of people of property, taken down a peg. Christophe was in the water. Everybody did their best to duck him.

They did not come down upon him all at once. One tried first, to spy out the land. Christophe made no response, and he struck more lustily. Others followed, and then the whole gang of them. Some joined in the sport simply for fun, like puppies who think it funny to leave their mark in inappropriate places. They were the flying squadron of incompetent journalists, who, knowing nothing, try to hide their ignorance by belauding the victors and belaboring the vanquished. Others brought the weight of their principles and they shouted like deaf people. Nothing was left of anything when they had passed. They were the critics—with the criticism which kills.

Fortunately for Christophe, he did not read the papers. A few devoted friends took care to send him the most insulting. But he left them in a heap on his desk and never thought of opening them. It was only towards the end of it that his eyes were attracted by a great red mark round an article. He read that his *Lieder* were like the roaring of a wild beast; that his symphonies seemed to have come from a madhouse; that his art was hysterical, his harmony spasmodic, as a change from the dryness of his heart and the emptiness of his thought. The critic, who was well known, ended with these words:

"Herr Krafft as a journalist has lately given astounding proof of his style and taste, which roused irresistible merriment in musical circles. He was then given the friendly advice rather to devote himself to composition. But the latest products of his muse have shown that this advice, though well–meant, was bad. Herr Krafft should certainly devote himself to journalism."

After reading the article, which prevented Christophe working the whole morning, naturally he began to look for the other hostile papers, and became utterly demoralized. But Louisa, who had a mania for moving everything lying about, by way of "tidying up," had already burned them. He was irritated at first and then comforted, and he held out the last of the papers to her, and said that she had better do the same with that.

Other rebuffs hurt him more. A quartette which he had sent in manuscript to a well–known society at Frankfort was rejected unanimously and returned without explanation. An overture which an orchestra at Cologne seemed disposed to perform was returned after a month as unplayable. But the worst of all was inflicted on him by an orchestral society in the town. The *Kapellmeister*, H. Euphrat, its conductor, was quite a good musician, but like many conductors, he had no curiosity of mind. He suffered (or rather he carried to extremes) the laziness peculiar to his class, which consists in going on and on investigating familiar works, while it shuns any really new work like the plague. He was never tired of organizing Beethoven, Mozart, or Schumann festivals: in conducting these works he had only to let himself be carried along by the purring of the familiar rhythms. On the other hand, contemporary music was intolerable to him. He dared not admit it and pretended to be friendly towards young talent; in fact, whenever he was brought a work built on the old lines—a sort of hotch–potch of works that had been new fifty years before—he would receive it very well, and would even produce it ostentatiously and force it upon the public. It did not disturb either his effects or the way in which the public was accustomed to be moved. On the other hand, he was filled with a mixture of contempt and hatred for anything which threatened to disturb that arrangement and put him to extra trouble. Contempt would predominate if the innovator had no chance of emerging from obscurity. But if there were any danger of his succeeding, then hatred would predominate—of course until the moment when he had gained an established success.

Christophe was not yet in that position: far from it. And so he was much surprised when he was informed, by indirect overtures, that Herr H. Euphrat would be very glad to produce one of his compositions. It was all the more unexpected as he knew that the *Kapellmeister* was an intimate friend of Brahms and others whom he had maltreated in his criticisms. Being honest himself, he credited his adversaries with the same generous feelings which he would have had himself. He supposed that now that he was down they wished to show him that they were above petty spite. He was touched by it. He wrote effusively to Herr Euphrat and sent him a symphonic poem. The conductor replied through his secretary coldly but politely, acknowledging the receipt of his work, and adding that, in accordance with the rules of the society, the symphony would be given out to the orchestra immediately and put to the test of a general rehearsal before it could be accepted for public hearing. A rule is a rule. Christophe had to bow to it, though it was a pure formality which served to weed out the lucubrations of amateurs which were sometimes a nuisance.

A few weeks later Christophe was told that his composition was to be rehearsed. On principle everything was done privately and even the author was not permitted to be present at the rehearsal. But by a generally agreed indulgence the author was always admitted; only he did not show himself. Everybody knew it and everybody pretended not to know it. On the appointed day one of his friends brought Christophe to the hall, where he sat at the back of a box. He was surprised to see that at this private rehearsal the hall—at least the ground floor seats—were almost all filled; a crowd of dilettante idlers and critics moved about and chattered to each other. The orchestra had to ignore their presence.

They began with the Brahms *Rhapsody* for alto, chorus of male voices, and orchestra on a fragment of the *Harzreise im Winter* of Goethe. Christophe, who detested the majestic sentimentality of the work, thought that perhaps the "Brahmins" had introduced it politely to avenge themselves by forcing him to hear a composition of which he had written irreverently. The idea made him laugh, and his good humour increased when after the *Rhapsody* there came two other productions by known musicians whom he had taken to task; there seemed to be no doubt about their intentions. And while he could not help making a face at it he thought that after all it was quite fair tactics; and, failing the music, he appreciated the joke. It even amused him to applaud ironically with the audience, which made manifest its enthusiasm for Brahms and his like.

At last it came to Christophe's symphony. He saw from the way the orchestra and the people in the hall were looking at his box that they were aware of his presence. He hid himself. He waited with the catch at his heart which every musician feels at the moment when the conductor's wand is raised and the waters of the music gather in silence before bursting their dam. He had never yet heard his work played. How would the creatures of his dreams live? How would their voices sound? He felt their roaring within him; and he leaned over the abyss of sounds waiting fearfully for what should come forth.

What did come forth was a nameless thing, a shapeless hotch–potch. Instead of the bold columns which were to support the front of the building the chords came crumbling down like a building in ruins; there was nothing to be seen but the dust of mortar. For a moment Christophe was not quite sure whether they were really playing his work. He cast back for the train, the rhythm of his thoughts; he could not recognize it; it went on babbling and hiccoughing like a drunken man clinging close to the wall, and he was overcome with shame, as though he had himself been seen in that condition. It was of no avail to think that he had not written such stuff; when an idiotic interpreter destroys a man's thoughts he has always a moment of doubt when he asks himself in consternation if he is himself responsible for it. The audience never asks such a question; the audience believes in the interpreter, in the singers, in the orchestra whom they are accustomed to hear as they believe in their newspaper; they cannot make a mistake; if they say absurd things, it is the absurdity of the author. This audience was the less inclined to doubt because it liked to believe. Christophe tried to persuade himself that the *Kapellmeister* was aware of the hash and would stop the orchestra and begin again. The instruments were not playing together. The horn had missed his beat and had come in a bar too late; he went on for a few minutes, and then stopped quietly to clean his instrument. Certain passages for the oboe had absolutely disappeared. It was impossible for the most skilled ear to pick up the thread of the musical idea, or even to imagine that there was one. Fantastic instrumentations, humoristic sallies became grotesque through the coarseness of the execution. It was lamentably stupid, the work of an idiot, of a joker who knew nothing of music. Christophe tore his hair. He tried to interrupt, but the friend who was with him held him back, assuring him that the *Herr Kapellmeister* must surely see the faults of the execution and would put everything right—that Christophe must not show himself and that if he made any remark it would have a very bad effect. He made Christophe sit at the very back of the box. Christophe obeyed, but he beat his head with his fists; and every fresh monstrosity drew from him a groan of indignation and misery.

"The wretches! The wretches!..."

He groaned, and squeezed his hands tight to keep himself from crying out.

Now mingled with the wrong notes there came up to him the muttering of the audience, who were beginning to be restless. At first it was only a tremor; but soon Christophe was left without a doubt; they were laughing. The musicians of the orchestra had given the signal; some of them did not conceal their hilarity. The audience, certain then that the music was laughable, rocked with laughter. This merriment became general; it increased at the return of a very rhythmical motif which the double–basses accentuated in a burlesque fashion. Only the *Kapellmeister* went on through the uproar imperturbably beating time.

At last they reached the end (the best things come to an end). It was the turn of the audience. They exploded with delight, an explosion which lasted for several minutes. Some hissed; others applauded ironically; the wittiest of all shouted "Encore!" A bass voice coming from a stage box began to imitate the grotesque motif. Other jokers followed suit and imitated it also. Some one shouted "Author!" It was long since these witty folk had been so highly entertained.

When the tumult was calmed down a little the *Kapellmeister*, standing quite impassive with his face turned towards the audience though he was pretending not to see it—(the audience was still supposed to be non–existent)—made a sign to the audience that he was about to speak. There was a cry of "Ssh," and silence. He waited a moment longer; then—(his voice was curt, cold, and cutting):

"Gentlemen," he said, "I should certainly not have let *that* he played through to the end if I had not wished to make an example of the gentleman who has dared to write offensively of the great Brahms."

That was all; and jumping down from his stand he went out amid cheers from the delighted audience. They tried to recall him; the applause went on for a few minutes longer. But he did not return. The orchestra went away. The audience decided to go too. The concert was over.

It had been a good day.

Christophe had gone already. Hardly had he seen the wretched conductor leave his desk when he had rushed from the box; he plunged down the stairs from the first floor to meet him and slap his face. His friend who had brought him followed and tried to hold him back, but Christophe brushed him aside and almost threw him downstairs;—(he had reason to believe that the fellow was concerned in the trick which had been played him). Fortunately for H. Euphrat and himself the door leading to the stage was shut; and his furious knocking could not make them open it. However the audience was beginning to leave the hall. Christophe could not stay there. He fled.

He was in an indescribable condition. He walked blindly, waving his arms, rolling his eyes, talking aloud like a madman; he suppressed his cries of indignation and rage. The street was almost empty. The concert hall had been built the year before in a new neighborhood a little way out of the town; and Christophe instinctively fled towards the country across the empty fields in which were a few lonely shanties and scaffoldings surrounded by fences. His thoughts were murderous; he could have killed the man who had put such an affront upon him. Alas! and when he had killed him would there be any change in the animosity of those people whose insulting laughter was still ringing in his ears? They were too many; he could do nothing against them; they were all agreed—they who were divided about so many things—to insult and crush him. It was past understanding; there was hatred in them. What had he done to them all? There were beautiful things in him, things to do good and make the heart big; he had tried to say them, to make others enjoy them; he thought they would be happy like himself. Even if they did not like them they should be grateful to him for his intentions; they could, if need be, show him kindly where he had been wrong; but that they should take such a malignant joy in insulting and odiously travestying his ideas, in trampling them underfoot, and killing him by ridicule, how was it possible? In his excitement he exaggerated their hatred; he thought it much more serious than such mediocre people could ever be. He sobbed: "What have I done to them?" He choked, he thought that all was lost, just as he did when he was a child coming into contact for the first time with human wickedness.

And when he looked about him he suddenly saw that he had reached the edge of the mill–race, at the very spot where a few years before his father had been drowned. And at once he thought of drowning himself too. He was just at the point of making the plunge.

But as he leaned over the steep bank, fascinated by the calm clean aspect of the water, a tiny bird in a tree by his side began to sing—to sing madly. He held his breath to listen. The water murmured. The ripening corn moaned as it waved under the soft caressing wind; the poplars shivered. Behind the hedge on the road, out of sight, bees in hives in a garden filled the air with their scented music. From the other side of the stream a cow was chewing the cud and gazing with soft eyes. A little fair–haired girl was sitting on a wall, with a light basket on her shoulders, like a little angel with wings, and she was dreaming, and swinging her bare legs and humming aimlessly. Far away in a meadow a white dog was leaping and running in wide circles. Christophe leaned against a tree and listened and watched the earth in Spring; he was caught up by the peace and joy of these creatures; he could forget, he could forget. Suddenly he clasped the tree with his arms and leaned his cheek against it. He threw himself on the ground; he buried his face in the grass; he laughed nervously, happily. All the beauty, the grace, the charm of life wrapped him round, imbued his soul, and he sucked them up like a sponge. He thought:

"Why are you so beautiful, and they—men—so ugly?"

No matter! He loved it, he loved it, he felt that he would always love it, and that nothing could ever take it from him. He held the earth to his breast. He held life to his breast:

"I love you! You are mine. They cannot take you from me. Let them do what they will! Let them make me suffer!... Suffering also is life!"

Christophe began bravely to work again. He refused to have anything more to do with "men of letters"—well named—makers of phrases, the sterile babblers, journalists, critics, the exploiters and traffickers of art. As for musicians he would waste no more time in battling with their prejudices and jealousy. They did not want him? Very well! He did not want them. He had his work to do; he would do it. The Court had given him back his liberty; he was grateful for it. He was grateful to the people for their hostility; he could work in peace.

Louisa approved with all her heart. She had no ambition; she was not a Krafft; she was like neither his father nor his grandfather. She did not want honors or reputation for her son. She would have liked him to be rich and famous; but if those advantages could only be bought at the price of so much unpleasantness she much preferred not to bother about them. She had been more upset by Christophe's grief over his rupture with the Palace than by the event itself; and she was heartily glad that he had quarreled with the review and newspaper people. She had a peasant's distrust of blackened paper; it was only a waste of time and made enemies. She had sometimes heard his young friends of the Review talking to Christophe; she had been horrified by their malevolence; they tore

443

everything to pieces and said horrible things about everybody; and the worse things they said the better pleased they were. She did not like them. No doubt they were very clever and very learned, but they were not kind, and she was very glad that Christophe saw no more of them. She was full of common sense: what good were they to him?

"They may say, write, and think what they like of me," said Christophe. "They cannot prevent my being myself. What do their ideas or their art matter to me? I deny them!"

* * * * *

It is all very fine to deny the world. But the world is not so easily denied by a young man's boasting. Christophe was sincere, but he was under illusion; he did not know himself. He was not a monk; he had not the temperament for renouncing the world, and besides he was not old enough to do so. At first he did not suffer much, he was plunged in composition; and while his work lasted he did not feel the want of anything. But when he came to the period of depression which follows the completion of a work and lasts until a new work takes possession of the mind, he looked about him and was horrified by his loneliness. He asked himself why he wrote. While a man is writing he never asks himself that question; he must write, there is no arguing about it. And then he finds himself with the work that he has begotten: the great instinct which caused it to spring forth is silent; he does not understand why it was born: he hardly recognizes it, it is almost a stranger to him; he longs to forget it. And that is impossible as long as it is not published or played, or living its own life in the world. Till then it is like a new–born child attached to its mother, a living thing bound fast to his living flesh; it must be amputated at all costs or it will not live. The more Christophe composed the more he suffered under the weight of these creatures who had sprung forth from himself and could neither live nor die. He was haunted by them. Who could deliver him from them? Some obscure impulse would stir in these children of his thoughts; they longed desperately to break away from him to expand into other souls like the quick and fruitful seed which the wind scatters over the universe. Must he remain imprisoned in his sterility? He raged against it.

Since every outlet—theaters, concerts—was closed to him, and nothing would induce him to approach those managers who had once failed him, there was nothing left but for him to publish his writings, but he could not flatter himself that it would be easier to find a publisher to produce his work than an orchestra to play it. The two or three clumsy attempts that he had made were enough; rather than expose himself to another rebuff, or to bargain with one of these music merchants and put up with his patronizing airs, he preferred to publish it at his own expense. It was an act of madness; he had some small savings out of his Court salary and the proceeds of a few concerts, but the source from which the money had come was dried up and it would be a long time before he could find another; and he should have been prudent enough to be careful with his scanty funds which had to help him over the difficult period upon which he was entering. Not only did he not do so; but, as his savings were not enough to cover the expenses of publication, he did not shrink from getting into debt. Louisa dared not say anything; she found him absolutely unreasonable, and did not understand how anybody could spend money for the sake of seeing his name on a book; but since it was a way of making him be patient and of keeping him with her, she was only too happy for him to have that satisfaction.

Instead of offering the public compositions of a familiar and undisturbing kind, in which it could feel at home, Christophe chose from among his manuscripts a suite very individual in character, which he valued highly. They were piano pieces mixed with *Lieder*, some very short and popular in style, others very elaborate and almost dramatic. The whole formed a series of impressions, joyous or mild, linked together naturally and written alternately for the piano and the voice, alone or accompanied. "For," said Christophe, "when I dream, I do not always formulate what I feel. I suffer, I am happy, and have no words to say; but then comes a moment when I must say what I am feeling, and I sing without thinking of what I am doing; sometimes I sing only vague words, a few disconnected phrases, sometimes whole poems; then I begin to dream again. And so the day goes by; and I have tried to give the impression of a day. Why these gathered impressions composed only of songs or preludes? There is nothing more false or less harmonious. One must try to give the free play of the soul." He had called his suite: *A Day*. The different parts of the composition bore sub–titles, shortly indicating the succession of his inward dreams. Christophe had written mysterious dedications, initials, dates, which only he could understand, as they reminded Mm of poetic moments or beloved faces: the gay Corinne, the languishing Sabine, and the little unknown Frenchwoman.

Besides this work he selected thirty of his *Lieder*—those which pleased him most, and consequently pleased the public least. He avoided choosing the most "melodious" of his melodies, but he did choose the most characteristic. (The public always has a horror of anything "characteristic." Characterless things are more likely to please them.)

These *Lieder* were written to poems of old Silesian poets of the seventeenth century that Christophe had read by chance in a popular collection, and whose loyalty he had loved. Two especially were dear to him, dear as brothers, two creatures full of genius and both had died at thirty: the charming Paul Fleming, the traveler to the Caucasus and to Ispahan, who preserved his soul pure, loving and serene in the midst of the savagery of war, the sorrows of life, and the corruption of his time, and Johann Christian Guenther, the unbalanced genius who wore himself out in debauchery and despair, casting his life to the four winds. He had translated Guenther's cries of provocation and vengeful irony against the hostile God who overwhelms His creatures, his furious curses like those of a Titan overthrown hurling the thunder back against the heavens. He had selected Fleming's love songs to Anemone and Basilene, soft and sweet as flowers, and the rondo of the stars, the *Tanzlied* (dancing song) of hearts glad and limpid—and the calm heroic sonnet To Himself (*An Sich*), which Christophe used to recite as a prayer every morning.

The smiling optimism of the pious Paul Gerhardt also had its charm for Christophe. It was a rest for him on recovering from his own sorrows. He loved that innocent vision of nature as God, the fresh meadows, where the storks walk gravely among the tulips and white narcissus, by little brooks singing on the sands, the transparent air wherein there pass the wide–winged, swallows and flying doves, the gaiety of a sunbeam piercing the rain, and the luminous sky smiling through the clouds, and the serene majesty of the evening, the sweet peace of the forests, the cattle, the bowers and the fields. He had had the impertinence to set to music several of those mystic canticles which are still sung in Protestant communities. And he had avoided preserving the choral character. Far from it: he had a horror of it; he had given them a free and vivacious character. Old Gerhardt would have shuddered at the devilish pride which was breathed forth now in certain lines of his *Song of the Christian Traveler*, or the pagan delight which made this peaceful stream of his *Song of Summer* bubble over like a torrent.

The collection was published without any regard for common sense, of course. The publisher whom Christophe paid for printing and storing his *Lieder* had no other claim to his choice than that of being his neighbor. He was not equipped for such important work; the printing went on for months; there were mistakes and expensive corrections. Christophe knew nothing about it and the whole thing cost more by a third than it need have done; the expenses far exceeded anything he had anticipated. Then when it was done, Christophe found an enormous edition on his hands and did not know what to do with it. The publisher had no customers; he took no steps to circulate the work. And his apathy was quite in accord with Christophe's attitude. When he asked him, to satisfy his conscience, to write him a short advertisement of it, Christophe replied that "he did not want any advertisement; if his music was good it would speak for itself." The publisher religiously respected his wishes; he put the edition away in his warehouse. It was well kept; for in six months not a copy was sold.

* * * * *

While he was waiting for the public to make up its mind Christophe had to find some way of repairing the hole he had made in his means; and he could not be nice about it, for he had to live and pay his debts. Not only were his debts larger than he had imagined but he saw that the moneys on which he had counted were less than he had thought. Had he lost money without knowing it or—what was infinitely more probable—had he reckoned up wrongly? (He had never been able to add correctly.) It did not matter much why the money was missing; it was missing without a doubt. Louisa had to give her all to help her son. He was bitterly remorseful and tried to pay her back as soon as possible and at all costs. He tried to get lessons, though it was painful to him to ask and to put up with refusals. He was out of favor altogether; he found it very difficult to obtain pupils again. And so when it was suggested that he should teach at a school he was only too glad.

It was a semi–religious institution. The director, an astute gentleman, had seen, though he was no musician, how useful Christophe might be, and how cheaply in his present position. He was pleasant and paid very little. When Christophe ventured to make a timid remark the director told him with a kindly smile that as he no longer held an official position he could not very well expect more.

It was a sad task! It was not so much a matter of teaching the pupils music as of making their parents and themselves believe that they had learned it. The chief thing was to make them able to sing at the ceremonies to which the public were admitted. It did not matter how it was done, Christophe was in despair; he had not even the consolation of telling himself as he fulfilled his task that he was doing useful work; his conscience reproached him with it as hypocrisy. He tried to give the children more solid instruction and to make them acquainted with and love serious music; but they did not care for it a bit. Christophe could not succeed in making them listen to it; he had no authority over them; in truth he was not made for teaching children. He took no interest in their floundering; he tried to explain to them all at once the theory of music. When he had to give a piano lesson he

447

would set his pupil a symphony of Beethoven which he would play as a duet with her. Naturally that could not succeed; he would explode angrily, drive the pupil from the piano and go on playing alone for a long time. He was just the same with his private pupils outside the school. He had not an ounce of patience; for instance he would tell a young lady who prided herself on her aristocratic appearance and position, that she played like a kitchen maid; or he would even write to her mother and say that he gave it up, that it would kill him if he went on long bothering about a girl so devoid of talent. All of which did not improve his position. His few pupils left him; he could not keep any of them more than a few months. His mother argued with him; he would argue with himself. Louisa made him promise that at least he would not break with the school he had joined; for if he lost that position he did not know what he should do for a living. And so he restrained himself in spite of his disgust; he was most exemplarily punctual. But how could he conceal his thoughts when a donkey of a pupil blundered for the tenth time in some passages, or when he had to coach his class for the next concert in some foolish chorus!—(For he was not even allowed to choose his programme: his taste was not trusted)—He was not exactly zealous about it all. And yet he went stubbornly on, silent, frowning, only betraying his secret wrath by occasionally thumping on his desk and making his pupils jump in their seats. But sometimes the pill was too bitter; he could not bear it any longer. In the middle of the chorus he would interrupt the singers:

"Oh! Stop! Stop! I'll play you some Wagner instead."

They asked nothing better. They played cards behind his back. There was always someone who reported the matter to the director; and Christophe would be reminded that he was not there to make his pupils like music but to make them sing. He received his scoldings with a shudder; but he accepted them; he did not want to lose his work. Who would have thought a few years before, when his career looked so assured and brilliant (when he had done nothing), that he would be reduced to such humiliation just as he was beginning to be worth something?

Among the hurts to his vanity that he came by in his work at the school, one of the most painful was having to call on his colleagues. He paid two calls at random; and they bored him so that he had not the heart to go on. The two privileged persons were not at all pleased about it, but the others were personally affronted. They all regarded Christophe as their inferior in position and intelligence; and they assumed a patronizing manner towards him. Sometimes he was overwhelmed by it, for they seemed to be so sure of themselves and the opinion they had of him that he began to share it; he felt stupid with them; what could he have found to say to them? They were full of their profession and saw nothing beyond it. They were not men. If only they had been books! But they were only notes to books, philological commentaries.

Christophe avoided meeting them. But sometimes he was forced to do so. The director was at home once a month in the afternoon; and he insisted on all his people being there. Christophe, who had cut the first afternoon, without excuse, in the vain hope that his absence would not be noticed, was ever afterwards the object of sour attention. Next time he was lectured by his mother and decided to go; he was as solemn about it as though he were going to a funeral.

He found himself at a gathering of the teachers of the school and other institutions of the town, and their wives and daughters. They were all huddled together in a room too small for them, and grouped hierarchically. They paid no attention to him. The group nearest him was talking of pedagogy and cooking. All the wives of the teachers had culinary recipes which they set out with pedantic exuberance and insistence. The men were no less interested in these matters and hardly less competent. They were as proud of the domestic talents of their wives as they of their husbands' learning. Christophe stood by a window leaning against the wall, not knowing how to look, now trying to smile stupidly, now gloomy with a fixed stare and unmoved features, and he was bored to death. A little away from him, sitting in the recess of the window, was a young woman to whom nobody was talking and she was as bored as he. They both looked at the room and not at each other. It was only after some time that they noticed each other just as they both turned away to yawn, both being at the limit of endurance. Just at that moment their eyes met. They exchanged a look of friendly understanding. He moved towards her. She said in a low voice:

"Are you amused?"

He turned his back on the room, and, looking out of the window, put out his tongue. She burst out laughing, and suddenly waking up she signed to him to sit down by her side. They introduced themselves; she was the wife of Professor Reinhart, who lectured on natural history at the school, and was newly come to the town, where they knew nobody. She was not beautiful; she had a large nose, ugly teeth, and she lacked freshness; but she had keen, clever eyes and a kindly smile. She chattered like a magpie; he answered her solemnly; she had an amusing frankness and a droll wit; they laughingly exchanged impressions out loud without bothering about the people round them. Their neighbors, who had not deigned to notice their existence when it would have been charitable to help them out of their loneliness, now threw angry looks at them; it was in bad taste to be so much amused. But they did not care what the others might think of them; they were taking their revenge in their chatter.

In the end Frau Reinhart introduced her husband to Christophe. He was extremely ugly; he had a pale, greasy, pockmarked, rather sinister face, but he looked very kind. He spoke low down in his throat and pronounced his words sententiously, stammeringly, pausing between each syllable.

They had been married a few months only and these two plain people were in love with each other; they had an affectionate way of looking at each other, talking to each other, taking each other's hands in the presence of everybody—which was comic and touching. If one wanted anything the other would want it too. And so they invited Christophe to go and sup with them after the reception. Christophe began jokingly to beg to be excused; he said that the best thing to do that evening would be to go to bed; he was quite worn out with boredom, as tired as though he had walked ten miles. But Frau Reinhart said that he could not be left in that condition; it would be dangerous to spend the night with such gloomy thoughts. Christophe let them drag him off. In his loneliness he was glad to have met these good people, who were not very distinguished in their manners but were simple and *gemuetlich*.

* * * * *

The Reinharts' little house was *gemuetlich* like themselves. It was a rather chattering *Gemuet*, a *Gemuet* with inscriptions. The furniture, the utensils, the china all talked, and went on repeating their joy in seeing their "charming guest," asked after his health, and gave him pleasant and virtuous advice. On the sofas—which was very hard—was a little cushion which murmured amiably:

"Only a quarter of an hour!" (*Nur ein Viertelstuendchen.*)

The cup of coffee which was handed to Christophe insisted on his taking more:

"Just a drop!" (*Noch ein Schlueckchen.*)

The plates seasoned the cooking with morality and otherwise the cooking was quite excellent. One plate said:

"Think of everything: otherwise no good will come to you!"

Another:

"Affection and gratitude please everybody. Ingratitude pleases nobody."

Although Christophe did not smoke, the ash–tray on the mantelpiece insisted on introducing itself to him:

"A little resting place for burning cigars." (*Ruheplaetzchen fuer brennende Cigarren.*)

He wanted to wash his hands. The soap on the washstand said:

"For our charming guest." (*Fuer unseren lieben Gast.*)

And the sententious towel, like a person who has nothing to say, but thinks he must say something all the same, gave him this reflection, full of good sense but not very apposite, that "to enjoy the morning you must rise early."

"*Morgenstund hat Gold im Mund.*"

At length Christophe dared not even turn in his chair for fear of hearing himself addressed by other voices coming from every part of the room. He wanted to say:

"Be silent, you little monsters! We don't understand each other."

And he burst out laughing crazily and then tried to explain to his host and hostess that he was thinking of the gathering at the school. He would not have hurt them for the world, And he was not very sensible of the ridiculous. Very soon he grew accustomed to the loquacious cordiality of these people and their belongings. He could have tolerated anything in them! They were so kind! They were not tiresome either; if they had no taste they were not lacking in intelligence.

They were a little lost in the place to which they had come. The intolerable susceptibilities of the little provincial town did not allow people to enter it as though it were a mill, without having properly asked for the honor of becoming part of it. The Reinharts had not sufficiently attended to the provincial code which regulated the duties of new arrivals in the town towards those who had settled in it before them. Reinhart would have submitted to it mechanically. But his wife, to whom such drudgery was oppressive—she disliked being put out—postponed her duties from day to day. She had selected those calls which bored her least, to be paid first, or she had put the others off indefinitely. The distinguished persons who were comprised in the last category choked with indignation at such a want of respect. Angelica Reinhart—(her husband called her Lili)—was a little free in her manners; she could not take on the official tone. She would address her superiors in the hierarchy familiarly and make than go red in the face with indignation; and if need be she was not afraid of contradicting them. She had a quick tongue and always had to say whatever was in her head; sometimes she made extraordinarily foolish remarks at which people laughed behind her back; and also she could be malicious whole–heartedly, and that made her mortal enemies. She would bite her tongue as she was saying rash things and wish she had not said them, but it was too late. Her husband, the gentlest and most respectful of men, would chide her timidly about it. She would kiss him and say that she was a fool and that he was right. But the next moment she would break out again; and she would always say things at the least suitable moment; she would have burst if she had not said them. She was exactly the sort of woman to get on with Christophe.

Among the many ridiculous things which she ought not to have said, and consequently was always saying, was her trick of perpetually comparing the way things were done in Germany and the way they were done in France. She was a German—(nobody more so)—but she had been brought up in Alsace among French Alsatians, and she had felt the attraction of Latin civilization which so many Germans in the annexed countries, even those who seem the least likely to feel it, cannot resist. Perhaps, to tell the truth, the attraction had become stronger out of a spirit of contradiction since Angelica had married a North German and lived with him in purely German society.

She opened up her usual subject of discussion on her first evening with Christophe. She loved the pleasant freedom of conversation in France, Christophe echoed her. France to him was Corinne; bright blue eyes, smiling lips, frank free manners, a musical voice; he loved to know more about it.

Lili Reinhart clapped her hands on finding herself so thoroughly agreeing with Christophe.

"It is a pity," she said, "that my little French friend has gone, but she could not stand it; she has gone."

The image of Corinne was at once blotted out. As a match going out suddenly makes the gentle glimmer of the stars shine out from the dark sky, another image and other eyes appeared.

"Who?" asked Christophe with a start, "the little governess?"

"What?" said Frau Reinhart, "you knew her too?"

He described her; the two portraits were identical.

"You knew her?" repeated Christophe. "Oh! Tell me everything you know about her!..."

Frau Reinhart began by declaring that they were bosom friends and had no secrets from each other. But when she had to go into detail her knowledge was reduced to very little. They had met out calling. Frau Reinhart had made advances to the girl; and with her usual cordiality had invited her to come and see her. The girl had come two or three times and they had talked. But the curious Lili had not so easily succeeded in finding out anything about the life of the little Frenchwoman; the girl was very reserved; she had had to worm her story out of her, bit by bit. Frau Reinhart knew that she was called Antoinette Jeannin; she had no fortune, and no friends, except a younger brother who lived in Paris and to whom she was devoted. She used always to talk of him; he was the only subject about which she could talk freely; and Lili Reinhart had gained her confidence by showing sympathy and pity for the boy living alone in Paris without relations, without friends, at a boarding school. It was partly to pay for his education that Antoinette had accepted a post abroad. But the two children could not live without each other; they wanted to be with each other every day, and the least delay in the delivery of their letters used to make them quite ill with anxiety. Antoinette was always worrying about her brother, the poor child could not always manage to hide his sadness and loneliness from her; every one of his complaints used to sound through Antoinette's heart and seemed like to break it; the thought that he was suffering used to torture her and she used often to imagine that he was ill and would not say so. Frau Reinhart in her kindness had often had to rebuke her for her groundless fears, and she used to succeed in restoring her confidence for a moment. She had not been able to find out anything about Antoinette's family or position or her inner self. The girl was wildly shy and used to draw into herself at the first question. The little she said showed that she was cultured and intelligent; she seemed to have a precocious knowledge of life; she seemed to be at once naive and undeceived, pious and disillusioned. She had not been happy in the town in a tactless and unkind family. She used not to complain, but it was easy to see that she used to suffer—Frau Reinhart did not exactly know why she had gone. It had been said that she had behaved badly. Angelica did not believe it; she was ready to swear that it was all a disgusting calumny, worthy of the foolish rotten town. But there had been stories; it did not matter what, did it?

"No," said Christophe, bowing his head.

"And so she has gone."

"And what did she say—anything to you when she went?"

"Ah!" said Lili Reinhart, "I had no chance. I had gone to Cologne for a few days just then! When I came back—*Zu spaet*" (too late).—She stopped to scold her maid, who had brought her lemon too late for her tea.

And she added sententiously with the solemnity which the true German brings naturally to the performance of the familiar duties of daily life:

"Too late, as one so often is in life!"

(It was not clear whether she meant the lemon or her interrupted story.)

She went on:

"When I returned I found a line from her thanking me for all I had done and telling me that she was going; she was returning to Paris; she gave no address."

"And she did not write again?"

"Not again."

Once more Christophe saw her sad face disappear into the night; once more he saw her eyes for a moment just as he had seen them for the last time looking at him through the carriage window.

The enigma of France was once more set before him more insistently than ever. Christophe never tired of asking Frau Reinhart about the country which she pretended to know so well. And Frau Reinhart who had never been there was not reluctant to tell him about it. Reinhart, a good patriot, full of prejudices against France, which he knew better than his wife, sometimes used to qualify her remarks when her enthusiasm went too far; but she would repeat her assertions only the more vigorously, and Christophe, knowing nothing at all about it, backed her up confidently.

What was more precious even than Lili Reinhart's memories were her books. She had a small library of French books: school books, a few novels, a few volumes bought at random. Christophe, greedy of knowledge and ignorant of France, thought them a treasure when Reinhart went and got them for him and put them at his disposal.

He began with volumes of select passages, old school books, which had been used by Lili Reinhart or her husband in their school days. Reinhart had assured him that he must begin with them if he wished to find his way about French literature, which was absolutely unknown to him. Christophe was full of respect for those who knew more than himself, and obeyed religiously: and that very evening he began to read. He tried first of all to take stock of the riches in his possession.

He made the acquaintance of certain French writers, namely: Thedore–Henri Barrau, Francois Petis de la Croix, Frederic Baudry, Emile Delerot, Charles–Auguste–Desire Filon, Samuel Descombaz, and Prosper Baur. He read the poetry of Abbe Joseph Reyre, Pierre Lachambaudie, the Duc de Nivernois, Andre van Hasselt, Andrieux, Madame Colet, Constance–Marie Princesse de Salm–Dyck, Henrietta Hollard,

Gabriel–Jean–Baptiste–Ernest–Wilfrid Legouve, Hippolyte Violeau, Jean Reboul, Jean Racine, Jean de Beranger, Frederic Bechard, Gustave Nadaud, Edouard Plouvier, Eugene Manuel, Hugo, Millevoye, Chenedolle, James Lacour Delatre, Felix Chavannes, Francis–Edouard–Joachim, known as Francois Coppee, and Louis Belmontet. Christophe was lost, drowned, submerged under such a deluge of poetry and turned to prose. He found Gustave de Molinari, Flechier, Ferdinand–Edouard Buisson, Merimee, Malte–Brun, Voltaire, Lame–Fleury, Dumas pere, J.J. Bousseau, Mezieres, Mirabeau, de Mazade, Claretie, Cortambert, Frederic II, and M. de Voguee. The most often quoted of French historians was Maximilien Samson–Frederic Schoell. In the French anthology Christophe found the Proclamation of the new German Empire; and he read a description of the Germans by Frederic–Constant de Rougemont, in which he learned that " *the German was born to live in the region of the soul. He has not the light noisy gaiety of the Frenchman. His is a great soul; his affections are tender and profound. He is indefatigable in toil, and persevering in enterprise. There is no more moral or long–lived people. Germany has an extraordinary number of writers. She has the genius of art. While the inhabitants of other countries pride themselves on being French, English, Spanish, the German on the other hand embraces all humanity in his love. And though its position is the very center of Europe the German nation seems to be at once the heart and the higher reason of humanity.*"

Christophe closed the book. He was astonished and tired. He thought:

"The French are good fellows; but they are not strong."

He took another volume. It was on a higher plane; it was meant for high schools. Musset occupied three pages, and Victor Duray thirty, Lamartine seven pages and Thiers almost forty. The whole of the *Cid* was included—or almost the whole:——(ten monologues of Don Diegue and Rodrigue had been suppressed because they were too long.)—Lanfrey exalted Prussia against Napoleon I and so he had not been cut down; he alone occupied more space than all the great classics of the eighteenth century. Copious narrations of the French defeats of 1870 had been extracted from *La Debacle* of Zola. Neither Montaigne, nor La Rochefoucauld, nor La Bruyere, nor Diderot, nor Stendhal, nor Balzac, nor Flaubert appeared. On the other hand, Pascal, who did not appear in the other book, found a place in this as a curiosity; and Christophe learned by the way that the convulsionary *"was one of the fathers of Port–Royal, a girls' school, near Paris..."* [Footnote: The anthologies of French literature which Jean–Christophe borrowed from his friends the Reinharts were:

I. *Selected French passages for the use of secondary schools*, by Hubert H. Wingerath, Ph.D., director of the real–school of Saint John at Strasburg. Part II: Middle forms.—7th Edition, 1902, Dumont–Schauberg.

II. L. Herrig and G.F. Burguy: *Literary France*, arranged by F. Tendering, director of the real–gymnasium of the Johanneum, Hamburg.—1904, Brunswick.]

Christophe was on the point of throwing the book away; his head was swimming; he could not see. He said to himself: "I shall never get through with it." He could not formulate any opinion. He turned over the leaves idly for hours without knowing what he was reading. He did not read French easily, and when he had labored to make out a passage, it was almost always something meaningless and highfalutin.

And yet from the chaos there darted flashes of light, like rapier thrusts, words that looked and stabbed, heroic laughter. Gradually an impression emerged from his first reading, perhaps through the biased scheme of the selections. Voluntarily or involuntarily the German editors had selected those pieces of French which could seem to establish by the testimony of the French themselves the failings of the French and the superiority of the Germans. But they had no notion that what they most exposed to the eyes of an independent mind like Christophe's was the surprising liberty of these Frenchmen who criticised everything in their own country and praised their adversaries. Michelet praised Frederick II, Lanfrey the English of Trafalgar, Charras the Prussia of 1813. No enemy of Napoleon had ever dared to speak of him so harshly. Nothing was too greatly respected to escape their disparagement. Even under the great King the previous poets had had their freedom of speech. Moliere spared nothing, La Fontaine laughed at everything. Even Boileau gibed at the nobles. Voltaire derided war, flogged religion, scoffed at his country. Moralists, satirists, pamphleteers, comic writers, they all vied one with another in gay or somber audacity. Want of respect was universal. The honest German editors were sometimes scared by it, they had to throw a rope to their consciences by trying to excuse Pascal, who lumped together cooks, porters, soldiers, and camp followers; they protested in a note that Pascal would not have written thus if he had been acquainted with the noble armies of modern times. They did not fail to remind the reader how happily Lessing had corrected the Fables of La Fontaine by following, for instance, the advice of the Genevese Rousseau and changing the piece of cheese of Master Crow to a piece of poisoned meat of which the vile fox dies.

"May you never gain anything but poison. You cursed flatterers! "

They blinked at naked truth; but Christophe was pleased with it; he loved this light. Here and there he was even a little shocked; he was not used to such unbridled independence which looks like anarchy to the eyes even of the freest of Germans, who in spite of everything is accustomed to order and discipline. And he was led astray by the way of the French; he took certain things too seriously; and other things which were implacable denials seemed to him to be amusing paradoxes. No matter! Surprised or shocked he was drawn on little by little. He gave up trying to classify his impressions; he passed from one feeling to another; he lived. The gaiety of the French stories—Chamfort, Segur, Dumas pere, Merimee all lumped together—delighted him; and every now and then in gusts there would creep forth from the printed page the wild intoxicating scent of the Revolutions.

It was nearly dawn when Louisa, who slept in the next room, woke up and saw the light through the chinks of Christophe's door. She knocked on the wall and asked if he were ill. A chair creaked on the floor: the door opened and Christophe appeared, pale, in his nightgown, with a candle and a book in his hand, making strange, solemn, and grotesque gestures. Louisa was in terror and got up in her bed, thinking that he was mad. He began to laugh, and, waving his candle, he declaimed a scene from Moliere. In the middle of a sentence he gurgled with laughter; he sat at the foot of his mother's bed to take breath; the candle shook in his hand. Louisa was reassured, and scolded him forcibly:

"What is the matter with you? What is it? Go to bed.... My poor boy, are you going out of your senses?"

But he began again:

"You must listen to this!"

And he sat by her bedside and read the play, going back to the beginning again. He seemed to see Corinne; he heard her mocking tones, cutting and sonorous. Louisa protested:

"Go away! Go away! You will catch cold. How tiresome you are. Let me go to sleep!"

He went on relentlessly. He raised his voice, waved his arms, choked with laughter; and he asked his mother if she did not think it wonderful. Louisa turned her back on him, buried herself in the bedclothes, stopped her ears, and said:

"Do leave me alone!..."

But she laughed inwardly at hearing his laugh. At last she gave up protesting. And when Christophe had finished the act, and asked her, without eliciting any reply, if she did not think what he had read interesting, he bent over her and saw that she was asleep. Then he smiled, gently kissed her hair, and stole back to his own room.

* * * * *

He borrowed more and more books from the Reinharts' library. There were all sorts of books in it. Christophe devoured them all. He wanted so much to love the country of Corinne and the unknown young woman. He had so much enthusiasm to get rid of that he found a use for it in his reading. Even in second–rate works there were sentences and pages which had the effect on him of a gust of fresh air. He exaggerated the effect, especially when he was talking to Frau Reinhart, who always went a little better than he. Although she was as ignorant as a fish, she delighted to contrast French and German culture and to decry the German to the advantage of the French, just to annoy her husband and to avenge herself for the boredom she had to suffer in the little town.

Reinhart was really amused. Notwithstanding his learning, he had stopped short at the ideas he had learned at school. To him the French were a clever people, skilled in practical things, amiable, talkative, but frivolous, susceptible, and boastful, incapable of being serious, or sincere, or of feeling strongly—a people without music, without philosophy, without poetry (except for *l'Art Poetique*, Beranger and Francois Coppee)—a people of pathos, much gesticulation, exaggerated speech, and pornography. There were not words strong enough for the denunciation——of Latin Immorality; and for want of a better he always came back to *frivolity*, which for him, as for the majority of his compatriots, had a particularly unpleasant meaning. And he would end with the usual couplet in praise of the noble German people,—the moral people ("*By that,*" Herder has said, "*it is distinguished from all other nations.*")—the faithful people (*treues Volk ...*

Treu meaning everything: sincere, faithful, loyal and upright)—*the People par excellence*, as Fichte says—German Force, the symbol of justice and truth—German thought—the German *Gemuet*—the German language, the only original language, the only language that, like the race itself, has preserved its purity—German women, German wine, German song ... "*Germany, Germany above everything in the world!*"

Christophe would protest. Frau Reinhart would cry out. They would all shout. They did not get on the less for it. They knew quite well that they were all three good Germans.

Christophe used often to go and talk, dine and walk with his new friends. Lili Reinhart made much of him, and used to cook dainty suppers for him. She was delighted to have the excuse for satisfying her own greediness. She paid him all sorts of sentimental and culinary attentions. For Christophe's birthday she made a cake, on which were twenty candles and in the middle a little wax figure in Greek costume which was supposed to represent Iphigenia holding a bouquet. Christophe, who was profoundly German in spite of himself, was touched by these rather blunt and not very refined marks of true affection.

The excellent Reinharts found other more subtle ways of showing their real friendship. On his wife's instigation Reinhart, who could hardly read a note of music, had bought twenty copies of Christophe's *Lieder*—(the first to leave the publisher's shop)—he had sent them to different parts of Germany to university acquaintances. He had also sent a certain number to the libraries of Leipzig and Berlin, with which he had dealings through his classbooks. For the moment at least their touching enterprise, of which Christophe knew nothing, bore no fruit. The *Lieder* which had been scattered broadcast seemed to miss fire; nobody talked of them; and the Reinharts, who were hurt by this indifference, were glad they had not told Christophe about what they had done, for it would have given him more pain than consolation. But in truth nothing is lost, as so often appears in life; no effort is in vain. For years nothing happens. Then one day it appears that your idea has made its way. It was impossible to be sure that Christophe's *Lieder* had not reached the hearts of a few good people buried in the country, who were too timid or too tired to tell him so.

One person wrote to him. Two or three months after the Reinharts had sent them, a letter came for Christophe. It was warm, ceremonious, enthusiastic, old–fashioned in form, and came from a little town in Thuringia, and was signed "*Universitaets Musikdirektor Professor Dr. Peter Schulz.*"

It was a great joy for Christophe, and even greater for the Reinharts, when at their house he opened the letter, which he had left lying in his pocket for two days. They read it together. Reinhart made signs to his wife which Christophe did not notice. He looked radiant, until suddenly Reinhart saw his face grow gloomy, and he stopped dead in the middle of his reading.

"Well, why do you stop?" he asked.

(They used the familiar *du*.)

Christophe flung the letter on the table angrily.

"No. It is too much!" he said.

"What is?"

"Read!"

He turned away and went and sulked in a corner.

Reinhart and his wife read the letter, and could find in it only fervent admiration.

"I don't see," he said in astonishment.

"You don't see? You don't see?..." cried Christophe, taking the letter and thrusting it in his face. "Can't you read? Don't you see that he is a '*Brahmin*'"?

And then Reinhart noticed that in one sentence the *Universitaets Musikdirektor* compared Christophe's *Lieder* with those of Brahms. Christophe moaned:

"A friend! I have found a friend at last!... And I have hardly found him when I have lost him!..."

The comparison revolted him. If they had let him, he would have replied with a stupid letter, or perhaps, upon reflection, he would have thought himself very prudent and generous in not replying at all. Fortunately, the Reinharts were amused by his ill–humor, and kept him from committing any further absurdity. They succeeded in making him write a letter of thanks. But the letter, written reluctantly, was cold and constrained. The enthusiasm of Peter Schulz was not shaken by it. He sent two or three more letters, brimming, over with affection. Christophe was not a good correspondent, and although he was a little reconciled to his unknown friend by the sincerity and real sympathy which he could feel behind his words, he let the correspondence drop. Schulz wrote no more. Christophe never thought about him.

* * * * *

He now saw the Reinharts every day and frequently several times a day. They spent almost all the evenings together. After spending the day alone in concentration he had a physical need of talking, of saying everything that was in his mind, even if he were not understood, and of laughing with or without reason, of expanding and stretching himself.

He played for them. Having no other means of showing his gratitude, he would sit at the piano and play for hours together. Frau Reinhart was no musician, and she had difficulty in keeping herself from yawning; but she sympathized with Christophe, and pretended to be interested in everything he played. Reinhart was not much more of a musician than his wife, but was sometimes touched quite materially by certain pieces of music, certain passages, certain bars, and then he would be violently moved sometimes even to tears, and that seemed silly to him. The rest of the time he felt nothing; it was just music to him. That was the general rule. He was never moved except by the least good passages of a composition—absolutely insignificant passages. Both of them persuaded themselves that they understood Christophe, and Christophe tried to pretend that it was so. Every now and then he would be seized by a wicked desire to make fun of them. He would lay traps for them and play things without any meaning, inapt *potpourris*; and he would let them think that he had composed them. Then, when they had admired it, he would tell them what it was. Then they would grow wary, and when Christophe played them a piece with an air of mystery, they would imagine that he was trying to catch them again, and they would criticise it. Christophe would let them go on and back them up, and argue that such music was worthless, and then he would break out:

"Rascals! You are right!... It is my own!" He would be as happy as a boy at having taken them in. Frau Reinhart would be cross and come and give him a little slap; but he would laugh so good–humoredly that they would laugh with him. They did not pretend to be infallible. And as they had no leg to stand on, Lili Reinhart would criticise everything and her husband would praise everything, and so they were certain that one or other of them would always be in agreement with Christophe.

For the rest, it was not so much the musician that attracted them in Christophe as the crack–brained boy, with his affectionate ways and true reality of life. The ill that they had heard spoken of him had rather disposed them in his favor. Like him, they were rather oppressed by the atmosphere of the little town; like him, they were frank, they judged for themselves, and they regarded him as a great baby, not very clever in the ways of life, and the victim of his own frankness.

Christophe was not under many illusions concerning his new friends, and it made him sad to think that they did not understand the depths of his character, and that they would never understand it. But he was so much deprived of friendship and he stood in such sore need of it, that he was infinitely grateful to them for wanting to like him a little. He had learned wisdom in his experiences of the last year; he no longer thought he had the right to be overwise. Two years earlier he would not have been so patient. He remembered with amusement and remorse his severe judgment of the honest and tiresome Eulers! Alas! How wisdom had grown in him! He sighed a little. A secret voice whispered: "Yes, but for how long?"

That made him smile and consoled him a little. What would he not have given to have a friend, one friend who would understand him and share his soul! But although he was still young he had enough experience of the world to know that his desire was one of those which are most difficult to realize in life, and that he could not hope to be happier than the majority of the true artists who had gone before him. He had learned the histories of some of them. Certain books, borrowed from the Reinharts, had told him about the terrible trials through which the German musicians of the seventeenth century had passed, and the calmness and resolution with which one of these great souls—the greatest of all, the heroic Schutz—had striven, as unshakably he went on his way in the midst of wars and burning towns, and provinces ravaged by the plague, with his country invaded, trampled underfoot by the hordes of all Europe, and—worst of all—broken, worn out, degraded by misfortune, making no fight, indifferent to everything, longing only for rest. He thought: "With such as example, what right has any man to complain? They had no audience, they had no future; they wrote for themselves and God. What they wrote one day would perhaps be destroyed by the next. And yet they went on writing and they were not sad. Nothing made them lose their intrepidity, their joviality. They were satisfied with their song; they asked nothing of life but to live, to earn their daily bread, to express their ideas, and to find a few honest men, simple, true, not artists, who no doubt did not understand them, but had confidence in them and won their confidence in return. How dared he have demanded more than they? There is a minimum of happiness which it is permitted to demand. But no man has the right to more; it rests with a man's self to gain the surplus of happiness, not with others."

Such thoughts brought him new serenity, and he loved his good friends the Reinharts the more for them. He had no idea that even this affection was to be denied him.

 * * * * *

He reckoned without the malevolence of small towns. They are tenacious in their spite—all the more tenacious because their spite is aimless. A healthy hatred which knows what it wants is appeased when it has achieved its end. But men who are mischievous from boredom never lay down their arms, for they are always bored. Christophe was a natural prey for their want of occupation. He was beaten without a doubt; but he was bold enough not to seem crushed. He did not bother anybody, but then he did not bother about anybody. He asked nothing. They were impotent against him. He was happy with his new friends and indifferent to anything that was said or thought of him. That was intolerable.—Frau Reinhart roused even more irritation. Her open friendship with Christophe in the face of the whole town seemed, like his attitude, to be a defiance of public opinion. But the good Lili Reinhart defied nothing and nobody. She had no thought to provoke others; she did what she thought fit without asking anybody else's advice. That was the worst provocation.

All their doings were watched. They had no idea of it. He was extravagant, she scatter–brained, and both even wanting in prudence when they went out together, or even at home in the evening, when they leaned over the balcony talking and laughing. They drifted innocently into a familiarity of speech and manner which could easily supply food for calumny.

One morning Christophe received an anonymous letter. He was accused in basely insulting terms of being Frau Reinhart's lover. His arms fell by his sides. He had never had the least thought of love or even of flirtation with her. He was too honest. He had a

Puritanical horror of adultery. The very idea of such a dirty sharing gave him a physical and moral feeling of nausea. To take the wife of a friend would have been a crime in his eyes, and Lili Reinhart would have been the last person in the world with whom he could have been tempted to commit such an offense. The poor woman was not beautiful, and he would not have had even the excuse of passion.

He went to his friends ashamed and embarrassed. They also were embarrassed. Each of them had received a similar letter, but they had not dared to tell each other, and all three of them were on their guard and watched each other and dared not move or speak, and they just talked nonsense. If Lili Reinhart's natural carelessness took the ascendant for a moment, or if she began to laugh and talk wildly, suddenly a look from her husband or Christophe would stop her dead; the letter would cross her mind; she would stop in the middle of a familiar gesture and grow uneasy. Christophe and Reinhart were in the same plight. And each of them was thinking: "Do the others know?"

However, they said nothing to each other and tried to go on as though nothing had happened.

But the anonymous letters went on, growing more and mores insulting and dirty. They were plunged into a condition of depression and intolerable shame. They hid themselves when they received the letters, and had not the strength to burn them unopened. They opened them with trembling hands, and as they unfolded the letters their hearts would sink; and when they read what they feared to read, with some new variation on the same theme—the injurious and ignoble inventions of a mind bent on causing a hurt—they wept in silence. They racked their brains to discover who the wretch might be who so persistently persecuted them..

One day Frau Reinhart, at the end of her letter, confessed the persecution of which she was the victim to her husband, and with tears in his eyes he confessed that he was suffering in the same way. Should they mention it to Christophe? They dared not. But they had to warn him to make him be cautious.—At the first words that Frau Reinhart said to him, with a blush, she saw to her horror that Christophe had also received letters. Such utter malignance appalled them. Frau Reinhart had no doubt that the whole town was in the secret. Instead of helping each other, they only undermined each other's fortitude. They did not know what to do. Christophe talked of breaking somebody's head. But whose? And besides, that would be to justify the calumny!... Inform the police of the letters?—That would make their insinuations public...—Pretend to ignore them? It was no longer possible. Their friendly relations were now disturbed. It was useless for Reinhart to have absolute faith in the honesty of his wife and Christophe. He suspected them in spite of himself. He felt that his suspicions were shameful and absurd, and tried hard not to pay any heed to them, and to leave Christophe and his wife alone together. But he suffered, and his wife saw that he was suffering.

It was even worse for her. She had never thought of flirting with Christophe, any more than he had thought of it with her. The calumnious letters brought her imperceptibly to the ridiculous idea that after all Christophe was perhaps in love with her; and although he was never anywhere near showing any such feeling for her, she thought she must defend herself, not by referring directly to it, but by clumsy precautions, which Christophe did not understand at first, though, when he did understand, he was beside himself. It was so stupid that it made him laugh and cry at the same time! He in love with the honest little woman, kind enough as she was, but plain and common!... And to think that she should believe it!... And that he could not deny it, and tell her and her husband:

"Come! There is no danger! Be calm!..." But no; he could not offend these good people. And besides, he was beginning to think that if she held out against being loved by him it was because she was secretly on the point of loving him. The anonymous letters had had the fine result of having given him so foolish and fantastic an idea.

The situation had become at once so painful and so silly that it was impossible for this to go on. Besides, Lili Reinhart, who, in spite of her brave words, had no strength of character, lost her head in the face of the dumb hostility of the little town. They made shamefaced excuses for not meeting:

"Frau Reinhart was unwell.... Reinhart was busy.... They were going away for a few days...."

Clumsy lies which were always unmasked by chance, which seemed to take a malicious pleasure in doing so.

Christophe was more frank, and said:

"Let us part, my friends. We are not strong enough."

The Reinharts wept.—But they were happier when the breach was made.

The town had its triumph. This time Christophe was quite alone. It had robbed him of his last breath of air:—the affection, however humble, without which no heart can live.

III. DELIVERANCE

He had no one. All his friends had disappeared. His dear Gottfried, who had come to his aid in times of difficulty, and whom now he so sorely needed, had gone some months before. This time forever. One evening in the summer of the last year a letter in large handwriting, bearing the address of a distant village, had informed Louisa that her brother had died upon one of his vagabond journeys which the little peddler had insisted on making, in spite of his ill health. He was buried there in the cemetery of the place. The last manly and serene friendship which could have supported Christophe had been swallowed up. He was left alone with his old mother, who cared nothing for his ideas—could only love him and not understand him. About him was the immense plain of Germany, the green ocean. At every attempt to climb out of it he only slipped back deeper than ever. The hostile town watched him drown....

And as he was struggling a light flashed upon him in the middle of the night, the image of Hassler, the great musician whom he had loved so much when he was a child. His fame shone over all Germany now. He remembered the promises that Hassler had made him then. And he clung to this piece of wreckage in desperation. Hassler could save him! Hassler must save him! What was he asking? Not help, nor money, nor material assistance of any kind. Nothing but understanding. Hassler had been persecuted like him. Hassler was a free man. He would understand a free man, whom German mediocrity was pursuing with its spite and trying to crush. They were fighting the same battle.

He carried the idea into execution as soon as it occurred to him. He told his mother that he would be away for a week, and that very evening he took the train for the great town in the north of Germany where Hassler was *Kapellmeister*, He could not wait. It was a last effort to breathe.

* * * * *

Hassler was famous. His enemies had not disarmed, but his friends cried that he was the greatest musician, present, past and future. He was surrounded by partisans and detractors who were equally absurd. As he was not of a very firm character, he had been embittered by the last, and mollified by the first. He devoted his energy to writing things to annoy his critics and make them cry out. He was like an urchin playing pranks. These pranks were often in the most detestable taste. Not only did he devote his prodigious talent to musical eccentricities which made the hair of the pontiffs stand on end, but he showed a perverse predilection for queer themes, bizarre subjects, and often for equivocal and scabrous situations; in a word, for everything which could offend ordinary good sense and decency. He was quite happy when the people howled, and the people did not fail him. Even the Emperor, who dabbled in art, as every one knows, with the insolent presumption of upstarts and princes, regarded Hassler's fame as a public scandal, and let no opportunity slip of showing his contemptuous indifference to his impudent works. Hassler was enraged and delighted by such august opposition, which had almost become a consecration for the advanced paths in German art, and went on smashing windows. At every new folly his friends went into ecstasies and cried that he was a genius.

Hassler's coterie was chiefly composed of writers, painters, and decadent critics who certainly had the merit of representing the party of revolt against the reaction—always a menace in North Germany—of the pietistic spirit and State morality; but in the struggle the independence had been carried to a pitch of absurdity of which they were unconscious. For, if many of them were not lacking in a rude sort of talent, they had little intelligence and less taste. They could not rise above the fastidious atmosphere which they had created, and like all cliques, they had ended by losing all sense of real life. They legislated for themselves and hundreds of fools who read their reviews and gulped down everything they were pleased to promulgate. Their adulation had been fatal to Hassler, for it had made him too pleased with himself. He accepted without examination every musical idea that came into his head, and he had a private conviction, however he might fall below his own level, he was still superior to that of all other musicians. And though that idea was only too true in the majority of cases, it did not follow that it was a very fit state of mind for the creation of great works. At heart Hassler had a supreme contempt for everybody, friends and enemies alike; and this bitter jeering contempt was extended to himself and life in general. He was all the more driven back into his ironic skepticism because he had once believed in a number of generous and simple things. As he had not been strong enough to ward off the slow destruction of the passing of the days, nor hypocritical enough to pretend to believe in the faith he had lost, he was forever gibing at the memory of it. He was of a Southern German nature, soft and indolent, not made to resist excess of fortune or misfortune, of heat or cold, needing a moderate temperature to preserve its balance. He had drifted insensibly into a lazy enjoyment of life. He loved good food, heavy drinking, idle lounging, and sensuous thoughts. His whole art smacked of these things, although he was too gifted for the flashes of his genius not still to shine forth from his lax music which drifted with the fashion. No one was more conscious than himself of his decay. In truth, he was the only one to be conscious of it—at rare moments which, naturally, he avoided. Besides, he was misanthropic, absorbed by his fearful moods, his egoistic preoccupations, his concern about his health—he was indifferent to everything which had formerly excited his enthusiasm or hatred.

* * * * *

Such was the man to whom Christophe came for assistance, With what joy and hope he arrived, one cold, wet morning, in the town wherein then lived the man who symbolized for him the spirit of independence in his art! He expected words of friendship and encouragement from him—words that he needed to help him to go on with the ungrateful, inevitable battle which every true artist has to wage against the world until he breathes his last, without even for one day laying down his arms; for, as Schiller has said, *"the only relation with the public of which a man never repents—is war."*

Christophe was so impatient that he just left his bag at the first hotel he came to near the station, and then ran to the theater to find out Hassler's address. Hassler lived some way from the center of the town, in one of the suburbs. Christophe took an electric train, and hungrily ate a roll. His heart thumped as he approached his goal.

The district in which Hassler had chosen his house was almost entirely built in that strange new architecture into which young Germany has thrown an erudite and deliberate barbarism struggling laboriously to have genius. In the middle of the commonplace town, with its straight, characterless streets, there suddenly appeared Egyptian hypogea, Norwegian chalets, cloisters, bastions, exhibition pavilions, pot–bellied houses, fakirs, buried in the ground, with expressionless faces, with only one enormous eye; dungeon gates, ponderous gates, iron hoops, golden cryptograms on the panes of grated windows, belching monsters over the front door, blue porcelain tiles plastered on in most unexpected places; variegated mosaics representing Adam and Eve; roofs covered with tiles of jarring colors; houses like citadels with castellated walls, deformed animals on the roofs, no windows on one side, and then suddenly, close to each other, gaping holes, square, red, angular, triangular, like wounds; great stretches of empty wall from which suddenly there would spring a massive balcony with one window—a balcony supported by Nibelungesque Caryatides, balconies from which there peered through the stone balustrade two pointed heads of old men, bearded and long–haired, mermen of Boecklin. On the front of one of these prisons—a Pharaohesque mansion, low and one–storied, with two naked giants at the gate—the architect had written:

Let the artist show his universe,
Which never was and yet will ever be.

Seine Welt zeige der Kuenstler,
Die niemals war noch jemals sein wird.

Christophe was absorbed by the idea of seeing Hassler, and looked with the eyes of amazement and under no attempt to understand. He reached the house he sought, one of the simplest—in a Carolingian style. Inside was rich luxury, commonplace enough. On the staircase was the heavy atmosphere of hot air. There was a small lift which Christophe did not use, as he wanted to gain time to prepare himself for his call by going up the four flights of stairs slowly, with his legs giving and his heart thumping with his excitement. During that short ascent his former interview with Hassler, his childish enthusiasm, the image of his grandfather were as clearly in his mind as though it had all been yesterday.

It was nearly eleven when he rang the bell. He was received by a sharp maid, with a *serva padrona* manner, who looked at him impertinently and began to say that "Herr Hassler could not see him, as Herr Hassler was tired." Then the naive disappointment expressed in Christophe's face amused her; for after making an unabashed scrutiny of him from head to foot, she softened suddenly and introduced him to Hassler's study, and said she would go and see if Herr Hassler would receive him. Thereupon she gave him a little wink and closed the door.

On the walls were a few impressionist paintings and some gallant French engravings of the eighteenth century: for Hassler pretended to some knowledge of all the arts, and Manet and Watteau were joined together in his taste in accordance with the prescription of his coterie. The same mixture of styles appeared in the furniture, and a very fine Louis

XV bureau was surrounded by new art armchairs and an oriental divan with a mountain of multi–colored cushions. The doors were ornamented with mirrors, and Japanese bric–a–brac covered the shelves and the mantelpiece, on which stood a bust of Hassler. In a bowl on a round table was a profusion of photographs of singers, female admirers and friends, with witty remarks and enthusiastic interjections. The bureau was incredibly untidy. The piano was open. The shelves were dusty, and half–smoked cigars were lying about everywhere.

In the next room Christophe heard a cross voice grumbling, It was answered by the shrill tones of the little maid. It was dear that Hassler was not very pleased at having to appear. It was clear, also, that the young woman had decided that Hassler should appear; and she answered him with extreme familiarity and her shrill voice penetrated the walls. Christophe was rather upset at hearing some of the remarks she made to her master. But Hassler did not seem to mind. On the contrary, it rather seemed as though her impertinence amused him; and while he went on growling, he chaffed the girl and took a delight in exciting her. At last Christophe heard a door open, and, still growling and chaffing, Hassler came shuffling.

He entered. Christophe's heart sank. He recognized him. Would to God he had not! It was Hassler, and yet it was not he. He still had his great smooth brow, his face as unwrinkled as that of a babe; but he was bald, stout, yellowish, sleepy–looking; his lower lip drooped a little, his mouth looked bored and sulky. He hunched his shoulders, buried his hands in the pockets of his open waistcoat; old shoes flopped on his feet; his shirt was bagged above his trousers, which he had not finished buttoning. He looked at Christophe with his sleepy eyes, in which there was no light as the young man murmured his name. He bowed automatically, said nothing, nodded towards a chair, and with a sigh, sank down on the divan and piled the cushions about himself. Christophe repeated:

"I have already had the honor.... You were kind enough.... My name is Christophe Krafft...."

Hassler lay back on the divan, with his legs crossed, his lands clasped together on his right knee, which he held up to his chin as he replied:

"I don't remember."

Christophe's throat went dry, and he tried to remind him of their former meeting. Under any circumstances it would have been difficult for him to talk of memories so intimate; now it was torture for him. He bungled his sentences, could not find words, said absurd things which made him blush. Hassler let him flounder on and never ceased to look at him with his vague, indifferent eyes. When Christophe had reached the end of his story, Hassler went on rocking his knee in silence for a moment, as though he were waiting for Christophe to go on. Then he said:

"Yes.... That does not make us young again...." and stretched his legs.

After a yawn he added:

"... I beg pardon.... Did not sleep.... Supper at the theater last night...." and yawned again.

Christophe hoped that Hassler would make some reference to what he had just told him, but Hassler, whom the story had not interested at all, said nothing about it, and he did not ask Christophe anything about his life. When he had done yawning he asked:

"Have you been in Berlin long?"

"I arrived this morning," said Christophe.

"Ah!" said Hassler, without any surprise. "What hotel?"

He did not seem to listen to the reply, but got up lazily and pressed an electric bell.

"Allow me," he said.

The little maid appeared with her impertinent manner.

"Kitty," said he, "are you trying to make me go without breakfast this morning?"

"You don't think I am going to bring it here while you have some one with you?"

"Why not?" he said, with a wink and a nod in Christophe's direction. "He feeds my mind: I must feed my body."

472

"Aren't you ashamed to have some one watching you eat—like an animal in a menagerie?"

Instead of being angry, Hassler began to laugh and corrected her:

"Like a domestic animal," he went on. "But do bring it. I'll eat my shame with it."

Christophe saw that Hassler was making no attempt to find out what he was doing, and tried to lead the conversation back. He spoke of the difficulties of provincial life, of the mediocrity of the people, the narrow–mindedness, and of his own isolation. He tried to interest him in his moral distress. But Hassler was sunk deep in the divan, with his head lying back on a cushion and his eyes half closed, and let him go on talking without even seeming to listen; or he would raise his eyelids for a moment and pronounce a few coldly ironical words, some ponderous jest at the expense of provincial people, which cut short Christophe's attempts to talk more intimately. Kitty returned with the breakfast tray: coffee, butter, ham, etc. She put it down crossly on the desk in the middle of the untidy papers. Christophe waited until she had gone before he went on with his sad story which he had such difficulty in continuing. Hassler drew the tray towards himself. He poured himself out some coffee and sipped at it. Then in a familiar and cordial though rather contemptuous way he stopped Christophe in the middle of a sentence to ask if he would take a cup.

Christophe refused. He tried to pick up the thread of his sentence, but he was more and more nonplussed, and did not know what he was saying. He was distracted by the sight of Hassler with his plate under his chin, like a child, gorging pieces of bread and butter and slices of ham which he held in his fingers. However, he did succeed in saying that he composed, that he had had an overture in the *Judith* of Hebbel performed. Hassler listened absently.

"*Was?*" (What?) he asked.

Christophe repeated the title.

"*Ach! So, so!*" (Ah! Good, good!) said Hassler, dipping his bread and his fingers into his cup. That was all.

Christophe was discouraged and was on the point of getting up and going, but he thought of his long journey in vain, and summoning up all his courage he murmured a proposal that he should play some of his works to Hassler. At the first mention of it Hassler stopped him.

"No, no. I don't know anything about it," he said, with his chaffing and rather insulting irony. "Besides, I haven't the time."

Tears came to Christophe's eyes. But he had vowed not to leave until he had Hassler's opinion about his work. He said, with a mixture of confusion and anger:

"I beg your pardon, but you promised once to hear me. I came to see you for that from the other end of Germany. You shall hear me."

Hassler, who was not used to such ways, looked at the awkward young man, who was furious, blushing, and near tears. That amused him, and wearily shrugging his shoulders, he pointed to the piano, and said with an air of comic resignation:

"Well, then!... There you are!"

On that he lay back on his divan, like a man who is going to sleep, smoothed out his cushions, put them under his outstretched arms, half closed his eyes, opened them for a moment to take stock of the size of the roll of music which Christophe had brought from one of his pockets, gave a little sigh, and lay back to listen listlessly.

Christophe was intimidated and mortified, but he began to play. It was not long before Hassler opened his eyes and ears with the professional interest of the artist who is struck in spite of himself by a beautiful thing. At first he said nothing and lay still, but his eyes became less dim and his sulky lips moved. Then he suddenly woke up, growling his surprise and approbation. He only gave inarticulate interjections, but the form of them left no doubt as to his feelings, and they gave Christophe an inexpressible pleasure. Hassler forgot to count the number of pages that had been played and were left to be played. When Christophe had finished a piece, he said:

"Go on!... Go on!..."

He was beginning to use human language.

"That's good! Good!" he exclaimed to himself. "Famous!... Awfully famous! (*Schrecklich famos!*) But, damme!" He growled in astonishment. "What is it?"

He had risen on his seat, was stretching for wind, making a trumpet with his hand, talking to himself, laughing with pleasure, or at certain odd harmonies, just putting out his tongue as though to moisten his lips. An unexpected modulation had such an effect on him that he got up suddenly with an exclamation, and came and sat at the piano by Christophe's side. He did not seem to notice that Christophe was there. He was only concerned with the music, and when the piece was finished he took the book and began to read the page again, then the following pages, and went on ejaculating his admiration and surprise as though he had been alone in the room.

"The devil!" he said. "Where did the little beast find that?..."

He pushed Christophe away with his shoulders and himself played certain passages. He had a charming touch on the piano, very soft, caressing and light. Christophe noticed his fine long, well–tended hands, which were a little morbidly aristocratic and out of keeping with the rest. Hassler stopped at certain chords and repeated them, winking, and clicking with his tongue. He hummed with his lips, imitating the sounds of the instruments, and went on interspersing the music with his apostrophes in which pleasure and annoyance were mingled. He could not help having a secret initiative, an unavowed jealousy, and at the same time he greedily enjoyed it all.

Although he went on talking to himself as though Christophe did not exist, Christophe, blushing with pleasure, could not help taking Hassler's exclamations to himself, and he explained what he had tried to do. At first Hassler seemed not to pay any attention to what the young man was saying, and went on thinking out loud; then something that Christophe said struck him and he was silent, with his eyes still fixed on the music, which he turned over as he listened without seeming to hear. Christophe grew more and more excited, and at last he plumped into confidence, and talked with naive enthusiasm about his projects and his life.

Hassler was silent, and as he listened he slipped hack into his irony. He had let Christophe take the book from his hands; with his elbow on the rack of the piano and his hand on his forehead, he looked at Christophe, who was explaining; his work with youthful ardor and eagerness. And he smiled bitterly as he thought of his own beginning, his own hopes, and of Christophe's hopes, and all the disappointments that lay in wait for him.

Christophe spoke with his eyes cast down, fearful of losing the thread of what he had to say. Hassler's silence encouraged him. He felt that Hassler was watching him and not missing a word that he said, and he thought he had broken the ice between them, and he was glad at heart. When he had finished he shyly raised his head—confidently, too—and looked at Hassler. All the joy welling in him was frozen on the instant, like too early birds, when he saw the gloomy, mocking eyes that looked into his without kindness. He was silent.

After an icy moment, Hassler spoke dully. He had changed once more; he affected a sort of harshness towards the young man. He teased him cruelly about his plans, his hopes of success, as though he were trying to chaff himself, now that he had recovered himself. He set himself coldly to destroy his faith in life, his faith in art, his faith in himself. Bitterly he gave himself as an example, speaking of his actual works in an insulting fashion.

"Hog–waste!" he said. "That is what these swine want. Do you think there are ten people in the world who love music? Is there a single one?"

"There is myself!" said Christophe emphatically. Hassler looked at him, shrugged his shoulders, and said wearily:

"You will be like the rest. You will do as the rest have done. You will think of success, of amusing yourself, like the rest.... And you will be right...."

Christophe tried to protest, but Hassler cut him short; he took the music and began bitterly to criticise the works which he had first been praising, Not only did he harshly pick out the real carelessness, the mistakes in writing, the faults of taste or of expression which had escaped the young man, but he made absurd criticisms, criticisms which might have been made by the most narrow and antiquated of musicians, from which he himself, Hassler, had had to suffer all his life. He asked what was the sense of it all. He did not even criticise: he denied; it was as though he were trying desperately to efface the impression that the music had made on him in spite of himself.

Christophe was horrified and made no attempt to reply. How could he reply to absurdities which he blushed to hear on the lips of a man whom he esteemed and loved? Besides, Hassler did not listen to him. He stopped at that, stopped dead, with the book in his hands, shut; no expression in his eyes and his lips drawn down in bitterness. At last he said, as though he had once more forgotten Christophe's presence:

"Ah! the worst misery of all is that there is not a single man who can understand you!"

Christophe was racked with emotion. He turned suddenly, laid his hand on Hassler's, and with love in his heart he repeated:

"There is myself!"

But Hassler did not move his hand, and if something stirred in his heart for a moment at that boyish cry, no light shone in his dull eyes, as they looked at Christophe. Irony and evasion were in the ascendant. He made a ceremonious and comic little bow in acknowledgment.

"Honored!" he said.

He was thinking:

"Do you, though? Do you think I have lost my life for you?"

He got up, threw the book on the piano, and went with his long spindle legs and sat on the divan again. Christophe had divined his thoughts and had felt the savage insult in them, and he tried proudly to reply that a man does not need to be understood by everybody; certain souls are worth a whole people; they think for it, and what they have thought the people have to think.—But Hassler did not listen to him. He had fallen back into his apathy, caused by the weakening of the life slumbering in him. Christophe, too sane to understand the sudden change, felt that he had lost. But he could not resign himself to losing after seeming to be so near victory. He made desperate efforts to excite Hassler's attention once more. He took up his music book and tried to explain the reason, for the irregularities which Hassler had remarked. Hassler lay back on the sofa and preserved a gloomy silence. He neither agreed nor contradicted; he was only waiting for him to finish.

Christophe saw that there was nothing more to be done. He stopped short in the middle of a sentence. He rolled up his music and got up. Hassler got up, too. Christophe was shy and ashamed, and murmured excuses. Hassler bowed slightly, with a certain haughty and bored distinction, coldly held out his hand politely, and accompanied him to the door without a word of suggestion that he should stay or come again.

* * * * *

Christophe found himself in the street once more, absolutely crushed. He walked at random; he did not know where he was going. He walked down several streets mechanically, and then found himself at a station of the train by which he had come. He went back by it without thinking of what he was doing. He sank down on the seat with his arms and legs limp. It was impossible to think or to collect his ideas; he thought of nothing, he did not try to think. He was afraid to envisage himself. He was utterly empty. It seemed to him that there was emptiness everywhere about him in that town. He could not breathe in it. The mists, the massive houses stifled him. He had only one idea, to fly, to fly as quickly as possible,—as if by escaping from the town he would leave in it the bitter disillusion which he had found in it.

He returned to his hotel. It was half–past twelve. It was two hours since he had entered it,—with what a light shining in his heart! Now it was dead.

He took no lunch. He did not go up to his room. To the astonishment of the people of the hotel, he asked for his bill, paid as though he had spent the night there, and said that he was going. In vain did they explain to him that there was no hurry, that the train he wanted to go by did not leave for hours, and that he had much better wait in the hotel. He insisted on going to the station at once. He was like a child. He wanted to go by the first train, no matter which, and not to stay another hour in the place. After the long journey and all the expense he had incurred,—although he had taken his holiday not only to see Hassler, but the museums, and to hear concerts and to make certain acquaintances—he had only one idea in his head: To go....

He went back to the station. As he had been told, his train did not leave for three hours. And also the train was not express—(for Christophe had to go by the cheapest class)—stopped on the way. Christophe would have done better to go by the next train, which went two hours later and caught up the first. But that meant spending two more hours in the place, and Christophe could not bear it. He would not even leave the station while he was waiting.—A gloomy period of waiting in those vast and empty halls, dark and noisy, where strange shadows were going in and out, always busy, always hurrying; strange shadows who meant nothing to him, all unknown to him, not one friendly face. The misty day died down. The electric lamps, enveloped in fog, flushed the night and made it darker than ever. Christophe grew more and more depressed as time went on, waiting in agony for the time to go. Ten times an hour he went to look at the train indicators to make sure that he had not made a mistake. As he was reading them once more from end to end to pass the time, the name of a place caught his eye. He thought he knew it. It was only after a moment that he remembered that it was where old Schulz lived, who had written him such kind and enthusiastic letters. In his wretchedness the idea came to him of going to see his unknown friend. The town was not on the direct line on his way home, but a few hours away, by a little local line. It meant a whole night's journey, with two or three changes and interminable waits. Christophe never thought about it. He decided suddenly to go. He had an instinctive need of clinging to sympathy of some sort. He gave himself no time to think, and telegraphed to Schulz to say that he would arrive next morning. Hardly had he sent the telegram than he regretted it. He laughed bitterly at his eternal illusions. Why go to meet a new sorrow?—But it was done now. It was too late to change his mind.

These thoughts filled his last hour of waiting—his train at last was ready. He was the first to get into it, and he was so childish that he only began to breathe again when the train shook, and through the carriage window he could see the outlines of the town fading into the gray sky under the heavy downpour of the night. He thought he must have died if he had spent the night in it.

At the very hour—about six in the evening—a letter from Hassler came for Christophe at his hotel. Christophe's visit stirred many things in him. The whole afternoon he had been thinking of it bitterly, and not without sympathy for the poor boy who had come to him with such eager affection to be received so coldly. He was sorry for that reception and a little angry with himself. In truth, it had been only one of those fits of sulky whimsies to which he was subject. He thought to make it good by sending Christophe a ticket for the opera and a few words appointing a meeting after the performance—Christophe never knew anything about it. When he did not see him, Hassler thought:

"He is angry. So much the worse for him!"

He shrugged his shoulders and did not wait long for him.

Next day Christophe was far away—so far that all eternity would not have been enough to bring them together. And, they were both separated forever.

* * * * *

Peter Schulz was seventy–five. He had always had delicate health, and age had not spared him. He was fairly tail, but stooping, and his head hung down to his chest. He had a weak throat and difficulty in breathing. Asthma, catarrh, bronchitis were always upon him, and the marks of the struggles he had to make—many a night sitting up in his bed, bending forward, dripping with sweat in the effort to force a breath of air into his stifling lungs—were in the sorrowful lines on his long, thin, clean–shaven face. His nose was long and a little swollen at the top. Deep lines came from under his eyes and crossed his cheeks, that were hollow from his toothlessness. Age and infirmity had not been the only sculptors of that poor wreck of a man: the sorrows of life also had had their share in its making.—And in spite of all he was not sad. There was kindness and serenity in his large mouth. But in his eyes especially there was that which gave a touching softness to the old face. They were light gray, limpid, and transparent. They looked straight, calmly and frankly. They hid nothing of the soul. Its depths could be read in them.

His life had been uneventful. He had been alone for years. His wife was dead. She was not very good, or very intelligent, and she was not at all beautiful. But he preserved a tender memory of her. It was twenty–five years since he had lost her, and he had never once failed a night to have a little imaginary conversation, sad and tender, with her before he went to sleep. He shared all his doings with her.—He had had no children. That was the great sorrow of his life. He had transferred his need of affection to his pupils, to whom he was attached as a father to his sons. He had found very little return. An old heart can feel very near to a young heart and almost of the same age; knowing how brief are the years that lie between them. But the young man never has any idea of that. To him an old man is a man of another age, and besides, he is absorbed by his immediate anxieties and instinctively turns away from the melancholy end of all his efforts. Old Schulz had sometimes found gratitude in his pupils who were touched by the keen and lively interest he took in everything good or ill that happened to them. They used to come and see him from time to time. They used to write and thank him when they left the university. Some of them used to go on writing occasionally during the years following.

And then old Schulz would hear nothing more of them except in the papers which kept him informed of their advancement, and he would be as glad of their success as though it was his own. He was never hurt by their silence. He found a thousand excuses for it. He never doubted their affection and used to ascribe even to the most selfish the feelings that he had for them.

But his books were his greatest refuge. They neither forgot nor deceived him. The souls which he cherished in them had risen above the flood of time. They were inscrutable, fixed for eternity in the love they inspired and seemed to feel, and gave forth once more to those who loved them. He was Professor of AEsthetics and the History of Music, and he was like an old wood quivering with the songs of birds. Some of these songs sounded very far away. They came from the depths of the ages. But they were not the least sweet and mysterious of all.—Others were familiar and intimate to him, dear companions; their every phrase reminded him of the joys and sorrows of his past life, conscious or unconscious:—(for under every day lit by the light of the sun there are unfolded other days lit by a light unknown)—And there were some songs that he had never yet heard, songs which said the things that he had been long awaiting and needing; and his heart opened to receive them like the earth to receive rain. And so old Schulz listened, in the silence of his solitary life, to the forest filled with birds, and, like the monk of the legend, who slept in the ecstasy of the song of the magic bird, the years passed over him and the evening of life was come, but still he had the heart of a boy of twenty.

He was not only rich in music. He loved the poets—old and new. He had a predilection for those of his own country, especially for Goethe; but he also loved those of other countries. He was a learned man and could read several languages. In mind he was a contemporary of Herder and the great *Weltbuerger*—the "citizens of the world" of the end of the eighteenth century. He had lived through the years of bitter struggle which preceded and followed seventy, and was immersed in their vast idea. And although he adored Germany, he was not "vainglorious" about it. He thought, with Herder, that *"among all vainglorious men, he who is vainglorious of his nationality is the completest fool,"* and, with Schiller, that *"it is a poor ideal only to write for one nation."* And he was timid of mind, but his heart was large, and ready to welcome lovingly everything beautiful in the world. Perhaps he was too indulgent with mediocrity; but his instinct never doubted as to what was the best; and if he was not strong enough to condemn the sham artists admired by public opinion, he was always strong enough to defend the artists of originality and power whom public opinion disregarded. His kindness often led him astray. He was fearful of committing any injustice, and when he did not like what others liked, he never doubted but that it must be he who was mistaken, and he would manage to love it. It was so sweet to him to love! Love and admiration were even more necessary to his moral being than air to his miserable lungs. And so how grateful he was to those who gave him a new opportunity of showing them!—Christophe could have no idea of what his *Lieder* had been to him. He himself had not felt them nearly so keenly when he had written them. His songs were to him only a few sparks thrown out from his inner fire. He had cast them forth and would cast forth others. But to old Schulz they were a whole world suddenly revealed to him—a whole world to be loved. His life had been lit up by them.

* * * * *

A year before he had had to resign his position at the university. His health, growing more and more precarious, prevented his lecturing. He was ill and in bed when Wolf's Library had sent him as usual a parcel of the latest music they had received, and in it were Christophe's *Lieder*. He was alone. He was without relatives. The few that he had had were long since dead. He was delivered into the hands of an old servant, who profited by his weakness to make him do whatever she liked. A few friends hardly younger than himself used to come and see him from time to time, but they were not in very good health either, and when the weather was bad they too stayed indoors and missed their visits. It was winter then and the streets were covered with melting snow. Schulz had not seen anybody all day. It was dark in the room. A yellow fog was drawn over the windows like a screen, making it impossible to see out. The heat of the stove was thick and oppressive. From the church hard by an old peal of bells of the seventeenth century chimed every quarter of an hour, haltingly and horribly out of tune, scraps of monotonous chants, which seemed grim in their heartiness to Schulz when he was far from gay himself. He was coughing, propped up by a heap of pillows. He was trying to read Montaigne, whom he loved; but now he did not find as much pleasure in reading him as usual. He let the book fall, and was breathing with difficulty and dreaming. The parcel of music was on the bed. He had not the courage to open it. He was sad at heart. At last he sighed, and when he had very carefully untied the string, he put on his spectacles and began to read the pieces of music. His thoughts were elsewhere, always returning to memories which he was trying to thrust aside.

The book he was holding was Christophe's. His eyes fell on an old canticle the words of which Christophe had taken from a simple, pious poet of the seventeenth century, and had modernized them. The *Christliches Wanderlied* (The Christian Wanderer's Song) of Paul Gerhardt.

Hoff! O du arme Seele,
Hoff! und sei unverzagt.

Enwarte nur der Zeit,
So wirst du schon erblicken
Die Sonne der schoensten Freud.

Hope, oh! thou wretched soul,
Hope, hope and be valiant!

* * * * *

Only wait then, wait,
And surely thou shalt see
The sun of lovely Joy.

Old Schulz knew the ingenuous words, but never had they so spoken to him, never so nearly.... It was not the tranquil piety, soothing and lulling the soul by its monotony. It was a soul like his own. It was his own soul, but younger and stronger, suffering, striving to hope, striving to see, and seeing, Joy. His hands trembled, great tears trickled down his cheeks. He read on:

Auf! Auf! gieb deinem Schmerze
Und Sorgen gute Nacht!
Lass fahren was das Herze
Betruebt und traurig macht!

Up! Up! and give thy sorrow
And all thy cares good–night;
And all that grieves and saddens
Thy heart be put to flight.

483

Christophe brought to these thoughts a boyish and valiant ardor, and the heroic laughter in it showed forth in the last naive and confident verses:

Bist du doch nicht Regente,
Der alles fuehren, soll,
Gott sitzt im Regimente,
Und fuehret alles wohl.

Not thou thyself art ruler
Whom all things must obey,
But God is Lord decreeing—
All follows in His way.

And when there came the superbly defiant stanzas which in his youthful barbarian insolence he had calmly plucked from their original position in the poem to form the conclusion of his *Lied*:

Und obgleich alle Teufel
Hier wollten wiederstehn,
So wird doch ohne Zweifel,
Gott nicht zuruecke gehn.

Was er ihm vorgenommen,
Und was er haben will,
Das muss doch endlich Rommen
Zu seinem Zweck und Ziel.

And even though all Devils
Came and opposed his will,
There were no cause for doubting,
God will be steadfast still:

What He has undertaken,
All His divine decree—
Exactly as He ordered
At last shall all things be.

... then there were transports of delight, the intoxication of war, the triumph of a Roman *Imperator*.

The old man trembled all over. Breathlessly he followed the impetuous music like a child dragged along by a companion. His heart beat. Tears trickled down. He stammered:

"Oh! My God!... Oh! My God!..."

He began to sob and he laughed; he was happy. He choked. He was attacked by a terrible fit of coughing. Salome, the old servant, ran to him, and she thought the old man was going to die. He went on crying, and coughing, and saying over and over again:

"Oh! My God!... My God!..."

And in the short moments of respite between the fits of coughing he laughed a little hysterically.

Salome thought he was going mad. When at last she understood the cause of his agitation, she scolded him sharply:

"How can anybody get into such a state over a piece of foolery!... Give it me! I shall take it away. You shan't see it again."

But the old man held firm, in the midst of his coughing, and he cried to Salome to leave him alone. As she insisted, he grew angry, swore, and choked himself with his oaths. Never had she known him to be angry and to stand out against her. She was aghast and surrendered her prize. But she did not mince her words with him. She told him he was an old fool and said that hitherto she had thought she had to do with a gentleman, but that now she saw her mistake; that he said things which would make a plowman blush, that his eyes were starting from his head, and if they had been pistols would have killed her.... She would have gone on for a long time in that strain if he had not got up furiously on his pillow and shouted at her:

"Go!" in so peremptory a voice that she went, slamming the door and declaring that he might call her as much as he liked, only she would not put herself out and would leave him alone to kick the bucket.

Then silence descended upon the darkening room. Once more the bells pealed placidly and grotesquely through the calm evening. A little ashamed of his anger, old Schulz was lying on his back, motionless, waiting, breathless, for the tumult in his heart to die down. He was clasping the precious *Lieder* to his breast and laughing like a child.

* * * * *

He spent the following days of solitude in a sort of ecstasy. He thought no more of his illness, of the winter, of the gray light, or of his loneliness. Everything was bright and filled with love about him. So near to death, he felt himself living again in the young soul of an unknown friend.

He tried to imagine Christophe. He did not see him as anything like what he was. He saw him rather as an idealized version of himself, as he would have liked to be: fair, slim, with blue eyes, and a gentle, quiet voice, soft, timid and tender. He idealized everything about him: his pupils, his neighbors, his friends, his old servant. His gentle, affectionate disposition and his want of the critical faculty—in part voluntary, so as to avoid any disturbing thought—surrounded him with serene, pure images like himself. It was the kindly lying which he needed if he were to live. He was not altogether deceived by it, and often in his bed at night he would sigh as he thought of a thousand little things which had happened during the day to contradict his idealism. He knew quite well that old Salome used to laugh at him behind his back with her gossips, and that she used to rob him regularly every week. He knew that his pupils were obsequious with him while they had need of him, and that after they had received all the services they could expect from him they deserted him. He knew that his former colleagues at the university had forgotten him altogether since he had retired, and that his successor attacked him in his articles, not by name, but by some treacherous allusion, and by quoting some worthless thing that he had said or by pointing out his mistakes—(a procedure very common in the world of criticism). He knew that his told friend Kunz had lied to him that very afternoon, and that he would never see again the books which his other friend, Pottpetschmidt, had borrowed for a few days,—which was hard for a man who, like himself, was as attached to his books as to living people. Many other sad things, old or new, would come to him. He tried not to think of them, but they were there all the same. He was conscious of them. Sometimes the memory of them would pierce him like some rending sorrow.

"Oh! My God! My God!..."

He would groan in the silence of the night.—And then fee would discard such hurtful thoughts; he would deny them; he would try to be confident, and optimistic, and to believe in human truth; and he would believe. How often had his illusions been brutally destroyed!—But always others springing into life, always, always.... He could not do without them.

The unknown Christophe became a fire of warmth to his life. The first cold, ungracious letter which he received from him would have hurt him—(perhaps it did so)—but he would not admit it, and it gave him a childish joy. He was so modest and asked so little of men that the little he received from them was enough to feed his need of loving and being grateful to them. To see Christophe was a happiness which he had never dared to hope for, for he was too old now to journey to the banks of the Rhine, and as for asking Christophe to come to him, the idea had never even occurred to him.

Christophe's telegram reached him in the evening, just as he was sitting down to dinner. He did not understand at first. He thought he did not know the signature. He thought there was some mistake, that the telegram was not for him. He read it three times. In his excitement his spectacles would not stay on his nose. The lamp gave a very bad light, and the letters danced before his eyes. When he did understand he was so overwhelmed that he forgot to eat. In vain did Salome shout at him. He could not swallow a morsel. He threw his napkin on the table, unfolded,—a thing he never did. He got up, hobbled to get his hat and stick, and went out. Old Schulz's first thought on receiving such good news was to go and share it with others, and to tell his friends of Christophe's coming.

He had two friends who were music mad like himself, and he had succeeded in making them share his enthusiasm for Christophe. Judge Samuel Kunz and the dentist, Oscar Pottpetschmidt, who was an excellent singer. The three old friends had often talked about Christophe, and they had played all his music that they could find. Pottpetschmidt sang, Schulz accompanied, and Kunz listened. They would go into ecstasies for hours together. How often had they said while they were playing:

"Ah! If only Krafft were here!"

Schulz laughed to himself in the street for the joy he had and was going to give. Night was falling, and Kunz lived in a little village half an hour away from the town. But the sky was clear; it was a soft April evening. The nightingales were singing. Old Schulz's heart was overflowing with happiness. He breathed without difficulty, he walked like a boy. He strode along gleefully, without heeding the stones against which he kicked in the darkness. He turned blithely into the side of the road when carts came along, and exchanged a merry greeting with the drivers, who looked at him in astonishment when the lamps showed the old man climbing up the bank of the road.

Night was fully come when he reached Kunz's house, a little way out of the village in a little garden. He drummed on the door and shouted at the top of his voice. A window was opened and Kunz appeared in alarm. He peered through the door and asked:

"Who is there? What is it?"

Schulz was out of breath, but he called gladly:

"Krafft—Krafft is coming to–morrow...." Kunz did not understand; but he recognized the voice:

"Schulz!... What! At this hour? What is it?" Schulz repeated:

"To–morrow, he is coming to–morrow morning!...'

"What?" asked Kunz, still mystified.

"Krafft!" cried Schulz.

Kunz pondered the word for a moment; then a loud exclamation showed that he had understood.

"I am coming down!" he shouted.

The window was closed. He appeared on the steps with a lamp in his hand and came down into the garden. He was a little stout old man, with a large gray head, a red beard, red hair on his face and hands. He took little steps and he was smoking a porcelain pipe. This good natured, rather sleepy little man had never worried much about anything. For all that, the news brought by Schulz excited him; he waved his short arms and his lamp and asked:

"What? Is it him? Is he really coming?"

"To—morrow morning!" said Schulz, triumphantly waving the telegram.

The two old friends went and sat on a seat in the arbor. Schulz took the lamp. Kunz carefully unfolded the telegram and read it slowly in a whisper. Schulz read it again aloud over his shoulder. Kunz went on looking at the paper, the marks on the telegram, the time when it had been sent, the time when it had arrived, the number of words. Then he gave the precious paper back to Schulz, who was laughing happily, looked at him and wagged his head and said:

"Ah! well ... Ah! well!..."

After a moment's thought and after drawing in and expelling a cloud of tobacco smoke he put his hand on Schulz's knee and said:

"We must tell Pottpetschmidt."

"I was going to him," said Schulz.

"I will go with you," said Kunz.

He went in and put down his lamp and came back immediately. The two old men went on arm in arm. Pottpetschmidt lived at the other end of the village. Schulz and Kunz exchanged a few absent words, but they were both pondering the news. Suddenly Kunz stopped and whacked on the ground with his stick:

"Oh! Lord!" he said.... "He is away!"

He had remembered that Pottpetschmidt had had to go away that afternoon for an operation at a neighboring town where he had to spend the night and stay a day or two. Schulz was distressed. Kunz was equally put out. They were proud of Pottpetschmidt; they would have liked to show him off. They stood in the middle of the road and could not make up their minds what to do.

"What shall we do? What shall we do?" asked Kunz.

"Krafft absolutely must hear Pottpetschmidt," said Schulz.

He thought for a moment and said:

"We must sent him a telegram."

They went to the post office and together they composed a long and excited telegram of which it was very difficult to understand a word, Then they went back. Schulz reckoned:

"He could be here to–morrow morning if he took the first train."

But Kunz pointed out that it was too late and that the telegram would not be sent until the morning. Schulz nodded, and they said:

"How unfortunate!"

They parted at Kunz's door; for in spite of his friendship for Schulz it did not go so far as to make him commit the imprudence of accompanying Schulz outside the village, and even to the end of the road by which he would have had to come back alone in the dark. It was arranged that Kunz should dine on the morrow with Schulz. Schulz looked anxiously at the sky:

"If only it is fine to–morrow!"

And his heart was a little lighter when Kunz, who was supposed to have a wonderful knowledge of meteorology, looked gravely at the sky—(for he was no less anxious than Schulz that Christophe should see their little countryside in all its beauty)—and said:

"It will be fine to–morrow."

* * * * *

Schulz went along the road to the town and came to it not without having stumbled more than once in the ruts and the heaps of stones by the wayside. Before he went home he called in at the confectioner's to order a certain tart which was the envy of the town. Then he went home, but just as he was going in he turned back to go to the station to find out the exact time at which the train arrived. At last he did go home and called Salome and discussed at length the dinner for the morrow. Then only he went to bed worn out; but he was as excited as a child on Christmas Eve, and all night he turned about and about and never slept a wink. About one o'clock in the morning he thought of getting up to go and tell Salome to cook a stewed carp for dinner; for she was marvelously successful with that dish. He did not tell her; and it was as well, no doubt. But he did get up to arrange all sorts of things in the room he meant to give Christophe; he took a thousand precautions so that Salome should not hear him, for he was afraid of being scolded. All night long he was afraid of missing the train although Christophe could not arrive before eight o'clock. He was up very early. He first looked at the sky; Kunz had not made a mistake; it was glorious weather. On tiptoe Schulz went down to the cellar; he had not been there for a long time, fearing the cold and the steep stairs; he selected his best wines, knocked his head hard against the ceiling as he came up again, and thought he was going to choke when he reached the top of the stairs with his full basket. Then he went to the garden with his shears; ruthlessly he cut his finest roses and the first branches of lilac in flower. Then he went up to his room again, shaved feverishly, and cut himself more than once. He dressed carefully and set out for the station. It was seven o'clock. Salome had not succeeded in making him take so much as a drop of milk, for he declared that Christophe would not have had breakfast when he arrived and that they would have breakfast together when they came from the station.

He was at the station three–quarters of an hour too soon. He waited and waited for Christophe and finally missed him. Instead of waiting patiently at the gate he went on to the platform and lost his head in the crowd of people coming and going. In spite of the exact information of the telegram he had imagined, God knows why, that Christophe would arrive by a different train from that which brought him; and besides it had never occurred to him that Christophe would get out of a fourth–class carriage. He stayed on for more than half an hour waiting at the station, when Christophe, who had long since arrived, had gone straight to his house. As a crowning misfortune Salome had just gone out to do her shopping; Christophe found the door shut. The woman next door whom Salome had told to say, in case any one should ring, that she would soon be back, gave the message without any addition to it. Christophe, who had not come to see Salome and did not even know who she was, thought it a very bad joke; he asked if *Herr Universitaets Musikdirektor* Schulz was not at home. He was told "Yes," but the woman could not tell him where he was. Christophe was furious and went away.

When old Schulz came back with a face an ell long and learned from Salome, who had just come in too, what had happened he was in despair; he almost wept. He stormed at his servant for her stupidity in going out while he was away and not having even given instructions that Christophe was to be kept waiting. Salome replied in the same way that she could not imagine that he would be so foolish as to miss a man whom he had gone to meet. But the old man did not stay to argue with her; without losing a moment he hobbled out of doors again and went off to look for Christophe armed with the very vague clues given him by his neighbors.

Christophe had been offended at finding nobody and not even a word of excuse. Not knowing what to do until the next train he went and walked about the town and the fields, which, he thought very pretty. It was a quiet reposeful little town sheltered between gently sloping hills; there were gardens round the houses, cherry–trees and flowers, green lawns, beautiful shady trees, pseudo–antique ruins, white busts of bygone princesses on marble columns in the midst of the trees, with gentle and pleasing faces. All about the town were meadows, and hills. In the flowering trees blackbirds whistled joyously, for many little orchestras of flutes gay and solemn. It was not long before Christophe's ill–humor vanished; he forgot Peter Schulz.

The old man rushed vainly through the streets questioning people; he went up to the old castle on the hill above the town, and was coming back in despair when, with his keen, far–sighted eyes, he saw some distance away a man lying in a meadow in the shade of a thorn. He did not know Christophe; he had no means of being sure that it was he. Besides, the man's back was turned towards him and his face was half hidden in the grass. Schulz prowled along the road and about the meadow with his heart beating:

"It is he ... No, it is not he..."

He dared not call to him. An idea struck him; he began to sing the last bars of Christophe's *Lied*:

"*Auf! Auf!...*" (Up! Up!...)

Christophe rose to it like a fish out of the water and shouted the following bars at the top of his voice. He turned gladly. His face was red and there was grass in his hair. They called to each other by name and ran together. Schulz strode across the ditch by the road;

Christophe leaped the fence. They shook hands warmly and went back to the house laughing and talking loudly. The old man told how he had missed him. Christophe, who a moment before had decided to go away without making any further attempt to see Schulz, was at once conscious of his kindness and simplicity and began to love him. Before they arrived they had already confided many things to each other.

When they reached the house they found Kunz, who, having learned that Schulz had gone to look for Christophe, was waiting quietly. They were given *cafe au lait*. But Christophe said that he had breakfasted at an inn. The old man was upset; it was a real grief to him that Christophe's first meal in the place should not have been in his house; such small things were of vast importance to his fond heart. Christophe, who understood him, was amused by it secretly, and loved him the more for it. And to console him he assured him that he had appetite enough for two breakfasts; and he proved his assertion.

All his troubles had gone from his mind; he felt that he was among true friends and he began to recover. He told them about his journey and his rebuffs in a humorous way; he looked like a schoolboy on holiday. Schulz beamed and devoured him with his eyes and laughed heartily.

It was not long before conversation turned upon the secret bond that united the three of them: Christophe's music. Schulz was longing to hear Christophe play some of his compositions; but he dared not ask him to do so. Christophe was striding about the room and talking. Schulz watched him whenever he went near the open piano; and he prayed inwardly that he might stop at it. The same thought was in Kunz. Their hearts beat when they saw him sit down mechanically on the piano stool, without stopping talking, and then without looking at the instrument run his fingers over the keys at random. As Schulz expected hardly had Christophe struck a few arpeggios than the sound took possession of him; he went on striking chords and still talking; then there came whole phrases; and then he stopped talking and began to play. The old men exchanged a meaning glance, sly and happy.

"Do you know that?" asked Christophe, playing one of his *Lieder*.

"Do I know it?" said Schulz delightedly. Christophe said without stopping, half turning his head:

"Euh! It is not very good. Your piano!" The old man was very contrite. He begged pardon:

"It is old," he said humbly. "It is like myself." Christophe turned round and looked at the old man, who seemed to be asking pardon for his age, took both his hands, and laughed. He looked into his honest eyes:

"Oh!" he said, "you are younger than I." Schulz laughed aloud and spoke of his old body and his infirmities.

"Ta, ta, ta!" said Christophe, "I don't mean that; I know what I am saying. It is true, isn't it, Kunz?"

(They had already suppressed the "*Herr.*")

Kunz agreed emphatically.

Schulz tried to find the same indulgence for his piano. "It has still some beautiful notes," he said timidly.

And he touched them–four or five notes that were fairly true, half an octave in the middle register of the instrument, Christophe understood that it was an old friend and he said kindly,—thinking of Schulz's eyes:

"Yes. It still has beautiful eyes."

Schulz's face lit up. He launched out on an involved eulogy of his old piano, but he dropped immediately, for Christophe had begun to play again. *Lieder* followed *Lieder*; Christophe sang them softly. With tears in his eyes Schulz followed his every movement. With his hands folded on his stomach Kunz closed his eyes the better to enjoy it. From time to time Christophe turned beaming towards the two old men who were absolutely delighted, and he said with a naive enthusiasm at which they never thought of laughing:

"Hein! It is beautiful I... And this! What do you say about this?... And this again!... This is the most beautiful of all.... Now I will play you something which will make your hair curl...."

As he was finishing a dreamy fragment the cuckoo clock began to call. Christophe started and shouted angrily. Kunz was suddenly awakened and rolled his eyes fearfully. Even Schulz did not understand at first. Then when he saw Christophe shaking his fist at the calling bird and shouting to someone in the name of Heaven to take the idiot and throw it away, the ventriloquist specter, he too discovered for the first time in his life that the noise was intolerable; and he took a chair and tried to mount it to take down the spoil–sport. But he nearly fell and Kunz would not let him try again; he called Salome. She came without hurrying herself, as usual, and was staggered to find the clock thrust into her hands, which Christophe in his impatience had taken down himself.

"What am I to do with it?" she asked.

"Whatever you like. Take it away! Don't let us see it again!" said Schulz, no less impatient than Christophe.

(He wondered how he could have borne such a horror for so long.)

Salome thought that they were surely all cracked.

The music went on. Hours passed. Salome came and announced that dinner was served. Schulz bade her be silent. She came again ten minutes later, then once again, ten minutes after that; this time she was beside herself and boiling with rage while she tried to look unperturbed; she stood firmly in, the middle of the room and in spite of Schulz's desperate gestures she asked in a brazen voice:

"Do the gentlemen prefer to eat their dinner cold or burned? It does not matter to me. I only await your orders."

Schulz was confused by her scolding and tried to retort; but Christophe burst out laughing. Kunz followed his example and at length Schulz laughed too. Salome, satisfied with the effect she had produced, turned on her heels with the air of a queen who is graciously pleased to pardon her repentant subjects.

"That's a good creature!" said Christophe, getting up from the piano. "She is right. There is nothing so intolerable as an audience arriving in the middle of a concert."

They sat at table. There was an enormous and delicious repast. Schulz had touched Salome's vanity and she only asked an excuse to display her art. There was no lack of opportunity for her to exercise it. The old friends were tremendous feeders. Kunz was a different man at table; he expanded like a sun; he would have done well as a sign for a restaurant. Schulz was no less susceptible to good cheer; but his ill health imposed more restraint upon him. It is true that generally he did not pay much heed to that; and he had to pay for it. In that event he did not complain, if he were ill at least he knew why. Like Kunz he had recipes of his own handed down from father to son for generations. Salome was accustomed therefore to work for connoisseurs. But on this occasion, she had contrived to include all her masterpieces in one menu; it was like an exhibition of the unforgettable cooking of Germany, honest and unsophisticated, with all the scents of all the herbs, and thick sauces, substantial soups, perfect stews, wonderful carp, sauerkraut, geese, plain cakes, aniseed and caraway seed bread. Christophe was in raptures with his mouth full, and he ate like an ogre; he had the formidable capacity of his father and grandfather, who would have devoured a whole goose. But he could live just as well for a whole week on bread and cheese, and cram when occasion served. Schulz was cordial and ceremonious and watched him with kind eyes, and plied him with all the wines of the Rhine. Kunz was shining and recognized him as a brother. Salome's large face was beaming happily. At first she had been deceived when Christophe came. Schulz had spoken about him so much beforehand that she had fancied him as an Excellency, laden with letters and honors. When she saw him she cried out:

"What! Is that all?"

But at table Christophe won her good graces; she had never seen anybody so splendidly do justice to her talent. Instead of going back to her kitchen she stayed by the door to watch Christophe, who was saying all sorts of absurd things without missing a bite, and with her hands on her hips she roared with laughter. They were all glad and happy. There vas only one shadow over their joy: the absence of Pottpetschmidt. They often returned to it.

"Ah! If he were here! How he would eat! How he would drink! How he would sing!"

Their praises of him were inexhaustible.

"If only Christophe could see him!... But perhaps he would be able to. Perhaps Pottpetschmidt would return in the evening, on that night at latest...."

"Oh! I shall be gone to–night," said Christophe.

A shadow passed over Schulz's beaming face.

"What! Gone!" he said in a trembling voice. "But you are not going."

"Oh, yes," said Christophe gaily. "I must catch the train to–night."

Schulz was in despair. He had counted on Christophe spending the night, perhaps several nights, in his house. He murmured:

"No, no. You can't go!..."

Kunz repeated:

"And Pottpetschmidt!..."

Christophe looked at the two of them; he was touched by the dismay on their kind friendly faces and said:

"How good you are!... If you like I will go to–morrow morning."

Schulz took him by the hand.

"Ah!" he said. "How glad I am! Thank you! Thank you!"

He was like a child to whom to–morrow seems so far, so far, that it will not bear thinking on. Christophe was not going to–day; to–day was theirs; they would spend the whole evening together; he would sleep under his roof; that was all that Schulz saw; he would not look further.

They became merry again. Schulz rose suddenly, looked very solemn, and excitedly and slowly proposed the toast of their guest, who had given him the immense joy and honor of visiting the little town and his humble house; he drank to his happy return, to his success, to his glory, to every happiness in the world, which with all his heart he wished him. And then he proposed another toast "to noble music,"—another to his old friend Kunz,—another to spring,—and he did not forget Pottpetschmidt. Kunz in his turn drank to Schulz and the others, and Christophe, to bring the toasts to an end, proposed the health of dame Salome, who blushed crimson. Upon that, without giving the orators time to reply, he began a familiar song which the two old men took up; after that another, and then another for three parts which was all about friendship and music and wine; the whole was accompanied by loud laughter and the clink of glasses continually touching.

It was half–past three when they got up from the table. They were rather drowsy. Kunz sank into a chair; he was longing to have a sleep. Schulz's legs were worn out by his exertions of the morning and by standing for his toasts. They both hoped that Christophe would sit at the piano again and go on playing for hours. But the terrible boy, who was in fine form, first struck two or three chords on the piano, shut it abruptly, looked out of the window, and asked if they could not go for a walk until supper. The country attracted him. Kunz showed little enthusiasm, but Schulz at once thought it an excellent idea and declared that he must show their guest the walk round the *Schoenbuchwaelder*. Kunz made a face; but he did not protest and got up with the others; he was as desirous as Schulz of showing Christophe the beauties of the country.

They went out. Christophe took Schulz's arm and made him walk a little faster than the old man liked. Kunz followed mopping his brow. They talked gaily. The people standing at their doors watched them pass and thought that *Herr Professor* Schulz looked like a young man. When they left the town they took to the fields. Kunz complained of the heat. Christophe was merciless and declared that the air was exquisite. Fortunately for the two old men, they stopped frequently to argue and they forgot the length of the walk in their conversation. They went into the woods. Schulz recited verses of Goethe and Moerike. Christophe loved poetry, but he could not remember any, and while he listened he stepped into a vague dream in which music replaced the words and made him forget them. He admired Schulz's memory. What a difference there was between the vivacity of mind of this poor rich old man, almost impotent, shut up in his room for a great part of the year, shut up in his little provincial town almost all his life,—and Hassler, young, famous, in the very thick of the artistic movement, and touring over all Europe for his concerts and yet interested in nothing and unwilling to know anything! Not only was Schulz in touch with every manifestation of the art of the day that Christophe knew, but he knew an immense amount about musicians of the past and of other countries of whom Christophe had never heard. His memory was a great reservoir in which all the beautiful waters of the heavens were collected. Christophe never wearied of dipping into it, and Schulz was glad of Christophe's interest. He had sometime? found willing listeners or docile pupils, but he had never yet found a young and ardent heart with which he could share his enthusiasms, which sometimes so swelled in him that he was like to choke.

They had become the best friends in the world when unhappily the old man chanced to express his admiration for Brahms. Christophe was at once coldly angry; he dropped Schulz's arm and said harshly that anyone who loved Brahms could not be his friend. That threw cold water on their happiness. Schulz was too timid to argue, too honest to lie, and murmured and tried to explain. But Christophe stopped him:

"Enough?"

It was so cutting that it was impossible to reply. There was an icy silence. They walked on. The two old men dared not look at each other. Kunz coughed and tried to take up the conversation again and to talk of the woods and the weather; but Christophe sulked and would not talk and only answered with monosyllables. Kunz, finding no response from him, tried to break the silence by talking to Schulz; but Schulz's throat was dry, he could not speak. Christophe watched him out of the corner of his eyes and he wanted to laugh; he had forgiven him already. He had never been seriously angry with him; he even thought it brutal to make the poor old man sad; but he abused his power and would not appear to go back on what he had said. They remained so until they left the woods; nothing was to be heard but the weary steps of the two downcast old men; Christophe whistled through his teeth and pretended not to see them. Suddenly he could bear it no longer. He burst out laughing, turned towards Schulz and gripped his arm:

"My dear good old Schulz!" he said, looking at him affectionately. "Isn't it beautiful? Isn't it beautiful?"

He was speaking of the country and the fine day, but his laughing eyes seemed to say:

"You are good. I am a brute. Forgive me! I love you much."

The old man's heart melted. It was as though the sun had shone again after an eclipse. But a short time passed before he could utter a word. Christophe took his arm and went on talking to him more amiably than ever; in his eagerness he went faster and faster without noticing the strain upon his two companions. Schulz did not complain; he did not even notice his fatigue; he was so happy. He knew that he would have to pay for that day's rashness; but he thought:

"So much the worse for to–morrow! When *he* is gone I shall have plenty of time to rest."

But Kunz, who was not so excited, followed fifteen yards behind and looked a pitiful object. Christophe noticed it at last. He begged his pardon confusedly and proposed that they should lie down in a meadow in the shade of the poplars. Of course Schulz acquiesced without a thought for the effect it might have on his bronchitis. Fortunately Kunz thought of it for him; or at least he made it an excuse for not running any risk from the moisture of the grass when he was in such a perspiration. He suggested that they should take the train back to the town from a station close by. They did so. In spite of their fatigue they had to hurry, so as not to be late, and they reached the station just as the train came in.

At the sight of them a big man threw himself out of the door of a carriage and roared the names of Schulz and Kunz, together with all their titles and qualities, and he waved his arms like a madman. Schulz and Kunz shouted in reply and also waved their arms; they rushed to the big man's compartment and he ran to meet them, jostling the people on the platform. Christophe was amazed and ran after them asking:

"What is it?"

And the others shouted exultantly:

"It is Pottpetschmidt!"

The name did not convey much to him. He had forgotten the toasts at dinner. Pottpetschmidt in the carriage and Schulz and Kunz on the step were making a deafening noise, they were marveling at their encounter. They climbed into the train as it was going. Schulz introduced Christophe. Pottpetschmidt bowed as stiff as a poker and his features lost all expression; then when the formalities were over he caught hold of Christophe's hand and shook it five or six times, as though he were trying to pull his arm out, and then began to shout again. Christophe was able to make out that he thanked God and his stars for the extraordinary meeting. That did not keep him from slapping his thigh a moment later and crying out upon the misfortune of having had to go away—he who never went away—just when the *Herr Kapellmeister* was coming. Schulz's telegram had only reached him that morning an hour after the train went; he was asleep when it arrived and they had not thought it worth while to wake him. He had stormed at the hotel people all morning. He was still storming. He had sent his patients away, cut his business appointments and taken the first train in his haste to return, but the infernal train had missed the connection on the main line; Pottpetschmidt had had to wait three hours at a station; he had exhausted all the expletives in his vocabulary and fully twenty times had narrated his misadventures to other travelers who were also waiting, and a porter at the station. At last he had started again. He was fearful of arriving too late ... But, thank God! Thank God!...

He took Christophe's hands again and crushed them in his vast paws with their hairy fingers. He was fabulously stout and tall in proportion; he had a square head, close cut red hair, a clean–shaven pock–marked face, big eyes, large nose, thin lips, a double chin, a short neck, a monstrously wide back, a stomach like a barrel, arms thrust out by his body, enormous feet and hands; a gigantic mass of flesh, deformed by excess in eating and drinking; one of those human tobacco–jars that one sees sometimes rolling along the streets in the towns of Bavaria, which keep the secret of that race of men that is produced by a system of gorging similar to that of the Strasburg geese. He listened with joy and warmth like a pot of butter, and with his two hands on his outstretched knees, or on those of his neighbors, he never stopped talking, hurling consonants into the air like a catapult and making them roll along. Occasionally he would have a fit of laughing which made him shake all over; he would throw back his head, open his mouth, snorting, gurgling, choking. His laughter would infect Schulz and Kunz and when it was over they would look at Christophe as they dried their eyes. They seemed to be asking him:

"Hein!... And what do you say?"

Christophe said nothing; he thought fearfully:

"And this monster sings my music?"

They went home with Schulz. Christophe hoped to avoid Pottpetschmidt's singing and made no advances in spite of Pottpetschmidt's hints. He was itching to be heard. But Schulz and Kunz were too intent oh showing their friend off; Christophe had to submit. He sat at the piano rather ungraciously; he thought:

"My good man, my good man, you don't know what is in store for you; have a care! I will spare you nothing."

He thought that he would hurt Schulz and he was angry at that; but he was none the less determined to hurt him rather than have this Falstaff murdering his music. He was spared the pain of hurting his old friend: the fat man had an admirable voice. At the first bars Christophe gave a start of surprise. Schulz, who never took his eyes off him, trembled; he thought that Christophe was dissatisfied; and he was only reassured when he saw his face grow brighter and brighter as he went on playing. He was lit up by the reflection of Christophe's delight; and when the song was finished and Christophe turned round and declared that he had never heard any of his songs sung so well, Schulz found a joy in all sweeter and greater than Christophe's in his satisfaction, sweeter and greater than Pottpetschmidt's in his triumph; for they had only their own pleasure, and Schulz had that of his two friends. They went on with the music. Christophe cried aloud; he could not understand how so ponderous and common a creature could succeed in reading the idea of his *Lieder*. No doubt there were not exactly all the shades of meaning, but there was the impulse and the passion which he had never quite succeeded in imparting to professional singers. He looked at Pottpetschmidt and wondered:

"Does he really feel that?"

But he could not see in his eyes any other light than that of satisfied vanity. Some unconscious force stirred in that solid flesh. The blind passion was like an army fighting without knowing against whom or why. The spirit of the *Lieder* took possession of it and it obeyed gladly, for it had need of action; and, left to itself, it never would have known how.

Christophe fancied that on the day of the Creation the Great Sculptor did not take very much trouble to put in order the scattered members of his rough–hewn creatures, and that He had adjusted them anyhow without bothering to find out whether they were suited to each other, and so every one was made up of all sorts of pieces; and one man was scattered among five or six different men; his brain was with one, his heart with another, and the body belonging to his soul with yet another; the instrument was on one side, the performer on the other. Certain creatures remained like wonderful violins, forever shut up in their cases, for want of anyone with the art to play them. And those who were fit to play them were found all their lives to put up with wretched scraping fiddles. He had all the more reason for thinking so as he was furious with himself for never having been able properly to sing a page of music. He had an untuned voice and could never hear himself without disgust.

However, intoxicated by his success, Pottpetschmidt began to "put expression" into Christophe's *Lieder*, that is to say he substituted his own for Christophe's. Naturally he did not think that the music gained by the change, and he grew gloomy. Schulz saw it. His lack of the critical faculty and his admiration for his friends would not have allowed him of his own accord to set it down to Pottpetschmidt's bad taste. But his affection for Christophe made him perceptive of the young man's finest shades of thought; he was no longer in himself, he was in Christophe; and he too suffered from Pottpetschmidt's affectations. He tried hard to stop his going down that perilous slope. It was not easy to silence Pottpetschmidt. Schulz found it enormously difficult, when the singer had exhausted Christophe's repertory, to keep him from breaking out into the lucubrations of mediocre compositions at the mention of whose names Christophe curled up and bristled like a porcupine.

Fortunately the announcement of supper muzzled Pottpetschmidt. Another field for his valor was opened for him; he had no rival there; and Christophe, who was a little weary with his exploits in the afternoon, made no attempt to vie with him.

It was getting late. They sat round the table and the three friends watched Christophe; they drank in his words. It seemed very strange to Christophe to find himself in the remote little town among these old men whom he had never seen until that day and to be more intimate with them than if they had been his relations. He thought how fine it would be for an artist if he could know of the unknown friends whom his ideas find in the world,—how gladdened his heart would be and how fortified he would be in his strength. But he is rarely that; every one lives and dies alone, fearing to say what he feels the more he feels and the more he needs to express it. Vulgar flatterers have no difficulty in speaking. Those who love most have to force their lips open to say that they love. And so he must be grateful indeed to those who dare to speak; they are unconsciously collaborators with the artist.—Christophe was filled with gratitude for old Schulz. He did not confound him with his two friends; he felt that he was the soul of the little group; the others were only reflections of that living fire of goodness and love. The friendship that Kunz and Pottpetschmidt had for him was very different. Kunz was selfish; music gave him a comfortable satisfaction like a fat cat when it is stroked. Pottpetschmidt found in it the pleasure of tickled vanity and physical exercise. Neither of them troubled to understand him. But Schulz absolutely forgot himself; he loved.

It was late. The two friends went away in the night. Christophe was left alone with Schulz. He said:

"Now I will play for you alone."

He sat at the piano and played,—as he knew how to play when he had some one dear to him by his side. He played his latest compositions. The old man was in ecstasies. He sat near Christophe and never took his eyes from him and held his breath. In the goodness of his heart he was incapable of keeping the smallest happiness to himself, and in spite of himself he said:

"Ah! What a pity Kunz is not here!"

That irritated Christophe a little.

An hour passed; Christophe was still playing; they had not exchanged a word. When Christophe had finished neither spoke a word. There was silence, the house, the street, was asleep. Christophe turned and saw that the old man was weeping; he got up and went and embraced him. They talked in whispers in the stillness of the night. The clock ticked dully in the next room. Schulz talked in a whisper, with his hands clasped, and leaning forward; he was telling Christophe, in answer to his questions, about his life and his sorrow; at every turn he was ashamed of complaining and had to say:

"I am wrong ... I have no right to complain ... Everybody has been very good to me...."

And indeed he was not complaining; it was only an involuntary melancholy emanating from the dull story of his lonely life. At the most sorrowful moments he wove into it professions of faith vaguely idealistic and very sentimental which amazed Christophe, though it would have been too cruel to contradict him. At bottom there was in Schulz not so much a firm belief as a passionate desire to believe—an uncertain hope to which he clung as to a buoy. He sought the confirmation of it in Christophe's eyes. Christophe understood the appeal in the eyes of his friend, who clung to him with touching confidence, imploring him,—and dictating his answer. Then he spoke of the calm faith or strength, sure of itself, words which the old man was expecting, and they comforted him. The old man and the young had forgotten the years that lay between, them; they were near each other, like brothers of the same age, loving and helping each other; the weaker sought the support of the stronger; the old man took refuge in the young man's soul.

They parted after midnight; Christophe had to get up early to catch the train by which he had come. And so he did not loiter as he undressed. The old man had prepared his guests room as though for a visit of several months. He had put a bowl of roses on the table and a branch of laurel. He had put fresh blotting paper on the bureau. During the morning he had had an upright piano carried up. On the shelf by the bed he had placed books chosen from among his most precious and beloved. There was no detail that he had not lovingly thought out. But it was a waste of trouble: Christophe saw nothing. He flung himself on his bed and went sound asleep at once.

Schulz could not sleep. He was pondering the joy that he had had and the sorrow he must have at the departure of his friend. He was turning over in his mind the words that had been spoken. He was thinking that his dear Christophe was sleeping near him on the other side of the wall against which his bed lay. He was worn out, stiff all over, depressed; he felt that he had caught cold during the walk and that he was going to have a relapse; but he had only one thought:

"If only I can hold out until he has gone!" And he was fearful of having a fit of coughing and waking Christophe. He was full of gratitude to God, and began to compose verses to the song of old Simeon: "*Nunc dimittis* ..." He got up in a sweat to write the verses down and sat at his desk until he had carefully copied them out with an affectionate dedication, and his signature, and the date and hour. Then he lay down again with a shiver and could not get warm all night.

Dawn came. Schulz thought regretfully of the dawn of the day before. But he was angry with himself for spoiling with such thoughts the few minutes of happiness left to him; he knew that on the morrow he would regret the time fleeting then, and he tried not to waste any of it. He listened, eager for the least sound in the next room. But Christophe did not stir. He lay still just as he had gone to bed; he had not moved. Half–past six rang and he still slept. Nothing would have been easier than to make him miss the train, and doubtless he would have taken it with a laugh. But the old man was too scrupulous to use a friend so without his consent. In vain did he say to himself:

"It will not be my fault. I could not help it. It will be enough to say nothing. And if he does not wake in time I shall have another whole day with him."

He answered himself:

"No, I have no right."

And he thought it his duty to go and wake him. He knocked at his door. Christophe did not hear at first; he had to knock again. That made the old man's heart thump as he thought: "Ah! How well he sleeps! He would stay like that till mid–day!..."

At last Christophe replied gaily through the partition. When he learned the time he cried out; he was heard bustling about his room, noisily dressing himself, singing scraps of melody, while he chattered with Schulz through the wall and cracked Jokes while the old man laughed in spite of his sorrow. The door opened; Christophe appeared, fresh, rested, and happy; he had no thought of the pain he was causing. In reality there was no hurry for him to go; it would have cost him nothing to stay a few days longer; and it would have given Schulz so much pleasure! But Christophe could not know that. Besides, although he was very fond of the old man, he was glad to go; he was worn out by the day of perpetual conversation, by these people who clung to him in desperate fondness. And then he was young, he thought there would be plenty of time to meet again; he was not going to the other ends of the earth!—The old man knew that he would soon be much farther than the other ends of the earth, and he looked at Christophe for all eternity.

In spite of hit extreme weariness he took him to the station. A fine cold rain was falling noiselessly. At the station when he opened his purse Christophe found that he had not enough money to buy his ticket home. He knew that Schulz would gladly lead him the money, but he would not ask him for it.... Why? Why deny those who love you the opportunity—the happiness of doing you a service?... He would not out of discretion—perhaps out of vanity. He took a ticket for a station on the way, saying that he would do the rest of the journey on foot.

The time for leaving came. They embraced on the footboard of the carriage. Schulz slipped the poem he had written during the night into Christophe's hand. He stayed on the platform below the compartment. They had nothing more to say to each other, as usual when good–byes are too long drawn out, but Schulz's eyes went on speaking, they never left Christophe's face until the train went.

The carriage disappeared round a curve. Schulz was left alone. He went back by the muddy path; he dragged along; suddenly he felt all his weariness, the cold, the melancholy of the rainy day. He was hardly able to reach home and to go upstairs again. Hardly had he reached his room than he was seized with an attack of asthma and coughing. Salome came to his aid. Through his involuntary groans, he said:

"What luck!... What luck that I was prepared for it...." He felt very ill. He went to bed. Salome fetched the doctor. In bed he became as limp as a rag. He could not move; only his breast was heaving and panting like a million billows. His head was heavy and feverish. He spent the whole day in living through the day before, minute by minute; he tormented himself, and then was angry with himself for complaining after so much happiness. With his hands clasped and his heart big with love he thanked God.

* * * * *

Christophe was soothed by his day and restored to confidence in himself by the affection that he had left behind him,—so he returned home. When he had gone as far as his ticket would take him he got out blithely and took to the road on foot. He had sixty kilometers to do. He was in no hurry and dawdled like a school–boy. It was April. The country was not very far on. The leaves were unfolding like little wrinkled hands at the ends of the Hack branches; the apple trees were in flower, and along the hedges the frail eglantine smiled. Above the leafless forest, where a soft greenish down was beginning to appear, on the summit of a little hill, like a trophy on the end of a lance, there rose an old Romanic castle. Three black clouds sailed across the soft blue sky. Shadows chased over the country in spring, showers passed, then the bright sun shone forth again and the birds sang.

Christophe found that for some time he had been thinking of Uncle Gottfried. He had not thought of the poor man for a long time, and he wondered why the memory of him should so obstinately obsess him now; he was haunted by it as he walked along a path along a canal that reflected the poplars; and the image of his uncle was so actual that as he turned a great wall he thought he saw him coming towards him.

The sky grew dark. A heavy downpour of rain and hail fell, and thunder rumbled in the distance. Christophe was near a village; he could see its pink walls and red roofs among the clumps of trees. He hurried and took shelter under the projecting roof of the nearest house. The hail−stones came lashing down; they rang out on the tiles and fell down into the street like pieces of lead. The ruts were overflowing. Above the blossoming orchards a rainbow flung its brilliant garish scarf over the dark blue clouds.

On the threshold a girl was standing knitting. She asked Christophe to enter. He accepted the invitation. The room into which he stepped was used as a kitchen, a dining−room, and a bed−room. At the back a stew−pot hung over a great fire. A peasant woman who was cleaning vegetables wished Christophe good−day, and bade him go near the fire to dry himself. The girl fetched a bottle of wine and gave him to drink. She sat on the other side of the table and went on knitting, while at the same time she looked after two children who were playing at testing each other's eyes with those grasses which are known in the country as "thiefs" or "sweeps." She began to talk to Christophe. It was only after a moment that he saw that she was blind. She was not pretty. She was a big girl, with red cheeks, white teeth, and strong arms, but her features were irregular; she had the smiling, rather expressionless air of many blind people, and also their mania for talking of things and people as though they could see them. At first Christophe was startled and wondered if she were making fun of him when she said that he looked well and that the country was looking very pretty. But after looking from the blind girl to the woman who was cleaning the vegetables, he saw that nobody was surprised and that it was no joke—(there was nothing to joke about indeed).—The two women asked Christophe friendly questions as to whither he was going and whence he had come. The blind girl joined in the conversation with a rather exaggerated eagerness; she agreed with, or commented on, Christophe's remarks about the road and the fields. Naturally her observations were often wide of the mark. She seemed to be trying to pretend that she could see as well as he.

Other members of the family came in: a healthy peasant of thirty and his young wife. Christophe talked to them all, and watched the clearing sky, waiting for the moment to set out again. The blind girl hummed an air while she plied her knitting needles. The air brought back all sorts of old memories to Christophe.

"What!" he said. "You know that." (Gottfried had taught her it.)

He hummed the following notes. The girl began to laugh. She sang the first half of the phrases and he finished them. He had just got up to go and look at the weather and he was walking round the room, mechanically taking stock of every corner of it, when near the dresser he saw an object which made him start. It was a long twisted stick, the handle of which was roughly carved to represent a little bent man bowing. Christophe knew it well, he had played with it as a child. He pounced on the stick and asked in a choking voice:

"Where did you get this?... Where did you get it?" The man looked up and said:

"A friend left it here—an old friend who is dead."

Christophe cried:

"Gottfried?"

They all turned and asked:

"How do you know ...?"

And when Christophe told them that Gottfried was his uncle, they were all greatly excited. The blind girl got up; her ball of wool rolled across the room; she stopped her work and took Christophe's hands and said in a great state of emotion:

"You are his nephew?"

They all talked at once. Christophe asked:

"But how ... how do you come to know him?" The man replied:

"It was here that he died."

They sat down again, and when the excitement had gone down a little, the mother told, as she went on with her work, that Gottfried used to go to the house for many years; he always used to stay there on his way to and fro from his journeys. The last time he came—(it was in last July)—he seemed very tired, and when he took off his pack it was some time before he could speak a word, but they did not take any notice of it because they were used to seeing him like that when he arrived and knew that he was short of breath. He did not complain either. He never used to complain; he always used to find some happiness in the most unpleasant things. When he was doing some exhausting work he used to be glad thinking how good it would be in bed at night, and when he was ill he used to say how good it would be when he was not ill any longer....

"And, sir, it is wrong to be always content," added the woman, "for if you axe not sorry for yourself, nobody will pity you. I always complain...."

Well, nobody had paid any attention to him. They had even chaffed him about looking so well and Modesta—(that was the blind girl's name)—who had just relieved him of his pack had asked him if he was never going to be tired of running like a young man. He smiled in reply, for he could not speak. He sat on the seat by the door. Everybody went about their work, the men to the fields, the woman to her cooking. Modesta went near the seat, she stood leaning against the door with her knitting in her hands and talked to Gottfried. He did not reply; she did not ask him for any reply and told him everything that had happened since his last visit. He breathed with difficulty and she heard him trying hard to speak. Instead of being anxious about him she said:

"Don't speak. Just rest. You shall talk presently.... How can people tire themselves out like that!..."

And then he did not talk or even try to talk. She went on with her story thinking that he was listening. He sighed and said nothing. When the mother came a little later she found Modesta still talking and Gottfried motionless on the seat with his head flung back facing the sky; for some minutes Modesta had been talking to a dead man. She understood then that the poor man had been trying to say a few words before he died but had not been able to; then with his sad smile he had accepted that and had closed his eyes in the peace of the summer evening....

The rain had ceased. The daughter–in–law went to the stables, the son took his mattock and cleared the little gutter in front of the door which the mud had obstructed. Modesta had disappeared at the beginning of the story. Christophe was left alone in the room with the mother, and was silent and much moved. The old woman, who was rather talkative, could not bear a prolonged silence; and she began to tell him the whole history of her acquaintance with Gottfried. It went far back. When she was quite young Gottfried loved her. He dared not tell her, but it became a joke; she made fun of him, everybody made fun of him,—(it was; the custom wherever he went)—Gottfried used to come faithfully every year. It seemed natural to him that people should make fun of him, natural that she should have married and been happy with another man. She had been too happy, she had boasted too much of her happiness; then unhappiness came. Her husband died suddenly. Then his daughter,—a fine strong girl whom everybody admired, who was to be married to the son of the richest farmer of the district,—lost her sight as the result of an accident. One day when she had climbed to the great pear tree behind the house to pick the fruit the ladder slipped; as she fell a broken branch struck a blow near the eye. At first it was thought that she would escape with a scar, but later, she had had unceasing pains in her forehead; one eye lost its sight, then the other; and all their remedies had been useless. Of course the marriage was broken off; her betrothed had vanished without any explanation, and of all the young men who a month before had actually fought for a dance with her, not one had the courage—(it is quite comprehensible)—to take a blind girl to his arms. And so Modesta, who till then had been careless and gay, had fallen into such despair that she wanted to die. She refused to eat; she did nothing but weep from morning to evening, and during the night they used to hear her still moaning in her bed. They did not know what to do, they could only join her in her despair; and she only wept the more. At last they lost patience with her moaning; then they scolded her and she talked of throwing herself into the canal. The minister would come sometimes; he would talk of the good God, and eternal things, and the merit she was gaining for the next world by bearing her sorrows, but that did not console her at all. One day Gottfried came. Modesta had never been very kind to him. Not that she was naturally unkind, but she was disdainful, and besides she never thought; she loved to laugh, and there was no malice in what she said or did to him. When he heard of her misfortune he was as overwhelmed by it as though he were a member of the family. However he did not let her see it the first time he saw her. He went and sat by her side, made no allusion to her accident and began to talk quietly as he had always done before. He had no word of pity for her; he even seemed not to notice that she was blind. Only he never talked to her of things she could not see; he talked to her about what she could hear or notice in her blindness; and he did it quite simply as though it were a natural thing; it was as though he too were blind. At first she did not listen and went on weeping. But next day she listened better and even talked to him a little....

"And," the woman went on, "I do not know what he can have said to her. For we were hay–making and I was too busy to notice her. But in the evening when we came in from the fields we found her talking quietly. And after that she went on getting better. She seemed to forget her affliction. But every now and then she would think of it again; she would weep alone or try to talk to Gottfried of sad things; but he seemed not to hear, or he would not reply in the same tone; he would go on talking gravely or merrily of things which soothed and interested her. At last he persuaded her to go out of the house, which she had never left since her accident. He made her go a few yards round the garden at first, and then for a longer distance in the fields. And at last she learned to find her way everywhere and to make out everything as though she could see. She even notices things to which we never pay any attention, and she is interested in everything, whereas before she was never interested in much outside herself. That time Gottfried stayed with us longer than usual. We dared not ask him to postpone his departure, but he stayed of his own accord until he saw that she was calmer. And one day—she was out there in the yard,—I heard her laughing. I cannot tell you what an effect that had on me. Gottfried looked happy too. He was sitting near me. We looked at each other, and I am not ashamed to tell you, sir, that I kissed him with all my heart. Then he said to me:

"'Now I think I can go. I am not needed any more.'

"I tried to keep him. But he said:

"'No. I must go now. I cannot stay any longer.'

"Everybody knew that he was like the Wandering Jew: he could not stay anywhere; we did not insist. Then he went, but he arranged to come here more often, and every time it was a great joy for Modesta; she was always better after his visits. She began to work in the house again; her brother married; she looks after the children; and now she never complains and always looks happy. I sometimes wonder if she would be so happy if she had her two eyes. Yes, indeed, sir, there are days, when I think that it would be better to be like her and not to see certain ugly people and certain evil things. The world is growing very ugly, it grows worse every day.... And yet I should be very much afraid of

God taking me at my word, and for my part I would rather go on seeing the world, ugly as it is...."

Modesta came back and the conversation changed. Christophe wished to go now that the weather was fair again, but they would not let him. He had to agree to stay to supper and to spend the night with them. Modesta sat near Christophe and did not leave him all the evening. He would have liked to talk intimately to the girl whose lot filled him with pity. But she gave him no opportunity. She would only try to ask him about Gottfried. When Christophe told her certain things she did not know, she was happy and a little jealous. She was a little unwilling to talk of Gottfried herself; it was apparent that she did not tell everything, and when she did tell everything she was sorry for it at once; her memories were her property, she did not like sharing them with another; in her affection she was as eager as a peasant woman in her attachment to her land; it hurt her to think that anybody could love Gottfried as much as she. It is true that she refused to believe it; and Christophe, understanding, left her that satisfaction. As he listened to her he saw that, although she had seen Gottfried and had even seen him with indulgent eyes, since her blindness she had made of him an image absolutely different from the reality, and she had transferred to the phantom of her mind all the hunger for love that was in her. Nothing had disturbed her illusion. With the bold certainty of the blind, who calmly invent what they do not know, she said to Christophe:

"You are like him."

He understood that for years she had grown used to living in a house with closed shutters through which the truth could not enter. And now that she had learned to see in the darkness that surrounded her, and even to forget the darkness, perhaps she would have been afraid of a ray of light filtering through the gloom. With Christophe she recalled a number of rather silly trivialities in a smiling and disjointed conversation in which Christophe could not be at his ease. He was irritated by her chatter; he could not understand how a creature who had suffered so much had not become more serious in her suffering, and he could not find tolerance for such futility; every now and then he tried to talk of graver things, but they found no echo; Modesta could not—or would not—follow him.

They went to bed. It was long before Christophe could sleep. He was thinking of Gottfried and trying to disengage him from the image of Modesta's childish memories.

513

He found it difficult and was irritated. His heart ached at the thought that Gottfried had died there and that his body had no doubt lain in that very bed. He tried to live through the agony of his last moments, when he could neither speak nor make the blind girl understand, and had closed his eyes in death. He longed to have been able to raise his eyelids and to read the thoughts hidden under them, the mystery of that soul, which had gone without making itself known, perhaps even without knowing itself! It never tried to know itself, and all its wisdom lay in not desiring wisdom, or in not trying to impose its will on circumstance, but in abandoning itself to the force of circumstance, in accepting it and loving it. So he assimilated the mysterious essence of the world without even thinking of it. And if he had done so much good to the blind girl, to Christophe, and doubtless to many others who would be forever unknown, it was because, instead of bringing the customary words of the revolt of man against nature, he brought something of the indifferent peace of Nature, and reconciled the submissive soul with her. He did good like the fields, the woods, all Nature with which he was impregnated. Christophe remembered the evenings he had spent with Gottfried in the country, his walks as a child, the stories and songs in the night. He remembered also the last walk he had taken with his uncle, on the hill above the town, on a cold winter's morning, and the tears came to his eyes once more. He did not try to sleep, so as to remain with his memories. He did not wish to lose one moment of that night in the little place, filled with the soul of Gottfried, to which he had been led as though impelled by some unknown force. But while he lay listening to the irregular trickling of the fountain and the shrill cries of the bats, the healthy fatigue of youth mastered his will, and he fell asleep.

When he awoke the sun was shining: everybody on the farm was already at work. In the hall he found only the old woman and the children. The young couple were in the fields, sand Modesta had gone to milk. They looked for her in vain. She was nowhere to be found. Christophe said he would not wait for her return. He did not much want to see her, and he said that he was in a hurry. He set out after telling the old woman to bid the others good–bye for him.

As he was leaving the village at a turn of the road he the blind girl sitting on a bank under a hawthorn hedge. She got up as she heard him coming, approached him smiling, took his hand, and said:

"Come."

They climbed up through meadows to a little shady flowering field filled with tombstones, which looked down on the village. She led him to a grave and said:

"He is there."

They both knelt down. Christophe remembered another grave by which he had knelt with Gottfried, and he thought:

"Soon it will be my turn."

But there was no sadness in his thought. A great peace was ascending from the earth. Christophe leaned over the grave and said, in a whisper to Gottfried:

"Enter into me!..."

Modesta was praying, with her hands clasped and her lips moving in silence. Then she went round the grave on her knees, feeling the ground and the grass and the flowers with her hands. She seemed to caress them, her quick fingers seemed to see. They gently plucked the dead stalks of the ivy and the faded violets. She laid her hand on the curb to get up. Christophe saw her fingers pass furtively over Gottfried's name, lightly touching each letter. She said:

"The earth is sweet this morning."

She held out her hand to him. He gave her his. She made him touch the moist warm earth. He did not loose her hand. Their locked fingers plunged into the earth. He kissed Modesta. She kissed him, too.

They both rose to their feet. She held out to him a few fresh violets she had gathered, and put the faded ones into her bosom. They dusted their knees and left the cemetery without a word. In the fields the larks were singing. White butterflies danced about their heads. They sat down in a meadow a few yards away from each other. The smoke of the village was ascending direct to the sky that was washed by the rain. The still canal glimmered between the poplars. A gleaming blue mist wrapped the meadows and woods in its folds.

Modesta broke the silence. She spoke in a whisper of the beauty of the day as though she could see it. She drank in the air through her half–open lips; she listened for the sounds of creatures and things. Christophe also knew the worth of such music. He said what she was thinking and could not have said. He named certain of the cries and imperceptible tremors that they could hear in the grass, in the depths of the air. She said:

"Ah! You see that, too?"

He replied that Gottfried had taught him to distinguish them.

"You, too?" she said a little crossly.

He wanted to say to her:

"Do not be jealous."

But he saw the divine light smiling all about them: he looked at her blind eyes and was filled with pity.

"So," he asked, "it was Gottfried taught you?"

She said "Yes," and that they gave her more delight than ever before.... She did not say before "what." She never mentioned the words "eyes" or "blind."

They were silent for a moment. Christophe looked at her in pity. She felt that he was looking at her. He would have liked to tell her how much he pitied her. He would have liked her to complain, to confide in him. He asked kindly:

"You have been very unhappy?"

She sat dumb and unyielding. She plucked the blades of grass and munched them in silence. After a few moments,—(the song of a lark was going farther and farther from them in the sky),—Christophe told her how he too had been unhappy, and how Gottfried had helped him. He told her all his sorrows, his trials, as though he were thinking aloud or talking to a sister. The blind girl's face lit up as he told his story, which she followed eagerly. Christophe watched her and saw that she was on the point of speaking. She made a movement to come near him and hold his hand. He moved, too—but already she had relapsed into her impassiveness, and when he had finished, she only replied with a few banal words. Behind her broad forehead, on which there was not a line, there was the obstinacy of a peasant, hard as a stone. She said that she must go home to look after her brothers children. She talked of them with a calm smile.

He asked her:

"You are happy?"

She seemed to be more happy to hear him say the word. She said she was happy and insisted on the reasons she had for being so: she was trying to persuade herself and him that it was so. She spoke of the children, and the house, and all that she had to do....

"Oh! yes," she said, "I am very happy!" Christophe did not reply. She rose to go. He rose too. They said good–bye gaily and carelessly. Modesta's hand trembled a little in Christophe's. She said:

"You will have fine weather for your walk to–day." And she told him of a crossroads where he must not go wrong. It was as though, of the two, Christophe were the blind one.

They parted. He went down the hill. When he reached the bottom he turned. She was standing at the summit in the same place. She waved her handkerchief and made signs to him as though she saw him.

There was something heroic and absurd in her obstinacy in denying her misfortune, something which touched Christophe and hurt him. He felt how worthy Modesta was of pity and even of admiration,—and he could not have lived two days with her. As he went his way between flowering hedges he thought of dear old Schulz, and his old eyes, bright and tender, before which so many sorrows had passed which they refused to see, for they would not see hurtful realities.

"How does he see me, I wonder?" thought Christophe. "I am so different from his idea of me! To him I am what he wants me to be. Everything is in his own image, pure and noble like himself. He could not bear life if he saw it as it is."

And he thought of the girl living in darkness who denied the darkness, and tried to pretend that what was was not, and that what was not was.

Then he saw the greatness of German idealism, which he had so often loathed because in vulgar souls it is a source of hypocrisy and stupidity. He saw the beauty of the faith which Begets a world within the world, different from the world, like a little island in the ocean.—But he could not bear such a faith for himself, and refused to take refuge upon such an Island of the Dead. Life! Truth! He would not be a lying hero. Perhaps that optimistic lie which a German Emperor tried to make law for all his people was indeed necessary for weak creatures if they were to live. And Christophe would have thought it a crime to snatch from such poor wretches the illusion which upheld them. But for himself he never could have recourse to such subterfuges. He would rather die than live by illusion. Was not Art also an illusion? No. It must not be. Truth! Truth! Byes wide open, let him draw in through every pore the all–puissant breath of life, see things as they are, squarely face his misfortunes,—and laugh.

* * * * *

Several months passed. Christophe had lost all hope of escaping from the town. Hassler, the only man who could have saved him, had refused to help him. And old Schulz's friendship had been taken from him almost as soon as it had been given.

He had written once on his return, and he had received two affectionate letters, but from sheer laziness, and especially because of the difficulty he had expressing himself in a letter, he delayed thanking him for his kind words. He put off writing from day to day. And when at last he made up his mind to write he had a word from Kunz announcing the death of his old friend. Schulz had had a relapse of his bronchitis which had developed into pneumonia. He had forbidden them to bother Christophe, of whom he was always talking. In spite of his extreme weakness and many years of illness, he was not spared a long and painful end. He had charged Kunz to convey the tidings to Christophe and to tell him that he had thought of him up to the last hour; that he thanked him for all the happiness he owed him, and that his blessing would be on Christophe as long as he lived. Kunz did not tell him that the day with Christophe had probably been the reason of his relapse and the cause of his death.

Christophe wept in silence, and he felt them all the worth of the friend he had lost, and how much he loved him, and he was grieved not to have told him more of how he loved him. It was too late now. And what was left to him? The good Schulz had only appeared enough to make the void seem more empty, the night more black after he ceased to be. As for Kunz and Pottpetschmidt, they had no value outside the friendship they had for Schulz and Schulz for them. Christophe valued them at their proper worth. He wrote to them once and their relation ended there. He tried also to write to Modesta, but she answered with a commonplace letter in which she spoke only of trivialities. He gave up the correspondence. He wrote to nobody and nobody wrote to him.

Silence. Silence. From day to day the heavy cloak of silence descended upon Christophe. It was like a rain of ashes falling on him. It seemed already to be evening, and Christophe was losing his hold on life. He would not resign himself to that. The hour of sleep was not yet come. He must live.

And he could not live in Germany. The sufferings of his genius cramped by the narrowness of the little town lashed him into injustice. His nerves were raw: everything drew blood. He was like one of those wretched wild animals who perished of boredom in the holes and cages in which they were imprisoned in the *Stadtgarten* (town gardens). Christophe used often to go and look at them in sympathy. He used to look at their wonderful eyes, in which there burned—or every day grew fainter—a fierce and desperate fire. Ah! How they would have loved the brutal bullet which sets free, or the knife that strikes into their bleeding hearts! Anything rather than the savage indifference of those men who prevented them from either living or dying!

Not the hostility of the people was the hardest for Christophe to bear, but their inconsistency, their formless, shallow natures. There was no knowing how to take them. The pig–headed opposition of one of those stiff–necked, bard races who refuse to understand any new thought were much better. Against force it is possible to oppose force—the pick and the mine which hew away and blow up the hard rock. But what can be done against an amorphous mass which gives like a jelly, collapses under the least pressure, and retains no imprint of it? All thought and energy and everything disappeared in the slough. When a stone fell there were hardly more than a few ripples quivering on the surface of the gulf: the monster opened and shut its maw, and there was left no trace of what had been.

They were not enemies. Dear God! if they only had been enemies! They were people who had not the strength to love or hate, or believe or disbelieve,—in religion, in art, in politics, in daily life; and all their energies were expended in trying to reconcile the irreconcilable. Especially since the German victories they had been striving to make a compromise, a revolting intrigue between their new power and their old principles. The old idealism had not been renounced. There should have been a new effort of freedom of which they were incapable. They were content with a forgery, with making it subservient to German interests. Like the serene and subtle Schwabian, Hegel, who had waited until after Leipzig and Waterloo to assimilate the cause of his philosophy with the Prussian State—their interests having changed, their principles had changed too. When they were defeated they said that Germany's ideal was humanity. Now that they had defeated others, they said that Germany was the ideal of humanity. When other countries were more powerful, they said, with Lessing, that *patriotism is a heroic weakness which it is well to be without*" and they called themselves *"citizens of the world."* Now that they were in the ascendant, they could not enough despise the Utopias *"a la Francaise."* Universal peace, fraternity, pacific progress, the rights of man, natural equality: they said that the strongest people had absolute rights against the others, and that the others, being weaker, had no rights against themselves. It was the living God and the Incarnate Idea, the progress of which is accomplished by war, violence, and oppression. Force had become holy now that it was on their side. Force had become the only idealism and the only intelligence.

In truth, Germany had suffered so much for centuries from having idealism and no fame that she had every excuse after so many trials for making the sorrowful confession that at all costs Force must be hers. But what bitterness was hidden in such a confession from the people of Herder and Goethe! And what an abdication was the German victory, what a degradation of the German ideal! Alas! There were only too many facilities for such an abdication in the deplorable tendency even of the best Germans to submit.

"The chief characteristic of Germany," said Moser, more than a century ago, *"is obedience*." And Madame de Stael:

"They have submitted doughtily. They find philosophic reasons for explaining the least philosophic theory in the world: respect for power and the chastening emotion of fear which changes that respect into admiration."

Christophe found that feeling everywhere in Germany, from the highest to the lowest—from the William Tell of Schiller, that limited little bourgeois with muscles like a porter, who, as the free Jew Boerne says, *"to reconcile honor and fear passes before the pillar of dear Herr Gessler, with his eyes down so as to be able to say that he did not see the hat; did not disobey,"*—to the aged and respectable Professor Weisse, a man of seventy, and one of the most honored mea of learning in the town, who, when he saw a *Herr Lieutenant* coming, would make haste to give him the path and would step down into the road. Christophe's blood boiled whenever he saw one of these small acts of daily servility. They hurt him as much as though he had demeaned himself. The arrogant manners of the officers whom he met in the street, their haughty insolence, made him speechless with anger. He never would make way for them. Whenever he passed them he returned their arrogant stare. More than once he was very near causing a scene. He seemed to be looking for trouble. However, he was the first to understand the futility of such bravado; but he had moments of aberration, the perpetual constraint which he imposed on himself and the accumulation of force in him that had no outlet made him furious. Then he was ready to go any length, and he had a feeling that if he stayed a year longer in the place he would be lost. He loathed the brutal militarism which he felt weighing down upon him, the sabers clanking on the pavement, the piles of arms, and the guns placed outside the barracks, their muzzles gaping down on the town, ready to fire. Scandalous novels, which were then making a great stir, denounced the corruption of the garrisons, great and small: the officers were represented as mischievous creatures, who, outside their automatic duties, were only idle and spent their time in drinking, gambling, getting into debt, living on their families, slandering one another, and from top to bottom of the hierarchy they abused their authority at the expense of their inferiors. The idea that he would one day have to obey them stuck in Christophe's throat. He could not, no, he could never bear it, and lose his own self–respect by submitting to their humiliations and injustice.... He had no idea of the moral strength in some of them, or of all that they might be suffering themselves: lost illusions, so much strength and youth and honor and faith, and passionate desire for sacrifice, turned to ill account and spoiled,—the pointlessness of a career, which, if it is only a career, if it has not sacrifice as its end, is only a grim activity, an inept display, a ritual which is recited without belief in the words that are said....

His country was not enough for Christophe. He felt in himself that unknown force which wakes suddenly, irresistibly, in certain species of birds, at definite times, like the ebb and flow of the tides:—the instinct of the great migrations. As he read the volumes of Herder and Fichte which old Schulz had left him, he found souls like his own, not *"sons of the soil"* slavishly bound to the globe, but *" spirits, sons of the sun"* turning invincibly to the light wheresoever it comes.

Whither should he go? He did not know. But instinctively his eyes turned to the Latin South. And first to France—France, the eternal refuge of Germany in distress. How often had German thought turned to France, without ceasing to slander her! Even since seventy, what an attraction emanated from the town which had been shattered and smoking under the German guns! The most revolutionary and the most reactionary forms of thought and art had found alternately and sometimes at once example and inspiration there. Like so many other great German musicians in distress, Christophe turned towards Paris.... What did he know of the French? Two women's faces and some chance reading. That was enough for him to imagine a country of light, of gaiety, of courage, and even of a little Gallic boasting, which does not sort ill with the bold youth of the heart. He believed it all, because he needed to believe it all, because, with all his soul, he would have liked it to be so.

* * * * *

He made up his mind to go. But he could not go because of his mother.

Louisa was growing old. She adored her son, who was her only joy, and she was all that he most loved on earth. And yet they were always hurting each other. She hardly understood Christophe, and did not try to understand him. She was only concerned to love him. She had a narrow, timid, dull mind, and a fine heart; an immense need of loving and being loved in which there was something touching and sad. She respected her son because he seemed to her to be very learned; but she did all she could to stifle his genius. She thought he would stay all his life with her in their little town. They had lived together for years, and she could not imagine that he would not always be the same. She was happy: why should he not be happy, too? All her dreams for him soared no higher than seeing him married to some prosperous citizen of the town, hearing him play the organ at church on Sundays, and never having him leave her. She regarded her son as though he were still twelve years old. She would have liked him never to be more than that. Innocently she inflicted torture on the unhappy man who was suffocated in that narrow world.

522

And yet there was much truth—moral greatness—in that unconscious philosophy of the mother, who could not understand ambition and saw all the happiness of life in the family affections and the accomplishment of humble duties. She was a creature who wished to love and only to love. Sooner renounce life, reason, logic, the material world, everything, rather than love! And that love was infinite, suppliant, exacting: it gave everything—it wished to be given everything; it renounced life for love, and it desired that renunciation from others, from the beloved. What a power is the love of a simple soul! It makes it find at once what the groping reasoning of an uncertain genius like Tolstoy, or the too refined art of a dying civilization, discovers after a lifetime—ages—of bitter struggle and exhausting effort! But the imperious world which was seething in Christophe had very different laws and demanded another wisdom.

For a long time he had been wanting to announce his determination to his mother. But he was fearful of the grief it would bring to her, and just as he was about to speak he would lose his courage and put it off. Two or three times he did timidly allude to his departure, but Louisa did not take him seriously:—perhaps she preferred not to take him seriously, so as to persuade him that he was talking in jest. Then he dared not go on; but he would remain gloomy and thoughtful, or it was apparent that he had some secret burden upon his soul. And the poor woman, who had an intuition as to the nature of that secret, tried fearfully to delay the confession of it. Sometimes in the evening, when they were sitting, silent, in the light of the lamp, she would suddenly feel that he was going to speak, and then in terror she would begin to talk, very quickly, at random, about nothing in particular. She hardly knew what she was saying, but at all costs she must keep him from speaking. Generally her instinct made her find the best means of imposing silence on him: she would complain about her health, about the swelling of her hands and feet, and the cramps in her legs. She would exaggerate her sickness: call herself an old, useless, bed–ridden woman. He was not deceived by her simple tricks. He would look at her sadly in dumb reproach, and after a moment he would get up, saying that he was tired, and go to bed.

But all her devices could not save Louisa for long. One evening, when she resorted to them once more, Christophe gathered his courage and put his hand on his mother's and said:

"No, mother. I have something to say to you." Louisa was horrified, but she tried to smile and say chokingly:

"What is it, my dear?"

Christophe stammered out his intention of going. She tried to take it as a joke and to turn the conversation as usual, but he was not to be put off, and went on so deliberately and so seriously that there was no possibility of doubt. Then she said nothing. Her pulse stopped, and she sat there dumb, frozen, looking at him with terror in her eyes. Such sorrow showed in her eyes as he spoke that he too stopped, and they sat, both speechless. When at last she was able to recover her breath, she said—(her lips trembled)—:

"It is impossible.... It is impossible...."

Two large tears trickled down her cheeks. He turned his head away in despair and hid his face in his hands. They wept. After some time he went to his room and shut himself up until the morrow. They made no reference to what had happened, and as he did not speak of it again she tried to pretend that he had abandoned the project. But she lived on tenterhooks.

There came a time when he could hold himself in no longer. He had to speak even if it broke his heart: he was suffering too much. The egoism of his sorrow mastered the idea of the suffering he would bring to her. He spoke. He went through with it, never looking at his mother, for fear of being too greatly moved. He fixed the day for his departure so as to avoid a second discussion—(he did not know if he could again win the sad courage that was in him that day). Louisa cried:

"No, no! Stop, stop!..."

He set his teeth and went on implacably. When he had finished (she was sobbing) he took her hands and tried to make her understand how it was absolutely necessary for his art and his life for him to go away for some time. She refused to listen. She wept and said:

"No, no!... I will not...."

After trying to reason with her, in vain, he left her, thinking that the night would bring about a change in her ideas. But when they met next day at breakfast he began once more to talk of his plans. She dropped the piece of bread she was raising to her lips and said sorrowfully and reproachfully:

"Why do you want to torture me?"

He was touched, but he said:

"Dear mother, I must."

"No, no!" she replied. "You must not.... You want to hurt me.... It is a madness...."

They tried to convince each other, but they did not listen to each other. He saw that argument was wasted; it would only make her suffer more, and he began ostentatiously to prepare for his departure.

When she saw that no entreaty would stop him, Louisa relapsed into a gloomy stupor. She spent her days locked up in her room and without a light, when evening came. She did not speak or eat. At night he could hear her weeping. He was racked by it. He could have cried out in his grief, as he lay all night twisting and turning in his bed, sleeplessly, a prey to his remorse. He loved her so. Why must he make her suffer?... Alas! She would not be the only one: he saw that clearly.... Why had destiny given him the desire and strength of a mission which must make those whom he loved suffer?

"Ah!" he thought. "If I were free, if I were not drawn on by the cruel need of being what I must be, or else of dying in shame and disgust with myself, how happy would I make you—you whom I love! Let me live first; do, fight, suffer, and then I will come hack to you and love you more than ever. How I would like only to love, love, love!..."

He never could have been strong enough to resist the perpetual reproach of the grief–stricken soul had that reproach been strong enough to remain silent. But Louisa, who was weak and rather talkative, could not keep the sorrow that was stifling her to herself. She told her neighbors. She told her two other sons. They could not miss such a fine opportunity of putting Christophe in the wrong. Rodolphe especially, who had never ceased to be jealous of his elder brother, although there was little enough reason for it at the time—Rodolphe, who was cut to the quick by the least praise of Christophe, and was secretly afraid of his future success, though he never dared admit so base a thought—(for he was clever enough to feel his brother's force, and to be afraid that others would feel it, too), Rodolphe was only too happy to crush Christophe beneath the weight of his superiority. He had never worried much about his mother, though he knew her straitened circumstances: although he was well able to afford to help her, he left it all to Christophe. But when he heard of Christophe's intention he discovered at once hidden treasures of affection. He was furious at his proposing to leave his mother and called it monstrous egoism. He was impudent enough to tell Christophe so. He lectured him loftily like a child who deserves smacking: he told him stiffly of his duty towards his mother and of all that she had sacrificed for him. Christophe almost burst with rage. He kicked Rodolphe out and called him a rascal and a hypocrite. Rodolphe avenged himself by feeding his mother's indignation. Excited by him, Louisa began to persuade herself that Christophe was behaving like a bad son. She tried to declare that he had mo right to go, and she was only too willing to believe it. Instead of using only her tears, which were her strongest weapon, she reproached Christophe bitterly and unjustly, and disgusted him. They said cruel things to each other: the result was that Christophe, who, till then, had been hesitating, only thought of hastening his preparations for his departure. He knew that the charitable neighbors were commiserating his mother and that in the opinion of the neighborhood she was regarded as a victim and himself as a monster. He set his teeth and would not go back on his resolve.

The days passed. Christophe and Louisa hardly spoke to each other. Instead of enjoying to the last drop their last days together, these two who loved each other wasted the time that was left—as too often happens—in one of those sterile fits of sullenness in which so many affections are swallowed up. They only met at meals, when they sat opposite each other, not looking at each other, never speaking, forcing themselves to eat a few mouthfuls, not so much for the sake of eating as for the sake of appearances. Christophe would contrive to mumble a few words, but Louisa would not reply; and when she tried to talk he would be silent. This state of things was intolerable to both of them, and the longer it went on the more difficult it became to break it. Were they going to part like that? Louisa admitted that she had been unjust and awkward, but she was suffering too much to know how to win back her son's love, which she thought she had lost, and at all costs to prevent his departure, the idea of which she refused to face. Christophe stole glances at his mother's pale, swollen face and he was torn by remorse; but he had made up his mind to go, and knowing that he was going forever out of her life, he wished cowardly to be gone to escape his remorse.

His departure was fixed for the next day but one. One of their sad meals had just come to an end. When they finished their supper, during which they had not spoken a word, Christophe withdrew to his room; and sitting at his desk, with his head in his hands—he was incapable of working—he became lost in thought. The night was drawing late: it was nearly one o'clock in the morning. Suddenly he heard a noise, a chair upset in the next room. The door opened and his mother appeared in her nightgown, barefooted, and threw her arms round his neck and sobbed. She was feverish. She kissed her son and moaned through her despairing sobs:

"Don't go! Don't go! I implore you! I implore you! My dear, don't go!... I shall die.... I can't, I can't bear it!..."

He was alarmed and upset. He kissed her and said: "Dear mother, calm yourself, please, please!"

But she went on:

"I can't bear it ... I have only you. If you go, what will become of me? I shall die if you go. I don't want to die away from you. I don't want to die alone. Wait until I am dead!..."

Her words rent his heart. He did not know what to say to console her. What arguments could hold good against such an outpouring of love and sorrow! He took her on his knees and tried to calm her with kisses and little affectionate words. The old woman gradually became silent and wept softly. When she was a little comforted, he said:

"Go to bed. You will catch cold."

She repeated: "Don't go!"

He said in a low voice: "I will not go."

She trembled and took his hand. "Truly?" she said. "Truly?"

He turned his head away sadly. "To–morrow," he answered, "I will tell you to–morrow.... Leave me now, please!..."

She got up meekly and went back to her room. Next morning she was ashamed of her despairing outburst which had come upon her like a madness in the middle of the night, and she was fearful of what her son would say to her. She waited for him, sitting in a corner of the room. She had taken up some knitting for occupation, but her hands refused to hold it. She let it fall. Christophe entered. They greeted each other in a whisper, without looking at each other. He was gloomy, and went and stood by the window, with his back to his mother, and he stayed without speaking. There was a great struggle in him. He knew the result of it already, and was trying to delay the issue. Louisa dared not speak a word to him and provoke the answer which she expected and feared. She forced herself to take up her knitting again, but she could not see what she was doing, and she dropped her stitches. Outside it was raining. After a long silence Christophe came to her. She did not stir, but her heart was beating. Christophe stood still and looked at her, then, suddenly, he went down on his knees and hid his face in his mother's dress, and without saying a word, he wept. Then she understood that he was going to stay, and her heart was filled with a mortal agony of joy—but at once she was seized by remorse, for she felt all that her son was sacrificing for her, and she began to suffer all that Christophe had suffered when it was she whom he sacrificed. She bent over him and covered his brow and his hair with kisses. In silence their tears and their sorrow mingled. At last he raised his head, and Louisa took his face in her hands and looked into his eyes. She would have liked to say to him:

"Go!"

But she could not.

He would have liked to say to her:

"I am glad to stay."

But he could not.

The situation was hopeless; neither of them could alter it. She sighed in her sorrow and love:

"Ah! if we could all be born and all die together!" Her simple way filled him with tenderness; he dried his tears and tried to smile and said:

"We shall all die together."

She insisted:

"Truly you will not go?"

He got up:

"I have said so. Don't let us talk about it. There is nothing more to be said."

Christophe kept his word; he never talked of going again, but he could not help thinking of it. He stayed, but he made his mother pay dearly for his sacrifice by his sadness and bad temper. And Louisa tactlessly—much more tactlessly than she knew, never failing to do what she ought not to have done—Louisa, who knew only too well the reason of his grief, insisted on his telling her what it was. She worried him with her affection, uneasy, vexing, argumentative, reminding him every moment that they were very different from each other—and that he was trying to forget. How often he had tried to open his heart to her! But just as he was about to speak the Great Wall of China would rise between them, and he would keep his secrets buried in himself. She would guess, but she never dared invite his confidence, or else she could not. When she tried she would succeed only in flinging back in him those secrets which weighed so sorely on him and which he was so longing to tell.

A thousand little things, harmless tricks, cut her off from him and irritated Christophe. The good old creature was doting. She had to talk about the local gossip, and she had that nurse's tenderness which will recall all the silly little things of the earliest years, and everything that is associated with the cradle. We have such difficulty in issuing from it and growing into men and women! And Juliet's nurse must forever be laying before us our duty–swaddling clothes, commonplace thoughts, the whole unhappy period in which the growing soul struggles against the oppression of vile matter or stifling surroundings!

And with it all she had little outbursts of touching tenderness—as though to a little child—which used to move him greatly and he would surrender to them—like a little child.

The worst of all to bear was living from morning to night as they did, together, always together, isolated from the rest of the world. When two people suffer and cannot help each other's suffering, exasperation is fatal; each in the end holds the other responsible for the suffering; and each in the end believes it. It were better to be alone; alone in suffering.

It was a daily torment for both of them. They would never have broken free if chance had not come to break the cruel indecision, against which they were struggling, in a way that seemed unfortunate—but it was really fortunate.

It was a Sunday in October. Four o'clock in the afternoon. The weather was brilliant. Christophe had stayed in his room all day, chewing the cud of melancholy.

He could bear it no longer; he wanted desperately to go out, to walk, to expend his energy, to tire himself out, so as to stop thinking.

Relations with his mother had been strained since the day before. He was just going out without saying good–bye to her; but on the stairs he thought how it would hurt her the whole evening when she was left alone. He went back, making an excuse of having left something in his room. The door of his mother's room was ajar. He put his head in through the aperture. He watched his mother for a, few moments.... (What a place those two seconds were to fill in his life ever after!)...

Louisa had just come in from vespers. She was sitting in her favorite place, the recess of the window. The wall of the house opposite, dirty white and cracked, obstructed the view, but from the corner where she sat she could see to the right through the yards of the next houses a little patch of lawn the size of a pocket–handkerchief. On the window–sill a pot of convolvulus climbed along its threads and over this frail ladder stretched its tendrils which were caressed by a ray of sunlight. Louisa was sitting in a low chair bending over her great Bible which was open on her lap, but she was not reading. Her hands were laid flat on the book—her hands with their swollen veins, worker's nails, square and a little bent—and she was devouring with loving eyes the little plant and the patch of sky she could see through it. A sunbeam, basking on the green gold leaves, lit up her tired face, with its rather blotchy complexion, her white, soft, and rather thick hair, and her lips, parted in a smile. She was enjoying her hour of rest. It was the best moment of the week to her. She made use of it to sink into that state so sweet to those who suffer, when thoughts dwell on nothing, and in torpor nothing speaks save the heart and that is half asleep.

"Mother," he said, "I want to go out. I am going by Buir. I shall be rather late."

Louisa, who was dozing off, trembled a little. Then she turned her head towards him and looked at him with her calm, kind eyes.

"Yes, my dear, go," she said. "You are right; make use of the fine weather."

She smiled at him. He smiled at her. They looked at each other for a moment, then they said good–night affectionately, nodding and smiling with the eyes.

He closed the door softly. She slipped back into her reverie, which her son's smile had lit up with a bright ray of light like the sunbeam on the pale leaves of the convolvulus.

So he left her—forever.

* * * * *

An October evening. A pale watery sun. The drowsy country is sinking to sleep. Little village bells are slowly ringing in the silence of the fields. Columns of smoke rise slowly in the midst of the plowed fields. A fine mist hovers in the distance. The white fogs are awaiting the coming of the night to rise.... A dog with his nose to the ground was running in circles in a field of beet. Great flocks of crows whirled against the gray sky.

Christophe went on dreaming, having no fixed object, but yet instinctively he was walking in a definite direction. For several weeks his walks round the town had gravitated whether he liked it or not towards another village where he was sure to meet a pretty girl who attracted him. It was only an attraction, but it was very vivid and rather disturbing. Christophe could hardly do without loving some one; and his heart was rarely left empty; it always had some lovely image for its idol. Generally it did not matter whether the idol knew of his love; his need was to love, the fire must never be allowed to go out; there must never be darkness in his heart.

The object of this new flame was the daughter of a peasant whom he had met, as Eliezer met Rebecca, by a well; but she did not give him to drink; she threw water in his face. She was kneeling by the edge of a stream in a hollow in the bank between two willows, the roots of which made a sort of nest about her; she was washing linen vigorously; and her tongue was not less active than her arms; she was talking and laughing loudly with other girls of the village who were washing opposite her or the other side of the stream. Christophe was lying in the grass a few yards away, and, with his chin resting in his hands, he watched them. They were not put out by it; they went on chattering in a style which sometimes did not lack bluntness. He hardly listened; he heard only the sound of their merry voices, mingling with the noise of their washing pots, and with the distant lowing of the cows in the meadows, and he was dreaming, never taking his eyes off the beautiful washerwoman. A bright young face would make him glad for a whole day. It was not long before the girls made out which of them he was looking at; and they made caustic remarks to each other; the girl he preferred was not the least cutting in the observations she threw at him. As he did not budge, she got up, took a bundle of linen washed and wrung, and began to lay it out on the bushes near him so as to have an excuse for looking at him. As she passed him she continued to splash him with her wet clothes and she looked at him boldly and laughed. She was thin and strong: she had a fine chin, a little underhung, a short nose, arching eyebrows, deep–set blue eyes, bold, bright and hard, a pretty mouth with thick lips, pouting a little like those of a Greek maid, a mass of fair hair turned up in a knot on her head, and a full color. She carried her head very erect, tittered at every word she said and even when she said nothing, and walked like a man, swinging her sunburned arms. She went on laying out hey linen while she looked at Christophe with a provoking smile—waiting for him to speak. Christophe stared at her too; but he had no desire to talk to her. At last she burst out laughing to his face and turned back towards her companions. He stayed lying where he was until evening fell and he saw her go with her bundle on her back and her bare arms crossed, her back bent under her load, still talking and laughing.

He saw her again a few days later at the town market among heaps of carrots and tomatoes and cucumbers and cabbages. He lounged about watching the crowd of women, selling, who were standing in a line by their baskets like slaves for sale. The police official went up to each of them with his satchel and roll of tickets, receiving a piece of money and giving a paper. The coffee seller went from row to row with a basket full of little coffee pots. And an old nun, plump and jovial, went round the market with two large baskets on her arms and without any sort of humility begged vegetables, or talked of the good God. The women shouted: the old scales with their green painted pans jingled and clanked with the noise of their chains; the big dogs harnessed to the little carts barked loudly, proud of their importance. In the midst of the rabble Christophe saw Rebecca.—Her real name was Lorchen (Eleanor).—On her fair hair she had placed a large cabbage leaf, green and white, which made a dainty lace cap for her. She was sitting on a basket by a heap of golden onions, little pink turnips, haricot beans, and ruddy apples, and she was munching her own apples one after another without trying to sell them. She never stopped eating. From time to time she would dry her chin and wipe it with her apron, brush back her hair with her arm, rub her cheek against her shoulder, or her nose with the back of her hand. Or, with her hands on her knees, she would go on and on throwing a handful of shelled peas from one to the other. And she would look to right and left idly and indifferently. But she missed nothing of what was going on about her. And without seeming to do so she marked every glance cast in her direction. She saw Christophe. As she talked to her customers she had a way of raising her eyebrows and looking at her admirer over their heads. She was as dignified and serious as a Pope; but inwardly she was laughing at Christophe. And he deserved it; he stood there a few yards away devouring her with his eyes, then he went away without speaking to her. He had not the least desire to do so.

He came back more than once to prowl round the market and the village where she lived. She would be about the yard of the farm; he would stop on the road to look at her. He did not admit that he came to see her, and indeed he did so almost unconsciously. When, as often happened, he was absorbed by the composition of some work he would be rather like a somnambulist: while his conscious soul was following its musical ideas the rest of him would be delivered up to the other unconscious soul which is forever watching for the smallest distraction of the mind to take the freedom of the fields. He was often bewildered by the buzzing of his musical ideas when he was face to face with her; and he would go on dreaming as he watched her. He could not have said that he loved her; he did not even think of that; it gave him pleasure to see her, nothing more. He did not take stock of the desire which was always bringing him back to her.

His insistence was remarked. The people at the farm joked about it, for they had discovered who Christophe was. But they left him in peace; for he was quite harmless. He looked silly enough in truth; but he never bothered about it.

* * * * *

There was a holiday in the village. Little boys were crushing crackers between stones and shouting "God save the Emperor!" (" *Kaiser lebe! Hoch!*"). A cow shut up in the barn and the men drinking at the inn were to be heard. Kites with long tails like comets dipped and swung in the air above the fields. The fowls were scratching frantically in the straw and the golden dung–heap; the wind blew out their feathers like the skirts of an old lady. A pink pig was sleeping voluptuously on his side in the sun.

Christophe made his way towards the red roof of the inn of the *Three Kings* above which floated a little flag. Strings of onions hung by the door, and the windows were decorated with red and yellow flowers. He went into the saloon, filled with tobacco smoke, where yellowing chromos hung on the walls and in the place of honor a colored portrait of the Emperor–King surrounded with a wreath of oak leaves. People were dancing. Christophe was sure his charmer would be there. He sat in a corner of the room from which he could watch the movement of the dancers undisturbed. But in spite of all this care to pass unnoticed Lorchen spied him out in his corner. While she waltzed indefatigably she threw quick glances at him over her partner's shoulder to make sure that he was still looking at her; and it amused her to excite him; she coquetted with the young men of the village, laughing the while with her wide mouth. She talked a great deal and said silly things and was not very different from the girls of the polite world who think they must laugh and move about and play to the gallery when anybody looks at them, instead of keeping their foolishness to themselves. But they are not so very foolish either; for they know quite well that the gallery only looks at them and does not listen to what they say.—With his elbows on the table and his chin in his hands Christophe watched the girl's tricks with burning, furious eyes; his mind was free enough not to be taken in by her wiles, but he was not enough himself not to be led on by them; and he growled with rage and he laughed in silence and shrugged his shoulders in falling into the snare.

Not only the girl was watching him; Lorchen's father also had his eyes on him. Thick–set and short, bald–headed—a big head with a short nose—sunburned skull with a fringe of hair that had been fair and hung in thick curls like Duerer's St. John, clean–shaven, expressionless face, with a long pipe in the corner of his mouth, he was talking very deliberately to some other peasants while all the time he was watching Christophe's pantomime out of the corner of his eye; and he laughed softly. After a moment he coughed and a malicious light shone in his little gray eyes and he came and sat at Christophe's table. Christophe was annoyed and turned and scowled at him; he met the cunning look of the old man, who addressed Christophe familiarly without taking his pipe from his lips. Christophe knew him; he knew him for a common old man; but his weakness for his daughter made him indulgent towards the father and even gave him a queer pleasure in being with him; the old rascal saw that. After talking about rain and fine weather and some chaffing reference to the pretty girls in the room, and a remark on Christophe's not dancing he concluded that Christophe was right not to put himself out and that it was much better to sit at table with a mug in his hand; without ceremony he invited himself to have a drink. While he drank the old man went on talking deliberately as always. He spoke about his affairs, the difficulty of gaining a livelihood, the bad weather and high prices. Christophe hardly listened and only replied with an occasional grunt; he was not interested; he was looking at Lorchen. Christophe wondered what had procured him the honor of the old man's company and confidences. At last he understood. When the old man had exhausted his complaints he passed on to another chapter; he praised the quality of his produce, his vegetables, his fowls, his eggs, his milk, and suddenly he asked if Christophe could not procure him the custom of the Palace. Christophe started:

"How the devil did he know?... He knew him then?"

"Oh, yes," said the old man. "Everything is known ..." He did not add:

"... when you take the trouble to make enquiries."

But Christophe added it for him. He took a wicked pleasure in telling him that although everything was known, he was no doubt unaware that he had just quarreled with the Court and that if he had ever been able to flatter himself on having some credit with the servants' quarters and butchers of the Palace—(which he doubted strongly)—that credit at present was dead and buried. The old man's lips twitched imperceptibly. However, he was not put out and after a moment he asked if Christophe could not at least recommend him to such and such a family. And he mentioned all those with whom Christophe had had dealings; for he had informed himself of them at the market, and there was no danger of his forgetting any detail that might be useful to him. Christophe would have been furious at such spying upon him had he not rather wanted to laugh at the thought that the old man would be robbed in spite of all his cunning (for he had no doubt of the value of the recommendation he was asking—a recommendation more likely to make him lose his customers than to procure him fresh ones). So he let him empty all his bag of clumsy tricks and answered neither "Yes" nor "No." But the peasant persisted and finally he came down to Christophe and Louisa whom he had kept for the end, and expressed his keen desire to provide them with milk, butter and cream. He added that as Christophe was a musician nothing was so good for the voice as a fresh egg swallowed raw morning and evening; and he tried hard to make him let him provide him with these, warm from the hen. The idea of the old peasant taking him for a singer made Christophe roar with laughter. The peasant took advantage of that to order another bottle. And then having got all he could out of Christophe for the time being he went away without further ceremony.

Night had fallen. The dancing had become more and more excited. Lorchen had ceased to pay any attention to Christophe; she was too busy turning the head of a young lout of the village, the son of a rich farmer, for whom all the girls were competing. Christophe was interested by the struggle; the young women smiled at each other and would have been only too pleased to scratch each other. Christophe forgot himself and prayed for the triumph of Lorchen. But when her triumph was won he felt a little downcast. He was enraged by it. He did not love Lorchen; he did not want to be loved by her; it was natural that she should love anybody she liked.—No doubt. But it was not pleasant to receive so little sympathy himself when he had so much need of giving and receiving. Here, as in the town, he was alone. All these people were only interested in him while they could make use of him and then laugh at him. He sighed, smiled as he looked at Lorchen, whom her joy in the discomfiture of her rivals had made ten times prettier than ever, and got ready to go. It was nearly nine. He had fully two miles to go to the town.

He got up from the table when the door opened and a handful of soldiers burst in. Their entry dashed the gaiety of the place. The people began to whisper. A few couples stopped dancing to look uneasily at the new arrivals. The peasants standing near the door deliberately turned their backs on them and began to talk among themselves; but without seeming to do so they presently contrived to leave room for them to pass. For some time past the whole neighborhood had been at loggerheads with the garrisons of the fortresses round it. The soldiers were bored to death and wreaked their vengeance on the peasants. They made coarse fun of them, maltreated them, and used the women as though they were in a conquered country. The week before some of them, full of wine, had disturbed a feast at a neighboring village and had half killed a farmer. Christophe, who knew these things, shared the state of mind of the peasant, and he sat down again and waited to see what would happen.

The soldiers were not worried by the ill–will with which their entry was received, and went noisily and sat down at the full tables, jostling the people away from them to make room; it was the affair of a moment. Most of the people, went away grumbling. An old man sitting at the end of a bench did not move quickly enough; they lifted the bench and the old man toppled over amid roars of laughter. Christophe felt the blood rushing to his head; he got up indignantly; but, as he was on the point of interfering, he saw the old man painfully pick himself up and instead of complaining humbly crave pardon. Two of the soldiers came to Christophe's table; he watched them come and clenched his fists. But he did not have to defend himself. They were two tall, strong, good–humored louts, who had followed sheepishly one or two daredevils and were trying to imitate them. They were intimidated by Christophe's defiant manner, and when he said curtly: "This place is taken," they hastily begged his pardon and withdrew to their end of the bench so as not to disturb him. There had been a masterful inflection in his voice; their natural servility came to the fore. They saw that Christophe was not a peasant.

Christophe was a little mollified by their submission, and was able to watch things more coolly. It was not difficult to see that the gang were led by a non–commissioned officer—a little bull–dog of a man with hard eyes—with a rascally, hypocritical and wicked face; he was one of the heroes of the affray of the Sunday before. He was sitting at the table next to Christophe. He was drunk already and stared at the people and threw insulting sarcasms at them which they pretended not to hear. He attacked especially the couples dancing, describing their physical advantages or defects with a coarseness of expression which made his companions laugh. The girls blushed and tears came to their eyes; the young men ground their teeth and raged in silence. Their tormentor's eyes wandered slowly round the room, sparing nobody; Christophe saw them moving towards himself. He seized his mug, and clenched his fist on the table and waited, determined to throw the liquor at his head on the first insult. He said to himself:

"I am mad. It would be better to go away. They will slit me up; and then if I escape they will put me in prison; the game is not worth the candle. I'd better go before he provokes me."

But his pride would not let him, he would not seem to be running away from such brutes as these. The officer's cunning brutal stare was fixed on him. Christophe stiffened and glared at him angrily. The officer looked at him for a moment; Christophe's face irritated him; he nudged his neighbor and pointed out the young man with a snigger; and he opened his lips to insult him. Christophe gathered himself together and was just about to fling his mug at him.... Once more chance saved him. Just as the drunken man was about to speak an awkward couple of dancers bumped into him and made him drop his glass. He turned furiously and let loose a flood of insults. His attention was distracted; he forgot

Christophe. Christophe waited for a few minutes longer; then seeing that his enemy had no thought of going on with his remarks he got up, slowly took his hat and walked leisurely towards the door. He did not take his eyes off the bench where the other was sitting, just to let him feel that he was not giving in to him. But the officer had forgotten him altogether; no one took any notice of him.

He was just turning the handle of the door; in a few seconds he would have been outside. But it was ordered that he should not leave so soon. An angry murmur rose at the end of the room. When the soldiers had drunk they had decided to dance. And as all the girls had their cavaliers they drove away their partners, who submitted to it. But Lorchen was not going to put up with that. It was not for nothing that she had her bold eyes and her firm chin which so charmed Christophe. She was waltzing like a mad thing when the officer who had fixed his choice upon her came and pulled her partner away from her. She stamped with her foot, screamed, and pushed the soldier away, declaring that she would never dance with such a boor. He pursued her. He dispersed with his fists the people behind whom she was trying to hide. At last she took refuge behind a table; and then protected from him for a moment she took breath to scream abuse at him; she saw that all her resistance would be useless and she stamped with rage and groped for the most violent words to fling at him and compared his face to that of various animals of the farm–yard. He leaned towards her over the table, smiled wickedly, and his eyes glittered with rage. Suddenly he pounced and jumped over the table. He caught hold of her. She struggled with feet and fists like the cow–woman she was. He was not too steady on his legs and almost lost his balance. In his fury he flung her against the wall and slapped her face. He had no time to do it again; some one had jumped on his back, and was cuffing him and kicking him back into the crowd. It was Christophe who had flung himself on him, overturning tables and people without stopping to think of what he was doing. Mad with rage, the officer turned and drew his saber. Before he could make use of it Christophe felled him with a stool. The whole thing had been So sudden that none of the spectators had time to think of interfering. The other soldiers ran to Christophe drawing their sabers. The peasants flung themselves at them. The uproar became general. Mugs flew across the room; the tables were overturned. The peasants woke up; they had old scores to pay off. The men rolled about on the ground and bit each other savagely. Lorchen's partner, a stolid farm–hand, had caught hold of the head of the soldier who had just insulted him and was banging it furiously against the wall. Lorchen, armed with a cudgel, was striking out blindly. The other girls ran away screaming, except for a few wantons who joined in heartily. One of them—a fat little fair girl—seeing a gigantic

538

soldier—the same who had sat at Christophe's table—crushing in the chest of his prostrate adversary with his boot, ran to the fire, came back, dragged the brute's head backwards and flung a handful of burning ashes into his eyes. The man bellowed. The girl gloated, abused the disarmed enemy, whom the peasants now thwacked at their ease. At last the soldiers finding themselves on the losing side rushed away leaving two of their number on the floor. The fight went on in the village street. They burst into the houses crying murder, and trying to smash everything. The peasants followed them with forks, and set their savage dogs on them. A third soldier fell with his belly cleft by a fork. The others had to fly and were hunted out of the village, and from a distance they shouted as they ran across the fields that they would fetch their comrades and come back immediately.

The peasants, left masters of the field, returned to the inn; they were exultant; it was a revenge for all the outrages they had suffered for so long. They had as yet no thought of the consequences of the affray. They all talked at once and boasted of their prowess. They fraternized with Christophe, who was delighted to feel in touch with them. Lorchen came and took his hand and held it for a moment in her rough paw while she giggled at him. She did not think him ridiculous for the moment.

They looked to the wounded. Among the villagers there were only a few teeth knocked out, a few ribs broken and a few slight bruises and scars. But it was very different with the soldiers. They were seriously injured: the giant whose eyes had been burned had had his shoulder half cut off with a hatchet; the man whose belly had been pierced was dying; and there was the officer who had been knocked down by Christophe. They were laid out by the hearth. The officer, who was the least injured of the three, had just opened his eyes. He took a long look at the ring of peasants leaning over him, a look filled with hatred. Hardly had he regained consciousness of what had happened than he began to abuse them. He swore that he would be avenged and would settle their hash, the whole lot of them; he choked with rage; it was palpable that if he could he would exterminate them. They tried to laugh, but their laughter was forced. A young peasant shouted to the wounded man:

"Hold your gab or I'll kill you."

The officer tried to get up, and he glared at the man who had just spoken to him with blood–shot eyes:

"Swine!" he said. "Kill me! They'll cut your heads off."

He went on shouting. The man who had been ripped up screamed like a bleeding pig. The third was stiff and still like a dead man. A crushing terror came over the peasants. Lorchen and some women carried the wounded men to another room. The shouts of the officer and the screams of the dying man died away. The peasants were silent; they stood fixed in the circle as though the three bodies were still lying at their feet; they dared not budge and looked at each other in panic. At last Lorchen's father said:

"You have done a fine piece of work!"

There was an agonized murmuring; their throats were dry. Then they began all to talk at once. At first they whispered as though they were afraid of eavesdroppers, but soon they raised their voices and became more vehement; they accused each other; they blamed each other for the blows they had struck. The dispute became acrid; they seemed to be on the point of going for each other. Lorchen's father brought them to unanimity. With his arms folded he turned towards Christophe and jerked his chin at him:

"And," he said, "what business had this fellow here?"

The wrath of the rabble was turned on Christophe:

"True! True!" they cried. "He began it! But for him nothing would have happened."

Christophe was amazed. He tried to reply:

"You know perfectly that what I did was for you, not for myself."

But they replied furiously:

"Aren't we capable of defending ourselves? Do you think we need a gentleman from the town to tell us what we should do? Who asked your advice? And besides who asked you to come? Couldn't you stay at home?"

Christophe shrugged his shoulders and turned towards the door. But Lorchen's father barred the way, screaming:

"That's it! That's it!" he shouted. "He would like to cut away now after getting us all into a scrape. He shan't go!"

The peasants roared:

"He shan't go! He's the cause of it all. He shall pay for it all!"

They surrounded him and shook their fists at him. Christophe saw the circle of threatening faces closing in upon him; fear had infuriated them. He said nothing, made a face of disgust, threw his hat on the table, went and sat at the end of the room, and turned his back on them.

But Lorchen was angry and flung herself at the peasants. Her pretty face was red and scowling with rage. She pushed back the people who were crowding round Christophe:

"Cowards! Brute beasts!" she cried. "Aren't you ashamed? You want to pretend that he brought it all on you! As if they did not see you all! As if there was a single one of you who had not hit out his hand as he could!... If there had been a man who had stayed with his arms folded while the others were fighting I would spit in his face and call him: Coward! Coward!..."

The peasants, surprised by this unexpected outburst, stayed for a moment in silence; they began to shout again:

"He began it! Nothing would have happened but for him."

In vain did Lorchen's father make signs to his daughter. She went on:

"Yes. He did begin it! That is nothing for you to boast about. But for him you would have let them insult you. You would have let them insult you. You cowards! You funks!"

She abused her partner:

"And you, you said nothing. Your heart was in your mouth; you held out your bottom to be kicked. You would have thanked them for it! Aren't you ashamed?... Aren't you all ashamed? You are not men! You're as brave as sheep with your noses to the ground all the time! He had to give you an example!—And now you want to make him bear everything?... Well, I tell you, that shan't happen! He fought for us. Either you save him or you'll suffer along with him. I give you my word for it!"

Lorchen's father caught her arm. He was beside himself and shouted:

"Shut up! Shut up!... Will you shut up, you bitch!"

But she thrust him away and went on again. The peasants yelled. She shouted louder than they in a shrill, piercing scream:

"What have you to say to it all? Do you think I did not see you just now kicking the man who is lying half dead in the next room? And you, show me your hands!... There's blood on them. Do you think I did not see you with your knife? I shall tell everything I saw if you do the least thing against him. I will have you all condemned."

The infuriated peasants thrust their faces into Lorchen's and bawled at her. One of them made as though to box her ears, but Lorchen's lover seized him by the scruff of the neck and they jostled each other and were on the point of coming to blows. An old man said to Lorchen:

"If we are condemned, you will be too."

"I shall be too," she said, "I am not so cowardly as you."

And she burst out again.

They did not know what to do. They turned to her father:

"Can't you make her be silent?"

The old man had understood that it was not wise to push Lorchen too far. He signed to them to be calm. Silence came. Lorchen went on talking alone; then as she found no response, like a fire without fuel, she stopped. After a moment her father coughed and said:

"Well, then, what do you want? You don't want to ruin us."

She said:

"I want him to be saved."

They began to think. Christophe had not moved from where he sat; he was stiff and proud and seemed not to understand that they were discussing him; but he was touched by Lorchen's intervention. Lorchen seemed not to be aware of his presence; she was leaning against the table by which he was sitting, and glaring defiantly at the peasants, who were smoking and looking down at the ground. At last her father chewed his pipe for a little and said:

"Whether we say anything or not,—if he stays he is done for. The sergeant major recognized him; he won't spare him. There is only one thing for him to do—to get away at once to the other side of the frontier."

He had come to the conclusion it would be better for them all If Christophe escaped; in that way he would admit his guilt, and when he was no longer there to defend himself it would not be difficult to put upon him the burden of the affair. The others agreed. They understood each other perfectly.—Now that they had come to a decision they were all in a hurry for Christophe to go. Without being in the least embarrassed by what they had been saying a moment before they came up to him and pretended to be deeply interested in his welfare.

"There is not a moment to lose, sir," said Lorchen's father. "They will come back. Half an hour to go to the fortress. Half an hour to come back.... There is only just time to slip away."

Christophe had risen. He too had been thinking. He knew that if he stayed he was lost. But to go, to go without seeing his mother?... No. It was impossible. He said that he would first go back to the town and would still have time to go during the night and cross the frontier. But they protested loudly. They had barred the door just before to prevent his going; now they wanted to prevent his not going. If he went back to the town he was certain to be caught; they would know at the fortress before he got there; they would await him at home.—He insisted. Lorchen had understood him:

"You want to see your mother?... I will go instead of you."

"When?"

"To–night."

"Really! You will do that?"

"I will go."

She took her shawl and put it round her head.

"Write a letter. I will take it to her. Come with me. I will give you some ink."

She took him into the inner room. At the door she turned, and addressing her lover:

"And do you get ready," she said. "You must take him. You must not leave him until you have seen him over the frontier."

He was as eager as anybody to see Christophe over into France and farther if possible.

Lorchen went into the next room with Christophe. He was still hesitating. He was torn by grief at the thought that he would not be able to embrace his mother. When would he see her again? She was so old, so worn out, so lonely! This fresh blow would be too much for her. What would become of her without him?... But what would become of him if he stayed and were condemned and put in prison for years? Would not that even more certainly mean destitution and misery for her? If he were free, though far away, he could always help her, or she could come to him.—He had not time to see clearly in his mind. Lorchen took his hands—she stood near him and looked at him; their faces were almost touching; she threw her arms round his neck and kissed his mouth:

"Quick! Quick!" she whispered, pointing to the table, He gave up trying to think. He sat down. She tore a sheet of squared paper with red lines from an account book.

He wrote:

"My DEAR MOTHER: Forgive me. I am going to hurt you much. I cannot do otherwise. I have done nothing wrong. But now I must fly and leave the country. The girl who brings you this letter will tell you everything. I wanted to say good–bye to you. They will not let me. They say that I should be arrested. I am so unhappy that I have no will left. I am going over the frontier but I shall stay near it until you have written to me; the girl who brings you my letter will bring me your reply. Tell me what to do. I will do whatever you say. Do you want me to come back? Tell me to come back! I cannot bear the idea of leaving you alone. What will you do to live? Forgive me! Forgive me! I love you and I kiss you...."

"Be quick, sir, or we shall be too late," said Lorchen's swain, pushing the door open.

Christophe wrote his name hurriedly and gave the letter to Lorchen.

"You will give it to her yourself?"

"I am going," she said.

She was already ready to go.

"To–morrow," she went on, "I will bring you her reply; you must wait for me at Leiden,—(the first station beyond the German frontier)—on the platform."

(She had read Christophe's letter over his shoulder as he wrote.)

"You will tell me everything and how she bore the blow and everything she says to you? You will not keep anything from me?" said Christophe beseechingly.

"I will tell you everything."

They were not so free to talk now, for the young man was at the door watching them:

"And then, Herr Christophe," said Lorchen, "I will go and see her sometimes and I will send you news of her; do not be anxious."

She shook hands with him vigorously like a man.

"Let us go!" said the peasant.

"Let us go!" said Christophe.

All three went out. On the road they parted. Lorchen went one way and Christophe, with his guide, the other. They did not speak. The crescent moon veiled in mists was disappearing behind the woods. A pale light hovered over the fields. In the hollows the mists had risen thick and milky white. The shivering trees were bathed in the moisture of the air.—They were not more than a few minutes gone from the village when the peasant flung back sharply and signed to Christophe to stop. They listened. On the road in front of them they heard the regular tramp of a troop of soldiers coming towards them. The peasant climbed the hedge into the fields. Christophe followed him. They walked away across the plowed fields. They heard the soldiers go by on the road. In the darkness the peasant shook his fist at them. Christophe's heart stopped like a hunted animal that hears the baying of the hounds. They returned to the road again, avoiding the villages and isolated farms where the barking of the dogs betrayed them to the countryside. On the slope of a wooded hill they saw in the distance the red lights of the railway. They took the direction of the signals and decided to go to the first station. It was not easy. As they came down into the valley they plunged into the fog. They had to jump a few streams. Soon they found themselves in immense fields of beetroot and plowed land; they thought they would never be through. The plain was uneven; there were little rises and hollows into which they were always in danger of falling. At last after walking blindly through the fog they saw suddenly a few yards away the signal light of the railway at the top of an embankment. They climbed the bank. At the risk of being run over they followed the rails until they were within a hundred yards of the station; then they took to the road again. They reached the station twenty minutes before the train went. In spite of Lorchen's orders the peasant left Christophe; he was in a hurry to go back to see what had happened to the others and to his own property.

Christophe took a ticket for Leiden and waited alone in the empty third–class waiting room. An official who was asleep on a seat came and looked at Christophe's ticket and opened the door for him when the train came in. There was nobody in the carriage. Everybody in the train was asleep. In the fields all was asleep. Only Christophe did not sleep in spite of his weariness. As the heavy iron wheels approached the frontier he felt a fearful longing to be out of reach. In an hour he would be free. But till then a word would be enough to have him arrested.... Arrested! His whole being revolted at the word. To be stifled by odious force!... He could not breathe. His mother, his country, that he was leaving, were no longer in his thoughts. In the egoism of his threatened liberty he thought only of that liberty of his life which he wished to save. Whatever it might cost! Even at the cost of crime. He was bitterly sorry that he had taken the train instead of continuing the journey to the frontier on foot. He had wanted to gain a few hours. A fine gain! He was throwing himself into the jaws of the wolf. Surely they were waiting for him at the frontier station; orders must have been given; he would be arrested.... He thought for a moment of leaving the train while it was moving, before it reached the station; he even opened the door of the carriage, but it was too late; the train was at the station. It stopped. Fire minutes. An eternity. Christophe withdrew to the end of the compartment and hid behind the curtain and anxiously watched the platform on which a gendarme was standing motionless. The station master came out of his office with a telegram in his hand and went hurriedly up to the gendarme. Christophe had no doubt that it was about himself. He looked for a weapon. He had only a strong knife with two blades. He opened it in his pocket. An official with a lamp on his chest had passed the station master and was running along the train. Christophe saw him coming. His fist closed on the handle of the knife in his pocket and he thought:

"I am lost."

He was in such a state of excitement that he would have been capable of plunging the knife into the man's breast if he had been unfortunate enough to come straight to him and open his compartment. But the official stopped at the next carriage to look at the ticket of a passenger who had just taken his seat. The train moved on again. Christophe repressed the throbbing of his heart. He did not stir. He dared hardly say to himself that he was saved. He would not say it until he had crossed the frontier.... Day was beginning to dawn. The silhouettes of the trees were starting out of the night. A carriage was passing on the road like a fantastic shadow with a jingle of bells and a winking eye.... With his face close pressed to the window Christophe tried to see the post with the imperial arms which marked the bounds of his servitude. He was still looking for it in the growing light when the train whistled to announce its arrival at the first Belgian station.

He got up, opened the door wide, and drank in the icy air. Free! His whole life before him! The joy of life!... And at once there came upon him suddenly all the sadness of what he was leaving, all the sadness of what he was going to meet; and he was overwhelmed by the fatigue of that night of emotion. He sank down on the seat. He had hardly been in the station a minute. When a minute later an official opened the door of the carriage he found Christophe asleep. Christophe awoke, dazed, thinking he had been asleep an hour; he got out heavily and dragged himself to the customs, and when he was definitely accepted on foreign territory, having no more to defend himself, he lay down along a seat in the waiting room and dropped off and slept like a log.

* * * * *

He awoke about noon. Lorchen could hardly come before two or three o'clock. While he was waiting for the trains he walked up and down the platform of the little station. Then he went straight on into the middle of the fields; It was a gray and joyless day giving warning of the approach of winter. The light was dim. The plaintive whistle of a train stopping was all that broke the melancholy silence. Christophe stopped a few yards away from the frontier in the deserted country. Before him was a little pond, a clear pool of water, in which the gloomy sky was reflected. It was inclosed by a fence and two trees grew by its side. On the right, a poplar with leafless trembling top. Behind, a great walnut tree with black naked branches like a monstrous polypus. The black fruit of it swung heavily on it. The last withered leaves were decaying and falling one by one upon the still pond....

It seemed to him that he had already seen them, the two trees, the pond ...—and suddenly he had one of those moments of giddiness which open great distances in the plain of life. A chasm in Time. He knew not where he was, who he was, in what age he lived, through how many ages he had been so. Christophe had a feeling that it had already been, that what was, now, was not, now, but in some other time. He was no longer himself. He was able to see himself from outside, from a great distance, as though it were some one else standing there in that place. He heard the buzzing of memory and of an unknown creature within himself; the blood boiled in his veins and roared:

"Thus ... Thus .. Thus ...”

The centuries whirled through him.... Many other Kraffts had passed through the experiences which were his on that day, and had tasted the wretchedness of the last hour on their native soil. A wandering race, banished everywhere for their independence and disturbing qualities. A race always the prey of an inner demon that never let it settle anywhere. A race attached to the soil from which it was torn, and never, never ceasing to love it.

Christophe in his turn was passing through these same sorrowful experiences; and he was finding on the way the footsteps of those who had gone before him. With tears in his eyes he watched his native land disappear in the mist, his country to which he had to say farewell.—Had he not ardently desired to leave it?—Yes; but now that he was actually leaving it he felt himself racked by anguish. Only a brutish heart can part without emotion from the motherland. Happy or unhappy he had lived with her; she was his mother and his comrade; he had slept in her, he had slept on her bosom, he was impregnated with her; in her bosom she held the treasure of his dreams, all his past life, the sacred dust of those whom he had loved. Christophe saw now in review the days of his life, and the dear men and women whom he was leaving on that soil or beneath it. His sufferings were not less dear to him than his joys. Minna, Sabine, Ada, his grandfather, Uncle Gottfried, old Schulz—all passed before him in the space of a few minutes. He could not tear himself away from the dead—(for he counted Ada also among the dead)—the idea of his mother whom he was leaving, the only living creature of all those whom he loved, among these phantoms was intolerable to him.

He was almost on the point of crossing the frontier again, so cowardly did his flight seem to him. He made up his mind that if the answer Lorchen was to bring him from his mother betrayed too great grief he would return at all costs. But if he received nothing? If Lorchen had not been able to reach Louisa, or to bring back the answer? Well, he would go back.

He returned to the station. After a grim time of waiting the train at last appeared. Christophe expected to see Lorchen's bold face in the train; for he was sure she would keep her promise; but she did not appear. He ran anxiously from one compartment to another; he said to himself that if she had been in the train she would have been one of the first to get out. As he was plunging through the stream of passengers coming from the opposite direction he saw a face which he seemed to know. It was the face of a little girl of thirteen or fourteen, chubby, dimpled, and ruddy as an apple, with a little turned–up nose and a large mouth, and a thick plait coiled around her head. As he looked more closely at her he saw that she had in her hand an old valise very much like his own. She was watching him too like a sparrow; and when she saw that he was looking at her she came towards him; but she stood firmly in front of Christophe and stared at him with her little mouse–like eyes, without speaking a word. Christophe knew her; she was a little milkmaid at Lorchen's farm. Pointing to the valise he said:

"That is mine, isn't it?"

The girl did not move and replied cunningly:

"I'm not sure. Where do you come from, first of all?"

"Buir."

"And who sent it you?"

"Lorchen. Come. Give it me."

The little girl held out the valise.

"There it is."

And she added:

"Oh! But I knew you at once!"

"What were you waiting for then?"

"I was waiting for you to tell me that it was you."

"And Lorchen?" asked Christophe. "Why didn't she come?"

The girl did not reply. Christophe understood that she did not want to say anything among all the people. They had first to pass through the customs. When that was done Christophe took the girl to the end of the platform:

"The police came," said the girl, now very talkative. "They came almost as soon as you had gone. They went into all the houses. They questioned everybody, and they arrested big Sami and Christian and old Kaspar. And also Melanie and Gertrude, though they declared they had done nothing, and they wept; and Gertrude scratched the gendarmes. It was not any good then saying that you had done it all."

"I?" exclaimed Christophe.

"Oh! yes," said the girl quietly. "It was no good as you had gone. Then they looked for you everywhere and hunted for you in every direction."

"And Lorchen?"

"Lorchen was not there. She came back afterwards after she had been to the town."

"Did she see my mother?"

"Yes. Here is the letter. And she wanted to come herself, but she was arrested too."

"How did you manage to come?"

"Well, she came back to the village without being seen by the police, and she was going to set out again. But Irmina, Gertrude's sister, denounced her. They came to arrest her. Then when she saw the gendarmes coming she went up to her room and shouted that she would come down in a minute, that she was dressing. I was in the vineyard behind the house; she called to me from the window: 'Lydia! Lydia!' I went to her; she threw down your valise and the letter which your mother had given her, and she explained where I should find you. I ran, and here I am."

"Didn't she say anything more?"

"Yes. She told me to give you this shawl to show you that I came from her."

Christophe recognized the white shawl with red spots and embroidered flowers which Lorchen had tied round her head when she left him on the night before. The naive improbability of the excuse she had made for sending him such a love–token did not make him smile.

"Now," said the girl, "here is the return train. I must go home. Good–night."

"Wait," said Christophe. "And the fare, what did you do about that?"

"Lorchen gave it me."

"Take this," said Christophe, pressing a few pieces of money into her hand.

He held her back as she was trying to go.

"And then...." he said.

He stooped and kissed her cheeks. The girl affected to protest.

"Don't mind," said Christophe jokingly. "It was not for you."

"Oh! I know that," said the girl mockingly. "It was for Lorchen."

It was not only Lorchen that Christophe kissed as he kissed the little milkmaid's chubby cheeks; it was all Germany.

The girl slipped away and ran towards the train which was just going. She hung out of the window and waved her handkerchief to him until she was out of sight. He followed with his eyes the rustic messenger who had brought him for the last time the breath of his country and of those he loved.

When she had gone he found himself utterly alone, this time, a stranger in a strange land. He had in his hand his mother's letter and the shawl love–token. He pressed the shawl to his breast and tried to open the letter. But his hands trembled. What would he find in it? What suffering would be written in it?—No; he could not bear the sorrowful words of reproach which already he seemed to hear; he would retrace his steps.

At last he unfolded the letter and read: "My poor child, do not be anxious about me. I will be wise. God has punished me. I must not be selfish and keep you here. Go to Paris. Perhaps it will be better for you. Do not worry about me. I can manage somehow. The chief thing is that you should be happy. I kiss you. MOTHER.

"Write to me when you can."

Christophe sat down on his valise and wept.

* * * * *

The porter was shouting the train for Paris.

The heavy train was slowing down with a terrific noise. Christophe dried his tears, got up and said:

"I must go."

He looked at the sky in the direction in which Paris must be. The sky, dark everywhere, was even darker there. It was like a dark chasm. Christophe's heart ached, but he said again:

"I must go."

He climbed into the train and leaning out of the window went on looking at the menacing horizon:

"O, Paris!" he thought, "Paris! Come to my aid! Save me! Save my thoughts!"

The thick fog grew denser still. Behind Christophe, above the country he was leaving, a little patch of sky, pale blue, large, like two eyes—like the eyes of Sabine—smiled sorrowfully through the heavy veil of clouds and then was gone. The train departed. Rain fell. Night fell.

Printed in the United States
216569BV00003B/24/A

Kessinger Publishing's Rare Reprints

Thousands of Scarce and Hard-to-Find Books

- Americana
- Ancient Mysteries
- Animals
- Anthropology
- Architecture
- Arts
- Astrology
- Bibliographies
- Biographies & Memoirs
- Body, Mind & Spirit
- Business & Investing
- Children & Young Adult
- Collectibles
- Comparative Religions
- Crafts & Hobbies
- Earth Sciences
- Education
- Ephemera
- Fiction

- Folklore
- Geography
- Health & Diet
- History
- Hobbies & Leisure
- Humor
- Illustrated Books
- Language & Culture
- Law
- Life Sciences
- Literature
- Medicine & Pharmacy
- Metaphysical
- Music
- Mystery & Crime
- Mythology
- Natural History
- Outdoor & Nature
- Philosophy

- Poetry
- Political Science
- Psychiatry & Psychology
- Rare Books
- Reference
- Religion & Spiritualism
- Rhetoric
- Sacred Books
- Science Fiction
- Science & Technology
- Social Sciences
- Symbolism
- Theatre & Drama
- Theology
- Travel & Explorations
- War & Military
- Women
- Yoga

Download a free catalog and search our titles at: www.kessinger.net

KESSINGER
PUBLISHING

ISBN 1-4191-2738-1

9 781419 127380